THE COLLECTED POEMS *of* JOHN HEWITT

IF I SHOULD BE REMEMBERED AFTER THIS . . .

If I should be remembered after this,
pray providence it be by happy men
who do not feel the skull behind the kiss,
the bony knuckles round the rusting pen,

but summon from the stiff archaic words
a heart whose pulse in its best moments was
free on the wing, as natural as the birds,
as clear and common as the year's first grass.

For I was nourished by the normal year,
leafmould and frosted clod and sudden rain,
and though a sick age ran its steep career
the quiet voices were not all in vain.

CONTENTS

PART I

COLLECTED POEMS 1929–86

November 1930	Is appointed as an art assistant at the Belfast Museum and Art Gallery; meets the painter W.J. (Billy) McClughin, who becomes a lifelong friend.
1931	Holidays in Paris.
1931–2	The Hewitt family spends summer holidays on the Isle of Man.
1932	W.J. McClughin introduces Hewitt to the painter John Luke, who becomes a close friend; Hewitt attends a diploma course in Manchester, the first one of its kind to be organised by the Museums Association.
Autumn 1932	At the Rodin exhibition in the Belfast Museum and Art Gallery, Hewitt gives explanatory talks to visitors, one of whom is a young woman he recognises as 'the youngest of the three daughters of a genial little widow who had been very friendly with my parents for many years [who] had gone to Canada . . . some years previously and now was enjoying her first holiday back home' ('A North Light'). This was Roberta Black. (In her journal Roberta Black records that the meeting took place in 1933.)
Summer 1933	Hewitt and Roberta Black attend the summer school of the Independent Labour Party at Welwyn Garden City, where they meet, among others, the Chinese poet Shelley Wang, the Bradford socialist Fred Jowett and Fenner Brockway.
7 May 1934	John Hewitt and Roberta Black marry in the Registry Office, Great Victoria Street, Belfast. At this time Roberta is secretary of the Belfast Peace League, which the Hewitts helped to found, and both are members of the British Civil Liberties Union and the Left Book Club. Their first home is a flat at 45 Malone Road. In September they honeymoon in Paris.

1927–9	Attends teacher training course at Stranmillis College, Belfast.
1928	His earliest published poems appear, some pseudonymously, in left-wing newspapers and periodicals such as the *Irishman*, the *Workers' Voice* and the *New Leader*.
	He attends the open sessions of the Trades Union Congress in the Grosvenor Hall, Belfast, and meets R.M. Fox, author of *Smoky Crusade*.
	David McLean's Progressive Bookshop opens in Union Street, and Hewitt is a regular customer.
	Hewitt and three other poets – Ralph Meredith, a science student at Queen's University, Paddy Fisher, a medical student, and Graeme Roberts, an assistant in the Central Library, Belfast – found a typescript journal of stories and verse, with the title *Iskra* (the spark), in homage to Lenin.
c. 1928–30	Hewitt belongs to a secular society that meets in the Labour Hall, York Street, and he frequently speaks at meetings of the men's fellowship of the York Street Non-subscribing Presbyterian Church, which was open to all creeds and classes and discussed a wide range of subjects.
1929	Contributes poetry and prose to the Queen's University periodical the *Northman* and has a poem published in AE's *Irish Statesman*.
	Accompanies his father on a trip to Paris.
	At the annual conference of the Northern Ireland Labour Party, he acts as a delegate of the Belfast City branch.
1929–30	Final year at Queen's University Belfast.
10 July 1930	Graduates from Queen's University with a BA in English.
Summer 1930	Has a holiday trip to Paris.

1914–21	Family holidays are spent at Portstewart (July 1914), Brown's Bay, Islandmagee (spring 1917), Donaghadee (July 1918), Islandmagee (1919 and 1921), and other places.
1919	Hewitt is present at demonstrations during the shipyard workers' strike for a forty-four-hour week.
c. 1919–20	Hewitt is deeply impressed by Professor Cizek's exhibition of Austrian children's art at the Old Museum, Belfast.
1919–20	Attends the Royal Belfast Academical Institution, but leaves after one year.
1920–4	Is educated at Methodist College, Belfast, where he is a keen cricketer. In his last year, with matriculation behind him, he is given permission to attend art classes at the College of Technology. Throughout this period, and later, Hewitt accompanies his father to meetings in the Gaiety Cinema, the Ulster Hall, and at the Custom House steps, hearing a wide range of speakers.
1923	Hewitt's paternal grandfather dies.
Spring–Summer 1924	Hewitt begins to write poetry.
Autumn 1924	Enters Queen's University Belfast to read English.
1926	Hears Dr Alexander Irvine, author of *From The Bottom Up* and *My Lady of the Chimney Corner*, lecture in Belfast.
July 1927	Accompanies his father on a holiday trip to Belgium, visiting Ghent, Bruges, Brussels and Ostend.
15 September 1927	Hewitt's sister Eileen marries Norman Todhunter.
November–December 1927	An exhibition of British art, organised by Sir Joseph Duveen, visits Belfast and provokes controversy in the local press; Hewitt writes a number of letters to the *Belfast Evening Telegraph*.

BIOGRAPHICAL CHRONOLOGY

1839	Hewitt's paternal grandmother, Jane Redpath, is born near Kilmore, County Armagh.
1841	Hewitt's paternal grandfather, John Hewitt, is born near Kilmore, County Armagh.
1858	John Hewitt and Jane Redpath marry; shortly afterwards they move to Glasgow.
1873	Robert Telford Hewitt, the poet's father, is born in Glasgow.
1877	Elinor Robinson, the poet's mother, is born in Belfast.
1885	Hewitt's paternal grandparents return to Belfast.
1898	Hewitt's maternal grandfather dies.
12 July 1900	Robert Hewitt and Elinor Robinson marry by special licence at Bangor, County Down.
20 February 1902	Eileen Hewitt, the poet's sister, is born in Belfast.
30 October 1904	Roberta Black, the poet's future wife, is born in Larne, County Antrim.
28 October 1907	John Harold Hewitt is born at 96 Cliftonpark Avenue, Belfast.
January 1910	Hewitt's paternal grandmother dies.
1912–16	The Hewitt family spends frequent holidays at Mrs Hewitt's brother John's house at Ballyholme, near Bangor, County Down, where her mother also lives. The young John Hewitt spends the entire winter of 1915–16 there.
c. 1912–19	Hewitt is educated at Agnes Street National School, the Methodist elementary school where his father is principal.
c. 1913–14	Hewitt hears Jim Larkin address a Labour meeting in Belfast, and hears Sir Edward Carson at a gathering at Six Road Ends.

NOTE

The following notes summarise some basic textual procedures in the present volume, particularly in relation to spelling and punctuation.

I have retained:

1 certain archaic or idiosyncratic spellings, where they occur, such as shew, rime, plow, plowman, plowshare, yowe, craytur, Kelt, Keltic, Elisabeth, landskip, squareset;

2 alternate spellings of proper names, for example, Oisin/Ossian, Colmcille/Columcille, and spellings such as Concobar, Gilwirra and Glenarriffe;

3 Hewitt's practice in some poems where he has opted for a minimum of punctuation, for example, 'Antrim April', 'Lyric' ('Chestnut and beech . . .'), 'Hand over hand', 'Man fish and bird', 'Spring of the year', 'The storm', 'For R.', 'Camaradas y compañeros', 'Mist', 'Awareness of time', 'Corncrake', or in poems such as 'Et tu in Arcadia vixisti', 'The man from the mountains' and 'Tiphead', where the punctuation is unusual but seems to me justifiable in terms of the content;

4 forms such as ev'n, conf'rence, th'iambic, th'Apprentice Boys, which, however clumsy, are usually intended to maintain a particular syllable count.

I have, however, made the following alterations:

5 corrected obvious spelling errors and occasionally revised punctuation where it seemed to be inaccurate or confusingly ambiguous;

6 modernised spellings such as agen, thro', tho', and forms such as talkd, lovd, ragd, plannd, except in a few instances where the sound is arguably an echo of the sense;

7 reprinted foreign words in italics, but not dialect words such as brairded, freets, sheugh, girning, or Irish words absorbed into dialect, such as airt, grugach, and ceilidhe (or céilí);

8 omitted Hewitt's dating of poems by year in *The Day of the Corncrake: Poems of the Nine Glens* (1969), *Out of My Time* (1974) and elsewhere.

FRANK ORMSBY
BELFAST 1991

PREFACE

This volume brings together, for the first time, all the poems John Hewitt published during his lifetime, with a supplementary selection of previously unpublished work drawn from his manuscript notebooks. I have arranged this material in three main sections, the third in the form of an appendix.

Part I reprints all Hewitt's books and pamphlets and the contents are ordered chronologically by date of publication. Where a poem is reprinted without alteration in more than one collection, I have placed it in its original context; where Hewitt revised a poem from an earlier collection for inclusion in a later, I have included the later version only, in its appropriate place, and recorded the revisions in the Notes to this volume. I have chosen this method of organisation, rather than a chronological ordering by date of composition, for two particular reasons. First, Hewitt's collections *Time Enough: Poems New and Revised*, *The Rain Dance: Poems New and Revised*, *Mosaic*, *Loose Ends* and *Freehold and Other Poems* contain a considerable number of reworkings and recastings of earlier poems, published and unpublished; this would make a chronological ordering by date of composition extremely unwieldly. Second, in any case, it seems to me preferable to retain the poet's own organisation of particular books and pamphlets, though even this has not been possible in every instance.

A broad chronological picture is, however, useful and I have attempted, in Appendix II, to provide one.

Part II contains a selection from the thousands of unpublished poems in Hewitt's manuscript notebooks. The selection procedure was largely subjective. These are the poems which, for various reasons, stood out initially and continued to appeal to me on subsequent readings. The translations represent an enterprise comparatively rare in Hewitt's poetry; the love poems have an uninhibited quality more common in the notebooks than in the published work and the group as a whole is, I think, likely to enrich a reader's sense of Hewitt and the range of his concerns.

Appendix I reprints the poems Hewitt published in periodicals but never collected in book or pamphlet form. Of the earliest of these – the socialist and romantic verses of the late 1920s and early 1930s – Hewitt himself declared: 'None of them was really any good' (interview, *Quarto*, no. 7, 1980–1). I have, however, chosen to gather them in an appendix on the grounds that, for all their inadequacies as poetry, they represent an important post-juvenalia phase in his development and may, for that reason, be of interest to the general reader and the scholar. The remaining poems in Appendix I complement Hewitt's collected work from the 1930s to the 1980s.

ACKNOWLEDGEMENTS

I gratefully acknowledge the help of the following individuals and institutions:

John Hewitt's executors, Dr Keith Millar and Deirdre Todhunter, who gave generously of their time and were unfailingly supportive;

the staff of the Library, University of Ulster at Coleraine, particularly Joe McLaughlin, Frank Reynolds and Eileen Tyrell;

the staff of the Public Records Office of Northern Ireland;

the staff of the Central Library, Belfast, the Library, Methodist College, Belfast, particularly Paul Fry, the Library, Queen's University Belfast, the Library, the Royal Belfast Academical Institution, particularly R.W. McMurray and Elaine Patterson, the Linen Hall Library, Belfast, and the National Library of Scotland;

the library staff of the *Belfast Telegraph* and the *Irish Times*;

the Ulster Folk and Transport Museum, particularly Clifford Harkness, and Gráinne Loughran and Marian McCavana, BBC broadcasting archive assistants;

Sound Archives, RTE, particularly Dr Peter Doyle;

the Ulster Museum, particularly Angela Reid;

S. Brown and Brian Baird, Stranmillis College, Belfast;

Professor Marcus Wheeler, Department of Slavonic Studies, Queen's University Belfast, and Professor Ronnie Buchanan, Institute of Irish Studies, Queen's University Belfast;

the Poetry Book Society, particularly Martha Smart;

the Publications Department of the World Council of Churches, particularly Heather Stunt;

Jean Craig, John, Renee and Siobhán Kilfeather, Alfred Lyner, Jack McCann, Ciaran McKeown and Michael J. Murphy, all of whom knew John Hewitt well and talked illuminatingly about him;

all those who gave practical help and support, in particular Karen McAteer, Terence Brown, Tom Clyde, Seamus Deane, Mary Denver, John Gamble, Conor Macauley, D.J. Madill, Denis Mahon, Colin Meir, Michael Murray and Brian Walker;

the Blackstaff Press;

and, not least, the Arts Council of Northern Ireland for a bursary to assist with research.

APPENDIX I

UNCOLLECTED POEMS 1928–86

Autumn 1934	Hewitt helps to found the Ulster Unit, a progressive art group, with John Luke, Colin Middleton and others, and acts as secretary to the unit; the group rents Locksley Hall, Belfast, for its one and only exhibition, held before and after Christmas, and Hewitt writes the foreword to the catalogue. His friendship with Middleton dates from this time. Meets Alexander Irvine at the Labour Hall, York Street.
21–8 June 1935	The Hewitts holiday on Rathlin Island.
Summer(?) 1935	Hewitt, having already attended courses in Manchester and Liverpool in the early 1930s, attends a Museums Association course in Bristol.
August 1936	The Hewitts attend the summer school at the Adelphi Centre at Langham, near Colchester, meeting John Middleton Murry, George Orwell, Rayner Heppenstall and others; they are also involved in the National Council of Civil Liberties' investigation of the Special Powers Act.
October(?) 1936	The Hewitts move to 15 Westland Drive, Belfast.
Spring 1937	Hewitt takes part in a meeting at the Brown Horse (McGlade's), Library Street, Belfast, with George Hill, Joe Sherlock and Edward Boyle, which leads to the founding of the *Irish Democrat*; he acts as literary editor for a time and contributes articles and reviews under the pseudonym 'Richard Telford'. He acts as literary editor of *Forum*, a literary supplement to a short-lived newspaper, *Irish Jewry*.
January 1938	Shelley Wang comes to Belfast to speak at a public meeting in the Ulster Hall on 'Aid for China' and stays with the Hewitts for some ten days.

Spring 1938	Hewitt attends a Museums Association course in Edinburgh, and Roberta helps found Edenderry Nursery School.
September 1938	A group of Basque refugee children arrives in Belfast to give a series of concerts under the auspices of the NI Joint Committee for Spanish Relief, raising money for the maintenance of Basque children in England. Two of them, Laura Martinez and Aurora Breton Perez, stay with the Hewitts at Westland Drive. Laura returns in January 1939 and remains with the Hewitts until the early summer of that year.
Spring 1939	The Hewitts move from Westland Drive to a flat at 123 Crumlin Road, Strangemore Terrace, Belfast, and later rent a house at 14 Shandarragh Park, Belfast.
3 July 1939	Hewitt is among the first group ever to be awarded the Diploma of the Museums Association; the award is based on courses attended, practical tests, a written examination, and a thesis on 'The problems of a provincial gallery'.
Autumn 1939	Attempts to join the British Army, but as a local government officer, he is in a reserved occupation and can only be accepted if he resigned his post; his patriotism is, however, 'more provisional than headlong' ('A North Light'). Later he responds to a press notice asking graduates to apply for commissions, but is rejected because he has had no OTC experience. Among those who stay with the Hewitts during 1939 is James Bertram, author of *North China Front.*
1939–45	Lectures on art, Marxism and other subjects at army camps and stations all over Northern Ireland, an experience

	that influences the development of his regionalist ideas.
Autumn 1940	The Hewitts move to a flat at 18 Mountcharles, University Road, Belfast. Visitors and guests there include Forces personnel of all ranks, among them writers such as Rayner Heppenstall, Emmanuel Litvinoff, Paul Potts and the Australian poet John Manifold, all stationed in Northern Ireland; Hewitt joins the local civil defence organisation, based in Donegall Pass.
1941	Roberta Hewitt helps to found Frederick Street Nursery School.
1942	Hewitt reads Lewis Mumford's books *The Culture of Cities* (1938) and *A Faith for Living* (1940), and the volume *Cities in Evolution* (1915) by Patrick Geddes, titles that extend and confirm his regionalist outlook at this time.
1943	Hewitt is a founder member of the Committee for the Encouragement of Music and the Arts (NI). His association with CEMA continues until 1957, during which period he serves as a member of the board, and the standing and art committees, and is chairman of the art committee for six years.
1 April 1943	Hewitt is promoted to chief assistant in the Belfast Museum and Art Gallery.
September 1943	*Conacre* is privately published.
December 1944	*Compass: Two Poems* is privately published.
18 July 1945	Hewitt's father dies.
1945–6	Hewitt serves as an associate editor of the periodical *Lagan*.
May 1946	The Hewitts, having spent numerous holidays in Cushendall from 1940 onwards, rent a cottage at Tiveragh (or Tieveragh), outside the village, the gate lodge of a convent, formerly Glenville House. They continue renting the lodge until 1965.

	Hewitt becomes a member of the BBC (NI) Advisory Council, serving until 1950.
February 1948	Visits Glasgow to give a talk to Scottish PEN and attends a Van Gogh exhibition; meets Hugh MacDiarmid.
November 1948	*No Rebel Word* is published by Frederick Muller.
September 1949	Acts as delegate to the PEN Conference in Venice; meets Edwin and Willa Muir there. The Hewitts visit Paris on their way home.
1950	Becomes deputy director and keeper of art at the Belfast Museum and Art Gallery.
10 July 1951	Is awarded an MA degree by Queen's University Belfast, for his thesis 'Ulster poets, 1800–1870'.
c. 1951–2	Befriends the folklorist Michael J. Murphy, who was then living at Layde near Cushendall.
1953	Applies for the directorship of the Belfast Museum and Art Gallery, but is denied the post, largely because of his radical and socialist ideals.
1953–7	Acts as art critic for the *Belfast Telegraph*, under the pseudonym 'MacArt', and as drama and art critic for the *Irish Times.*
13 January 1954	Hewitt's verse play *The Bloody Brae* is broadcast on BBC radio, Northern Ireland Home Service (NIHS); attends PEN Conference in Amsterdam, visiting Haarlem, Leyden and other places.
1955	Attends PEN Conference in Vienna.
1956	*Those Swans Remember: A Poem* is privately published.
March 1957	Hewitt moves to Coventry to become art director of the Herbert Art Gallery and Museum. The Hewitts live for some months in a council flat at 320 Purcell Road, then at 27B Radford Road. Later they buy 5 Postbridge Road, where they live until 1972.

	Hewitt becomes poetry editor of *Threshold*, continuing until 1962.
	Hewitt's verse play *The Bloody Brae* is performed by the Lyric Players, shortly after the Hewitts move to Coventry.
4–7 April 1958	The Hewitts take part in a CND march from Trafalgar Square to Aldermaston.
22 October 1958	Hewitt's mother dies.
1959	Beltona Records, a subsidiary of Decca, issues a gramophone record, *Poetry of Ireland*, on which the readers are Richard Hayward, Hewitt and Eithne Dunn.
13–20 February 1959	Visits Dresden as part of a group representing Coventry on the anniversary of the Allied raids, 13–14 February 1945.
Winter 1959	Visits Yugoslavia.
1960	Is elected to the Irish Academy of Letters.
June 1960	The Hewitts visit Rome and Florence.
10–26 May 1961	The Hewitts travel to Italy again, visiting Florence, Rome, Milan; they also go to Sicily (Palermo, Agrigento, Erice and other places).
15 August 1961	Delivers lecture on William Allingham at Yeats Summer School, Sligo.
7–18 June 1962	Makes a trip to Warsaw for Polish national museum centenary, also visiting Krakow, Auschwitz, Katowice, Posnan and other places.
13–27 July 1963	The Hewitts visit Czechoslovakia.
1963–4	Hewitt works on his unpublished autobiography 'A North Light'.
12–26 July 1964	The Hewitts visit Yugoslavia (Belgrade, Sarajevo, Split and other places).
22 September–7 October 1966	The Hewitts visit Greece and the Cyclades (Athens, Mykonos and other places).
1967	*Tesserae* is published by Festival Publications, Queen's University Belfast; *The Poems of William Allingham* (a selection), edited and introduced by Hewitt, is published by Dolmen Press.

30 September–13 October 1967	The Hewitts travel to Sicily, visiting Monte Pellegrino, Agrigento, Montelepre and other places.
August 1968	*Collected Poems 1932–1967* is published by MacGibbon and Kee.
1969	*The Day of the Corncrake: Poems of the Nine Glens* is published by The Glens of Antrim Historical Society.
April 1969	The Hewitts buy 11 Stockman's Lane, Belfast, as a preparation for his retirement.
2–16 August 1969	The Hewitts visit Hungary (Budapest, Lake Balaton and other places).
September–October 1969	The Hewitts visit Paris, with a day trip to Rotterdam.
1970	*The Planter and the Gael* (with John Montague) is published by the Arts Council of Northern Ireland to coincide with the poets' tour of the province, 23–30 November; they give readings in Ballymena, Coleraine, Derry, Omagh, Enniskillen, Armagh and Belfast.
1971	*An Ulster Reckoning* is privately published.
15–27 March 1971	The Hewitts visit Athens, Crete and Rhodes.
October 1972	Hewitt retires as art director of the Herbert Art Gallery and Museum, Coventry; he and Roberta return to Belfast to live at 11 Stockman's Lane.
September 1973	The Hewitts visit Turkey (Istanbul, Ankara, Kayseri and other places).
1974	*The Chinese Fluteplayer* and *Scissors for a One-Armed Tailor: Marginal Verses 1929–1954* both privately published.
4 July 1974	Hewitt is awarded an honorary degree of Doctor of Letters by the New University of Ulster.
October 1974	*Out of My Time: Poems 1967–1974* is published by Blackstaff Press.
November 1974	*Rhyming Weavers and Other Country Poets of Antrim and Down*, edited and

	introduced by Hewitt, is published by Blackstaff Press.
1975	Hewitt is elected vice-president of the Irish Academy of Letters.
24 February 1975	Hewitt's sister Eileen dies.
6–20 September 1975	The Hewitts visit the USSR (Moscow, Leningrad, Tashkent, Bukhara, Samarkand, Dushanbe and other places).
19 October 1975	Roberta Hewitt dies.
1976	Is appointed first writer-in-residence at Queen's University Belfast, a post he holds until 1979.
	Colin Middleton is published by the Arts Council of Northern Ireland.
8–23 May 1976	Visits Italy (Rome, Assisi and other places).
November 1976	*Time Enough: Poems New and Revised* is published by Blackstaff Press.
November 1977	*Art in Ulster I* is published by Blackstaff Press.
1978	Hewitt visits Italy in the company of Jean, Colin and Ian Craig.
19 November 1978	*I Found Myself Alone*, a short film on Hewitt's life and work, made by Landseer Productions for the Arts Council of Northern Ireland, is premiered at the Queen's Film Theatre, Belfast.
	John Luke 1906–1975 is published jointly by the Arts Councils of Ireland.
December 1978	*The Rain Dance: Poems New and Revised* is published by Blackstaff Press.
1979	Hewitt is elected first president of Northern Ireland Fabian Society.
	Refuses offer of an OBE.
1980	Audio Arts, London, issues *Substance and Shadow*, a cassette recording of Hewitt reading his poetry.
February 1980	*Kites in Spring: A Belfast Boyhood* is published by Blackstaff Press.
September 1980	Visits Paris with John and Renee Kilfeather.

22–9 March 1981	Hewitt visits southern Spain with his nephew Keith Millar (Granada, Cordoba, Seville and other places).
17–27 August 1981	Visits Paris with the Kilfeathers.
September 1981	*The Selected John Hewitt*, edited by Alan Warner, is published by Blackstaff Press.
November 1981	*Mosaic* is published by Blackstaff Press.
September(?) 1982	Hewitt's third visit to Paris in the company of the Kilfeathers.
1 March 1983	Hewitt is made a freeman of the city of Belfast.
April 1983	*Loose Ends* is published by Blackstaff Press.
8 July 1983	Hewitt is awarded the degree of Doctor of Literature (*honoris causa*) by Queen's University Belfast.
1984	Is awarded the Gregory Medal by the Irish Academy of Letters; Peadar O'Donnell makes the presentation. *The Day of the Corncrake: Poems of the Nine Glens* (revised edition) is published by The Glens of Antrim Historical Society.
March 1986	*Freehold and Other Poems* is published by Blackstaff Press.
May 1986	His verse play *The Bloody Brae* is performed by the Lyric Players, Belfast.
27 June 1987	John Hewitt dies in Belfast.
November 1987	*Ancestral Voices: The Selected Prose of John Hewitt*, edited by Tom Clyde, is published by Blackstaff Press.
1988	First John Hewitt International Summer School takes place at St MacNissi's College, Garron Tower, County Antrim.

Among the earliest surviving papers in John Hewitt's hand are two transcriptions, dated 4 October 1922. One is of Walter Savage Landor's four-line 'Finis':

> I strove with none, for none was worth my strife;
> Nature I loved, and next to Nature Art;
> I warmed both hands before the fire of life;
> It sinks and I am ready to depart.

And the other is the final stanza of W.E. Henley's 'Invictus'. It is not clear whether these neat copies are part of a set of handwriting exercises, or whether the fifteen-year-old Methodist College schoolboy is already beginning to choose his poetic models, or both. Two years later, in his final months at Methody, and during the summer before he entered Queen's University Belfast, Hewitt wrote the first poems of a creative span that was to last for over sixty years.

There was nothing half-hearted about Hewitt's early commitment to verse. He once revealed in interview (*Acorn*, no. 7, Autumn 1964) that in 1924 alone he produced over six hundred poems, and the work preserved in his notebooks for the period 1924–30 shows him responding to a wide range of influences and experimenting with a comprehensive variety of forms. These notebooks are worth summarising for the evidence they provide of his formative literary exemplars, the breadth of his early reading and the rich multiplicity of accents and cadences that became part of his poetic voice. He began as a practitioner of free verse – 'old lollopy stuff' (interview, *Quarto*, no. 7, 1980–1) in the mode of Walt Whitman. Thereafter he filled the notebooks with sonnets, ballads, dramatic lyrics and monologues; exercises in consonant rhyme and assonance, French rhyme, rime royal, *terza rima*, the heroic couplet, the octosyllabic couplet, blank verse, alliterative verse; poems in the 'In Memoriam' stanza, the Spenserian stanza, the 'Christabel' metre, the metaphysical style, the 'Nineties' style; triolets, *chansons*, villanelles, rondeaux, roundels, ballades; satires, dialect poems (Negro and Irish), Christmas carols, Negro spirituals, adaptations and translations, 'poetic trifles'. This work is heavily derivative. Among the models named in the notebooks are William Blake, George Crabbe and William Morris; many of the ballads are imitations of James Macpherson's 'Ossian' poems and the Border Ballads; the sonnets bear the mark of Dante Gabriel Rossetti in particular (between September 1926 and March 1927 Hewitt wrote a series of eighty-three Rossettian sonnets); the dramatic monologues show the influence of Robert Browning; and the diction and mannerisms of poets such as W.B. Yeats and Humbert Wolfe are discernible in the lyrics. To this list might be added the names of Oscar Wilde and those Georgian poets whose work appeared in Ernest Benn's The Augustan Poets series, especially John Drinkwater.

As may be surmised from this summary of influences, much of Hewitt's earliest work has a strongly literary-romantic flavour. Some titles from the early notebooks indicate the favoured mode: 'The ballad of the Wandering Jew, after the antient manyere', 'How Caedmon first sang, writ out in short by Robert of Whitby, monk', 'Marie, courtesan of Paris, to Sir Guy du Cri Bruyant, in prison', 'Ballade of Joachim de Flores, on the eve of his martyrdom, to Jean de Parme'. Equally prominent, however, is a strain of socialist verse which takes as its subjects class inequality, poverty and injustice, strikes, pickets, unemployment, municipal and national elections, and international affairs, much of it reflecting the beginnings of the Depression period. One writer in particular dictated the development of both these strands in Hewitt's work. The poet records how, while a student at Queen's University, he borrowed ten shillings from his mother to buy a five-volume second-hand set of William Morris's *The Earthly Paradise* (1868–70), poems based on classical and northern European legends, and how this formidable collection made Morris his 'first, lifelong love among the poets' (Radio Éireann broadcast, 18 February 1975). Inevitably, *The Earthly Paradise* led him to Morris's propagandist *Chants for Socialists* (1884–5), to *A Dream of John Ball* (1888), Morris's prose tale of the medieval monk who dreamed of social justice and who was a leader of the English peasants' revolt, to *News from Nowhere* (1891), a portrait of an ideal society characterised by equality and compassion, and to lectures such as 'How I became a socialist'. Hewitt's debt to Morris is a complex one: he notes also that Morris's romantic verse brought him to Yeats and that when he went to work in the Belfast Museum and Art Gallery, some of Morris's lectures in *Hopes and Fears for Art* (1882) and *Signs of Change* (1888) 'provided the basis for [his] sense of social stability, and [his] ideas for a just organisation of human needs and fulfilments' (Radio Éireann broadcast, 18 February 1975).

Hewitt did not, of course, *discover* socialism in the writings of William Morris. These writings represent an articulation and confirmation of values the poet had already acquired from his Methodist background and his socialist father, Robert Telford Hewitt, who counted Keir Hardie, trade unionist James Larkin, and R.J. Campbell, author of *The Christian Commonwealth*, among his heroes. Time and again in the poetry John Hewitt pays tribute to and reflects the shaping influence of this liberal, patient, undogmatic man who 'unequivocably stood/for quality of life and brotherhood,/without defiance, in all charity/towards those who in themselves were not yet free' (*Freehold*), and whose 'wise discipline' Hewitt continually aspired to. It was on his father's bookshelves that he found, not only the works that stimulated his interest in literature and art, but also the 'strong thread' of an English radical tradition that was to be part of the 'fabric' of his philosophy and outlook for the rest of his life: the main threads were the Diggers and Levellers who had sought to bring about a social revolution during the English Civil War, the writings of Thomas Paine and William Cobbett, the Chartists who had campaigned in the 1840s for workers' votes, as well as John Ball and Morris's utopian socialism. It was, too, in the 1920s and early 1930s that Hewitt heard leading socialists of the day, such as John Wheatley, one of the pioneers of council housing, Shaphurji Saklatvala, the Indian communist MP for Battersea, Dr Alexander Irvine, James Maxton, Colonel Josiah Wedgwood, Commander C.H. Kenworthy, George Buchanan and Campbell Stephen speak at various venues in Belfast.

As a committee man, writer of letters to newspapers and delegate to the Irish National Teachers' Organisation, Hewitt's father also embodied what Morris called 'practical socialism', and there is no doubt that the socialist verse which Hewitt had published at the end of the 1920s is informed by a similarly 'practical' impulse. In poems such as 'The songs I sing' and 'To a modern Irish poet' (which rejects the Celtic Twilightery of the early Yeats), there is a reaction against the sumptuous self-indulgence of his literary-romantic verse, in favour of the 'flaming slogan's challenge fit for use'; in others, the guilt is that of the idealistic 'little bourgeois' or 'Mr Faintheart Middleclass' aware of their privileges but clinging to a vision of equality. Appropriately, many of these poems appeared (between 1928 and 1932) in publications such as the *Irishman*, an Irish Labour Party journal 'for all who work and think', and its successor, the *Watchword*, the official organ of the Irish Trades Union Congress and the Irish Labour Party; in the communist newspaper the *Workers' Voice* (pseudonymously); in *Vanguard*, the *Freethinker*, the *New Leader*, the *New Age* and *New Britain*. During the same period Hewitt's more romantic verse found its chief outlet in the Queen's University publication the *Northman*.

The fabric of Hewitt's early socialism had several other durable strands. *The Cry for Justice* (1915), an anthology of social-protest literature, edited by the American novelist Upton Sinclair, provided inspirational verse models other than Morris. Another exemplar was Vachel Lindsay, whose work Hewitt discovered in the late 1920s in the pages of Louis Untermeyer's anthology *Modern American Poetry* (1925); Lindsay was a poet he admired for 'a ready sympathy with any good or unpopular cause, a pity for the passage of the primitive before the grinding insolent machine, an invincible faith in the ultimate triumph of vision and justice', a poet for whom 'the oppressed Negro of the South, the tramp-harvester of Kansas, or the lousy vagrant in the hostel ward, were alike partakers in a transfigured world and inheritors of a glittering Jerusalem' (*Northman*, vol. 3, no. 5, 1932).

'I've come under a tremendous number of influences . . . They've been peppering me like hailstones' (*Quarto*, no. 7, 1980–1), Hewitt remarked and no account of the making of the poet would be complete without reference to Arthur Waley's *One Hundred and Seventy Chinese Poems* (1918), which Hewitt read at the end of the 1920s. Waley's translations suited a part of Hewitt's temperament 'because they were pallid and quiet and undemonstrative but clear and direct in their statement' (*Quarto*, no. 7, 1980–1). In 'A North Light', he comments that 'the quiet, undramatic tone, the even texture, the significant abstraction from experience of natural phenomena, the awareness of landscape, and man-in-landscape . . . were qualities which I admired and which I must half-consciously have attempted to reproduce'.

Hewitt records that the first book of poems he ever bought was *Songs from the Shipyards* (1924) by the shipyard poet Thomas Carnduff, whose verse appeared regularly in the *Belfast Evening Telegraph* (*Belfast Telegraph*, 24 November 1958). When Hewitt began writing verse in 1924, however, he knew little or nothing about other poets from the north of Ireland, living or dead. He had learned Lady Dufferin's 'The lament of the Irish emigrant' at Agnes Street National School and 'The burial of King Cormac' by Sir Samuel Ferguson at Methodist College, but was ignorant of the fact that these poets 'were any closer to [him] than Wordsworth or Tennyson' (*Belfast Telegraph*, 24 November 1958). Then, about 1925, he heard Richard Hayward (who had once played the cello in the Hewitts' house) broadcasting poems from his collection *Love in Ulster and Other Poems* (1922), and Hayward's work directed him to that of the best-known Ulster poet of the period – the linen manufacturer Richard Valentine Williams, who published under the pseudonym Richard Rowley. On the shelves of the North Belfast Branch Library, Oldpark Road, Hewitt discovered not only Rowley's *The City of Refuge and Other Poems* (1917), *City Songs and Other Poems* (1918), *Workers* (1923), *County Down Songs and Others* (1924) and *The Old Gods and Other Poems* (1925), but also Joseph Campbell's *The Mountainy Singer* (1909) and *The Rushlight* (1906). Campbell's 'The ninepenny fidil', 'The silence of unlaboured fields' and 'I will go with my father a-ploughing' have, Hewitt wrote in 1958, been 'mine for so long that if I live to be a havering old man I shall likely claim to have written them myself' (*Belfast Telegraph*, 24 November 1958). Campbell lived in the south of Ireland at this time, as did a number of other northern poets with whose work Hewitt was becoming acquainted: Moira O'Neill, best known for her *Songs of the Glens of Antrim* (1900), Elizabeth Shane, author of the popular 'Wee Hughie', Alice Milligan and George Russell (AE). A friend of Robert and Elinor Hewitt sat with Russell on a committee in Dublin and his name was familiar in the Hewitt household as a pioneer of the co-operative movement. Hewitt and his friends at Queen's University, however, knew him as a poet and editor, and Hewitt considered it a breakthrough when his poem 'Christmas Eve' was published by AE in the *Irish Statesman* in 1929. Another productive experience was hearing R.M. Henry review R.N.D. Wilson's *The Holy Wells of Orris* on radio in 1927; Wilson's collection 'brought by its imagery and rhythms, the whole Yeatsian school of poetry to our doorstep and somehow provided a point of contact with the richer literature of the other part of the nation' (*Belfast Telegraph*, 24 November 1958).

At this point in Hewitt's development he also became aware of Ulster novels such as Olga Fielden's *Island Story* (set in Islandmagee, where the Hewitt family had spent a number of holidays during the poet's boyhood), and of local prose writers such as Forrest Reid, Robert Lynd, St John Ervine and Shan F. Bullock, as well as the work of various Ulster dramatists. Hewitt's own prose, published in the pages of the *Northman*, was stimulated by wider, more eclectic reading: James Joyce, Liam O'Flaherty, Morris, Wilde's *De Profundis* (1905) and works such as *The Roadmender* (1902) by Michael Fairless and *Mr Weston's Good Wine* (1927) by T.F. Powys, which 'seemed to our clique one of the great works of the age' ('A North Light').

Much of Hewitt's early poetry is both international and specifically Irish in its concerns. There are unpublished poems in his notebooks which respond to the fall of Shanghai in March 1927, the Conservatives' Anti-Trade Union Bill of May 1927, the case of Sacco and Vanzetti, 'murdered on the twenty-third day of August, nineteen twenty-seven by the legal minions of American capital, after years' imprisonment', Lindberg's flight across the Atlantic, the outlawing of war by the League of Nations in September 1927, and the lynching of a Negro in Whitesburg, Kentucky, in November 1927. At the same time he and his university friends were caught up in what he calls 'a vague sense of romantic Irish Nationalism, with Oisin and Connolly, Maeve and Maud Gonne bright in the sky' ('No rootless colonist', *Aquarius*, no. 5, 1972). This strain is evident in poems such as 'Erin's sorrow ended: a hope', in which Kathleen Ni Houlihan emerges from her tomb and her 'sister of the north' approaches her 'Enlightened growing as each old hate dies,/Remembering now the kinship of her race'. In 'Mona' we find the nineteen-year-old Hewitt lamenting the deterioration of the Irish race into grasping huxterism, dreaming of 'ancient Manannan/of Oisin and of Finn', and vowing 'To serve the cause of my own land/with tongue or sword of steel'. There is a group of Irish ballads, dated 1925 – 'Heber and Heremon', 'The harper from the sea', 'Galbina's lover' and others – and when Hewitt looks at the *Mona Lisa* (in one of his earliest poems inspired by art), he is moved to think not only of Cleopatra, Helen, Venus and Haidee weeping for Juan, but also 'Our own Erin's Deirdre'. Closer to home and only marginally less starry-eyed are the dialect poem 'The Antrim man' and (interesting as a forerunner of 'Ulster names') one entitled 'An exercise in proper names', which moves from praise of English place names to:

But Ulster leads as ever, my own land,
  With magic spells o' faery woven webs –
Magheramorne, Carnlough and Cushendal [*sic*].

These poems both blend and contrast strikingly with Hewitt's early socialist verse, which is also, to an extent, sentimentally romantic, but charged with anger and compassion. The settings are mostly Belfast, as perceived or experienced by the young Hewitt in the late 1920s and early 1930s, the themes are those of international socialist writing. So in the poem 'To the memory of James Connolly', an admired Irish socialist and a martyr of the Easter rising of 1916 is commemorated in terms that elevate him to the status of a Christ-figure who died for universal brotherhood, and in 'The song of the shipyard men', Thomas Carnduff meets William Morris, as it were, at the gates of Harland and Wolff. Urban 'Ireland', specifically Belfast, may be said to be the subject of many of these poems, but more often than not the city and country remain unidentified, are located among the many places blighted by poverty and injustice, among the many battlefields where the class struggle takes place.

Hewitt's sense of Ireland and his own corner of it extends and deepens throughout the 1930s – though his preoccupation with the subject seems, in retrospect, tentative and exploratory. For example, two of the most notable treatments, 'Ireland' and the dramatic poem *The Bloody Brae*, did not appear in book form for a long time after they were written. Furthermore, the sequence 'Uladh', written in July, August and September 1934, and a revised, extended version of the same work, 'The Red Hand: a poemosaic', on which Hewitt probably worked in the mid- to late 1930s, were never published, though some sections appeared as separate poems; these sequences provide evidence of an early, not-quite-realised ambition to write a comprehensive 'Ulster' poem.

'Ireland', written in February 1932, published in the *Listener* in May 1932 and in the anthology *Poems of Tomorrow* (1935), is not included in Hewitt's first full-length collection, *No Rebel Word* (1948), but he places it prominently at the beginning of *Collected Poems 1932–1967* (1968). It contrasts interestingly with a number of key developments in Hewitt's later work. The speaker in the poem is a descendant of the Celts who bemoans the complacent insularity of the Irish and sees them as the bitter remnant of a wandering, conquering people, 'dying out/in terrible harshness in this lonely place', their patriotism is dismissed as ingrown and misguided, their self-congratulatory attachment to a rainy, sterile place as a refusal of more vital impulses, a 'forgotten longing for the sea/ that cries far out and calls us to partake/in his great tidal movements round the earth'. If we are to take the speaker as Hewitt (that is, if the poem is not to be read as a dramatic monologue spoken by a Celt), his identification with the Irish and his portrayal of them as primarily Celtic indicates that he has not yet begun to consider in any depth the complexities of ancestry and identity which inform some of his best and best-known poems, though the line 'We are not native here or anywhere', taken out of context, might serve as an epigraph for a central quest in Hewitt's *oeuvre.* Furthermore, the presentation of rural Ireland as a combination of rock, bleak beach and barren bog is one that Hewitt revises fruitfully before the end of the decade as he discovers Rathlin Island, the Glens of Antrim and other parts of the north. The images of defeated exile and hard transatlantic sidewalks and the image of the sea calling are poignantly complicated and complemented by some of Hewitt's 'Coventry' poems, particularly 'An Irishman in Coventry', with its concluding lines:

> Yet like Lir's children banished to the waters
> our hearts still listen for the landward bells.

In June 1935, Hewitt and his wife Roberta spent a week on Rathlin Island, his first extended experience of a part of Ulster that was to nourish his poetry for some forty years, and returned to Belfast at a time of violent sectarian riots. They had been married for over a year; both had helped found and were active in the Belfast Peace League at a period when the threat of war in Europe increased by the month; Hewitt had been working for five years as an assistant in the Belfast Museum and Art Gallery and had, during the summer of 1935, been to Bristol on a Museums Association course. He was in the mood to take stock and the immediate result was his poem 'The return', written in September 1935 but not published until 1944. Rathlin provides escape from a 'loud year vibrant with cross-trumpet calls' which, despite its successes and satisfactions, requires the kind of 'nurture' and 'succour' the island's serenity offers, though the return to Belfast, the 'city of our dreadful night', is a challenge to hope. Hewitt's trip, alone, to Bristol gives him sustaining images of human endurance and creativity – 'the touch of immortality/upon the things of death' – to set against the threat of violence and destruction. The poem moves with a tentative confidence towards a conviction that art and positive action matter, and concludes with the image of Hewitt and his wife travelling into the uncharted future:

> . . . at bidding of this uncouth compass,
> though no more than a needle stuck in a straw,
> and floating in a shaking bowl of water.

'The return', though somewhat inert as poetry, is the precursor of poems such as 'The ruins answer', *Conacre*, *Freehold*, 'The colony',

'Variations on a theme' and 'Bifocal in Gaza', in which Hewitt the lyricist rises to a more sustained consideration of his stance and attitudes at particular points in his life. Already present, too, is the impulse (strong also in *Freehold* and a number of longer unpublished poems) to invoke admired friends and exemplars, living and dead.

Hewitt's work as an art assistant in the Belfast Museum and Art Gallery played a significant part in broadening what he describes as his 'local imaginative mythology' ('No rootless colonist'). His duties included 'looking after portraits and relics of notable men of Planter stock', such as the American presidents of Ulster descent. It was, however, the 'sad, long-jawed painting of James Hope and the faded daguerrotype of Mary Ann McCracken' which 'proved themselves icons of greater charismatic power' ('No rootless colonist') and kindled in Hewitt an abiding enthusiasm for the radical Presbyterianism of the late eighteenth century. One consequence of this engagement with the local historical past was the writing of *The Bloody Brae: A Dramatic Poem* (finished in 1936, broadcast in 1954 and published in *Threshold* magazine in 1957), Hewitt's most considered treatment up to that point of the troubled history of Planter and Gael in the north of Ireland. The subject is a 'legendary and largely fictitious' massacre of Catholics by Cromwellian soldiery at the Gobbins, Islandmagee, County Antrim, in January 1642. John Hill, an aged soldier racked by guilt about the murder of a young woman and her child, is forgiven by her ghost but also taxed with having indulged his guilt rather than striven to promote tolerance in others. The poem is a morality on the nature of responsibility and the necessity to escape from the destructive cycles of atrocity and revenge. John Hill (the initials are perhaps significant), a third-generation Planter, expresses in terms that anticipate 'The colony' and 'Once alien here' the conviction that his people have established a claim to live side by side with the native Magees:

> This is my country; my grandfather came here
> and raised his walls and fenced the tangled waste
> and gave his years and strength into the earth.
> My father also. Now their white bones lime
> the tillage and the pasture. Ebb and flow
> have made us one with this.

He is also unhappily aware, however, that 'whenever the Irish meet with the Planters' breed/there's always a sword between and black memories for both'. Hill does have a vision of how 'mercy' and 'kindness' might have woven the threads of the different traditions into a glittering, colourful web and *The Bloody Brae* constantly celebrates such redeeming dreams and impulses while registering the protagonists' lack of illusions. Bridget Magee, Hill's victim, acknowledges how strongly persistent and harshly disabling is the desire for revenge and though she forgives Hill she speaks with moving awareness of the irretrievable consequences of his action:

> . . . I am dead
> who might have mothered crowding generations:
> for good or ill you altered the shape of things.

In addition, the drama of remorse and forgiveness has a certain fragility beside the offhand ruthlessness and intransigence of the second soldier, Malcolm Scott.

A number of other poems with local subjects and settings originated during the period 1932–9. Some, such as 'Mary Hagan, Islandmagee, 1919' (1932), 'An Island folk tale' (1935), 'MacDonnell's question' (1936), 'Ulster names' (1936) and 'The Curfew Tower' (1938), remained in Hewitt's notebooks for many years; others, such as 'The hired lad's farewell' (1932), 'Mourne Mountains' (1937) and 'Load' (1937), appeared in magazines shortly after they were written. Throughout the period, however, the discernible poetic influences are non-Irish and Hewitt's breadth of reading is constantly reflected in his work. The unpublished sequence 'Uladh', for example, invokes Hugh MacDiarmid in its opening section; *The Bloody Brae* owes much to the historical verse plays of Gordon Bottomley, particularly *Towie Castle* and *Marsaili's Weeping*, in which guilt, the exorcising of a violent historical heritage, and the need for forgiveness are key themes; Edward Thomas presides over 'The neglected lane', Robert Frost over 'The hired lad's farewell', Ezra Pound over 'Mauberley's son: a summary', T.S. Eliot over 'Tiphead' and W.H. Auden over 'Prelude to an ode for Barnum'. Hewitt recalls discovering the work of the Auden generation in Michael Roberts's anthology *New Signatures* (1932) and expresses a particular enthusiasm for C. Day Lewis's collection *The Magnetic Mountain* (1933) (*Quarto*, no. 7, 1980–1). There is also evidence in Hewitt's notebooks of a brief flirtation with surrealist verse.

Many of the preoccupations detailed here – and, indeed, their immediate background – may be seen as paving the way for the next notable phase in Hewitt's development, his interest in the concept of regionalism. Historical circumstances played a significant role. Hewitt's travels had already taken him to Belgium, London, Paris, Manchester, Liverpool, Bristol and Edinburgh and to socialist summer schools at Welwyn Garden City and Langham, but with the outbreak of war in 1939 travel abroad was heavily restricted and even a trip to the Republic of Ireland required a special permit: 'I felt very enclosed and segregated, and then my thinking turned inwards' (*Quarto*, no. 7, 1980–1), Hewitt comments and he goes on to summarise his regionalist fervour as 'a reaction to the isolationism of the war years'. The Hewitts began to discover the Glens of Antrim, where they took holidays at all seasons from 1940, finally, in May 1946, renting a cottage outside Cushendall, County Antrim, which they were to retain until 1965. In Belfast Hewitt took employment (for which he waived all fees) with the Department of Extra-Mural Studies at Queen's University, travelling to army camps throughout Antrim, Down and Armagh to lecture on art and Marxism (this after the entry of the USSR into the war on the side of the Allies), and visiting Derry, for the first time, to select exhibits for a display of arts and crafts by civil defence personnel. He also visited Kilmore in County Armagh, where his Planter ancestry had first settled, and had two brief holidays with Roberta in County Donegal, where they explored The Rosses and took a boat trip to Aranmore.

Hewitt's deepening sense of the topography and landscape of Ulster made him doubly receptive to the ideas he found in Lewis Mumford's books *The Culture of Cities* (1938) (which Hewitt read for the first time in 1942) and *A Faith for Living* (1940). Prompted by Mumford's work, he sought out earlier literature with a regionalist slant, such as Frédéric Mistral's *Memoires* (translated 1907), the works of Frédéric Le Play, with his emphasis on 'place', 'work' and 'folk' as the basic unities of the region, and the writings of Patrick Geddes, particularly the volume *Cities in Evolution* (1915). In retrospect Hewitt identified an element of socialist utopianism in his regionalist philosophy, though it lay 'nearer perhaps the frontier of possibility than many of the more romantic and highly coloured concepts with which that indispensable dream-scape is studded' ('A North Light'), and he expresses a particular debt of gratitude to Victor Branford's *Science and Sanity* (1923), which 'by its emphatic presentation of the necessary constellation of Hearth, Workshop, Marketplace, Cloister as the *foci* for the Good City, has with the compulsions of its grand simplifications, kept me from straying too far from social realities when I air my dreams in public' ('A North Light').

The dreams and the realities had many a public airing. Evangelist, propagandist and hard-headed realist, Hewitt set about spreading the gospel of regionalism in articles, reviews, broadcasts, lectures and letters to the press. Lewis Mumford wrote of 'a dynamic emotional urge, springing out of a sense of frustration on one hand and a renewed vision of life on the other', and Hewitt embraced the concept on every level – intellectual, emotional, imaginative and practical. In his essay 'Regionalism: the last chance', he summarises its essential purpose and appeal:

> Regionalism is based upon the conviction that, as man is a social being, he must, now that the nation has become an enormously complicated organisation, find some smaller unit to which to give his loyalty. This unit, since the day of the clan is over and that of the large family is passing, must be grounded on something more than kinship. Between these limits lies the region; an area which possesses geographical and economic coherence, which has had some sort of traditional and historical identity and which still, in some measure, demonstrates cultural and linguistic individuality.

A further distillation of these ideas occurs in the much later essay, 'No rootless colonist' (1972):

> Since the world about us is so vast and complex, strangled by bureaucratic centralisation – 'apoplexy at the centre, paralysis at the extremities' – we must seek for some grouping smaller than the nation, larger than the family, with which we could effectively identify, with which we could come to terms of sympathetic comprehension, within which our faculties and human potentialities could find due nurture and proper fulfilment. In a word, the region, an area of a size and significance that we could hold in our hearts.

Regionalism as propounded by Mumford and others offered attractive opportunities for the local expression of universal impulses in, for example, politics and the arts. It was part of Hewitt's vision that regional loyalties might transcend sectarian division in Northern Ireland and that the Protestant majority in the north would come to realise themselves 'for the first time, not Britain's pensioners or stranded Englishmen and Scots, being instead a group living long enough in Ireland to have the air in their blood, the landscape in their bones, and the history in their hearts, and so, a special kind of Irish themselves, they could with grace make the transition to federal unity' (draft of a letter to John Montague, spring 1964), with the Republic of Ireland, as well as with the other main regions of the British Isles.

Inevitably, also, Hewitt perceived regionalism as a potentially galvanising force in the arts and the arts as a natural embodiment of the regional ideal. Aware of literary developments in Scotland and Wales, he sought, in his essay 'The bitter gourd: some problems of the Ulster writer' to analyse 'the problems and cleavages for which we can find no counterpart elsewhere in the British archipelago', lamenting the difficulty of establishing a vital literary tradition in 'an extroverted, stubborn, inarticulate society with well-defined material values and, for the most part, a rigid creed'. He asserts that the Ulster writer 'must be a rooted man, must carry the native tang of his idiom like the native dust on his sleeve: otherwise he is an airy internationalist, thistledown, a twig in a stream'. In 'The bitter gourd' Hewitt is at pains to give his regionalism a valid, international context, by no means 'airy', to look outwards as well as inwards, finding arguments and parallels in, for example, the relationship between Canada and the United States of America, the position within Canada of French Quebec, the lives of Swinburne, Tolstoy, Yeats, Joyce, Grant Wood, William Sidney Mount, Dvořák and Hugh MacDiarmid, and quoting Robert Frost's poem 'The gift outright', about the colonial dilemmas of New England, as a paradigm of the Ulster poet's dilemma. He is also adamant that the local writer must have 'ancestors not just of the blood but of the emotions', with the same 'quality and slant of mind'. Many of Hewitt's prose writings and broadcasts throughout the 1940s and early 1950s and some of his poems from the same period (the 'Roll call' section of *Freehold*, for example) are bent on discovering and identifying a whole host of such ancestors, not only writers and artists, but also naturalists, scientists, foreign diplomats, and the Presbyterian radicals of the 1798 period. He both extends his personal myth and provides a comprehensive basis for regional pride.

So, for example, he salutes the devotion of the United Irishman weaver James Hope 'to the cause of Irish working-class freedom' (*Northern Star*, January 1944), his grasp of 'economic truth' and recognition that 'the national struggle was emphatically a class struggle'; he celebrates the writer Francis Davis as a 'voice consistently for tolerance and the values of the free spirit' (Northern Ireland Home Service broadcast, 4 February 1948), and the educationist Vere Foster, who 'spent himself and his fortune . . . waging a long personal war against Poverty and Ignorance' (Northern Ireland Home Service broadcast, 2 December 1949); he praises the deist John Toland for his 'lifelong battle against intolerance and superstition'; he cites the example of young Frederick Richard Chichester, Earl of Belfast, who delivered a series of lectures on poetry to raise funds for the Mechanics' Institute and wrote songs to be sold in aid of famine relief, as a man 'whose values were those of the imagination and the creative spirit, an urgent person of immediate goodwill' (Northern Ireland Home Service broadcast, 13 January 1950).

Hewitt's energies as a cultural activist found many other outlets during the 1940s. In addition to being a founder member of the Committee for the Encouragement of Music and the Arts (CEMA), an organisation in which he served as a committee man for some fourteen years, he was an associate editor of the literary magazine *Lagan*, which had a strongly regional flavour, a leading light in the Belfast branch of PEN and a lecturer with the Workers' Educational Association. During the war years the Hewitts' flat in Mountcharles in Belfast was a meeting place for literary servicemen stationed in and around the city, and towards the end of the decade we find Hewitt not only researching Ulster poetry of the period 1800–70 at Queen's University, but contributing a series of articles on poetry and folk tradition (as well as a poem, 'The lint pulling', written specially for the series) to the *Ulster Young Farmer*, giving careful criticism to readers who submitted their own work and invoking the Ulster 'weavers, bleachers, craftsmen, small farmers, sometimes even tramps of the roads, who took to poetry as naturally as thrushes to singing' (*Ulster Young Farmer*, May 1948). It was, of course, also during this decade that Hewitt published his first pamphlets, *Conacre* (1943) and *Compass: Two Poems* (1944), privately published, and his first full collection of poems, *No Rebel Word* (1948), as well as contributing the long poem *Freehold* to *Lagan* (1946).

Hewitt regarded the poems *Conacre*, *Freehold* and the later 'Homestead' (1949) as constituting a trilogy. Already, in *The Bloody Brae* (1936),

'Once alien here' (March 1942) and 'The Glens' (September 1942), he had begun to negotiate the crosscurrents in which the liberal Ulsterman of Planter stock finds himself caught. The speaker in these poems is sufficiently rooted in the province to feel 'native' in his 'thought' and insists that his ancestry have, by constructive hard work, established certain claims. He is aware also of the dispossessed natives' 'savage history of wrong' and tentatively desires to make amends, while conscious that the conciliatory impulse may not be entirely adequate in the circumstances. He is sensitive to the older indigenous tradition, though suspicious of its predominant Catholicism, and yearns to achieve an individuality that partakes of both traditions and expresses both, yet he encounters at every turn the 'many fences' between colonist and native.

This search for equilibrium and an abiding place – not only in a divided province but also in a world at war – is present, too, as the titles suggest, in the trilogy *Conacre*, *Freehold* and 'Homestead', though it is more broadly based in these poems. The term 'conacre' describes 'the letting by a tenant for a season, of small portions of land ready ploughed and prepared for a crop' (OED) and the speaker in the poem of that name articulates a profound sense of dislocation; he is out of touch with the skills of his rural ancestry but not at home in the city where he lives, finding fulfilment there only in books and random encounters. The couplets move with a restless, unsettled energy as the city dweller, who is a countryman at heart yet acknowledges his debt to the city and perhaps regrets that it is not a source of inspiration, conducts an obsessive dialogue with himself. The city leaves his 'quiet depths unmeasured still', whereas the countryside, particularly the Glens of Antrim, has yielded moments of almost mystical intensity. The destruction of the city would cause Hewitt little grief, he tells us, for all his debt to it, 'For what was good [there] can be better still', and he posits an unpolluted, idyllic rurality. Again we are drawn into the poem's essential dynamic, its play of passionate assertion and romantic vision against the cautious procedures of argument, reflection ('you may argue', 'if scholars' words be trusted', 'one may urge') and rigorous self-assessment. Hewitt gives due weight to the fact that man has left a constructive, benevolent mark on the landscape too, and attacks his own timidity, complacency and malice, his dependence on 'the comfortable pace/of safe tradition'. Once more the mood shifts; he checks his outburst of 'coarse introspection' and ponders on how a meditation that began in a spirit of nothing more than 'gentle sentiment' (a description the reader is likely to find surprising) and self-exploration has become a poem about 'human history and its wry concerns'. He perceives what the shifts and balancings of his own meditation have enacted, 'that definition means comparison/and that we find our lightest words demand/a cosmos weighed within a human hand', and that thought and action are, finally, a 'groping for the infinite'. Again the meditation changes gear: there is a retreat from the madness or cynicism to which such extreme introspection might lead and a movement towards resignation and serenity; it is the orderly withdrawal of one who is neither 'saint nor fool', the 'happy man who seldom sees/the emptiness behind the images/that wake [his] heart to wonder'. In this section of the poem the note of trust and the concepts of love, home, happiness are dogged by images of emptiness, bloody ghosts, madness, lost origins; yet they persist into the lines:

> This is my home and country. Later on
> perhaps I'll find this nation is my own;
> but here and now it is enough to love
> this faulted ledge, this map of cloud above.

Though the theme of dislocation pervades the poem, the issue raised here is introduced with unconvincing abruptness and remains undeveloped. The reference to 'this mad island crammed with bloody ghosts' and the 'forgotten coasts/our fathers steered from' cannot quite dispel the impression of some half a dozen lines strayed from a related but different poem.

The remainder of *Conacre* follows the same pattern as the earlier sections but seems curiously diffuse. Hewitt returns to the nourishing marvels of landscape and season with the impulse of one who would make joy his theme, were it not for the 'troubled heart'. He goes on to insist that, far from being 'drunk on pastoral', he has an unsentimental sense of the squalor and meanness of country life; but balances this 'too savage' view with recollections of the 'friendly doors and hearths of Donegal' and, among others, the man

> who calls the hare and badger both his friends,
> yet turns no back on progress, dreaming still
> of the broad tractors sweeping up the hill,
> and the great binder worked by equal men,
> lifting its swathes of fat collective grain.

This partly resolves the tension earlier in the poem between the 'mad machines' and a pre-industrial countryside and prepares for the dying fall with which the poem ends, its mood one of hope and contentment, the itch of contradiction no longer troublesome, passion and rage 'hushed in perspectives of the Golden Age'.

The title of Hewitt's sequel to *Conacre*, *Freehold*, suggests a more confident sense of absolute inheritance and the poem is, on one level, his most substantial attempt to define his stance and values. It had its beginnings in 1939 and accumulated throughout the early 1940s: a first version of section three, 'Townland of peace', appeared in *The Bell* (1944) and the entire poem, thoroughly revised, in *Lagan* (1946). The theme of inheritance is prefigured in the opening section. The death of Hewitt's father prompts both a 'sapflow' of grief and a meditative *gravitas* as the poet approaches his thirty-eighth birthday. He is aware of a closer bond with Roberta, feels that he has learned patience, kindness and tolerance and that his 'ambitious mind [is] content with less'. Yet this serenity is by no means static, it is complemented by a deepening sense of purpose, the search (central also to 'The return' and *Conacre*) for growth and meaning and a richly textured existence among the vagaries of chance and mortality. There are further echoes of 'The return' and *Conacre* as the Hewitts return to the city and its 'mad engines' after a visit to the Glens of Antrim and Hewitt celebrates the natural world that has given them delight and inspiration. He is plagued, however, by a lonely sense of the distances between them and all country dwellers, mindful of the 'thorny hedge of thought and speech' and of their peripheral status as holidaymakers in a place where the only companionship they can expect is from the 'wild things'. The focal point of the opening section ('Feathers on turf') is a description of how the Hewitts sheltered from a storm in the ruins of Orra Lodge; the gutted house, with its vestiges of former habitation, affects the poet both as a symbol of a war-torn world and a place where a 'war-purged passion stirs'; he identifies it with his own 'grief-gutted heart', experiences a moment of liberation from time and place, perceives that moment as a 'watershed/between the man I now am and the lad/I grew from', and is prompted to a retrospective exploration which is not simply a stock-taking but will be a basis for the next stage of his journey. Though sensitive to the potentially reductive nature of such an enterprise, he has a desire 'to set in ordered rhythmic line/the values I discover now are mine'.

The second section of *Freehold* ('The lonely heart') begins with a tribute to Hewitt's father – 'the greatest man of all the men I love' – a most moving love poem to one whose personality and values form the basis of the poet's freehold-inheritance. Robert Telford Hewitt is depicted as an enlightened city schoolmaster, a generous, dignified socialist who translated his belief in human brotherhood into modest, effective action. The portrait is animated by vividly affectionate recollections of jokes, gestures, habits, and by Hewitt's sense that his father, though 'not alone', was, for all his devotion to brotherhood and the respect of hundreds, essentially lonely at heart. Hewitt sees himself as rasher, less tolerant than his father, but learning something of the older man's wisdom. His father's principal legacy is an enabling optimism:

> And when my faith in man is ebbing low,
> I summon heart again at thought of him.

The portrait ends on a more ambiguous note in which legacy and loss mingle. Hewitt constantly has the impulse to share 'the little victories/for life and art and human decencies' with his father, but his agnosticism will not allow him to believe with conviction that the dead man exists anywhere and he must resign himself to the absence of the 'translucent mind' that radically transformed such victories.

Hewitt then acknowledges a second key element in his heritage, the sense of ancestry he acquired from his paternal grandfather John, who, he tells us, 'made me know my race':

a stubborn Irishry that would recall
the famine's curse, the farm that was too small,
yet with a faith protestant that denied
the hope of mercy to the papist side,
tongue-loose with stories of the Ninety-Eight,
yet proud the British Empire is so great.

Having touched on these paradoxes and complexities of the Planter tradition in Ulster, Hewitt goes on to make, as it were, a kind of confession. He recalls a visit to a Catholic church 'to see the sculpture and admire the glass' and his sense on the occasion that he might have lit a candle there in an extra-denominational spirit, a 'single flame to sway with all the other/small earnest flames against the crowding gloom/ which seemed that year descending on our time'. 'Not this [his] father's faith', however; the sectarian element in his inheritance triumphs and he leaves the church as he had come, 'a protestant,/and all unconscious of my yawning want'. He now regrets the possibilities refused and claims to have achieved greater tolerance for the symbols humanity finds to 'succour grief'. The section culminates in an embracing of the nonsectarian brotherhood espoused by the poet's father and in marvellous, encompassing images of the human situation and our 'continuity/with being's seamless garment':

O windblown grass upon the mounded dead,
O seed in crevice of the frost-split rock,
the power that fixed your root shall take us back,
though endlessly through aeons we are thrust
as luminous or unreflecting dust.

Section three, 'Townland of peace', opens with a visit to Kilmore, County Armagh, one of the homes of Hewitt's Planter forefathers. The journey is partly a search for serenity in time of war ('I stepped clean out of Europe into peace'), partly a quest to satisfy 'some need of roots'. What he finds is a world of 'natural diligence' that has forgotten its 'old turbulence', despite the evidence of a violent history that is never far from the surface. There is a warm imaginative recovery of his grandfather John's boyhood around Kilmore, a mode of existence the warriven world has lost, though Hewitt concedes that humanity may adjust to 'new societies of earth and steel'. One of the most haunting images in Hewitt's prose emerged from this journey; in his autobiographical essay 'Planter's Gothic' he writes:

> When I discovered, not long ago, that the old Planter's Gothic tower of Kilmore Church still encloses the stump of a round tower and that it was built on the site of a Culdee holy place, I felt a step nearer to that synthesis [of the Scots, English and Irish elements in his make-up]. It is the best symbol I have yet found for the strange textures of my response to this island of which I am a native. I may appear Planter's Gothic, but there is a round tower somewhere inside, and needled through every sentence I utter.

County Armagh has other attractions for the poet: his friends the poet W.R. Rodgers and the painter John Luke live there – Rodgers as Presbyterian minister at Loughgall, Luke and his mother at Knappagh, as refugees from Belfast – and his encounters with them give the journey the additional, unquantifiable 'warm logic of a testament/by which since then my better moments move,/assured of certainties I need not prove'. The journey inspires Hewitt to one of the most stirring realisations in his verse of his regionalist convictions (indeed, the concluding section of 'Townland of peace' was published as a separate poem with the title 'Regionalist'). He sings the region's claims 'against the anthill and the beehive states', stakes his personal claim to Ulster as his own 'corner of the universe', to 'crooked roads and accidental flowers' to 'food unpoisoned, unpolluted air':

> But these small rights require a smaller stage
> than the vast forum of the nations' rage,
> for they imply a well-compacted space
> where every voice declares its native place,
> townland, townquarter, county at the most,
> the local word not ignorantly lost
> in the smooth jargon, bland and half alive,
> which wears no clinging burr upon its sleeve
> to tell the ground it grew from, and to prove
> there is for sure a plot of earth we love.

In the confident surge of its concluding thirty-odd lines, 'Townland of peace' represents a compelling synthesis of the lyrical and didactic impulses in Hewitt's verse.

The section of *Freehold* which follows, 'The glittering sod', is in some ways the least immediately personal in the poem and closest in spirit to Hewitt's propagandist prose writings on regionalism. He speaks here more as the proud representative of a vital tradition than on his own behalf. For much of the section 'we' replaces 'I' as the dominant pronoun and there is a sense of Hewitt marshalling forces for a concerted drive towards regional identity. Again there is an insistence on the pioneering work of the Planters, again Hewitt invokes the qualities and values of those he admires. The shared experiences and folk traditions of Ulster are seen as more enduring than the annals of bloodshed between Planter and Gael. The shaping influence of place as a local strength and as a basis for growth is perceived as extending beyond the province, a feature of Ulster emigrants, 'from Alexander Irvine back to Columcille' (two of the brightest stars in Hewitt's personal galaxy). The reference to emigrants is one of a number of ways in which Hewitt again places the region in a wider context. Ulster was settled by foreigners and must, Hewitt argues, continue to be receptive to outside influences. The whole section, with its elements of blueprint and manifesto, is a demonstration of the poet's Planter spirit (and of the practical spirit of his father) in action; he urgently enjoins that there is much to learn about the region, much to do to promote its progress, and posits an enlightened work ethic which includes town and country, economics and the arts and crafts. The section rises to a strongly utopian, universal vision of 'an ordered state,/rock-based and fertile', which is 'scaled to offer, for individual growth,/the peace of age, the ecstasies of youth', and ends with Hewitt confirming his roots. There is an emotional homecoming, previously resisted or sidetracked, now welcomed with a transforming sense of inevitability.

'Roll call', originally the final part of *Freehold* but omitted from the version in *Freehold and Other Poems* (1986), arises naturally out of the preceding sections but is somewhat programmatic, a kind of holdall into which Hewitt crams a variety of kindred spirits. In a fifteen-line section of 'The glittering sod', excised from the version published in book form, Hewitt had already named the naturalist John Templeton, the deist John Toland and the United Irishman James Hope as luminaries in the Ulster pantheon; in 'Roll call' he conscripts a number of his contemporaries such as Rodgers, Luke, the artist Colin Middleton, the human geographer and folklorist Estyn Evans, all of whom he regarded as helping to give Ulster a literary, artistic and folk identity, builders of a house the next generation would not find 'cold and unfriendly and anonymous'.

Conacre and *Freehold* are generally recognised as high points in Hewitt's work; 'Homestead' (1949), the final poem of the trilogy, has been comparatively invisible. It begins, as 'Roll call' ends, with an image of a house. The speaker in the poem, a shadowy figure less perceptibly 'Hewittish' than the speakers in *Conacre* and *Freehold*, is preparing to build an austere, practical shelter that is both a 'dwelling, and . . . an outcrop, part of the place'. It will be a haven for the speaker and those close to him – not an ark, because the Ark became an abandoned wreck, but a structure to survive storm and darkness in the way rocks survive an ice age. The tone is of one who has been preparing to build for a long time and the 'homestead' he contemplates is both a durable physical structure and a symbolic home for the spirit. He thinks, for example, of Easter, with its Christian and seasonal associations of resurrection and renewal, as a time that might stimulate him and endow him with the skill to begin, and elects Oisin, both poet and man of action, a resurrected embodiment of the power of pagan myth, as his symbol. Reading a translation from the Old Irish of a dispute between the practical, pragmatic farmer Dan Lavery and the poet Gillwirra MacCartan, a confrontation between 'humble regard for the disciplines of sap and frost' and 'the proud step in tradition of handling words', he finds the tension in his own 'cloven nature' brought sharply into focus. In the second section of the poem a multitude of voices suggest alternative courses of action. The practical advise renting 'a corner/in some durable place' as a sensible option to building a house that may not be finished before the storm and will require constant repairs; others seem to recommend the attractions of different civilisations, from the ancient Greek to the modern American; yet others encourage a defeatist inaction or promote a nebulous, ornamental existence that has the insubstantiality of a mirage. The speaker rejects these and is all the more determined to achieve an unvarnished simplicity; his house will combine hospitality with the spirituality and creativity of the monastic tradition and an Emersonian self-sufficiency; it will be a joyful place for the young, and 'Oisin MacCartan' and Dan Lavery (vision and action, imagination and practicality, the opposing and complementary elements present in Hewitt's work from the start) will be equally at home there:

> The stonework will be simple, honest and sturdy,
> not showy, not even neat, but built to last.
> I go today to the quarry to tryst the stones.

'Homestead' is more intellectual, less directly emotional in its procedures than *Conacre* and *Freehold*; it pursues a quest for synthesis and stability that is both local and universal into the realm of myths and symbols that define some of our deepest tensions and longings. Hewitt abandons the rhyming couplets of the earlier poems for a more flexible blank verse in which the weight of image and symbol ballasts and is lightened by a meditatively colloquial note – a mode entirely appropriate to the content and an integral dimension of it.

As Hewitt himself conceded in later years, his region was not so much Ulster as the north-east corner of it along with Belfast and parts of County Armagh. The Hewitts never returned to Rathlin Island but their association with the Glens of Antrim from 1940 onwards was crucial to the poet's developing awareness of the land, the folk and their idiom. About seventy of his published poems, most notably those collected in *The Day of the Corncrake: Poems of the Nine Glens* (1969, revised edition 1984), are recognisably about his experience of north-east Antrim. In his own view, this association 'had so deep a significance on thought and feeling and particularly on my verse, that without it I should have been another kind of person, another kind of poet' ('A North Light'). Again, in a draft foreword, dated 1970, intended for a history of the Cushendall area by Hugh Alexander Boyd (not published), Hewitt writes:

> No other area in my native province has been so nourishing to my senses, my imagination and my heart; not even the hill-hooped Belfast where I was born or the apple orchards of Armagh where my people first settled in this island.
>
> Thirty years and more have permitted me to know and make verse of this landscape and its folk in every season. From the twisted mouth of the Dall river inland by Ballyemon, past Lurigedan and Tievebulliagh, to Barard and Trostan, to the mist beyond, from the falling waters of Drumnasole to the Mass Rock in the Craigagh Woods, I can fairly claim familiarity with hill and house and wallstead, with cairn and boulder.

On one level, the budding nature poet among whose earliest writings were descriptions of the sky as seen from his window in Cliftonpark Avenue and who had spent the first thirty or so years of his life in the semi-rural environs of the Crumlin Road, Cliftonville Road and Cavehill Road areas of north Belfast, now blossomed.

There were productive influences other than landscape and people. In the late 1920s and early 1930s, Hewitt, then involved in the secularist movement, was reading not only periodicals such as the *Freethinker* and the publications of the Rationalist Press Association, but a wide range of books on comparative religion, popular archaeology, folklore and mythology, including Sir James Frazer's *The Golden Bough*. 'Thereafter,' Hewitt wrote, 'I saw the Christian story in its proper context among the Fertility Myths of the fertile crescent' (ms. among Hewitt's papers). With folklore he discovered himself 'oddly at home, perhaps because Jung had told us what we had in mind' and found it 'easier to believe in Finn MacCool than in Goliath'. So a range of 'images, ideas, propositions which lay beyond or outside proof, or to which [he] could not fairly give intellectual assent, were thrust back over the threshold where imaginative acceptance begins' to emerge, of course, in numerous poems, most specifically in 'Those swans remember'. 'Years later,' he continues, 'my experience of the Glensfolk and the Glens provided the idiom and the setting which my reading had been unable to supply, and when Michael J. Murphy [the folklorist] became my friend . . . the whole web of myths, charms, beliefs, practices gave a greater depth and a richer grain to my appreciation and understanding of my people and my country and myself.' Another significant catalyst was William Wordsworth. Around 1940 Hewitt acquired a pocket edition of *The Prelude*, which, he acknowledged, 'made it possible for [him] to live in and to realise that landscape, those people, with an intensity [he] had never known before' (Radio Éireann broadcast, 18 February 1975). It was during this period also that Hewitt read Estyn Evans's study *Irish Heritage: The Landscape, the People and their Work* (1942) and praised Evans for 'seeing the whole subject in the light of his wide knowledge of other societies' (review, *The Bell*, August 1942), singling out his 'fresh dialectical way of showing man shaped by and as shaping his physical environment'.

In many of the Glens poems Hewitt is content to be observer and listener, a fascinated outsider with a folklorist's urge to preserve local stories, history and dialect, as well as a painterly impulse to portray the countryside and its inhabitants; in others we find him lending a hand in the hayfield and the potato field; but it is to the distance between himself and the people of the Glens that he obsessively returns. In 'Sunset over Glenaan', for example, he finds among the descendants of the defeated Irish and Scots Gaels 'a peace and speech' not to be found among his own 'inland Planter folk', but goes on to speculate that this may represent the working out of some ancestral Planter guilt, or embody the way 'the unchristened heart of man/still hankers for the little friendly clan/that lives as native as the lark or hare'.

In some poems he depicts the Glens as complementing the city rather than as a pastoral alternative to it; the 'honey of the city hive' sustains his brain and body, but he looks to the country for 'nurture of the heart' and in 'Gathering praties' wonders whether there is 'some meander of [his] country blood' which in the course of the work 'runs gracious, happy to be used'.

In poems such as 'The Glens', 'May altar', 'When the bell rings in the steeple . . .' and 'The priest goes through the motions of the play . . .', Hewitt is most sharply conscious of the barrier of religion. The Catholic girls flocking to Confirmation ('May altar') are being received into a 'faith and haven' he salutes but sheers away from; his yearning is for 'the pagan thorn/that none dare break a spray from'. In the original version of 'The Glens' he professes to fear Catholicism 'as we have always feared/the lifted hand between the mind and truth', though for *The Selected John Hewitt* (1981) he substituted 'the lifted hand against unfettered thought', on the grounds that the original was 'arrogant' and 'gave offence to kindly and gentle Catholics' (*Quarto*, no. 7, 1980–1). In 'The hill-farm' he stands outside a farmhouse, eavesdropping on a recital of the rosary, a form of devotion he thinks of as being 'easy as breathing, natural/as birds that fly, as leaves that fall' but alien to his 'breed and mind'; the poem ends with Hewitt's sense that he 'still stood/far from that faith-based certitude,/here in the vast enclosing night,/outside its little ring of light', where the intimations of defiant stance in the verb 'stood' are muted by the lonely vulnerability and feeling of exclusion in the lines that follow. The Hewitt who 'hankers for the pagan thorn' or stands 'under the unchristened tree' is more confidently at home in the vicinity of Oisin's grave; in 'Rite, Lubitavish, Glenaan' he proclaims himself 'of the Irishry/by nurture and by birth', in touch with the pre-Christian past, and in 'Ossian's grave, Lubitavish, County Antrim' he professes to accept the legend or the historical theory about the grave's provenance, as head or heart dictates, finding, however, that on this occasion Oisin, the enduring myth and symbol, has the stronger appeal.

The same people who are perceived at times as 'faith-constricted' ('When the bell rings in the steeple . . .') are, at others, admired for their sturdy independence (in, for instance, 'The Volunteer' ['For his long working life an engineer . . .'] and 'For any women who pass this house'). In 'Fame' and 'The Ballad' ('I named a ballad round a sparking fire . . .') Hewitt acknowledges the power and validity of folk poetry as a kind of collective memory, communicating in a way his own cannot; his related reverence for local idiom and dialect is tactfully and unpatronisingly expressed in 'On the use of dialect words', though his well-intentioned attempts to incorporate such words in his own poetry – as in 'The fairy thresher' – have an uncomfortably self-conscious quality.

The best of the Glens poems are faithful to their locale and discover what is universal in it. Best of all, perhaps, is the poignant 'O country people', in which Hewitt uses direct, tentative address to enact the kind of communication he forlornly recognises is not possible. The poem is permeated by profound respect for what is most vital in folk culture and an elegiac realisation that the poet cannot hope to become 'even a phrase or a story which will come/pat to the tongue, part of the tapestry/of apt response, at the appropriate time'. The language itself (pat – part – tapestry – apt – appropriate) is an act of homage to intricacies the poet sees as ultimately beyond him. Nevertheless, it is the hill-farmer of the Glens, 'a master of the tasks his years allow', who stands as one of the defining and sustaining symbols in Hewitt's work, surviving disasters, taking risks, producing with a minimum of fuss, as the poet would hope to, 'good sustenance for other hearts than his' ('Ars poetica').

In his essay 'No rootless colonist' Hewitt records how, at the end of 1949 (actually, during the first week of January 1950) he found himself working in the cottage at Cushendall 'on three new poems . . . switching, as the spirit seized [him], from one to the other and back again'. This 'strange gust of verse-making' produced 'O country people' and the obscure but compelling 'Man fish and bird', in which he delves into the personal and ancestral subconscious and explores the potential limitations of perception and creativity, using the seven-day framework of the Genesis myth. By the end of the week he had also written what he describes in the same article as 'the definitive statement of my realisation that I am an Ulsterman' – the dramatic monologue 'The colony'.

The speaker in the poem is a colonist who remembers the violence and injustice of the original colonisation, wishes to make what amends he can to the dispossessed natives and offers a tentative vision of colonist and native living side by side in mutually beneficent harmony; more confidently, he asserts that he and his kind

. . . have rights drawn from the soil and sky;
the use, the pace, the patient years of labour,
the rain against the lips, the changing light,
the heavy clay-sucked stride, have altered us;
we would be strangers in the Capitol;
this is our country also, nowhere else;
and we shall not be outcast on the world.

The application to Ulster is obvious, but the method of the poem encourages broader human and historical perspectives, dramatising the consequences of colonialism and the problems of the liberal conscience.

By 1950 Hewitt had served for twenty years in the Belfast Museum and Art Gallery, was assistant director there and had high hopes of being appointed director when the incumbent retired. In 'From chairmen and committee men, Good Lord deliver us' he tells the story of how, in 1953, he was denied the post on the casting vote of the unionist chairman of the appointing committee, having been 'branded both as communist and pro-Catholic . . . My years of gallery experience, my education, my long practice as lecturer on art, my reputation, such as it was, as broadcaster, my service on cultural committees, these lay outside the reckoning.' Four years later, after a period of depression and recovery, Hewitt was appointed director of the Herbert Art Gallery and Museum in Coventry, and so began a new phase in his professional and creative life.

Hewitt describes the move to Coventry as 'one of the best things that ever happened to me' (*Quarto*, no. 7, 1980–1). The city offered an exciting challenge for a man of his energies and ideals: it was rebuilding after the devastating air raids of 1940 and 1941, had an enlightened Labour council, offered an opportunity to develop a new art gallery which as yet possessed no collection and was situated within easy reach of London, Stratford and Oxford. The city had a cosmopolitan aura, having attracted people from all over Britain, and, as Hewitt remarked in an interview at the time, had a climate in marked contrast to the 'ingrown parochialism' of Ireland, a climate in which 'emotions, ideas and beliefs are accepted for what they are and are never challenged on mere obscurantist grounds' (*Standard*, 5 June 1959). Furthermore, the social idealism of the city planners had given emphasis to 'such concepts as the comprehensive principle in education, the insistence on contemporary design in structure and lay-out, the use of the most up-to-date methods in construction, but, above all, to a watchful awareness of human needs and aspirations, for childhood, maturity and age' (Introduction to *Coventry: The Tradition of Change and Continuity*, 1966). Coventry, which had by 1966 established international links with twenty-two towns on three continents, creating abundant opportunity for cultural exchange, had come to stand as 'a symbol for the undefeated determination of men of goodwill', and the new cathedral gave witness to the world of 'the necessity for reconciliation and mutual forgiveness among men of every belief and colour'. It is clear that the constants and continuities of Hewitt's philosophy had found a natural home in the Midlands of England, despite the fragmented nature of the society there and the comparative absence of local literary activity.

There were, too, unexpected opportunities for Hewitt to extend his personal myth. He discovered that the Hewitt family had figured prominently in the history of Coventry. In the fourteenth century John Hewitt, mason, had been employed by the council to arbitrate in matters relating to the maintenance of property; in the sixteenth century another namesake had painted scenery and props for the Coventry Miracle Plays; and in the eighteenth century another had been mayor, so that the Planter in Hewitt could savour a good-humouredly romantic sense of homecoming.

Comparatively few of the published poems Hewitt wrote during his fifteen years in Coventry are directly about his experience there, but those that are express certain tensions. The cultural energies that flourished in Belfast in the 1940s and 1950s take new directions and we find him writing occasional poems to mark, for example, the opening of the Belgrade Theatre (1958) and the reopening of the Whitefriars (1970), but though he evinces a determination not to struggle with his past, 'locked in an angry posture with a ghost,/but, striding forward, trust the shrunken thigh' ('Jacob and the angel'), more often than not the Coventry poems reflect the exile's yearning to adapt and an ache of loss that is more than mere nostalgia. 'The mainland', for instance, which delineates the complex inter-relationship between Ireland and England, colony and colonising people, ends with the ambiguous image of the colonial descendant who returns to the place of origin 'to find it rich in all but what he sought'. 'An Irishman in Coventry' (1958), written in Hewitt's second year abroad, is informed by much rawer emotions: having whole-heartedly embraced the promise of the developing city, the poet is stirred by his presence at an Irish gathering in the Midlands into an impassioned outburst of pained bitterness and loss, in which agonies of kinship and difference, the release of personal grievance and a vision of Irish history culminate in the orphaned patience and dignity of the exile awaiting the summons home. 'The search' (1967) expresses this tension with the sad objectivity of one who has now been in Coventry for ten years; the 'you' which replaces the 'we' of the opening stanza intimates some indeterminate middle ground where all dislocated humanity is stranded. Despite the consideration that they have returned to an 'older place whose landmarks are [theirs] also', exiles are essentially strangers:

> Yet you may not rest here, having come back,
> for this is not your abiding place, either.

These four poems are perhaps the best to emerge from Hewitt's Coventry phase but a number of others reflect his perennial concerns. Observing the *Prunus* and Japanese cherry flowering, 'fragile but assertive' in suburban gardens, Hewitt thinks of them as settlers' flowers and awaits the blossoming of the tougher, less ornamental chestnut and laburnum, associating the latter in particular with his 'grandmother's garden/in another country' ('Suburban spring in Warwickshire'). His elegy 'J.B. Shelton (1876–1958), the Coventry antiquarian' commemorates its subject not only as custodian of the past but as a city-lover who retains something of his rural ancestry. A gymkhana in the Midlands prompts reflections on how the ancient migrations westward of Asian settlers have dwindled to 'a huddle/of jodhpurs and hurdles' ('The riders'), and when Hewitt visits Compton Wynyates in Warwickshire for the second time, he is less concerned with its aristocratic history than with 'the squat headstones of labouring folk,/humble, enduring' ('Compton Wynyates, Warwickshire').

Hewitt once wrote that he had 'experienced a deep enduring sense of our human past before the Lion-Gate of Mycenae and among the Rolright Stones of the Oxfordshire border' ('No rootless colonist'). From the summer of 1927, when he accompanied his father on a trip to Belgium, until his final trips to Paris in the early 1980s, the poet was an inveterate traveller. As private individual, as member of PEN and as director of the Herbert Art Gallery and Museum, he visited Holland, Poland, Austria, Germany, Italy, Hungary, Czechoslovakia, Yugoslavia, Sicily, Greece, Spain, Turkey and the USSR, and his travel poems, though not generally among his best, reflect his internationalism, his receptivity to other cultures, as well as that sensitivity of observation and awareness of wider contexts for which he admired Estyn Evans. The thirty or so travel poems among his published work, many of them written during his years in Coventry, and the poems that reflect more obliquely the effect of his travels, relate interestingly to the more 'local' aspects of his regionalism and give a more immediate dimension to his continuous, lifelong journeys in the realms of international literature and art.

The most extended group of travel poems arose out of the Hewitts' visit to Greece and the Cyclades in the autumn of 1966 and was first published in the pamphlet *Tesserae* (1967). When, in Corinth, they find themselves not only tuned imaginatively to the voice of Saint Paul but also 'listening for the liquid syllables/of an older oracle' ('Old Corinth'), we think of the poems about Oisin's grave at Lubitavish. Indeed, Oisin and Cuchullain spring to Hewitt's mind at Mycenae and Epidaurus, though it is only beside a dark-green olive grove that he feels 'somehow strangely at home,/receiving, open, myself' ('Mycenae and Epidaurus'). At Delos, 'in the groin of Mount Cygnus' ('Delos'), he has intimations of human antiquity, the human saga, and in 'Vida, Mykonos' and 'To Piraeus' the historical, mythological past comes into immediate, timeless focus. Unlike those visitors to classical Greece in 'Homestead', who come home 'with nothing of worth to declare' that the speaker in that poem 'needed to hear', Hewitt returns enriched; indeed, the Greek poems might almost be an act of reparation for the speaker's apparently offhand treatment of the classical tradition in 'Homestead', though he does pay tribute in that poem to what has endured of Greek philosophy and literature. In a similar way the poem 'Whit Monday', in which Hewitt recalls the Confirmation of young girls in a Polish chapel in 1962 and is moved to a form of secular prayer that 'providence' or 'dialectic' or 'whatever name/men put upon time's enginery, permit/this scene to re-enact itself, the same,/so long as any heart finds grace in it', might be read on one level as a mellower version of 'May altar'. Listening to the Yiddish poet Itzik Manger, Hewitt has confirmed yet again the importance of 'ghetto-phrases, idioms' ('Remembering a conversation: Itzik Manger at the PEN Conference, Edinburgh, 1950') – in this case for an understanding of Chagall's paintings – and comes to see 'the nation in the man', while in 'Strangers and neighbours' he atones for certain superficial prejudices of his youth ('The song of the shipyard men' begins 'Oh Jews, an' lords, an' moneymen,/They're vampires one an' all'), rediscovering the Jews of his Cliftonpark Avenue childhood. He is able to do so partly through the experiences of visiting Auschwitz, 'Kafka's Prague' and the Portuguese synagogue in Amsterdam. And in 'Et tu in Arcadia vixisti' it is, perhaps, partly his visits to Greece and Sicily, the cradles of pastoral, that help to release into poetry a memory from his honeymoon in Paris in September 1934 so movingly epiphanic that he had not, he states in 'A North Light', previously dared to write about it.

Such poems show us the 'open, receiving' Hewitt who can gain from his friend the Chinese poet Shelley Wang a perpective on his own 'clumsy Western thought'; who, stopping at some anonymous border crossing, has a chastening confirmation of how the landscape transcends man-made boundaries ('The frontier'); who acknowledges (as in 'Conversations in Hungary, August 1969') the historical home truths to be learned in foreign places; who, most tellingly of all, is led to a repeated recognition of the restlessness of the human condition (in, for example, 'The search').

The Hewitts continued to rent their cottage at Cushendall until 1965 and visited Ireland every year, so that Ireland in general and Ulster in particular remained the chief source of Hewitt's inspiration during the Coventry years. The month of September 1969 was especially productive. 'Conversations in Hungary, August 1969' records how the Hewitts, on holiday near Lake Balaton, heard for the first time that in the aftermath of serious sectarian riots in Belfast and Derry, British troops had been drafted into Northern Ireland. Hewitt's poetic response was the booklet *An Ulster Reckoning* (1971), written entirely in September. In the foreword he registers his mistaken impression, held until the events of August 1969, of 'a growing tolerance between the historic communities', and quotes John Montague's description of him as 'the first (and probably the last) deliberately Ulster Protestant poet', concluding: 'That designation carries a heavy obligation these days.'

In the twenty poems that follow, themes familiar in Hewitt's poetry in the 1940s and 1950s resurface in a context of crisis. His Planter rights are obstinately restated in 'An Ulsterman' and he presents himself as 'caught in the crossfire of [a] false campaign' in a 'maimed', 'creed-infected', 'ruptured' island ('The dilemma'). He registers the viciously circular nature of the violence, recollecting ominous episodes in his own experience from as far back as the 1920s and notes that the very streets in Belfast that were his 'childhood's precinct' ('Street names') are still the scene of bloodshed. The ruling unionist class in Ulster is indicted for its calculated use of sectarianism to maintain power and in a diffuse but effective poem, 'The coasters', Hewitt points an accusing finger at the complacencies and skin-deep liberalism of the bourgeoisie. Self-accusation is the predominant note in 'A Belfastman abroad argues with himself'; having endured the 'venom' and survived the 'sneers' of Belfast, he might have stayed 'and kept one corner clear for decency'. Two poems in *An Ulster Reckoning*, 'The tribune' and 'The well-intentioned consul', adopt the same historical paralleling used in 'The colony'; in a poem entitled 'Parallels never meet', Hewitt then rejects the procedure as artificial, inappropriate, somehow untrue to the 'coarser texture' of 'reality'. The dream kindled in Hewitt by his father that 'all people should be free' and its regionalist expression in the 1940s and 1950s as a vision

> . . . that on our glens,
> our little fields, our artless shabby towns
> might break some generous light of common sense,
> and men of will wake eager to renounce
> our sad past and its sick corollary ('Demagogue')

is seen as practically extinguished. Yet despite the fact that Northern Ireland is a state where reforming zeal is enough to bring down a prime minister ('The well-intentioned consul'), Hewitt can still muster a hopeful admiration for radical youth, especially when imbued with the egalitarian spirit of Wolfe Tone ('Agitator'), and still counsels peace, tolerance, goodwill ('Memorandum for the moderates'). The booklet ends, however, with W.R. Rodgers's idea that 'the Hare must need the Hound/ as surely as the Hound must need the Hare' and Hewitt's fear that 'the chase continues, with no end in sight' ('The iron circle').

The poems in *An Ulster Reckoning* have an undeniable urgency and their sincerity is not to be doubted, but too often they give the impression of instant, unmediated response and of recourse to rhetoric and imagery that the poet has used more effectively elsewhere. The crisis in Northern Ireland has not quite revitalised old themes and it is generally true that Hewitt's most enduring poems about the Troubles pre-date 1969. Nevertheless, a number of successful later poems should be mentioned here. The same year that saw the publication of *An Ulster Reckoning* produced 'Bogside, Derry, 1971', which interprets the riots in that city as a reaction to 'the long indignities/the stubborn core within each heart defies', and 'The scar', in which Hewitt makes a resonant lyric of an episode that had been part of his family heritage since childhood, his great-grandmother's generous response to a sufferer from famine fever and her consequent death; Hewitt insists that this act 'conscribed [him] of the Irishry for ever':

> Though much I cherish lies outside their vision,
> and much they prize I have no claim to share,
> yet in that woman's death I found my nation;
> the old wound aches and shews its fellow scar.

'Neither an elegy nor a manifesto' (1972) is a plea that we 'bear in mind' ('remember' is too loaded a word in Ireland) the victims and casualties of violence; the 'Postscript, 1984' to Hewitt's earlier poem 'Ulster names' adds several place names associated with atrocities, points on a 'tarnished map . . . not to be read as pastoral again'; and in 'Colonial consequence', Hewitt's final poem in the mode of 'The colony', the speaker and others watch administrators from the mainland come and go and feel 'no whit the wiser than [they] were before'.

'Although it is my native place/and dear to me for many associations,/ how can I return to that city/from my exile among strangers?' ('Exile'), Hewitt asked in 1969. He had, however, already bought a house in Belfast that year and return he did in 1972, having reached retirement age. He and Roberta settled in Stockman's Lane and lived there for the rest of their lives. Hewitt's profile as a poet was high in Ireland at that time: his *Collected Poems 1932–1967* had appeared in 1968, *An Ulster Reckoning* had been widely reviewed, and he had at the end of 1970 toured the province with John Montague in a series of poetry readings sponsored by the Arts Council of Northern Ireland under the title 'The Planter and the Gael'. His return coincided not only with a period of civil upheaval but also with a resurgence of cultural activity unparalleled since the 1940s; James Simmons had founded the *Honest Ulsterman* magazine in 1968, the Blackstaff Press, which was to publish practically all of Hewitt's subsequent books, had been founded in 1971, a new generation of Ulster poets (including Seamus Heaney, Derek Mahon, Michael Longley, James Simmons and Seamus Deane) had already published in book form and yet another (which included Ciaran

Carson, Paul Muldoon, Tom Paulin and Gerald Dawe) had begun to emerge.

It was for Hewitt a period of unprecedented public recognition and creative output. By the end of the 1970s he had been awarded an honorary degree by the New University of Ulster (1974), elected vice-president of the Irish Academy of Letters (1975), served as the first writer-in-residence at Queen's University Belfast (1976–9), and the Arts Council of Northern Ireland had commissioned a film, *I Found Myself Alone* (1978), on his life and work. He had also edited and introduced the anthology *Rhyming Weavers and Other Country Poets of Antrim and Down* (1974), published monographs on his friends Colin Middleton (1976) and John Luke (1978) and the survey *Art in Ulster 1* (1977); in addition, two pamphlets of poems, *The Chinese Fluteplayer* and *Scissors for a One-Armed Tailor* (both published privately in 1974), and three full collections, *Out of My Time* (1974), *Time Enough* (1976) and *The Rain Dance* (1978), had appeared, and he had written the one hundred and seven sonnets that make up *Kites in Spring: A Belfast Boyhood* (1980). This pattern continued into the 1980s: in the last seven years of his life Hewitt published *Mosaic* (1981), *Loose Ends* (1983), *The Day of the Corncrake: Poems of the Nine Glens* (revised edition, 1984) and *Freehold and other Poems* (1986), had a cassette recording of his poems released under the title *Substance and Shadow* (1980) and had his verse play *The Bloody Brae* performed at the Lyric Players Theatre, Belfast (1986); he also saw the appearance of *The Selected John Hewitt* (edited by Alan Warner, 1981) and the preparation of *Ancestral Voices: The Selected Prose of John Hewitt* (edited by Tom Clyde), issued shortly after his death in 1987. During this decade his awards included an honorary degree from Queen's University Belfast (1983) and the Gregory Medal of the Irish Academy of Letters (1984), and he was made a freeman of the city of Belfast (1983).

The final phase of Hewitt's poetic career is primarily one of salvage and consolidation. Though he continues to produce notable new work, much of his energy goes into the revision and recasting of earlier poems, published and unpublished, and the quarrying of publishable material from his manuscript notebooks. *Scissors for a One-Armed Tailor*, for example, is subtitled 'Marginal Verses 1929–1954'; *Time Enough* and *The Rain Dance* are both designated 'Poems New and Revised'; *Mosaic* and *Loose Ends* present a similar blend of old and new and *Freehold and Other Poems* collects for the first time in book form a verse play written fifty years previously and a long poem written in the 1940s. Hewitt's impulse to recover and re-explore his formative years takes an autobiographical direction in his most extended run of new poems, *Kites in Spring: A Belfast Boyhood.* Poem after poem presents a character or episode familiar from Hewitt's earlier work (including his autobiographical prose); comparatively few of the individual poems add significantly to our factual knowledge of Hewitt's earliest years but the poems have a dramatic immediacy not generally characteristic of the prose and accumulate to give a more coherent picture of what was previously fragmented.

It is also noticeable in the work published during Hewitt's final phase that he is, though still frequently circumspect, more emotionally direct than before. The release of feeling in earlier poems such as 'Ghosts', 'The little death', 'The lonely heart' section of *Freehold*, 'Betrayal' and 'No second Troy' is untypical of this usually reticent poet – untypical, at least, of his published work. In 'Clogh-Oir, September 1971' Hewitt describes himself as reluctant to name the stirrings of love, slow to 'yield words/for the dialectic of the heart', but he does, in fact, find abundant words for this dialectic in a number of his manuscript notebooks, especially those which date from the time of his meeting with and early marriage to Roberta Black. Whether his reticence in such matters was temperamental, a reluctance to expose his most personal feelings in print, or whether consideration for Roberta and others played a part, are imponderables. Whatever the case, it is true that in the 1970s and 1980s Hewitt shows greater willingness to make his love poems public. In *Conacre* and *Freehold*, 'A country walk in March', 'A country walk in May' and many other poems Roberta is a loved but shadowy companion, whereas among the lyrics at the end of *The Chinese Fluteplayer* we find Hewitt declaring 'I'd squander all the skill I've stored/to give you half a glimpse of her' ('The lyric sonorously rhymed . . .'), confessing that he is obsessed 'by such complexities of love/as tremble in [her] gentle breast' ('I turned my touch to Campion . . .') and celebrating 'her heart's hair-triggered miracle' ('I've known her turn from bitter phrase . . .'). Even in these mannered verses the woman's presence is elusive and it is perhaps significant that they are followed by the poem 'For R.', which seems to imply that Roberta is so woven into his poetry that she is inextricably part of its fabric.

Though two of these poems ('The lyric sonorously rhymed . . .' and 'For R.') appeared in magazines, it took Hewitt several decades to collect them in pamphlet form. 'I turned my touch to Campion . . .' dates from the 1930s, 'The lyric sonorously rhymed . . .' and 'I've known her turn from bitter phrase . . .' belong to the 1940s and 'For R.' had its origins in the 1950s. Roberta's death in 1975 prompted the moving 'A birthday rhyme for Roberta' (published at the beginning of *Time Enough* in 1976), in which Hewitt mourns that the one who 'had shared the spring/and summer of [his] love' has missed his 'late harvesting', though even this is an older poem given new direction. It was, however, in *The Rain Dance* (1978) that Hewitt released the most harrowing of all his love poems, the five 'Sonnets for Roberta (1954)' – the last two of which were, in fact, written in 1956. In this sequence, which reflects the traumas, for Hewitt and his wife, of the period after his application for the directorship of the Belfast Museum and Art Gallery was rejected and before the move to Coventry, the formality of the sonnet form strains and crackles with the pressure of self-accusation, remorse, compassion, uncertainty about the future. Hewitt castigates his self-absorption and the emotional neglect that has reduced his wife to 'some mere chattel-thing of cloth and wood', and perhaps stripped his own verses of 'a richer texture and a warmer tone'; he pleads for forgiveness so that they may rebuild their house from the débris (a recurrent image in Hewitt's poetry) and begin again the 'dialogue of love'.

Inevitably, Hewitt's sense of his own mortality, always well developed, increases as he grows older, as relatives and in-laws die and as he resurrects the past in *Kites in Spring*. His father continues to haunt him 'from within' ('My father's ghost'), prompting heartfelt lyrics of loss and recovery, and he writes movingly of his mother, his sister Eileen, his brother-in-law by marriage Andrew Millar, his uncles, his paternal grandfather, and others, such as Dorothy Roberts, to whom he had been engaged around 1930 (in 'Hesitant memorial'). Hewitt depicts the approach and arrival of death as piteous, clumsy, aimless, crude and lonely, and he is not disposed to be comforted by visions of an afterlife. Nevertheless, his final collection strikes a predominantly affirmative note, not only in the questing spirit and humane perspectives of *Freehold* and *The Bloody Brae*, as fresh and relevant as when Hewitt wrote them, but also in the presence of other loved ghosts – William Morris, John Toland, 'the sturdy folk, the nameless and the named,/the vertical men who never genuflected,/the assertors, the protesters' ('Roseblade's visitants and mine'), and in the tentatively confident mood of lines such as these from 'Bifocal in Gaza':

> So as I venture along the narrow years
> a brighter road than ever I have known
> beckons my eager step now and tomorrow,
> and I can only pray all senses join
> in life more precious now, more perilous.

Belfast is the setting of 'Bifocal in Gaza' and it is a feature of Hewitt's final phase, from *An Ulster Reckoning* onwards – prompted in part by his return to the city – that the background is more frequently urban than in any of his work since his earliest socialist verse. This is particularly true of *Kites in Spring*, which re-creates a middle-class city childhood in and around Cliftonpark Avenue, the street names becoming part of his lexicon for the first time. The poet who had 'paced [his] thought by the natural world' ('Because I paced my thought') and who had once written that he would have few regrets if Belfast returned to the swamp, now finds himself redrawing a dissolving map, reconstructing without sentimentality areas and aspects of the city that have largely disappeared. It is interesting that in 1980 Hewitt revised his poem 'The ruins answer' (first published in 1944), addressing again, with even more cautious optimism than originally, the problem of how to build a better society and reiterating some of his most cherished values.

Though Hewitt's addiction to the sonnet form is undiminished and he not only recasts earlier poems in their original, traditional forms but also continues to use rhyme and half-rhyme, the collections of his final fifteen years show the poet who had begun as a disciple of Whitman developing the more relaxed, flexible mode he had practised intermittently in poems such as 'The return', 'Those swans remember' and 'Homestead'. It is touching to find Hewitt writing in one of his final notebook sonnets:

> I like my lines in faltering syllables
> that had before followed the measured gait
> of older craftsmen, meditative, wise
> in weather, season, time of day, or else,
> when mood unlatched, flowed with a sudden spate,
> and once a decade sparked a bright surprise.

This is the last of many comments in Hewitt's verse on his own temperament and poetic voice. These comments frequently contain elements of diffidence, self-effacement, regretful awareness of his own limitations; he judges himself to be a poet who has, 'obedient to [his] sober thought,/ disdained the riper curves of rhetoric' ('Ars poetica'), one who 'mourns for his mannerly verses/that had left so much unsaid' ('A local poet'); he can find himself plodding, undemonstrative and unadventurous in life and in poetry. Yet he is also at times pleased to claim for his poetry the plain, practical qualities of crafts like carpentry, ploughing or building ('Ars poetica'), to note that he is still 'equipped/for report, comment, comparison' ('On the canal') and has the capacity to 'gently revel in [his] joys,/despite the prohibitions curt/sedate decorum still deploys' ('Variations on a theme'). In one of his best-known 'manifesto' poems, the concise and memorable 'I write for . . .' he declares:

> I write for my own kind,
> I do not pitch my voice
> that every phrase be heard
> by those that have no choice:
> their quality of mind
> must be withdrawn and still,
> as moth that answers moth
> across a roaring hill.

This constitutes a confident claim for the strength of the quiet voice, for all its apparent fragility.

There is, of course, an extent to which Hewitt's assessment of his limitations is accurate. Even his most devoted advocates would concede that there are tracts of his verse that are at best worthy, at worst dull, and that he can be predictable, patronising and self-congratulatory. He gives the impression of being a poet who rarely surprises himself (though his own estimate of 'once a decade' is much too severe) and readers might wish that his sense of humour found more frequent outlet in his poems. Considering his belief in and often well-deserved reputation for craftsmanship, he is surprisingly prone to clumsy syntax, mixed metaphors and ungrammatical structures, and 'th'iambic tick-tock' ('Music lessons') of his verse can be too monotonously insistent. At times he strikes a cadence or turns a phrase that would not be out of place in Sir Arthur Quiller-Couch's *Oxford Book of Victorian Verse* (1912), though this is perhaps less a fault than a deliberate flouting of fashion and a fidelity to his first loves in poetry.

Hewitt's shortcomings, however disabling to particular poems, seem insignificant when measured against the scale, tenacity and integrity of some sixty years' work. Much of his poetry is troubled into utterance by the tensions and paradoxes of a particular fractured culture; he attempts more comprehensively than any other Irish poet to define that culture and in doing so transcends the particulars. His best poems embody the constants and variables of the human condition: man as social being and isolated individual, man as capable of intelligent choice and victim of chance, the struggles of the individual conscience and the necessary rigours of dissent, the endlessly exacting, endlessly revitalising search for equilibrium and for the myths and symbols by which he and others might aspire to more vibrant, useful lives. His work pursues the earthly paradise, a dynamic encounter of vision and reality in which passionate pragmatism and vigilant idealism rehearse their elusive synthesis against a backdrop of human imperfection.

Hewitt's prose writings and poems have passed into our imaginative and intellectual freehold, carrying with them the history, people, art and literature that became part of his. Edna Longley comments that his 'cross-sectarian ideal of regionalism [not only] energised writers, painters and general cultural activity during the post-war period [but] recovered ancestral voices and provided some of the basis for a second take-off in the Sixties', and the leading poets of the 1960s generation in particular have paid tribute to his example. Michael Longley commemorates him as a poet who 'held out the creative hand rather than the clenched fist [and] made himself heard in a land of bellowers without raising his voice'. Seamus Heaney's obituary appreciation of Hewitt notes that he 'outstrips the categories we keep invoking for him, such as "doyen of the Ulster poets" or "conscience of the Planter tradition"' and becomes instead 'the universal poet'. Heaney anticipates the potentially enduring nature of this universality. Hewitt, he writes, is now 'blessed by that grace that devolves upon all good poets at the moment of their death. It is then, when the person has been withdrawn, that the work seems stronger than ever.'

It is one measure of the coherence of Hewitt's writings that there are numerous lines and verses among his poems that suggest themselves as potential epigraphs and epitaphs for the man and his work. My own choice is the previously unpublished lyric 'If I should be remembered after this . . .', written when Hewitt was in his late thirties, in which he asks to be recalled as 'a heart whose pulse in its best moments was/free on the wing, as natural as the birds' and expresses the conviction that 'the quiet voices were not all in vain'. Equally appropriate would be certain passages from *Freehold*, or the brief 'I write for . . .', or the concluding stanza of 'Because I paced my thought'. This last, in which an image from William Morris, memoirs of Labour Party summer schools in the 1930s and a detail from Giorgio Vasari's life of the painter Giovanni Cimabue are transmuted into resonant symbols true to both actuality and the imagination, is one of the 'best moments' in Hewitt's poetry – doubly poignant now that the life has been 'withdrawn', doubly powerful in its embodiment of how the work and its values survive:

. . . I stake my future
on birds flying in and out of the schoolroom window,
on the council of sunburnt comrades in the sun,
and the picture carried with singing into the temple.

FRANK ORMSBY
BELFAST, 1991

PART
I

COLLECTED POEMS
1929–86

CONACRE

'Conacre: in Irish land system; the letting by a tenant for a season, of small portions of land ready ploughed and prepared for a crop'

OED

What itch of contradiction bids me find
no prompting satisfactions for my mind
to make verse of, between grey house and house,
save when moon rising through the sooty boughs
recalls familiar frames, or when in spring
one blackbird fills the longer evening,
but like a tippler, urgently must go
to taste pine-resined air and mark below
moss-cumbered boles the yellow flowers in spate,
or just to gaze at grass across a gate?

I sleep above a flagged resounding street,
and men from shops deliver all I eat.
I burn cart coals and breathe the gritty airs,
and rock in trams about my brisk affairs.
My father also. Last of all my kin
to live beneath a thatch and not within
tall walls was one whose birth goes back from now
well over a hundred years. The scythe and plow
are alien to my grasp. I cannot tell
the weather's chance by glance or oracle.
How far an acre spreads I scarcely guess;
no crop's yield offers sign I may assess.

What lore I have is harvested with care
from buckram books, or sometimes here and there
from talkative old men who pause to crack
on sunny bank or from the sagging back
of mare heeled home from shoeing. I have tried
to key my jargon to the man beside
my elbow at the bar on market day,
but though I strive to turn the talk the way
my hunger clamours, he will not be led
and fobs me off with politics instead.
Why not then seize the virtue in my luck,
and make my theme the riveters who struck

the other day for solidarity,
or take a derrick simply as a tree
and praise a puddle that contains the sky
for all the boots and wheels that clatter by?

The lonely person looking for a nod
along the street; the old man dazed with God
howling his gospel, hoarse with prophecy;
the laden soldier with his family
dragging towards the train; the shuffling throng
that turn cold shoulders on the busker's song;
the polished horses with the quiet van
that breasts a wave of lifted hats; the man
who, stumped or blinded, squats beside his cap
and props a motto on his greasy lap;
frost's flourish on the pavement; hissing snow
that thumps like sugar on the steps below;
old walls in morning sunlight; spiking shower
of summer rain on dust; the plume and power
of narrow chimney in the sunset sky;
the bridge-baulked jets of steam as trains go by;
nostalgic hoot from ships that slip by night
down the dark channel: these by sound and sight
make up the world my heel and nostril know,
but not the world my pulses take for true.

But somehow these close images engage
the prompt responses only, pity, humour, rage,
and leave the quiet depths unmeasured still;
whereas the heathered shoulder of a hill,
a quick cloud on the meadow, wind-lashed corn,
black wrinkled haws, grey tufted wool on thorn,
the high lark singing, the retreating sea –
these stab the heart with sharp humility
and prick like water on the thirsty wrist
in hill-spring thrust, when hot sun splits the mist
among dark peatstacks on long boggy plains,
such as lie high and black between the Glens,
or on the crown of Garron struck by sun
to emerald or rain-wrapped. I have won,
by grace or by intention, to delight
that seems to match the colours mystics write
only in places far from kerb or street.

For memory's sake indulgent I repeat
the marvel of that dawn when you and I
rose when the stars commanded all the sky,
and on the dry road under the windless firs
heard the first bird that stirs before light stirs,
and took the steep lane to the brackened crest,
and stood to see the water's dark unrest,
wet to the knees with dew and shivering,
and watched a black shag cross with hurried wing
close to the surface of the roaring bay.
We waited for the sun. To the east there lay
a cloud that hid its rising. Quickly one by one
the stars were snuffed. We waited for the sun.
Above cold Garron's cape in lucid air
one star remained. The sky was high and bare,
save for that cloudbank, growing golden now,
and little scattered gusts in bush and bough
troubled the dry leaves, rasped the thistle crown
ripe with the autumn. Where the wrack was brown
small sea fowl started on their sleek routine.
The peak of Lurigedan now was green
in brighter light, but still the sun delayed.

We turned disheartened. Suddenly you said
and pointed, 'Look.' Behind above the trees
a crook-necked heron flapped with patient ease
and passing over, flew ahead as if
slow missile aimed at Scotland. Down the cliff
chagrined we took our way. The hour was gone
that should have marked the coming of the dawn.

We reached the dewcrisp sand and turned again;
the wakened world still lacked the noise of men,
though in the nearest house blue smoke began
to mingle with the leaves. A rabbit ran
over the salt short grass. The grazing sheep
came stumbling from the hedges lame with sleep
to browse along the rough. And then at once
we strode to where the river cuts the stones
after a lazy drift, bog-brown and slow
between steep banks where grey-leaved salleys grow,
and saw a speckled gannet poise on wing
to fall like hurtling pebble from a sling,

deadly as David, clean and pitiless
as later sparrowhawk for wren's distress
we ran to check from havoc in the hedge
half-hid by nettles at the first tee's edge.
Then turning for a last look at the sea,
we gasped amazed. The thing we came to see
had happened when our foolish backs were turned.
The cloud had lifted and below it burned,
hot brass upon the water, a bar of sun
like moon fantastic, and the job was done.
Our little world was younger by a day,
and we paced proudly home the longer way,
aware of every freshly spiring scent
as benediction and as sacrament.

For once a day was ours, possessed entire
till a dark world should narrow to a fire
and porridge steaming and a friendly book
beneath the lamp, and one to share a look
or hear a passage read with quiet joy.
A day was ours wherein we could employ
the active senses undiverted, free
for touch of bark and taste of blackberry,
till sleep unvexed should bless the dreamless head,
until tomorrow brought the postman's tread.

My mind such nurture seeks, dissatisfied
with the long hours my passion or my pride
determines I shall fill with rhetoric
of Paul Cézanne or hostels for the sick,
and the expounding of a tedious text,
how affirmation breeds the sure negation next.
Regard the thimbles: point to where it is
and shew beneath the third the nimble synthesis.

Even the storied objects of my trade,
the golden brooch, the pot, the long bronze blade,
the mammoth's tooth, the weasel's skeleton,
the public portrait and the lettered stone
can strike no certain spark: though now and then
I wake to kinship with the beasts and men
who walked a younger earth, were proved unfit,
and ended as we end for all our wit.

I'd give the collar of an Irish king
for one wet catkin jigging loosely in the spring,
when I am weary of the labelled bird
and want the song and not the Latin word.

It's life I need and grasp, that careless spends,
yet offers its unnumbered means as ends;
not growth and death: together they are one
for all beneath the sun and for the sun.

Life, you may argue, surely intervenes
between the crashing of the mad machines
and the bound bales. The back-yard cat at least
still carries out the motions of a beast,
and life still ripples down each yawning paw.

You see the tooth and may provoke the claw.
The pallid urchin, half his years in height,
no less than bramble dwarfed for lack of light,
provides the text you travel far to seek
one June weekend or warm September week,
and is beside you if you fix your eyes
on smaller shapes than attitudes of skies.

Then take this city. In a decent street
I opened eyes and found both tongue and feet.
Its windows and its walls, its doors and stones
have tailored this close flesh upon my bones,
and what of me is honest debt to it
I care not to assess or to admit.
And yet should these high chimneys tumble down,
the gantries sag and fall, and nettles crown
the festered mounds of rust above the marsh,
and herons nest, and kittiwakes cry harsh
over the banks where bridge and rigging met,
there is but little that I should regret.
For what was good here can be better still,
the spring-gilt whin upon the blunt-browed hill
with no raw villas smoking at its foot,
the flapping leaves no longer drenched with soot,
the little stream uncoffined now of brick
clean running where it drifted black and thick
with oil and rag to carry out to sea
th'excreted silt of mill and factory.

If scholars' words be trusted, we have been
too long untutored for the coarse machine
to bid our pulses march to beat of loom,
or find salvation in a stuffy room;
too many hills are calcined in our bones
for us to rest content on paving stones.

I would not raise a hand to bring a state
magnificent in art, in commerce great,
with the smooth comfort of its concrete squares
superbly measured out in equal shares,
where there was left no single ragged line
of twisted thorn or resin-oozing pine
where boys may light a fire, and for a day
slough off two thousand years in naked play.

But one may urge that in the landscape loved
the hedge and copse the use of man has proved;
by patient years the countryside has grown
friendly in sod and timber; even stone
battered by water, shattered by the frost
in dyke and kiln gives more than weather cost.

You would escape from brick but not too far.
You want the hill at hand familiar,
the punctual packet and the telephone,
that you may not be lonely when alone.

I nod assent, no dusty pioneer
complaining that the road has come too near,
but one who needs the comfortable pace
of safe tradition. Reckon from my face
and its smooth lazy cheeks, the close-set eyes,
the tight-shut mouth aggressive that belies
the hand that scarce dare push a latchless gate,
and you will gauge me hero in debate
who funks decisions nor will shift his hams
save to applause for savage epigrams
which skim a laugh and leave mistrust behind
that one so harsh insists he still is kind –
I warp and wrench the canvas that was meant
for nothing more than gentle sentiment
with this coarse introspection. I began

these verses to discover why a man,
townbred and timid, should attain to peace
with outworn themes and rustic images,
and now I find the shifting meaning turns
on human history and its wry concerns.
I should have guessed what other men have known,
that definition means comparison,
and that we find our lightest words demand
a cosmos weighed within a human hand,
and that our logic must be stretched to include
the coral insect, cancer in the blood,
the crazy atom, and the crocodile,
the twitching nerve that's knotted to a smile,
and that the simple shock at spilling salt
implies the murdered prophet in the vault,
the grave da Vinci's mural and the plans
that left hand drew to father bombing planes.
For every act is like that ivory sphere
some turbaned rascal carved in high Kashmir
that holds another and another yet,
till eye blurs groping for the infinite.
The surfaces of life are safer stuff;
if weather tear the husk it is enough.
Should we persist and split the final pod,
who knows if it reveal the seed of God?

Yet this way madness or a cynic mind
that in Yeats' ditch hears blind man thumping blind
and laughs because the splashing slime is cool
on the hot brow.

But neither saint nor fool,
rather a happy man who seldom sees
the emptiness behind the images
that wake my heart to wonder, I derive
sufficient joy from being here alive
in this mad island crammed with bloody ghosts
and moaning memories of forgotten coasts
our fathers steered from, where we cannot go
the name's so lost in time's grey undertow.

This is my home and country. Later on
perhaps I'll find this nation is my own;

but here and now it is enough to love
this faulted ledge, this map of cloud above,
and the great sea that beats against the west
to swamp the sun.

                    No single season's best.
I think in autumn, when the seed's afield,
the year is crowned. But black in winter, stilled
by a clean frost, the trees are lovelier;
and then in spring, with song and sap astir,
I touch a peak of joy that lasts until
the hawthorn in the quarry-gutted hill
brims the warm air, or from a cairn-tipped mound
the whole loughside is an enchanted ground
with crowded fruit, and dazzled waters spread
layer after layer of gold, and overhead
the weary rooks are burnished as they come
through yellow light laboriously home.

Once in a summer, stepping slow again
through the lush homage of a shadowed lane
with one released from privacy of pain
remarking with now unimprisoned eyes
the shepherd's purse, the barren strawberries,
just where the ruts run in past pillared stone
the mossy foot-track to the stream goes down,
there on a tall beech close against the sky
an evening thrush was calling stridently,
lost in the leaves at first, discovered on
the utmost branch, his breast toward the sun;
no nestlings' clamour and no rivals' threat
to vex his peace with danger or with debt,
he simply sang and sang for naked zest,
shouting the mellow sun down the submissive west.

We stood to marvel, silent at his skill;
the cruising bee in clover too was still.
So, thought I in that instant, should my art
make joy its theme, were but the troubled heart
released from anger, severed from dismay
for the last hour of my declining day.

It is not that like Goldsmith I recall
some shabby Auburn with a crumbling wall

seen through the sparkling lens of exile grief
that gilds the lily of a child's belief;
nor that like Crabbe I must for evermore
compulsive seek the miserable shore
or the neat laurels by the patron's door
that scarred his youth. For no man's pensioner,
I pick and choose whom I shall greet with 'Sir';
nor that like stricken Cowper safe from view
I seek God's mercy in the morning dew:
nor that a foolish fancy cheats my mind
of moon-faced folk incorrigibly kind,
who mouth slow proverbs and whose hands are deft
in many a woodcut-illustrated craft.

No tweed-bright poet drunk in pastoral
or morris-dances in the legion hall
I know my farmer and my farmer's wife,
the squalid focus of their huxter life,
the grime-veined fists, the thick rheumatic legs,
the cracked voice gloating on the price of eggs,
the miser's Bible, and the tedious aim
to add another boggy acre to the name.

And yet this is too savage.
I recall
the friendly doors and hearths of Donegal,
the red heels in the ash, the turf blown ripe
tonged up and held to light the broken pipe,
and the stooped father mingling puff with puff,
talking of labour when the world was rough
in lowland barns or where the track was thrust
across the range or through the prairie dust;
and I remember one who sat and swayed
in island kitchen till we were afraid
of ghost or grugach for she filled the glen
with shadowy forms of fierce fanatic men
and left us for the midnight's rainy squall
to hobble past them with a tugging shawl;
or that deaf man who stopped us on a bridge
across the lough-end where no tree or hedge
covers the tilted slabs of rain-grained stone,
and in slow phrases bellowed one by one
offered a chance of poaching if I'd care,
then, pressing more, if I'd the heart to dare.

Now after twenty years I recollect
old Brennan scrawny, long and freckle-necked,
padding the floor with thick and matted sock
and stretching to adjust the German clock,
and as he winds, gazing with tireless eyes
on the framed picture of his famous prize –
a bull, a cup, a man beside the bull –
the day he won, the cup was splashing full:
and that slow man who loves the faery thorn,
and never fails to fork new cribs of corn
for his few heifers when the old year ends,
who calls the hare and badger both his friends,
yet turns no back on progress, dreaming still
of the broad tractors sweeping up the hill,
and the great binder worked by equal men,
lifting its swathes of fat collective grain.
So in this hope which harbours all I love
as rain-chill fist slips grateful into glove,
as the soft plastic gathers from the mould
a strength by its loose atoms unforetold,
I rest content. No contradictions vex
the single mind unfriended, or perplex
the will that finds no longer life to waste
so clear the path imperative is traced;
the heart's conscripted with its plunging blood;
the place is past for wilful attitude;
so ends my passion, ends my lonely rage,
hushed in perspectives of the Golden Age.

from

COMPASS

TWO POEMS

TO ROBERT TELFORD HEWITT

Here at these verses' head I write your name
who gave me breath, and set the leaping flame
of social justice in my wayward heart.
In all I say or do the wiser part
is but your impulse working in the blood,
for quality of life and brotherhood.

THE RETURN

The gulls began at daybreak in the mist,
gliding a smooth adagio astern.
Intent on it they slowly dropped aside,
then, with a hurry, flapped back into place.

The scarts, the cormorants, upon each buoy
sat still, aloof, averting their long heads,
repeated stencil of black silhouette;
I'd taken a bet with myself I'd find them there.

Day brightening, and the mist being thin and torn,
a flock of rooks from the woods at Clandeboye
passed safe and high above our bobbing track.

Over the spume and welter of the wake
I flung my scraps of bread, and the screaming started,
the rival hunger and the pedantic skill,
disdaining jostle for swoop of dignity;
always life poised upon the edge of pain.

The quiet that had come upon my spirit,
since at the flat Meare field I'd found my place
in the strait film of man's immortal stride,
was cut to flicker. Superimposing shots

set me at angles with a marvellous sky:
Rathlin, the Westlight, and the tall black stacks,
the hurtling puffins and the guillemots,
rocketing past our faces into the surge:
Dunanrooey, mounded fort of sword-girt kings:
and, cresting a small hill, a heron surprised,
trailing off with offended arrogance;
the oystercatcher's eggs you found on a ledge
when the frightened parents cried in a narrowing circle;
and down by Ushet Lough a sparrowhawk
striking the gull's breast in a flurried fury.

A year more packed and nurtured than any before,
now brought to the bench and challenged for its worth
by this brief English sojourn and the return,
the sharpened retrospect and the foreign touchstone
to shatter the ore along the threads of gold;
first daily use of living out my love,
existence that before was spent in snatches
with cold and lonely intervals of self;
learning a mind, judging a spirit's tension,
sail shortening for the weather of the mood:
trusting one side of an arch to hold love's keystone.
That span is steady. Lay the trowel by.

A loud year vibrant with cross-trumpet calls,
rally to art, a hand, a voice for beauty,
a bitter tongue for what I took as fraud,
verse jogging close at elbow to be uttered,
but brushed aside to whimper into dreams;
to spear a strident error, or lift a banner
of mercy and justice in a smoky room:
war imminent, and its black wing unnoticed
by careless gapers at a showy neon,
but threat so dread for those who watched the skyline
that you and I dare not delay to give
what little craft we had, to rouse and warn them:
skirmish with those false prophets bleating gently
the crazy circle of daft circumstance,
and the oversimple chart of easy rescue:
an electric day with that high-volted rebel,
who has battered the walls of folly with his head
for longer than I've cried upon this planet:

your fevered weeks alone of rash endeavour,
to raise a beacon for the night-bewildered
who rather love this darkness than your light.

Name me the faces rocking in the shadow:
the white tired face of the exile German woman,
behind her gentle words the whip and pistol
working relentless murder to her hopes,
and menacing the gestures we had known
of friendship laced with thongs of argument
that is treasured only in its jeopardy;
the grim, good-humoured face of the dramatist,
talking of Thoreau, Synge and Anton Chekhov,
encountered in the rain of an Irish June,
yet bright with a ripe wisdom and gay courage;
the rough-cut face, the strong mouth eloquent,
of the one major prophet of the north,
betrayed a little into vanity,
flattered to silence on his stormy dream;
the ivory sculpture of the ageless woman,
who rallied her sex to freedom and saw it lost,
and turned to rally a class to win it back;
the hooded features' mumble over the peat
of Neil the Piper and the grugach's cry.

Not one of these but gave us strength and wisdom,
wisdom through pity, strength through reverence.
And when the world's walls trembled to engulf us,
we had the strength to face the poised disaster,
and cry salute to the clean stars beyond.

Yet for our nurture and our spent wits' succour
we hurried to an island, Rathlin, knowing,
hooped by steel cliffs and circled by the ocean,
islands are wellheads of the world's salvation.

There, men at peace, in fields, or driving cattle,
women at doors, and children brown and shy,
sheep on the hills, the mare with a stumbling foal,
the sick calf in the corn, the stacks of sods,
the white road with each lough a bright surprise,
Craigmacaggan, Mullyroger, Ally, Ushet,
the charlock-yellow barley, the warm sweet beans,

and the perpetual crying of the birds,
brought back clear joy and merry sanity.

Not once a social conscience troubled us.
Leaning on rocks, or perched precarious
on the stone walls between bare field and field,
we let the free heart flutter till it found,
up near the sun, a happy sky of light.

So we decided what our days must mean,
sustenance of sense and steady growth to ripeness,
hands, eyes and wits bound slaves to poetry;
the briefest pain to be the oyster's grit.

This then decided, fresh in a salty squall,
we tacked for home and raced small ragged clouds.
But in the city of our dreadful night
men fought with men because of a threadbare flag,
or history distorted in temper.

                                        In the streets
crowds brandished the blunt slogans of their hate,
drove from their midst the strangers of a creed,
and set the lithe flame licking up the curtain.

So we were thrust back out of the lair of light
into the flickering gloom.

                                    The wounded wits
played on the broken bottles of despair,
struck the tin cans of helpless misery,
and poetry was smothered by the drums.

Brief, for a moment, we grasped the hem of Peace . . .

Along the mirror river by the trees,
the tansy's golden buttons, and the shells
of a new mollusc bitted the bounding heart
back to a new track of promised permanence.
There too a field of corn in heavy sheaf,
brown gold against blue shadow of green tree,
steadied the shifting pattern of belief.

But the old battles still were left unwon:
men driven from their homes to beg for shelter
or seize it.

All authority impotent,
before the frantic chalk marks on the wall.

What hope, we thought then, for the foolish people,
what hope for our desire to bring them life,
abundant life; first for the body's need,
then for the heart's?

The broader field of time
brought hushed concern for maps, the league's delay,
the bullfrog leader and the bearded king,
widening to a net to mesh the world,
narrowing to a personal decision,
that must be made to keep the core of self
not flashing off at wheelwhirl of event.

I remembered one who went to die in France,
hating the war and wishing only to paint,
but dreading more the pointed finger and gibe,
and what his son might think when he had grown.
Remembered, too, that deft hand with the brush,
glad to slop filth and human excrement,
rather than crack his fleas in a frontline trench,
or have his sensitive wits scraped bare with suspense.

Then when to Bristol, town of Chatterton,
I went alone, intent upon my trade,
camp follower of the wayward feet of men,
hoarder of trifles scattered by the road,
of things well made and broken or half made,
strainer of cinders, winnower of dust,
preserver of the shards, keeper of names,
lackey of time, ostler of the Apocalypse –
suddenly there descended over me
sense of the instant's mergence into time,
my plight no more or less on the rims of space
than the busy gestures of Cabot, father and son,
lading the little vessel for adventure,
ruling their course and ticking off the crew,

Burke's rhetoric, or the dreams of a western heaven
blueprinted by Robert Southey and his friends.

I walked those streets aware of older streets
before the black glass and the chromium;
Corn Street, Wine Street, Red Lodge, Christmas Steps,
Paragon Terrace built with the price of slaves,
and the famous Gothic of St Mary Redcliffe.

And when chance sent me jolted to the south,
over the Mendip hills by Cheddar Gorge,
Westhover, Westhay, crossing the River Brue,
the thing was plainer. Life was eternal life:
the windfalls littered in the tufted grass,
the bigger apples netted in a heap,
men milking in the meadows, twisty roads,
red roofs of tiles, stacks thatched with yellow straw:
life was eternal, involving every instant.
Change creed or state; apples of Somerset
make cider to be drunk by living men.

At Meare, in a wind-whipped field as flat as bog
(my Antrim eye had noted, so it proved),
there had been dug a magic hole through time
revealing a crisscross raft of oak and alder
and silver birch with the bark not rotted yet,
where men had wrought and sung before Christ's birth:
the nail-scored pot, bonecomb, smooth ring of jet,
the blade now shattered and the amber beads,
the baked clay hearth and the bars of hammered iron.

Man has gone on, endured the incidence
of Rome and Caesar, lived to see the end
of woad and crucifixion, Thor and Zeus:
if not men individual with these faces,
jaws set so, brows this angle, eyes this colour,
man has gone on, essential man, the Maker,
the double man, destroyer in his blood,
charring the wood and heaping hills of slag,
smearing a plain with slums, and firing the whin;
yet out of his nature making something lovely;
a bronze blade meant to kill, but leaf-precise.

Always the touch of immortality
upon the things of death; the mark of life
on things with else no secondary meaning.
For it is not the wars that we remember
but the chiselled face, the brooch, the silver bugle,
the temple, and the sonnet: these are Man.

And knowing this, I thought of the things I care for.
I knew my choice was the choice of life and good:
though men still choose the way of death and evil,
life in them works denial of their waste
through the superb economy of art,
cleaves through their chaos with a feathered joy.
A faith men murdered thousands for may leave
a symbol life's the richer for, a ritual
recovered, that may waken a lost sense.

I saw how the two engines of my thought
and being, despite the clogging grease of self,
beat in the right direction.
First, positive action gearing the destroyer,
crushing the rocks for basis, digging clear
the level path for justice, the paved way
for mercy: tentative effort following
of sheer creation out of my sense-fed scope,
leaving the things I love no poorer for
my loving them, and adding where I can
my touch of life, of life articulate
through me, a particular focus of memories.

So, at the ship's stern as I fed the gulls,
appraising each swift arabesque of hunger,
I grew aware of the conflict of my being,
the interplay of memory and thought,
and having the dialectic in my sinews,
was eager for the resolving synthesis.

I wrote these words out, ever recognising
the shifting lights I missed in definition,
yet sure the fumbling pattern was not worthless,
that I or you in dark days coming after
might not despair because of the uncharted
but move at bidding of this uncouth compass,
though no more than a needle stuck in a straw,
and floating in a shaking bowl of water.

from

NO REBEL WORD

THE TOUCH OF THINGS

I know the touch of things: the play of mind
upon the smooth or ragged surfaces:
have reached rich ecstasy merely by thought
sent skating over glaciers of sense:
admire in a logical, intellectual way
the pattern a tree makes leaning across a window.

But these remain outside me. Light and shade
move over them, and change them, alter thought
till I become a strange anthology
bound by no thread save of a nimble wit,
and find no fabric for my spirit's house.

If life's to mean full fist and riper wisdom
these things must turn to blood, to blood and muscle,
till lash of eye is April rain transmuted
and lift of knee the sun on Antrim cliffs.

Then when I set a flock of dreams adrift
they will be pigeons wandering at will,
not paper boats blown in among the reeds,
or helter-skelter down the spated streams,
but have small eager beings of their own
to plane or circle to any possible cloud,
and then with homesick hearts come back to me.

ONCE ALIEN HERE

Once alien here my fathers built their house,
claimed, drained, and gave the land the shapes of use,
and for their urgent labour grudged no more
than shuffled pennies from the hoarded store
of well-rubbed words that had left their overtones
in the ripe England of the mounded downs.

The sullen Irish limping to the hills
bore with them the enchantments and the spells
that in the clans' free days hung gay and rich
on every twig of every thorny hedge,
and gave the rain-pocked stone a meaning past
the blurred engraving of the fibrous frost.

So I, because of all the buried men
in Ulster clay, because of rock and glen
and mist and cloud and quality of air
as native in my thought as any here,
who now would seek a native mode to tell
our stubborn wisdom individual,
yet lacking skill in either scale of song,
the graver English, lyric Irish tongue,
must let this rich earth so enhance the blood
with steady pulse where now is plunging mood
till thought and image may, identified,
find easy voice to utter each aright.

GLENARRIFFE AND PARKMORE

Go to Glenarriffe if you'd know this Antrim,
from Waterfoot's wide street of lime-washed walls
with the broad sandbank where the children play
and the gulls cry among the billowy washing.

Go to Glenarriffe, take the rising road,
the curving road that hugs the northern slope,
that winds and clambers up among the trees
and spreads the little valley flat below:
the corn and grazing trim and limited
by the dark lines of hedges: here and there
the grey gleam of a lane from farm to farm,
the houses white and slated neat as toys:
the river like a restless snake that darts
from cover of the clotted map of growth.
The valley's other side is ribbed with streams
that fall and hang like broken rods of glass
unheard against the greater central roar.
The road still urges up till on the right
your eye is level with wet boles of trees
and on the left, below, a well of air,

often mist-curdled, rimmed with pointed firs.
Then suddenly the way is bracken-banked
where hazels clothe the steepening slope with green,
and turning left across a high stone bridge,
the glen lies wide to the east and to the sea.
Through closer tangle hearing louder now
the water roar: above its breathless fall
the river is a bog-brown mountain stream
cruising and cresting over rocks and moss.

You reach the open country. Wide and bare
the rounded hills spread far as eye can draw,
with great turf stacks built wedge-like to the west,
in farther fields not easily defined
if stacks or cattle grazing in the mist:
a place man never tilled or cut for hay,
the seasons only marked by snow or sun.

The raw earth gashed with water cups the sky,
with grey clouds moulded cold and desolate,
where shaggy mountain sheep, great black-faced sheep,
browse in the raincombed grass or shelter close
to the stone walls that march along the hills.
Here is the lonely station of Parkmore,
deserted now, grass rank along the track,
hardly a tree, a dwelling here and there
grim as a fortress in debated land,
with pens well fenced but empty like a fair
with the bright stir gone from its naked stalls.
Maybe a mare with foal a lighter brown
will gallop to a gap to see who passed.

The road dips westward. Suddenly you come
on narrow fields of corn fantastic green
in the broad landscape where no colour is bright:
houses well thatched, with elder bush and fowl,
replace the grey bleak barns where shepherds live,
more numerous; you may count five at once.

The earth grows friendly with well-hedged fields,
knee-deep cows moving in the seeded grass,
shorn sheep, neat-headed, lacking the curled horn,
and children staring over a privet fence.

Trees shade the road awhile: slowly running brooks
brushing the long grass edges as they flow;
haystacks broad based, and flax wind buffeted;
potatoes flowering; beans in heavy leaf.
Earth wears the shapes of use in colour and curve.

You reach the frontier at the swollen Ravel;
a well-tilled country prosperous and mild,
the heart contented now and riding easy,
secure in the slow customary things
that man has set against the rock and fallow:
but you already know it a lesser joy
than the bare moors beneath a heavy sky
where rock and sheep and stream are timeless forms,
and Finn may raise his cry on any hill.

So you have travelled far from Waterfoot,
not marked in metres but in rhythm of pulse:
the heart uplifted with the mounting trees
and falling waters, scooped out of the air
and gapped beneath you as you stop to look;
uplifted from the transience of life
and held at level of hushed ecstasy
as if with gull's straight keel you pass
to the vast silence of unmastered earth.

THE SPLENDID DAWN

On the bare platform cold beneath the lamps
that spilled their cones of dismal light, I stood,
straining my wind-vexed eyes, my ears for shrill
train's evidence that coasts the darker shadow
we know for northern shore of that drab bay.

The water spread a dull and leaden surface
between me and the mounded island bulk.

With growing light the web of mud emerged,
the mats of sodden turf, the tangled wrack
lively with birds that rose and wheeled away
with harsh, hurt, bitter cries or settled back,
dark, restless shapes upon the hissing slime.

Then suddenly to feeling, not to time,
for time has ceased to matter to my mood,
daybreak began with colour in the sky
that colder yet had held itself aloof
from the raw, wind-whipped and unkindled earth,
and all at once a marvellous dawn appeared,
angry with sailors' warnings, spears of gold,
and burning clouds that set the world afire,
a dawn too splendid and too vast for one
lonely and cold in an unfriendly place.

ANTRIM APRIL

Over the bright green rich with buttercups
where in the level light of evening
each frightened lamb distinctly limned with gold
frolicked heraldic on the scroll of spring
a low mound moated with a brambled ditch
topped by small plough-patch of brown broken sods
upon its brow among the nettled stones
goats peering round like old priapic gods
the wild crab apple with no petal yet
but hinting crimson promise tangled arms
of cherry spiked with froth for cruising bees
the sycamore well banked for summer swarms
the blackthorn bushes delicately masked
beside the sky-deep stream abrim with rain
yoke flecks on whin the lilting larches hung
with light green plumes along the tufted lane
this was in Clady walking with my friend
remarking damson gay the misty crest
of beeches tall above the dove-grey house
at April's end when Antrim's loveliest
somewhere in Europe men were locked in war
and rocked to crush us from their tilted peak
we spoke of urgent things like poetry
but there were certain things we did not speak.

POEM IN MAY

May afternoon with birds in every bush
and the hot walls forgotten, I surrender

my tired mind, callous with slack rhetoric
and close to terror at the sick world's plight,
to this clean kingdom vehement with life
that does not need my wrist to crank its gears
but marks its rich and independent hours
with ebb and flow of perfume and of colour,
its little threads of being, chords of motion,
as restlessly complex as evening swarm
of summer midges by a drifting stream.

I lay my senses bare, uncritical,
to be possessed, enjoyed, and laid aside,
and taken up enhanced another time,
not only by my avaricious mind,
but by the swift sensations that themselves
have schooled a surer temper of response.

The life about me, from the humming ground
its gay green gemmed with yellow pimpernel,
with bracken still involved, its rusted whorls
as fat as caterpillars, to the trees
heavy with blossom, thick with singing leaves,
and the high sky a quivering dome of light,
so overcrowds the senses that I sink
into a friendly pantheistic dream
that offers healing and eternity,
secure from pain, did not the diligent
and plodding mind, not yet relaxed, insist
on small half-hearted efforts to define
the interwoven strands, the elements
that fused, create a unity beyond
the simple aggregation of their sum:
the chaffinch with his sturdy string of notes
that quavers at the end beyond his reach;
the limestone-loving neat forget-me-not
close to my toe; the moss that cracks the rock
the frosts have menaced, on whose ragged edge
I hoist my limbs; the sycamore above
that holds a birdsong still anonymous
to my poor essay, counterpointed by
the chiffchaff's seesaw pulsing monotone,
and all the sounds and colours that surround
the hard stone of my heart like endless rings
a pebble wakens in a sleepy pond.

THE LITTLE GLEN

Step off the road and in a hollow place
too rough for lovers, seldom vexed by children
until the clustered blackberries are ripe,
the blackthorn blossom and the gaudy whin
offer a dappled interval of peace.
A slow stream curbed at every little fall
by drifted leaves, and shrinking down the stones
that tilt, clay caked, for lack of recent rain,
maps out the ragged path you still may take
between the tall and ivy-smothered trees.
The broad grass swathes are rich with violet
long-stemmed by struggle to achieve the sun,
and glossy kingcup lavish of its gold,
and, banked along the whittled hawthorn hedge,
the gay wood sorrel with its blunted leaf,
and the neat stitchwort with its taper blades.
The noisy rooks pass over, and you may
pace undiverted through the netted light
as silent as a thrush with work to do.

FIRST CORNCRAKE

We heard the corncrake's call from close at hand,
and took the lane that led us near the noise;
a hedged half-acre, flanked by sycamore,
was his small wedge of world. We crouched and peered
through the close thorn. The moving cry again
swivelled our gaze. Time whispered in the leaves.
A tall ditch-grass blade rocked as a languid bee
brushed the dry sliver with a rasping wing.

In silence still we watched; a careless heel
smashing a twig husk, grating on the grit,
and winning for itself a warning glance.
Then, when strung patience seemed about to yawn
as if the world demanded leave to move
on its slung reeling pitch about the sun,
I saw a head, a narrow pointed head
stirring among the brown weed-mottled grass
as the monotonous and edgy voice
kept up its hard complaint. I held the spot

in a fixed gaze. The brown head disappeared,
was seen in seconds in another clump,
and for a blessed moment, full in sight
the brown bird, brighter than the book foresaw,
stood calling in a little pool of grass.
I moved a finger and you shared the joy
that chance till then had never offered us.

It would have been a little grief to know
this punctual cry each year, and yet grow old
without one glimpse of him that made the cry.
The heart still hankers for the rounded shape.

THE ALDER STICK

Cutting an alder branch to shape a stick,
I peeled the thick bark off green strip by strip;
like bitten apple the white wood turned red,
rust-red of beech leaf not of cherry or lip;
and as I wrought it, pausing now and then
to balance on my fingers or to swing,
feeling its strength along my arm, I thought
men fools to name this wood a useless thing,
good only for the props and piles whereon
to heap their brittle walls of stone and brick.
Its red blood stained my hands. The mark remains.
I have gained something more than plodding stick.

SEPTEMBER LULL

This house well fenced with alder, sycamore,
and beech that was a flickering copse of song
from the grey hour before the wakened day
was brimmed with wing-beat and the work of birds
until the last rook left the empty sky
knows only now the strong winds blustering
and the sharp batteries of the gusty rain.

This is the ebb of birdsong. You may see
a startled robin scuffle in the hedge
and hear no more than curlews passing over
the bare wet hill between you and the light.

I TURN TO TREES

I turn to trees: these trees are metaphors
for some green truth that traps and taps the sun,
not merely in my own and lonely mind
but in that part of life all beings share
which seizes from the end results of sense
the flow, the pulse, the continuity,
that even gives the forked divided man
the mute coherence that a shadow throws.

These are not merely allegorical trees,
fictions for fashion, counters for a game,
worth this and this by usage and agreement.
These mortal trees have immortality
lively in sap and acid. When I walk
my heel is always on a withered leaf.

NOVEMBER WOOD

Walking today beneath the bankrupt trees,
the long grass grey and shabby, and the tracks
glazed with the rain, defeat seems absolute.

Here where the berries bred defiance of
bramble's defence in depth, shrunken and black
a few remain on winter-shrivelled bush,
that if you reach a hand and touch the tongue
are tasteless drops of water round a seed.
The seasons of the leaves are stratified;
the first, save for the ribs, dispersed in clay,
the later layers gone rotten but intact,
and crisp on top, the silver sycamore.

On a dead trunk brought down by falling years
are mats of moss, soft to the cheek and dry,
with little crocus-threads of hanging flowers,
and all the thorn trees sheathed and smothered in
a fur of lichen lifeless to the touch,
through which hard haws thrust out on their dark stems,
their shape and colour both irrelevant
to the dead textures of the muffled twigs.

This wood wears death beyond the season's death;
the tax of time has sapped its capital.

Infrequent thistle and ground ivy here
still signal life amid a world's despair.

EAST ANTRIM WINTER

Wet roads between black hedges, and a sky
faint yellow-green with sunset, ribbed by trees
all stripped to twigs. Unregimented, loose,
rooks flap for home with slow and easy beat
from the dark furrows that this morning's plough
ripped over the bleached stubble. At the bridge
the glutted ripples crowd beneath the arch,
each spined with light like twinkling stickleback,
or idly turn aside and coast the stones
that held the withered lichen since the floods
of August draped each nape with wisps of straw.
White in the distance in the dayli'gone
move fists and faces, metal to the light
the cycle's wheel-rims and a swinging can.
Only a lonely blackbird cries aloud,
near hand but out of sight.

Sun's tide recedes,
then darkens as a cap of cloud descends;
but no lamp wakens in the scattered farms.
The moon will rise on a defeated world.

THE HIRED LAD'S FAREWELL

The farm boy, only older than myself
by two tanned years, sighed like a grandfather,
shifted his ragged body on the stack,
and plucked a longer straw. With chin on knees,
I sat not looking at him, gazing out
beyond the lime-washed pillars at the yard,
where a late hen that'd strayed all afternoon,
ran clucking back and scraping round the door.
From the open byre came swish of lazy tails
and noisy breathing till a bucket fell.

Rooks gathered in the dark elms near the house.
The sun's last crested torch set earth aflame

till stack and hedge were smouldering in a haze.
Tomorrow I'll be going home again . . .
For two months now Sandy and I had been
close friends and comrades in this country life.
I had learned much from him. More than I will
ever learn in so short a time. Today,
I walk more wisely for the knowledge he gave,
know lore of cow and horse, of crop and root,
that brims my heart up when a screaming train
tears through green acres from town to smoky town.

He'd learned from me a scrap or two of verse,
the names of foreign places and strange tribes,
and something of three men who have given life
a richer texture by their simple words,
and how to hold a bat, or toss a lob,
that gave more trouble than my overarm.
We both were changed through meeting with each other.
We would not ever be just quite the same.

Now life became the thing I'd heard men curse,
had used us each for each, then sundered us.
In three months' time the lad would go to sea,
an older cousin promised that last year . . .
for all his people always went to sea
though bred in a country place of corn and flax
and early familiar with the ways of cattle.
For their small meadows stumbled to the sea's edge
and broke in cliff and shingle to the waves.
And brine was on the hay the creatures munched,
giving a tang to the milk. They spread brown kelp
over the dug fields at the proper time
and got good crops: as good as any dung;
while blackhead gulls screamed in the plowman's wake.

He would go to sea for thirty or forty years
then settle down, a lighthouse keeper or pilot,
at some lost crumbling cliff-foot round the coast;
but never again go back to work on the land:
no more to the end than window box of lilies.
It seemed a foolish thing to lose his wisdom,
hard-mastered skill he spent his boyhood getting,
only to turn his hand to rope and shovel;

and eat tinned pork and biscuit, who knew how
to slit hog's throat, or stack the heavy sheaves.

Tomorrow then I'd sit in the farmer's trap
on labelled box and wave a nervous hand,
while Sandy'd stand peering over the trampled hedge
just where the heifer broke through yesterday.
And after I'd not see him any more,
unless maybe an Indian typhoon
fling me into a bar in Singapore,
or at some quayside walking to the train
I'd catch a glimpse of him through an open port.
But here we were on the stack's top, very still.
Old Brennan's black bull roared. The moyley cow,
that was Jane's pet, lowed quietly back to him.
The shadows of the elms and stacks spread out.
What sun was left shone on the tips of stubble:
a curlew or some other wandering bird
cried from the lough. Far off an engine hooted.

Tomorrow I was going home for good,
and even if I came again next year
he would be gone. I thought of friendly things,
of our antics on the hayfloat, or picking up
hard little windfalls bitter in the mouth,
or scrambling in the rafters after a nest,
or crawling on our bellies after beans,
or whipping up the pony or whacking pigs
till their red buttocks quivered as they ran.
But it was useless.
                                I was going home
and Sandy here was going away to sea.

He never was at best a clever talker,
even with the family round the kitchen table.
At least his eyes were full of comradeship
and pity at the parting. I had been
the first boy to run with him as a friend,
for he'd no brothers or sisters, was an orphan,
and always was a sort of hired lad
out working for his keep to sullen people.

Now he was going away, a hired lad,
indentured to the sea till time should end.

And I was going home to a city of brick
to bind myself to a desk and a shelf of books . . .

The sun set sharp behind the Antrim ridge,
and there was one star over Muldersley Hill.
I shall not be more sad at any death.

THE BROTHERS

We saw him first stretching for blackberries,
a tall and shambling lad with an English tongue,
and, knee high, by his side a tiny boy,
tow-headed, munching what his brother plucked.

Then after, urgent in the driving rain,
downhill towards the village, once again
we passed them coming up; the little child
well wrapped against the weather in his car,
the tall lad pushing silent, his wet hair
flat on his brow. He answered our salute,
and thrust on aimless, snapping over twigs
the ceaseless gale had flung upon the road
with muddy leaves reversed and fuchsia flowers.

At noon, at dusk, we've seen the moving pair
ignoring weather and the time of day,
resting no more than birds rest, by a bush
or for a moment by the six-barred gates
these farmers guard their fields with.

When the day
seems all propitious we shall stop to talk,
and they shall answer in their separate ways
why they are bound so to these hilly roads,
and what their world is like, and who may be
the other strange inhabitants besides
the heavy heron with the floppy wings,
the black rooks homing to the smoky trees
and the small robin on the whitewashed post.

MINOTAUR

What savage world is this when folk to live
must lace their boots and walk across the sea,

or gut their summers with the herring fleet,
spending their senses, wearing bone and hide
on the hard harvest beds or hefts of picks
and posting life in little packets home?

We hurried to the pier to catch the boat,
Willy Bonar's boat that goes to Aranmore,
were early, waited sitting on a box
with dry claws in the corner. Down the steps
the green tide struck and fell in little rills,
and the rope tautened, tethered to the boat
below us rocking as its ribs were slapped
and tiny worms of light made scribbling dance
flickering along the curving underside.

The long bare quay was empty and the rails
truckless and rusted. Then a young man came,
lively and trim, his left hand in his pocket,
hatless with flagging flannels to his shoes,
nodded good day and slippered down the steps,
stretched to the boat and lightly leaped on board,
shifted a hatch and tinkered in the square
of hollow deck, his shoulders out of sight.

Gazing to sea we saw a moving shape
too slow for shag and much too far away,
lost in the dip and trough, but coming in
with clearer definition gradually:
a small boat with two figures at the stern,
a dirty sail upon a stumpy mast.

Our lazy glances swung to watch the sky,
a sprawl of bundled clouds that carried rain
from the high bulk of Aranmore across
the flat green islands that lie in between
our rocky world's edge and that misted shape
and must be threaded through on a rolling swell.

The boat approached – an old man and a girl –
the sail was lowered, and a splashing oar
geared its momentum with familiar skill.
It bumped the steps, was tied, and they came up
after a parley with the lad who now
had found a tongue beyond mere courtesies.

They stopped with us and passed the time of day,
located us by speech, although we lacked
the lilting Irish phrase, as Irish too;
and talked a little of the distant war,
and if our house still stood and how we'd fared:
then hurried off, the old man with a box
and the young girl with hat and leather case,
her Midland destination on her lips
and twenty island years on hands and cheeks.

We rose and moved a little. Bonar next,
a broad-faced fellow with a grey cloth cap,
saluted us, and so we went aboard,
avoiding cones of rope and the lashed mast.
They spoke some words. The young man nimbly stretched
from the high bow and loosened the wet knot
round the stone pillar. Bonar with an oar
fended us off. The engine volleyed out
its random quickfire, and the stench of oil
subdued the herring smell that had become
accepted climate for our enterprise.
Then Bonar's brown left hand controlled our turn.
We passed the near-hand reef and headed clear
for the rough water running north to south,
saw to the north the great seas breaking white,
and to the south the surf on Islandcrone.

The steady engine needing no more care,
the young man sprawled at last beside the hatch,
his left arm hanging by his side, the hand
gloved but disclosing wrist of bone or wood.
We gasped at it amazed, remembering
with shock that all the nimble things he'd done –
stretching and vaulting, tugging rope and spar –
had been accomplished with a deft right arm
which we had watched but never realised.
We turned to Bonar, whose good-natured voice
grated a whisper, answering our thought:
'He lost his left arm working on a farm
last year in England when a binder caught it
and nearly pulled his bloody shoulder out.
He always was a bugger for machines . . .'
And then as if an afterthought, he added,
'And so he can't go back like the rest of them.'

So, as we hit the channel, and the swell
swiftly thrust back the rocks on either side
and the stone houses with no stir of life
save for the silent gulls and screaming gulls,
the urgent shag that wave-high crossed our bows
and one grey heron quiet on a stone,
we held in one hurt thought the tragedy
of this harsh rim of Europe in the west.

This is a savage country for the young,
and yet the old have little bitterness,
but give a kindly word for strangers when
a child or dog reports that they are here.

They curse the barren soil, the narrow fields,
as though it were a ritual, and then
summon their years to witness that the world
has bred no better people than their kin.

THE WITCH

A bunch of wrack was hung inside the porch
with frost of salt upon it, and the man
who lived within came out and looked at it
each morning for what weather was to be.
Then he went in and blew the ashen turf
and swung the kettle over the new glow
and called to the sick woman in the bed.

He was a bearded man, with puckered face
above his sailor's jersey: but his age
was far outside a small boy's aimless guess
and not worth asking, with so many things
he had to tell of ships and foreign ports.

He'd sit outside, a dish between his feet,
and drop the cleaned potatoes into it,
piling the parings on another dish,
talking of Newfoundland and Liverpool
and men he'd served with. Then he'd cross the road
and hurl the parings over the sea wall
among the tins and splintered lobster pots
for gulls to scatter. Then he would go in

to make the dinner, and I'd walk away
kicking a ball among the drying nets.

I saw the woman once. My mother'd sent me
to fill a bucket at the gushing pipe,
and I was coming back not spilling it.
I looked in at the seaweed in the porch
when suddenly the half-door snapped its latch,
a little figure in a faded shawl
bowed on a stick, with little skinny legs,
came shuffling out. I saw her crazy face
yellow and dirty, with brown burning eyes
like all the witches in my picture books.

I stopped in fright. She opened her creased mouth
and mumbled something that I could not hear
and didn't want to.
                    When I found my strength
I dropped the bucket and ran straight for home.

Next day the sailor would not speak to me.

THE SWATHE UNCUT

As the brown mowers strode across the field
shapes fled before them thrusting back the grain,
till in a shrinking angle unrevealed
the frightened hare crouched back, the last at bay,
for even the corncrake, blind in his dismay,
had found the narrow safety of the drain.

And so of old the country folk declared
the last swathe holds a wayward fugitive,
uncaught, moth-gentle, tremulously scared,
that must be, by the nature of all grain,
the spirit of the corn that should be slain
if the saved seed will have the strength to live.

Then by their ancient ritual they sought
to kill the queen, the goddess, and ensure
that her spent husk and shell be safely brought
to some known corner of beneficence,
lest her desired and lively influence
be left to mock the next plough's signature.

So I have figured in my crazy wit
in this flat island sundered to the west
the last swathe left uncut, the blessed wheat
wherein still free the gentle creatures go
instinctively erratic, rash or slow,
unregimented, never yet possessed.

LYRIC

Let but a thrush begin
or colour catch my eye,
maybe a spring-woke whin
under a reeling sky,

and all at once I lose
mortality's despair,
having so much to choose
out of the teeming air.

HAY

Already summer crested, the decline,
the surf of blossom fails, the high green tide
hangs lulled at full. The sullen midnight's line
of silver light has its precarious hour.
A weariness now drowses on the flower
that into seed or apple has not died.

The swallows that were urgent in the eaves
turn wing less deftly. None shall pause to see
untutored fledglings fluster in the leaves.
Only the hay cut wet and laid in rows
achieves that rich and aromatic close
the heart demands for all maturity.

THE LITTLE LOUGH

There in a bare place, in among the rocks,
grey rounded boulders shouldered from the ground,
where no field's big enough to yield three stacks
and corn grows on a fistful of black land,
is a small narrow lake, narrow and brown,

with whistling rushes elbowed here and there
and in the middle is a grassy stone
that heron or some other wanderer
will rest on darkly. Sometimes there will rise
a squawking mallard with a startling spray,
heading far inland, that the swift eyes lose
in the low mist that closes round the day.

Though many things I love should disappear
in the black night ahead of us, I know
I shall remember, silent, crouching there,
your pale face gazing where the rushes grow,
seeking between the tall stems for the last
black chick the grebe is cruising round to find,
my pointing finger showing it not lost
but sheltered only from the ruffling wind.

LYRIC

Chestnut and beech
sycamore and willow
with one chill touch
of autumn are yellow.

Even the alder
slanting over the river
is cold and older
than you shall be ever

who hold a thought
with a simple passion
shall last through drought
to the rainy season.

SONNET IN AUTUMN

During this silence, innocent of song,
concerned with faces, places, shapes of stone,
things thrusting hands out, eager to be known,
forms true at distance, proving to be wrong
on close sensation, I have lost the long
withdrawal of the sap, the undertone

of leaf's retreat. The heedless rose has blown
unmarked, unneeded in the hooting throng.

I turn today then from the published mask,
the attitude commended, phrase assayed,
the imminent insistence of the task,
because the hard bright berries of the haw
report an older, an austerer law,
a season older, suddenly afraid.

SONNETS IN OCTOBER

Now striding through the reaped and withered year;
the stacks black in the fields, the stubble grey,
and the red sun at either end of day
slipping through mist, one star at twilight clear,
but later lost in a thronged hemisphere,
the children's voices shriller in their play,
the sycamore's broad rags that sprawl and splay
bring back the hours that make October dear.

For closely scan the twigs these leaves have spurned,
and you shall see the black buds on the tips
that urge their way toward repeated springs,
and yet before that consummation's earned
there are the days when breath shall feather lips
with the true songs that only winter sings.

Now who dare say in autumn: this is new-
ripeness and leaf-fall, harvest of desire,
the year's grey phoenix nested on the pyre,
the choking smoke that lets the phoenix through,
the spring-lipped hopes that to fruition drew
and now in rich satiety retire.
Yes, fling these withered words upon the fire;
yet say of autumn that they still are true.

For in October born, my veins have kept,
whatever men with lens and blade deny
about the implications of the blood,
a sober joy that, squirrel-curled, has slept
till wakened by the flame in leaf and wood
for all the coloured summers crowding by.

LEAF

O fall of the leaf I am tired,
with this sunset let me be still.
The tips of the stubble are fired
by the slanted blade of the sun
sheathing his flame in the hill.
Let me smoulder so and be done.

The withered leaf tumbles and turns
over lazy islands of air,
more lovely now as it burns
than when it was green overhead.
Let me draw from autumnal despair
the strength to be tired without dread.

The pigeons, a dozen and two,
take a half-mile circle of light:
they are washed in the green and the blue
and the delicate gold of the sky.
Let me narrow in on my night
with that effortless certainty.

LOAD

Today we carted home the last brown sheaf
and hooked the scythe against the dry barn wall:
the yellow border's on the chestnut leaf,
the beech leaf's yellow all.

Tomorrow we must bring the apples in,
they are as big as they shall ever be:
already starlings eager to begin
have tasted many a tree.

And in the garden, all the roses done,
the light lies gently, faint and almost cold,
on withered golden-rod and snapdragon
and tarnished marigold.

FROST

With frost again the thought is clear and wise
that rain made dismal with a mist's despair,

the raw bleak earth beneath cloud-narrowed skies
finds new horizons in the naked air.
Light leaps along the lashes of the eyes;
a tree is truer for its being bare.

So must the world seem keen and very bright
to one whose gaze is on the end of things,
who knows, past summer lush, brimmed autumn's height,
no promise in the inevitable springs,
all stripped of shadow down to bone of light,
the false songs gone and gone the restless wings.

THE MASK

The grey efficient masks rock home by bus,
peering at print, are hung in hall with hat
or left in bathroom mirrors overnight
till soap and razor slick them on again.
Bland mask smirks over knife and glancing cup,
ticking new scores to sympathetic mask
lettered inside domestic mother-size:
but rubber tightens with a slapping snap,
the wearer fumbles, mumbles, disappears;
is found by rose bed puffing at a pipe
or silent-slippered, tripping after bowls,
the old creased shiny mask with sagging jowl
lifted from peg beside the torn tweed coat.

THE HAPPY MAN

The happy leave no clues. The frightened man
peers backward to the taws behind the door,
the shattered flowerpot, the embezzled change.
The cynic wears the laminated boot
he limped with round the twilit cinder track.
The rebel always carries on his back
the roaring master or the prim-lipped aunt.
The sprawling signature curves back in time.
But when the happy man has left the room
we only can recall the instant's spur
that woke his laughter or provoked his smile.
We cannot prove how he was taught to laugh.

THIS THEN MY COUNTRY

This then my country, not parturient,
but boulder-sterile, cragging harsh and bare,
not the round-bellied meadow indolent,
or the healed gashes of the loving share.

My stock, if head's a measure, otherwise
legged ample acres, taut with eager growth;
cocked eye for manifesto in the skies,
and by the Corn God thrusting made their oath:
but by the westward gust were plucked and flung
across two waters to an alien ground;
there set about familiar tasks of dung
and furrow till the flow again was found.

Lettered on page, the way they came and went,
my restless fathers, tapes a tidal curve;
the shapes of history, rise or fall per cent
insisting motive for the leap or swerve,
in them was not such, but decision made:
a man upon a gate or by a fire,
tired of his ailing father or his trade,
or eager for the body of his desire.

So out and on, until the growing thing
that rooted us to earth's fierce pumping flow,
the hidden light that swilled the loins with spring
and warmed the chill heart walled with sky and snow,
the growing thing was shattered, broken clean.
There is no seed or crop to know my hand.
No sod responds. Thought wanders spare and lean
across the whin and heather of my land.

GHOSTS

I have no ghosts.
My dead are safely dead:
my grandfather reading the paper, my grandmother
fumbling in cupboards, my uncle with his clubs
standing idly, his left hand licked by the dog,
or walking rapidly talking of Mark Twain.

These are flat pictures flickering in the mind
with focus narrowing, widening, blurring, lost.
They are not repeating these acts on another plane,
and when they did them they were not shadows of things
but suffering creatures moving with pain or joy.

They survive now only in the brittle thoughts
of a dwindling group of people.
                                        If I could
gather the scattered colours and shapes and words
that are left in minds of a dozen friends growing old
any manikin I'd make would never stir.

The winter evening reading and asking questions
while my grandfather straightened his tasselled cap
and gave the answer, had surely spun a cable
that should hold when the hesitant flesh had disappeared.
I knew his mind and mocked him and loved him well;
he knew my rash opinions and jeered at them.

Yet he is dead and has not whispered a word,
or shifted a glass of water on a table.
I even begin to forget the sound of his voice.

Died first to the active senses, dying again
to the senses in memory, touch and hearing are gone;
only a listless eye remembers his face.

THE LITTLE DEATH

in memory of Shelley Wang, Chinese poet and patriot,
died in Honan, 1939

I cannot cheat my thought. I remember too well
his bland smooth face by the hearth, his cigarettes,
his explanation of the characters,
the firm fist with the brush held vertical,
his glinting glasses laminated thick;
his way of speaking of his early days,
his wise grandfather, ways of making tea,
Confucius, soya beans, and Mao Tse-tung,
his interest in my clumsy Western thought.

My spirit grew beneath his influence
as seedling sprouts in cinematograph,

waving uncertain arm and alternating
with night and morning, suddenly abrupt,
jostling the big rough grains of earth aside
and stretching towards the warmth that wakened it.

He was a quiet man, a humble scholar,
compact of wisdom, courage, tolerance,
a gentle poet, even of our hills,
making a lovely stanza as he passed,
disliking our coarse literal arts' conceit
and setting style and reason against despair.

For all his greatness life could offer him
only a little death in a vast campaign,
a manuscript unpublished and a book
of badly printed verse on wartime paper.
Yet I do not think he would have understood
that sick word failure. There are other words . . .

INTERIM

Henceforth my slow skill I must only spend
to phrase affection, or to mourn a friend;
to state the convolutions of my thought
in quiet verse deliberately wrought,
leaving the coloured crags' romantic line
for humbler acre fairly mapped as mine:
stranger to passion, never strongly moved
to those emotions use has not approved;
responsive to the year's flow, spring and fall,
saluting winter at the end of all:
yet hoping that in twenty years I'll find
wisdom like Marvell's comfortable mind,
and that my thought and action prove to be
secure in similar integrity.

THOSE SWANS REMEMBER
A POEM

for Austin Clarke

I

The symbols jostle for their breathing space,
elbow each other like a football crowd,
whereas that crowd should split and offer place
to let them enter singly down the track,
where the green field awaits the play of grace,
the uncommitted gestures of the proud,
before the whistle launches pack on pack,
and the high stands give tongue, responsive, loud.

There should be that slow, stately ritual
when courteous gestures lob or toss the ball
in genuflection to the earnest game
which waits above the arena to descend,
while those that watch may still give each his name
and the opposers speak as friend with friend.

II

But in an instant this strained simile
falls like a wattled fence before the flood,
the shouting waves of image urgently
thrust toward the shores of consciousness to be
identified, defined and understood.

III

Name them as they appear or disappear
in this close huddle. Phoenix, Unicorn,
the Tiger, Hawk, the Ram, the Bull, the Deer,
the Hound and Hare miraculously born
to be each other's shadow, Heron, Swan,
Gannet and Badger, flickering Bat and Owl,
the White Horse by the river with its foal,
the moon-raged Lion. Set the scene for dawn,
for noon or sunset, for eternity,
whatever tint that takes when it shall come.
Pluck harp; strike fiddle; beat the single drum;
let bagpipes grieve, and bid the trilling fife

lift in the wind that fills the banners out:
this is the stage and circus of my life,
that's aimed at drama, that may end in rout.

The Tiger first, Blake's Tiger, which was led
leashed in a dream forewarning, pleading pity,
companioned by the Lion, glaring red,
from the high rocks, upon the empty city;
city of ruins, fallen columns, squares
that nothing save the ant or lizard cross;
town with the foundered gables, where the stairs
scale the cracked plaster and torn wallpaper;
that town intact, untenanted, where still
the traffic lights propose, approve, deny
safe transit to the goggled messenger
with gloved despatch of empty victory.

The first whelps lambs – the paradox is clear –
black-faced and crying on the lonely moss,
the striding shepherd, searching, finds them here,
Good Shepherd of the print, Saint Christopher,
knee-deep in glazes over the shut door;
the staff, the crook, the crozier, the cross
mid most of three, skull-rooted, that same tree
which stood by Eden's streams. Yet why should oak,
or elm or beech mean less than sycamore,
than chestnut, or than alder, hazel, thorn,
hawthorn and blackthorn both, though these with rime
are more song-sodden than the bee-thronged lime?

Oak is for use, is for humanity,
is of and for the English, even though
Colmcille loved his Derry long ago,
is sawn and staved and curved and carved to meet
the hands' demands. The chanting Druid folk,
for all their spells, have left it but a tree,
its nature yielded to its purposes,
though these be wide as sprawl of rimless seas
or strictly ordered as a one-way street.

The hawthorn's dense with magic, twisted, thick,
unlucky to the house, but worth a wish
above the springwell spreading; sycamore,
though neatly turned by lathe to simple dish,

is the immortal nest of that small man
who wished to see Christ plain above the press;
blackthorn is blackthorn winter, the black stick
breaking in blossom; it may also be
the resurrection; but the merry haws,
lavish on spray, foretelling winter dearth,
draped with dragged tufts of lint and varnished straws,
declare that, to the Man Above, the earth
is no mere once-wound toy which tirelessly
must slot and mesh until the worn spring breaks;
yet, of the woody creatures, hazel wakes
the oldest wonder, clean, unchristened, free
of any burdened guilt or prick of treachery.
Its forked twigs twist for water rightly held,
for water is its kin and answers it:
it keeps its nature not as oak when felled
that turns to timber eager for the tool;
the lithe rods still are hazel, bent or split:
but still for ever by the mountain pool
the Hazel leans, whose nuts all knowledge hold,
all knowledge older than man's scrabbling wit,
and in due season drop out of the air
into the water waiting; slow and cold
the Salmon of All Knowledge waits to eat,
its ancient nurture, each close kernel's meat.

The nuts drop in the pool: the Salmon there
is wisest of all creatures, old and wise,
who equally can hope and fear outstare
with the cold focus of unblinking eyes:
this, from the ancient legendry I share
simply by breathing in the drifting air
near the swift waters of a mountain glen,
and with it, knowledge also, of the kind
that jingles in the pockets of the mind,
but has the smallest currency with men.

This Salmon of All Knowledge is the same
in napkin woven, scratched upon the sand
and quickly smoothed away with idle shoe;
which is the signal for the Secret Name.
When you are friendless in a heathen land
shew this, and thou'lt be taken by the hand

to where we meet together, we, the few,
who know the parable and understand.

This is the Phoenix also, that which came
westward from time, the self-engendered flame
when the swept leaves are burnt, foreshadowing,
through the coiled smoulder, the green fires of spring.
This Phoenix, by some mythologic twist,
splits into Eagle rising from the smoke
and the singed Scorpion scuttling from the blaze;
yet each, in turn, the emblem of Saint Luke,
saint of my season, my evangelist
of those that wrote Christ's story in four ways,
and Scorpio, my sign, the jagged tongued,
who is himself the cause by which he's wronged.

And in the autumn, swifts and swallows gone,
there passes overhead the urgent swan
to inland waters stretching neck and wing,
till driven down the shoreward slope again
by the first bugles of returning spring.
Those swans, remember, lacked the golden chain,
yet linked the dark Aegean to the Moyle,
daring the whistling winds and crossing slow
the painted roof of Michelangelo,
past Tara's grass and the wrecked Trojan spoil.

Already the Three Rivers are conjoined
that found in springs upon the haunted hills
their first begetting: ledges, clefts and sills
could not divert them from this meeting place,
conjunction of their colours in one point,
as white they say's epitome of hues
the rainbow signals to the stricken world,
so webbed and stressed it has nor time nor use
for any truth so anciently unfurled.

Minerva's owl, harsh fowl of prophecy,
a ghost mid tree boles. Hawk and gannet mine,
more mine the plunging gannet than the hawk,
who take that plummet as a secret sign,
swift in intention, slowly, in disdain,
wheeling upon the purpose. More than he,
the flagging heron rising from the pool

or stilted on a stone beside the sea;
I too obey an old and lonely rule.

The White Horse now comes pounding down the slope
to stop beside the black star-bubbled stream,
a Saxon totem; part of Plato's trope;
the Dutch king's charger; ballad-maker's theme;
True Thomas saddled; when the firm girth broke
and Oisin tumbled in among his years,
that like grey nettles waited for his fall,
and Patrick mobbed him with his praying folk,
the white horse turned and fled with twitching ears
and left the small man lonely, last of all
the Fenians, Oisin blinking through his tears;
Oisin pursued by Patrick's nagging words,
the old hawk harried by the croaking birds.

The hawk Oisin, and Colm the angry dove,
begin a flight which takes me high and far
across grey waters under a bright star
to where all skills may live in quiet love,
but as tides clash between the cliff and cape
back through the thresh the salmon all return,
pause at the weir and in light's leaping shape
achieve the inland loughs where they were born,
so Oisin came as his heart bade him come
to face the change and challenge of his home.

The hawk is drawn, clear, firm and angular,
among the wings of angels on the page
where the lines join in one unending band,
though interlaced and interwoven far
beyond the skill and art of mortal hand,
in stream's meanders such as salmon trace;
though tangles seem to knot in monster's rage,
the whole's inscribed with cold and laboured grace.
But closer to the heart, the lithe white cat
that rubbed its shoulder on the scribe's worn shoe
till he thrust by the missal he was at,
and jotted down those stanzas, sharp and true,
on cats and poets, moves across the page,
clenched in intention, focused on its aim,
to let the paws' ten syllables engage
upon its prey, yet keep alive the game.

Lions there are, the Lion of Saint Mark,
proud-breasted with the standard in his paw;
the leaping salmon; and a writhing horde
that never tumbled out of Noah's Ark,
that all men fear but no man ever saw;
but not the twilight badger. He will stay
till crack of twig or even whispered word
send him down headlong to his tunnelled den,
the swiftest comment on the race of men.

The deer alarmed will also start away,
the deer so shy that were protective once,
when Patrick strode among them through the king s
wide scattered camp with his companions,
invisible as if with seraph wings
his passage had been masked, will start away,
leaping to cover; but the unicorn
returns at certain times to dip his horn
in the foul pool that it be rendered clean
for those who drink hereafter. Therefore pray
the unicorn, that white and gentle beast,
that he come back again. Yet if he come,
the lion, still opposing, must appear
with tilted crown, recruiting sergeant's drum –
O white and gentle creature, come not near,
but through the shadows delicately pass
between the dark pool and the moonlit grass.

That emblem's known: but where were ever found
these brave supporters matched each side a shield?
Should but the quick hare turn to face its hound
the mortal laws of heraldry must yield
to a new order; water then should burn,
and oil quench fire, and man grow young and gay,
and the tumultuous ages backward turn
to the first birdsong of the primal day,
the Tiger and the Lamb together play.

from

TESSERAE

HAND OVER HAND

Some time now I have felt outside life
floating like a padded man
on a slack cable round his capsule
with neither pull nor drag.

Dangerous to continue the slow
limbs flexing not gesturing.
One measures things by standing near them
and reaching towards them.

This billowing freedom threatens to
smother me with euphoria.
Hand over hand eagerly I crawl
back to uncertainty.

BETRAYAL

I had a nurse when I was very small –
God only knows how we afforded her,
teachers' salaries being what they were.
Yet we lacked nothing much that I recall.

I loved her well. She always wore a hat,
and prammed me out along the afternoon,
from vast adventures coming home too soon.
My careless chatter put an end to that.

I learned to talk apace. One fated day
my father asked me if the park was fun.
The simple truth was that our steady run
was to a crony's house a mile away,
where I was loosed from harness and let out
to tumble with my cronies on the floor,
while one of our tall seniors went next door
and brought back six black bottles they called stout

and sweeties for the children. So I told
that we had been where stout and ladies were.
My father called the nurse in, being fair,
and, though he talked a long time, did not scold.

She combed my curls next day and went away,
and I was broken-hearted for a week.
That you should always think before you speak
was something which I learned a later day.

NO SECOND TROY

Later, more mother's help than mine alone,
our nurse returned, and choked affection woke;
the private games renewed, the secret joke,
each tense with eager effort to atone.

She took my hand now I had grown so much,
and walked safe places with me, never more
to knuckle on that friendly open door.
There was great comfort in that rough hand's touch;
to bath, dry, button me and comb my hair,
set straight the ship's name on my ribboned cap,
to hoist me sleepy on her shiny lap,
and hug me safely past the squeaking stair.

One night there was a row. A shouting man
leaned on our gate and called her out by name,
he tossed a bottle on the green sod's span
to shame our house before the neighbourhood.
This final insult was too much to take:
my father said for her sake, for our sake,
she'd better give up living here, for good.

When she was gone, my questing mother found,
beneath the thick flock mattress of her bed,
long rows of empty bottles neatly spread.
Next time the dust-cart had a clinking sound.

PAVANE FOR A DEAD PROFESSOR

A sad-faced, heavy scholar
who, in spite of exemplary diligence,

had published very little
and that in 'obscure journals',
when the chance came
and the young men were away at the wars,
was invited or proposed himself
to write one in a series
of popular handbooks.

This was 'his apogee':
'His scholarship bore fruit.'
He smiled, in the street,
and scarcely limped at all.

He read a paper soon after
to a small literary society
of which I was then a member,
on Claudel or Valéry –
I forget which.

A sonorous clergyman present,
congratulating him, 'spoke at some length'
of Eluard, vaguely recollecting
a translation current at that time,
and not realising the difference.

I have not read or heard of the scholar
for many years:
his book in the popular series
has long been superseded and replaced
by another manual,
'more in keeping with
the climate of opinion'.

I should find it difficult
to lay my hands on a copy.

VIDA, MYKONOS

Each morning in the soft prismatic light,
with blue peaked cap, close-hunkered chin to knee,
on granite step the old man faced the sea,
as satin smooth, streaked amber, opal, white.
You'd hear the vessel throbbing out of sight;

then round the chapelled headland it would slide
over broad ripples, engine-stilled, to slew
'gainst tiny pier, a man and boy its crew;
boy at the tiller; man along the side
tossing a rope. Grandfather, father, son,
three necessary generations met.
Barefoot the boy would leap ashore and run
up the steep path, while from the tangled net
the catch was shaken, basketed, and won.

MYKONOS

This dun-coloured island, dry and coarse as a cinder,
with no past to speak of, let alone sing,
anchored in the pulsating shadow
of that holy place, Delos.

Humped-up out of the dark water,
with steep granite edges,
not low in the gunwale or nearly awash,
like its neighbour, with history.

Not a single broken column
with the fluted drums disjointed like vertebrae,
nor mutilated torso, boulder-big,
to ballast it.

Delos may fill some with a strange sadness
at the presence of shadowy crowds
in the narrow streets, in the *agora,*
slippering over the ruined mosaics.

Mykonos is a suburb of the hot moon,
the threshing floors on the slopes, shallow craters.
Man has not been here long
and may leave tomorrow.

Even that proud old woman in black,
high on her wide-laden donkey,
brown face shawled, dark eyes bright,
is only passing this way.

DELOS

Delos in the bright sea-light,
tufted with pillars, coupled or alone;
ripples lapping tideless where the slaves crouched;
the sleek row of lions crystal as melting sugar;
the Italian *agora* with its chattering voices
scarcely stilled yet;
the stone man and woman, headless, who must endure
eternity together, pompously, with no comment;
the frogs floating like sticks in the deep cisterns;
only the small neat lizards
flicking among the dressed stones
can change or choose direction.

But in the groin of Mount Cygnus,
that tremendous little hillock,
in the cleft of the propped slabs,
above the bone-dry watercourse and the parched grass,
stand for a moment and accept
not the Helladic prelude, the Periclean opera,
or the Hellenistic epilogue,
but the whole saga of your kind.

MYCENAE AND EPIDAURUS

Across the scorched stubble among the grey olives
the thin black goats and the old woman with the distaff
inhabited a landscape hard and simple,
but impossible to share.

On the broken hillside with the dry-stone
walls and the deep-paddocked grave-pits,
Cuchullain and Oisin leaped suddenly to mind;
and I could have joined in the shouting
as the small clouds of chariot-dust
exploded up the long slope –
could have joined in the loud chant
as the shod-wheels sparked in the rutted stone,
for a poem's span,
too absolute to be endured longer.

But only near the dark green grove
with the pine-scent and the light airs

among the fronded fans,
was I somehow strangely at home,
receiving, open, myself;
tiered far back in that pin-drop theatre
or beside the square pit
with its shock-therapy of snakes.

CAPE SUNION

Empty stage-set on the headland
shouldered above the dark Aegean,
the gestures, the arias to be guessed:
a galley rowed them to another place,
less obviously theatrical,
more plausible, more convenient.

Banal Technicolor poster in 3-D
beckoning tourists from uneasy climates,
soliciting attitudes and cameras,
with sunlight sensuous on white marble,
with carefully composed and autographed ruins,
and a well-placed sunset.

Yet these stones were once dragged down
along those contour-flanking tracks
that run back to the land's heart:
they were brought here for a purpose,
and now, in their abandonment, serve
another purpose no less important.

OLD CORINTH

Sweating under the intense Corinthian sun,
climbing up the slabbed street between rows of ruins,
the synagogue knee-high, the shop turned church
with the crumbling fresco, like an open byre,
we endured the harsh breath of Roman authority;
hung round the *agora* to hear if Paul should speak
once more of charity against the harsh brass
of the light and the glinting stones,
avoiding the stripped abrupt temple pillars,
arrogant in defeat.

But down in the cool shadow of the Perene Fountain
we stepped carefully over the tilted flagstones,
and leaned for a long time over the low parapet,
gazing into the little caves under the arches,
listening for the liquid syllables
of an older oracle.

from

COLLECTED POEMS 1932–1967

IRELAND

We Irish pride ourselves as patriots
and tell the beadroll of the valiant ones
since Clontarf's sunset saw the Norsemen broken . . .
Aye, and before that too we had our heroes:
but they were mighty fighters and victorious.
The later men got nothing save defeat,
hard transatlantic sidewalks or the scaffold . . .

We Irish, vainer than tense Lucifer,
are yet content with half a dozen turf,
and cry our adoration for a bog,
rejoicing in the rain that never ceases,
and happy to stride over the sterile acres,
or stony hills that scarcely feed a sheep.
But we are fools, I say, are ignorant fools
to waste the spirit's warmth in this cold air,
to spend our wit and love and poetry
on half a dozen peat and a black bog.

We are not native here or anywhere.
We were the Keltic wave that broke over Europe,
and ran up this bleak beach among these stones:
but when the tide ebbed, were left stranded here
in crevices, and ledge-protected pools
that have grown salter with the drying up
of the great common flow that kept us sweet
with fresh cold draughts from deep down in the ocean.

So we are bitter, and are dying out
in terrible harshness in this lonely place,
and what we think is love for usual rock,
or old affection for our customary ledge,
is but forgotten longing for the sea
that cries far out and calls us to partake
in his great tidal movements round the earth.

TURF-CARRIER ON ARANMORE

The small boy drove the shaggy ass
out of the yard along the track,
rutted between two dry-stone walls,
his errand guessed from half-built stack.
Barefoot he tripped behind its tail,
too shy to lag and stride with us:
an older lad would match our pace
and snatch some topic to discuss.
He swung his switch, a salley rod,
his bleached head glinting in the sun,
but only flicked his ragged thighs
and pattered nonchalantly on.

We spoke no word. The boy, the ass,
the rutted path across the bare
unprofitable mountainside,
were native to this Druid air.
But, as we followed, rag and patch,
the string which braced each splintered creel,
the bald, rubbed flank, the hooves unshod,
growing awry and down-at-heel,
so woke our pity, I pronounced
a bitter sentence to condemn
the land that bred such boys and beasts
to starve the beauty out of them.

The small boy heard, not quite my words,
but, rather say, my angry tone;
a bright blush warmed his sunburnt neck;
he struck a sharp and jolting bone,
and turned the ass with prod and cry
through the first gap that caught his glance,
although the ruts roamed on ahead
to meet the bog's black-trenched expanse,
misjudging my intent and sure
that we were proud and critical.
Your father's beast is very dear,
if you are poor, if you are small.

SWAN

The swan I see upon the sullen water
is Leda's lover and a child of Lir,

moves slowly now encumbered by the verses
remembered from a half-forgotten year.

The very whiteness that its cold reflection
sinks to a lower key to hold subdued
is white of cloud and snow and wall and collar,
is colour scumbled over the dark wood.

Its feathers are the feathers of a gull
stuck in short turf beside a guzzling lamb.
Its hard eyes are unfriendly as the glance
of the tall stranger in the crowded room.

The bent neck swaying and the flat dark beak
are stretched neck, hissing beak, when I was small,
anxiously waiting till they cruised away,
to let me guide my fleet home with a pole.

Substance and light provide the unthumbed clay;
my eyes find textures for my memory's shape.
This is no kin of any swan you see;
this is the swan that comes before I sleep.

BECAUSE I PACED MY THOUGHT

Because I paced my thought by the natural world,
the earth organic, renewed with the palpable seasons,
rather than the city falling ruinous, slowly
by weather and use, swiftly by bomb and argument,

I found myself alone who had hoped for attention.
If one listened a moment he murmured his dissent:
this is an idle game for a cowardly mind.
The day is urgent. The sun is not on the agenda.

And some who hated the city and man's unreasoning acts
remarked: He is no ally. He does not say that
Power and Hate are the engines of human treason.
There is no answering love in the yellowing leaf.

I should have made it plain that I stake my future
on birds flying in and out of the schoolroom window,
on the council of sunburnt comrades in the sun,
and the picture carried with singing into the temple.

TWO IRISH SAINTS

I SAINT PATRICK

So Patrick once, striding the flogging weathers,
and hoisting hills with fire, took kings to task,
proud only as a man who bears a mask
to glaze his wound against the cynic fingers,
brought Christ to Eire better than the others
who, baffled, oared the yeasty billow's risk,
and grated back on limestone, pale, loquacious;
for he died blest and lies in his own shadow.

Yet loud with Leary, dominant with Druids,
passing with stags tall-antlered down the valley,
was happy only when his text-vexed eyes
saw the flat lough from Slemish as before,
how long ago the boy stood with the swine,
and dreamt of Christ's bright sandals in the heather.

II COLMCILLE

Of Colmcille, blood-arrogant and royal,
spilling a war like a flung fist of cards,
throwing his purple round the threatened poets,
and taunting the slow king with lettered vellum,
too much remains within the veins and sinews
of this mad people, turbulent and rash,
the knuckled swift intolerance, the tongue
too ready with the rasped malicious words.

Rather for succour, think of that far island:
the patient fellows singing in the byre,
the small world scooped and narrowed to an Eden,
whence, daily, he would pass, with blessing fingers,
spadesmen, mason, dark man beating metal,
to print the tide's track with his sharpened ribs.

FROM A MUSEUM MAN'S ALBUM

My trade takes me frequently into decaying houses,
house not literally in the sense of gaping roof,
although often with the damp maps of wallpaper in the attic
and the pickle of plaster on the cellar shelf:
but house usually represented by a very old woman

who bears a name once famous for trade or wealth
or skill or simply breeding,
and is the last of that name.

Take, for instance, the tall large-knuckled woman in tweeds
whose grandfather was an artist of repute,
and had his quarrel with the Academy
and wrote his angry letters, and marginal notes
on those from his friends and patrons. (O pitiful letters,
I keep your copies safely in a metal drawer.)
Her mother had been part of the caravan
he trundled through Europe, eloquent, passionate, poor.

Now she offers us a few early copies
made in his student days when Rubens hit him
like a boy's first cigar;
a badly cracked, circular head of a girl
with flowers on a balcony, from his Roman days;
a thick bronze medal from the Exposition;
and a beaded chair-cover made by her grandmother.

She will die in a boarding house.

•

I remember, too, the small stout woman well,
her white hair brushed up in a manner
which was then out of fashion but has been in it again,
her deafness and her gentle smile,
her way of talking as if her words
were like the porcelain in her cabinets.
The substance of her conversation has gone blurred:
something of Assisi and Siena and Giotto
and the children singing at evening
and mist coming up the valley, and, I think, bells.

I remember, too, her shelves of books;
Okey, Henry James, Berenson, Vernon Lee,
and a number of popular manuals
like Chaffers on Pottery Marks;
and the maiolica plaque of a smiling head,
and the large glossy photograph of Mussolini
on the mantelpiece.

She was a widow, and I remember thinking it odd
that she displayed no photograph of her nephew
who was at that time a Cabinet Minister.

She died later at another address,
and left us her ceramics, but her books were to be
divided among the friends who used to come in
for an evening's bridge in the winter –
that is, all except the green-bound Chaffers
which came to us with the ceramics.

Another, younger, a spinster, led me up to an attic,
offering antlered heads, and a ship in a bottle,
and an ivory rickshaw model.

She panted a little after climbing the stairs,
and sat on a leather trunk to get her breath,
and pointed out a golden photograph
of her tall brother who died of a fever in Siam
after his first leave home.

She was giving up the house to go and live
in a larger one among trees, left by her aunt,
and in the family at least two hundred years.

I selected a rough-edged book in wooden covers,
watercolours on worm-holed rice paper, with unstuck silk
– a series of Chinese tortures of prisoners.

THE GREEN SHOOT

In my harsh city, when a Catholic priest,
known by his collar, padded down our street,
I'd trot beside him, pull my schoolcap off
and fling it on the ground and stamp on it.

I'd catch my enemy, that errand boy,
grip his torn jersey and admonish him
first to admit his faith and, when he did,
repeatedly to curse the Pope of Rome;

schooled in such duties by my bolder friends;
yet not so many hurried years before,

when I slipped in from play one Christmas Eve
my mother bathed me at the kitchen fire,

and wrapped me in a blanket for the climb
up the long stairs; and suddenly we heard
the carol singers somewhere in the dark,
their voices sharper, for the frost was hard.

My mother carried me through the dim hall
into the parlour, where the only light
upon the patterned wall and furniture
came from the iron lamp across the street;

and there looped round the lamp the singers stood,
but not on snow in grocers' calendars,
singing a song I liked until I saw
my mother's lashes were all bright with tears.

Out of this mulch of ready sentiment,
gritty with threads of flinty violence,
I am the green shoot asking for the flower,
soft as the feathers of the snow's cold swans.

FIRST SNOW IN THE GLENS

When the winter sky, snow-ominous, crowds in,
here at the wood's edge is the world's end;
the valley cockcrow, the bleat of sheep on the hills
hint of a wider stage, like friendly rumours,
but our immediate place is an island in time.

Chopping the twigs on a stump till the dull blood sang
(my arm beats still with the unaccustomed labour)
I too was a warm oasis–island of joy,
watching the first light flakes, and hearing the leaves,
dry on the hard ground, whisper salutation,
hearing the robin's chirr, and following
the wren's intentions in a bare thorn hedge;
for no large life, this hour, shall intersect
my patient curves; since even the hooded hag
tying her faggot of kindling, garrulous,
and John MacNaghten, that slow friendly lad,
clumping up the lane to his snares in the whins,

and at a distance, striding through slant flakes,
a man, not seen before, with bag and gun,
have the same lease and something of the nature
of rocking branch, of blackbird, bluetit, wren.

BLESSING

To love or pity is easy, if pity, if love
come limping with mangled paw or moan in the trap;
it is, at times, proper to pity the photograph.
But the tired stout woman with the soiled white glove,
the girl with acne and glasses and nervous laugh,
the smiling mongol with the schoolboy's cap
appeal in vain for the saint's neurotic caress.
We must always aim the fingers we raise to bless.

COLOUR

Moved to the blessing of colour
because of the marvellous whin
and over the clay-fleshed plowland
the young corn brairded green,
I name each colour for blessing,
for blessing's the grace of delight;
the bud the leaf and the blossom
till I rise to the mercy of white.
I bless the cloud and the seagull,
the blackthorn and hawthorn bless,
the lamb and the farmer's daughter
in her Confirmation dress.

REVENANT

He has come back, as some expected, and may be heard
if you are one of us or know the password,
talking to friends in committee rooms, any evening,
making small trials of strength to shew he is well;
they say that later he intends to visit the new branches.

Some move ponderously now, assured of their judgement,
would propose a spectacular showdown
with the officials. But he forbids all this.

Some sit smiling on benches warm in his light
and cannot be urged to stir and plan for tomorrow.

Others do not believe it is he, and stay away
ostentatiously, claiming they know the facts.

I have gone once and listened, and know it is he,
but feel he was ill-advised to come back again.
This complicates the business.

After a week
of utter agony I had clarified my mind and braced my heart,
and from then on could have faced any circumstance,
and indeed can yet, if I hold to the stubborn truth
that he was killed, and most of us ran away.

AGENDA

Already I recognise signs that the trouble has started.
There are those who demand a formal constitution,
and others with them would summon a conference
with delegates and their credentials and badges,
with chairmen and secretaries, amendments, resolutions.
This is the way to destruction, or worse, to success
and titles and salaries and patronage.

When we were together first none spoke of standing orders
or committees or the functions of office-bearers.
There were no office-bearers – we were a bunch
of rough-tongued peasants caught in a marvellous moment
and gripped by the power of our Leader, and when he had gone
we splintered back to our individual selves.
I admit that those selves were changed because of the sojourn.

I think that he meant to warn us against organisation
by asking our cleverest man to handle the money
and letting us see what happened to him and to it.

I should like to encounter some of the older people again;
I'd like to learn how they'd fared in the years that followed:
they'd remember things I remember, and might even help me
to recollect things I'd forgotten. A young man
with an educated voice read carefully over

the notes he'd made for a pamphlet for propaganda
and wondered why, at the end, I could only nod.

LANDSCAPE

For a countryman the living landscape is
a map of kinship at one level,
at another, just below this, a chart of use,
never at any level a fine view:
sky is a handbook of labour or idleness;
wind in one airt is the lapping of hay,
in another a long day at turf on the moss;
landscape is families, and a lone man
boiling a small pot, and letters once a year;
it is also, underpinning this, good corn
and summer grazing for sheep free of scab
and fallow acres waiting for the lint.
So talk of weather is also talk of life,
and life is man and place and these have names.

THE RAM'S HORN

I have turned to the landscape because men disappoint me:
the trunk of a tree is proud; when the woodmen fell it,
it still has a contained ionic solemnity:
it is a rounded event without the need to tell it.

I have never been compelled to turn away from the dawn
because it carries treason behind its wakened face:
even the horned ram, glowering over the bog hole,
though symbol of evil, will step through the blown grass with grace.

Animal, plant, or insect, stone or water,
are, every minute, themselves; they behave by law.
I am not required to discover motives for them,
or strip my heart to forgive the rat in the straw.

I live my best in the landscape, being at ease there;
the only trouble I find I have brought in my hand.
See, I let it fall with a rustle of stems in the nettles,
and never for a moment suppose that they understand.

THE CROSSING

Following the white horse of the famous legend we shall cross,
certainly with some, but no very considerable loss:
for it is shallow here, or the foe would not defend this place;
upstream there are cataracts, below it is like a mill-race.
This is the ford, the crossing; it is here or nowhere else
that we may approach the walled city with its anxious bells.
See! The leader is up. He beckons. His horse leaps with eagerness.
Take your weapons only. There will be no time now to dress.

Do not worry about the leader. He is a symbol only.
He is a small man. His eminence keeps him lonely.
There is no richness in his character. That does not matter.
You will not need to learn the jargon of his whims to flatter.
He is himself a purpose – he does not exist outside it –
which is to mount the legendary horse and ride it
across the river to the bell-walled town, and that
latter part of his purpose is also ours. His hat
bobs up and down with feathers we need not salute.

It is well for our expedition that he does not travel on foot,
for he is, as I say, a small man, and might be lost
in the scrimmage and scuffle before we had crossed,
and in the muddle without the pointing of his sword
some might mistake direction, some step without a word
into the potholes on either side – already the bugle peals.
I shall proceed carefully, keeping clear of the neat white heels.

HOMESTEAD

I

It is time now for me to build a house
to be a shelter in the rough days,
with a bare hearth where one could kindle a fire
and dry his duds and boil his small pot;
a house which, seen, will be recognised
as a dwelling, and yet an outcrop, part of the place,
not obtrusive, wrong, abrupt or irrelevant;
yet no archaic folly waiting for ivy,
nor ruin asking scholars to stroke its face.

I require such a fabric to house my troubles –
and not mine only, but yours and the best of my friends';

the girl in bright shorts lilting from tennis,
the tired man pale in the sun, the skipping child,
the artist pacing his mind, the young poet waiting
to be introduced over the ring of faces,
and the writer too, when he can be rid of the faces,
the dark woman marking the clay with string,
and the lad heeling the mare home at dusk.

When I number these, the foolish image arises
of a blunt, wallowing ark and a sloping plank,
but the timbers on Ararat stick up through the snow,
and none visit it now to claim a snapshot.

There will be no flood. I take my stand on that:
dirty weather for sure, and the failing of light,
and many exposed must die before the spring;
but there are rocks which smash the raindrop
and score the glacier's bottom, surviving as rocks,
and they can be balanced together to meet my need.

I thought at Easter, climbing through the whins,
that out of the rising sun and the redolent earth
some wisdom might pass into the prone bones
with the skill and the will to start effective building:
the power of Christ seasonal only as nature,
proposing heady spurts of activity,
and long yawning sprawls of compelled idleness.

Oisin, I said, is my symbol, that shadowy man,
warrior and bard returning again and again
to find the Fenians forgotten and unforgotten,
rising when bidden on the young men's lips
to face defeat and go down and sleep in their cave.
Oisin, who baffled Patrick, his older faith
tougher than the parchment or the string of beads:
Oisin after the Fenians.

                                        Straight in my hand
the young priest thrust the words of the old dispute
of big Dan Lavery with Gillwirra MacCartan,
the flat-foot, red-necked farmer, the reed-voiced bard,
the calloused knowledge of one, the poise of the other,
the humble regard for the disciplines of sap and frost,
the proud step in tradition of handling words

spoke to my cloven nature. The answer will come,
for MacCartan is Oisin also. Yeats was Oisin.
The dinted symbols rust in the crumbling tower,
but Oisin is not there now. I saw Yeats carried
to the wailing of bagpipes through the wind-washed town,
and watched Oisin elbow back through the holiday crowd,
going the opposite way as we followed the hearse.
I have seen him since, can tell you where he whispers
among the salleys and the blood-bright holly;
but Lavery bids the musicians make simple songs
to haul his tractor out of the sucking bog,
using harsh words to blame all intricate music.

Yet it's Oisin also after Patrick's legions;
the vestments fray and tarnish, the crafty man
makes a show of genuflection, but in his heart
still rises to the rhythms his Fenians knew.

II

Yet those, familiar with business, suggest instead
of building for myself and taking the risk
of not having finished in time for the breaking storm,
unable to afford first-quality stuff,
and having to spend the rest of my fretted days
in minor repairs, in lurching from crisis to crisis
as the wall bulges, the chimney smokes, the snow
drifts under the slates and spreads in a nasty stain,
or fungus thrusts the splintering boards aside,
finding myself standing alone, bankrupt, unroofed:
they suggest, instead, I try to rent a corner
in some durable place. The Parthenon's features
beam from the glossy pages selling a cruise,
battered, it's true, but above ground; Sophocles, Plato,
pediment, naos and volute – the orders endure,
the tall chipped philosophy, the swinging hexameters –
I cannot explain that the former tenants died
of a swift anaemia, that the Greeks were spivs
selling freedom in packets from under the counter,
the little erotic stones to the Roman contractors,
that those who lodged under the lintel and then came home
had nothing of worth to declare that I needed to hear.

I have read the reports with care; there is nothing in them
that speaks to our condition. We might as well

hire a loincloth and hunker among the tombs,
or paddle in the Ganges, stepping over the corpses,
or dangle our legs from the beams among the pigeons.

Others say, in the Empire State there are vacant rooms
high over the scarves of gas and the flashing traffic;
a wise man there could be close to the naked stars,
and breed his mind on austerities till it is lean
and leaping and eager to move among their orbits.
But the earth quivers at times, the plaster trickles.
I'd rather have my heels on the friendly ground,
and not be caught between floors in the elevator
when rumour or fear flings its bolas at my head.

Others, sad-hearted, remark: Why trouble? The house will fall;
it is the nature of stone to fall and lie;
the shrinking heart of the cinder will draw all in;
this is the core and condition of existence.
I, in my day, have seen many mansions perish
slowly with gifts and bequests, with cobwebbed antlers,
or opening to noise and flame like a marvellous flower,
to smoulder in the heaped ash for a year
till the willowherb rejoicing claimed the scorched earth.

I have seen men step limping out of the rubble
and look round for the cool shadow of a spire
before they look up to see if there's one left standing.
Another, too, pants over the arid land
in search of some other ecclesiastical shadow;
when I saw him last he was slicing a stiff-curved cactus.

I have known a man ask offers for a mirage
glinting white in the light with fountains and arbours.
One fellow who bought it told me, without smiling,
the virtue of a mirage is in not having frontiers;
it can be where you say it is: you can take it with you.

No. There is nothing for it but to build right here
in rough-cut stone and spread a roof of scraws.
Maybe a coal tit will nest here or a houseleek flower,
or toadflax bind the stones with its little threads,
or a fox trotting stop to sniff round the doorpost.

There will be no conveniences. Only life.
I shall leave space at the lane's end for a bus to turn,

and a field for the city boys to camp in summer;
but for a long time yet not many will travel
from the paved ways. I shall always hang a cup
on the old thorn above the spirting pipe
for any thirsty passer too shy to knock
or in a hurry to find a stance for his easel
or aiming for the hills with his vasculum.

I shall often remember the Walden Pond,
and the grey beehive cells of the tonsured men
busy with the seasons and a quill
and talking to God across the assenting grass.
And spitting in the ash at the heel of the year,
the latch will rattle and Oisin MacCartan will enter
with his old familiar stories of passion and action;
and when I've been there awhile its name will flourish;
the young women and the young men will know its name
and gather to ceilidhe there in the winter evenings.
Although their laughter'll be quick their words will be slow,
their gestures as easy as breathing. Then one blessed night
Dan Lavery too will come, having heard of the crack,
to sit on a stone in the corner and puff his pipe
and maybe even join in the oldest chorus.

The stonework will be simple, honest and sturdy,
not showy, not even neat, but built to last.
I go today to the quarry to tryst the stones.

O COUNTRY PEOPLE

O country people, you of the hill farms,
huddled so in darkness I cannot tell
whether the light across the glen is a star,
or the bright lamp spilling over the sill,
I would be neighbourly, would come to terms
with your existence, but you are so far;
there is a wide bog between us, a high wall.
I've tried to learn the smaller parts of speech
in your slow language, but my thoughts need more
flexible shapes to move in, if I am to reach
into the hearth's red heart across the half-door.

You are coarse to my senses, to my washed skin;
I shall maybe learn to wear dung on my heel,
but the slow assurance, the unconscious discipline

informing your vocabulary of skill,
is beyond my mastery, who have followed a trade
three generations now, at counter and desk;
hand me a rake, and I at once, betrayed,
will shed more sweat than is needed for the task.

If I could gear my mind to the year's round,
take season into season without a break,
instead of feeling my heart bound and rebound
because of the full moon or the first snowflake,
I should have gained something. Your secret is pace.
Already in your company I can keep step,
but alone, involved in a headlong race,
I never know the moment when to stop.
I know the level you accept me on,
like a strange bird observed about the house,
or sometimes seen out flying on the moss
that may tomorrow, or next week, be gone,
liable to return without warning
on a May afternoon and away in the morning.

But we are no part of your world, your way,
as a field or a tree is, or a spring well.
We are not held to you by the mesh of kin;
we must always take a step back to begin,
and there are many things you never tell
because we would not know the things you say.

I recognise the limits I can stretch;
even a lifetime among you should leave me strange,
for I could not change enough, and you will not change;
there'd still be levels neither'd ever reach.
And so I cannot ever hope to become,
for all my good will toward you, yours to me,
even a phrase or a story which will come
pat to the tongue, part of the tapestry
of apt response, at the appropriate time,
like a wise saw, a joke, an ancient rime
used when the last stack's topped at the day's end,
or when the last lint's carted round the bend.

MAN FISH AND BIRD

Bird fish and man
I cannot fly into the sun

but I can carry the sun in my head
I cannot dive cavorting
over and round the submerged rocks and in the water
but the circumambience of space
whether full of water, air or particles of sand,
I can contain
I can also contain it empty.

I cannot sit in that chair
when the man is sitting there
but I can contain the chair, the man sitting
and my sitting where the man is sitting therefore
I am bird fish and man and the circumambience.

This is the first day.

I can carry man fish and bird to the mountain top
I can lie in a dark place and be full of light
I can say to the man be fish and he fins among the firs
I can say to the fish be bird
and it will build a nest beside a crab.

This is the second day.

I can take words to cover
the man fish and bird
I can write the words, writing
Green Man Yellow Fish Red Bird
and the green man is spring
pushing fingers, then his whole hands and wrists
through the wet mould;
and the yellow fish leaps out of the waters
and the darkness becomes dawn;
and the red bird calls the yellow fish back to the sea
and darkness resumes
but the red bird is also my heart crying against the darkness
and may also beak out of the rocks with dawn in its call.

This is the third day.

I can tell the green man I understand him
and ask him to answer my questions
I can feed the yellow fish with the ants' eggs of my affection
letting it lip my palm and vanish away with a swift curve
I can tell the red bird to cry dawn in lonely places
and I can stand lonely and inhabited at the same time
in doubt and in understanding.

This is the fourth day.

When my mind is clenched
I can bid these creatures inhabit the circumambience
but when I sleep entering the darkness
that darkness becomes their circumambience and their liberty
and the green man is my father
and the yellow fish far back in my generations
and the red bird is a moment I had forgotten
a moment of grief or humiliation.

And this is the fifth day.

I can come down from the mountain and ask the people
Have you heard the answers of the Green Man
Have you seen the Yellow Fish pass this way
Did you feed it and speed it on its journey
Did the Red Bird cry to you in your loneliness.

And many will say No we saw or heard nothing.

And others will say The Man who answered was white
and the Fish you call Yellow was not yellow: it was
the colour of this handkerchief or this flag
and the Bird was most certainly not Red
A red bird is a monster. The Bird
was yellow Not the Fish. Indeed
it was not a bird at all it was
a feathered serpent or a cockatrice.

And some will say Yes we heard the answers
the Green Man made but fail to understand them
and the Yellow Fish passed so quickly we caught only a glimpse
and the Red Bird cried yesterday but across the frontier
tomorrow it may cry nearer

and two will say Yes we heard the Green Man
answering the Green Man's questions
but the Yellow Fish gave no hint of his intentions
and the Red Bird flew down out of a piece of Chinese needlework.
And one will say Hallo Green Man
and, Yellow Fish you have returned already
and Red Bird I bid you welcome. You are needed
to cry light against the shadow here.

This is the sixth day.

When my mind can no longer because of age
or mishap clench within itself the circumambience
and the man and the fish and the bird
I shall lie down in shadow which will deepen into darkness
and the man will sit in his chair
and I shall sit in his chair and be in his mind
and the green man of the split sod
and the yellow fish will turn and turn in swift curves
in the globe of his skull
peering out of his eyes in passing
and the red bird will fly shouting out of his mouth.

This is the seventh day
Man Fish and Bird.

THE COLONY

First came the legions, then the colonists,
provincials, landless citizens, and some
camp-followers of restless generals
content now only with the least of wars.
Among this rabble, some to feel more free
beyond the ready whim of Caesar's fist;
for conscience' sake the best of these, but others
because their debts had tongues, one reckless man,
a tax absconder with a sack of coin.

With these, young law clerks skilled with chart and stylus,
their boxes crammed with lease-scrolls duly marked
with distances and names, to be defined
when all was mapped.
When they'd surveyed the land,
they gave the richer tillage, tract by tract,
from the great captains down to men-at-arms,
some of the sprawling rents to be retained
by Caesar's mistresses in their far villas.

We planted little towns to garrison
the heaving country, heaping walls of earth
and keeping all our cattle close at hand;
then, thrusting north and west, we felled the trees,

selling them off the foothills, at a stroke
making quick profits, smoking out the nests
of the barbarian tribesmen, clan by clan,
who hunkered in their blankets, biding chance,
till, unobserved, they slither down and run
with torch and blade among the frontier huts
when guards were nodding, or when shining corn
bade sword-hand grip the sickle. There was once
a terrible year when, huddled in our towns,
my people trembled as the beacons ran
from hill to hill across the countryside,
calling the dispossessed to lift their standards.
There was great slaughter then, man, woman, child,
with fire and pillage of our timbered houses;
we had to build in stone for ever after.

That terror dogs us; back of all our thought
the threat behind the dream, those beacons flare,
and we run headlong, screaming in our fear;
fear quickened by the memory of guilt
for we began the plunder – naked men
still have their household gods and holy places,
and what a people loves it will defend.
We took their temples from them and forbade them,
for many years, to worship their strange idols.
They gathered secret, deep in the dripping glens,
chanting their prayers before a lichened rock.

We took the kindlier soils. It had been theirs,
this patient, temperate, slow, indifferent,
crop-yielding, crop-denying, in-neglect-
quickly-returning-to-the-nettle-and-bracken,
sodden and friendly land. We took it from them.
We laboured hard and stubborn, draining, planting,
till half the country took its shape from us.

Only among the hills with hare and kestrel
will you observe what once this land was like
before we made it fat for human use –
all but the forests, all but the tall trees –
I could invent a legend of those trees,
and how their creatures, dryads, hamadryads,
fled from the copses, hid in thorny bushes,
and grew a crooked and malignant folk,

plotting and waiting for a bitter revenge
on their despoilers. So our troubled thought
is from enchantments of the old tree magic,
but I am not a sick and haunted man . . .

Teams of the tamer natives we employed
to hew and draw, but did not call them slaves.
Some say this was our error. Others claim
we were too slow to make them citizens;
we might have made them Caesar's bravest legions.
This is a matter for historians,
or old beards in the Senate to wag over,
not pertinent to us these many years.

But here and there the land was poor and starved,
which, though we mapped, we did not occupy,
leaving the natives, out of laziness
in our demanding it, to hold unleased
the marshy quarters, fens, the broken hills,
and all the rougher places where the whin
still thrust from limestone with its cracking pods.

They multiplied and came with open hands,
begging a crust because their land was poor,
and they were many; squatting at our gates,
till our towns grew and threw them hovelled lanes
which they inhabit still. You may distinguish,
if you were schooled with us, by pigmentation,
by cast of features or by turn of phrase,
or by the clan names on them which are they,
among the faces moving in the street.
They worship Heaven strangely, having rites
we snigger at, are known as superstitious,
cunning by nature, never to be trusted,
given to dancing and a kind of song
seductive to the ear, a whining sorrow.
Also they breed like flies. The danger's there;
when Caesar's old and lays his sceptre down,
we'll be a little people, well outnumbered.

Some of us think our leases have run out
but dig square heels in, keep the roads repaired;
and one or two loud voices would restore
the rack, the yellow patch, the curfewed ghetto.

Most try to ignore the question, going their way,
glad to be living, sure that Caesar's word
is Caesar's bond for legions in our need.
Among us, some, beguiled by their sad music,
make common cause with the natives, in their hearts
hoping to win a truce when the tribes assert
their ancient right and take what once was theirs.
Already from other lands the legions ebb
and men no longer know the Roman peace.

Alone, I have a harder row to hoe:
I think these natives human, think their code,
though strange to us, and farther from the truth,
only a little so – to be redeemed
if they themselves rise up against the spells
and fears their celibates surround them with.
I find their symbols good, as such, for me,
when I walk in dark places of the heart;
but name them not to be misunderstood.
I know no vices they monopolise,
if we allow the forms by hunger bred,
the sores of old oppression, the deep skill
in all evasive acts, the swaddled minds,
admit our load of guilt – I mourn the trees
more than as symbol – and would make amends
by fraternising, by small friendly gestures,
hoping by patient words I may convince
my people and this people we are changed
from the raw levies which usurped the land,
if not to kin, to co-inhabitants,
as goat and ox may graze in the same field
and each gain something from proximity;
for we have rights drawn from the soil and sky;
the use, the pace, the patient years of labour,
the rain against the lips, the changing light,
the heavy clay-sucked stride, have altered us;
we would be strangers in the Capitol;
this is our country also, nowhere else;
and we shall not be outcast on the world.

THE STOAT

Walking in the warmest afternoon
this year has yielded yet, through slopes of whin

that made the shadows luminous, and filled
the slow air with its fragrance, we went down
a narrow track, stone-littered, under trees
which with new leaf and opening bud contrived
to offer a green commentary on light;
and as we wondered silent, stone by stone,
on lavish spring, a sudden volley broke,
a squealing terror ripped through twig and briar,
as a small rabbit pawing at the air
and stilting quickly thrust full into view,
clenched on its rump a dark-eyed stoat was viced,
shaped in its naked purpose to destroy.
We stopped. I stepped across. Before a stick
could fall in mercy, its harsh grip released,
the crouched stoat vanished, and the rabbit ran
whimpering and yelping into the thick grass.
Something had happened to the afternoon;
the neighbourly benevolence of spring
was shattered with that cast of violence;
and as we turned to follow the steep track,
it seemed no inconsistent codicil,
that in the mud a broken shell should loll
in equal speckled parts, and on a stone,
a little yoke, a golden sixpence, lay,
a fallen sun in a wrecked universe.

THE WATCHERS

We crouched and waited as the day ebbed off
and the close birdsong dwindled point by point,
nor daring the indulgence of a cough
nor the jerked protest of a weary joint;
and when our sixty minutes had run by
and lost themselves in the declining light
we heard the warning snuffle and the sly
scuffle of mould, and, instantly, the white
long head thrust through the sighing undergrowth,
and the grey badger scrambled into view,
eager to frolic carelessly, yet loth
to trust the air his greedy nostrils drew;
awhile debated with each distant sound,
then, settling into confidence, began
to scratch his tough-haired side, to sniff the ground

without the threat of that old monster, man.
And as we watched him, gripped in our surprise,
that moment suddenly began to mean
more than a badger, and a row of eyes,
a stony brook, a leafy ditch between.
It was as if another nature came
close to my knowledge, but could not be known;
yet if I tried to call it by its name
would start, alarmed, and instantly be gone.

CORRIDOR

Mazed in a splay of lonely corridors,
anonymous as a hospital, innocent
of number, name or arrow, windowless,
I padded under bulbs
of bright unlidded light. What people passed
were deaf and slippered, and in uniforms
with neither rank nor grade. When I spoke
they gave no heed. My fingers found no touch.
I paused at shut doors, flush, bare, featureless,
that took my rapping knuckles as blotting paper
takes the blurred letters backwards. When I ran,
it was the same anonymous corridor
that I continued in. So I stopped to listen
for any elevator's whirr or grind,
but no sound came or passed. Where three ways forked,
I stood to hear my heart make up its mind,
and as I took the left-hand corridor
a slow door opened and I saw the king,
the dead, the bearded king, my boyhood's king.
I'd heard he was a gruff but kindly man,
so I approached him. When he turned to me
it was the little bald Prime Minister
who took my offered hand.
I saw the hand that answered, recognised
that wide curved thumb, that finger ring-tattooed,
and so I met my father five years dead.

A RHYME FOR BLAKE

There's nothing so weak as a lamb's first cry
in a sudden hush when the wind's gone by;

yet the crying lamb with the tottering stride
in season may sultan a mountainside,
and turn a black face and a baleful glare
on the lonely traveller passing there.

From lamb to ram, from innocence
to the horn-proud lust that has no pretence,
is too wide a stride for my mind to take;
so I sometimes pause on a mountain track,
and say to the devil that glowers at me –
Did He who made the lamb make thee?

THE GAP

Fencing a rough place on the mountain
where the stirk was killed,
he took a chill and came home shivering,
refused the doctor, enduring the wide bed
a few hours longer than usual;
for a week now he has sat
on a chair to the right of the hearth,
spitting against the turf and lighting his pipe,
reading the children's schoolbooks, and hearing reports
of how they are managing to save the hay without him,
as one day
they shall have to manage everything.

TORCELLO

The muddy shallow waters, tired and old,
without the strength to break in white of spray,
cry through the rushes, while our ripples fray
and lapse against the land; and we are poled
along the ditches in the tarnished gold
of an unreal Adriatic day.
And still our eyes, that caught from far away,
among the tilted sticks, the bell tower's bold
and vertical assurance, are intent
on that fixed mark in time, which yet shall stand,
now darkness comes upon our days again,
the symbol of an old drowned continent
where on the last rood of remaining land
faith still outfaced the mutinies of men.

HEDGEHOG

Outside my senses, known as printed words,
as tinted woodcut half a life ago,
the crouching hedgehog on the roadside sward
epitomised in spike and panting flank
the world of things I know and do not know.

True to the legend, when I threatened it,
the ball defensive coiled before my eyes;
the twitching snout, the small pathetic hands
withdrew and left me utterly expelled,
no longer free of Adam's paradise.

Patient I waited till the fear was spent,
and watched the waking from that little death,
a fellow creature native to my sod,
nervous and mortal, meant to be alive,
and eager for the purposes of breath.

RITE, LUBITAVISH, GLENAAN

Above my door the rushy cross,
the turf upon my hearth,
for I am of the Irishry
by nurture and by birth.

So let no patriot decry
or Kelt dispute my claim,
for I have found the faith was here
before Saint Patrick came.

The healing well by Rachray's cliff
that answers to the tide,
the blessing of the gentle bush
deep in my pulse abide.

Before men swung the crooked scythe,
I flung my hook with care,
and from the stook-lined harvest field
bore off the platted hare.

And yesterday as I came down
where Oisin's gravestones stand,

the holly branch with berries hung
thrust upright in my hand.

A COUNTRY WALK IN MARCH

for R.H. and E.N.C.

A sudden mildness, like the heart of May,
though two months early, set us on our way,
you, me, our friend the quiet botanist,
some small leaf aromatic in his fist:
and, as we walked, our resolution chose
the same gay round we'd paced in muddy shoes,
we two together, half a year before,
when windy autumn was a steady roar
of tossing treetops, and bright squalls of rain
cuffed the last leaves and chattered down the lane.

But though the memoried colours of the fall
stood ready to be summoned at our call,
we found each instant, to our open eyes,
was lit with recognition and surprise;
on each side of the way the world was rich,
field after field, with furrow, bush and ditch,
all brimmed with marvel to invoke our care;
and flowering currant warm upon the air;
the neat-foot trotting of the nimble sow
from our approach; the black-faced mountain yowe
with the quick lamb that shewed its Leicester sire
in length of nose and tail; the squawking choir
of guinea fowl with harsh pump-handle note,
and the horned ram with brambles round his throat.

We paused to watch and praise that yellow bird,
the yorlin, far less often seen than heard,
perched for a golden moment on the black
bare twigs of thorn before song called him back
to his high bush where, dark against the sky,
he scarce shewed feather you could name him by.

We plucked the nettletops and took away,
for flavour's sake, a single leaf of bay
over the low wall where the slope begins
to edge the tameness out with blossomed whins.

We passed stacked sacks of praties on the sward,
and loosed the last gate tethered by a cord,
and where, before, the jolted ruts were full
of lime-white water and a shallow pool
marked where tracks parted to the left and right,
our rutted wits were flushed with sound and sight;
hosted or single each thing visible
rang for attention sudden as a bell:
the lonely droning bee; the talking crowd
of black rooks rising in a flapping cloud
from the red furrows; and the curlew, high,
calling for rain because the hills were dry;
close primrose tuft and loose dog violet
on the sunned bank, and where the sheugh was wet
the hanging hart's-tongue with the rusted rim;
the last dark wrinkled haw that, tough and grim,
held up its head against the first green leaf;
the knotted ivy like a hieroglyph
round the bowed ash-bole; and above the burn
th'elusive wagtail that would not return
till we had gone; and, rusting in the briars,
strange shapes of metal, hooks and jagged shears,
flung by, one summer, when the work was done,
and the lean sheep leapt naked in the sun;
wallflowers in blossom on the gable top,
and sods with trailing stems, a shaggy crop,
along the gutter of a sagging roof;
the dry crisp mud that held the print of hoof
clean as a moulder's pattern. Each of these
was faced as facts or framed as similes,
as fancy offered or withdrew from each
the grace of silence or the gift of speech:
the trails of wool gave fingers itch to spin –
the tall pale reeds begged jars to posture in.

But still for me, of all the tangled sight,
the deepest implications came by right
from straggling beards torn off a heavy load
of scutched lint which had joggled down this road,
and left its Lear-sad tatters wedge by wedge,
spiked on each dragging corner of the hedge,
since we were here before. At once they brought
the swift stiff memories of the aching thought

when we had stumbled out across the hill
and tugged the coarse lint, beet by beet, until
the field was cleared, and, in the evening dew,
with weary limbs, we hunkered by the bru,
and gulped the brown stout down, with honour earned;
but in a wink the recollection turned
to the sad wonder if in any place
my passing leaves a more enduring trace,
and if the verses that I rush to print
are worth as much as these stray wisps of lint.

THE OWL

With quiet step and careful breath
we rubbered over grass and stone,
seeking that soft light-feathered bird
among the trees where it had flown.
The twisting road ran down beside
a straggling wood of ash and beech;
between us and the shadowed trees
a wire fence topped the whin-spiked ditch.
We stood and gazed: the only stir
of dry leaves in the topmost boughs;
the only noise now, far away,
the cawing of the roosting crows.
And as we watched in waning light,
our clenched attention pinned upon
that empty corner of the wood,
it seemed the quiet bird had gone.

Then when the light had ebbed to dusk
you moved a hand and signalled me:
I saw the little pointed ears
beside a tall and narrow tree.
A further signal, and I moved
in wide half-circle to surprise
that little feathered sheaf of life
that watched you watch with steady eyes.
But when I came by easy stealth,
at last, within a yard or two
the brown bird spread enormous wings
and rose and quietly withdrew.
And we were left to carry home
a sense no mortal will devised,

that, for one instant out of time,
we had been seen and recognised.

FOR A SEPTEMBER AFTERNOON OF UNEXPECTED BRIGHTNESS

The afternoon had opened like a rose:
the fallen leaves lay still; no others fell.
Time, like that golden moment when the bell
holds its round note before the dying close,
seemed being, not becoming. Even those
whose movement and direction briskly spell
the city's ordered habit, capable
and urgent, by their gestures spoke repose,
and not intention only. For this hour,
all unexpected in the failing year,
they peopled the warm world as if by right,
each natural and easy as a flower
that needs no courage and can know no fear,
because it is inheritor of light.

THE TUMBLING SPORE

They set their angels dancing on a pin,
surnamed the humours, smelt the witches out,
foretold the fate of crops or kings by omens,
by doves or conjugations of the stars,
and out of that dark language made bright song
and schooled their fingers to give life to stone.

The props gone from these images, we find
a narrowed plinth to raise conjecture on,
devising all as race of tumbling spores
or raindrops lurching round a leaden box,
and so our songs are scrannel, difficult,
and what our gloved hands touch to rubble turns.

THE CHILD, THE CHAIR, THE LEAF

I take the unity my senses offer
such as of birdsong out to hearing's rim
and known beyond to light's edge, moving on

and coming over, or stars reported by
men with no names to clothe their words with style,
yet which, uncoloured, pass as true as stone
or taste and texture of the well-tried leaf.

Since touch, sight, hearing and the other two
have bettered by response to what revolves
around my centre and have trenched it far
beyond the little jet that was my life,
I take without dismay what pebbles fall
or slates flick over it, knowing they will drop
through drift of depth far deeper than the self.

My world's no sphere, for there are surfaces
which fail in rondure, places when my sense
admits a quagmire or a green-slimed trough
where I lack skill to step or strength to pluck
the sucked heels upward;
yet these are part of it, of the account
that I draw up and keep for settlement.

This shook me once that one, a cripple child,
loved by no mother, given another's love
not warm with kind but aimed, deliberate,
which, in a space of months with some expense
of will and resolution, turned the wry bone
in life's way straighter, should, an hour unwatched,
strike a sharp death in squalid accident,
and all that social-love deliberate
run twelve ways wasted in th'indifferent dust:
for I could sieve no metaphor from this
would lift the heart against adversity.

The cripple child, not allegorical,
summons no symbol or shining archetype,
that like charged metal draws the grains of ore
to shapely pattern in its fans of force,
or even accretions palpable in bulk:
a twig snapped off by shoulder lurching past;
a straw snatched up and dropped by witless pigeon
between the pavement and the porte-cochere;
a smashed brick on deserted building site –
not even this last, for this has overtones

of Babylon and tablets – nor a leaf
launched into shadow from a sunny branch.

For take the reason in the falling leaf
and measure it against that falling child
and there's an atom split that opens more
than all the pounding physicists contrive.
Who'd love a leaf and tie its brittle stem
against the twig it grew from, that it face
the driven crystal and survive till spring?
A wiser hand would lay it in a book:
it would lie sad there, wisp of sentiment,
a fragment of a life, no more a leaf.

Take any common object, say, a chair,
a chair compiled of leaping particles
(such is the schoolman's fiction of the day)
will last so long as needed being chair:
have I here answer to my falling child?
Dare name who needed and define the need
as one could list the uses of a chair?
Or were the spinning particles required
to ease some balance elsewhere out of line?

Let no one mock me for my ignorance;
I grip the data that my wits provide,
and try the answers: if they cancel out
that is the answer; and I know the sum.

THE SPECTACLE OF TRUTH

A masterly lens-polisher,
pride of his guild in Amsterdam,
once linked two crystals rim by rim
whose mutual strength should make all clear;
and when he clapped them to his eyes
they proved so purging to the sight
that all seemed as the last Assize,
in the strict justice of the light.

He saw the burgomaster stand
beneath the towering Westkirk's porch,
and like a candle in a church

he held his small soul in his hand:
one housewife bent above her tub,
one pinned white linen on the line,
and whether shift or bridal robe,
bright as their sheets their spirits shone.

He saw the flowering barges glow,
the men aboard seemed bowed in prayer,
and at the stalls across the square
where nameless figures come and go,
all stood for judgment, stirring not,
hand held to mouth or hand at side;
and he could tell from where he sat
that this was wicked, this was good.

Then while he marvelled at the sight,
a breathless moment or an hour,
his rocking heart grew still and sure
that charity was more than light,
that, gazed at through the perfect glass,
this shining scene was bright and false,
the men, the houses and the trees,
mere patterned shapes on painted tiles;

and while he fixed his mind on truth,
time and the world were ice and stone,
so if he'd have them move again
and air thaw out in noisy breath,
he'd have to lay the lenses by,
and turn once more upon the street
his old decaying mortal eye,
desiring it, despising it.

THE MUNICIPAL GALLERY REVISITED, OCTOBER 1954

Brisk from the autumn of the sunlit square,
to overbrim a day already full,
because some exhibition drew me there,
the mannered essays of the latest school,
I stumbled into history unaware,
pausing a moment in the vestibule,
among the crowding presences again,
facing disarmed the stone and metal men:

O'Leary brooding in his long bronze beard,
out of the saga now, a king remote;
the tense faun, Shaw, by Rodin's marble spared
the pitiful declension of his thought:
and Stephens only known as overheard
billowed on ether, or as what he wrote,
a small grimacing urchin looking lost,
too wry and various for any ghost:

George Russell, then, my fellow countryman,
a lad this, as of seventy years ago;
you could not tell from this slight beardless one
that this was he who, in day's afterglow,
saw timeless creatures on gay errands run,
for there's no lettered label here to show
what scale or scope this stripling promised us;
no note here, either, of the sculptor, Hughes:

and this, the bold-jawed orator in bronze,
torch of rebellion, fanned by roaring crowds –
clutching my father's hand, I saw him once,
when heaven seemed scarcely higher than the clouds,
muster his dispossessed battalions –
who guttered his bright flame in smoky feuds;
but there's no name here either: you must guess
what passions forged these features with what stress:

another, named at least, a comely face
scorched to the skull and ardour of a saint,
a legend she, of time-surmounting grace:
verse ambers her beyond all scathe or taint,
and she's safe there; though in this silent place
false patination of the flaking paint,
indifferent as weather, has defaced
what should long since have been in metal cast.

And as I moved among these images,
nameless or named, still emblems of the power
that wrought a nation out of bitterness,
and gave its history one triumphant hour,
my heart, dejected, wondered which of these
may hold a meaning that will long endure,
for, see, before me, threatening, immense,
the creeping haircracks of indifference.

THE TWISTED HEART

I have seen camels at the outer gate,
and muttering shepherds have come running by,
gapped in their breath by thoughts of being late.
Already dawn flares up the lower sky
and with small cries the roof-birds congregate,
ruffle and stir as though about to fly.
The yawning servant pokes the ashy grate;
I pass the window with a wary eye,
for all my terror, carefully sedate.
I would have no one turn suspiciously
to track me through the yard. Affairs of state
demand a certain slow solemnity;
and past that door ajar our futures wait,
unseen as yet, but signalled by a cry,
exactly as the ancient scrolls relate.
But what or who I hope to meet, and why,
is still the subject of an old debate:
with twisting heart I enter silently.

It may be, after all, the stories lie
and here within's our judgment and our fate,
to bring all down in ruin equally:
the walls above this little town of late
have weathered low that once were strong and high,
and every man among us seems to wait
with empty words and gestures, anxiously,
some end to all, some avalanche or spate
of crowding waters out of prophecy,
to tumble past and leave all desolate.
I twist my heart between that infant cry
and the tall camels at the outer gate.

THE HEART OF JOY

The silence of the world's despair
hung round proud Caesar's empty day,
and though with drum and trumpet blare
he sought to drive the fear away,
the silence flooded back again
into the lonely hearts of men.

The legions marched; the circus roared,
but with a shudder at the heart;
the feasters thumped upon the board,
but that despair would not depart;
the silence of the world's despair
lay like an ocean everywhere.

And most men moved as puppets move,
though here and there, one seemed to wait
some sign or spectacle to prove
a core of justice in his fate;
yet not by science or by art
could any ease the stricken heart.

But on a winter midnight, far
from Caesar's tossed and troubled bed,
a shining choir, a sudden star,
a messenger light-garmented,
called down to kings and simple men
to bid them fill their hearts again;

for, in a village stable near
the Child was born whose Grace should bring
an end to man's despair and fear,
a Maiden's Son, and Heaven's King;
for God himself has taken on
Man's tribulations in His Son.

And so the point where time began,
flows back and forward from was there,
where mortal as the bravest man,
God faced the ultimate despair;
no other means could he employ
to prove the heart of life is joy.

THE HABIT OF MERCY

Only that lone man in the stone tower by the rough
Western Ocean consistently holds to the tragic view.
We others have our sops and varieties of anodyne:
despair at three in the morning surrenders to sleep;

the implications of the serious bulletin are swept away
by the prim whisk of the scholar or the loose mop of the clown;

the dragging swing of the band is the quickest exit of all,
for a sentimental sadness is like a warm small rain.

Even the most thoughtful and sensitive find their comfort
in the ultimate assured triumph of the suffering God,
writhing on his cross, pegged firm by nails, and moaning,
later to be accorded victorious trumpets.

Surely, by analogy, we assert, our positive pains –
scalds, burns, disappointments, frustrations, griefs –
will earn us, properly scaled to our relative statures,
accolade, garland or medal or clasp of the hand.

Suppose, for argument's sake, that Calvary was a defeat;
God faced the permitted evil and found it too much,
not merely too much for his creatures, too much for himself –
Man's honesty's kept the forsaken cry in the record –
then there's no hope save in enduring and trying by small
gestures of love and pity to publish the habit
of mercy from man to man. For the great world beyond us
has terror and horror enough to be faced and accepted.

I had thought that the parasites gorged in the animal's tears
are sufficient challenge to any with easy answers.

OSSIAN'S GRAVE, LUBITAVISH, COUNTY ANTRIM

We stood and pondered on the stones
whose plan displays their pattern still;
the small blunt arc, and, sill by sill,
the pockets stripped of shards and bones.

The legend has it, Ossian lies
beneath this landmark on the hill,
asleep till Fionn and Oscar rise
to summon his old bardic skill
in hosting their last enterprise.

This, stricter scholarship denies,
declares this megalithic form
millennia older than his time –
if such lived ever, out of rime –

was shaped beneath Sardinian skies,
was coasted round the capes of Spain,
brought here through black Biscayan storm,
to keep men's hearts in mind of home
and its tall Sun God, wise and warm,
across the walls of toppling foam,
against this twilight and the rain.

I cannot tell; would ask no proof;
let either story stand for true,
as heart or head shall rule. Enough
that, our long meditation done,
as we paced down the broken lane
by the dark hillside's holly trees,
a great white horse with lifted knees
came stepping past us, and we knew
his rider was no tinker's son.

THE RESPONSE

for Jill and Brenda

The sleeping dog before the stove
whimpered and twitched as in distress,
then eased back to a deeper dream.
In the next room the two girls slept,
the diaries of a busy day,
of hills and sheep and barking waves,
large-lettered with laconic care.

Some moments after the dog's cry
the younger girl tossed restlessly
and whistled a few straggling notes;
and I, who have known mind to mind
signal without the flags of speech,
and took that as an added grace
affection grants to sympathy,
stood suddenly upon the shore
of a new continent of sense
that's mapped beneath our coarser world,
where, not in the tormented throes
in which each lonely spirit strives
with broken splinters of the self,
being, like water, finds its shape

no longer bottled into selves,
but flowing, tidal, out of time,
and vast as ocean's unity.

THE FRONTIER

At the frontier the long train slows to a stop:
small men in uniform drift down the corridor,
thumb passports, or withdraw for consultation;
the customs officers chalk the bags and leave us to shut them.

We pass here into another allegiance,
expect new postage stamps, new prices, manifestoes,
and brace ourselves for the change. But the landscape does not alter;
we had already entered these mountains an hour ago.

JACOB AND THE ANGEL

I wrestled with my father in my dream,
holding my ground though he strove powerfully,
then suddenly remembered who we were,
and why we need not struggle, he and I;
thereat desisted. Now the meaning's clear;
I will not pause to struggle with my past,
locked in an angry posture with a ghost,
but, striding forward, trust the shrunken thigh.

THE MAINLAND

The island people first were mainland people
shouldered from crowded valley to the beach;
some even afloat before the outsiders came
with emblem and ultimatum of invaders
heavily armoured in rumour, invincible.

Always they were the young, the loose of foot,
could grab the few tools handy, bundle up
the little earthen gods, the lamps, the flints,
the pots of seed laid by for the next spring.

Occasionally awe might clear a space
for a grandfather who knew every star

and all the rimes for luck and love and labour,
but this was seldom. Children, goats and women
left little room enough for the rowers' knees.

And so departed while the drift of smoke
from the torched thatches hung a day's march off.
The only choice then was from the known landmarks
into the sunset out of the fierce noon.

When seven generations had been buried
in island earth and all was planted well,
the hill tribes broken and the hill names kept,
a long while since, the story should have ended,
the island now a nation, its people one;
but legends of the mainland still persist
in hearthside talk and rags of balladry:
and now and then a man will test their truth
by sailing back across the ancient track
to find it rich in all but what he sought.

AN IRISHMAN IN COVENTRY

A full year since, I took this eager city,
the tolerance that laced its blatant roar,
its famous steeples and its web of girders,
as image of the state hope argued for,
and scarcely flung a bitter thought behind me
on all that flaws the glory and the grace
which ribbons through the sick, guilt-clotted legend
of my creed-haunted, godforsaken race.
My rhetoric swung round from steel's high promise
to the precision of the well-gauged tool,
tracing the logic in the vast glass headlands,
the clockwork horse, the comprehensive school.

Then, sudden, by occasion's chance concerted,
in enclave of my nation, but apart,
the jigging dances and the lilting fiddle
stirred the old rage and pity in my heart.
The faces and the voices blurring round me,
the strong hands long familiar with the spade,
the whiskey-tinctured breath, the pious buttons,
called up a people endlessly betrayed

by our own weakness, by the wrongs we suffered
in that long twilight over bog and glen,
by force, by famine and by glittering fables
which gave us martyrs when we needed men,
by faith which had no charity to offer,
by poisoned memory, and by ready wit,
with poverty corroded into malice,
to hit and run and howl when it is hit.
This is our fate: eight hundred years' disaster,
crazily tangled as the Book of Kells;
the dream's distortion and the land's division,
the midnight raiders and the prison cells.
Yet like Lir's children banished to the waters
our hearts still listen for the landward bells.

THE KNIFE

We've always been unlucky with our tramps.
That old man with long sack on his back,
trudging to Ballyvoy, proved a dry stick,
though the setting was pure Synge, hill, road and sea –
his phrases stale, his gossip irrelevant.
Even old Mearns, who lay in his small hut
dead for a week before anyone noticed,
was only, for me, a drunk man roaring home,
holding on to the bushes, his pension spent,
glimpsed briefly late on Fridays; his unremarked death,
like a frog in a tussock or a bird in the heather,
drably consistent with his neutral life.

The tramps in England here have proved no better:
they live without letters; they are full of complaints.
Their talk is dull; their travelling has gathered
no vivid berry of phrase, no quartz-vein's sudden light.
A blind man's talk can be more evocative.

Like hikers or soldiers on leave, they thumb their ways,
making distance covered the measure of success,
breakfast the common yardstick of quality.
The man we lifted, but sent on his way again,
when we ran into flood water and stalled the car,
was monosyllabic and surly.
When he was gone, we found he had left behind

a little cloth bag containing his capital,
a lady's black left-hand glove, a prayer book, some thread,
an empty tin and a knife.
There's maybe a story in this worth teasing out,
but I lack that kind of pity. I carry the knife, now,
the scouts' type, far larger than I need,
a sort of penance, keeping its blade bright;
but only rarely do I ever think
of a tramp somewhere, moping and grieving
over his beggared luck, without that glove, the knife.

MASS

The church is small and well designed,
its woodwork clean, its altar neat;
the only things to vex the mind
those gaudy Stations of the Cross.
Three altar boys with nimble feet
flit round the fringes of the Mass.

The priest in vestments finely wrought
moves clever hands in graceful prayer,
so habited there seems no thought,
no effort, when he spins to bless
the hats and heads that bow to share
the mumble and gabble of the Mass.

Yet, rising from the altar rail
after the priest had passed the Bread,
a slight young fellow, shabby, pale,
with downcast eyes and palms pressed close,
moves down the aisle with dreamer's tread
rapt in the Mystery of the Mass.

WHIT MONDAY

The small girls hurried to the hilltop church,
their confirmation dresses fluttering
in the late sun. Before the shadowed porch
neat-fingered mothers knotted lace and string
and pinned each floral coronet in place;
while the dark-suited fathers stood apart,

pride and affection on each polished face:
it seemed as though some play were poised to start,
when the last swift had scoured the humming air.

Yet this was Poland, and the time was now;
and I, who pray too seldom, felt a prayer
take all my will, that providence allow,
or dialectic, or whatever name
men put upon time's enginery, permit
this scene to re-enact itself, the same,
so long as any heart finds grace in it.

COLLECTOR'S CHOICE

Not comprehending half the Chairman says,
hoping it flatters, is not ironical,
Janos, remembering, scans the gallery,
the platform's height gives clearance.

There's the Mortgage Picture, there, by the door.
Your native village. Mortgaged, brought enough
to float you past that rock where others floundered
and some went down. Paid back every penny
when the storm blew out. A picture is money.
Better than money. Keeps its shape and size.
The famous Balkan landscape-master gave it
to Mother before she married. Born there, too.
They'd been to the wooden school together.
Did the war wreck it? What's it used for now?

That jar with roses was extravagance.
Beside, a bargain, picked out of a dozen.
With his wife sick, the painter wanted cash.
Next, an exchange on the critic's advice.

The Chairman introduces the Minister,
hard to follow also, head down, reading.
A name to drop at the club.
You could call those investments, all well chosen.
Liking comes first. You should never buy
for the artist's name alone like an autograph.
That was a present you never gave:
the man it was meant for proved too clever;

lost more than a picture by his cleverness.
So the collection grew. Pictures were asked for;
lent by, lent by, ran through the catalogues.
On committees by now, a name getting known
by dealers, curators, artists.
Every picture a story, a page of life,
since in the long night in the blacked-out train
you touched the roll of canvas under the blanket,
crossing the frontier with it, out of danger.

Hands clap. The Minister turns and bows.
Janos wipes damp fingers on cool linen,
searching the faces for answering affection,
unsure and shy. You too would be unsure,
and smile and hug the shoulder of anyone
kind enough to wait, if your world had vanished,
and you were left alone with the need for living
and finding bread and friendship to feed your hunger,
if you had known the sausage in the park,
the tired feet eased in the enamel basin.

The speeches are over. Applause. Shifting of feet.
The platform party descends. Janos also,
hoping to hoard the handshake against the pogrom;
tomorrow's photograph should be evidence.

THE WHEEL

I remember that wooden wheel on the kitchen shelf
beside the boot-trees and the copper pans,
last relic of my uncle's ornithopter,
flogged up three feet once by its threshing wings.
Left in its shed to rot, this was preserved,
the polished steering wheel, while my uncle turned
to lesser inventions, like the invisible hinge
recalled now as the line-block illustration
of a prospectus leaflet, and the patent churn
stacked long with rods and golf clubs under the stairs.

I loved my uncle, loved his darting newts
on their aquarium-island, his bottled snakes
in bathroom cupboard, his pigeons in the attic,
the little eagle he carved, his mandolin,

the two great seashells lying inside the fender,
the long walks with him carrying nets and jars.

But when I was ten years old a family row
thrust him into hurt silence, and never again
I crossed the threshold of that teeming mind.
My father too was hurt, so I took the side
duty ordered, as if the flesh were cut
with a quick knife. And so, with one hand since,
I have explored the surfaces of life.

I had forgotten him and his house for years,
my brisk unconscious coffining his face,
convinced my maimed gait was normality,
until today the old wound cried again;
chance-glancing through a book on aeroplanes,
I paused to study one blurred photograph
of a gigantic dragonfly on wheels,
a dark man with a high collar steering it,
and underneath it his name; the smaller type
providing the dimensions and the date,
main chord, flexing portion, trailing edge.

LAKE BLED, SLOVENIA

The lake at Bled. Trees thick to water's edge.
Castle on bulging cliff. An island church.
Electric bulbs in swags. White-jacketed
waiters with foaming trays.

Big-breasted mothers in sunglasses. Men
in shorts. Old men, dark-suited, with wide hats.
Old women in black dresses. Brown and bare
children on sandalled feet.

Postcard of tourists' paradise. A dream
the blunt-cars hurried here to realise.
Accept the noon-Utopia. Accept,
you too, the workers' state.

THE MODELLED HEAD

for Eric Elmes

My friend the sculptor modelled the large head,
cast it in polyester, metal-grained.

It did not flatter, roughing the smooth cheeks
in search for planes, declensions, light and shadow,
making a feature of the fleshy nose,
catching the eyes but coarsening the tight mouth.

When I turned it round to observe the profile,
it brought my father's face at once to mind,
dead twenty years, the sculptor never knew him,
my sober father, that just, quiet man.
So it must touch some essence, reach some truth.

Set in the public gallery with the bronze
figures and faces by accomplished hands,
it stood beyond me, representative,
a period head wearing the date of style.
There I have left it to submit to judgement;
some name it at a glance, some hesitate;
too young perhaps, expressing one mood only,
correct for the hair, the chin, the hooded eyes.

Within myself I already sense a change:
with it there I have been liberated;
my life of strong opinions, vanities,
is held contained, sealed off from chance of time;
this was that stubborn, unforthcoming fellow,
dogmatic in assertion and dissent,
staunch democrat but curt with nodding neighbours,
short of talk's small change, in love with words;
and I am left with these alternatives,
to find a new mask for what I wish to be,
or to try to be a man without a mask,
resolved not to grow neutral, growing old.

THE WORD

Gathered in the dark pub at the Basin
after a long slow Sunday on the canal,
seeing back yards for houses, grass-stems for meadows,
we sat on benches at a long narrow table,
drinking our pints, deciphering from the gloom
the brown walls' plaster, low ceiling tongue-and-groove,
kippered with time, tin notices, varnished calendars,
high wooden settles each side the empty fireplace.

We listened to the locals by the window,
sitting where they could see all come by water,
talking of locks and cutts and narrow boats
and the strong men who worked them, giants all.
One fat old fellow, leaning on his belly,
buoyed up the conversation, propped with nods,
prompted by those who knew his stories well,
eager to hear them told for our amazement,
spun a wide net of words that coiled and sprawled,
looped with genealogies and seasons,
and out of the tangle one word slithered bright:
Bedlam, he said, where one lock keeper went,
after some practical joke or accident –
Bedlam meaning Hatton, the County Asylum.
And at that clanging word old Rowlandson
was instantly there in the corner, gripping his pad
and sketching like mad the listening faces round us,
the glazing bars, the scrubbed table, the fat old man.

THE PET SHOP

I never had the luck to keep a pet:
canary, rabbit, kitten, all were tried.
When she went mad, my father drowned the cat;
the rabbit fretted, the canaries died.

So, though my legs grew longer than my years,
I had no pup to race me round the hills.
The very sticklebacks brought home in jars,
within the week were furred with fishy ills.

But when, on Saturdays, we went to town,
my chums and I, one window drew our gaze:
glass tanks of snakes and lizards green and brown;
white mice and piebald mice on sawdust trays;
dumb tortoises; a haughty cockatoo;
bright-feathered bantams picking in the grit;
quick ferrets sniffing straw for something new,
and pigeons jerking on pink, clockwork feet.

Among the crowd that idled round the door,
you'd sometimes see a fellow slip his hand
into a hidden pocket to withdraw
a cowering lark or linnet contraband.

MY GRANDMOTHER'S GARTER

I never really liked my mother's mother;
she was too stiff and hard:
a single kindly word from those puckered lips
I never heard.

Slim, handsome, straight as a rush, her soft hair white,
smooth-skinned and fresh of cheek,
with purple ribbons threaded in jet-beaded cap,
always in black;

those who knew her acknowledged her the regent
of her grim Methodist God.
The little lead figures on the drawing-room piano
would, when you blew on them, nod.

Possessive of her house and six grown-up children,
she worshipped her eldest son,
but found the fast anchor of her long widowhood
in the second, John.

She faulted and quarrelled with every servant girl
until, in tears, she left,
suspected of trying to seduce the master,
accused of theft.

After twenty years he married, escaped and died
untimely, that good man.
So, when the house was sold and the young widow pensioned,
her travels began.

Each daughter's home, in turn, became her haven,
till restlessness set in.
The disagreements flared to rows; she packed her trunks,
and moved again,

keeping her children in perpetual turmoil,
a disruptive element,
leaving a trail of misunderstanding and malice
everywhere she went.

Yet she always had a pouch in her garter,
stuffed with snippets of clipped verse;

Tennyson, Whittier, Longfellow, George MacDonald,
the guineas in her purse.

And when at last she died there was scant mourning;
her eldest son already dead,
the family had poured its load of sorrow
over that noble head.

Yet, though I did not like her, nor she me, swearing
I'd come to a bad end,
remembering that satin pouch of poems,
I clasp her bony hand.

EAGER JOURNEY

My mother's father, when he came to die,
summoned his house to join him, singing clear
his road to Glory: this, obediently,
they, with schooled voices, did, well versed in praise,
for Methodists were people without fear
of Hell, or doubt of Their Redeemer's Grace.

That first time it was difficult for them
to hold their grief in balanced harmony,
claiming death gate to joy's Jerusalem,
while their brave father struggled with his pain;
but, when the crisis ebbed, relieved to see
the steady breath restored, they wept again.

For days he wrestled, weakening, called for song
when the end beckoned, falling back in sleep
each time God failed to answer. Far too long
d pitiful a vigil for his kin;
nurse was mustered, so that they might keep
some grip on time, some rhythm of discipline.

One afternoon, slipped down to fetch his tray,
quickly returned, she found him sprawling dead
athwart the tumbled blankets' disarray,
the man who never once had failed a friend,
alone now on that eager journey sped,
not one hosanna trumpeting the end.

A VICTORIAN STEPS OUT

One summer Sunday in the old Queen's time,
to evening service, for a social mile,
with ribboned bonnet, dolman, muff, umbrella,
leading her adult family with style,
Grandmother strode, a straight-backed matriarch:
her retinue reserved, responsible,
nodding where proper courtesy required,
as nicely judged as etiquette could spell,
a smile conferred on those whom they knew well.

Then, swinging from behind and catching up,
a band, along the cobbles, pounded by,
with drum and brass and frequent tambourine,
Booth's braided cohort, crimson banners high:
and, after them, the penitential few,
stiff-necked among the roughly jostling crowd,
bullies and blowens from the darkest slums,
raddled with liquor and damnation-proud,
their gestures mocking and their jeering loud.

To the quick consternation of her kin,
my grannie left the pavement, took her place
beside the blessed, tall among the shawls
her ribboned bonnet and her lady's face;
keeping in step the patent-leather boots
with broken boots. Alarmed, her daughters prayed
that none they cared for much should see her now,
gentility's decorum disarrayed,
their hugged pretensions utterly betrayed.

Yet what could you expect? In church itself,
you'd never know what blushes she might start;
one dreadful day she told the minister
his sermons never shook one sinner's heart.
But in that brash, excited company,
my grannie marched serene, until she came
to the church gate and stopped, her cheeks alight
with something other than her children's shame,
all self-consumed in that exultant flame.

WITH E.M.F. ON 28TH DECEMBER 1965

I can see him, in his cloth cap,
standing beside the car,
admiring the large winter sun,
a bright orange balloon in the deep white mist,
behind the black frosted twigs:

and after, in the tiny church,
when I read aloud the baroque epitaph
for some bustling Queen Anne functionary
below the draped urn on the wall,
his chuckling comment was
'wretched fellow';
the speaker himself eighty-seven next Saturday,
and by no means wretched.

TO PIRAEUS

He must have come aboard at Tinos
when it was growing dark,
for at Mykonos he was neither
on the gangway at the pier
nor on the ladder from the bobbing boats:
a strong small barrel-built man
with a grey-stubbled cannonball head
and a farmer's moustache.

He seemed not to know anybody
in the elbowing drift of passengers
where most knew many.

Sitting opposite us below deck,
he set a paper bag on the fixed table,
and, opening it, displayed
thick cuts of bread, two brown eggs and an apple
with some salt in a twist of tissue paper.

Munching slowly, he picked
the shells off, fleck by fleck:
and after the salted eggs were eaten and the bread
he began to peel the apple

with a broad-bladed knife
firm in a deliberate hand,
blunt fingers, square thumb.

He turned and offered a slice of apple
to the foreign lady who had brought no provender,
which, thanking him, she declined.
When the long coil of peel was dropped,
and the crumbs and eggshell fragments
tidily swept with the heel of his hand
into the paper bag,
he crushed it and put it in his pocket,
taking out, almost with the same gesture,
his tasselled string of beads,
amber cubes with rounded corners,
and began manipulating them
in the traditional manner.

Trying hard, I could not imagine
aboard which ship in Homer's catalogue
he might have served.
Yet I would feel safe
travelling to the moon with him.

from

THE DAY OF THE CORNCRAKE

POEMS OF THE NINE GLENS

1969

LATE SPRING

Old Trostan holds his snow among the clouds,
waiting, they say, for one last fall to clear
the last of winter from the first of spring.
For it is middle April, and by now
the busy corncrake should be on his ground,
whetting his voice among the upland whins,
till the low meadows offer him a home
with grass enough to loiter in secure;
but neither corncrake nor the cuckoo yet
is evident against the noisy winds
that roar among the hardly budded trees.
Larks may be heard in lulls or gaps of storm,
and blackbirds in the hedge which does not hide
their nesting traffic. But the little flowers
are few and tardy; and the shaggy yowes
hobble and stagger, snuffing, tuft by tuft,
the withered slivers, seeking the new grass;
and the young lambs, dropped late by custom here
to miss the snowdrift and the frosty star,
crouch in the shelter of the whistling thorn.
Only the whin with blossom keeps its date
– and yet there's always, somewhere, whin in bloom –
so though we praise, it's scarcely evidence,
and hold our greeting for the merry bird,
the yellowhammer trying out its song.

APRIL AWAKE

Lark-bright the air; the light
from leafing hedge and willow
was faceted with white
of blackthorn and whin-yellow.

The climbing sun made light
of the purple-shadowed furrow;
white was the lime, and white
the horse that dragged the harrow.

HAYMAKING IN THE LOW MEADOW

The rain held off. They came to turn the laps
to let the light wind dry them. Every year,
when all the fields, save this, are safely stacked,
the weather breaks and the lapped hay will lie
in its dark bundles day by dismal day,
won only piecemeal by quick spurts of work
because the mounting tide of crowding duty –
pulling, dubbing, spreading the wet lint,
or cutting the ripe corn, or drawing turf
from the high moss home, fills every day
that's free of rain or only gapped with showers.
Now, before corn's ready and the lint
can wait a day or two, they take this chance.
It is a Sunday. It is afternoon.
No loss of virtue's risked. Earth's needs are prime,
and older than the Mass they heard this morning.
Then on the tossed laps they spread out at ease,
cup the small flame to light the half-burnt fag,
or roll and talk and watch the changing sky
as the grey cloud flows slowly down the glen.
We join them now and slip into the talk
as cautious bathers first dip toe and foot
before they dare the stranger element.
Then the tall farmer with his leaping dogs,
heard just above the road, busy with sheep,
strides over, stoops to handle the coiled hay,
and, straightening, declares for instant action.
We rise and take his orders, lift the laps,
and drop them shaken in a circled heap,
then fork them up to him as slow he rises,
tramping and turning on the growing rick.
His brother then hives off with two or three
to start his own rick half a field away.
I stab and twist and hoist and carry high
and toss my burden in its wanted place,
and stab again, until occasion comes

to turn the twister for the long grass rope
which binds the rocking stack. The other man
with defter help has beaten us and now
already has a new foundation spread.
There's little talk today. Not silence though,
for who can work with others and hold his tongue?
But not the slow, full-laden conversation
that, on a dry day, gives to every wisp
of hay or oats the word which must be said,
the prickly proverbs plucked from hedge and bush.
This was the fourth year we had laboured here
in the same fields. I knew what to expect,
for there's but little change from field to field,
and hardly any change from year to year,
but I was wrong. The rain was far too close
to let the patient ritual continue;
already on my forearms and my brows
the small beads gathered, finding each a hair.
When the fourth rick was bound, it was the end,
and on the laps we passed to reach the gate
the bright rain glistened. They would have to wait.

FOOTING TURF

Footing turf on high Barard, the hip
of that long mountain, Trostan, it was cold
and wet, and every hair on sleeve or wrist
was globed with water, and the tangled grass
shod each chill foot with moisture. The whole world
was narrowed to a little dripping cave
walled by the weather and the bleat of sheep,
but when a gust of wind blew off the roof
the sky was clear and bright, and miles away,
down the landslope towards the quiet sea,
the day-long sun shone on the haymakers.

SUNSET OVER GLENAAN

As the vague sun that wrapped the mellow day
in a grey haze hangs red, about to drop
behind the western mountain rim, I stop
to name the peaks along their dark array,
for these are more than mountains shouldered clear

into the sharp star-pointed atmosphere,
into the sunset. They mark out and bound
the utmost limits of my chosen ground;
beyond them, and beyond the heather and moss
that only lonely roads and shepherds cross,
lie the fat valleys of another folk
who swarmed and settled when the clansmen broke
and limped defeated to the woody glens.

These inland Planter folk are skilled in toil,
their days, their holdings, so well husbanded,
economy has drilled the very soil
into a dulled prosperity that year
by reckoned year continues so; but here
the people have such history of wars,
that every hilltop wears its cairn of dead
and ancient memories of turbulence,
clan names persisting in each rocky stead.
They take life easier on their hillside farms,
with time to pause for talk, remembering
they'll be outlasted by the marching stars,
and, though there may be virtue still in charms,
no man dare be too sure of anything.

My breed is Planter also. I can shew
the grey and crooked headstones row on row
in a rich country mastered long ago
by stubborn farmers from across the sea,
whose minds and hands were rich in husbandry,
and who, when their slow blood was running thin,
crowded in towns for warmth, and bred me in
the clay-red city with the white horse on the wall,
the jangling steeples, and the green-domed hall.

Inheritor of these, I also share
the nature of this legendary air,
reaching a peace and speech I do not find
familiarly among my kin and kind.
Maybe, at some dark level, grown aware
of our old load of guilt, I shrink afraid,
and seek the false truce of a renegade;
or is it that the unchristened heart of man
still hankers for the little friendly clan
that lives as native as the lark or hare?

And though to keep my brain and body alive
I need the honey of the city hive,
I also need for nurture of the heart
the rowan berries and the painted cart,
the bell at noon, the scythesman in the corn,
the cross of rushes, and the fairy thorn.

GATHERING PRATIES

We gathered praties in the upper field
above the road, below the booley mounds,
and the red bracken with its bobbing scuts –
a long four-acre field, half pale with stubble,
half lengthwise ribbed with drills the digger broke
in slow dark showers of mould.

We bent and picked
and flung the tubers, if the proper size,
into the slatted basket, if too small,
into a bucket. When these both were full
we tipped the first into the narrow heaps
to be earthed over later, kind by kind,
Kerr's Pinks and Arran Victors as they came;
the bucket-load was poured into a sack
to serve the feeding for the stock at home.

The strong wind brought its slanted squalls of rain,
some light enough to work through, some too fierce,
which set us running for the low thorn hedge.
Then the half-buried praties daubed with mud
were cold and wet to handle, slithering
from the numb slipping fingers to their place,
till the next drill was scattered clean and dry.

Bend down and pick and fling, each throw a choice;
then the full basket carried to its pit,
and the full bucket tilted in its sack,
till shout of invitation brought us over
to the thorn hedge, and sweet tea from a can
and griddle bread with butter smeared in lumps.

Then raising heavy limbs, relaxed and warm,
into the wind's way and the failing light,

to bend and lift and throw with steady aim
and move through the slow ritual once more.

This till the moon came up, and Pat and Jimmie
began to earth the pits up, which would lie
through the long winter gloom like mounded graves,
narrow and ancient and anonymous.

I left them at the labour and came home,
stiff-jointed, tired, with that slow careful stride
I've learnt already or which lay involved
in some meander of my country blood,
and now runs gracious, happy to be used;
and as I walked, more body than a mind,
my clay-brown fingers felt the weight and pressure
of the round tuber gripped against the palm.
Lord, when we die and our poor minds are bared,
round what strange objects are they clenched and set?

MAY ALTAR

In every farmhouse through the thorn-white Glens
this is the season when the little girls
put on white dresses, veils and tinsel wreaths,
and flock to Confirmation. Three swift years
it is since Rose was dressed and photographed;
now her two younger sisters are received
into that faith and haven I salute
but sheer away from. In the smoky kitchen
the little posies on the cupboard's top,
pale lady's-smock and blowsy rhododendron,
are set out neatly in the six glass jars,
and in the midst there stands, on this May altar,
the chipped and battered statue of the Virgin,
but my heart hankers for the pagan thorn
that none dare break a spray from and bring in.

COUNTRY TALK

Partly from reading the books and hearing the plays,
and partly because it has happened to us now and then,
we expect the cadenced phrase and the singular image
when we stop to talk in the Glens with a casual person.

Such things have become our estate, like that metaphor
of the lively mare that 'took lightning out of the road';
but more often the wisest have no more style than a sod.

You will remember that woman whose house we passed,
the last house close to the road going up to the moss,
the whitewashed gable a lattice of flashing leaves,
and across the yard and over the shallow stream
a squad of children calling and running about;
and you said, 'You have a lovely wee family here',
and she, 'Och well, they have all their features, thank God.'

And that famous day when the national leader came
to attend the commemoration along the coast,
stopping for lunch at the convent, the village crammed,
we met the long-boned old man on the mountainy road,
and I said, 'You didn't go down to see him come in?'
'He didn't come up to see me, why should I go down?'
and strode with his one-man republic back to the hills.

THE BOOLEYS

Crackling on burnt whin, springing over moss,
stopping to search our memories for the names
of little unfamiliar flowers, we sought,
over the rough-grassed hillside in the warmth
of a June morning, for the twin earth-circles
the map shewed for this townland, Ballyvooley.

Once a brown mare led off her tall fawn foal,
and grazing cattle lurched across our path,
larks singing in the light, and sinister rooks
plotting in heather what to do in corn;
and in one place a pause to chart our steps
where cannavaun shook out its warning tufts.

Then suddenly we found our whin-bright mounds,
small neat earth-circles, each a lake of rushes,
where centuries ago the young folk came
to pasture their scragged cattle all the summer
on lush warm slopes above the growing corn
where the old people yawned for their return.

I thought, and surely you thought, somehow these
laboriously raised, forgotten rings
were richer than the lichened walls of castles,
held cleaner memories than those of kings
and their blood-sodden tapestries of guilt,
and were unhaunted places, full of blessing.

THE BALLAD

I named a ballad round a sparking fire,
the children squatting on the hobs, the mother
busy with cans; the husband turned his knife
in the pipe-ash and said: 'I knew the man
that wrote it years ago. He was a tramp
and beat about the roads here.' Then he spoke
a stanza from it in the singsong way
that things are learnt by heart and not by head.

I queried further. Aye, the names were right.
There was a smiddy once, and yon's the place
they saw the Yeos come riding from, and ran
to warn the blacksmith. Then the mother told
how once the tramp begged shelter in the house,
and how her mother sat with him all night
beside the warm fire singing song for song.

The father nodded, knowing the tale well;
the clustered children listened with bright eyes,
and so the ballad and its poet started
on five new journeys through the mounting years:
and I whose care is set on riming words
felt a sharp jag of envy and of pride.

THE WAKE

We snicked the latch where one was dead,
constrained by ancient courtesy;
the open coffin on the bed
shewed us the man we'd come to see.

We gave our greetings to the gloom;
I found a seat against the wall;

my wife was hustled to 'the room'
where women were foregathered all.

Since turf and wick gave feeble light,
the crouching shapes seemed much the same;
with anxious ear and questing sight
I sought to join each shape and name.

Of stock and weather was the talk,
of harvests fabulously great –
the distances men used to walk –
the dangers of our pampered state.

Then one would rise and say good night,
and one who stood would take his chair;
the smoking turf would flicker bright
with each fresh gust of chilly air.

Then suddenly the only sound
would be of crickets at the grate;
and James would reach and hand around
tobacco on a dinner plate.

GLENAAN

I have come by lonely Orra round the glen
and stopped with men at turf upon the moss,
or had a good hour's crack with surfacemen
about the snowstorm and the heavy loss
of sheep that winter seven years ago,
for in that place this is the theme to broach,
just as at Carry Lough you are bound to know
the tragic story of the foundered coach.

But farther down the glen you'll see a slipe
pulling the lint to dub, or scythes in corn,
but you'd no more discourse with any man
than dare to tell him that his oats are ripe,
or that the haws crowd thick upon the thorn,
for comers have no errand in Glenaan.

INSTEAD OF AN ELEGY

This was a friendly man I nodded to,
returning his slow greeting. I had planned,

some day, when omens offered, to engage
the turning meshes of our separate minds
and run, thereafter, smoother for his pace;
for he was master most of skills I lack.
But now it is too late. He put away
saw and chisel and spokeshave on the bench.
The boats he made will ride both tide and storm
for years yet; other hands will draw them up
to the short turf, to pull the copper nails
and wedge new boards in; their names will change
as they are bartered round this rocky coast
to silt at last below some harbour wall.

He laid his fiddle later in its box
that once was famous for jig and reel
at feis or ceilidhe, when they came for miles
to hear him draw his bow across the strings.
And I who whittle words and whistle tunes
will so continue, uneasily aware
of all I missed in never knowing him,
yet no more sure I shall not have failed again
when the next craftsman lays his tools aside.

THE VOLUNTEER

For his long working life an engineer
on the deep water, at the end he came
still single, pension-armed, to settle here
where he was known, the last to bear his name.
He found a little cabin in a field
above the village, but not far away,
and, since but scarce the comfort it could yield,
he travelled to the village every day.

When war broke on the world, he named each coast,
each port remembered. When the shadows grew
with the lost vessels and the seamen lost,
he felt affronted at the ease he knew,
and with stiff fingers, unaccustomed, wrote
to the Head Office, saying he was well
and fit as any engineer afloat
to sign and serve for any offered spell.

He told them in the village what he'd done:
they hid their smiles, declaring solemnly
that war itself could not be rightly won
till he was safely back again at sea.
The weeks of waiting let the joke grow thin,
though now and then a man or two still pressed,
'No letter, John? They don't deserve to win.'
And we all wished they'd let the matter rest.

But one black week, when all the bulletins
were bomber raids, retreats and fallen towns,
the postman found the shack among the whins,
and handed in a letter to announce
that John's name had been added to the list,
and when a berth came vacant they would wire.
John bore the letter in a trembling fist,
and read it twice at every neighbour's fire.

HALLOWEVE: A GLENSMAN SPEAKS

As we came up the brae last night at twelve,
after a ceilidhe down at Ballybrack,
a wild coarse night of storm with scuds of rain
and a gale roaring over Tieveragh,
I said in fun: 'A poor night for the fairies;
they'll not stir far, for all it's Halloweve.
And then we crossed the stile at our old neighbour's;
a wallstead of a place where that man lives,
with not a soul to lift a pot for him.
A cross wee man, our neighbour; off and on,
he's closed that stile against us out of spite,
and threatened law about the right of way;
but I don't heed him; for a stile's a stile
and strong enough for juries. From the lane
we saw his front door open to the world
and, in beyond, the low room door was wide,
and a big fire was blazing on the hearth,
but not a sign of him as we stepped by;
and we both thought it odd a man should keep
his house broad open on a night like this;
a man not known to look for visitors.

COMPANY

Leaving our hearth at midnight for his own
up the steep winding brae, our neighbour paused
beyond the gate to weigh the chance of rain;
an old man this, our neighbour, when we come,
with trees between us and a noisy stream,
who lives alone, and follows his slow craft
of joinery, at clock case, chair or churn;
his front door shut; his workshop open wide
to wandering dog or sunshine from the south
or the farm children from across the hill.

Beneath the high bright stars the old man paused
to name tomorrow's weather, and we heard,
out of the empty darkness of the earth,
a corncrake calling loudly, if ear judged right,
in the low meadow now the grass is deep.

'The first I've heard the year,' the old man said.
'They're getting scarcer now than times ago.
I always like to hear him, for his cry
is right good company.' And then, 'Good night.'
He turned and plodded up the winding lane
to his dark house behind the fuchsia hedge,
and left me, thinking, under the far stars,
how one could measure another's loneliness.

FOR ANY WOMEN WHO PASS THIS HOUSE

This shuffling fellow, old Tom McAteer,
was, in his prime, a roaring engineer
who drove his ship through gale and hurricane
to the world's sleety ends and back again.
When she was docked and he had drawn his pay,
with drink and women he made holiday.

Now over eighty, in his tin-roofed shack,
high in the hills behind the ocean's back,
he still must cackle, seeking in the fire
the dancing antics of his old desire.
So, if you meet him on the mountain road,

slow with his oil can or some other load,
forgive him if his fingers grip your arm;
his winks and nods will do you little harm.
Too few of us, this side of Lethe's stream,
have followed an unprofitable dream
with such devotion, such abandonment –
perhaps it was for this that he was sent.

CUSHKIB FAIR

One gable towards the road, one towards the slope
that meets the shoulder of the storied hill,
door facing east, well out of the winds' way,
which funnel steady from the great bare glens,
sparse trees about it and a sprawl of walls,
a quarry pit and a burn across the road,
this house was once a noisy family
of tall sons famous for their endless sport,
horseplay with harness, ballads, dances, games,
glad to be living, even if they knew
the acres were too few to hold them long.

The only daughter changed her faith and married
a seaman from a glen five miles away,
left home and church to follow another pad.
Then, one by one, the brothers took their bundles
and stepped out from the farm among the hills;
some to marry or die, some to grow old
by distant waters. When the father died,
only the eldest son was left at home
to keep his mother and endure the land's
stubborn and grudging yield of root and stem.
He'd run with horses long, had a way with them;
rich in skills and charms, his aid was begged
from Drumnasole beyond to Carry Mountain.

The house was quiet now. When her man was drowned,
he brought his sister home with her two small girls
to nurse the bedfast mother. When she died,
the sister stayed as woman of the house.

The girls grew up and married, going off,
one to the village, one across the sea.

Brother and sister, older, let the land,
leaning on pensions and the quarter's rent,
achieved a frugal comfort for the house,
which, though not, at set times like Halloween,
roaring with games and laughter, yet was known
as a good hearth to ceilidhe at, for still
the brother had his stories running on
and his old way with horses, and the sister
was a noted talker, eager for all news.

But as the years blew past, the brother grew
odd in his manner, furtive; if he saw you
out on the road, he'd step behind a bush
till all was clear; and after the Great Snow
that smothered drifts of yowes in every glen,
his breathing bothered him: he took to bed,
was up and down, and then he did not get up,
but lay for months, and died before the stone
had turned the warm side up. St Patrick's Eve,
the country came to wake him; men and boys
smoking round the hearth, with one dim lamp
above the open coffin; the women sat,
with the old sister, talking, in the room.
And next day, when the Fair was at its crest,
we buried him, and laid within that grave
half of the wonders of the countryside,
the load of stories, pocketful of charms
of the last hoarder of the old tradition.

The house is empty now. The farm is sold.
The sister's gone to join her daughter's throng,
and all is ended. It will serve as store
for seed potatoes, meal and implements
to keep the land in temper. But the walls
will never again hear that man telling how
the bright sun danced at Easter over Garron,
and never again grow shadowy with dancers
gathering at Cushkib at Halloween.

THE BELL

Here in the hill-rimmed house
where the angelus bell is heard,

when the wind's from the south or west,
as clear as the nearest bird,

today, because the wind
is strong from another airt,
and the rain beats loud on the earth,
you must listen deep in your heart

for the sound of that baffled bell;
yet the chaffinch on the thorn
still offers his ripple of notes
to the tips of the brairding corn.

THE HILL-FARM

My errand brought me once again
along the steep road, down the lane;
and through the long and stumbling dark
there was no cry, no welcome bark
announced my nearing. All was still
from lamp in glen to star on hill.
The door was shut, but curtained light
thrust muffled challenge to the night.
Then at the porch I stopped and stood
to muster courage to intrude,
for, as I paused, I overheard
the rise and fall of rhythmic word,
a voice, the mother's, giving clear
the rosary, the evening prayer,
and, mumbling on a lower key,
the voices of the family
responding and repeating, each
with adult or with childish speech,
the invocations running on,
with, now and then, a smothered yawn.

At each Hail Mary, Full of Grace,
I pictured every friendly face,
clenched in devotion of a kind
alien to my breed and mind,
easy as breathing, natural
as birds that fly, as leaves that fall;
yet with a sense that I still stood
far from that faith-based certitude,

here in the vast enclosing night,
outside its little ring of light.

THE BRAES O' LAYDE

The Danes were here. The forts above the road
are still called after them, and down by Layde
you can point out the port their longships used
when they left Ireland after their last raid.

A seaman from the Glens in Denmark once
went strolling, when his ship was dry in dock,
among the market stalls and pens to judge
the famous Danish quality of stock.

So he discoursed, by chance, a countryman
who had a run of English at his call,
and, in the talk between them, it came out
the sailor man belonged to Cushendall.

The farmer laughed and said: 'A box at home
is filled with wills and deeds my fathers made;
and I know rightly from what's handed down
it's cold the night about the braes o' Layde.'

FAME

We gathered in the joiner's rock-floored shop
when the dew falling gave us leave to stop
our tedious struggle with the meadow hay,
for it was half-roads home, and anyway
old Pat was glad to take a holiday
from his slow careful labour at a barrow
that well could wait for finishing tomorrow.

So talk began about the weather's way,
the law on catch-dams, and the cost of hay,
but travelled headlong like a roaring burn
which finds a salley branch excuse to turn
to left or right that it enjoy its course
a little longer. So the joiner spoke
of certain ancient glensmen, hardy folk,

whose skill in mountain tracks could leave a horse
tied to a twisting road an hour behind,
and never need to halt for second wind.
Among them one who travelled every day
from here to Cargan twelve long miles away
yet never gave the foreman any chance
to call him late or idle: and one night
went back again to Cargan for a dance,
for old-time dances were his chief delight.

Then Tom, the farmer, told of tramps and herds
who cut across the moss as light as birds,
and won their wagers, drinks for all the house,
a bright half-sovereign or a brimming glass.

Most of these names and deeds were strange to me
who have no lease to this folk memory;
so searching through my thoughts that I might find
some phrase or word an ember in each mind
which, blown on, might well prove my right to share
in the warm kinship of this friendly air,
there'd been a poem I had heard about;
I'd made enquiries, found the poet's niece
and spoke to her, so she had copied out
as much as she remembered of the piece,
eleven verses that her uncle made.
Though known as poet, equal in his trade
of village butcher to the very best
that ever killed a beast and skinned and dressed
a carcase for the table, cow or sheep.
Though seldom printed, many poems keep
his name and wit remembered miles around:
this that I speak of praised the storied Glens
in phrases apt enough for better pens.

My friends responded, and my hope was crowned
with lively recognition, for my bard,
I was to learn, was something of a card,
a noted drinker, wakening on straw
and making fifty pounds before the night,
not always keeping quite within the law.

In Cushendun, one Fair Day, on the strand,
they'd seen him rolling, full, upon the sand,

so full 'the tide was in among his feet';
or when, accosted for a small deceit,
he 'hung a long face on him' and denied
the accusation till he nearly cried.

This being somehow off familiar ground,
I sought to bring the conversation round
to topics more acceptable to me,
so I kept harping on the poetry,
to set another bard against my man,
better than Dan McGonnell, Stoddard Moore,
once celebrated as the Rhyming Tramp,
who took as invitation any lamp
from hill-farm window or across half-door
to call or ceilidhe, paying for his keep
with endless verses till the household dropped asleep.

But the hill-farmer held beyond dispute
his man the first. McGonnell never could,
with all his wits, make anything as good
as the ballad of the Smith of Tieveragh;
that was a poem for you. 'Henry Pat',
McGonnell's best, was not the beat of that,
though with its points, for every hit was clear –
still, all the parties he was tilting at
were dead and gone this many's a long year;
but yon's the smiddy, yon's the very place
the blacksmith led the Yeos their useless chase;
and where John Kane's land marches with Leamore –
this is a thing ye didn't know before –
a gate the blacksmith made is swinging yet.

Then sudden fooled by my own self-regard,
who am a more sophisticated bard
than either Dan McGonnell or old Moore,
I thought to lure them into realising
the higher altitude, the deeper note
when schooled and printed poets such as I sing,
compared to these that rimed and chimed by rote.
So, cutting in across the anecdote,
'Moira O'Neill is better known,' I said,
'than any other poet of the Glens.
Her verse is quoted, and what's more, it's read;

she sells her thousands where we're glad of tens.'
I tried a brief quotation just to shew
they'd other poets that they ought to know.
'Och aye, ye mean the young Miss Higginson
stayed with Miss Ada round by Cushendun.
She was a decent girl. I seen her when
they held the first big feis here at the Bay,
and Roger Casement brought the Rathlin men.
She writ a book of pomes, I heard them say.'

from

THE PLANTER AND THE GAEL

GLOSS, ON THE DIFFICULTIES OF TRANSLATION

Across Lock Laig
the yellow-billed blackbird
whistles from the blossomed whin.

Not, as you might expect,
a Japanese poem, although
it has the seventeen
syllables of the haiku.
Ninth-century Irish, in fact,
from a handbook on metrics,
the first written reference
to my native place.

In forty years of verse
I have not inched much further.
I may have matched the images;
but the intricate wordplay
of the original – assonance,
rime, alliteration –
is beyond my grasp.

To begin with, I should
have to substitute
golden for *yellow*
and *gorse* for *whin*,
this last is the word we use
on both sides of Belfast Lough.

CONVERSATIONS IN HUNGARY, AUGUST 1969

I

In a back garden at Lake Balaton,
the lamp above the table veiled with flies,

strangers, we sat to watch the full moon rise,
our host, Miklos, a friendly writer, known
from essays in a foreign magazine;
his ready English made us feel at home,
yet fresh-plucked peaches, jar of Cuban rum
confirmed the alien nature of the scene.

The eager talk ran on from book to play,
to language, politics. Then, suddenly,
he leaned to ask: 'You heard the bulletin?'
And added, with no pause for our reply:
'Riots in Northern Ireland yesterday;
and they have sent the British Army in.'

II

Our friends in Budapest
days later also, puzzled, queried why,
when the time's vibrant with technology,
such violence should still be manifest
between two factions, in religion's name.
It is three hundred years since, they declared,
divergent sects put claim and counterclaim
to arbitration of the torch and sword.

We tried to answer, spoke of Arab, Jew,
of Turk and Greek in Cyprus, Pakistan
and India; but no sense flickered through
that offered reason to a modern man,
why Europeans, Christians, working-class,
should thresh and struggle in that old morass.

III

So failing there, we turned to history;
the savage complications of our past;
our luckless country where old wrongs outlast,
in raging viruses of bigotry,
their first infection; certain tragedy
close-heeled on hope, as by the Furies paced;
blight in the air, and famine's aftertaste,
frustration, guilt, and fear, and enmity.

Our keen friends countered with ironic zest:
your little isle, the English overran –

our broad plain, Tartar, Hapsburg, Ottoman –
revolts and wars uncounted – Budapest
shows scarce one wall that's stood two hundred years.
We build to fill the centuries' arrears.

from

AN ULSTER RECKONING

AN ULSTERMAN

This is my country. If my people came
from England here four centuries ago,
the only trace that's left is in my name.
Kilmore, Armagh, no other sod can show
the weathered stone of our first burying.
Born in Belfast, which drew the landless in,
that river-straddling, hill-rimmed town, I cling
to the inflexions of my origin.

Though creed-crazed zealots and the ignorant crowd,
long-nurtured, never checked, in ways of hate,
have made our streets a byword of offence,
this is my country, never disavowed.
When it is fouled, shall I not remonstrate?
My heritage is not their violence.

THE DILEMMA

Born in this island, maimed by history
and creed-infected, by my father taught
the stubborn habit of unfettered thought,
I dreamed, like him, all people should be free.
So, while my logic steered me well outside
that ailing church which claims dominion
over the questing spirit, I denied
all credence to the state by rebels won
from a torn nation, rigged to guard their gain,
though they assert their love of liberty,
which craft has narrowed to a fear of Rome.
So, since this ruptured country is my home,
it long has been my bitter luck to be
caught in the crossfire of their false campaign.

AN ULSTERMAN IN ENGLAND REMEMBERS

Here at a distance, rocked by hopes and fears
with each convulsion of that fevered state,
the chafing thoughts attract, in sudden spate,
neglected shadows from my boyhood years:
the Crossley tenders caged and roofed with wire,
the crouching Black and Tans, the Lewis gun,
the dead lad in the entry; one by one
the Catholic public houses set on fire;
the anxious curfew of the summer night,
the thoroughfares deserted, at a door
three figures standing, till the tender's roar,
approaching closer, drives them out of sight;
and on the broad roof of the County Gaol
the singing prisoners brief freedom take
to keep an angry neighbourhood awake
with rattled plate and pot and metal pail;
below my bedroom window, bullet-spark
along the kerb, the beat of rapid feet
of the lone sniper, clipping up the street,
soon lost, the gas lamps shattered, in the dark;
and on the paved edge of our cinder-field,
intent till dusk upon the game, I ran
against a briskly striding, tall young man,
and glimpsed the rifle he thought well concealed.
At Auschwitz, Dallas, I felt no surprise
when violence, across the world's wide screen,
declared the age imperilled: I had seen
the future in that frightened gunman's eyes.

IN THIS YEAR OF GRACE

The night-sky red, crackle and roar of flame,
the barricades across the ruined street,
the thump of stones, the shots, the thudding feet;
as mob greets mob with claim and counterclaim,
each blames the other, none accepts the blame,
for fears entrenched will not permit retreat,
when creed and creed inhospitably meet,
and each child's fate's foreshadowed in its name.

So fare our cities in this year of grace,
sick with old poisons seeped from history;

frustration on one side, the other fear
sodden with guilt. To their embattled place
the stubborn masters cling, while year by year
from this infection no man's blood runs free.

STREET NAMES

I hear the street names on the radio
and map reported bomb or barricade:
this was my childhood's precinct, and I know
how such streets look, down to the very shade
of brick, of paintwork on each door and sill,
what school or church nearby one might attend,
if there's a chance to glimpse familiar hill
between the chimneys where the grey slates end.

Yet I speak only of appearances,
a stage unpeopled, not the tragic play:
though actual faces of known families
flash back across the gap of fifty years;
can these be theirs, the children that today
rage in the fetters of their fathers' fears?

AN ULSTER LANDOWNER'S SONG

I'm Major This or Captain That,
MC and DSO.
This Orange Lily in my hat
I sometimes wear for show,

so long as I can walk my dogs
around the old estate,
and keep the Fenians in their bogs,
the peasants at the gate.

I meet my tenants, decent men,
in Lodge, on market day,
and all seems safe till, now and then,
they start a small affray.

They stirred up an unwelcome noise,
it set my nerves on edge,

that day they beat those girls and boys
across Burntollet Bridge,

with journalists and cameras there
to send in their reports.
The world no longer seems to care
for healthy country sports.

FABLES FOR STORMONT

In Mrs Shelley's story, Frankenstein
made his own monster–master. Change the name
from that of man to party and the shame
needs no crude pen to mark or underline.
For generations, sign and countersign
secured the winnings of their wicked game;
now brawling zealots whom they dare not blame,
bred in black covens, blast the neat design.

That other fable may be more exact;
when the magician left for Camelot,
he laid his book aside. The foolish boy,
though he had often watched his master's act,
misread the gestures proper to employ,
when all he hoped for was to fill the pot.

THE COASTERS

You coasted along
to larger houses, gadgets, more machines,
to golf and weekend bungalows,
caravans when the children were small,
the Mediterranean, later, with the wife.

You did not go to church often,
weddings were special;
but you kept your name on the books
against eventualities;
and the parson called, or the curate.

You showed a sense of responsibility,
with subscriptions to worthwhile causes

and service in voluntary organisations;
and, anyhow, this did the business no harm,
no harm at all.
Relations were improving. A good
useful life. You coasted along.

You even had a friend or two of the other sort,
coasting too: your ways ran parallel.
Their children and yours seldom met, though,
being at different schools.
You visited each other, decent folk with a sense
of humour. Introduced, even, to
one of their clergy. And then you smiled
in the looking glass, admiring, a
little moved by, your broadmindedness.
Your father would never have known
one of them. Come to think of it,
when you were young, your own home was never
visited by one of the other sort.

Relations were improving. The annual processions
began to look rather like folk festivals.

When that noisy preacher started,
he seemed old-fashioned, a survival.
Later you remarked on his vehemence,
a bit on the rough side.
But you said, admit it, you said in the club,
'You know, there's something in what he says.'

And you who seldom had time to read a book,
what with reports and the colour supplements,
denounced censorship.
And you who never had an adventurous thought
were positive that the church of the other sort
vetoes thought.
And you, who simply put up with marriage
for the children's sake, deplored
the attitude of the other sort
to divorce.
You coasted along.
And all the time, though you never noticed,
the old lies festered;

the ignorant became more thoroughly infected;
there were gains, of course;
you never saw any go barefoot.

The government permanent, sustained
by the regular plebiscites of loyalty.
You always voted but never
put a sticker on the car;
a card in the window
would not have been seen from the street.
Faces changed on the posters, names too, often,
but the same families, the same class of people.
A minister once called you by your first name.
You coasted along
and the sores suppurated and spread.

Now the fever is high and raging;
who would have guessed it, coasting along?
The ignorant-sick thresh about in delirium
and tear at the scabs with dirty fingernails.
The cloud of infection hangs over the city,
a quick change of wind and it
might spill over the leafy suburbs.
You coasted too long.

MEMORANDUM FOR THE MODERATES

Speak peace and toleration. Moderate
your tone of voice, and everywhere avoid
what might provoke. Good will must be deployed
in efforts to restore our balanced state.
To long-held views sincere give proper weight;
one brief rash word and all might be destroyed.
Ignore that man who prates of Marx or Freud:
we know what lies behind this old debate.

This is your duty as a citizen:
hold firmly to it, deaf to cynic sneers.
Few will recall the names of any dead;
with luck the fire will die away for years;
the men in power will still be solid men,
and, like them too, you will have kept your head.

THE TRIBUNES

After the tumult and conflagration in the city
three tribunes were appointed by the senate
to discover the roots of the unrest.

When their report was read,
the tribunes, being fair-minded men,
blame was laid
on the mob with torches and the zealots
who had roused them,
and on the Thebans within the gates
(adding, since they were just, that
the Thebans were in fact denied citizenship),
but especially accusing the young men
who had spoken for freedom in the marketplace
and those who had resisted
the burning of the houses.

They remarked also
that the militia
had, once or twice, used
excessive force in quelling
the young men and the Thebans.

THE WELL-INTENTIONED CONSUL

Eased into the succession
by the ailing aged consul,
because of his house
respected among the patricians,
the realities of his office
slowly possessed his mind:
how to make lasting peace with Thebes
and admit
those Thebans who lived within the city
into free citizenship,
in spite of their loyalty to Thebes
and their false gods.

In this he was foolhardy,
for the patricians
had so used the threat of Thebes

to keep the people docile
that the people believed them
and distrusted all Thebans,
and the patricians, some of them,
swore by their own fears.

So he spoke in the senate of good will
and forbearance and peace
within the city and beyond its borders
and of forgetting old chronicles.

But when it became known
that he had sent and received emissaries,
the people shouted that he had betrayed the city,
and the patricians, angered since he was one of them,
that he had betrayed the senate also.
So the consular office was stripped from him
and given to his kinsman.

The merchants who had applauded his promise
stood silent while the unrest grew,
while the mob rushed out with torches
and set fire to the Theban houses,
the little houses in the Western Quarter.

PARALLELS NEVER MEET

Events in my native province now
twist my heart, threatening
any future I had planned.

To find focus for my taut feelings,
I thrust all back into a remote setting,
dressing the circumstances
in the properties of antiquity,
allegorising the actions and the actors,
finding Peloponnesian parallels
for the arrogant soothsayer,
the time-server, the ambitious knave,
the stupid, the buffoon, the cynic,
the just man without courage.

But they trip and flounder in their togas;
the classical names are inappropriate,

deflecting by their associations and resonance,
giving a rhetorical inflation
to their ignorance and banality.
Reality is of a coarser texture;
the scene collapses absurd,
lath and canvas.

But the heartbreak remains,
the malice and the hate are palpable,
the flames authentic,
the wounds weep real blood
and the future is not to be foretold.

PRIME MINISTER

We've seen that worried face upon the box
and watched the hesitations of his mind;
a decent man, he seems, no crafty fox
like some who went before, or lurk behind.
Yet pedigree supplies a flinty core
to his opinions; they were always right,
since his old Jacobean ancestor
burnt out the clans in many a bloody fight.
So, Captain or Colonel or Knight-in-arms,
his class has always gripped the power they took.
Now he admits the overdue reforms,
accepts them blandly for the statute book.
But one thing sticks. Dare he repudiate
the bigot rabble lodged in party hate?

DEMAGOGUE

Compulsive preacher, large, and loud of voice
in octaves of abuse, invective, hate;
a Samson self-ordained, his strength destroys
whatever justified our canting state,
since his chief skill is to articulate
the smouldering terrors and the prejudice
that makes our heritage a dubious freight
which, now exposed, is seen for what it is.
No long time since we dreamed that on our glens,
our little fields, our artless shabby towns

might break some generous light of common sense,
and men of will wake eager to renounce
our sad past and its sick corollary –
he breaks that hope across his broadcloth knee.

MINISTER

Not one of your tall captains bred to rule,
that right confirmed by school and army list,
he went to school, but not the proper school.
His family tree will offer little grist
to any plodding genealogist;
his father's money grew from making shirts.
But with ambition clenched in his tight fist,
and careful to discount the glancing hurts,
he climbed to office, studiously intent,
and reached the door he planned to enter, twice
to have it slammed by the establishment.
A plight that well might sympathy command,
had we not watched that staff of prejudice
he'd used with skill turn serpent in his hand.

AGITATOR

She may be rash, may flounder now and then,
driven by rage and pity to excess;
but in a country where the bravest men
no more than point a finger at distress,
yet lack the will to alter anything,
save at an inching pace, by compromise,
this girl is most imprudent, she will rise
to any challenge circumstance may bring.

Her qualities are youth's, but Irish youth –
though round the earth her generation stirs.
So, cutting through to reach the simple truth,
she spoke for 'people of no property'.
Thus Tone addressed them once; now it is hers,
that phrase, the warrant of her ancestry.

EXILE

Although it is my native place
and dear to me for many associations,

how can I return to that city
from my exile among strangers?

These people I now live among
are friendly in the street
and quiet in the evenings
around their own hearths.
And I grown old
do not wish to shuffle
through the rubble of my dreams
and lie down in hope's ashes:
the Phoenix is a fabulous bird.

A BELFASTMAN ABROAD ARGUES WITH HIMSELF

Admit the fact, you might have stood your ground
and kept one corner clear for decency,
making no claims, but like a friendly tree
offering shade to those who'd gather round.
You should have spoken when that evil man
first raised his raucous shout, to all who lied
given the lie direct, that little clan
who later marched for justice, joined with pride.

Now, from safe distance, you assert your right
to public rage. This town is, after all,
where I was born and lived for fifty years.
I knew its crooked masters well by sight,
endured its venom and survived its sneers.
I scratch these verses on its flame-scorched wall.

THE IRON CIRCLE

to the memory of the late W.R. Rodgers

Here, often, a man provoked has said his say,
stung by opinion or unjust event,
and found his angry words, to his dismay,
prop up his adversary's argument,
for bitterness is not allowed to die,
is fanned and fuelled, in this crazy land:

the brandished gun demands a gun's reply;
hate answers hate, our crest the Bloody Hand.

My friend, who followed coursing on this ground,
and sought its lore and logic everywhere,
suggested once, the Hare must need the Hound
as surely as the Hound must need the Hare.
In my mood now I fear that he was right:
the chase continues, with no end in sight.

from

THE CHINESE FLUTEPLAYER

SPRING OF THE YEAR

In April the spring of the year
it was the spring of the world
white with the bleating of larks
and the singing of the lambs
flowers in the ditches galore
lime on the harrowed mould
the buds and the stems like corks
with sap bottled ready-to-burst
in froth or dribble with flames
the bright sun varnished with frost.

BLACK AND WHITE

A blackbird flew to a hawthorn bush
and brushed a flutter of petals down;
they tumbled and turned like a flurry of snow
and settled slow on the waiting stone.

And, if that blackbird, all summer through,
could sing so long as there's light to see,
he would never fling a song as bright
as that lyric flight from the hawthorn tree.

SPARROWHAWK

The rooks rose cawing noisily with fright,
flapping the firs to motion, scattering
loose twigs unmeshed, in mad eccentric flight
from the sharp terror of this sudden thing.
Shot-straight and crying out his savage trade,
beneath the rocking nests that terror flew.
Although he seemed to like the stir he made,
the sparrowhawk had something else to do.

THE STORM

My gate is swinging by one hinge
twigs are scattered on the pavement
the withered chrysanthemums
have daubed themselves with mud
the lake has a feathery edge
the old grasses make a dry sound
and I think of my Chinese friend
on a ship going home.

FROM THE CHINESE OF WANG LI SHI

The Mourne Mountains like a team of bears
tumbling into the sea,
the embroidered fields like a monk's patched cloak
spreading their skirts to every door,
the peasants leisurely allowing
the chickens and dogs to wander at will
the bare trees standing silent
entangle the stranger's dream.

AUGUST 1939

On this day of crisis
when men march
and the avalanche waits for the shout
I try to make better English
of Wang's literal translation of verses
about the evening moon and the East Lake
by a Ming poet
painted on a small bowl
in the museum.

CHINESE FLUTEPLAYER

The small bronze figure lips a silent flute,
and stillness spreads about him like a lake;
he stands there out of time, and once you look
you are involved, released from mortal state,
because all sense is channelled into sight.
See how light strikes and strokes his rounded brow

and pauses on his dreaming-lidded eyes –
this shell of metal sings for ever now.

THE LYRIC SONOROUSLY RHYMED . . .

The lyric sonorously rhymed
with chimed device of bardic school
was never yet by man designed
to match the weather of her mood.
The sonnet moving to its close
with golden octave, pause and clinch,
was never woven yet to hold
those well-marked brows, that lifted chin.
And though I've spent ten years or more
on stanza's shape and ways of words,
I'd squander all the skill I've stored
to give you half a glimpse of her.

I TURNED MY TOUCH TO CAMPION . . .

I turned my touch to Campion
and fingered through his *Booke of Ayres;*
the griefs of his orpharion,
his madrigals' remote despairs
moved not at all or scarce could move,
my eager mind was so possessed
by such complexities of love
as tremble in your gentle breast.

I'VE KNOWN HER TURN FROM BITTER PHRASE . . .

I've known her turn from bitter phrase
to bring a smile across her face
when someone comes by chance event
to whom she is indifferent;
for only I am target of
the hard bombardment of her love,
and therefore none but I can tell
her heart's hair-triggered miracle.

FOR R.

How much of you is in my verse
another age deserves to say
detect the detail and disperse
the clouds that round the gathered day.

No more for me to pluck who plant
who needs nine lives to spell which grow
only whisper what I want
and name which bird could wear the snow.

So love me this it is not long
the bone shew through the grey remark
the other meaning of which song
that with one star consumed the dark.

from

SCISSORS FOR A ONE-ARMED TAILOR

MARGINAL VERSES 1929–1954

SURVIVAL

The libraries are bulged and ballasted
with poems of which only the pages and the binding have lasted:
they cram the shelves, the formidable fate
of the grey mouse gnawing towards his doctorate.

It is wiser to attempt a simple song
with an easy tune that does not last too long;
for, paradoxically, simplicity survives,
and short songs often have the longest lives.

THE LISTENER

People are too noisy, too loud;
they rip across my listening
with gabble, chatter, raucous salutation;
less often they sing.

I have painfully to become adjusted
anew, each time,
to the bluebottle in the geranium,
and the invisible bees in the lime.

NAME AND NUMBER

When Adam named the crowding beasts
that had no names before,
creation's second act threw wide
a bright and beckoning door.

But Noah numbered them in pairs
to stow them in the ark;
when all were numbered, all were in,
and all inside was dark.

ECCE HOMO

He took every job now
brought to the door,
the mould-board, the table,
the churn and the oar,
for Joseph was feeble,
his vision poor.

But her maiden secret
she dared not tell,
though he looked, at the bench
where the sunlight fell,
so like his tall father
Gabriel.

PROVIDENCE 1

White roses shatter, overblown,
by the breath of a little wind undone,
yet the same air passing scarcely stirs
the tall dark green perpetual firs.

PROVIDENCE 2

The beetle near my foot
tempts providence in me;
my inadvertent boot
is God's own mystery.

PROVIDENCE 3

The fish flopped on my shoes,
turned up a chilly eye,
its back a silver bruise,
mouth oozing bloodily.

So, while I cut more bait
and wiped my scaly rod,
I mused on chance and fate,
and, somehow, pitied God.

IN THE ROSSES

The hospitable Irish
come out to see who passes,
bid you sit by the fire
till it is time for Mass.

The room is bare, the bed
is shabby in the corner,
but the fine talk is ready
and the wide hearth is warm.

PASSION

The tall man spilled his cards
and stood up with a cry
as hard words started harder
and insults leapt on lies.

I scorned in sudden flash
my caution learnt at school
and cursed the fate makes passion
the privilege of fools.

TRIAD

Three things that men might scorn,
weak fragile things indeed
that bear the great world's bulk:
the thin green blade of corn,
the thin grey housewife's thread,
the thin white jet of milk.

TRIAD

Three sounds of peace and rich increase:
the lowing of calf-heavy cow;
the hammer's blow; the swishing mould
each side of the dividing plough.

NEW JERUSALEM 1

In easy days I joined my voice with them
who prophesied a new Jerusalem,
nor dreamed the outcome of the years should be
a far more terrible Gethsemane.

EPITAPH FOR A CONSCRIPT, 1940

I go to seek the peace we could not save
because we left it to the fool and knave,
will maybe find instead my father's grave.

COLD WARRIOR:
ANZAC DAY, 1946

With rotund word and bloated epithet
he slobbers through his venomous alphabet
and will not cease from his blood-boltered spells
though ghosts still gibber round the Dardanelles.

NEW JERUSALEM 2

Though men may clamour 'Why delay?
We want this visioned state today',
take care you do not offer them
some jerry-built Jerusalem.

MINOR POET'S DILEMMA, 1940

Caught in my prime in pitiful disaster,
my world's walls gape atilt, about to fall:
where must I turn for comfortable master
to fill the hush of terror's interval?

Say – Edward Thomas, who, when earth was breaking,
brooding on vole and hawthorn, deathward went,
or Roman Landor, brave at eighty, making
immortal quatrains of pure sentiment?

LILIBULERO

An old song wanders round
on some lost errand sent;
till great occasion's found
its melody is lent
to innocent event,
which once in high debate
had lashed a government
and overturned the state.

SECOND FRONT: DOUBLE SUMMERTIME, JULY 1943

The crazy clock two hours astray
defies the angle of the sun,
yet accurately ticks away
the dripping minutes one by one
that heap their grains to reach the date
our nibbled pencils testify,
and all the guns of Europe wait
for all the men who are to die.

BREASTPLATE

Take from the mind its little bitterness
and the vexations which encompass it:
release the warm capacity to bless,
the sense of, somehow, being infinite.

The dangers round our days are like the rain
that falls on good and evil equally.
Only the fool, the privately insane,
wears the assurance of his victory.

GRIEF

I thought when the grave was sodded,
and the carriage came back to the door,
and the sick man's bed was empty,
I could endure no more.

But the heart is a tougher metal,
it can carry beyond belief
a proud and ancient escutcheon,
etched by the acid of grief.

EMILY DICKINSON

When I, the easy one, was hurt
as never hurt before
I fumbled back through files of verse
for one who suffered more.

But all the poets' proverbs slept
as dry as my swept brain,
save that sweet witch who knew at once
my idiom of pain.

GRIEF

When men lie down for ever
and names their tombstones take,
the mind accepts the reason
but fears the heart may break.

Yet though life signs its verdict
on every breast and thigh,
it adds a kindly codicil
that grief must also die.

MOTHER AND SON

After this encounter the usual residue,
the particle undissolved, the teeth on edge.
Weaning was perhaps the shock. When the nipple withdrew,
we stepped uncertainly out of the Golden Age.

The womb that is rid of its load will sometimes yearn
for the friendly fullness, the natural miracle;
but the mother no more than the son can never learn
that, forgiven, we need to forgive the separate will.

BOY SEEN IN A BUS JOURNEY

Boy with the frail romantic grace,
the lustrous eyes, the wind-brushed hair,
your face recalled the poet's face,
and instantly I was aware
of what sick years could lie ahead –
not even with verse for your relief –
of heartbreak and the spittle red
upon the sodden handkerchief.

EPITAPH TO A MAN NOT DEAD

This weary body long served kindly use,
powered by a steady engine of good sense;
and if the bolts and tappets rattled loose,
it was that journey's length and violence.

R.K.

Houseboy, then cook's assistant, went to sea,
endured a year, now quietly at home
companions age and does embroidery,
in an old house where letters never come.

W.R.R.

This country parson with the corncob pipe
has secret vices, has been known to write
pun-cluttered verse like Hopkins overripe,
and read Krafft-Ebbing very late at night.

S.S.K.

A boy, he rode with telegrams.
A man, delivered postcards and letters,
with good or bad news impartially,
or merely neutral information.

Now at eighty,
with joints stiff from so much exercise,

he tilts tables at séances, seeking
a special message for himself.

B.O.W.

The man's a bag of wind, the critics sneer,
I nod assent, but smile my inward doubt:
for lack of bellows many a friendly fire
that warms us yet had long ago gone out.

R.P.M.

Affection would his vivid likeness give,
but in what rigid quatrain could it catch
that ripe curled lip, the drawled affirmative,
the surreptitious glances at his watch?

MIRROR

No actor with cupboard full of masks,
I use the mirror strictly as a tool,
knowing my face too well to set it tasks,
like looking cynical or masterful.

I never mouth in mirrors, do not speak,
only, at times, I signal with my hand,
not merely to adjust the lathered cheek,
but that the man within should understand.

SCISSORS FOR A ONE-ARMED TAILOR

The beggar, when I hurried to the door,
began the usual whine, this lack of pence
no fault of his; just luck, this being poor.
I told him that he needed no defence.

I dared to venture: did he play or sing,
or maybe write great poems on events?
Aye, all of that; but more than anything,
he'd greater notions than ten parliaments.

He mentioned some. I found a cast-off shirt
and fumbled coppers for his doss-house bed,
his white beard grey with thirty counties' dirt
and seventeen inventions in his head.

IN A SUBURBAN AVENUE

The young girl slacks the leash and lingers while
her brown pup checks the gatepost by its smell,
aware she must not interrupt or tug
him from the ritual of the lifted leg.
Yet all the while her prim and virgin heart
hugs memories of the boys who pay her court,
but my lewd mind suggests her frantic state
if they should lift their legs against her gate.

OCEAN, 1940

I sit here gazing at the tranquil bay
as slow waves curl and crumple on the shore,
and grieve for all the things I dare not say,
they have been said so many times before.

GREY AND WHITE

Grey sea, grey sky
two things are bright;
the gull-white foam,
the gull, foam-white.

MIST

On the bare moorland
across the brown heather
the cry of the curlew
reels out of the mist,
and the blur on my lenses
the light on my lashes
the chill in my heart is
from more than the mist.

ON A JANUARY TRAIN JOURNEY

Gulls at the plough's tail and rooks in the fallow, the
turnip field's empty of hoof or of bird;
only the ploughman who humours his horses, a
child with a milk can, with none for a third.

Hedges are naked and rain's in the ditches;
maybe a goat on the bank as we pass;
whin-tips are golden, but bracken is rusty, and
sheep stumble over the wind-clotted grass.

NOW IN THE SPRING

Now in the spring a man dare not be still,
there are so many things that must be done,
reports the brain must file from ear and eye
of cellulose and salt and chlorophyll,
the accurate ballistics of the sun,
bird's decibels, chromatics of the sky.

APRIL

How can a man by naming call to mind
this Antrim landscape, fallow, harrowed, ploughed,
the broken clods, the parallels defined
by violet shadows on a warm red clay,
bright green of new-leafed hawthorn, ringing loud
with all the small birds of an April day?

MID-APRIL

Mid-April now. Ploughed land is light
with dust of lime. The sowers stride
across the clods. The blossom's white
of blackthorn by the quarry side.

The shafted sunlight on the whin
sets slopes aflame with gold galore;
and tadpole-odysseys begin
across the lint-hole's shallow floor.

JULY

This is the ebb of birdsong. Only now
the yellow yorlin drips his rippled notes,
and the unmated corncrake chides the moon,
where once there scarcely was a vacant bough,
when in unnumbered leaves a thousand throats
were busy with necessities of June.

SKYPIECE

After a blatant dawn of red and gold,
the wind wiped off the clouds and left the sky
as clear as a glass of water and as cold,
and the dead moon was like a blind man's eye.

WINTER DAY

From the first light when in the upland field
the tractor roared beyond the tall black trees,
turning the bleached grass to a quilt of clay,
till in the dusk the robin sang concealed
and the young moon ran headlong in the breeze,
this winter day has been a happy day.

ALIEN HARVEST

I cross a laboured plot of ground
where skilful men with spade and graip
through weary years of use have found
the comfort of recurring shape.

I break the sods of my slow mind
with tools that some old craftsman wrought,
yet when the yield is cut, I find
a harvest alien to my thought.

BLEEZE

The laden senses cram my mind,
I wait on wisdom yet unsaid;

in Rose McDonnell's phrase, I find,
'it taks a bleeze to harn the bread.'

RAINDROP

One said, because I saw the leaf
that clutched the raindrop to its heart,
'You're ignorant of Europe's grief.
You wander in a world apart.'
He did not see within that drop
the round earth lying small enough
for my grave thought to lift it up
and know it without hate or love.

I WRITE FOR . . .

I write for my own kind,
I do not pitch my voice
that every phrase be heard
by those who have no choice:
their quality of mind
must be withdrawn and still,
as moth that answers moth
across a roaring hill.

from

OUT OF MY TIME

POEMS 1967–1974

THE SEARCH

for Shirley and Darryl

We left the western island to live among strangers
in a city older by centuries
than the market town which we had come from
where the slow river spills out between green hills
and gulls perch on the bannered poles.

It is a hard responsibility to be a stranger;
to hear your speech sounding at odds with your neighbours';
holding your tongue from quick comparisons;
remembering that you are a guest in the house.

Often you will regret the voyage,
wakening in the dark night to recall that other place
or glimpsing the moon rising and recollecting
that it is also rising over named hills,
shining on known waters.

But sometimes the thought
that you have not come away from, but returned,
to this older place whose landmarks are yours also,
occurs when you look down a long street remarking
the architectural styles or move through a landscape
with wheat ripening in large fields.

Yet you may not rest here, having come back,
for this is not your abiding place, either.

The authorities declare that in former days
the western island was uninhabited,
just as where you reside now was once tundra,
and what you seek may be no more than
a broken circle of stones on a rough hillside, somewhere.

ERICE, WESTERN SICILY

Walled hilltop, islanded in sea-mist
blown in from Trapani's water-grid,
in sun, above the turning road
pine-scented; under the heraldic arch,
past the skew bell tower, the shanked porch,
close streets cobbled in pattern, houses blank,
their high fronts shuttered. I look, furtive,
for flicked cloak, lifted forearm, expect to hear
the dagger clatter, patter of feet retreating,
hearken for lute-serenade, instead
offered only simple chirp,
the cage high, chin-high near door ajar.
What kind of bird? you ask. The lean woman
calls it *uccello, uccello,* repeatedly,
smiling, firm with our stupidity.

Guessing by corners, alleyways, inclinations,
step into the crammed bowl, *Centro*;
expect stall-awnings, coloured stuffs,
cowled procession with long candles, chanting;
but find three dozen Fiats – my count – jammed close
like hogs in pen, and stout men lighting cigarettes
outside the Banco di Sicilia.
What business is here to transact?
What merchandise? What ducats pass?

MONTELEPRE

On Hare Mountain, Giuliano's lair,
where steep road cuts abruptly round
perched streets strung with iron balustrades,
past the pastry-cooks' which wears,
blotched and weathered, the partners' names,
left by sudden bend to the new café;
at the town's frayed end we dismount.

We hand our lire to the bandit's sister
who rings the register, deft with coins.
The tiny mother, white hair knot-dragged,
in old woman's black, with bird-black eyes,
suddenly refuses the tourist's lens.

Although I know the café was built and paid for
with magazine articles, newspaper interviews,
that film, I salute her pride.

Outside, between petrol pumps, I gaze
down the abrupt slope cutting the bend
to squalid back, side of pastry-cooks',
notice electric-flex like swung-bridge from café
sagging six feet over filthy scree
of plastic containers, cartons, spilled rubbish,
and wonder, idly, how the current is charged.

THE LONG BRIDGE

for Keith

This must have been before, say, 1840,
before the long bridge was taken down
or collapsed, with its twenty-one cracked
arches, and the new one, with four, called
after the young queen, was set in its place.

A man approached the bridge slowly,
carrying his old father on his back.
The old man said: 'Set me down here;
down here, on the bridge wall.
The workhouse is a brave step yet.'
The man stopped and eased down his load;
and the old man said: 'It was here
I set my father down on this journey.'

I heard this from the son of the man,
the grandson of the old man, aged himself.
Clearly, it was part of his reality;
he believed every word of it.

Yet, as he was telling me, I realised
it was no more than a variant
of the Balkan folk tale
of the peasant dragging his old father
through the orchard by his beard or beating him
(I am acquainted with both versions)
and the old man crying: 'Far enough.

It was here by the third tree
that I stopped punishing my father.'
Perhaps it sounds more dramatic
in the Serbo-Croat.

FROM THE TIBETAN

In my native province when I was young
the lamas were presumed to be dishonest,
not because they were more wicked than the rest
but their calling gave them more scope.

They were not expected to be philosophers
or poets, for they were not educated persons;
theories were as inconceivable as books
in their satchels. All they were asked
was to provide certain familiar noises
on fixed occasions of the calendar,
spinning the wheels with ritual fervour
and chanting of 'The Emperor's Tunic'
and 'The Great Wall of China'.

For the rest of their time it was anticipated
that they should work hard rewarding their families,
promoting their nephews, replenishing their stores,
and accepting presents from contractors.
Traditionally, all this was to be done with a show
of cordiality, with handclasps, salutes,
conspicuous finger-signals and audible passwords:
the effect which it was desired to produce
being that of reluctant necessity
for complicated manoeuvre.

Now I am older and live in the suburbs of the capital,
I find that the lamas here are very much the same,
save that the rewarding, promoting, replenishing, is
done on their behalf by a permanent secretariat,
leaving them more time to devote to the illusion
of exercising power: this forces them to acquire
a more sophisticated vocabulary; indeed,
one or two of them have written books:
in my native province this
would have been looked upon with disfavour,
for we are a simple people.

CAROL SINGERS

for Deirdre

Why should it stir me, when, each face intent,
the Christmas children sing my childhood back,
clustered with hollied memories, innocent,
that lie discarded on my lonely track?

The walk in frost and darkness to the church,
doubling my steps to match my father's stride,
the greetings and the handshakes in the porch –
he held that faith, I think, until he died.

That faith, that story, half the stuff of art,
the myth, the magic of the Holy Child –
why should such sadness gather round my heart,
when every sense reports it unfulfilled,
its terms decayed, its uses out of date
as easel-painting or my classroom slate?

LEGEND IN HIS OWN LIFETIME

No role in peace for such a restless captain,
as he was not over-bright, a small sinecure;
chief instrument of expression that fast car
reckless he flogged daily from and to
his bungalow out in the country.

I saw him once in a club, bigger than any;
the place full of strangers after the match.
One, scrum-half's brother, with flushed face,
lurched round, needling people.

Setting his collared glass on a wet table,
the large hero stood a moment in the posture
of a stage-thinker [*Thinks*], stepped over to him,
grabbed the long tie in his left hand, hauled it tight,
and, measuring carefully with head tilted back,
smashed vast right against the hoisted jaw.
The struck man dropped.
The legend-in-his-own-lifetime raised the window
and shouted down to the street for an ambulance.

Such precision. Such violence.

In the village he roared through going home
there is a blind corner, a right-hand gable.
The villagers said, each time the great tyres screeched,
that the hero, some day, would smash himself up.

One night the fast car crashed into the gable;
the two streets nearest woke with the noise,
but nobody went out to see what had happened.
They knew well enough he had killed himself,
and nobody there liked him, the hero.
He was certainly dead by the first light
when the policemen prised him from the wreck.

War-hero, decorated, still remembered
where clubmen meet, a legend in his own lifetime,
someone has written a paperback about him,
with little space for more than his war exploits
which were, in fact, remarkable.

SUBURBAN SPRING IN WARWICKSHIRE

for Lilac

First then the *Prunus* and the Japanese cherry,
fragile but assertive before the year warms up;
appropriate to this suburb, these houses
and their people, not native here,
but forcing quick colour, short-lasting,
out of a thin topsoil.

Rather I wait for the chestnut flowering
and the dripping laburnum blossoms;
for the chestnuts later will yield
the spiky fruit with the ivory kernels,
and, for small boys, the knuckled challenges:

and the pale gilt laburnum recalls
the small tree which hung beside the fence,
where you could climb over to play
with your friends next door:
its pods I was warned against, repeatedly.
I was seven then:
it was my grandmother's garden,
in another country.

COMPTON WYNYATES, WARWICKSHIRE

for Beatrice and Ralph

The alabaster gentry, hacked and battered,
and, after, dropped into the moat:
five Tudor Comptons, one more than the four
who had spurred down the steep slope of Edgehill.

The church where they had lain, beside the great house,
was wrecked. Altar, font, smashed. Not the tower;
a tower will stand against what force spills a wall,
though one might climb to tip the coping off.

Dredged up when the moat was earthed, the effigies,
in twenty years, came home, when the church was rebuilt.
Last summer I noted all, the seventeen hatchments,
the classical tablet, the box-pews. This time

I chose rather to loiter in the June sun,
musing on the squat headstones of labouring folk,
humble, enduring, among clover, buttercups,
the seeding grasses, the rain-beaded grass.

ET TU IN ARCADIA VIXISTI

for Roberta

You woke me, rising – this in Paris once –
I watched you stepping – thirty years ago –
to the long window. Many such we've since
unshuttered back from narrow streets below,
but on no more than stir of wheel or foot –
as, finger-signalled, following, I stood
beside you, heeding, drifting up, a flute-
like music, blown through the clean hollow wood,
while, leaning, a dark lad against the wall
played to the splay of goats about his knees,
strayed, so it seemed, from classic pastoral,
an instant's magic – never ours in Greece,
when, later, older, or in Sicily,
we stood, at dawn, beside the tideless sea.

W.R. RODGERS

(1909–1969)

So we shall never hear him any more,
the slow low voice that wandered on and on,
slipping or looping from outrageous pun
to some split atom of semantic lore,
where sparking opposites would generate
a flash of wit or wisdom, to restore
the faith on which affection bade you wait
for glimpses of the poet loved before.

Within that kind, exasperating man,
devious and gentle, there were grappled fast
the same tense opposites. He was my friend,
and through his talk, for thirty years, there ran
a theme – the Hare – which seemed to have no end:
now that wild creature is run down at last.

AN HOUR WITH E.M.F. AT NINETY

for May and Robert

I sat with Morgan Forster for a while,
rug round his knees, long narrow hands on lap,
head tilted bird-like, quick to frown or smile,
as I reported whimsical mishap
or light encounter, in my day's routine:
then moved to tell – I gauged his interest
how Kenneth Clark, last night upon the screen,
described the ancient values driven west,
cliff-ledged like gannets, over the rough sea –

Then Morgan murmured, 'But Byzantium –
has Clark forgotten?' I named hastily
his reasons why that culture stayed at home,
gripped by the marvel that we still could find
an edge of sharpness in that gentle mind.

A MINOR VICTORIAN PAINTER

A bright scene; a summer morning,
dew on the deep grass. The bearded man

in corduroy stands before his easel
and as he paints, he sings;
at the bend of a Warwickshire stream
heavy with foliage and reflections
green, its surface still, except
for dip of swallow, broken ring.

At intervals he lays down his brush
beside the paintbox on the stool
and pads across to one or other
of the young men at their canvasses,
the brush-stroke demonstrated,
the difficult transition resolved,
the encouraging nod, he strides
back to his own adventure.

Then bread and beer under cool oak;
pipes are lit, and the smoke drifts
among the hanging leaves, as they talk
of Ruskin and truth to nature;
and the high sun moves over,
puts the shadows on the other side,
making ready the subjects
for the long afternoon.

A NEIGHBOUR'S FUNERAL

The day of the funeral we noticed,
as we drove past the house,
that the wreaths and sprays,
with their polythene wrappings removed,
were set out on the front grass
in a neat pattern.

At the service in the crematorium,
not a word that the clergyman said
shewed any personal acquaintance
with the dead man or with death.
There are buttons behind the lectern
for organ music and closing the curtains.

A week later a letter was handed round,
starred with capitals, from the widow,
thanking the neighbours for their floral tribute.

FIRST FUNERAL

Once when I was only eight or nine
and could not yet recall any
death as personal, my dead
were then a long way distant,
buried in the green foothills, a far
journey, once a year for short legs,
I went with my mother 'to have
a look at her father's grave'.

Assured of her direction, she paced
the paths between the granite kerbs
and the twisted rods of iron, till we came
to the gilt-lettered black marble . . .
While she was busy and I waited,
with only my grandfather there
the stone was quickly read,
a dark bare-headed dozen gathered
and four men put a bright coffin on clay,
two avenues away, beside
a pillar with a half-draped urn.
A small white-bearded man stepped forward,
and in the wind, the fresh west wind from
the high green hills, his beautiful voice
came gusting towards us,
Scots and sad and terrible.

My mother, standing still, whispered,
'It's John Pollock of St Enoch's.
I'd love him to bury me
when my time comes.'

I was only eight or nine
yet I remember the scene,
the hills, the stones, the clay,
and hearing the words, and my thinking
that what my mother said was strange,
for she would never die.

THE MOON

Now from our village we regard the moon
prime satellite, that some have visited,

a place like Venice but more surely dead,
with less to offer at its broadest noon
than thirty seconds here in any June;
its sole surprise the black sky overhead;
this, after all the peering poets said,
will mean no more than buoy or bollard soon.

Now stripped of mischief if it's glimpsed through glass,
a neutral disc hereforth, although its light
lays waning magic on tree-shadowed grass,
that fabulous tub of myth and metaphor
still rules the seas with undiminished might
and daily hurls the tides against the shore.

MIDDLE INFANT

for Eileen

I sat on the long form
and sponged my slate
while the terrible Miss McCleery
wagged her cane in front.
The smell of jerseys, crumbs, ink,
the sound of screeching chalk
and the firmly shut windows
established her kingdom.

A Middle Infant now,
released from the chanting tiers,
I was edging my way
out into life.
The years would give me
height, words, problems;
she, in her black tight carapace,
would stay there for ever.

THE RIDERS

Driving to Long Buckby down the byroads,
the ploughed fields brown in the March sun,
the tall dark trees not yet in leaf;
black-faced sheep in a paddock

with small negro-lambs at heel,
we passed a hedged field on the right
full of girls and ponies,
the girls with peaked velvet caps
and large numbers pinned across their shoulders,
the horseboxes in a corner near the gate
like a camp of watchmen's huts.
The mounts with their riders were
crossing and recrossing the turf
in a medley of legs, fidgety,
the trials not yet started.

And I marvelled how far
the sure-footed ponies had carried us
from the heart of Asia across
a continent
to these offshore islands,
and the time it all took,
to end here in a huddle
of jodhpurs and hurdles.

THE TURBAN

After swift blizzard and strong frost,
light skies urge thaw. Redemption marred,
gutters ooze slush. The shovelled tracks
cross-furrow the Precinct, vacant now
with shops' half-day, where sparse black trees,
crotched with white swabs and tufts, shake down,
wind-fingered, sprays of crystal mist.

An aged Sikh fists broken crusts
from narrow paper bag and steps
back as he scatters; a grey stream
of bustling pigeons nudge his boots;
his long beard streaked, his turban
pale violet, more subtle shade
than any other colour here.

THE DISTANCES

Driving along the unfenced road
in August dusk, the sun gone from

an empty sky, we overtook
a man walking his dog on the turf.

The parked car we passed later,
its sidelights on, a woman
shadow in the dark interior
sitting upright, motionless.

And fifty yards farther a runner
in shorts pacing steadily;
and I thought of the distances
of loneliness.

ST ROSALIE: MONTE PELLEGRINO

High up the steep dark mountain
the warm cave with the enormous candles,
an unremarkable baroque church
leaning against its glowing mouth.
The tall candles were bought in
the gay stalls where the cars turn,
and carried up the long steps
like ivory wands,
to socket and melt with wagging flames,
each in a puddle of hot wax
that glinted like the wet streaks
down the smeared walls, metal-flanged.

Beyond the first, lower room with the
spinney of flames, the congregation
crammed, kneeling with bead-strung fingers
or shouldered, shuffled
beside, round the glass tank
holding the marble sleeping girl
afloat in a pool of rings,
brooches, coins, medallions.

As the priest, Mass-vestmented,
spoke of sanctity, marriage,
religion, the family –
that much I caught from his words –
a dark-suited, bull-necked young man
and a sallow girl in bride's white

elbowed towards the glass box to lay
her wilting bouquet upon it.

DISASTER ON THE BOX

At this moment lava travels
down the long Sicilian slope:
in Anatolian rubble a limb
twitches, then stiffens.
                                        Vineyards
overwhelmed; ash in the mouth;
cinders for picking over
for seeds of a new life,
of market, mosque, harvest,
always on the edge of hunger.

Rage, pity, shake us as the camera pans;
but acceptance reasserts
our rationality. We will step
tiptoe tomorrow anxiously
over this perilous earth-crust
briefly, as the logic of this slips,
for we accept the nature of things,
from our minds, which are not equipped
to weep or bleed.
                                        The skinny old
woman in black watches her wall
collapse as boulders tumble, stones pour
irresistibly down, a bright door-
key hanging at her lean hip.

WILLIAM J. MCCLUGHIN
(1900–1971)

This slow, private man, a paradigm
of small singular disasters,
misfortune-prone, shut off from life
by his own nature, unaligned
with any faction. Tragedy
demands a noble stature marred,
the tall potential flawed and felled,
gift's promised offering betrayed.

A certain gift for colour, tone,
offered some memorable themes,
paper selected, brush contrived,
the proven pigments organised,
but throttled these with theory,
close-printed words, discussion, thought,
which only eked a few filled frames,
the niggard yield of thwarted skill.

That such constricted feeling, will,
which swaddled, smothered all, was fixed
in some involved astrology,
supposes an elaborate
system beyond his scale. To set
that cracked jaw badly, split that skull,
hobble his years with penury,
argues a lack of mercy somewhere.

MY UNCLE

My Uncle, the little girl calls him
who comes in to visit my wife,
when games are going unfair, or she falls out
with her friends.

He walks past here at all hours, a small man,
his white head bent on narrow shoulders,
plodding rapidly, intent, always going
hatless, from or to the house where he sleeps.

I gave him a lift once up from town –
the occasion of our only conversation –
we talked holidays, it being near that season;
and he remarked that, the previous summer,
for the Coventry Fortnight
he had been to Iceland.

And immediately I thought
of the harsh bare landscape,
and the helmeted warriors,
and the laughter in the great halls,
of Kiertan brought dead to Bathstead
and the tearless Gudrun
standing over the body.

My Uncle trots for ever,
clenched in his silent dream,
beset by a household of sturdy children,
a loud deaf sister and her cheerful husband,
and a hidden, aged mother.

THE BURNT POST

There's a pub here called *The Burnt Post*;
I find the name somewhat disconcerting.
The Phantom Coach is easy; it
is not far from the crematorium.
The Saracen's Head a few miles out
in the country and *The Turk's Head*
in the town remind me that
the English are an old nation
and remember the talk of men
back from the Crusades.
The Fox and Grapes must refer to
some Aesopian folk tale.
But *The Burnt Post,* its charred
echo notched with tomahawks,
is more difficult to explain.
I have seen the name on old maps
when this city's suburbs
were a scatter of hamlets.

Maybe it began with
some small misadventure
like the accidental burning-
down of a thatched dwelling –
the Protestant Martyrs
were immolated elsewhere –
and survived as a landmark
for waggoners and packmen,
as now, for friends with cars.

THE ROMAN FORT

for Peggy and George

The site decoded from the air
at ground level confirmed, with this hill

easily defensible in an elbow of the river;
a steep escarpment wooded
to the north; the river broader once;
those ploughed fields marsh.

After stripping the sods, by scrutiny
of discoloured soils they were able
to mark out with string and pegs
the granary, the barrack-block,
the centurion's quarters,
dig out the water tank, the cess pit,
and set up the eastward rampart of turves,
topping it with a palisade
after the Roman fashion.

A scatter of coins, pieces of metal, shards,
gave the span of its occupation;
a mustering post for Vespasian's legions
protecting the straight roads, the Fosse Way,
when the barbarians swarmed.

This high timber gateway which you now see
was recently constructed, erected by soldiers
using the old Roman methods
as a practical workshop exercise.

Like the Romans also, they may shortly receive
further experience in a beleaguered colony,
for, daily, public prints and moving pictures
bring evidence of the stubborn barbarians.

BOGSIDE, DERRY, 1971

Shielded, vague soldiers, visored, crouch alert;
between tall houses down the blackened street
the hurled stones pour hurt-instinct aims to hurt,
frustration spurts in flame about their feet.

Lads who at ease had tossed a laughing ball,
or, ganged in teams, pursued some shouting game,
beat angry fists against that stubborn wall
of faceless fears which now at last they name.

Night after night this city yields a stage
with peak of drama for the pointless day,
where shadows offer stature, roles to play,
urging the gestures which might purge in rage
the slights, the wrongs, the long indignities
the stubborn core within each heart defies.

THE SCAR

for Padraic Fiacc

There's not a chance now that I might recover
one syllable of what that sick man said,
tapping upon my great-grandmother's shutter,
and begging, I was told, a piece of bread;
for on his tainted breath there hung infection
rank from the cabins of the stricken west,
the spores from black potato-stalks, the spittle
mottled with poison in his rattling chest;
but she who, by her nature, quickly answered,
accepted in return the famine-fever;
and that chance meeting, that brief confrontation,
conscribed me of the Irishry for ever.

Though much I cherish lies outside their vision,
and much they prize I have no claim to share,
yet in that woman's death I found my nation;
the old wound aches and shews its fellow scar.

CLOGH-OIR: SEPTEMBER 1971

for Roberta

Requested journey to a planned occasion,
a poet's praising, bronze-unveiling, lecture,
thrust us, not expecting, through small places
where you had lived sharp fragments of your past,
your childhood past, among grave strangers,
urged country air and fare for your pale face,
from the grey street a farmhouse holiday;
but found it not all skipping in the sun,
fenced with unanticipated tasks,
helping about the place, with the new baby,

dishes to scour, bed-making, hearth to sweep;
Sunday trap-drive to Meeting over a shop,
where, starched with faith, a stiff sect rallied:
so you recalled as road's turn woke,
shop-name, corner, signpost, milestone noted.

As we threaded, beads on our brisk line,
the folk-rhyme placenames, Augher, Clogher,
we paused at Clogher, short of Fivemiletown,
and strolled uphill its long tidy street
to St Macartan's, that plain church,
early eighteenth century, Anglican,
with walled churchyard's battered crosses; inside
the inner porch, papered with prints, frames, faces,
Clogh-Oir, stripped of its gold, oracle-
stone kings once heeded, one of the Three
Sacred Stones when queens sunned at Aileach.

Time truant, all the past foregathered,
myth, legend, history, yours, mine, ours,
but, strongest whisper, it was your own
that answered you, and stirred for me, with love,
who seldom name such stirrings, or yield words
for the dialectic of the heart.
Standing there, I saw the lonely child
with the black tossing head, the dark brows,
as intense and definite as now,
as palpable, now, musing by my side,
close in a vivid murmuring congregation
among queens, heroes, bards, kneeling peasants,
immortally assembled, that child's face
known before time struck, known for ever,
stuff of the fabric whereof I am made.

MARY HAGAN, ISLANDMAGEE, 1919

She wore high sea-boots and a wave-dowsed skirt,
a man's cloth cap, a jersey, her forearms freckled,
wind-roughened her strong face; with the men
she hauled the boat up, harsh upon the shingle,
and as they hauled they called out to each other,
she coarse as the rest. A skinny twelve-year-old,

pale from the city, watched this marvellous
creature, large-eyed, from my sun-warmed boulder.

I cannot remember her at any time
tossing the lapped hay, urging home the cattle,
or stepping out on a Sunday: she exists
in that one posture, knuckles on the gunwale,
the great boots crackling on the bladderwrack;
one with Grace Darling, one with Granuaile.

THE FAIRY THRESHER

for Michael J. Murphy

That winter night round the blazing turf,
the children on the hobs, the talk ran on,
most from the farmer and his sister Kitty,
his wife not holding much with superstitions,
to rhyme and ramble through familiar stories
of ghosts and fairies, witches, blinks and spells.

For instance, when a cub, the man himself
joined with his brother to herd cattle in,
and a stirk turned and would not be compelled,
when it had strayed across the wee stone bridge,
to follow the others, and a neighbour stood
to mock their efforts till they gave it up,
and he said, laughing, she'll come back all right
when that wee man there goes away,
a wee man threatening by the door of the byre,
seen only by the neighbour and the stirk.

The sister told how once between the lights
in the next house up the road a woman answered
a tap on the half-door, and peering over, saw
a wee old woman standing in the street
who begged her please to empty no more pots
across the bru, for she'd come to lodge there,
and all her family were nearly drowned.

The farmer launched into another tale
of how a man, a famous storyteller,
to whom all happened, who was always present

when freets appeared, one midnight in Glenaan,
carrying in his fist a smouldering turf
which, blown to flame, would better any torch
to clear his homeward steps across the fields,
heard a strange creature girning in the sheugh
and blew on his turf and by its light made out
a wee man with his face where his arse should be,
and charged towards him, thrusting the red turf
into the scowling face, whereat the creature
let out a yell and tore into the hedge,
its speed a hare's, its loud howl murderous.

This, told with vigour and economy,
was new to me. I though of Bosch and Breughel,
and wondered by what roads the tale came here
over Europe, out of the Dark Ages;
but thought it something out of character
with the old forts and thorns and fairy rings,
and distant singing heard and fiddle music
and dancing light on hillsides, which I take
as proper to the ambience of the Glens
and the dim twilight of the tweedy poets.

The father faltered, as it seemed abashed
by his bold coarseness in that company
of children and his womenfolk and us.
But suddenly the sister swept the talk
to charms and hedgerow cures dropped out of use,
for chin-cough and for cleaning of the blood,
that kept the people healthy years ago.
Thereat the brother at this hint began
a rambling story of a man he knew
dead twenty years or more, lived birdalone,
who had a charm for erysipelas, sprains –
with well-attested instances of each –
with nobody that he could pass it to.
He'd got it from an aunt, his father's sister,
and had been sworn to hand it to a niece,
for its transmission had to be from male
to female and to male, alternately
by generation, a secret always held
within that family only. But his niece
was out in Boston. It could not be written.

He could not travel. She would not come back.
So ended what was known from Druid times.

His wife, the mother of the listening weans,
recalled a story that they loved to hear,
a mother's story, how a widow left,
her corn unthreshed, her children infants, heard
a flail thump in the night, and peering out
to thank some kindly neighbour, saw a shadow,
a little shadow, flit across the yard.
And in the light when she went out she found
the clean corn heaped in the middle of the floor.
And next night she heard the flail again,
this time a fall of snow that smeared the ground
exposed the track of feet from barn to gate;
the light impression shewed the feet were small
and bare from heel to toe. So she went down
and bought a pair of shoes in the village shop
to match the little feet that she had measured,
smaller feet than any of her brood.
She set them out beside the flailing floor,
and, waiting late, the third night heard a cry,
a cry of utter anguish and despair
would break your heart to hear it, and she saw
the little shadow running from the barn,
giving his grief these pitiable words,
'She's paid me off – she's given me my wages',
repeated as he ran and dying out
into the darkness of the wall of hills.

We nodded, expectation satisfied:
the children chanted together, 'She's paid me off.
She's paid me off. She's given me my wages' –
they'd only held their tongues till their mother finished:
this was a tale their children would remember,
and a boy or a girl might some day understand.

ART ROOM IN A CITY SCHOOL

for Colin Dick

His class released, he guided us with care
round the drab art room crammed with crooked screens

and littered tables, pointing here and there
where joy's surprise surmounted frugal means:
the Tyger with the more than Blake-like glare
in linocut; the bright imagined scenes
a loaded brush presents of cows and trees;
a batik-rainbow wrought with candle grease;
the roughly scissored textures which contrive,
from hoarded scraps of fabric, to compose
an underwater world which seems alive
with hovering monsters; and this card which shews,
in careful lines crosshatched, acorn or leaf,
or some small object clenched in its repose.

ON THE GRAND DUBLIN CANAL: MUSING ON THE 'TWO NATIONS' THEORY

for Anne and Dermod

Leaning forward, I watch how the
dark trees, the blossom-loaded hedges,
the stiff grasses, the bent grasses and
their exact reflections, fall behind
while the clouds, as we move, a tone darker
in their translation to water, run on ahead.

I look up to observe some way in front
a humpbacked bridge arch over and contain,
in an oval, a neat-hilly landscape
which presents no originality
in its naively obvious composition.

Black and white cattle you could see
anywhere graze in adjacent
fields or along the tow-path.
The only unusual element
is that the occasional cottage
shews the hipped, round thatch
which is traditional on this
side of the Black Pig's Dyke.

ON THE CANAL

for Norman

Slower now, less sure of my footing,
tired sooner, I must estimate

new response, reluctant sinew,
kerb's height, speed of approaching traffic.
Yet used response to written words, to
intended shapes, to coded messages,
floods in the freeways still; I am equipped
for report, comment, comparison.

Loitering here aboard, aware
of early June's colours, odours, sounds,
where broad meadows margin the canal,
senses assemble, mind accepts;
happy and alert, I can contain
my world and time, reaching out to touch
the smooth grooves the tow-ropes scored
in the long prime of that old stone bridge.

AT SHOTTERY, ANNE HATHAWAY'S COTTAGE

for Peggy and Joe

Admiring the rustic
garden, the fat thatch,
trailing after tourists
through the famous cottage,
inspecting the glazed pots,
the grain of the scrubbed boards,
climbing up the toy stairs,
lowering our heads for
the dark beams in the attic;
no presence,
empty as an exhibit
in a folk museum.

So sadly we stepped out
into the sunlight,
and paced the green sward
through the narrow orchard
littered with windfalls.

And at the last low hedge
overlooking the wide field
we saw a brown hare skip
in and out of the furrows,

paying no attention,
far beyond our reach:
we nodded to each other,
the point taken.

THE GERIATRIC WARD

Bald this, hunched, jaw on fist,
or, ten-fingered, palps pate;
silent that, strains, leaning
to conjure monsters
from tap or counterpane.

Others rigid sit,
absent with empty eyes;
or, prone, sigh, call out,
at times cry quietly,
or moan continually.

One, at his own distance, nips
numb thumb and forefinger,
if he can grip it, at
saltcellar, napkin,
holding on to something.

THE KING'S HORSES

After fifty years, nearly, I remember,
living then in a quiet leafy suburb,
waking in the darkness, made aware
of a continuous irregular noise,
and groping to the side window to discover
the shadow-shapes which made that muffled patter
passing across the end of our avenue,
the black trees and the streetlights shuttering
a straggle of flowing shadows, endless, of horses.

Gypsies they could have been, or tinkers maybe,
mustering to some hosting of their clans,
or horse-dealers heading their charges to the docks,
timed to miss the day's traffic and alarms;
a migration the newspapers had not foretold;

some battle's ragged finish, dream repeated;
the last of an age retreating, withdrawing,
leaving us beggared, bereft
of the proud nodding muzzles, the nervous bodies;
gone from us the dark men with their ancient skills
of saddle and stirrup, of bridle and breeding.

It was an end, I was sure, but an end of what
I never could tell. It was never reported;
but the echoing hooves persisted. Years after,
in a London hotel in the grey dawn
a serious man concerned with certain duties,
I heard again the metal clatter of hooves staccato
and hurriedly rose to catch a glimpse of my horses,
but the pace and beat were utterly different:
I saw by the men astride these were the King's horses
going about the King's business, never mine.

GLENDUN ON A WET JULY DAY

for Peggy and Andrew

Today the misty hills are filled with water:
the Dun runs brown round stones and over stones,
or amber over gravel – a bleached branch
stranded by spate beside a swaying foxglove
rooted in stony splinters – loud it sounds,
brimming the air with rush and splash and chatter,
and, over, under these, an endless roar;
foam-white at boulder's damming, ramming froth
in the sharp crevices abrupt, it hurries
along the glen-foot past the dripping trees
and the combed grasses and the beaded whins.

The sounds of running water are its own;
its nature's patient, pliant to all use,
but not its voices, not its coloured shapes,
may offer easy symbols, metaphors,
or simply pleasure, going its own way.

ON READING TERENCE DE VERE WHITE ON LANDOR

He says that old men fool themselves by claiming
they have the qualities they clearly lack:

so one believes he's noble, open-handed,
wise in all ways of others, all-forgiving . . .
another's sure he kept the ship afloat
by his own shrewdness, till that chance wave struck.
Landor loved art and hung his walls with trash,
sat cinder-gazing, with scorched, battered hands.

Now shuffling, drifting to the terminus,
I know I'm timid, proud, intolerant,
ripe with the ready tear, too sharp of tongue,
with theories primed for every attitude
that proves me right, but surest most of this,
the man men see is not the man I am.

THE LAGAN IN OCTOBER

remembering Frederick W. Hull
(1867–1953)

October's end, a blue still sky;
rust-red, flame-red, yellow of all shades,
tall trees hold autumn's moment clenched;
the hedges, grasses, dry and pale
beside the river, drifting, a dark glass
with muted, deep reflections;
and from each branch, each twig above,
singly stiff leaves launch out
to drop and float in the bright air,
gently to reach their place
on earth, on water, moving with slow flow,
eddied or rafted by chance-circumstance,
on tow-path layered and crisp,
at hedge-foot heaped in swathes,
chestnut, lime, beech, oak, hawthorn, ash,
broad fans or crumpled tokens, rags of summer,
the prime of that green landscape over now.
From years back I recall an elderly man,
he was tall and deaf but friendly,
who came each season to that place
to note its changing colours
with a quick, loving brush, and how it was
autumn which rinsed his vision, roused his heart
to exaltation in the visible world
till his little panels, six by eight,

brimmed with quiet joy.
And as the leaves fall, as
the tireless water moves,
their motion making stillness absolute,
I toss a pebble in the stream,
remembering him;
the widening ring of ripples my tribute
like a distant lift of the hand
to a generous friend.

CULTRA MANOR: THE ULSTER FOLK MUSEUM

for Renee and John

After looking at the enlarged photographs
of obsolete rural crafts, the bearded man
winnowing, the women in long skirts
at their embroidery,
the objects on open display, the churn,
the snuff-mill, the dogskin float,
in the Manor House galleries,
we walked among the trees to the half-dozen
re-erected workshops and cottages
transported from the edge of our region,
tidy and white in the mild April sun.

Passing between the archetypal round pillars
with the open five-barred gate,
my friend John said:
'What they need now, somewhere about here,
is a field for the faction fights.'

DEDICATION OF 'THE RHYMING WEAVERS'

for G. Brendan Adams,
honorary archivist of the Ulster Folk Museum

None in our day has to such sure effect
defined the textures of our tangled speech;
from barony and borough drawing each
well-handselled thread, that we may learn respect
for the rich colours of each dialect;
this, given ready usage, yet might teach
our tense minds to unclench, and, open, reach

across the gap that sunders sect from sect.
So take this tapestry of prose and rhyme,
the prose is mostly mine, the rhymes belong
to weaver, ploughman, blacksmith, from that time
before the schoolhouse tamed their lively tongue,
when spinning wheel and loom were at their prime
and every townland earned its name in song.

NEITHER AN ELEGY NOR A MANIFESTO

for the people of my province
and the rest of Ireland

Bear in mind these dead:
I can find no plainer words.
I dare not risk using
that loaded work, Remember,
for your memory is a cruel web
threaded from thorn to thorn across
a hedge of dead bramble, heavy
with pathetic atomies.

I cannot urge or beg you
to pray for anyone or anything,
for prayer in this green island
is tarnished with stale breath,
worn smooth and characterless
as an old flagstone, trafficked
with journeys no longer credible
to lost destinations.

The careful words of my injunction
are unrhetorical, as neutral
and unaligned as any I know:
they propose no more than thoughtful response;
they do not pound with drum-beats
of patriotism, loyalty, martyrdom.

So I say only: bear in mind
those men and lads killed in the streets;
but do not differentiate between
those deliberately gunned down

and those caught by unaddressed bullets:
such distinctions are not relevant.

Bear in mind the skipping child hit
by the anonymous ricochet;
the man shot at his own fireside
with his staring family round him;
the elderly woman
making tea for the firemen
when the wall collapsed;
and the garrulous neighbours at the bar
when the bomb exploded near them;
the gesticulating deaf-mute stilled
by the soldier's rifle in the town square;
and the policeman dismembered
by the booby-trap in the car.

I might have recited a pitiful litany
of the names of all the dead:
but these could effectively be presented
only in small batches,
like a lettered tablet in a village church,
valid while everyone knew everyone,
or longer, where a family name persists.

Accident, misfortune, disease, coincidence
of genetic factors or social circumstance,
may summon courage, resolution, sympathy,
to whatever level one is engaged.
Natural disasters of lava and hurricane,
famine or flood in far countries, will evoke
compassion for the thin-shanked survivors.

Patriotism has to do with keeping
the country in good heart, the community
ordered with justice and mercy;
these will enlist loyalty and courage often,
and sacrifice, sometimes even martyrdom.
Bear these eventualities in mind also;
they will concern you forever:
but, at this moment, bear in mind these dead.

TIME ENOUGH

POEMS NEW AND REVISED

A BIRTHDAY RHYME FOR ROBERTA

October 1904–October 1975

For ease of heart and mind
I estimate each stride,
and, lurching forward, find
the landmarks still abide
though senses be decayed,
blurred sight and muffled sound.
Yet yesterday I strayed
on acorn-gravelled ground
to find October true
by each diminished sense,
perpetually new
as grace or innocence.

But now not with me there
picking the coloured leaves,
was she I thought must share
the thistles and the sheaves
when this late harvesting
my husbandry may prove,
as she had shared the spring
and summer of my love.

SUBSTANCE AND SHADOW

There is a bareness in the images
I temper time with in my mind's defence;
they hold their own, their stubborn secrecies;
no use to rage against their reticence:
a gannet's plunge, a heron by a pond,
a last rook homing as the sun goes down,
a spider squatting on a bracken-frond,
and thistles in a cornsheaf's tufted crown,

a boulder on a hillside, lichen-stained,
the sparks of sun on dripping icicles,
their durable significance contained
in texture, colour, shape, and nothing else.
All these are sharp, spare, simple, native to
this small republic I have charted out
as the sure acre where my sense is true,
while round its boundaries sprawl the screes of doubt.

My lamp lights up the kettle on the stove
and throws its shadow on the whitewashed wall,
like some Assyrian profile with, above,
a snake, or bird-prowed helmet crested tall;
but this remains a shadow; when I shift
the lamp or move the kettle it is gone,
the substance and the shadow break adrift
that needed bronze to lock them, bronze or stone.

THE SHEEP SKULL

As we came up the steep familiar lane,
famous for berries, brimmed with meadowsweet,
and bright with rosehips in season, every rut
was stiff with frost and rigid as a bone;
and in the dead red bracken at one side
a sheep skull lay exposed, as though the year
had yielded all, had nothing more to hide,
and shaped this symbol to make all things clear.

We stopped. You poked your stick into the hole
the spine had entered, raised the sculpture up:
my left hand took it in a steady grip,
my right drew off a horn with easy pull;
then, with more labour, we dislodged its twin
and dropped the bare mask back into the grass.
One horn for powder dry when foes draw in,
and one to toast each danger as we pass.

FUNCTION

No longer now the attitude's high profile,
the strutting mind, the wet prophetic eye,

the coiffured nimbus, the rapt coterie,
the bland hand's blessing off the steering wheel;
the poet now must pace the common level,
be member of, as active as may be,
this board or that, must move responsibly
when clashing systems gather for a fall.

Must also potter, each strict sense intent,
chalk-up and check the score of rights and wrongs,
know by quick instinct what's significant
in draper's thumb or drover's gift of tongues;
yet find his surest sod, for all his care,
'twixt parachuting seed and punctual star.

THE FOOL'S CAP

1

Instructed by my mother, father, friends,
books, pictures, how all names with objects go,
I understand that what I see depends,
not on what's actual, but on what I know.
I know green in its multitudes, on trees,
in grasses, growing things, when seen by day.
Of blue I am unsure; through all degrees
light scumbled over black space must be grey,
and sky is never blue, all say it is,
yet any shade-card shews how far they're out:
we pick our path among appearances,
and wisdom safely lies in cautious doubt.

2

But otherwise there is some common ground;
I handle words convention keeps in use;
communication easier all round
avoids the esoteric and abstruse,
and what I have no key to I must guess,
hoping my guess makes sense to someone else
and usually find that, more or less,
his mind and mine keep to their parallels.

3

With young folk now the old distinctions blur;
you know no more than that it's girl or boy;
till either speak, it's risky to infer
or fix on which reactions to deploy.
Long trouser legs and coloured shirt and beads
offer no help now, though a welcome beard
supplies the information which one needs
if the response should properly be geared.

4

I saw a man once in a blacked-out bus,
wearing a fool's cap like some monstrous cone;
he seemed more frightening than ridiculous,
one of those clowns James Ensor made his own.
He moved. At once his peaked conductor's cap
was a white circle under bluish light;
it was a trick of vision set that trap,
my educated wits confused my sight.

THE SPRING RESTORED

They wanted water. Once there'd been a spring,
their succour in that distant summer's drought
where thick hedge buffers hay and corn apart,
a lucky flick of memory'd pick it out.
With only hints to hone his reckoning,
he gripped the hook and went to make a start.

Close by the hedge, among the meadowsweet,
beyond the last swathe that the scythe would mow,
with pollen-speckled fist he slashed his way
with stride and stroke deliberating, slow,
through falling stems that parted at his feet,
as the crazed earth laid bare its cheek of clay.

Glance ratified, he recognised the place
by taller ash tree, wider thrusting whin,
dragged out the dead dry bushes, bough by bough,
breasted the hidden ditch and slithered in,
but rustling bracken smothered every trace
of the bright tunnel that had snaked below.

With random swing now, jarring steel on stone,
he ripped the lush grass off the upper side,
glimpsed threads of liquid trickle from a sod,
as though the spring had burrowed hard to hide,
but could not hug the secret long its own
when the whole ground was glutted where he trod.

Then, pawing round the pale roots at his knees,
chilled fingers found the wettest sod of all,
which signalled that the spring was pressing near,
through some lost crevice in the deep chalk wall,
and, scraping back the muck, he could release
an urgent jet to spirt and volley clear.

As ready evidence where certitude
required no firmer sanction, he searched out
a foot-long pipe and half a dozen stones,
that once had been the spout, that propped the spout,
and a thick slab of black and sodden wood,
the floor that held the bucket steady once.

Choosing what mossy flints best plugged the space,
thumbing the soft mould round, and wedging in
the crusted metal nearly as before,
he saw the baffled element begin,
now it had come to the remembered place,
to dribble, splutter, readily to pour.

With sweat-smeared brow and knuckles bramble-scored,
he straightened back, his effort gratified,
watching clear water's crystal arch and fall,
his sinews' tiredness armatured with pride,
for, though a tiny spring had been restored,
somehow the act was allegorical.

A SEASIDE TOWN

We went where we had often been when young,
to test for happiness: the promenade's
Victorian bay windows parched for paint;
the unfrequented station's padlocked gates;
the whitewashed lighthouse basking on its cliff.
Rimmed by black rocks, on scanty fans of sand,

a few shrill children waded, bucketed,
and wagtails flickered in beached bladderwrack.

But still that magic spring; below high tide
sweet water issued unobtrusively,
and a woman clambered down to fill her pail,
its permanence accepted; here before
the lighthouse winked its warning, and family men
owned season tickets for those summer trains.

IN A LURGAN PUB

Three men in a Lurgan pub by chance;
the old prizefighter with a raddled face,
forever sparring, dancing on neat feet,
between steps rocking, sodden, waiting a treat;
along the bar, and smiling on his stool,
the hand-tattooist, last to have that skill,
his incredible masterpiece a crucifixion
needled across and down some young priest's back;
and third, amused, not mocking, the tall poet,
his thought and utterance haunted by a stammer,
who'll find the studied breath, the safe short line,
to make some sense of his chance companions.

DUNGANNON CATTLE MARKET

In the concrete shed among the calves,
dribbling, shaky, sad eyes to the wall,
we classed them by colour, closed for Charollais,
grey, fawn, white, confirmed in this
by fresh-faced dealer fluent with their merit,
fast-growing, fine for beef. The Japanese
have been enquiring. With good listeners
he seized his chance, asked with diffidence
if we'd take a bit of paper from him,
out of his inside pocket, a tract apiece.
Then launched into his theme, how old Tom Paine
the atheist (untrue, Paine was a deist)
died in despair (apocryphal at best),
and how there'd been another man he knew
had two sons 'both far gone in wickedness',

called them to his bed before he died,
for the convincing Christian example.

His talk ran all on death and how to die
to be assured of everlasting life.
Yet, as he spoke, his rough hand stroked the flank
of a grey calf whose purpose was its death,
and all round roared the beasts that were to die.
In some barbaric faiths they eat their gods.

J.B. SHELTON (1876–1958), THE COVENTRY ANTIQUARIAN

A friendly, ripe old man, full-charged with tales
of ancient trades and offices of state,
hoarder of buttons, rich in hand-cut nails,
the chronicler of ruined wall and gate;
there is no man among us, now he's gone,
will know as he did what a story's here;
who'll date the shattered pot, the whittled bone,
when holes are dug with no John Shelton near?

Yet, though he hugged this city to his heart,
and scattered knowledge with a sower's hand,
when trudging mercy-bent down Bayley Lane,
his ploughman's pace bespoke another art
of well-pleached hedge, and red, straight-furrowed land
and barn stout-timbered, crammed with clean threshed grain.

PETER PERI (1899–1967)

Sculptor, Quaker, Communist

His studio's bed and stove staked narrow space,
shelved round with débris of his art's demands;
round-shouldered, slouched, with acid-grimy hands,
black beret on bare skull, a rabbi's face;
if short, conspicuous in any place
save ghetto or bazaar, he still commands,
though dead, hereafter notice, for he stands
a stubborn symbol of his exile race.

A lad in Pest, to Paris, to Berlin,
in endless flight to London, at his tail
a vulnerable vanity was tied;
sworn hierophant of peace he could not win,
of peopled sculpture fashion doomed to fail,
for comradeship he suffered, quarrelled, died.

NICOLAI, COURIER IN BELGRADE

Our toothless chauffeur with the rubber face
had certain words he loved to toss about;
he'd lift a warning finger up and shout
'Moment', or 'Protocol', with droll grimace;
and by that gesture fixed our proper place,
deserving more than diplomat's address,
bourgeois indeed, but human none the less,
though whence we'd come might well be outer space.

He badgered clerks, advised the manager,
admonished waiters, telephoned his son
to come and see what comradeship could mean.
He tucked us in the train for Graz with care,
and when his final offices were done,
conferred on each a foil-wrapped tangerine.

REMEMBERING A CONVERSATION: ITZIK MANGER AT THE PEN CONFERENCE, EDINBURGH, 1950

He looked more like an Arab than a Jew,
threadbare and gaunt in that bland conference;
who'd nominated him we never knew,
his friendly smile an absolute defence.
'Of Yiddish poets,' Leftwich said, 'the best
we've had for ages, high and lyrical.'

As slow in step we climbed the castle's crest
our sprawling talk looped round to Marc Chagall.
'To understand his paintings you should know
the ghetto-phrases, idioms, they translate;
the fiddlers upside down in trees or snow
where lovers, roses, cows proliferate . . .'

And as he webbed his bright words, I began
to realise the nation in the man.

STRANGERS AND NEIGHBOURS

The Jews of my childhood were
resident strangers and neighbours;
not like the flash gypsies
once a year with clothes pegs, lace and luck,
or the occasional organ-grinders
with earrings and beautiful parrots;
they lived among us doors away.

You recognised their features as foreign
and exaggerated their accent,
holding your nose with thumb and forefinger,
knew their names, Weiner, Eban, Lantin,
surprised at some with off-key names
like Gordon or Ross.

Though you played readily enough
with their youngsters after school,
you did not, as with your best friends,
run in and out of their houses,
which, anyway, smelt of hot olive oil.

They were often handsome when young,
but frequently ran to fat,
quickly losing their looks.
The grown men seldom had comfortable feet;
I thought they walked tired
because of their ancestor, the Wandering Jew,
with the black hat and the greasy ringlets.

They followed no handicraft or trade
except that of baking bread,
unleavened bread, their special biscuit
which a boy brought round once a week
on a bicycle. For the rest
they lent out money to poor people,
sold articles on instalments,
oblong objects wrapped in American cloth
like pictures, so we called them Pickey Jews.

They kept their Sunday on Saturday,
had a feast they called the Passover
and a silly New Year, not at the New Year,
called their flat-flooted minister
Rabbi; he wore a long beard.
Their coffins were cheaply constructed
of onion boxes and thin black cloth.

I have never been to Palestine,
Israel, where they are native,
so I do not know if labour
has made them more like us
or like the leathery peasants
I have seen in other countries,
bending in the large fields.
But I remember that the dark,
florid wives of the more prosperous
were demanding and loud in shops
and very conspicuous;
I cannot imagine what
a nation of these would be like.

Nevertheless, I have been to Auschwitz,
once when a delegate,
have passed through the prison gate
with the cast-iron Freedom motto,
walked along the straight paths round
the barracks of undressed brick.
(The Nazis blew up the furnace before they left.)
And I have felt my heart turn
and my eyes burn dry beyond tears
at the swathes and billows of human hair
in the long museum showcase,
inextricably tangled like a
vast sombre sand-churning wave,
grizzled tufts, plaits, ringlets,
blond, brown, black, lank, curling;
the cropped heads of that harvest
long gone into the furnace.

And once in Kafka's Prague, I
went into the ancient synagogue,
an architectural eccentricity,
a tiny Gothic Jewish church,

shrine not of saint but the Golem,
and, nearby, stepped where I could
among the close-stacked headstones
where the bony centuries huddle under the
bulging turf of the miniature graveyard
so many dead are poured into it:
and so I have some pity and much respect
for a patient enduring people.

When we found the famous Portuguese
synagogue in Amsterdam shut,
it was opened for us by the caretaker's
daughter that winter morning.
Inside the cold shell I saw
the grimy woodwork and the tarnished
candelabra, neglected as if
it was no longer a holy place.
So I was surprised when my friend,
who is not an orthodox Jew,
fumbled round the shelves and benches
until, in a corner, he found
a dusty skullcap, and carefully
put it on his bare head.

AS YOU LIKE IT

The hurried meeting called for Law Reform
assembled slowly. Someone fetched the key,
and there were four of us, for twenty minutes,
setting the chairs in order, clearing tables.
The friendly chairman introduced himself,
found us an ashtray, shewed us circulars
not yet despatched, which summed its decent aim.

When half a dozen dribbled in, it started.
Thanking us two as representative
of those who'd rallied to last year's appeal,
the chairman outlined why we'd come together,
called for the dapper secretary's report.
That neat man with the black moustache went through
the correspondence briskly, the replies,
refusals blunt or sharp, evasions bland
from those who wanted time to reconsider,
since to some ascending public men

our project had its queasy overtones;
posters, petitions; arguments for both
and cautious warnings; deputations, letters
to editors or paid advertisements,
and which might be the more immediate use.

We studied our associates, strange till now;
the tall man like a burly front-row forward,
the quiet workingman with collar and tie,
that fat lad whose brave jokes gave light and air,
the whispering friends who shared some private gossip,
those silent by the window . . . It could have been
some sports committee, a debating club . . .

Then two slim girls in slacks came clomping in
on those high hooves they love now, with bare arms,
and little golden chains about their throats.

I tried to place them unsuccessfully,
not among any urgent for reform –
in my long days I've learned the stereotypes,
for civil rights, for workers' unity,
for the free mind against the book-shut mind,
for rage against oppression somewhere else –
which of these urges I could not decide
impelled these youngsters, till, at last, they spoke
with rough-rasped workshop voices – they were lads
linking with us against our laggard law
which leaves them unpermitted, out of step.

I thought instinctive that they posed an image
not to our serious purpose, giggling, coy . . .
I have some feeling for the loneliness,
the pathos of the homosexual,
friendless among the hugging families,
waiting, with frustrate hope, for one to love
whose destiny's the same; the furtive posture
poised against rebuff, against taboo.

Here was no protest powered by indignation.
This was play-acting; this was dressing up,
hardly amusing, childish, dissonant.

Yet, as my thought swerved, suddenly I recalled
the great boy-actors of the Bankside Globe

I'd read about but scarcely visualised,
tripping their maiden-steps to marvellous verse
that Shakespeare, Jonson, Webster wrote for them.
That dark chap there could have been Celia,
his fair friend, heart-high, sportive Rosalind,
boy playing lovesick lass disguised as boy,
with all those sparking ambiguities;
but that dimensions's lost. They have no play
save what they wring from their wry circumstance,
though this town still has bloody tragedies.

And, if it seems like farce, I am unfair;
their brittle miming primes my resolution
to pin my stubborn pledge to principle.
They have their quaint quirks – that is one of mine.

THE LAST CALL

He had outlived his day, old Papworth said;
at eighty-five, that is indeed a fact,
and all his friends, or nearly all, were dead.
His books were gone now or were safely packed
for quick disposal when he'd go himself.
He still kept three or four for memory's sake –
he gestured towards the almost empty shelf –
an hour a day's the most his eyes could take.

You'll have a glass of sherry? Sweet or dry?
He hobbled out, brought bottle, glasses, back,
and set them on the table carefully;
that near his hand was cracked and deeply chipped:
he filled mine to the brim, his past the crack;
a braver sherry I have never lipped.

THE FAIRY-MAN AT LAYDE

Michael J. Murphy

D'ye know your man that's come to live at Layde?
Ye'll see him steppin' this road after Mass;
he'll always stop where other ones would pass –
for why? He follows a peculiar trade;
he's after stories country people made

of skeagh-bush, and forth and hungry grass.
He'll turn the talk, the quiet way he has,
to freets and grugachs and the whole brigade
of notions hosted round the cottage hearth
when old ones cracked in winter, ferlies all,
gone with their four bones back into the earth,
or drifted like dead leaves within the mind,
until his whisper stirs them, and you find
some smouldering word sparks up the far recall.

THE HEN AND THE COCK: A GLENS FOLK RHYME

I lay six eggs, says the Hen –
I lay six eggs, I lay six eggs,
and I still run barefoot.

I've been to Yorkey, says the Cock –
I've been to Yorkey. I've been to Corkey,
and I can't find a boot to fit you.
So what can I do? So what can I do?

The clucking hen runs barefoot still,
and the cock complains that she spurns him;
yet you'll never find either gone over the hill
on any class of a journey,
unless to the fair in the well of a cart
or strung by the heels in a van:
for everyone knows that rhyme by heart
but the Egg and Poultry man.

AN ISLAND FOLK TALE

'Father O'Haire,' said the girl to the priest,
'a lawyer's letter this mornin'
says a rich American uncle of Da's
has left him the half of his fortune.

'Now a house on a hill with a view like this,
with the Island stretchin' before us,
needs the weight of a name would make folk look up,
nor ever afford to ignore us.

'My mother and me has talked it all out,
Mount Grand is the name we've decided.
We'd be grateful now if your Reverence
was the first of the neighbours applied it.'

'If that is your will,' the young priest said,
'it's myself will be glad to begin it.
The name of this house, from now on, is Mount Grand,
and the heart of poverty in it.'

NINETEEN SIXTEEN, OR THE TERRIBLE BEAUTY

Once, as a boy of nine, he heard his teacher
back from his interrupted holiday,
a red-faced, white-haired man, repeating wildly
all he had seen of Dublin's rash affray:

'The abandoned motor cars, the carcases
of army horses littering the street . . .'
No more remains of all he must have told them
of that remote, ambiguous defeat.

It took those decades crammed with guns and ballads
to sanctify the names which star that myth;
and, to this day, the fierce infection pulses
in the hot blood of half our ghetto-youth.

Yet, sitting there, that long-remembered morning,
he caught no hint he'd cast an ageing eye
on angled rifles, parcels left in doorways,
or unattended cars, he'd sidle by.

ENCOUNTER NINETEEN TWENTY

Kicking a ragged ball from lamp to lamp,
in close November dusk, my head well down,
not yet aware the teams had dribbled off,
I collided with a stiffly striding man.

He cursed. I stumbled, glimpsing his sharp face,
his coat brushed open and a rifle held
close to his side. That image has become
the shape of fear that waits each Irish child.

Shock sent each reeling from the light's pale cone;
in shadow since that man moves out to kill;
and I, with thumping heart, from lamp to lamp,
still race to score my sad unchallenged goal.

FOR ANY IRISHMAN

Your face, voice, name will tell
those master of such scholarship,
as the veins of a pebble
readily encapsulate
an exact geology,
the lava flows, the faults,
the glacial periods,
the sediments which formed
and grip us locked and rocked
in the cold tides that beat
on these disastrous shores.

NORTHERN SPRING

After a crazy winter
when garden flowers went mad,
blossoming at Christmas,
a cold spell, snow at Easter,
drew the expected line.

But taking trees as signals,
for flowers are fickle witnesses,
I had watched the blunt twigs daily,
and felt an honest promise
in buds' painted ends.

With May, trees in the gardens,
in the avenues, in the parks,
are vivid with young clean green
and I, older, soiled, thought sadly
of each spring's innocence,

wishing we could imitate –
let spring renew us like the year –
a silly notion, you might say,
but not without its poignancy
in this time-tortured place.

'THE LASS OF RICHMOND HILL', OR THE ROYAL GARDEN PARTY

I remember that Garden Party
in June of the Festival Year.
The steps down from the Parliament House
were roped off, but we milled on the lawns,
and a military band played all afternoon
on the gravelled plateau at the top.

The Queen – Queen Mother now – appeared,
and as she stepped and turned her head, smiling,
and gently moved her right hand, as she stepped
on high heels down the stone-cascade,
I remember admiring that woman's poise,
as we crowded in and gaped across the ropes,
hoping to catch and hoard a smile or a nod.

At that moment the uniformed band played
'The Lass of Richmond Hill',
a gay lilt and appropriate it seemed;
it was a pleasant occasion.

But I also remember wondering
if many among us had ever heard
that when the United Irishmen marched in
to Antrim town that other June day,
the young men in green jackets, the leaders,
tried to sing 'The Marseillaise',
the proper anthem for revolutions,
and none of the pikemen-peasants knew it
and few of the Belfast artisans had heard it;
so their steps got into a tangle as they straggled.
But Jemmy Hope, that reliable man
who never postured, rallied all
by striking up 'The Lass of Richmond Hill',
which most knew anyway.
So, in step together, they swung
down the long street to meet the enemy.

The irony of it is
that this song was written
by Leonard McNally, the ugly little lawyer,
defender in the courts of the United Men,

proved by State papers, long after,
to have been a Castle informer.

How many at the Garden Party remembered
and enjoyed the complicated ambiguity?
Yet there must have been among those present,
some with forefathers in the rabble
scattered after the skirmish.

When I see the Queen Mother on the box
or in a colour supplement,
I sometimes think of 'The Lass of Richmond Hill',
of Leonard McNally and Jemmy Hope,
and you and me, my dear,
at the Royal Garden Party.

IRISH GLASS

We are careful never to
say 'Waterford' or 'Cork' or
'Dublin' where these are not marked,
but simply 'Irish', with a
whimsical smile, dis-
claiming any precision
in our expertise.

These then you may take (the hand
makes an inclusive gesture)
as typical: the boat-shaped
salad bowl with the turned o-
ver rim, on the square foot, set
rather crooked, the squat jug;
the heavy barrel-

like decanter with the three-
ringed collar; the cutting deep
in 'strawberries', in 'prisms', full
of light. Not 'the bluish tinge'
which is a shopman's fable,
giving the false impression
of ready knowledge.

Made certainly in Ireland
by Englishmen avoiding

the House of Commons duty
on the metal, and only
then, till 'the economic
balance' tilted, when they fol-
lowed the profit home.

Typical it may be, in
that the deep cutting, the weight,
were appropriate to the
randy squire with his high boots,
his card tables, his candles,
and his stucco flaking in-
to the encroaching bog.

Reinvented for tycoons
furnishing their tables to
entertain Common Market
guests, they offer evidence
that we are conscious we have
a 'cultural heritage'
of 'glittering masterpieces
born in white hot fire'.

MY FATHER'S DEATH IN HOSPITAL

I

Unshaven, gaping-jawed, with muffled brain,
blurred meanings tangled through infrequent phrase,
with stricken features, with unfocused gaze,
in that long tedium as the senses wane;
so death rose slowly, brimming cell and vein,
thick in his throat through which the choked breath thrust,
like a clogged pump, the doomed crew's dwindling trust,
as the hulk shudders and dips down again.

Then when light lapped along the polished wood
as shadows crept before its gradual brush,
and father, mother, son, were each alone,
death took him roughly; with a sudden gush
the slack mouth belched its black and clotted flood,
and instantly the man we loved had gone.

II

From this out all's at odds. Can this rough death,
wombed in his being, be his closest heir?
Each struggling throe, ungainly, ill to bear,
denied his nature and betrayed his breath,
who, with an unassertive dignity,
through a long life so evidently stood
for mercy and the freely chosen good
by which all men in mercy must be free.

But this harsh phantom gripping in the dark,
its every gesture cruelly defined,
cuffing and jostling him to this crude end,
offered no signals to pace out and mark
the brave submission of a firm-set mind:
death should be welcome as a waiting friend.

MY FATHER'S GHOST

My father dead, the prince among my dead,
has never come again except in dream,
unless the word that jangles in my head,
reminding me, rebuking me's from him;
never his palpable presence or his face,
his ink-ringed finger or his broad-splayed thumb –
yet, when I've since stood in some famous place,
I've always thought I'll tell him he must come.

It never was his wish to play planchette
or tilt a table; once I asked him why,
and I recall his confident reply,
so I have never tried. I'd rather let
my pulses keep the quiet discipline
that, if he haunts, he haunts me from within.

E.H. (1877–1958)

She was my harbour, larder,
and my lexicon.
I ran to her for shelter.
She filled my plate with food.
I learnt my letters from the tins

she lifted from the shelf.
These twenty letters hint my debt.

THE DRIFT OF PETALS

Firm-footed, small, she thrust my pram
its endless uphill, downhill way,
intent on country air.

I can recall our sheltering
beneath a hawthorn in a lane,
a dark cloud dowsed the sky.

And as we watched the slanting drops
a drift of petals settled on
my buttoned coverlet.

A wide road now that lane, with cars;
the hedges rooted out; the fields,
on either side, built-up.

And of that moment what survives
in these numb syllables, except
an old man's gratitude?

A GREAT EVENT

A great event when I was small
was when a heavy carthorse fell,
for, running to the spot, I'd find
a ready gang had gathered round,
eager with gesture and advice
on the best remedies for ic-
y surfaces, for slipping stones,
for buckled axles, broken bones.

The carter'd kneel upon its head,
while someone grabbed a sack to spread
under the threshing rims of steel.
The girths and harness loosed, they'd haul,
slow inch by inch, the cart away,
its shafts, one fractured, sprung agley.

With panting flank and frightened eyes
the creature would attempt to rise
by scramble, slither, heave and strain.
The carter, clutching bit and rein,
would bawl to warn all crowding near
to step back there, to stand well clear.

Then stuttered struggle, hoof and hock,
there'd be safe footing on that sack.
The horse would stand and shiver with
air clouded out of shaken mouth.
A nosebag looped on ears and head
would quieten the quadruped;
and we would hurry home to tell
how, after danger, all was well.

THE MILE-LONG STREET

The long-mile street you trudge to school,
past factory walls and painted sills,
house doors, curtains, little shops,
that padlocked church with lettered board,
was staged and starred with asterisks.
First, harness-shop that flashed with brass,
bits, stirrups, bridles, whips and reins,
huge blinkers for shy animals,
round its door, the leather smells;
farther, under a large sign
which spelt that strange word Farrier,
an open gateway offered you
hammer on anvil, the sharp taste
of scorched horn hissing;
and, farther still, a narrow door,
with glint of straw, warm tang of hay;
scatter of grains fanned round the step
brought the flapping pigeons down.

If you were rich and had a mind
to buy yourself a little horse,
he could be saddled, shod and fed,
and never need to leave that street.

I REMEMBER

After the Schools' Broadcast,
the listening class asked questions.
My pocket money? Comics? Sweets?
Did I remember the names
my sister gave her dolls?
And was it better then?
And when did I decide
to become a professional poet?

I fumbled with my answers
using too many words,
unable to conjure back
the shy and lonely child
snipping his paper-figures,
aligning his lead regiments,
dreaming of icebergs, blizzards,
the lost *Titanic*, Captain Scott.

THE COLLEGE FENCE

At the morning break
the senior boys in twos and threes marched down
the practice-field to the dark wooden fence.
We dare not follow, dare not imitate,
scattered before them with our ragged games;
they towered among us, vast, invincible.
A leg's length off the fence and all in step,
each thrust against it with a lifted foot,
then turned, swimmer's twist, to stride away;
a ritual reserved for those great men,
the hulking heroes of the First Fifteen,
Prefects, Athletes, Cricketers.
Heroes all, we lisped their names with awe,
and when chance errand promised leave to speak,
we stammered hesitant,
admitting our small value, our respect;
later claimed status in our little clans,
reporting in vernacular our luck –
'I told Bull Alley, Smellie wanted him,'
bidding the prefect seek the Science Master.

In the crowded sixty years since then,
I never met one of them anywhere,
glimpsed few guessed names in printed paragraphs;
they must be aged men now, any alive.
That fence is down; a tall plain-featured block
houses the swarming children, covers that field,
the custom and its course forever gone.

DIPTERA

Walking along the tow-path,
we encountered a young man
in jeans, with a knapsack,
swishing his long-shafted net
among the nettles and grasses.

Stopping, I asked if he
were taking a sample-census.
He was, he explained,
an entomologist
in the local museum.

I remarked that I had worked there
for almost thirty years,
about twenty years ago.
He asked me my name,
and in what department.

I have read somewhere
in a popular book
on natural history,
that *Diptera* have
very short lives.

AWAY MATCH: JUNE 1924

We crammed one compartment and crowded the windows,
denying the master all hope of a place,
the First Eleven with Tom as our scorer,
the bags on the rack of leather and baize.
Exams all over, the summer term ending,
this was the crown of my halcyon days.

Met by their captain and solemn committee,
we walked to the school in the morning sun,
changed our togs in the chilly pavilion,
gratefully swallowed the milk and the bun,
switched several names in the batting order,
and larked around till the coin was spun.

I was one of the opening batsmen,
not for my style or the runs I might make,
but rightly because I was safe and steady,
defensive, a difficult wicket to take.
The bowler handed his cap to the umpire
and loosened his arm with a slow off-break.

All has altered. That world has gone under.
Those still living are sober and staid,
retired from pulpit or general practice,
or worried and bald in some withering trade.
One, tripped up on the rim of a scandal,
took his life when he felt betrayed.

But I remember that bright June morning,
the locals perched on the low stone wall,
the bowling-screen and, beyond in the valley,
full-leafed sycamores glittering tall,
and, far away in the Palace Barracks,
the stirring thrill of a bugle call:

the flight of pigeons, the cockcrow distant,
the bruised-grass smell from the well-spiked heel,
the pock and knock of the maiden over,
the snick to leg and the quick appeal;
the hour is noon and our score is twenty,
the bell in the tower is beginning to peal.

That age went under; disaster struck it:
we had no skills to keep it alive.
My innings's end was prophetic omen,
when what I meant for a cover-drive
shot straight through the slips like a skimming swallow
to the small swift hands of Kenny Five.

Idyllic the setting: the myth spored from paper;
our school-story values never were true:

hardly half of our team were boarders;
neither the bats nor the pads were new;
but a cricket cap somewhere in a cupboard
has the year embroidered in white on blue.

THE FADED LEAF:
A CHAPTER OF FAMILY HISTORY

I could have been no more than three years old,
if dates are matched, when my grandmother died,
my father's mother, so what I recall
is partly drawn from album photographs
or that, historic, on our mantelpiece.

Pale pointed face, the straight hair parted,
a middle parting dragged to the pierced ears;
dark searching eyes – the pock-marked cheeks
reported, passing, in my elders' talk,
as common enough in her generation.
I cannot tell if I ever touched her face:
black dress puckered, a round cameo;
hands folded only when she dozed,
or sat to have her picture taken.

I some time later learnt that she was blunt
in her plain speech,
even in her ready generosity:
my parents in those days were poor enough –
a teacher's pay at ninety pounds a year
not much comfort when paid quarterly.
Her brisk assistance, unabashed by tact,
settled the matter by a searching question.

Rising early, seeing her men off,
husband and the son who hadn't married,
with a warm breakfast in them,
if my mother called, by ten o'clock
the house was tidy, the dishes washed,
the black range shining, the fire red,
no ash inside the bright steel fender,
the old woman dozing beside it, dressed;
awake, her hands at the quilting frame.

There was a quilt made of my uncle's ties
made me think of Joseph in the Bible.

A hospitable woman, my father told me.
Some book a roving Yankee preacher wrote
named that house for welcome in Belfast.
There had been music with three singing sons,
harmonium, piano, mandolin,
a phonograph with turning cylinders
lasted till I marvelled how it worked.

I know no tune she loved to hum or hear,
no book she cherished; no opinion
of the world's ways, of the times' great men –
not like her husband John who hated Gladstone
because he murdered Gordon at Khartoum,
disliked Bradlaugh, saw General Tom Thumb,
consider Buller a coward, Redvers Buller,
joined the Volunteers to scare off the French –
my sister's daughter has that photograph –
the old shako lay on the wardrobe top,
the pom-pom loose, a toy. I still consider
Buller a coward, skulking in his tent.

No shape of words, no sound of her voice,
but to my sister, once, 'Ladies never whistle',
folk memory, maybe, of the crowing hen.
Yet she was kind, gave me a fleecy coat
that cheered my heart when I had chickenpox,
my hot cheeks plastered with windmill crosses.

A country girl, two years older than her man,
they fled to Glasgow after his father married
a lass of seventeen, the house too small,
ill-matched the women in it, with fretting roles.
They shipped on Christmas Eve; the sea was rough.

In a high close bore eleven children
and saw five die in infancy.
Mothered half a dozen of their cousins
that handsome John, her brother, dropped in her lap,
sailing on the first of his hundred trips
across the Atlantic to make his fortune,
selling his little farm to buy wide acres,

their mother dead, or fled with her fancy man.
I met that John, the aged patriarch,
beautifully bearded, tall and gaunt –
he should have been a prophet with such looks
or the rheumatic Walt, the good grey poet –
in a small farm somewhere; in his house
a young embarrassed woman made us tea;
she guessed we guessed she warmed the cold old bones.
My steady grandfather without complaint
fed the flock that my grandmother scrubbed,
for any child was seized and scrubbed, they said.
He neither smoked nor drank, resigned his Lodge
when liquor was voted in, and he the Master;
the faded sash, in a drawer, survived for years.

Returned in twenty years, a better job,
still at his trade, to Ireland, found a house,
and waited at the quayside. She came down
the gangway with a dead child in her arms,
died of convulsions – so our story has it –
when the ship's siren rocked the Broomielaw,
six others trailing after, two girls, four boys –
my father, my three uncles, I knew them men.
His urgent task before they were settled
was finding a burial plot for that dead child.
So we were earthed where none before was laid
at the town's edge, under a green hill.

I know that grave, the headstone; the text
I am proud of, for its honesty:
We all do fade as a leaf: no easy hope,
no sanctimonious, Pentecostal phrase,
simply a natural image for the fact.
I've written verses of the falling leaf.

The house I knew came later, not the first,
nor second as I reckon, the third or fourth,
in the same crowded wedge of streets,
a clean-faced street of brick, respectable;
that is her context, her reality,
the kitchen range, the high-shelved copper pans,
the picture in the parlour by my uncle.

A town's slowly mortal: known families
ebbed from the decent dwellings which broke down
to common lodging houses, doorless shells,
swarming with ragged children, idle men,
dishevelled women talking at the doors.

In time the planners pulled their drawings out,
the great bulldozers smashed the scabby walls,
and the next street, the next, till all's now down
or newly built. The name has vanished
from every list or map. There must be few
recall John Hewitt lived there, or his wife,
and few if any other than I remember
Jane Redpath, my grandmother, that good woman.
That was the text: *We all do fade as a leaf.*

A MOBILE MOLLUSC

He learned, as a dissenter, he must be
a man who'd never fail to speak his mind,
eager to challenge, readily resigned
to leave all free as he himself was free;
yet, in assertion of that liberty,
still to a stance of arrogance inclined,
a mobile mollusc of a special kind
that finds and foots his rock in any sea.

So, snug within his metaphoric shell,
he edged along the indifferent cliffs with care,
the senses sorting out directions well,
not heeding signals he mistrusted from
insistent tides that headed straight for Rome,
Moscow, Peking, New York, or anywhere.

ORIENTATIONS

The Flat Earth folk will lift their eyes,
for God's above and Hell's below;
an unconvincing exercise
to those of us who think we know
Australia's on the other side
of this small wrinkled spinning sphere.

The Milky Way vast aeons wide,
our sun comparatively near.

Yet when I test the changing sky
by metaphor of bell or cup –
to explicate the mystery –
I need my world the right way up,
and so I'm always more at home
on the round floor of Shelley's dome.

NOURISH YOUR HEART

Nourish your heart through all the ports of sense;
let sight's salute constrain them to come in
that furtive lurk in shadow; let touch spin
her dragging spider-threads with diligence,
no anchor-cable these, a net to freight,
meshed close as flesh, from the reluctant tide
the veering atomies: let the rest provide
all they can bundle through each closing gate.

See you miss nothing proffered. Name and store
and set in order all. Let nothing be
a toy too small, a trophy overpast
the weighing palm that reckons less or more;
for all you know, or I know, these must last
the slow attritions of eternity.

A LOCAL POET

He followed their lilting stanzas
through a thousand columns or more,
and scratched for the splintered couplets
in the cracks on the cottage floor,
for his Rhyming Weavers fell silent
when they flocked through the factory door.

He'd imagined a highway of heroes
and stepped aside on the grass
to let Cuchullain's chariot through,
and the Starry Ploughmen pass;
but he met the Travelling Gunman
instead of the Galloglass.

And so, with luck, for a decade
down the widowed years ahead,
the pension which crippled his courage
will keep him in daily bread,
while he mourns for his mannerly verses
that had left so much unsaid.

THE RAIN DANCE

POEMS NEW AND REVISED

FOR A MOMENT OF DARKNESS OVER THE NATIONS

The black cloud
is a happy portent
for dwellers in the drylands
waiting for the monsoon.

You there,
take up your dusty prayer-wheel.
As for me, I shall stand up
and begin the Rain Dance.

THE ROMANTIC

When the first white flakes
fall out of the black Antrim sky
I toboggan across Alaska.

When a friend falls ill
I rehearse the funeral oration;
since I am for completeness,
never having learned to live at ease
with incompleteness.

1957–1972

Not his that gaunt mask. Fool's comparison.
No Florence his sick town.
Yet there was exile once after a defeat,
and years spent walking through an alien place
among bland strangers kinder than his kin,
and then there was return –
as some translated poet wrote –

to this betraying, violent city
irremediably home.

NOVEMBER PARK

November dusk, at four o'clock,
I walk in the deserted park;
the tight-lipped trees are still; the mist
has scarcely drawn its gauze aside
since light at eight leaked hint of day.

The season's in autumnal mood,
the epoch's end, to every sense
the cadence of the dying fall,
as empty as the bowling green
that waits, indifferent, for play.

MY OWN AND NOT MY OWN

Here with approaching age
a stranger in the land,
forgive me if I rage
or clench my empty hand,
because the tasks I planned,
the hopes that held my aim,
appear and disappear,
the same and not the same,
down each diminished year.

My hair grows grey; the lines
across my features crawl;
yet these predicted signs
still signally appal;
this certainty is all.
And in the looking glass
appear and disappear
my lonely father's face,
the coarser face I wear.

No path has dipped or turned
exactly as it should,
or as I had been warned.

Confronting ill-and-good
had I but understood,
I might have been content
to shew, and to be shewn,
conjointly each event
my own and not my own.

THE END OF THE WORLD

Tents pegged, the beds unrolled,
pitched on the high moraine
we're given time enough
by this unsetting sun
to cram our waking hours
with necessary work,
though sometimes sweating hard,
black fists of midges irk.

Our small ship in the sound,
fast-cabled, floats secure.
Against the lambent sky
the tall peak's tipped with fire.
As if with mescalin
the light brings far bergs near.
The radio gone dead,
there's nothing we need hear.

First then to plot our route
along that broken slope,
sharpening the disciplines
of toe and fingertip;
and, if we reach the top
before this long day's done,
we'll have achieved our goal,
the last peak scaled by men.

Yet, if too difficult,
well beaten we return,
we still may wait the end
lodged here on this moraine,
no whit affronted more,
with no more sense of shame
than those who squat among
the rubble of their time.

AFTER READING *SONNETS* BY REV. CHARLES TURNER (1864) AND *THE NEW DAY*, SONNETS BY DR T. GORDON HAKE (1890)

Sonnet beloved of doctors, clergymen,
whose taste, whose mental habit's not averse
to small-scale essays of a leisure pen,
I too have slipped my pence in your tight purse.
Keeper of art, my working will involved
some cautious thought, some cheerful exposition
of certain questions never to be solved,
a ready fluency the prime condition;
with the coiled dangers which such use affords
for shifty wit's distortions in dispute,
or theory's bland selective unconcern.
So, to the sonnet's riming net of words,
with its syllabic disciplines, I turn
to mark what I'd remember or salute.

ROME SUNDAY, JUNE 1960

Expectant faces brimmed the waiting square,
their Holy Father breasted his high sill;
incessant roars of greeting rocked the air
and swept with pigeons round each pinnacle.
The Holy Father spoke; the world stood still,
secure within the comfort of his care;
ev'n I, conditioned not to bend my will
to any dogma, felt that grace was there.

We'd stood an hour, midmost the rustling crowd,
on a plinth's vantage, critical, withdrawn
from fumbled cameras and rosaries,
yet, for that instant's mercy, we are proud,
and count among the moments of our peace,
we shared the blessing of that good Pope John.

WILLIAM CONOR RHA, 1881–1968

So, Conor, take our thanks for what you've done
not through those harsh abstractions whose despair

of finding teeming earth forever fair
strip to a disc what we would face as sun,
nor lost in lonely fantasies which run
through secret labyrinths and mazes where
the dream-drenched man must find but few to share
the tortured forms his agonies have won.
Not these for you, but by your kindly skill,
the women gathered at some neighbour's door,
the shabby men against a windowsill –
the pity and the laughter of the poor –
stir the dull heart and prop the flagging will,
by mercy made more humble than before.

You, Conor, were the first of painting-men
whose art persuaded my young eyes to see
the shapes and colours which gave quiddity
to the strange bustling world about me then;
and if I would recall those days again,
yours are the shadows which companion me,
the shawled girls linked and stepping merrily,
the heavy-footed tread of Islandmen.
But now the years have blown that world away,
and drugged our days and dreams with violence,
your loaded canvasses may still provide,
in face of fear and hate, brave evidence
our people once knew how to pray and play,
and, laughing, take life's buffets side by side.

AQUARIUM

A challenge to my verbalising mind,
I coasted round the new aquarium,
convinced, since to my ears all fish are dumb,
the risks of dialogue were thrust behind.
I sought to take each movement as abstract
or, angled to its purpose, practical;
for either mode's consistent with the fact
than fish no creature looks more functional.

Yet as I gazed, the old obsessive search
for binding epithet brought its reproach
that I could find none riper than *striped* Perch
or *pink-finned* Rudd or *pallid-silver* Roach,

grabbing at *gravel-hugging* Gudgeon, and
glum Tench, to drag my leaky net to land.

THE POET'S TRADE

Of those ambitions which incited me
were caps in certain games, when I was young,
but even better still, to preach among
the palm-thatched huts remote, but best to be
grave leader of my folk that they be free,
with heart compassionate and healing tongue;
yet to one other, lesser, longest clung,
to find a voice I owned in poetry.

Though my account with hope is overdrawn
by those smug creditors, pride, indolence,
comfort and caution, I am not afraid,
so much else spent, discarded, shed upon
time's mazy track, to hold, at life's expense,
I never have denied the poet's trade.

POETRY, THEN . . .

*is an imitation of Nature by a pathetic
and numerous speech. Let us explain it.*

(The Advancement and Reformation of
Modern Poetry, *John Dennis, 1701*)

Let us explain it. Consider if it is
a simple hobby like collecting stamps
or vintage cars or crazy artefacts,
investments all, the best least numerous,
or annual sky-blue travels which result
in tedious evenings with transparencies;
a game like Patience with none opposite;
relief from ledger's prose; a substitute
for childhood's dreams; a quiver of quotations;
solipsist's rainbow looking glass; a drug
to ease the taut moods, shrilly echoing,
whose stretched pitch threatens snapped hysteria,
a pipe; a glass, or some blue sedative.

No. Poetry's an exercise, a way,
an attitude, a holding of the mind
like a vast radar-dish alert to life,
propping the five ports open, welcoming,
to Nature, Human Nature, time, this moment.
All other ports are fogged or overgrown;
the laser beam of utter intellect
bounces predicted signals from the moon.

You cannot trace the painter's muddled chart,
for he is lost too, where, before, he saw,
setting a frame around experience,
tracking waves' echo in the tossing hills,
the tides' rhythm in the seasons, on the pulse,
who now but scribbles in the running sand
his ephemeral, pathetic signature.

The east wind hardens, and the worried priests
swarm and buzz and disperse from the holy place,
in deeper confusion than when they droned in
to hoist their rainbow over quaking bog.

The politician's fingers plugging hole
by hole, each jetting mischief, cannot point,
being too stiff and cold: the barometer's
become his compass. The philosopher
scissors his reasons through the floating web,
starving the spider, shattering the threads.

For Poetry bogs quake, sands run, the moon
races through clouds yet slowly changes shape,
the dyke breaks and the flood laps bench and spire,
later to offer twig for the new song;
the spider settles on Blake's open palm.

ARS POETICA

1

Press on the thought till every word is proved
by evidence of sense; let no phrase fly
unballasted, but high as trees are high
that hold the sap still in the utmost leaf:

only of what you've cherished claim you loved,
and know the heart-scald if you'd name the grief.

This was my craft and discipline. I wrought
along the grain as with a steady tool,
its clean edge tempered and allowed to cool;
no surface scored by any wristy trick,
I have, obedient to my sober thought,
disdained the riper curves of rhetoric.

With what I made I have been satisfied
as country joiner with a country cart
made for a like use, fitting part to part,
built to endure all honest wear and tear
so long as needed, till it's laid aside
to flake and splinter back to earth and air.

My symbol's master was that solid man,
that slow and independent carpenter,
lord of an acre, no man's pensioner,
fixed in a place which knew his proper skill,
not waited on like chance of rain or sun,
but like a quarry or a spring-fed well.

But there were instants when that symbol failed,
when what I made stood idle; no one came
to buy or beg its use. Then I would blame
both time and place and thrust my tools aside
to find my hands a calling better scaled
to fill the empty pockets of my pride.

Or I would say: Not yours the time's demands.
Your heart's grown callous. Let the truth be told.
The savaged child, the lonely old and cold,
the hungry mother, beggared refugee,
the prisoner for conscience, in all lands,
utter blunt challenge to all poetry.

What word of yours can ever succour these?
Give life and purpose to a workless lad?
The hearthless house? Restore the strength they had
to the smashed fingers? For the prisoners
break down the bars? For mercy pray, and peace,
for that unravished kingdom rightly theirs?

Which one of these, if chance should let him spell
your wisest verse, would surely recognise
the certain comfort in your grave replies
to the harsh questions time has set your heart?
If you can frame the questions, it is well;
if not, you are defeated from the start.

2

Let the mind grasp the symbol which has grown
out of the thresh and welter of my words,
as somehow in spring's gale of singing birds
the grateful ear plucks out a single call,
not richest in its range, or of subtlest tone,
that offers core and melody of all.

That symbol now's the farmer on his ground,
hill-farmer with his yowes upon the moss,
and his brown horses moving slow across
the steep glen-acres with the jolting plough.
At any hour or season he'll be found
a master of the tasks his years allow.

He does not ask, before he casts his seed,
that it be pencilled in who'll use each grain,
and when the red cart climbs the long white lane
with cargoed lint, his slow thought does not run
beyond the scutch-mill, that it be decreed
the finished web serve such or such a one.

And there are times, too, when his labour's lost,
by misadventure lost, by flood or drought
or heavy snowstorm when the lambs are out,
or by world-accidents of war or trade.
He takes his chances, reckons all the cost,
repairs his reaper or rehafts his spade.

So be the poet. Let him till his years
follow the laws of language, feeling, thought,
that out of his close labour there be wrought
good sustenance for other hearts than his.
If no one begs it, let him shed no tears,
five or five thousand – none will come amiss.

ON READING WALLACE STEVENS' *COLLECTED POEMS* AFTER MANY YEARS

Put this artificer of *chiaroscuro*
on the high shelf with all those phrase-bound poets,
padded with pedant's resonance, ballooned
with bouncing echoes of their paladins.

Give me, instead, the crisp neat-witted fellows,
sharp and laconic, making one word do,
the clipped couplet, the pointing syllables,
the clean-beaked sentence, the exact look.

OCTOBER-BORN

Anxious for verse to come with apt release
for jangled motions of a restless mind,
when the dejected heart may find its peace
at anchorage restored,
subsumed when startling word
makes crystal of an image ill-defined,

I searched about the hills for seven days,
strode over stubble, marked the southward wing,
combed through the lull in birdsong for a phrase,
clear challenge, bright retort,
surprising, of a sort
to split the stone and bid the first jet spring.

When I was here before, the symbols stood
ready for naming, prompting the rash tongue
to shape the sounds which, later, understood,
gave nurture to the heart,
or, rich with time, seemed part
of the world's wisdom when the world was young.

I tell them over, but no answers come
from branch-high cuckoo or from brairding corn;
no owl calls now; no heather-bleat will drum;
for feather, perfume, flower,
have served their natural hour,
and berries thicken on the brightening thorn.

October-born, with autumn I am gay
as any summer propertied with bees,
and may again be so another day;
but, in this trough of time,
when the forsaken lime
holds no more hosting than the rest of trees,

I have not learned to wait or fix my thought
on emblems well devised to represent –
like veering twig in tumbling waters caught –
life's endless drift and flow
our baffled senses know
only when focused on some still event.

THE GLENS OF ANTRIM

I've drawn this landscape now for thirty years,
longer, if scribbles count, from lower ground,
as, climbing to the crest of it, I've found
the changing vesture which each season wears,
striding one hillside; how the hour appears
in rain, in snow, or when the valley's drowned
in drifting mist, or with bright blossom crowned,
the whin-gilt peak rebukes the sun's arrears.

And I have drilled my pen to draw each sign
which peoples time and place within this frame
with plough and harrow, reaper, or the line
of stooped men pulling lint, that when the night
draws darkness over you may mark and name
each lonely homestead by its steady light.

THE GLEN OF LIGHT

This open glen's so brimmed with air and light
that space itself has body, palpable;
between the steep fields rimming left and right,
this seems the deep cup of a crystal well.

Ribbed by green hedges, shadow-sharpened, clear,
grazing and grain their varied textures tilt;
the small sheep on the mountain flank appear
like rough burrs stitched into a billowed quilt.

Too full this sense. This eye's no mortal lens,
clouding with time and thought. Reality
must wear the colours of this innocence;
else how could creature-man creation see?

GARRON TOP

Here on this headland sheer a thousand feet
with the broad moorland rippling to the cliff
on every side save one where it runs back
till sight surrenders it to simple shapes
of cloud and mountain: no other world exists
than this we traverse, its inhabitants
the grazing sheep alert, the wheeling gull,
the small grey linnets starting from the grass
and swaying on the bracken their bright songs.
And no more mark of man than, long since passed,
a ruined wallstead with its sheltered trees
in southern hollow, and across the slope
a dry-stone wall in fretted silhouette;
the flowers are few, the moss anonymous;
all here's abstracted to the elements.

We somehow pause for complementary forces
to match the bare simplicities of sense:
thunder, cloudburst, fundamental storm,
some vast bird crying or some screaming beast
roused from the lairs of myth and memory,
but no voice fiercer than the linnet's falls
upon the bowed will or the waiting heart.

EASTER FLOCK

There in the meadow where we'll lap the hay
between next August's showers, this Easter Day
the ewes move slowly, each attended by
her lamb, her twins, or on the warm grass lie
content beside them. Gilding that dream of peace,
the slant-sun limns the rim of every fleece.

Were I to straddle fence and stride across,
I should add nothing; one would rise and toss

a warning bleat; the archipelago
of floating islands would drift off and flow
into a tense but momentary lull,
till I had passed beyond them, in each skull,
the sparking batteries of alarm adjusted
to secret range where strangers may be trusted,
while tactics of evasion and defence
poise mobilised around their innocence.

So let them hold, unroused, this Easter peace,
for neither they nor I have longer lease
of quiet: yet their presence offers me
a mood to share and bask in, which will be
an image to enrich my secret thought,
true to my sense and parable enwrought.

THE BLOSSOMED THORN

That lateness of the season here
allows the thorn to blossom now;
in opulent but brief career
each single bough is bent on show.

Once passing with a troubled mind
I saw one bush of all in flower
that had a presence of a kind
my senses had no sequel for.

As gazing at it long I stood,
a strange awareness stirred within,
not of my flesh becoming wood
and stinging where the buds begin,

but of a flowing universe
that poured and streamed towards the tree,
swept with a magnet's silent force
into the One Reality.

The sluicing earth, the rushing sky
seemed thrusting into twig and spray;
to hoard my risked identity
I had to pluck myself away.

FAILED IMAGE

With summer over, all unparalleled
for cloud and downpour, pallid sunless days,
expectantly we paced familiar ways,
holding our hearts in check that had rebelled,
with the tense hope we'd see our dread dispelled,
the golden sheaves immortally in place,
remarked by Breughel, that same state of grace
which Palmer pictured, which Traherne beheld.

But here, where we had pledged us to expect
the harvest's image endlessly renewed,
bright as the berries on the bird-rife thorn,
through rotting sheaves the thistles of neglect
thrust ragged spikes or, purple-crested, stood
in the pale acres of unripened corn.

THE THRESHING

In the wan sun of a December day,
when the chill earth seems waiting for the spring,
and only running waters hurrying
down every slope have very much to say,
there is a chance you'll maybe also hear,
when the west wind allows, the thresher's drone,
a nameless noise if not already known;
if known, a signal for the rounded year.

Till now the seasons, toward completion brought,
lacked this last note, this coda to the creed
by which the ploughman, sower, reaper wrought
that seed-time and its harvest shall not fail,
since men on broken soil flung broadcast seed
and threshed the tufted sheaves with thumping flail.

THE LETTERED SNOW

We spend our swift years learning how to read
new languages our urgent senses need;
first sentences, then coded syllables,
then, with assurance, the brief sign that spells

a family's, a people's history,
by tilt of stone or silhouette of tree.

But this day, walking in the sunlit snow,
we trace a script as yet we scarcely know;
pressure of boot and shoe, the clean tyre's tread
were readily identified and read;
the horse's dented crescent, deep-plunged track
of the quick dog that leapt and bounded back.
Then, with attention and close scholarship,
we scrutinised the blurred hoof's splay and grip,
argued along the little slithered lane
from hedge to stack which looped and came again,
postulating rodents as the cause,
confirmed by crisp cast of the small-toed paws;
but what that bird we have no skill to guess
which crossed this sward, this brittle wilderness,
and where it flew to, where it rested warm
in last night's bitter east of driving storm,
for all here's undeciphered cuneiform.

THE TINKER'S ANSWER

The tinker sat beside his driftwood fire
on the side-sward. His caravan was drawn
close to the ditch. The pony and the horse
grazed quietly at hand. A greyhound lay
beside his master; and the tinker's woman
sprawled near him, but withdrawn a little way.
Two boys with sun-flaxed fringes which bespoke
their gypsy-habit played piggie on the road,
and half a dozen bantam fowl picked round
the hessian-covered bundles and the boxes
which basked in that momentary gasp of air
before returning to the jolting gloom.

In the afternoon, when we had passed before,
only the boys were stirring; the taller lad
had parleyed with us, said his father and mother
were down at Waterfoot, should be back by five,
and took our kettle, promising the job
finished by six, or, for certain, half-past six.

Now it was after six, we stopped to ask,
but recognising the kettle between his knees,
still turned and hammered, you enquired again.
How soon will it be ready? The tinker paused,
and turned to the woman, telling her how long,
in words we couldn't catch. She answered for him,
'In twenty minutes, love, or half an hour.'
The tinker then resumed his hammering,
and we walked slowly down the brae to fill
the minutes up. And as we strolled, I thought
of that queer nomad family, not sorry
that, in the fissures and the crevices
of an ordered state, all taped and registered,
there should be those who run outside the rules,
taking their time from the sky. As I recalled
item by item of their inventory,
I realised how each was functional
as any fabrication of this age:
the hound for rabbits, the bantams portable,
even the children's game was such as two
could play without a third, its implements
pared from a splintered box-lid anywhere.

Some say these are not gypsies, but, instead,
are the last pockets of artificers
who've kept the itinerant pattern of our crafts,
mason and smith, tailor, carpenter,
in a poor countryside of scattered dwellings;
others believe them driven onto the roads
when the police crowbars had unroofed the walls,
four generations since, and so survive
in a hard world which yields no roof since then.

You take your choice. My choice is ordered by
that tinker's face averted from our question.
And his wife's answer for him; something old
and proud and tribal lingers in that gesture:
an ordinary workman's glad to talk,
to share, not stand aloof from what he does
or who he does it for, no ritualist,
but a plain fellow talking to plain men.

A pink-jowled old professor long ago,
his platform entrances preceded by

a straight-back porter with a pile of books
all to be opened when quotation orders,
gave us a lecture once on his theory
that the great ballads all began in the east
and came across the world by caravan,
the swarthy gypsies were their carriers.
But I had not the heart to ask my tinker
if he'd known Thomas the Rhymer or Johnny Faa,
or was one of the wild Sweeneys of Raphoe.

THE TRUE SMITH OF TIEVERAGH

There is a ballad rooted in the Glens
about a rebel smith the Yeos pursued,
and every stanza's badged with local names
from Trostan's shadow to the Craigagh wood.

We heard it in the kitchen at Cloughglass,
where Pat McDonnell pounded out its rhymes.
I later put the incident in verse,
and had it printed in the *Irish Times.*

Heard it again by asking Michael Leech,
a tall hill-farmer with rough-stubbled cheeks,
beyond there in Glenarriffe, in that house
Paul Nietsche borrowed for those showery weeks.

The bard who wrote the ballad – Struthers Moore –
was a known tramp who beat about the Glens;
his booklet came to hand one Lammas Fair,
and being scarce, it cost me eighteen pence.

The ballad's in the booklet, but the words
vary from glen to glen, to prove for sure
that it's the common property of all,
and only sped along by Struthers Moore.

He died in Ballycastle years ago,
but is remembered yet, if you'd enquire
in any little house among these hills,
in any house still shews a gleed of fire.

It's always called 'The Smith of Tieveragh';
there was a smiddy once below that hill,

and if you'd ask a man who knows his ground,
he'd point you out the wallstead of it, still.

But that was Duncan More's, not Kennedy's;
the ballad's got it wrong. The pikes were made
somewhere along Glenarriffe or Red Bay,
not here at Tieveragh. Another trade
was Duncan More's; he armed no living man,
but could both sock a plough or shoe a mare.
In Ballyvooley there's a gate he hung
that's hardly, if at all, the worse for wear.

But living at the foot of Tieveragh
our Duncan More had neighbours of a kind
a man will not admit, whatever else
he thinks about them in his private mind.

For neighbours, he'd the wee folk of the hill
and shoed their gentle horses when they came,
for he was friendly with them, let them sport
among his feet when they proposed a game.

And if he wished to turn another rood,
there on the slope, he'd drive the long spade in
and bid them face it in what airt they pleased,
so be it he'd not trouble thorn or whin
that they had planted for their proper use.
And when he came back, rolling, from the town
they'd tug his coat the way he had to go,
or see him happed and safely bedded down.

This was, some say, before the war was lost,
when the Scotch fairies beat the Irish clan,
and rivers all ran blood into the sea;
this others will dispute, and name a man,
or maybe an old woman, or a place
where someone, nameless, certainly since then
has come on wee folk at their midnight play
and heard them speak like decent Irishmen.

Last night, with others round our cottage fire,
an old man told us this that I commit
to paper now. Perhaps in fifty years
folklore collectors may take note of it.

Let me add this brief word, that old man is
our nearest neighbour, following the trade
of joiner, making churn staves, wheels and shafts
for carts as far apart as Cloughs and Layde.
He made a zinc-lined lid to cap the well
that rises there beside the hawthorn tree,
and twines and interweaves the trailing twigs
that careless fingers risk no penalty.
He lives alone above that gentle bush,
and few the strangers ever chap his door,
but I still wonder if, from dusk to dawn,
he has as many calls as Duncan More.

THE SEEDSMAN

(J.H., 1841–1922)

Pacing that sunburnt lane, on either side
those straw-pale tussocks stiff and mummified
by summer's parching, oddly brought to mind
my father's father who could name each kind
simply by touch that were all grass to me –
like bush, like hedge, a landscape property –
a skill I envy yet can never share,
his namesake but his disenfranchised heir.

Then sudden I recalled that I myself
can finger swift along the crowded shelf,
quick to the textures of the home-spun verse
of weavers, ploughmen, the last harvesters
of that rich word-hoard vivid long ago,
when seasons marked the time and it ran slow;
a lonelier knowledge I may add to, still,
with no son's son to envy me my skill.

THE BOAT-BUILDER'S CAULKING IRONS

When you hefted them you knew at once
that they had been made for the hand,
size, weight, the feel of them and the shape,
beautifully adjusted
to the palm of the hand and the clasping fingers,
but remote as a flaked flint-axe

from any of your purposes;
a deprivation, a lameness,
something lost for ever
in the grasses of that pastoral garden
beside the streams of Paradise
we were driven from generations ago.

FIRST RIDE

My Uncle Dick, my mother's youngest brother,
gave me my first ride in a motorcar.
I can recall the bustle and excitement
of that particular bright morning,
the high machine at the gate
with the big brass lamps,
and my uncle cranking the handle,
his floppy cap, his goggles above its peak,
his cowboy's gauntlets;
and Aunt Bertha – she died at ninety the other day –
and my mother – dead twenty years –
with coloured scarves – I remember them as mauve –
tying down their brimmed hats, and veils,
though veils were not unique to this occasion –
my grandmother's bonnet was always anchored with hatpins –
and the clambering up to the padded seats
and the hood folded down at the back
like a loosely furled sail;
and the doors banged shut –
with a cab-door sound which used to mean
going to the railway station on holidays –
and everybody talking all at once
as fence-high we floated,
after explosions and jerks,
between the blossoming hawthorn walls
of that June morning;
and my uncle's masterly skill in navigating
through a drift of straggling froth-muzzled cattle,
and men with tall horses drawing to one side,
and children in pinafores, at gates, waving –
as I myself used to do,
when a motorcar passed along
the avenue where I lived in town.

We were on holiday here, at Ballyholme,
staying with my grandmother,
but of myself I have no memory,
what I looked like, where I sat;
it seems not that I observed this event,
but somehow contained it.

MISS MURDOCH

In the small classroom
next to the girls' yard
our teacher kept the front bench free
to rest her bad leg on.

So I think of her seated,
Queen Victoria in profile,
her left arm rests on the bench-back,
her right hand keeps time

to our multiplication
tables, repetition of placenames,
or offers the nimble fist-signs
for tonic sol-fa.

THE BEASTIE

The man beside me in the country bus
had a small hessian sack upon his lap
which stirred and heaved with more than traffic's sway;
a red-faced countryman, his chequered cap,
tweedy and new, marked this a special day.

He saw me looking at the twitching cloth
and watched the puzzle puckering my brow,
and chuckled to himself. I had to ask.
'It's a grey ferret, mad wi' hunger now.'
The flint-hard eyes belied his genial mask.

To demonstrate this truth, he poked a hole;
a pink wet nose peeped out like fingertip.
'If you'd be up at Kells you'd see the set.
Since Monday not a morsel's crossed his lip.
He'll hae tae work the day for all he'll get.'

SUMMER PARK

When unexpected sun beat day-long down
the people drifted to the evening park,
cramming the benches, nodding to the flowers,
or flat on grass drew lids against the light;
the running children's voices rolled like hoops
over the shadows of the sycamores;
the old men left the shelter and the draughtboard
to play their games with walking sticks in dust,
and on the rough turf where the paths fray out,
the football bounced erratic on dry clay.
Assertive finches independent sang,
and one high blackbird on a conifer
said without words what everybody felt,
while some sat simply smiling at the world.

A FATHER'S DEATH

It was no vast dynastic fate
when gasp by gasp my father died,
no mourners at the palace gate,
or tall bells tolling slow and wide.

We sat beside the bed; the screen
shut out the hushed, the tiptoe ward,
and now and then we both would lean
to catch what seemed a whispered word.

My mother watched her days drag by,
two score and five the married years,
yet never weakened to a cry
who was so ready with her tears.

Then, when dawn washed the polished floor
and steps and voices woke and stirred
with wheels along the corridor,
my father went without a word.

The sick, the dying, bed by bed,
lay clenched around their own affairs;
that one behind a screen was dead
was someone's grief, but none of theirs.

It was no vast dynastic death,
no nation silent round that throne,
when, letting go his final breath,
a lonely man went out alone.

ON CHOOSING SOME VERSES FOR MY SISTER'S CREMATION

I learned to catch her quiet murmuring,
my pain-clawed sister on her tilted bed,
her pinned knee hoisted in a canvas sling,
the loose tubes dropping near her weary head.

The sense was plain. The friendly minister
had talked with her, knew how she'd like it planned,
appreciated what her feelings were –
I'd read some poem she would understand.

I nodded my assent, my punished thought
a chill black wind, a storm of screaming birds,
not at that instant to be quelled or caught
in any net of comfortable words;

but this injunction I could not deny,
I was to read a poem at the end,
when we were gathered there to bid goodbye
to wife, grandmother, mother, sister, friend.

So I have wrought these verses for her sake
who shared what love and nurture both demand;
if, you'd imagine, somewhere, she's awake,
this is the poem she would understand.

ON COLINWARD: THE SCATTERING

In May, late, under an open sky
with drifts of cloud that scarcely flecked
a film of shadow over
the noon-warm landscape, half a county wide,
great cargoes of whin-gold
heaped on each neighbouring hillock;
on the bare hill-flank
where uncertain feet must tread

the yielding surfaces
of that long tussocked slope
we stood, we four –
husband, daughter, brother, brother's wife –
to give my sister's ashes
to the bright gentle air,
to blow and flicker in the light,
to fall like sand, like pollen, on
last year's withered grasses,
this year's thrusting stems,
on blossomed sprays of lady's-smock,
on tiny bilberry bushes,
on primroses half hid.
Nearby a lark rose singing;
a distant beast lowed somewhere.

Sudden hush
in the wind's whisper
cupped single cockcrow far away.
A slow bee loitered past.

A fitting place for dust
to start again its journey.

BELOW THE MOURNES IN MAY

The landscape's upper frame was bounded by
the sinuous edge of the dark mountains:
the middle distance, foothill-filled,
in rough places gay mounds of whin
yolk-yellow on the turf;
hawthorn breaking surf-like on the hedges,
long ribs of dry-stone wall holding apart
the black-faced ewes, the scattered lambs,
from the black-and-white cattle grazing
on the rounded skyline of each field,
and overall, birdsong generous.

I considered the other little images waiting
for the nature-poet – violets,
primroses, stitchwort, vetch,
herb Robert lurking in the grassy fringes
of an untrod lane – a proliferation
of minute, appropriate detail.

And, though gazing wider,
I could only recall, not closely
identify, the exact whereabouts
of the guidebook-noted monuments –
that tripod dolmen like a sculptured beast,
the cashel round the souterrain –
I accepted these as inevitable
chapter headings of my country's past,
suggesting its social and economic patterns.

Then I remembered that the nature-poet
has no easy prosody for
class or property relationships,
for the social dialectic,
the stubborn tenure of the small farm,
the billowed hillsides of timber
brimming the high-walled demesnes.

So I was anxiously responsive
to the fresh graffiti on the gables
of roofless cottages at the next crossroads,
for these reported something
of more immediate significance
than the stump of that round tower beside the church,
the shattered box of grey stones
surmounting the Anglo-Norman motte.

THE BLUE LIAS INN

Under black oak beams which seemed original
with the usual brasses of a country pub,
I asked the blond woman behind the bar
how old the house was.

A hundred and sixty years, the oldest part,
a farmhouse then, with outbuildings;
but inconvenient, for all its size,
three bedrooms only, and it has a ghost;

a farm labourer, they say, who comes around
padding the passages silently
from March until October, not in winter;
I thought this very odd,

for in my own country, in County Antrim,
farm hands were hired in November and May.
I must find out when hiring fairs
were held then in Warwickshire.

Otherwise, the woman behind the bar
and her husband who, she says,
has glimpsed that lurching ghost,
have been misled by somebody.

MONASTERY, TOURLIANI, MYKONOS

To the dry island's dead centre
the old bus shuddered, jolted, swerved
abrupt at corners, missing rocks,
no green thing in that parched brown land,
white the square dovecotes of each farm,
white the toy chapels for the saved
seafarers, each on its own hill,
on saints' days briefly visited.
Maybe, in cleft, grey bushes cower,
treeless else bare tundra's spread
dun-brown, burnt-brown cinder of time.
At last then, hills tilt, slope to cup –
not cup, shallow saucer – crazed with stone
fences in the quick closing dusk.

Across flat dust Anomera's
backdrop of houses, one white row,
where bus slews in, the driver greets
the group of watching statuary,
women black-hooded, dark-faced men.

Dismounting for the half-hour stop,
turn on heel for the sought place;
peeping dome, bell tower thrusting, sound
of dripping water. Face black door,
twist ring, step into shadowed yard,
gawk at that hedged bell tower carved
with stocky saints in low relief,
well-fountained water, then a second
door to church now. In its dark womb
tall candles wavered, blue, ensconced.

Breathing cold air, lost, we notice
smudged leaflet which, when fingered, held
close to near wick, black-lettered facts.
Reading slow. The slight young priest
black as deep shadow, skullcap, beard,
slippered to elbow, beckoned. The
screen thick with bible stories, spelt,
we follow the moving shadow to
closet of holy lumber, icons,
sheepskin folios: a wooden
dish clattered with our timid coins.

We followed the quick soles, found stairs,
stood on whitewashed parapet near
the round stone tent, as the last light
dribbled to the dead cinder's rim.
There silence resignation peace,
like nothing else on earth, a place
as empty as the moon till now,
empty of hope, belief, fear, poised
at the dead centre of the heart.

THE MAN FROM THE MOUNTAINS

A man I once met
where I was a foreigner
and could not speak his tongue
told me as much as I needed to know
sitting at a café table
about his life.

From the mountains as a lad –
he pointed vaguely up
diagrammed the journey
and stamped with swinging arms –
he came to town for work –
this he shewed by moving his forearms
beating with his fists
describing circles and spirals with a finger
to indicate the nature of it –
The machinery was noisy –
hands over ears –

Then the war – he aimed and fired
with a shut eye and puffing lips
and swooping hands gave me
attacking enemy planes –
He ran away to the mountains (hills?)
and hid (slept?) – cheek on hand's back –

Caught by the enemy
after a lengthy search –
he lifted cups and plates
and peered under and round them
running fingers demonstrated the long chase –
He was caught, exhausted –
here he pants and holds his wrists together –
taken with five others to be shot –
index finger of the other hand, himself –
They fell in the repeated volleys –
One-Two-Three, Four-Five-Six –
he supplied the necessary noises –
Wounded he fell, lay still,
and after a while crawled away
when the enemy had marched off –
this he shewed also.

Thanking heaven – an upward glance –
for he was a Catholic
here in this Communist country –
he crossed himself rapidly with
nimble surreptitious fingers.

He had a son – hand held chest high –
grown now – hand raised to brow –
he would telephone him to come and meet me –
miming Telephoning, Son Coming, Meeting –

I shook hands with the son
and praised his father, my good friend,
with expansive gestures,
I who before had simply nodded slowly
or shaken my head.

IN THE LENIN LIBRARY, DUSHANBE

Having been shewn, with innocent pride,
the illuminated Arabic manuscripts

by famous scribes unknown to us,
the many illustrated translations
of the *Rubaiyat*,
and the discarded volumes presented
by the British Library Association,
we were conducted to
the Director's office.

A dish of grapes, a coffeepot,
coffee cups, and a platter,
paved and piled with rings of bread,
were reflected in
the polished table top.

When we explained that, shortly,
we should be having our evening meal
at the Intourist Hotel,
the interpreter said firmly
that it would be discourteous not
to break bread with the Director.

When we were each introduced
and seated round the table,
that neat man in the sports shirt
picked up the bread and
broke it into fragments,
and handed them to us.

The biblical phrase, the gesture,
reminded me instantly
how, earlier that day,
driving up the steep road
to the foothills of the Pamirs,
our bus drew aside,
allowing a great flock of sheep to pass,
coming down for the winter
from the upland pastures,
and the shepherd who led them
halted to let them drink
among the splashed stones of
the rushing, shallow, mountain-river.

The breaking of bread and the shepherd
leading his flock come out of
what was once our Holy Book;

but here the grass was blond, straw-coloured,
and the waters were not still.

CAMARADAS Y COMPAÑEROS

Once years ago
we listened to Bilbao
on headphones after midnight

found Albacete on the map
pronounced Barcelona properly

applauded the red-sashed boys
and the blue whirling skirts of the jota
the innocent fife and drum

argued for and against the Anarchists
or slipped an unobtrusive note
to a secretive comrade collecting
for the International Brigade

maybe even stood a drink
to a gruff-voiced laughing Basque
from the rusting ship at the docks.

That is all long over now.
It was only for a short while;
we have forgotten if it lasted years or months.
The pages of the atlas turn.
We have momentarily memorised
many other placenames,
hear foreign stations more easily.

But sometimes
a name slips back to mind
from a book or magazine
like Jarama or Guadalajara
or a fragment of song
like the scent of an exotic flower
of the merry muleteers
or the formal dance of the spinners.

Or maybe an elderly man in a crowd
catches your eye, flashes a grin

and clenches his fist shoulder-high,
he fought in Spain and imagines
we remember it.

SONNETS FOR ROBERTA (1954)

I

How have I served you? I have let you waste
the substance of your summer on my mood;
the image of the woman is defaced,
and some mere chattel-thing of cloth and wood
performs the household rites, while I, content,
mesh the fine words to net the turning thought,
or eke the hours out, gravely diligent,
to drag to sight that which, when it is brought,
is seldom worth the labour, while you wait,
the little loving gestures held at bay,
each mocking moment inappropriate
for pompous duty never stoops to play;
yet sometimes, at a pause, I recognise
the lonely pity in your lifted eyes.

II

If I had given you that love and care
I long have lavished with harsh loyalty
on some blurred concept spun of earth and air
and real only in some bird or tree,
then you had lived in every pulse and tone
and found the meaning in the wine and bread
who have been forced to walk these ways alone,
my dry thoughts droning always on ahead.
Then you had lived as other women live,
warmed by a touch, responsive to a glance,
glad to endure, so that endurance give
the right to share each changing circumstance,
and yet, for all my treason, you were true
to me, as I to something less than you.

III

And, by that act of giving, my slow hand
conditioned to the habit, might, in time,
have earned a better captain in command

and turned to finer purpose many a rhyme,
saving my thought for you that has been bound
to twig and feather or to figured stone,
and from that happy discipline have found
a richer texture and a warmer tone
for the bare verses which my plodding thought
must always shape of each reported sense;
and at some even moment of my day
I might at last have known emotion brought
to some authoritative eloquence
for the heart's hurry and the heart's delay.

IV

To such a gap as this our love has come
that, when I speak, you doubt the words I use,
and doubt no less those moments I am dumb,
till silence is no more than bitter truce.
I am not crass enough to heap the blame
on other shoulders than my own. I know
it was my selfish and forgetful aim
shaped blade and edge to drive a cruel blow
to your tense heart, though not by willed intent,
which, while it seems beyond your wit's belief,
had set you safe above all chance event,
fixed in the sober fabric of my life,
enriching its drab textures, lightening
its sombre autumn with remembered spring.

V

Take the intention then and let me live
a wiser creature for my foolishness,
and from these aching hurts you must forgive
achieve a bold capacity to bless
this meagre mortal circumstance has bound
to your mortality while breath endures,
for in this posture only may be found
the grace and peace inevitably yours.

For I need mercy much, and blessing more,
if, from the débris of my squandered days
your hand and mine should these four walls restore,
beacon and haven in this briery maze,

and, disciplined by guilt's diminished pain,
our dialogue of love begin again.

THE SHORTENED DAY

After uncounted days of drought and flood,
a tired, parched season and a spate of rain
in splashing torrents dismally withstood,
autumnal peace approaches us again;
the dark streams full, the trees in disrepair,
the fields past labour ready for the spring;
but, in October light, the brightened air
brings new dimensions for our comforting.

The landmarks have not perished with our hopes;
the hills remain; the constellations turn;
the raking sun-shafts on the western slopes
shew hidden contours we have yet to learn;
and, grateful, we stand ready to obey
the brave compulsions of the shortened day.

THE LAST SUMMER,
FOR ROBERTA (1975)

Deck-chaired in our back yard among your flowers,
bee-rifled poppies, tall *Impatiens*
in delicate blossom, triggers not yet set –
we brought its seeds first from Glendun,
a rank weed by the stream-side, of no repute
in any gardener's handbook, dear to me –
and rose of Sharon in a golden bush,
thrift with mop-heads on bare stems,
carnations tattered past their noon still sweet,
delphiniums, *Oxalis, Mimulus,*
in all their coloured companies . . .
We draw the sunlight in to warm our bones
against the creaking months, nor vex our wits
for metaphors to flourish round their names
or sprig our myth of being where we are.

These flowers are free of ambiguity
or other function than their single lives.

Our senses are not focused to accept
more than here is offered; we accept
the momentary excellence, content
with mood, with instant, knowing all will pass.

OLD MEN SITTING

Shew me a man who's seemingly at peace
with a game, a gadget, or merely listening
to others talking, to the band in the park;
he is himself, no more nor less than that.

Yet watch the same man talking at the bar,
or walking where he's seen; he's another person.
Through his eye's corner an observer peers,
assessing the performance, its success.

He is friend, stranger, wit, professional,
sportsman or artist, any but himself.
Each mask's a trick he's hardly conscious of,
or only if he deems you've guessed his play.

But old men sitting may not be at peace;
they are already absent from themselves;
when their eyes moisten, it's the chilling air
or a speck of dust that smarts a small boy's eye.

EXPECTANCY

Do all men wait like this for breaking light
or, tired of waiting, turn to stem the time
with jerking gestures and a swab of words,
till grown to numbness, they are content at last
to accept the twitching nerves and the stung lids?

Can one wait worthy, cramming his creeled hours
with fists for justice, brimmed with fair intentions,
flexing his wits deliberate with toys,
and knowing them for that, and running again
when signals beckon out or seem to beckon?

Is that old man, with all his tasks thrust by,
content, bemused, or brinked on weariness,
so drugged with rumours from the beaconed shore,
or gorged on glimpses, guesses, intuitions,
he has no will or power to do aught else?

I wait here for this light in my own fashion,
not lonely on a rock against the sky,
but as the men who bred me, in their day,
as men in country places still, have time,
working in some long field, to answer you.

KITES IN SPRING

A BELFAST BOYHOOD

A HAPPY BOY

This is the story of a happy boy,
born in this place while yet the century
scarce offered hint we'd not by now enjoy
a tolerant and just society
through wise congruence of our people's choices;
the path seemed clear, and only for a time
would some, deflected by ancestral voices,
posture and mouth in bigot pantomime.

The map dissolves. Familiar town decays.
No man can ever walk these ways again,
blind to the brooding of the coming storm,
and pacing towards apocalyptic days;
and yet his boyish hope was never vain;
if it seems foolish now, it still stands firm.

THIS NARRATIVE

This narrative's made up of what he knew
from elders' talk as use considered fit;
what he himself experienced is true
as memory's hidden censor edits it.
For, later on, he proved a myth-maker
as most men are, but conscious none the less
whatever happened him must take its share
in shaping what he hoped would best express –
when held in judgement by his living peers
and those who after come – the man he was,
intending kindness, trying to be just
in thought and act, desiring that the years
should yield his quiet verses some applause
before they end in radiated dust.

THE UNNECESSARY DREAD

My mother had three brothers, each one died
when he had touched or passed into his prime,
as if by law of nature turned aside
before they'd paused on that plateau of time.
Their father, well before them, had gone out
and six grown children left; as if the genes
put length of life perpetually in doubt,
if not the will, some weakness in the means.

Structured like them with body's bone and blood,
I grew into a dread I'd share their fate;
this stirring slowly as each year withstood
approached my undivulged but drastic date:
yet from my father's cells the messages
were coded with a disregarded ease.

MY UNCLE WILLY

The first to go was William. I recall
the winter night we learned that he had died,
the quick tyres crackling on the ice outside.
My mother held him Prince Imperial,
his school renowned when he was principal,
his bachelor's degree the family's pride.
Though deep the grief, the lamentation wide,
I was not marshalled to the funeral.

He left a widow, daughter and two sons.
Aunt Margaret threat of penury defied;
her resolution all their needs supplied
and saw them safely adult, proud of her.
To that commended man I never once
stood close enough to gauge his character.

MY UNCLE JOHNNY

In Bangor, brother John the bachelor
stayed with his widowed mother many a year.
Gun runner, golfer, well-read engineer,
he married late and left to live next door.
A child, I wondered what he married for
when everything a man could wish was here,
house, garden, mother, dog, pipe, book were near,
and, not too far, the golf links and the shore.

I can't recall his bride. The hedge was high
between our gardens. Yet she was a thief
to steal our uncle from us. Suddenly,
when influenza swept in lethal tide,
her nursing of him was to our belief
incompetent; he never should have died.

UNCLE DICK AND AUNT BERTHA

The youngest of them, Richard, had a wife,
Aunt Bertha, with no child to complicate
their singular enjoyment of their state;
it seemed, all ways, an enviable life.
I loved to sit in their high motorcar
with big brass headlamps, wind their gramophone
to play me Peter Dawson's baritone;
but otherwise I envied from afar.

Never so close as when he lay upstairs,
a corpse unlidded, and I stood alone,
I set myself the bravest of my dares,
and touched his cold nose – cartilage and bone –
to feel it yield. I've kissed chill brows since then,
taking my leave of those not seen again.

YEAR OF GRACE AND MY GREAT-GRANDFATHER

In eighteen fifty-nine, that Year of Grace,
when Christ's keen ploughshare broke faith's fallow land
with fearful husbandry few could withstand,
till every cottage seemed a stricken place;
then thousands troubled, trembled to embrace
salvation from their Saviour's nail-pierced hand,
daring to spurn sly Satan's least demand,
and rise hereafter to God's Halls of Praise.

My mother's mother, Ellen Harrison,
farmer's young daughter from around Wolfhill,
fell prostrate with her family, and rose
redeemed by mercy, all of them save one,
their cheerful father, unrepentant still,
who could not take the path these tremblers chose.

MY GREAT-GRANDFATHER'S REFUSAL

They gathered round in prayer, had preachers brought
to strive and wrestle with his stubborn will,
smote him with texts and sermons, and besought
his darkened heart to recognise its ill,
showed kin and neighbours all admitting still
their perilous state, the succour Jesus wrought,
but he unwitting of one wicked thought
could feel nor urge nor need grief's tears to spill.

They urged: 'By one last effort you may bring
your soul to Glory. You are skilled in song,
a song for Zion then. God's grace is strong.'
But when he lifted up his voice to sing
he found the songs they prayed for lilt into
the hearthside ballads in his heart he knew.

MY GRANDMOTHER ROBINSON

My mother's mother, born in forty-two,
saw bearded husband die of Bright's disease.
Of his brass foundry all I ever knew,
those bright Napoleons on the mantelpiece.
Each night he had to lean upon the gate
to light his pipe, for none dare smoke indoors.
Church-going, comely, critical, sedate,
deep down my terror of her still endures.

When walking with her in a summer lane,
I plucked a frothy flower, admiring it;
but she, whose ready word was to forbid,
asserted her peremptory disdain,
and in her crispest tones my error chid.
'Throw it away, child; it is cuckoo spit.'

THE TEACHER'S RESIDENCE

My Uncle William was made principal
of a town school, a Church appendage then –
such a condition once was general,
still is, when ordered by stout mitred men.
His family, my father's, worshipped there,
a meeting house for Methodists who came
to heed long sermons, testify with prayer,
and sing their hearts out in their Saviour's Name.

Associated with that school, a house
some distance off, the Teacher's Residence.
Unmarried, William brought his family
to live with him, which circumstance allows
a sober comfort, next to no expense,
and fixed the birthplace later meant for me.

96 CLIFTON PARK AVENUE
AND THE ROBINSONS

Fourth in a five-house terrace, stucco-faced,
three storeys, a bay window, patch of grass,
red tiles to gate, the railings iron-cast,
respectable, no longer working-class
as their last house was, doorstep to the street.
That half-mile march to Church and Sabbath School
each Sunday with the family complete
was a parade far more than dutiful.

My mother and her elder sister taught
in William's school, untrained, sang in the choir,
or round the new piano sang at home;
their younger sister to the keyboard brought
rich resonance. At times they'd light the fire,
and have a party in the drawing room.

GRANDFATHER ROBINSON DIES IN 1898

That summer noonday, zenith, was too brief.
I can't now estimate its length in years;
the decade, months or days subsumed in grief,
incapsulated in the family's tears,
when their proud father died, still at his prime,
after repeated crises of disease,
brought them together, singing, on their knees,
while he, the bravest, led them every time
to chorus into Glory. He lived on.
They could not face that music, weakening,
called in a nurse to guard him in their stead;
till, once, when she to fetch his tray had gone,
death took him swiftly without signalling;
when she returned she found him songless, dead.

THE SCATTERING

Time telescoped. My mother in two years
married her Robert. William found a bride.
Richard botched up a couple of careers.
John built a house in Bangor to provide
his mother with a home at last secure,
no lodger in a Teacher's Residence.
His sisters, till they married, must endure
their mother's eager ear for Providence.

John for himself assumed his father's role,
to be the anchor of that widowed life,
changing the foundry with his swift control
to prosper in the latest heating gear,
surrendered all to this, a hoped-for wife,
a Whitworth scholar with a bright career.

MY PARENTS' COURTSHIP

I never asked or heard enough to know
if there was anything they might have done
contrary to the omens. If you go
to the same church, sing in the choir, have fun
at the same soirées, if both families
are friendly, socially are similar,
should liking strike, it will mature with ease,
that only untoward circumstance might mar.

This was my parents' fortune. They were married,
he twenty-seven, she claimed twenty-one.
Affection, I observed, between them carried,
with no attrition, two score years and five;
no ragged thread in that close fabric spun,
their love ran deep and undemonstrative.

THE WEDDING PRESENT

My grandmother adored the great Miss Boyd
whose teashop based her brave authority,
was, with my parents' marriage, overjoyed
that her friend's wedding present all should see.
But, largesse from a liquor licensee,
the gift was tarnished, so my father vowed,
and straight returned it; conscience disallowed
that kindly woman's generosity.

There was a row, of course; my grandmother
was much affronted by her son-in-law,
her friend insulted, so she felt abused
by this crass act which so diminished her.
Despite the tempered weapons which she used
his rigid stance abated not a straw.

UNCLE SAM AND AUNT EDIE

Aunt Edith married Sam, an amateur
footballer – Daddy Martin to the crowd –
bland, affable and confidently loud,
his tasselled caps with braid provided sure
proof of his art. In business prospering,
already posted Justice of the Peace,
a listed sponsor, climbing by degrees,
the mayoral lamp-posts no unlikely spring.

Their house was large and in a leafy park,
a grand piano and a motorcar;
they entertained performers from afar;
my cousins' Christmas seemed a Noah's Ark.
But when war ended, business fell apart;
Sam bankrupt, still unvanquished extrovert.

AUNT CIS AND UNCLE TOM

My mother's elder sister married Tom,
a country lad turned city schoolmaster –
as so it seemed half my relations were –
lived in an avenue some distance from
our hub and centre. I was often there;
a childless house then. There I could remark
those graceful dancers drawn in poker-work
hung in the hall, their varnished pleasure share
with those tall velvet frames whose painted glass
was gemmed with gun dogs, water, tufted grass.
A friendly house since, till their daughter came,
for welcome child I stood as surrogate,
a kinship I could never after claim
when my small cousin stirred, a decade late.

ELLENDENE

In Bangor's eastward suburb, Ballyholme,
John's house was pitched, not in the older town
where buildings, dwellings, sweet shops shoulder down
to join the seafront where the trippers come,
but in a long, a new developed road,
one of the villas of those prosperous men
who travelled to Belfast and back again,
their families nested in each snug abode.

These villas, not manorial or vast,
were comfortable, every want supplied
by errand boys, by things which came by van;
what little happened there occurred inside,
except on Sundays when whole families passed
to pay due tribute to the Son of Man.

WHAT LITTLE HAPPENED THERE

What little happened there occurred inside.
I think at once of when the man next door
was carried in a blanket from the shore,
my elders nodded, whispered, 'Suicide',
as if some hushed affront to local pride
had been committed by some nameless one.
A horse that broke a necessary bone
on ice at home had a more dignified
dismissal when they shot him where he lay.
For this was drama, tragic, gravely stepped;
to this we groundlings gathered for the play,
and edging closer, to the kerbstone crept,
cowered into silence when the carter wept
and other horses dragged his cart away.

CARSON AT SIX ROAD ENDS

From Bangor I once went to Six Road Ends
with Tom and Cis. He must have carried me
much of the way. What age I was depends
on how one dates that meeting properly,
most likely six. We three were standing there,
facing the platform, draped, in its marquee.
The crowd was huge. Tom lifted me to see
Sir Edward Carson, with arm poised, declare –
for what he did declare I'd have to look
through old newspaper files, since all he said
has left no echo in my infant head –
yet I can swear I saw that famous face,
that right fist thrust in challenge or rebuke,
once and once only, at that time, that place.

MY GRANDMOTHER'S RESTLESSNESS

When John moved out Grandmother could foresee
her widowed loneliness too much to bear;
my sister first, and then our family were
compelled to come and keep her company.
So, for six months, that Bangor house was home,
a chapter vivid in my history;
the deeper tensions then not known to me,
I thought her stern and sometimes quarrelsome.

So we retreated. When my uncle died
the house was sold. Through her remaining years
that angry doting gypsy plagued her brood,
each shift a useless effort to provide
her lasting house, her bags brought down with tears,
her matriarchal right misunderstood.

THE TRICYCLE

Yet from those days three sights delighted me,
but never coinciding, each unique;
that thin-sparred, idle windmill you could see
three fields away, each day in every week;
in season, where two roads meet, in the wedge
they formed, a thresher's engine sometimes roared,
while clouds of gritty chaff spun up and soared
in endless fountain over the high hedge.

Symbols perhaps, interpret them who can,
or casual sightings, not unusual;
but one I treasure surely over all,
the regal spectre of that gaunt old man
slow urging up and gaily down the hill,
cranking, in leggings, his huge tricycle.

BALLOONS AND WOODEN GUNS

O it was lovely round that other house
where I was born and lived for thirty years.
Life surged about us. So that time appears,
dull intervals suppressed, in happy shows:
Italian organ-grinders, parrots, bears;
that blind old Happy Jimmy by himself;
the German bands; the Ulster Volunteers
with wooden guns; the women selling delph;
carts with balloons; great horses galloping,
their huge fire-engine brass and funnelled flames;
strung chestnuts every autumn; kites in spring;
girls skipping; slides and snowballs in the snow;
all those activities which bore the names
of May Queen, Kick-the-Tin, and Rally-O.

THE VOLUNTEER

My father's closest brother of his three
trained as an artist, by compulsion made
his living at the lithographic trade.
After adventures, Edinburgh, he
settled in Finchley with his family.
One Bangor holiday I saw him plain,
his tilted boater and his swagger cane,
a smiling man, he shared some jokes with me.

Months after war broke out he wrote to say
he had enlisted by deliberate choice,
not waiting for conscription, lest his boys
might think of that with shame some future day.
I still recall my father's countenance
that day we learned he had been killed in France.

MY BROOKLYN UNCLE

Thomas, the eldest brother, shipped across
the broad Atlantic where he found his bride,
a daughter of the firm, this proved no loss;
a Wall Street office was no crazy stride.
From her surname they took their son's first name,
and sent us stacks of photographs each year;
with office, house, rooms, cars, there would appear
that family face, the same and not the same.

After Depression, his Havana trip,
the sagging jowls subdued by surgeon's knife,
the blond son smiling in the partnership;
it seemed the sort of transatlantic life
which satirists make sport of; yet there were
those Christmas dollars for my grandfather.

MY FATHER'S MOTHER

I'm vague about my father's mother, Jane.
I was too young. She died in nineteen ten,
the first month of that year, which might explain
why I recall so little of her then,
some months past two. But others' memories
filled in some blanks. She had a pock-marked face.
That woolly coat she gave me long a prize.
Her house was known a hospitable place.

And all I ever heard's in character:
thrifty, rose early, working hard, her house
and person spotless, was most generous,
unprompted aid came readily from her.
With busy hands, her image still relies
on patchwork quilts made out of uncle's ties.

MY AUNT SARAH AND UNCLE JOE

A carpenter called Joseph Love, it's true,
married my father's sister, Sarah Jane.
With names like those some ballad should ensue
of rural passion, pastoral joy or pain.
Not so. He was a bright young workingman.
My father liked him. Later, scant of work,
they emigrated, settled near New York,
and from then on became American.

But once before, he with my father crossed
to Liverpool, to hear Keir Hardie speak,
returned committed both to Labour's cause;
I cannot reckon what that journey cost.
I've paid my dues and looked for no applause;
our New Jerusalem is still to seek.

LONSDALE STREET

My father's youngest brother stayed at home
with widowed father, all the others left.
I can record the treasures in each room
although the house is gone, that street bereft
of all but name. The rarest of bazaars –
the fender's conch shells, chair of prairie-grass
twisted in coils, newts, lizards tanked in glass,
live pigeons in the attic, snakes in jars,
the Orange sash, the Volunteer shako,
and Sandy's watercolours on the wall,
the frames of cork-pinned moths – all disappeared
into the limbo where such treasures go.
Gone too that wheel with which my uncle steered
his fabled ornithopter, vanished, all.

21ST SEPTEMBER 1912

This uncle, Sam, loved any aeroplane;
we went to see who'd win the Dublin Race,
but a whole afternoon of gusty rain
made any such event a wild-goose chase.
One autumn Saturday we found a place,
hedge-high, to watch a monoplane display
on the Balmoral Showgrounds' grassy space;
he held me up; inside the fence you'd pay.

Swooping and climbing, swinging quickly round,
the airman's deft control was magical.
Sudden he slipped, a stiff wing stabbed the ground.
At home that evening, when the paper came,
its Stop Press carried Harry Astley's name,
reporting he had died in hospital.

FIRST PANTOMIME

He took us to the Christmas Pantomime;
it was our first, this tale of Beanstalk Jack.
We'd heard the story told time after time,
so, though they danced and sang, I could keep track;
but Jack a girl, his mother a man, the cow
a man in front and one behind, seemed daft,
that clumsy canvas shape bulged anyhow –
it was small wonder other children laughed.

I liked the Giant's family on their stilts,
handing the dropped cap up from left to right,
but that was all, till, in my schoolbook years
those strolling players, Doran and his peers,
Caesar in togas and *Macbeth* in kilts,
for me first set the curtained stage alight.

THE MAGICIAN

So Uncle Sam was truly Prospero,
that house his island palace. There I shared
his marvels and his magic. Thence I'd go
with netted rods and jam-jars well prepared,
to pace the tow-path by the drifting stream,
or step through heather for the furtive moth.
I gaped to watch his magic-lantern beam
figure with life the hoisted tablecloth.

His nimble fingers thrilled the mandolin,
or strummed banjo. Once, with a pointed blade
he gouged a fist-sized eagle from tough oak.
He glittered through my days, a paladin
in all accomplished, nature's tricks his trade,
till one sad day, for me that dream-spell broke.

THE BREACH

Courting a widow, briefly, Grandfather
affronted, rowed with Sam, and fled to us.
My uncle bought himself a little house,
red-brick, suburban, shortly finding there
his next-door neighbour a spinster painting flowers.
Her house was larger; there was room to spare.
One house not two; it seemed good sense to share.
They married. It was no affair of ours.

Husband and wife now brinked on middle age,
they got a son, a sickly child soon dead.
Frankly my mother thought it very odd;
'A wonder of the world' was what she said.
Her carried words provoked my uncle's rage;
the row resulting closed that period.

CONSEQUENCES

Our houses parted as that shutter fell
in this same town. Not once I'd race again,
close on his heels, along a tufted lane,
net at the ready. Nevermore he'd spell
Darwinian theory from a mollusc shell,
nor cruel logic in the spider's skein.
Yet from that teeming mind there must remain
much which has made and kept me infidel.

He'd taught in Sunday School, had been expelled
for heresy, since Darwin's was his book;
from thence his reading went from bad to worse.
So, though I lost him early, I have held
close to that sceptic and enquiring look
at the old riddle of the universe.

ORCHARD COUNTRY

When my grandfather came to live with us
my past expanded, for he proffered me,
his lively mind so thronged and populous,
an open door to our own history.
That Armagh orchard country. Yea and Nay
of grave believers. How his mother died
of famine-fever caught the strangest way,
for that was not a famished countryside.
How his grandfather chafed the small child's hands,
chill from the snowballs – bringing life to yours
as he recalled. How Mark's, his father's, cures
healed creature's ills. How in those Planter lands
our name is hearth-rolled. Generation, place,
he gave you foothold in the human race.

SCOTTISH INTERLUDE

He had been born in eighteen forty-one,
just like the Prince of Wales, he'd always say.
The old Queen's reign had sixty years to run,
and with sound heart he would outlast her day.
An early marriage, John was seventeen,
Jane two years older. Mark then followed suit,
brought in a young step-mother, set the scene
for certain kitchen-friction in Clonroot.

So John and Jane, that fabled Christmas Eve,
set sail for Glasgow, huddled on the deck,
the voyage rough yet offering relief;
from then on they were long in coming back.
And so our Scottish sojourn then began
which gave a touch of tartan to our clan.

TEETOTAL MASTER

And in a Glasgow close they found their home.
His rustic fingers opened him a trade,
the seedsman's trade, and this conjunction laid
the table, made a bed for all who'd come.
First Mark, with eggs and chickens basketed,
to Broomielaw on deck; Jane's brother John
to stow his family, their mother fled,
leaving him free to travel farther on.

His youngsters swelled the growing family.
Jane fed and scrubbed the lot. Our John paid all,
nor bore his footloose kinsman any grudge;
accepted foreman's apt authority,
became a Volunteer lest war befall,
a teetotal Master, left his Orange Lodge.

THE RETURN (1885)

They had eleven children of their own;
five died in infancy, the last of these
a bundle in her arms as she stepped down
the dockside gangplank. It was no disease
but shock convulsive brought this startling end
when the ship's siren rocked the Broomielaw;
a tale I have no warrant to amend;
this was my namesake whom I never saw.

Back so to Ireland, working in Belfast
for better wages at his well-loved trade,
to this my natal city here at last
that long and looping pilgrimage was made.
It seems that at this pivot of our past
some fitting mortal tribute had been paid.

JENNY GEDDES

His talk composed a crowded tapestry
of people and events; the Queen's John Brown,
Tom Thumb's parade, the Golden Jubilee
and that wild night when the Tay Bridge blew down,
and Highland policemen called him out to see
if still the warehouse roof held, of Khartoum
where, through old Gladstone's wicked treachery,
the bible-searching Gordon met his doom.

Two stories he loved, often told with smiles –
I knew by heart the words which would be said –
one was of Jenny Geddes at St Giles
who hurled her creepie at the preacher's head,
the other of the ballot, when he'd quote
how the clerk asked, 'For whom d'you wish to vote?'

THE DOCTOR'S BAG

Old Doctor Ledlie brought me in his bag;
he had a king-like beard, a long frock coat.
And so, when other children used to brag
of flying storks, or, loud in chorus, vote
for cabbages or goosegab bushes as
the magic places where they first appeared,
I always thought mine was a higher class,
a doctor's bag and stout King Edward's beard.

Those summer months she waited for the day
the doctor'd fetch me, my small mother sped
to a secluded seat upon the bank
beside the Lough somewhere near Helen's Bay,
to fill her mind with lovely thoughts, she said;
for such thoughts I perhaps have this to thank.

METHODISTS

In those days always the School Manager
was the same man who ministered our church,
for we were Methodists; his tenure there
a four-year stint before he'd prowl in search
of lusher, greener pasture somewhere else;
if he were calculating, he might cruise
to comfortable pulpit, steeple, bells,
with blander sermons, softer cushioned pews.

Each year they met in Conference to agree
whose turn which was, who'd likely make a fuss
if sent to serve some rugged barony
or packed to corner which might prove his last,
and several times, when meeting in Belfast,
a kindly backwoods pastor stayed with us.

OUTSIDE THE CREEDS

By chance the minister when I was born
was just that fellow father rated least;
he could have been described, if with some scorn,
as 'looking like a barman, or a priest'.
White-headed, ruddy-jowled, in manner rude,
an overbearing sergeant on parade,
treating a teacher as a clerk unpaid
and clear where he subordinately stood.

So, when the time came for my christening,
my father knew that from a fist like his
the forehead-dabbing blessing which proceeds
would be no more than empty posturing.
In conscience then he gave the rite a miss,
and from that day I've stood outside the creeds.

MY NAMING

A woman, by my mother much admired,
had had two sons, Harold and Lancelot;
both names, but more the second, seemed inspired
by breeding and with taste, my mother thought.
This woman was a niece of that Miss Boyd
of whose famed teashop you've already heard,
and all within her sceptre's range enjoyed
the ticket for good taste which this conferred.

My father disagreed. Our names were plain,
honest, not flashy. John was good enough
for his own father, for her brother John;
a Lancelot would sound affected, vain;
but lest the child should crave an inch of cuff,
he'd maybe like a Harold, later on.

DOMESTIC HELP

At times we had a run of servant girls
from far-off places; one came from Conlig,
a widow's daughter, noisy, freckled, big,
whose broom whisked through the room in dusty whirls;
our cinders she called *chunners,* better swept
beneath the rugs and mats. Even more surprising,
once, round the room door where my parents slept,
poked her curl-tossing head with 'Who's for rising?'

There was another voiced her discontent
we did not dine on chicken every day
as she expected. Briefly entertaining,
their worth in work was scarcely evident,
it hardly met their pitiable pay;
my mother's fiction was they came for training.

THE ONE I LOVED

But there was one who was the paragon,
that separated wife who wore a hat –
I wrote some lines about her, later on –
nanny and mother's help. I marvel at
the love I bear her still, remembering
the comfort she provided, and her vice,
Strong Drink, that was, to us, a sinful thing.
She came to us, and stayed and left us, twice.

The first phase finished with that fatal trip
pramming me somewhere to her tippling friends,
not to the promised park. The second ends
when her drunk husband shouted at our gate.
Though she's secure in my heart's fellowship,
my love achieved its utterance too late.

THE NAMES WE USED

Then Mama, Papa, were the names we used,
far from this generation's Mum and Dad.
Some people, hearing us, were much amused,
for even then those terms their quaintness had.
The children in the streets cried Ma and Da,
those common, lazy, sheep-like syllables;
for them the youngest infant was the Ba,
the fitting adjunct to their bleating spells.

Yet even then I learned to gear my speech,
this for the home, this fitter for the street,
though still unconscious that there was for each,
confirmed by use, a syntax apposite;
as walking in the Glens much later on
I had to choose a stricter lexicon.

MY FIRST REPORTED WORDS

My first reported words were Ship, Boat, Water,
saluting from my pram, on hillside lane,
the gleaming Lough with its amazing scatter
of sails and steamers, hulls in shipyard plain.
This might have been a forecast I should follow
some wild career upon the Spanish Main;
but such predestination would prove hollow,
no lust for tossing waves I entertain.

I voyaged only on the Bangor Boat,
that paddle-urged, that broad leviathan,
with room to run from rail to rail and dote
upon the dipping gulls, or stand to scan
the green hills slipping past on either side
and wonder that my world should be so wide.

FOLK FOR TEA

With folk for tea, there in the dining room,
too shy to meet the unfamiliar guests,
and find myself the butt of strangers' jests,
I'd creep to seek the under table's gloom.
There was a lady once, with birthmarked face,
I was hauled out to greet. I gave a cry
and dived below; my infantile disgrace
became a text for future courtesy.

Among the boots and shoes I'd twist and toss
till, pressed by parents' coaxing, I'd comply,
crawl from my lair, strike attitudes, for one,
pose stiffly, hand in vest, Napoleon,
or find a floorspace readily to lie
with arms extended, Jesus on the Cross.

FIRST LETTERS

My letters I acquired from bottles, tins,
my mother handled from the pantry shelf,
her tact so gentle that it might convince
me almost I had learned them by myself:
Camp Coffee with its turbaned servitor,
and HP Sauce which pictured Parliament,
and others with no pictures to explore
where eye may tell you what the letters meant.

But better still, the others gone to school –
my father, sister – she'd sit down to knit
or sew or darn, and I'd draw up my stool
to tell her where my hero-self would fit
into the prompt-looped saga generous
which at this hour each day she spun for us.

THE DOUBLE-ENDED TRAM

I heard about but truly never knew
the old horse-trams with trace-boys for the hills,
though sometimes now and then my father'd show
the warning boards still left by certain sills.
Our trams were trolley-roped, electrical,
sparking at corner-points, and double-ended;
and at the terminus they'd swing and haul
the trolley round from which its rope depended.

The driver like the pilot of a ship
stood up in front and cranked his handle round;
the conductor punched the ticket for your fare;
but you would always try to make the trip
upstairs, where you could change the seat-backs round
and watch the whole town pass below you there.

SCARLATINA

That bag was opened in the top front room,
there on my parents' wide and friendly bed.
But later that apartment would assume
a private magic in the years ahead.
For six long weeks, when I had scarlet fever,
cut off and curtained from life's jolts and jars,
close-cosseted by mother's brisk endeavour,
I ate my meals, read books, played carpet-wars,
from Creasy's *Battles* plotting each campaign
with my lead regiments across the floor.
My neck-glands throbbed; his knife to ease the pain
the doctor promised, but, to be more sure,
we'd wait a week or two. The threat was vain;
the paste a friend named gave the unscarred cure.

SANCTUARY

This was, the days it lasted, grave suspense,
but of that illness I remember more
the disinfected sheet across the door,
the cold hands of the doctor, and the sense
of being with my mother on my own,
father and sister banished out of sight,
the morning sun, the coal fire red at night,
my mother tending me, and me alone.

There are some lines in Rilke, later read,
tell when boy's body's bound a prisoner
of illness, self's still plant has space to grow.
Those six weeks I was captive strangely sped
my stretching mind to wander everywhere,
returning taller with a world to know.

MY FATHER'S VOICE

Though Glasgow-born, a youngster in Belfast,
my father's voice along the telephone
had a Scots-tinctured timbre of its own,
an early echo from the Clydeside past
his daily speech would rarely demonstrate;
but the odd words I'd heard or underlined,
with sounds and fingers he would explicate;
lum hat and *pinkie* come at once to mind.

My native tongue is of my age and place,
articulated with deliberate care,
hinting of Scots a little, but at base
the Planter's patois. This now, I detect,
returned from years of absence, to my ear
has locally grown coarser in effect.

MY FATHER

With glinting pince-nez and a trimmed moustache,
my father faced life calmly confident.
In his first manhood doctrinaire and rash,
his manner mellowed quickly as he went
about his business, never with a purse
but with a pocket plucked from in relief
of any plea. No oath, however brief,
slipped from his lips at any slight reverse.

He'd been a cricketer, but gave it up
after he married, turned to golf instead,
but took no team-place let alone a cup.
On each fine forenoon Saturday he sped
to plod with fellow teachers round the links,
enjoyed the game, declined the clubhouse drinks.

A HOLY PLACE

I loved to watch him shave, his splayed thumb pressed
on chin upraised, to let the stropped steel skim
the fluffed froth off. I felt I could not rest
till, one day, I should share this rite with him;
such skill, such peril, such unerring grace.
This was my daily vigil none might share;
that morning bathroom was a holy place,
one celebrant, one breathless worshipper.

This finished, he'd begin a lesser rite,
scrubbing my face, my neck, my hands, my knees,
wholly engaging me, in sheer delight
my stance entranced by some repeated spell
from Aesop, from Lamb's *Shakespeare,* Kingsley's *Greece,*
Gould's *Book of Moral Lessons,* William Tell.

AN EYE FOR COLOUR

My mother played no games. She trimmed her hats;
her eye for colour was acutely true,
and with waxed tissue patterns to pursue,
her broad nib petalled paint on table mats.
Her tongue was lively, notable for use
of country phrases from her mother's youth,
quick, vivid, picturesque, not coarse or loose,
nor veering greatly from the simple truth.

She gobbled novels, magazines, the lot –
Strand, Nash's, John O'London, People's Friend.
She most of all admired George Eliot,
and George MacDonald's merits would maintain;
though she had read she did not recommend
Marie Corelli, Ouida, or Hall Caine.

MY MOTHER

A little woman when I knew her, stout,
as small but plumper than her sisters were,
before she married slight with hip-length hair;
feet firmly planted, stepping neatly out,
propelled her nimble movement everywhere.
Her features comely, her complexion fine,
her ankles when I glimpsed them, slim as mine;
she chose her costumes, hats, gloves, scarves, with care.

Once, at some distance from our house, at play
I saw her nearing, but as she passed by,
without a sound I pressed against the wall,
and gave no sign saluting her at all.
Later, at bedtime, I found tongue to say,
'You would be lovely, if you were *so* high.'

MY SISTER

My only sister, Eileen, always was
protective sister for a timid boy;
half-roads to Mother, she could still enjoy
my easy games, was quick with the applause
she saw I needed. When our parents went
to concert or to meeting, made my tea.
When bigger, rougher boys grew violent,
hers was the ready arm defended me.

And with the years her uses multiplied,
taught me, for instance, how to tie my shoe,
and headed me by candlelight to bed,
and only once reported when I lied.
I should have liked a brother, it is true,
but that was in addition, not instead.

PORTRAITS ON THE WALLS

The calendar behind my father's chair
was of King Edward on his quarterdeck –
I never questioned why he should be there,
although we did not own a Union Jack
to fly on loyal days like friends of mine –
but grim Jim Larkin on another wall,
and R.J. Campbell, snowy-haired, benign,
The Christian Commonwealth his urgent call:
unlikely icons joined in any room,
by what odd circumstance assembled here?
Not simply chance, some logic, I presume,
a lifetime's hidden logic, set the scene;
that grocer's gift which lasted past its year,
those portraits from some Labour magazine.

I LEARN ABOUT ART

Low on my father's shelves there lay this book,
a year's bound numbers of a magazine,
and through those pages often I would look
before I knew what strange new words could mean.
A man called Sparkes in monthly articles
printed a famous picture opposite
a diagram of curves or parallels,
the rhythms by which its artist structured it.

So I learned from these skeletal Landseers,
da Vincis, Turners, Michelangelos –
this trick surviving my unlettered years
would give my gallery days a running start –
along what simple lines sensation flows
which, with a master's wrist, attains to art.

LEAD SOLDIERS AND REGIMENTAL UNIFORMS

For years I mustered on our biggest table
my fighting regiments, not simply lead,
as the box-lid declared, but armed and able
to formulate the fiercest fight you'd read.
A bigger boy called Harry strolled around,
revealed his cards of coloured uniforms,
and pointing out what virtues there abound,
suggested they'd be mine on easy terms.

So he proposed, in fairness, I exchange
a single soldier for a single card –
almost a gift. I should not think it strange
he held his treasures in such high regard –
swop followed swop, till I had every bit
of cardboard, he my army, all of it.

LEAVING FOR HOLIDAY

The hour we fixed to leave for holiday
a horse and cab came clopping to the door.
The trunk was hoisted, roped the safest way;
we bundled in with lots of room for four.
The cabbie cracked his whip and gave a cry;
the brown horse drew us down the avenue.
We swayed in gloom and talked excitedly;
the holiday had started; it was true.

Down town to station. Whistles. Snorts of steam.
Scurry of porters. Jostling trippers crowd.
The trunk was lowered deftly; all was well.
Banged shut the cab door, sound unique and loud,
a sound I sometimes start at in a dream,
but not in dream, with that stale leather smell.

LATE SPRING, 1912

Late spring this year had its grave tragedies
when Captain Scott and his companions died,
when Oates, that quiet hero, stepped outside
where even polar bears and penguins freeze.
That vexed me sorely, but the saddest, worst,
was when we heard, incredulous, the news
our safe unsinkable *Titanic* burst,
ripped by sharp berg while on her maiden cruise.

We had been proud. As the *Olympic* was,
she had been built here. And the band still played.
But not for that end launched with such applause.
That day, when climbing on the Bangor train,
I heard a newsboy, spelt the bill displayed;
drowned now her hundreds, she'd not sail again.

I GO TO SCHOOL

I went to school when I was four or five,
the Infant School downstairs, one spacious room,
an empty mission hall you might assume,
did not mixed infants bring its gloom alive.
Long narrow desks and forms, and at the back
the high-tiered gallery where newcomers sit;
round and between the desks two ladies flit,
and Miss McCleery governs all, in black.

Tiered at the back, sit first with folded arms,
till cane-rapped regal order drives you down
to sit, desk-elbowed, on the shiny form,
alert to your tall lady's smile or frown,
place small blocks end to end, slate pencil grate
its spider's letters on the dark grey slate.

THE WAY TO SCHOOL

My sister walked me every day to school
till I grew taller than that infant class;
there then were splendid monuments to pass,
the corner butcher's, tiled with ram and bull,
the harness shop, its windows bright with brass,
whips, stirrups, saddles, and that leather smell,
and at the next street-crossing corner was
the Farrier's – a fancy name to spell –
scorched horn to sniff, the clanging anvil sound.
Then past some houses, sweet shops, to the door,
open and spilling grains upon the ground,
with jerking pigeons flapping, pecking round:
inside, that dark and sweet hay-scented store.
Who, with a little horse, could ask for more?

THE SCHOOL UPSTAIRS

I was promoted to the school upstairs;
two classrooms ground floor still, and the boys' yard,
to which at certain times our class repairs;
it was the last which held our best regard,
for there we'd squirt cool volleys from the tap
into the patch of sunlight on the wall
to spill its rainbow, drizzled over all;
or, from our pocket treasures we would swop,
in furtive market, marbles, penknife, ball.
The larger classroom, not with desks but forms,
was where we faced the pointer-prodded map
with rhythmic chant of placenames boldly known,
leaving the front form free, on teacher's terms,
to lay her bad leg on, for her alone.

THE BIG ROOM

The senior school seemed vast, an oblong space,
by the high platform cut down to a square,
the middle desks, with forms around the place;
there were at least six classes clustered there.
The pupils stood in circles, not in rows,
from blackboard puzzling what was to be done,
read from their lesson books the verse or prose
ordered in solo or in unison.

Those schoolroom odours were particular,
with chalk-dust, ink, crumbs, jerseys well endowed.
If you were lucky you might be allowed
to fill the ink-wells from an earthen jar,
or hand each book out by its owner's name
but teacher's pet's a title none would claim.

MY TEACHERS

My teachers then, old registers attest,
were certain maiden ladies. I recall
Miss Mary Murdoch, ancient, tubby, small,
that bad left leg in need of frequent rest,
and Maggie Thompson, lean, with greying hair,
by Uncle Willie courted for a time;
he married someone else, a heinous crime,
the guilt for which I felt she made me share.

And Annie Earls, with large and flashing teeth,
long-legged and tall, spray-spitting when distraught,
her glasses glinting, scolding, often kind.
Yet should I rake for ever down beneath
the wilted débris of those days, I'd find
I could not isolate one word they taught.

HIS MAJESTY'S INSPECTORS

Inspectors called at anxious intervals,
armed with the power to offer or deny,
assessing what takes place within these walls,
their labels for our teachers' quality;
this power conferred by those Commissioners
who lurked in Dublin, Starkie was their lord.
I thought of him crouched up his Castle stairs,
cloven of hoof, with fangs, with flaming sword.

His satraps, myrmidons, if they were small,
sucking their teeth and sniffing, questioning
about hard words, odd sums; if handsome, tall,
placing the paper basket on the table,
demanding that we draw the silly thing,
and with no rubbing out, if we were able.

A DOMINIE'S LOG

My father wrote his articles, reviews –
the postman brought him books – though now I'd say
that A.S. Neill is not the latest news,
his was the brightest star of many a day.
When those brave volumes of *The Dominie –*
His Log, Dismissed, In Doubt – dropped through the door –
his later books I'd name less certainly –
my father felt more surely than before
that he was right to head his romping class
to frolic in the quarry on Cavehill,
or march them to the baths to learn to swim.
Inspectors could not let such treason pass
when there were proper elements to fill
the squared timetable. They admonished him.

THOSE MORNING WALKS

But from these years I can remember still
my morning walks with Father down to school;
though coming back was different as a rule,
he stayed behind with those long forms to fill,
while I rushed home, a child intent on play
with any chum I possibly might find,
though walking with my father every day,
as man with man, gave me a striding mind.

We talked of everything, of Bible stories,
if they were true or false or possible.
What would Home Rule mean if it came about?
Why are some politicians known as Tories?
How many rainless days become a drought?
Could God our Father send a soul to Hell?

WHO WAS C.B. FRY?

This private class for one was every day
my seminar, my university,
my asking answered in a friendly way:
Where heaven was? Why leaves fall from a tree?
And rainbows, tides, eclipses, falling stars?
Who was Jack London? Who is C.B. Fry?
Why are they fighting in the Balkan Wars?
Why he called some words 'fossil poetry'? –
I found *Trench* later – and what did he think
of Mrs Pankhurst? 'Bluebird' Maeterlinck?
His answers framed to stretch my inching wit
he so contrived to set my doubts at ease.
I sometimes think romantically of it
as walking with the shade of Socrates.

GOING TO CHURCH

We went to church, by custom, not compelled,
and occupied the pew against the wall.
A preaching house, its galleon-pulpit held
the dominant position over all;
the organ pipes, the choir behind it tiered,
roared out the anthems only choirs can sing.
My father in the top back row appeared
when he had taken up the offering.

With hymns, with Bible readings, children's story,
next week's announcements as the plates passed round,
then sermon, exposition of the text
with scholarship which made it seem profound,
or, loudly shouted, sacrificial, gory,
to threaten us in this world with the next.

THE OPEN EYE

Those yawning mornings moored among the pews,
our creek of vantage once a month would yield
adventure in the current *Foreign Field*
which offered fancy freedom in a cruise
along the Congo; other voyages
promised pagodas, pigtailed Chinamen,
but with old Leopold's atrocities
I swore to be a missionary then.

We stood for hymns, bowed heads in prayer's appeal,
shut-eyed perhaps, but that I could not see,
all backs save choir's and preacher's turned to me.
Unlike some alien faiths, we did not kneel
or, genuflecting quickly, sit and rise . . .
Never in any church I've shut my eyes.

EVANGELIST

And now and then a loud evangelist
might come to plead, to threaten and alarm,
but though he'd thump the pulpit with his fist
the big thick Bible came to little harm.
It was in corrugated mission halls
the masters of this craft gained most success.
In our grandparents' days such strident calls
drew hundreds to surrender and confess,
rise penitent, redeemed, to step transformed
from pews where we now shifted, ill at ease;
no citadel of Satan here was stormed;
only that deaf old man in the front pew
habitually groaned upon his knees,
the last to Wesley's inspiration true.

ISAAC McKEOWN

This man, my mother said, with pony-cart
traversed the town to sell his cabbages,
his turnips, carrots. With but Christ to please
he travelled joyful with a lightsome heart.
Once, praying at the roadside out of town,
he stood entranced. The anxious pony stayed
two hours, they said, then turned and trotted down,
reporting home that Isaac was delayed.

At Watch Night service once, he shook my hand,
shortsighted, asked me how my brother was.
I thought him silly. Now I understand
how utterly beyond all mortal laws
he stood, the victor, needing no defence,
invulnerable in his innocence.

OUR AVENUE

Our avenue was long, a thoroughfare
for carts with coals, bread, milk, or passing through;
you'd risk no sprint across it, or but few,
so frequently those cartwheels trundled there.
Houses with tiny gardens set before –
some peopled with schoolteachers, ministers,
with civil servants, factory managers –
the largest with steep steps up to the door.

Yet faces, shapes, still fill the vivid frame,
the bearded doctor of divinity,
the huge bookmaker, the grey secretary,
for each had features, each had his own name;
but for romance, for mystery, I'd choose
the Rosenfields, the Weiners, our own Jews.

THE TWELFTH OF JULY

With orange sashes, flanked by shining blades,
to thund'ring drum, shrill fife and measured beat,
lodge after lodge, along the sounding street
the sober-suited company parades.
Their painted banners flaunt the bearded faces
of founding fathers, flicker an array
of famous fighters in embattled places
like Derry, Enniskillen, Dolly's Brae.

King William's high white horse steps daintily;
dripping Boyne water. Brave Duke Schomberg dies.
Queen hands a Bible to a turbaned black.
The broad silks sway and billow, tugging free
with jigging tassels, and are tethered back
with taut strings gripped by boys about my size.

THE ELEVENTH NIGHT

This marching season crested in July.
Gay bunting, arches, spanned streets; gables wore
fresh paint on pictures standing long before
as faded ghosts of last year's loyalty
which Orangemen maintain and celebrate:
'At Carrickfergus William steps ashore';
'Th'Apprentice Boys slam-to the Ferry Gate';
'The *Mountjoy* breaks the boom', and many more.

For weeks we haul and heap our horde of sticks
to build our bonfires. The Eleventh Night,
when summer dusk descends, sets them alight,
and blazing skyward like a Brahmin pyre.
We stay up late, till flames with ashes mix,
to leap across the embers of the fire.

THE RIVER STREETS

The side streets of my world in order ran
from Roe Street, Avonbeg, and Annalee
to Dargle, outer limit of my span,
whose lads about its corners taunted me.
Roe Street was quiet, swept, its pavements clean,
most children's fathers warders there, you'd say;
its doors had a shut look; at Halloween,
here were the bells to ring and run away.

But it was Avonbeg Street and its twin
where my chums swarmed; the closest then therein
were Walter, widow's son, who once displayed
such courage, when a tumble snapped his arm,
and John, the coachman's son, blond English lad –
that coach Miss Bruce's, pride of Thorndale Farm.

PORTSTEWART, JULY 1914

Portstewart. Nineteen fourteen. Willie's clutch –
our cousins, Cecil, Edna, Uncle, Aunt –
rented a house with us. There can't be much
remembered now which was significant:
the bathing pool, the jellyfish that stung,
and how the Chaplin film, unreeled, would fall
into an open basket; that is all,
that, and a chorus which the Pierrots sung.

The war broke out in Europe. Bishops blessed
the Austrians, the Russians. It was odd,
both benches hurled opposing prayers to God.
We thought that foolish, had more interest
in picnics at the strand, at Castlerock.
By August, back in Belfast, came the shock.

THE YCVS AND THE ULSTER DIVISION

Surprised one day, I watched Belfast's Lord Mayor
borne on gun-carriage, when Young Citizen
Volunteers in grey first took the air,
mere lads they looked, too soon they would be men.
And, some months later, we went down to see
our khaki soldiers marching to the docks
to sail away for France to keep us free;
our cheering then my memory often mocks.

For later still, as days limped past or flew,
the newsboys yelled hoarse tidings down the street
of Jutland's victory, Dardanelles' defeat,
and, propped on crutches, men in sloppy blue,
approached with awe, would tell us stories from
the shell-ploughed fields of Passchendaele and Somme.

BANGOR, SPRING 1916

In Bangor for some months I went to school;
I now have scanty memories of the place,
could point it out, but not describe one face.
One instant only was it colourful;
when Lord Clanmorris called, his face was pink
as was his shirt, his tie; his hair quite white.
The masters smirked and bowed and seemed to slink,
standing in silence we enjoyed the sight.

Headmaster, back from ruined holiday,
told once of Dublin and its Easter Week,
of the dead horses and abandoned cars.
But of the politics of that affray,
the seedbed and the source of future wars,
he certainly made no attempt to speak.

I STILL HAD A FRIEND

I once played truant, mitching round the rocks
beyond the Pickie Point, a dreary day.
An old man stopped to quiz. My luncheon box
had folding sides. I folded it away,
and coming home too late found that the news
had run before me with the paperboy
from my own class. I thought then: What's the use
of any plan a gossip might destroy?

My mother and grandmother were enraged.
I was sent up without my tea to bed;
my morning forecast promised no such end;
sobs stifled but the hurt still unassuaged.
Then Father came and sat beside me, read
some thrilling story. I still had a friend.

THE FILLED STOCKING

One Christmas Eve my grandmother fell ill,
staying at Dick's; my mother, first resort,
was begged by Bertha for her brisk support.
She left with Father's calm, ungrudged good will,
though he himself lay quinsy-stricken here,
the sock of hot salt tardy to relieve.
The crisis ours, the resolution clear;
tomorrow Christmas; this was Christmas Eve.

Mother had whispered where our presents were –
the top shelf of their wardrobe, as we found –
with these and other sundries from around
we sorted in the way to us seemed fair
and stuffed our stockings. With such enterprise
went tired to bed, to wake with feigned surprise.

THE CAROL SINGERS FROM THE CHURCH

Another Christmas wore its sprig of pride,
for, on its Eve, the carol singers came,
while dark endured, to stand and sing outside
Church members' houses. This year was the same.
It had been father's duty to go down
for doorstep greeting, giving alms as well,
but, ill again, to handle that half-crown
devolved on me, sole male responsible.

The long night dragged. I mustered all my powers
to meet the challenge. Often I could hear
far carols somewhere distant, drifting near,
till choirs passed laughing. These were none of ours.
I knew their sound and rose coin-palmed before
their grinning leader knocked upon the door.

BROWN'S BAY, ISLANDMAGEE, SPRING 1917

Once, with my mother and my grandmother,
conscribed to lend a hand, fetch water, go
on errands to the farm. Our cottage there
clung to a ridge, where certain hours would show,
steaming at dawn, returning, in a row,
the black minesweepers file, each evening.
While out in France we struck them blow for blow,
at Europe's edge here, we were hazarding
that U-boats kept the issue still in doubt.
One morning, tasks accomplished, for a stroll
I climbed the turf and rocks round Skernaghan,
and fifty yards off, swelling like a shoal,
sea-surface broke, a conning tower thrust out.
I scrambled, frightened, from the waving man.

LOST *ARGO*, ISLANDMAGEE, SUMMER 1919

I had a wooden boat to float and sail
on ponds in parks, and safe parts of the sea.
I named her *Argo,* after Jason's tale,
but never knew her age or history;
for father'd found her on some market stall
or in a junk shop, with a splintered case,
her masts and spars intact, so 'spite of all,
her broad hull kept a sturdy, buoyant grace.

Once, at the shore, where rim of tide-washed wrack
almost enclosed a bay, I set her course
to where my father'd meet and turn her back;
but, opposite the choppy gap, she stalled,
shivered and headed out, as if enthralled
by the far prospect of the Scottish shores.

THE DUSTCART

A dustcart anchored in our cinder field,
idle and empty stood from day to day;
with padlocks chained and stationary-wheeled,
it offered ready platform for our play.
We skirmished, stormed and boarded, sailed away,
Pitcairn or Treasure Island our far aim;
our lightweight silver medals on display,
we celebrated peace, another game.

Once, from the poop I tumbled, gashed my knee,
jagged and raw from such a fearsome drop.
My shipmates bore me to the chemist's shop
in Manor Street, where Mr Connolly
swabbed it with cotton wool and iodine:
on my left knee that scar's ghost still is seen.

THE 'FORTY-FOUR HOURS' STRIKE, 1919

There was the Strike; the shipyard engineers
would cut their working hours to forty-four;
their jingle threatened, 'Or we'll work no more.'
Then heady solidarity uprears;
the *Bulletin,* the Strike Committee's call;
we only saw that in the streets each light
went out, stayed out, as gasmen joined the fight;
for a tense week our strike was general.

My mother visited my grandmother,
at Edith's now; some miles she had to tramp,
with no trams running, there and back again.
And when at night, late, I expected her,
a swinging light approached. It soon was plain
it was my mother with a stable lamp.

READING

I learned to use the Public Library,
that red-brick haven which Carnegie built.
In bed, at table, I read avidly,
for in our house there was no blame or guilt
because 'you stuck your nose in some old book'.
Upstairs the landing held a well-filled case,
and when my books were read I'd often poke
through those my parents scattered round the place.

I borrowed *Coral Island,* Ballantyne,
but thought far more of Henty and Jules Verne,
loved Haggard, Conan Doyle and Stevenson;
but always prose; I never scanned a line
of any poem I had not to learn
save *Hiawatha,* that excepted one.

MUSIC LESSONS

I had piano lessons once a week,
that instrument then everybody knew;
my mother played and sang, my sister too,
my father made his cello grunt and squeak,
contesting Handel's *Largo.* Often then
friends tried a trio, friends at parties sung –
soprano ladies, tenor gentlemen –
and Tosti's parting hands were often wrung.

But I sat dumb: my ear was quite unskilled,
and *Hemy's Tutor* stumped my fingers' scope.
Miss Harrison, my sallow teacher, filled
the term's report with words which gave no hope,
and I was left, relieved, to carry home
th'iambic tick-tock of her metronome.

THE DRY SUMMER, ISLANDMAGEE, 1921

Those summer weeks of nineteen twenty-one
were hot and sunny all through long July.
Farm carts fetched water, for the pumps ran dry
as cracked clay crumbled in the day-long sun;
the bean stalks blackened, and the bluestone spray,
in rusty drums, stood at the furrow's end.
With farmboy Sandy, orphan, now my friend,
I played at cricket where they'd cut the hay.

Old Brennan had a bull, prizewinning, black;
men drove a heifer in, once, to be served –
an act I'd not seen spelled on any page –
and from the hayloft's vantage, I observed
his lifted forelegs grip her flanks and back.
Not yet fourteen, that hour I came of age.

MY FUTURE WIFE

These were the days I saw my future wife,
I not fourteen and she not seventeen:
that three years' gulf in time which gapped between
seemed more than could be leaped across in life.
She worked in town, the office of some mill,
came briefly down by noon each Saturday,
and left on Monday early, striding still
to catch the train across the long causeway.

In brilliant colours dressed, her wide black brows
above her small pale face, with kerchief tied,
I thought of her, as lovely as a rose,
to be saluted with admiring stare;
her student friend all company supplied
and in their walks no third had any share.

FREE MASON

My father joined the Masons later on,
took down the Bible, leafed to Chronicles
and studiously learned that part which tells
about the Temple built by Solomon.
Then, on the night he went to be enrolled,
in preparation for some awesome test,
he bathed, put on clean socks, and changed his vest,
but what then happened we were never told.

And every month he went there, year by year,
till I was old enough to think of it
and spoke to him of joining. He said No.
So, from then on, my path in life was clear;
unsworn, unbound for ever, I should go
a free man, freely, to the infinite.

PAID QUARTERLY

The tall dark handsome man who lived next door,
schoolmaster also, with his family
set out for better days across the sea.
My father, too, once dreamed some distant shore –
perhaps New Zealand – would reward him more,
for struggling on a teacher's salary
was punishing, with cheques paid quarterly;
but never once I thought of us as poor.

I never wanted much I could not have,
food, shoes, toys, books, and every Saturday
the pence for sweets and comics I required,
and in July we always went away.
But now I know my parents frugal, brave,
by true domestic loyalties inspired.

THE IRISH DIMENSION

With these folk gone, next door was tenanted
by a mild man, an Army Officer,
two girls, a boy, left in his quiet care,
his wife, their mother, being some years dead.
We shortly found that they were Catholics,
the very first I ever came to know.
To other friends they might be Teagues or Micks;
the lad I quickly found no sort of foe.

Just my own age. His Christian Brothers' School
to me seemed cruel. As an altar boy
he served with dread. His magazines were full
of faces, places, named, unknown to me.
Benburb, Wolfe Tone, Cuchullain, Fontenoy.
I still am grateful, Willie Morrissey.

THE KING CONCERNED

I saw King George in open carriage drive,
the Queen beside him, hosting from the dock.
We must at least be sixty, those alive,
who cheered that cortège round the Albert Clock.
The streets were crowded to the City Hall,
where he would open our new Parliament.
Although beside Queen Mary, he seemed small,
he was the King: it was a State Event.

Years after that, I read the speech he made –
Smuts drafted it: a wise, concerned appeal
that we surrender fear and end our strife,
and live together for the common weal –
and reading sadly, thought his hopes betrayed,
but never dreamed those hopes outlast my life.

GOING UP TO DUBLIN

My father almost every Easter went
as delegate to teachers' conference.
His fellows numbered far more eloquent,
dogmatic men, but few with cooler sense.
When, with Partition, Protestants hived off,
he stayed in loyalty to all his kind,
that they were teachers was to him enough,
to sect or party singularly blind.

He went to Cork, to Derry, Waterford,
to Dublin, liking Dublin best; he'd trained
at College, knew the Castle and the Coombe,
and to the end unconsciously retained
the old convention and the proper word
in 'up to' going, 'down from' coming home.

THE TROUBLES, 1922

The Troubles came; by nineteen twenty-two
we knew of and accepted violence
in the small streets at hand. With Curfew tense,
each evening when that quiet hour was due,
I never ventured far from where I knew
I could reach home in safety. At the door
I'd sometimes stand, till with oncoming roar,
the wire-cage Crossley tenders swept in view.

Once, from front bedroom window, I could mark
black shapes, flat-capped, across the shadowed street,
two policemen on patrol. With crack and spark
fierce bullets struck the kerb beneath their feet;
below the shattered streetlamp in the dark
blurred shadow crouched, then pattered quick retreat.

THE PRISONERS ON THE ROOF

A hundred yards along the other side
from where our house stood, ran the high gaol wall,
dark, grey and blank, with everything to hide
save at the clanging front gate where they call
with captured men in vans. So, once, just then,
the cells were crammed with gunmen – IRA;
their protest they asserted in a way
proclaimed, though they were captive, they were men.

For they had thrust and clambered to the roof,
and clattered, rattled chamber pot or pail –
all metal instruments they find in gaol –
to keep the town awake when all should sleep.
We heard the rumoured uproar, ran for proof;
and thought the ledge they danced on high and steep.

A CASE OF MISTAKEN IDENTITY

We heard a rumour, ran to swell the crowd
down at the far end of our avenue;
for in an empty house, a woman vowed,
a vicious gunman hid; it could be true.
Someone already had reported it;
the soldiers had arrived. A young man tried
the door, was warned, persisting, stepped inside.
The stout police sergeant urged us back a bit.

There was a burst of gunfire, sudden, clear;
we could not see but judged it very near.
The young man had run through to the back door
and opened it. And from the entry's end,
behind the houses, soldiers fired before
he'd chance to show he was not foe but friend.

AFTER THE FIRE

After a night when sky was lit with fire,
we wandered down familiar Agnes Street,
and at each side-street corner we would meet
the frequent public houses, each a pyre
of smoking rafters, charred, the floors a mass
of smouldering débris, sideboard, table, bed,
smashed counters, empty bottles, shards of glass,
the Catholic landlord and his family fled.

I walked that day with Willie Morrissey;
while I still feared all priests he was my friend.
Though clearly in the wrong, I would defend
his right to his own dark mythology.
You must give freedom if you would be free,
for only friendship matters in the end.

TWO SPECTRES HAUNT ME

Still from those years two incidents remain
which challenge yet my bland philosophy,
on this neat sheet leave dark corrosive stain,
which mars the dream of what I hope might be.
First, on the paved edge of our cinder field,
intent till dusk upon our game, I ran
by accident against a striding man
and glimpsed the shotgun he had thought concealed.

Then, once, I saw a workingman attack
a cycling sergeant. Whistle. Warning shout.
As if by magic plainclothes men sprang out,
grappled the struggler, carried, rammed his head
against a garden wall. I watched the red
blood dribble down his brow, his limbs grow slack.

ON DUNMORE'S WASTE

We had our cricket team, our football team;
our jerseys blue, our heroes, I should say,
were Glasgow Rangers, Linfield. Like a dream,
McCandless passed once, home on holiday.
On Dunmore's waste we strove with small success,
our goalposts bundled coats, all penalties
disputed – with no whitewash to express
the limits which the book of rules supplies.

At cricket every summer, on those fields
balls bounced or shot erratic on bare clay.
No word or mention any record yields
of our excitement every Saturday:
remembered names these syllables deploy,
McClean, MacManus, Maxwell, Dillon, Foy.

MY GRANDFATHER DIES, 1923

My father's father breasted his four score
till, stepping from a train, at eighty-one,
before it stopped, he cracked his collarbone,
and in the cottage hospital he wore
his bandages with courage. Every day
we called to see him. After several weeks,
though colour had not left his weathered cheeks,
his breathing bothered, but none bade us stay.

Next morning, going in, my father said,
'I'll speak to matron. Go you to his bed.'
The bright sun lacquered ceiling, floor and walls
with golden light. Then suddenly his head
dropped forward on his breast and he was dead,
as the ripe grain before the reaper falls.

CARNATIONS

They brought his coffin home and laid it on
the polished table in the dining room.
Though it was summer still, a mellow gloom
pervaded all, blinds down and curtains drawn.
Carnation wreaths – a little late that year –
lay round the open box when I stepped in;
I saw shirt-ruffles round the bearded chin;
the odour of those flowers was everywhere.

Once, long years after – I was seventy –
reading, companioned only by my thought,
a whiff of sweet carnations came to me.
It was that day the cleaning woman brought
a fistful in and thrust them in a vase –
I saw again that coffin, saw his face.

I LIE ALONE

I was promoted when Grandfather died,
taking his bed now in the top back room.
The mirrored wardrobe where he used to hide
his smuggled fruit still cidered its perfume.
I took all over, piled the mantel shelf
with books I owned, hung pictures on the wall
which I had been allowed to choose myself,
Murillo's *Shepherd* print, the crown of all.

I woke at dawn soon after, sensed he lay
beside me in the bed. I dared not stir,
but mused shut-eyed, how long I cannot say,
remembering he loved me in his way
as I loved him. No reason now for fear.
I reached my right hand out; no one was there.

from

THE SELECTED JOHN HEWITT

THE GLENS

Groined by deep glens and walled along the west
by the bare hilltops and the tufted moors,
this rim of arable that ends in foam
has but to drop a leaf or snap a branch
and my hand twitches with the leaping verse
as hazel twig will wrench the straining wrists
for untapped jet that thrusts beneath the sod.

Not these my people, of a vainer faith
and a more violent lineage. My dead
lie in the steepled hillock of Kilmore
in a fat country rich with bloom and fruit.
My days, the busy days I owe the world,
are bound to paved unerring roads and rooms
heavy with talk of politics and art.
I cannot spare more than a common phrase
of crops and weather when I pace these lanes
and pause at hedge gap spying on their skill,
so many fences stretch between our minds.

I fear their creed as we have always feared
the lifted hand against unfettered thought.
I know their savage history of wrong
and would at moments lend an eager voice,
if voice avail, to set that tally straight.

And yet no other corner in this land
offers in shape and colour all I need
for sight to torch the mind with living light.

from

MOSAIC

DEDICATION

for Mary O'Malley and the Lyric Players

I owe much thanks to players everywhere
who've placed such circumstance before my mind
I've often shed my momentary care
in rapt occasions of the richest kind:
the mad king and his fool; the broken man
who sees flame make the saint; the peevish pair
who wait beside the tree; the harridan
urging her creaking wheels beyond despair.

With all to thank I name in gratitude
and set among the best, of their own kind,
that little band upon their little stage
tempered to show, by that dark woman's mood,
O'Casey's humours, Lorca's sultry rage,
the Theban monarch's terror, fate-assigned.

THE PATH AHEAD

The spinney's sparse and thinner now,
bald earth, lank grass, as I pass through,
where leaves in generations once
made stepping soft for younger bones.

STYLE

Close-woven words my care,
I praised where praise seemed due,
and still had some to spare
for textures coarse and new,
till, sated, taste withdrew
from fashionable wear.

Now I must seek again
within my sceptic heart
those rhythms which should maintain
and pace my stride apart
with a slow measured art
irrevocably plain.

FOR STONECUTTERS

Select the stone. Incise the words
exactly marking time of year.
Cut deep or shallow as required.
Let light or shadow emphasise.

Define with kerb the viewer's stance.
Avoid abstractions large or small.
All value judgements flake or split.
The lettered stone's the metaphor.

THE IRON POT

At the cottage door, in the fat black pot,
brimmed with brown water, wisps of greasy fleece
steeping, waiting boiling, drying, carding,
later to be spun on treadled wheel
still now beside the hearth.

Tufts plucked off wire-fence barbs,
off brambles, hawthorn hedges,
all the summer in the fields
at other tasks when plodding home
when the warm world held its breath;
off the stiff sheep in the heather
after the hard winter.

I take the flat, square wooden bats
with their close rows of tilted teeth
to card and comb the images
which may be spun while light still lasts.

FONTANEL

on reading the shorter poems
of Michael Longley

The laughing bearded man,
genial, witty, fond of jazz,
seems to be an expansive
and sociable extrovert;
nevertheless he clutches
the convolutions of his mind,
refusing to liberate
the wren, the badger to follow
their purposes outside
the strict casket of his
intricate syllables.

I wait expectantly until
the badger lurches over
to nuzzle my slow boot,
offering his shy secret,
and the neat bird tightens,
then suddenly explodes in
a featherstorm of canticles.

MOSAIC

A man may objectively inherit
a role in history,
reluctantly or with devotion,
soldier, functionary, rebel,
engaging himself as an instrument
of required stability or urgent change.

But the bystanders accidentally involved,
the child on an errand run over by the army truck,
the young woman strayed into the line of fire,
the elderly person beside the wall when it fell
are marginalia only,
normally excluded from documents.

History is selective. Give us instead
the whole mosaic, the tesserae,
that we may judge if a period indeed

has a pattern and is not merely
a handful of coloured stones in the dust.

MEMORIAL SERVICE

When he has finished his address
alluding to the public virtues of the deceased
and bringing in a few references to life after death,
trite, unconvincing, exactly geared
to the understanding of his audience,
the bishop trips down from the pulpit.

After the prayers and the benediction,
tall in front of the long altar,
he leads the slow procession to the West Door
as the mourners peel from the pews
and join the shuffling queue.

There he stops, stands to one side,
and shakes hands as they are offered,
the widow, the married daughters, the sons-in-law,
the Mayoress and His Worship the Mayor
and the representatives of
neighbouring municipalities, local authorities,
distinguished by their chains of office,
remembering a great many faces and some names.

Finally, when all have been greeted with degrees
of sympathy, solemnity, warmth,
he retires to disengage from his finery
and the event,
and drives home for lunch with his large sister;
having duly played his part
in the memorial service
for a shrewd and very able fixer
who knew who to acknowledge, salute,
manipulate, and who to ignore
striding along the Town Hall corridor.

PRAGUE, OR NOVOTNY,
IF YOU REMEMBER HIM

In every classroom, hotel lobby,
public office, his photograph

faced from the wall, icon and emblem
of stable authority.

Dismissed from office, expelled from
the party, he trudged away
over the hill, into history
that will often be rewritten.

There are many others, remembered
each by a few, buried somewhere
because of his signature, his nod;
their names may be published some day.

I recall one, released, who met us
by arrangement at that hillside café
rehabilitated, re-enfranchised,
talking without rancour of his past friends.

His quiet, singular complaint was
that no one had apologised
for the lost years, or admitted
that they had ever been wrong.

MOSCOW MOMENT

In Moscow, wakening long past midnight,
high in a tall Intourist block,
distant, young voices in the dark
somewhere across, behind, among the bare cliffs,
fumbled uncertainly towards
a part-song, harmony,
gaining confidence, not very drunk.

A whistle-blast peremptory;
footsteps patter, scatter;
the song shuts abrupt;
then, after silence, farther off,
begins again with fewer voices,
trailing, diminished, lost.

The public statues within earshot
had momentarily unclenched their fists

and lifted their blunt bronze toes,
to stiffen back at the whistle-blast.

Next day, in Lenin's Tomb,
I could not swear
that the wax man had not winked at me.

AGRIGENTO, SICILY

Raw as a New Town,
the translation incomplete
from drawing board to site:
stark white blocks on a high ridge,
shoulder to shoulder, seen for miles
across the bone-dry country
harsh with stones, rocks, boulders,
tumbled, smashed in arid torrent-valleys.

Nearer, the tall blocks define themselves
within the century's familiar idiom –
offices, flats, garages, supermarkets;
it seems a moot point whether
they were being erected or demolished.

It is as if, flood-threatened,
the landfolk had drawn up, crowded
on their Ararat and stayed
though all water's gone, dribbled, seeped away.

On the other side a lower ridge
thrust down the wide plain to the far sea.
Mapped with temples, pillars, columns, débris;
a famous city once, Acras,
in the torn scrolls and papyrus.

Between them the wide landscape, ground-slope,
rimmed by rubble of both, rock-littered;
lacking blossom this season, the almond trees
writhe from, crouch over the parched clods,
beautiful, they say, in spring
as Acras once was.

THE MAN FROM MALABAR

Here in this Irish room
the man from Malabar
sits cross-legged on the floor
and beats his little drum;
though no drum's here to beat,
his mimicry is such
that we imagine it
as true for sight as touch.

To that accompaniment
he lifts a wavering song,
meandering along,
on some heart's errand sent,
a winding jungle track,
a dancing village mode,
swaying and falling back
as the dark fingers bid.

And somewhere on the rim
of that strange haunting cry
a cadence makes its way,
an old song wanders home,
to summon to the thought
a country crossroads fair –
a strain some singer caught
out of the misty air.

THE COVENANTER'S GRAVE

One day they argued whence their family name
and quizzed their father. 'Ayrshire,' he replied.
'Three hundred years ago a preacher came
to plant us in the Antrim countryside;
his grave's at Donegore.' The elder son
wondered aloud if there'd still be a trace –
that name – his name – upon some lettered stone –
to show that he had found the proper place.

He travelled there, and in the churchyard sought
among the stones, aware that someone stared,
a woman from that house beyond the gate.

Her peremptory challenge proudly brought
the name for which he searched, deliberate.
'Youse were a long time comin',' she declared.

VARIATIONS ON A THEME

1

It seems absurd I should avert
my ageing but admiring eyes
when shrunken hem of miniskirt
makes much of sculptured knees and thighs,
pretending to a shocked surprise.

That's sex, you say: well, if it is,
in paintings I've enjoyed the same,
nor taken my response amiss
which telegraphed no blush of shame
at Boucher's pink rococo dame.

For years, unclothed, the human form,
female preferred, but young and slim,
was long esteemed as beauty's norm,
till narrowed by romantic whim
to garden-nymph with missing limb.

Those naked marbles which the Greeks
flogged to the Romans by the score,
for centuries revered antiques,
though just as naked as before,
are stowed away and sought no more.

And from our modern galleries
the golden nudes no longer glow;
elsewhere young strippers throng to please –
as all who watch the papers know,
Godiva stole the Motor Show.

On hoardings, billboards, everywhere,
a cleavage sells a cigarette,
a navel, beach- or under-wear,
the more alluring when it's wet,
like dewdrop on violet.

Or so the anxious adman prays,
whose skills must push what most persuades,
convinced that titillation pays,
yet finds permissiveness invades,
defoliates his furtive glades.

2

Of galleries I've done my stint,
Palermo, Prague, Graz, Otterlo;
though ballasted with bales of print,
when once the great sensations flow
I hug my headlong vertigo.

So Saenredam, Chardin, Vermeer,
Kokoschka, Poussin, Palmer, Yeats,
supply those instants I'm aware,
beyond our trivial loves and hates
a final silent wisdom waits.

3

In Dresden years ago I saw
Conegliano's climbing child,
astounded Titian dared to draw
so much from this, each image filed
for new renditions, Titian-styled.

From here, beginning with the priest,
the steps, the crowd, he pilfered these,
yet their significance increased:
that basket-woman at her ease
turned sibyl in his masterpiece.

Thus are the moral rules of men
subsumed by Art's morality,
as Shakespeare's brisk unblotting pen
scored some old hack's calligraphy
with palimpsest of tragedy.

4

One day, before a canvas crammed
with country crafts and colours gay,
a Slovak landscape diagrammed,

across the sky a shepherd lay,
his long pipe lifted up to play.

I quizzed a group of children then
with pointing finger, playing fair;
they spelt each object back again,
but none among them could declare
what purpose spread the shepherd there.

Then, after silence infinite
I begged once more. A grubby boy
cried: sir, he plays the tune of It!
What better phrase could you employ
to symbolise Art's instant joy?

5

Though time should let my pictures fade,
as I grow feeble, shuffling, blind,
I must remember undismayed,
good fortune let me cram my mind
with masterpieces, signed, unsigned.

My only fear, I may forget:
the nerves and cells no longer play;
the plugs burn out, and leave a debt
my praising tongue cannot repay,
existence all one neutral grey.

6

So far the argument has run;
some questions begged, far more evaded.
Panofsky, Gombrich, Berenson,
I never braved the oceans they did,
but safe in shallow rock-pool waded.

Art now is girders, twisted, bright,
old engine innards, like as not,
fluorescent discs, a clanking light,
a huge black square with one blue spot,
the silkscreen of a printer's blot.

For cautious critics now define
a work of art as something said

to be just that; a coil of twine,
a plank with nails, a broken bed,
a tray of plastic gingerbread;

so long as someone nominates
object, assemblage, accident –
I'm not the only one who waits
the popping of each non-event,
and hopes it drops where Dada went.

Though honestly I must admit
these often shock my scrutiny
with mocking metaphors that fit
the menaces which underlie
our perilous ecology.

7

So I am back where I began:
I neither seek nor need defence,
knowing reality, for man
lives only through each active sense
which limits thoughts' circumference.

Accepting my conditioned wits
which structured all I've thought or felt,
and that sensorium which fits
within this body purpose-built,
I'll lightly hump my load of guilt,

and gently revel in my joys,
despite the prohibitions curt
sedate decorum still deploys,
and certainly shall not avert
my glance from any miniskirt.

8

I wrote these lines ten years ago,
what sparked them now is obsolete;
blue jeans and floppy dresses flow
across the quad, along the street;
the transformation is complete.

Surprised, in Communist Tashkent,
I've noticed with what grace and ease

the slant-eyed Tadjik typists went
to work in modern offices,
embroidered hems above their knees.

So, comforted by this, I knew,
though here at home I'm out of date
in this regard, some change is due
for fashioned needs must fluctuate,
while I'm serenely obstinate,

and cling to standards found and held
since in my father's magazine
some famous masterpieces spelled
in lines and curves with dots between
taught me what rhythm and structure mean.

So I must let these verses stand
though senses slacken year by year.
Only when earth spins, bare, unmanned,
a shrinking or exploding sphere,
will Art's last values disappear.

OUR SUNDAY SCHOOL TEACHER

I went in Bangor to the Sunday School
at Grandmother's behest; our teacher there
was daughter of a well-known minister;
white-haired and tall, I thought her beautiful,
her gestures elegant and most refined.
Selected Bible stories were our fare,
with praise for ready answers. She was kind;
but with one question I embarrassed her.

I'd read the story in the Book of Acts,
so I asked her what a eunuch was. She gave
a little gasp, and simply said, 'A slave',
which fails to take account of all the facts.
After the class, in innocence they came,
my cronies, and I told them – to my shame.

THE PSYCHOMETRIST'S REMARKABLE FORECAST

She took the belt I offered, closed her eyes,
some minutes meditated, slowly spoke,

as summoned in her trance, to our surprise
beyond sight's edge, she greeted phantom folk.
From her description Mother recognised
her father, her dead brother for a start.
By what their eager gestures signalised
the medium saw my future wrapped in Art.

At home we told my father. His dissent
was firm. Art was uncertain, as his brother'd found;
though what these wraiths proposed was kindly meant.
He'd better fix his aim on some profession –
I'd say, a teacher offered safer ground –
where he could step in family succession.

A GREAT HEADMASTER

Drawn daily in the dragnet of a horde
of dry frustrated creatures driven to teach,
where frail ambition, buckled back on each,
left even the fairest purposeless and bored,
I suffered most their pompous overlord,
his threatening prayers, his studied hearty speech,
his padding terror never out of reach,
seeding the grudges which my small heart stored.

We parted while I still lacked height and stance
to loose the arrows of my festering wrong,
and watch his quick contorting countenance
when what seemed feathered compliments became
the unexpected truth distilled so long
it stung like acid and it seared like flame.

A HOUSE DEMOLISHED

spring 1981

They might have waited had they been aware
that I still lived, before they knocked it down.
Bricked-up and blind, our terrace still stood there
as in so many streets in this sick town.
Sealed off from sight, rooms hugged bright memories,
the kitchen with its range, the dining room,
its coal fire lit for small festivities,

the room upstairs where singing friends would come.
And in the top front bedroom I was born;
familiar with each vivid place I grew
to manhood; every window, stair and door
led to the widening scene my senses drew.
Walls, woodwork shattered, textures shredded, torn,
those haunted corners hoard my dreams no more.

THE RUINS ANSWER

Our towns spill out, yet at the heart decay,
where, waking, many greet a workless day,
while signalled hopes, frustrations, enmities,
flicker before their famished eyes,
and in high flaking flat, in rotting street,
small vandals rally to engage
their hurt, their aimless rage,
while penury and age hug perilous retreat.

Yet still the structure stands, its fabric stayed
by simple acts of industry and trade,
while most fill core of their uncertain days
in customary ways,
as, unobserved, there hangs the poised event;
the radars fan, the missiles are deployed
some twitching finger may explode
to shatter all in the predicted accident.

What then for future's Europe, where we wait
dread's dire event which seems determinate,
and those unthinking, not involved in death,
must draw their threatened breath
till all can turn to life, released again,
repetitive in word and thought,
loving those gestures by their fathers taught,
essaying clumsy ready gestures of their own?

To let this be, though savaged, to survive
unregimented, lazy, talkative,
to build a world where one might catch a glance
and pause to join the dance,
sure of the proffered hand, the friendly touch,
where none shall find a crooked heart,

nor chide the man who walks apart
because they hope by now his silence makes them rich,

can we accept a politician's peace,
toothed with blunt saws and textbook instances,
ordered, statistical, benevolent
on careful precedent,
and not then find the avalanche of time
tilting its downward course these hundred years,
sped by our cynic fears,
will leave the crowded valley only its last name?

To bring this good life must we lean on prayer
to vast Computer programmed into care,
or by submission of our personal
sullen erratic will
to some tall-pyloned rigid discipline,
charged by a brilliant mind?
The ruins answer: truth may yet be found
in random drifting seed and not in lettered stone.

The lichened Christ, meshed in theology
which masks the timber of his riddled tree,
is hoisted so above our fumbling reach
we have no skill to touch
the human succour of that wounded side,
and cannot draw from that scarred face
the light of grace,
and must hang powerless till we choose a steeper road.

Shall science then release an instant light,
laying its harness on the shuddering might
of pounding waters to eradicate
our rooted lust and hate?
Weigh well the published evidence. The skill
that knows the scalpel's path to truth
may heal the broken mouth,
but leave the loosened tongue a crazy dream to tell.

Can Art make certain mercy walks with men?
Art can but jig according to the tune:
this man had fist and chisel poised to break
dumb stone awake;
a cynic prelate whipped him to his best:

and this plucked music from the planets once
at bidding of a witless prince;
these splendid images a fakir's myth expressed.

These fail us all. Art, intellect and prayer
can bring no succour from the dread-webbed air.
Now each man waits alone
for his blurred message on the telephone;
but when, with hope, the flood abates its power
and the still waters have lapped back,
who left shall venture from his rock
to name the weed-choked landmarks on the ocean's floor?

For all abides time's verdict good or bad
as feeble men's divided heart is bid;
so long forgotten now the loving will
you cannot hope to tell
what hope you or your children may expect
from this imperilled tenancy.
Already the sour fields in sickness lie,
savaged for profit once, now nettled with neglect.

Alone you cannot stem the tide of drought.
Walk soberly about your rented plot
and set the ways in order, tend with care
whatever roots and blossoms there.
Be happy to achieve a rounded shape
for hours and gestures of your family.
Graft your intentions to some fruiting tree,
and pray the slow hope grow like some sweet vintage grape.

Strive hard for this; but if disaster come,
sudden as flame or summoned by slow drum,
the high wall can no more than bramble hedge
check terror's creeping edge.
There still may gape your hearth against the sky,
not by fool's edict, bomber's load.
In that field which once crammed the threshing shed
the grey rush now resumes its rank dominion.

To win the life our aching needs define
we must accept some humble discipline;
we must unbuckle our stiff arrogance
and seize each proffered chance

to grapple textures to the hungry sense,
bidding the heart seek in the dream
some hidden whispered name
whereunder, singing, life's bright images advance.

We must bring every filament to birth
which glows with current of the pulsing earth
wherefrom, for all our notions, we derive
the right to live,
which will withdraw that right if we forsake
the logic of the seasons' round,
seizing with selfish hand
more seeming comfort than strict justice bids us take.

For the vain mind, still skill-less to devise
the sphere of truth from what each sense supplies,
shifts its rough freightage so, that way or this,
by wilful emphasis,
till the tense balance shivers out too far,
tips over, and we headlong fall,
our greedy cunning species all,
into the pit with the reluctant dinosaur.

How shall we gain that equipoise unless
we learn to take our blessing and to bless,
else on this shrinking cinder we must wait
the buffetings of fate?
For only in a fair society
can we contain our deep-veined violence,
and through invulnerable innocence
attain, sustain the peace which yet could be.

With only this for coda: that we find
a lexicon and syntax so aligned
to purge our feelings, clarify our thought,
the sound and sense enwrought,
that in communion we communicate;
for nowhere but in that society
can we, at last, be free,
necessity and nature of our human state.

THE NEGLECTED LANE

The farmhouse curtained neat,
grass in front, the privet trimly clipped,

the byre's and barn's new whitewash in the sun,
commended all in passing on the road,
well-doing folk must live here, thrifty people,
not like the squalid tenants here before.
Left, off the road, our lane turns,
high hawthorn hedges, nettle-edged each side,
thick swathes of seeding weeds unscythed and tall,
the tangled knapweed and the ragged thistle:
that lane which held its narrow spine of snow
for weeks beyond the last fall of the year.
The track grows muddy, squelching to a stream
with small clouds staining in the deeper places
we rouse in passing. Scarcely one firm stone.
The water spilling out of the tangled growth
into the tangled growth, with smudge like oil,
dark rainbow at the root, uncertainly
half following the path, half counter to it,
veining in ruts or spread to shallow puddles
in trodden places, for the lane runs down
to ford the stream above the waterfall,
brown, sluicing water over rounded stones;
to our left the cleft frogs mate in, to the right
the rush and fumble of the tumbling waters.

I'd liked this lane, remembering the snow,
the celandines, the walls of hawthorn blossom,
those grappled frogs watched once, that splashing dog
one day last autumn, bounding, standing, shaking.
I'd like it still if only it were dry,
but giving care to where my foot should go
puts all in jeopardy I have enjoyed,
diminished, distanced, altered with revisions,
nearly obliterated palimpsest.
So when I find my tread is over gravel
I scrape the worst mud off, and turn to ask,
'Why don't they do something about the lane?'

ON A COUNTRY BUS FORTY YEARS AGO

The bus is crammed with laden passengers
not pledged to journey far, who drift away
down wet lanes in the waning winter day

over high stiles, up avenues of firs.
The bus grows stuffy; every window blurs;
we judge hills traversed by our lurch and sway
till at each stop chill flakes gust in and play
round a diminished crew of travellers.

Then, at some village, swarming farm-boys board,
well warmed with liquor, laughing, talkative;
our isolation shed, we strain to give
what skew attention our cramped seats afford
to the loud round of jests their coarse wits keep,
while two behind speak low of snow and sheep.

THE CURFEW TOWER

1

That Curfew Tower in Cushendall
stands oddly individual,
a square stone tower, a hill beyond,
rising where the four roads joined
which we here call the Diamond:
not Norman, no vast edifice
ivied with epic centuries,
but dull and plain, anonymous,
a little castle, a tall house.

A loitering fellow told its name
but it was years before I came
to muster more about the man
in whose strange mind it all began,
whose dreams died with a feeble son
whom litigation battened on.

2

Francis Turnley, it appears,
found a fortune in five years
fifty more would fail to spend –
over fifty thousand pound –
ivory, jade or bars of gold,
the source of it was never told.
And whether he was tall or short
the narratives make no report.

Perhaps some canvas or lost bust
still hints his features through the dust,
imperious, benevolent,
as artist's skill makes evident,
building here, proposing there,
in his passionate character,
a larger house at Drumnasole,
a smaller one at Cushendall.
Good roads he planned. He built a school
at Carnlough. He sought to rule
over field and man and beast
like a nabob from the East,
blasted rocks and bored the way
which the Red Arch spans today.
Outside this village on each road
passing travellers must tread,
he set watchmen to prevent
tramps, beggars, tinkers who might taint
the air with fever, plague, disease
from fetid towns or villages.

3

He built this tower, a perfect square,
rising to forty feet or near,
in this New Town of the Glens
where the Bissets lorded once,
stipulating garrison
of one solitary man
armed with bayonet and gun,
with a pike and with a brace
of fine pistols in their case.
For this duty did decide
on one Daniel MacBride
who had fought at Waterloo,
now with little more to do
than to undertake to ring
the bell at nine each evening.
The dark room at the tower's square base
should serve as a detention place
where malefactors cool their heels
when gentle admonition fails.

4

He argued this and ordered that,
fanatic, kind, deliberate,
suggesting there should even be
a proselytes' society
of servant girls he'd hire out
to Papist farmers thereabout
to win them by good works and faith
from their superstitious path.
Drafting a fantastic will,
he left the house at Drumnasole
as a haven for th'insane,
under care of clergyman,
now in wiser circumstance,
who had been afflicted once.

He penned his book, kept in a box
under heavy hasps and locks
in a barred and shuttered room
into which none else might come,
with a rare intelligence
mustering the evidence
that the world had better be
ordered with equality
when man's foolish strivings cease
in a Universal Peace.
To publish this he willed they spend
his fortune wholly to this end.

Then he ordered them to write
on a rock at a great height
where the basalt slabs outcrop
Craig-a-Tinnel's heathy top,
in plain English and good Greek
certain words Saint Matthew spoke:
'When he sent the folk away
he went up the hill to pray
when the evening was come.'

This high-place was his heart's home,
here above the waterfall.
Now the place he loved is still
save for curlew, passing gull;

and there stands no lettered stone
to mark where Turnley prayed alone.
When time chilled that restless heart
the lawyers tore his will apart.

5

I have been to Drumnasole,
stood beneath the waterfall,
climbed the cliff those waters leap,
fern-hung ledge and mossy step,
to the hazels near the top,
passed through bracken out to whin
till bog-cotton tufts begin,
to find there revealed at once
no lettered rock among the stones.
Now none remembers that great heart
who dreamed th'engraver's chiselled art
should keep his plans and policies
as best hope for manly peace,
who always felt high places were
fit podium for his character.

6

The thankless generations run;
the other day a kinsman, John,
disclosed his eccentricity
in dreaming Ireland one and free,
and got a bullet for his pains
which smashed the windscreen, splashed his brains.

When you next pass Turnley's Tower,
on foot, awheel, in cushioned car,
slow down and spare a kindly thought
for that valiant man who wrought
for dreams, ideals vaster than
the ordinary hopes of man,
a symbol still for those who are
content to stay unpopular,
securely armoured in immense
insufferable innocence.

By good fortune kept alive
until eighteen forty-five,

he had the luck, it must be said,
in this daft land, to die in bed.

OCTOBER SONNETS

1

This is the season I think most of death
with hackneyed prompting of the fallen leaf,
with withered grass, the chill cloud-feathered breath,
the darkened mornings, sunlight pale and brief;
and at this time of year my dark spouse died;
after our forty years so close enwrought
it seemed absurd that she'd be thrust aside
to leave me lonely to my crippled thought.

For in October born we both had shared
whatever stars' aspect or circumstance
for the strange sequence of our days prepared,
only to find it pivoted on chance.
Let luck or lack intrude, there still must be,
for every mortal, the last certainty.

2

Of course, the gruffest prompting comes from age;
I've passed my biblical three score and ten
and realise I'll soon limp off the stage,
pausing to hear the prompter tell me when.
During that August holiday we went
and saw the new Pope show himself in Rome;
he was the third I'd seen by chance event,
since with good John we'd felt much nearer home.
This third man, humble, not by pomp beset,
younger than I, it seemed should be the last
I'd live to see, and registered regret.
It proved not so. That gentle pontiff passed;
on coloured box we've watched reaction bent
to kiss numb tarmac on each brisk descent.

3

I've seen no more than three loved persons die;
of those approaching death I've watched a few;
they ebb or drift in loneliness, or lie

inert within the carapace we knew.
But death's quick moment's final, ultimate,
never by any circumstance reversed;
the sudden lifting of the starting gate
or the split second the balloon is burst.

Yet how could these trite images presume
to yield the merest hint of what death meant?
It is an instant singular event,
that sudden absence in the silent room,
survivor's whisper, while the world outside
persists in its low roar, self-justified.

4

I saw my father die. For two long years
he had been stricken. Yet he could address,
if justice beckoned, letters to the press
when none but he found words to voice their fears;
and on that polling day, sustained by rage,
he hobbled on my sister's arm to vote
against that mountebank who'd changed his coat,
but not his rancour or his verbiage.

He died a few weeks later. We sat there,
my mother and myself, beside the screen –
in other verses I have sketched that scene,
assayed that sentence, showing it unfair,
sans justice, mercy, with no sort of plan
for the last hours of that bewildered man.

5

My dear spouse died – a tumour on the brain.
I gazed with pity on that shaven head,
so nun-like, quiet, on the smooth white bed.
We watched her breathing faintly. It was plain
she would not stay, would never more regain
that vivid being who so recently
had paced the Asian lanes and laughed with me
when hurtling back from Russia in the plane.

We sat together in the silent room,
our nephew Keith and I, both well aware
this was the end. We had few words to share.

This was the end, I thought, an end for whom?
For me, of love that living had increased
these more than forty years. The breathing ceased.

6

Her situation seemed a piteous thing,
my punished sister on her tilted bed,
her pinned knee hoisted in a canvas sling,
the loose tubes drooping round her weary head.
For years she'd sat or only stirred with pain;
nodding at times, or sleeping if at ease,
but quick to speak, though never to complain,
if someone's word should interest or please.

I loved her always, there ahead of me.
She loved her brother, equally would greet,
when he announced it, some small victory,
or laboured sullen under a defeat,
just as she took death's coming quietly,
making it seem an orderly retreat.

7

When my wife's sister's husband came to die
I took my turn to sit beside his bed
and watched that good mind wither in that head
which had contrived so much for decency,
for friendly wards wherein the sick might lie,
and nurses, doctors hospitably ply
their caring crafts and skills. But now instead
his bright wits flickered, weakened, rallied, fled
to crooning moments of his infancy.

This was an aimless and a clumsy end
for one whose strength was action, changed and lit
by rustic wisdom, dialect and wit;
a Trollope-addict, storyteller, friend.
If there is that Good Shepherd, as some say,
he might have led him home the Psalmist's way.

THE FREE FOOT

We used to see him, then a shambling lad,
emerging sudden through a thorny hedge

along the rushing stream, alert to dodge
back for the hidden salmon, or on the road
with shouldered sticks from the forbidden wood,
or striding briskly through the misty airs
of early morning to inspect the snares
with which he'd meshed the sleeping neighbourhood.

Now you will hear him, talking loud to his
dog or the child he carries on his back,
across three fields, still strolling through the whin
at any season; and for all your lack
of freedom, you take time to pity this,
the middle age of Huckleberry Finn.

SALUTE

Far off we saw them in the upland field,
the figures moving, the yellow wedge of corn;
counted the figures, giving each a name:
whistled and waved and hoped an answer came
through the bright evening air, if voice, maybe
confused in the dry rustle of the leaves,
if arm, then maybe misinterpreted
and gesture consequent upon their work –
and yet the numbers of the names and shapes
were well equated, any one of them
had right to answer us with voice or hand.

THE LITTLE HOUSE

Within, the little house was dark with hate
and anger smashed like glass against the floor,
while that grey heifer, dawn, paused at the gate
and a bird started singing near the door.

But two in that shut house were caught and bound
in a close grapple none could disengage,
and silence, after anger, tiptoed round
through the bright spikes and splinters of their rage.

Unsleeping, each alone in time's abyss,
dealt out the hurts and shuffled them again;

in anguish clenched, what could they do but miss
day coming gently through the leaves in rain?

SUNSET

Leafing through a book on Oriental art,
I remark a deft and elegant Chinese script
and remember Wang with the vertical brush
showing us how to write
the character for grass
and for sun-in-the-grass
in the pictorial style.
But he has gone now,
and I cannot salute him
even with the scratch and splutter
of my clumsy Western pen.

VIGIL

I wait for a meaning in the coming words,
sure as the earth of seasons, sure as a street
of the familiar tread of postman's feet,
or as a winter tree is sure of birds;
for earth is what the seasons happen to,
and in the branch's crotch a tattered nest
still wisps in wind, and, in the houses, you,
to whom th'expected letters are addressed.

LOOSE ENDS

FOR JEAN

Dear girl, dream daughter of the childless years –
known all your days – of such a surrogate,
of her too, hearthstone of my prime's estate,
staff, anchor, buttress, when beset by cares –
those forty vivid years none living shares –
till riven from me by a witless fate
when I most needed, older grown; so great
a sheaf of masks your single visage wears.

When, that bright day, chance brought beneath my roof
you and your sons, I snatched at the relief,
a sounding house to stem my lonely grief.
Now, six years later, with the daily proof
of this assuagement, to your bracing care
may these brief lines my lucky debt declare.

NORTH-WEST PASSAGE:
AN OLD MAN DYING

Tired now both mind and body, bearings loose,
he meshes into meaning now and then
when an old cog engages. If you press
it turns with logic. Let his attention wander,
it slips out of the true and spins away,
inventing sentences like 'It's a pity
the boy hadn't reached that stage before he was
challenged by the poetry . . .' I too
am challenged by the stubborn will of words
that, linked by their own law, communicate
an argument that seems an armature
for some new structure for the searching mind.
Which linked these words? Was he the unnamed boy?
And at what stage? And whose the poetry?
Is this some flicker of talk yesterday
when the page prompted and the verse leapt out
of its dead classroom context long forgotten?
Yet this spins free from any text we shared.

Ignoring his long illness and his weakness,
he's just returned who never left his bed,
proposes rising, calls to one not there,
or plucks the quilt blind-fingered, though grasps firm
for greeting or goodbye, accepting either:
shadow is substance, substance shadow, time
irrelevant, sound actual on what level.

The hulk's swamped. As the wheel whirls out of hand,
awash the vessel drifts in mountainous seas,
with tattered signals we've no skill to read.

THE REFERENCE

We hadn't met for six or seven years,
a slight lad then, his eyes, his mind shone bright
with dreams of social justice, of revolution;
his being stripped for action, his thought single,
clean as a bow strung tense for its intention;
with none of the crippling harness of the world
to halt or hobble him. Neither girls nor cars,
career nor hobby, love of success nor money,
trap of domestic comfort, to divert
his frank gaze from the first faint hint of dawn.

And I had envied him his youth, his dream,
my own dream not dissimilar but blurred
with too much reading, of liking, of indulgence
in what I always think my loyalties,
his sheer lack of self-interest, his open heart.

I'd known he'd crammed the six years' interval
with pickets, strike committees, protest meetings,
strident west and south at factory gates,
bannered now and then with demonstrations.
I'd seen his name thread through the flimsy sheets
I read at times to prick my sagging hopes,
signed to some blunt and turgid article
in the numb jargon of his rigid sect.
I'd thought the mould was set. He'd edge away
along the margin of my politics,
fixed, doctrinaire, among the gales of time
that whisk the wilting answers from our lips.

Then he arrived to ask my signature
as casually as one might beg a match
from someone passing, neighbour in a queue.
A man now, six years older, he had not lost
the brightness of the eyes, the friendly smile,
not puffed or stuffed with ready rhetoric,
glib-lipped with party clichés in his talk,
gentler perhaps, maybe a thought less urgent.
My envy now was spiced with admiration,
still undefeated, not grown cynical,
the dream survived intact, the trapping rocks
his course was mixed with had been navigated.

He knew the men he'd worked with, virtues, faults.
He hoped to stand aside now for a year
to weigh and finger his experience,
take stock, decide how best he could be used
and what he'd need to learn to meet that use.

So, for this once, he'd need a reference
to buy the time in this unvexing job
he'd fixed his mind on. So I signed the form.
Were he my son I should be satisfied.

THE PORTRAIT

Up the damp gravelled drive as the laurels dripped,
grating on pebbled level, turned to the steps;
the house itself solid Victorian,
built when the town grew linen-prosperous
along the loughside free of factory smoke,
compelled by purpose of my careful trade
to value and preserve what might be lost,
awarding names, suggesting destinations,
I came that chill, appointed winter morning.

I reached the steps. I pressed the bell and waited.
A woman opened, knowing why I'd come,
no fresh-cheeked country servant, no housekeeper,
the lady of the house by her demeanour,
a small neat woman in her middle years.
Welcomed, led to and left in the drawing room
till she returned with what I'd called to see,

my glance and step moved round, establishing,
by furniture and what was on the walls,
the tidemarks of the rippled generations,
the well-scuffed armchairs tasselled, the low sofa,
the well-worn carpet and some later rugs,
the tables, the piano piled with sheet music,
the rows of Scott and Dickens in the bookcase,
a steel engraving of that man at shoeing,
a watercolour of our native mountains
in the safe manner of ninety years ago,
a few Arundel prints in Oxford frames,
two, gilded, oval, of tinted shawl and whiskers,
flanking the mirror over the mantelpiece,
the marble clock stacked round with photographs
of tight-lipped officers from several wars,
a hockey team with cup and folded arms.

I said, when she came back and set the box
on a side table, fingering its wrapping cloth,
that I should not appear too curious,
turning to the window which faced the sea,
'That's a fine view you have, across the bay.'
'But from that other window,' she replied,
indicating with ring-fingered hand,
'you see the hill. That is the view we like.'
I turned and checked, rose garden, trellised wall,
rising abruptly to a timbered prospect,
bare cliff behind it, against the heavy sky.
'It must have been,' I said, 'say, last October,
a splendid sight with all those autumn tints.'
'But we prefer the look of it in spring' –
I took that as some family opinion
taken by a vote some Halloween –
'I hope the people after us will take care
of the plantation, and not let it go
to be a public park for children to ruin,
breaking the branches, pulling all the bluebells.'
Was then the place for sale? Already sold?
That's why she'd rung the office. Who were we
who liked the view: her husband, mother, sister?
The questions tangled. She'd unwrapped the box
and opened it. Examining the object,
lifting and turning, with my pocket lens
and jargon of technique, I followed through

the ritual of occasion to my sentence,
padding it out with ready parallels.
She listened, nodded, took it from my hand,
laid it in and closed the box again.

Our business ended, stepping to the door,
when she had offered coffee or a sherry
which I'd declined with press of other calls,
I spared a comment for the watercolour.
She told me nothing of its provenance;
it had no history; it was always there.

Along the passage my glance lingered on
a crayon portrait by a hand I knew,
familiar in these parts. The artist seldom
dated his work. His style had never altered.
I could not tell just when this had been drawn.
'He caught the likeness but completely missed
the personality. That young man there'
(she had me puzzled; nephew? cousin? kinsman?
not closer clearly with that adjective)
'is not, as he has drawn him, slightly built.
He is strong and broad; there is no doubt of that.'
My quick thoughts flickered; I could not relate
this dateless drawing to a time in her life,
or work out what relation she bore to it.
'This never would suggest the Armstrong shoulders.'
The notion shook me. Had he been a forward?
Or was such bulk the family male tradition?
Young in the drawing, what was his age now?

Checking my confusion, I followed her,
the unasked questions now dismissed for ever.
The last stride brought us to the broad front door;
she opened, thanked me, pointed to the right.
'You should go that way down; it's more direct.'

A DIFFICULT MAN

He was boring often with his laborious talk
describing some technical process in tedious detail,
though admittedly well briefed in his narrow reading;
annoying too in his stubborn postures, for instance,

not painting in watercolours because he was thinking in oils.
Even the meticulous manner in which he folded his scarf
before putting on his overcoat seemed surely designed
indefinitely to delay his overdue departure,
yet we liked him because he was honest and loyal.

One summer Sunday evening over forty years ago
when we had had a day's picnic at Donegore,
he got as far as outlining the church on the canvas board,
while we had chattered, picked wild flowers, read the headstones.
We missed the last bus home and had to walk to Parkgate
to catch a later bus by another route back to town,
and as we followed steadily the long slope of the land,
past houses with slated roofs and whitewashed gables,
corrugated rusty sheds and older thatched outbuildings,
hedges and trees and fields of potatoes and grazing
were still in the sidelong light of the setting sun,
he pointed out and named the coloured shadows
on roof, on gable, on pillar, on every surface,
in the dark furrows between the growing rows,
among the cut swathes of hay and the seeding grasses,
the colour of sunlight enriched by the colour of shadows;
not tedious now the instances, the repetitions,
demonstrating the features of the Impressionist Theory.
Because of that day I look always for colour in shadow;
very few, before or after, have taught me so much.

DRYPOINT

A final-year student at the Art School,
a gangling fellow loping in his stride,
his paintings skilful but derivative,
his experimental carvings clumsy,
only his drypoints – the copper plate in his pocket
to be drawn upon directly with the needle –
communicated a delicate personal vision,
those and one brief Imagist poem
about a hen and farm cart.

It was because of this last
he suddenly took me for an enemy.
I'd had it printed without asking his leave
in an ephemeral sheet a friend published.
He stumped in one evening without a word

– have you ever tried to speak
to one who remains obdurately silent? –
lurched round the shelves and walls gathering
his unframed canvases and wooden figures,
and clumped down the stairs for the last time.
The drypoints he could not remove
because I had paid him a few shillings for them.

Within the year he was dead;
I did not even know that he was ill.
I did not hear of this for several months,
and now, with others dead who knew him,
I do not know if anyone else remembers him.

I had learnt that it was not
the printing of the poem
which had annoyed him
but where it had been printed,
a circumstance I could not comprehend,
for most young poets like to see their verses
in print anywhere.

Framed now a long time,
his print of the ponderous sow
is among the few pictures in my possession
which I always keep somewhere at hand,
but the last line of the poem
is his best epitaph:
'the hen that laid away'.

THE TEST

Sped by the British Council
to study museum techniques,
the gentle little Indian
with the large dark mournful eyes
(thirty-two, curator, married, three children,
from a museum in Bengal)
paced the public galleries,
inspecting the picture store, the print room,
the workroom, the back stairs, the lift,
and returned to my office
where I waited for his questions.

One problem he raised with some seriousness:
'You have Indian workers employed here.
Were there no Englishmans waiting?'
I replied that after interviews
the best applicants were appointed,
those most suitable for our purpose,
carefully conscious that I made
no reference to race or colour.

He nodded a tepid approval,
his large dark eyes still mournful,
showing less enthusiasm
than I had expected.
'Did you not give them a taste?'
A split second permitted me
to grasp that he pronounced the word 'test'
with a diphthong.

Then he continued with deliberation:
'In these things there is often backdoorism.
A man may have a letter from the Minister.
If you make him a test
this is an advantage.'

Being Irish, from a tribal society myself,
I appreciated the difficulty, recalling
the scrum of backdoorists I had known
at home, both cunning and clumsy,
and thought that if this brown little man
had come to learn modern techniques
he certainly knew the old ones.

CALLING ON PEADAR O'DONNELL AT DUNGLOE

I remember striding through the August twilight
along a narrow lane from house to house;
a crowd of lads were hurling loud and shouting,
and once a black calf gave a mournful cry.

It seemed the long track round that we had taken
over a rough ground higher than the bog.
Three fields away foam topped the distant breakers.
Storm's opposition flogged us both dog-tired.

Then darkness dropped, and window after window
offered no trace of colour. We went on,
slow pacing now, and painfully admonished
by plaintive gulls above the ocean's din.

We reached the three small houses and the gate
which faced the place the drive swung to the right.
Now far too late to make our call we argued.
There was no blink of light in any room.

But halfway up the drive we glimpsed the writer
still working in the garden with his wife;
I shouted and he straightened up to answer,
and in the gloom his fine head glimmered white.

THE BALLAD

When I sought out the Cottage Hospital
basking in sun beside the village stream,
the matron absent, a smiling sister
led me upstairs to my aged woman
sitting by her bed,
her two companions prone;
one slept, the other stirred and smiled.

My aged woman peered, puckering her lids.
Loudly I named myself and when we met last.
She recognised but asked
had I been bearded then.
Sure of her ground now, slipped to Robbie Burns,
great-hearted poet, and one piece he wrote
about his latter end, addressing his Maker,
better than all.

Then with a smile, 'I put you
in the same room with him and those I like.
My memory's all in tatters. Here and there
I have my cameos. You wrote a poem
about the sunrise over the bay.'
That was nearly forty years ago,
part of a long poem on the place.
I knew her slightly then, a small woman,
behind the counter of her shop;
recalled the nature of our talk;

with frequent visits after
becoming my Sibyl of the Glens.

Proud but embarrassed,
I turned the talk to something else,
a topic I had tried with elderly folk
where a response was possible,
and phrased the title of that ballad
current in her youth among her kind;
I have called up frequent echoes
in places I'd thought likely,
those now over pension age
who share memories of our national past.

She knew it as I had expected;
the opening lines came easily, then limped;
then confidence found wings,
brisk verses followed, faltered . . .
a prose account filled in the missing lines.
Hands before her face,
she blamed her tattered memory;
'You can't put your own words for the poet's words,
for his words are the poem.'

Then snatching at a run the final stanzas,
lifted her white face and smiled,
took my hand, thanked me for calling,
for having made her day.
Humbly, moved, I left,
now more than her day made.

THE CLINK OF RHYME

A student here, from Ballintoy,
a laughing fair-haired country boy,
felt now and then fit to employ
his Sunday leisure
in turning verses to enjoy
poetic pleasure.

I showed him how with little cost
his thought was better far engrossed
in the blank verse of Robert Frost,
and as a duck

takes to the burn in which it's tossed
        he tried his luck.

The lines came supple, steady, clear,
true to the country atmosphere.
There was no flowery discourse here
        but honest phrasing;
and half a dozen times that year
        he sought my praising.

But once he read his verse o'er
to some oul' callaigh at her door
who had a name in three or four
        townlands for rhyming,
that he might hear how much he'd score
        by her skilled timing.

Awhile she listened to him dumb,
with not so much as Haw or Hum;
then, sucking at her toothless gum,
        she said, 'I think
I'd rather hae the thochts that come
        in lines that clink.'

FOLK CUSTOM

Our foolish neighbour farther up the hill,
already twice before the Bench, again
has earned more trouble with his private still
he wore a pad to like a well-trod lane,
running his neck into law's ready noose,
who only made poteen for table use.

It had been something if he'd flashed the stuff
at every céilí round the countryside
and from the eager orders cleared enough
to pay his debts or gain a second bride,
but he'd no better wit nor more to do
than stretch on Sundays full, along the bru.

It's not his misdemeanour that affronts;
we all have careless follies to confess;
be up before the Petty Sessions once,

and not a man will rate a haet the less:
it's that we know of smarter men that wrought
at stilling all their days were never caught.

MACDONNELL'S QUESTION

Raging on Duneneeny while the smoke
spired from the thatches round the boat-thronged bay –
across the treacherous sound of Corrie Vrecken,
where Brechan's fifty currachs were all swamped –
the bay of Rathlin, Raghery of the Oaks,
he stormed along the cliff-turf impotent,
while children, women, cattle, stores of grain
flared to the zenith by the English torch
and cannonry of Norris, Essex' man –
the cruel Drake was of that company;
the great Queen heard of it at Kenilworth –
this Sorley Boy, this Charley Yellowhair,
of Clan MacDonnell chief, Lord of the Route,
sixth son of Alexander of Cantyre,
vast troubler of that great Queen's deputies –
he could not write his name, but touched the quill
his secretary penned despatches with.

And where Sir Arthur Chichester kneels down,
facing his kneeling lady in that high tomb
in Carrickfergus, old St Nicholas' Church,
over the smaller effigy of Sir John
praying his pardon, MacDonnell stopped to gape –
James, son of Sorley, knighted by James the Sixth
a brave, courageous, hospitable fellow –
'Whar gat ye your heid, Sir John? I mind the day
I clippt it aff ye, when you'd hae ambushed me.'
Those footnote addicts, the historians,
assert this is some legendary fiction,
offering proper dates as positive proof,
and anyhow James never spoke in Scots
but in the Gaelic of the Western Isles.
I do not care. My heart takes it as true;
there's little justice enough in our history.

THE HOUSE ON THE HILL

This house built tall, half burnt and raised again
here on the round crest of an Antrim brae,

has earthed the dreams and schemes of many men
and watched far more than seasons pass this way.

For us then first the chief who turned his coat
when the old faith endured a cruel shock,
and in the dripping wood not too remote
a hunted priest served Mass upon a rock;
and with the loyal lining now displayed
new words were found to chip into the stone
that covers where the Papist bones were laid,
the details, dates and heraldry his own.

So the rough Gaels became fine gentlemen,
the place marked clearly on the coaching chart;
the gothic lodge, the drive, the high-walled garden,
the pillared gates bespoke this change of heart.
Then, by degrees of breeding's planned ascent,
the new age beckons, old clan shadows lift;
the flushed, wigged master drives to parliament,
or sets his wit against the wit of Swift.

The elder son succeeds, secure in state
pores over those long letters from Bengal,
stands bravely up to Grattan in debate
or prunes his roses on the trellised wall.
His two well-dowried daughters married soon,
into wide paddocks, artificial lakes.
This is Augustan peace. It is high noon.
The wager's now for ever-rising stakes.

Along the steep lane where the gate lodge broods
beneath the thorn, beside the shattered gate,
where only a lost traveller intrudes
or some snare-setting local working late,
there is a cottage just above the spring,
where a man standing by his workshop door
will, if you wait, remember everything
that happened to the big house long before.

He can recall when he was just a child
what older people told him of the place;
Castle, they called it, with great coaches styled
where trailing dresses swept with haughty grace.
He shuffles back among his eighty years

to times the house changed hands, from whom to whom;
the timber merchants' French carved screen, he hears,
is still the wonder of the drawing room,
left with much else after he sold it to
an admiral who bore a famous name –
it was a kinsman with another crew
whose rebel-death gave all that family's fame.

The wheel spins faster now. They come and go;
the Glasgow publican whose lucky bet
brought horses, grooms, till with a sudden blow
the moneylenders seized all for his debt.
It seems the house lay under some old curse,
for once fire gutted upper rooms inside,
just when the painters and the plasterers
had made all trim and tidy for a bride.

The man who bought it planned to renovate it,
planted new trees or had some cut away,
proved it too big, remotely situated,
its heavy upkeep more than he could pay.
The next, on city architect's report,
raised a blind wall to balance the left wing,
with castellated turrets, tennis court,
but never stayed to see a second spring.

There was a spell when what was once a home
became a lit hotel with board and sign,
and tweedy golfers, fishermen, would come
in motor roaring up the lane to dine;
and the rooms tangled ancient memories
with gramophones and jazz, all out of key
with gracious gestures and grave courtesies,
laced with gay Dublin Castle repartee.

The Church then purchased it. The lily pond
with squat Greek gods like opera-set or play,
the gravelled courtyard where the four-in-hand
brought word of Bunkershill or Castlereagh,
is seldom vexed by any other stir
than that of nuns whose dignity and grace,
whose hooded forms, lend quiet character
to what was once a change-tormented place.

Although the fabulous slab may still be found
amid the old graveyard's tussocked grass and stone
in that high house, a landmark miles around,
the Gael's faith slippers back to claim its own.

THIS ANTRIM AIR IN SUMMER

This country's air is cleansing to the heart;
Atlantic-fresh, and washed with spray and rain,
it leaps off leaves and blusters down the lane;
in frolic gusto sometimes spins apart
to pluck at peat-reek, bearing in its stride
that friendly tang across a sheltered glen;
whips flax-dam's ripples to a thrusting tide,
or heads the drifting swan's-down back again;
shaped by the running lines of crag and hill,
combs tossed bog-cotton tufts, lifts flagging crow,
stripping cloud's corner, clears the bare blue sky,
or, drunk on hawthorn, hoards the heat until,
startled at sudden thunder stumping by,
it cuffs the thistle with a rocking blow.

AUTUMN GALE

All day a strong gale rushed north-west by north,
herding stripped leaves in corners, wiping dry
the bare wet lanes, and over crumbled earth
spreading a crisper surface, scudding by
and flicking skirts of shadow on the ground,
till breath was an adventure bravely borne,
despite the bitter winter's forecast found
in crowded berries on the whistling thorn.

Then as the sun dropped down, his tilted light
raking the rocking treetops, the black crows
whirling in gusts were each that moment bright
against the wind's face as they sank or rose,
as this which seemed some March-fresh interval
played havoc with the season's dying fall.

THE OLD MILL-RACE

From the high stream the water poured and forced
an unstaunched torrent through the gaping boards

which fenced in better times the streams apart;
but now it struck the lower constant river
with such a jet there shot a fountainhead,
a crest of spray, which carried to the light
a bush of blossom white like a summer tree
wearing its golden tinctures of the sun
a trembling moment on its quivering twigs;
as suddenly becoming, these withdrawn,
a snowy bush that shivered with chill flakes.
O bush of hawthorn blossom, bush of snow,
holding frail shape of ever-shifting atoms,
must I spin also, lost, into the sea?

THE DESCENT

We slipped and slithered down the thick-timbered hill,
snatched branch which snapped like tinder, broke away,
struck heel on leaf imprinted flat on clay
which sledded us precipitate, until
fist fumbled tussock on a crumbling sill
and we dropped depths we'd not have dared in play,
groping, with twig-whipped face, through chequered day,
dislodging stones which bounded, rolled, fell still.

With aching ankles, sinews wrenched in fright,
stained fingers, palms streaked by grey, yielding moss,
we thrust through the last thicket and stood free
and, safe on sod secure, remarked the height
we'd lurched down, cancelled out, amazed to see
high pool of sky a heron soars across.

THE SOUTERRAIN

We cut the sod. We dug the heavy mould
to bare the stones which stronger folk have laid
over their tunnelled dwelling. Pick and spade
reminded shoulder, forearm, we grew old,
save for the lad whose easy gestures told
that this was something near his daily trade.
Absolved by age, the nodding farmer made
a ready bet we'd crack no crock of gold.

When the large stone was scraped, was bared to light
and shifted as the soil began to spill
in sandglass trickle slowly out of sight,
as the dark passage beckoned, deep and still,
for a hushed spell no crock of gold could buy
we brinked the silent pit of mystery.

PALIMPSEST

I pace these lanes where progress and decay
scribble wry palimpsest across the scene;
the raw byre gable shoulders concrete-clean
where once a reeking midden seeped away;
the tractor treads have sliced into the clay
but left a middle track still clover green;
once homesteads, now those wallsteads bulge and lean,
and nettles flower where children used to play.

And all those old men gone, those slow old men,
whose thumbs were thick with skills I could not share,
at loanen-end or gate, shall not again
foregather, nor at church door or the fair,
the shepherd, scythesman, blacksmith, carpenter,
as life drains surely down the tree-dark glen.

THE CHRISTMAS RHYMERS, BALLYNURE, 1941

an old woman remembers

The Christmas Rhymers came again last year,
wee boys with blackened faces at the door,
not like those strapping lads that would appear,
dressed for the mummers' parts in times before,
to act the old play on the kitchen floor;
at warwork now or fighting overseas,
my neighbours' sons; there's hardly one of these
that will be coming back here any more.

I gave them coppers, bid them turn and go;
and as I watched that rueful regiment
head for the road, I felt that with them went
those songs we sang, the rhymes we used to know,
heartsore imagining the years without
The Doctor, Darkie, and Wee Divil Doubt.

ENCOUNTER WITH R.J. WELCH, THE ANTIQUARY

On tram's top deck – in nineteen twenty-three –
as I sat reading in my usual way –
the passing townscape known familiarly,
there was no need to let attention stray –
a bearded man who sat beside me peered
at what I read. I smirked in some unease,
a Sitwell book, *Bucolic Comedies.*
His curiosity seemed undeterred.

'What are you reading?' Coolest of replies,
I showed him all the title page declares.
'Bucolic has to do with country things.
Reading in trams will ruin your young eyes.'
And with that warning suddenly he springs
out of his seat and rushes down the stairs.

THE HOUSE AT BALLYHOLME

I

This was my grannie's house, far different
from ours at home, much farther from the road,
with wide bay windows spaciously endowed,
a long path to the door, which bravely bent
right round the house, with gardens front and rear,
that at the front in summer sure to please
with scent and colour lavish everywhere,
that round the back half grass, half apple trees.

Yet from that richness my prime picture comes
with lion's cage, with caravan and clown,
with prancing horses, loud bassoons and drums,
as down those jolting pebbles to the gate
my father's shoulder bore my infant weight
when Duffy's Circus flourished into town.

II

I knew that place but never felt it mine,
paid frequent visits, often holidayed,
and lived there half a year when I was nine;
on those front steps my mitching was betrayed.

In spring I think of that laburnum tree
whose pods were poison; it was sinister;
that small back garden orchard was for me
a magic island, I was Crusoe there.

Within the walls my wits hold little more
than private cupboards where my grannie'd hide
and fumble over secrets hers alone,
red kitchen tiles, scrubbed table, the back door
at which the black dog Jim would twitch and moan,
mourning his master when our uncle died.

MY WIDOWED MOTHER

Ten years a widow, my old mother's mind
became fragmented; first the box played tricks
with horses in the hall; then she would find
comedians' features quickly intermix
with those of ancient friends, and once she thought
I was her husband, callous and inhuman
when quite regardless of her rights I'd brought
under her roof a young and comely woman.

We drove her to the Mental Hospital,
passing a new-built chapel on the way,
which noting, she considered 'well-behaved';
a shrewd remark, scant evidence at all
her envied choice of words had gone astray
which since my childhood held my wits enslaved.

BANDSTAND

Remark the empty bandstand in the park,
bird-droppings on the iron balustrade
and dead leaves in the corners. After dark
when the bell rings and rangers lock the gate
the lilting games the laughing children played
are little sleepy ghosts, and hardly wait
till the last footfall dies before they find
a quiet twig to hammock their repose,
and the quick birds are nested with their kind;
but sometimes when the wind gusts up and blows
dark clouds across and off the rocking moon,

between the gusts, in lulls within the storm,
you'll hear by chance a low drum-major tune
from shadowy men in moon-pale uniform.

FOR ROBERTA IN THE GARDEN

I know when you are at your happiest,
kneeling on mould, a trowel in your glove;
you raise your eyes and for a moment rest;
you turn a young-girl's face, like one in love.

Intent, entranced, this hour, in gardening,
surely to life's bright process you belong.
I wonder, when you pause, you do not sing,
for such a moment surely has its song.

THE HEDGEHOG: FOR R.

With shrewd snout the hedgehog
snuffles across the lawn
over the long shadows
of stilted hollyhock;
unpredicted presence,
its purposes unguessed,
threading a tiny life,
heart pulsing, hungry, warm,
slack spines dragging against
the prospering clover,
unresting, out of reach.

Its secret triggers set,
it seemed a symbol
for all timid strangeness,
all shy wildness, alert
to defend itself by
privacy, withdrawal;
a fellow creature lurked
within your heart and mine.

AT THE NEWSAGENT'S

I

At about 8.15 a.m.
a police reservist called

at the newsagent's
for his morning paper.

When he came out
he met a spray of bullets
which killed him and wounded
his companion waiting in the car.

One of the bullets cut a hole
in the upper panel
of the glass and metal door
which had closed behind him.

I go to this newsagent's
several times a week
to pick up my magazines
and buy pipe tobacco.

And every time
I push open that door,
though the shattered glass
has since been replaced,

I think fleetingly
of the bullet hole;
this, I suppose, might be considered
'an objective correlative'.

II

Colleagues of the murderer
or murderers – I do not know
how many guns were then fired –
captured, sentenced, imprisoned, insisted
that they were 'political prisoners';
and to assert the status they claimed
neither washed, shaved, nor cut their hair;
they wore no clothes except a blanket,
and smeared their cell walls with their shit.
This exercise was known as 'On the Blanket'
or 'The Dirty Protest'.

Some months later
ten of the younger prisoners

starved themselves to death
to sustain the protest.

None of these happenings,
widely communicated through
the popular media,
even flickers, however faintly,
among the reflecting grimaces
in that glass door.

THE BOMBED PUBLIC HOUSE

This was the pub where I once took that playwright
famous for broadcast brawl but witty sober.
He warned me going in he had no money,
and took a single pint of several offered.

This was the pub where I was called to meet
the foreign poet; when he asked my age
he kissed me on both cheeks and called me father.

This was the pub where the small bald barman
always called me Doctor or Professor
on my infrequent visits, being neither.

When this interior is restored, re-covered
with fashionable surfaces and textures,
will any mirror echo such reflections
or cushioned corner's covers bounce them back?

EXECUTIVES THIRD TIER

The morning after the seminar
I met a colleague whose glance I had caught
in that maze of programme budgeting,
input analysis and cost-effectiveness.

So, knowing my man, I stopped to enquire:
How are your parameters this morning?
Nearly frozen off. And your infrastructure?
I haven't quantified it yet.

And the two elderly Luddites
strode off to their separate departments,

smiling serenely, each caressing
the spanner in his pocket.

ADMINISTRATION

He is a knowing fellow who devotes
his busy pen to brisk peremptory notes:
Your Observations re; Consult; Discuss.
You should not think such scripts ridiculous;
our age's judgement is, he who creates
most memoranda, best administrates.
So paste these on the broad blind, slat by slat;
the battle orders of the bureaucrat.

BY AIR TO BIRMINGHAM ON A MID-JUNE EVENING

Lough Beg a sungleam, little Coney Island,
the Irish hedges powdered still
with blossom on blackthorn.

We have shot up
too quickly for my wits to draw
the comforting webs of association;
for the moment I take what my eyes offer.

The Unseen God,
who so has hoisted us out of time
and disengaged us from reality,
has already promised us
Speed, Altitude, Arrival back in time,
and foretold the weather of our coming.

Out of the mist over the city valley –
because of that mist pervasive
and the paths our past took,
I have never once been able to comprehend
my city from above and fix an image for it;
walking through, it breaks into fragments of existence,
mine and others I have knowledge of –
we cut through to a glacial landscape,
passing in sunlight over a near-white floor,
not brilliant white, not painter's gesso panel,

but rather grey of fleece, of sunwarm fleece,
a furrowed field of snow, its contours padded
with furrows of rounded clods
by some gigantic ploughshare tossed,
a stiff ocean of thumb-puttied waves –
I once had a ship model in a glass box
with painted putty waves, their crests
in series flecked with white for foam.

Here free by now
from flight's involvement, subjugation to
abrupt event, engined beyond me,
riding easy, the mind unbelts, unclenches,
and moves over experience
smoothly, slotting in sensation.

Our angle changes, the landscape tilts
as sometimes land spills off the board;
and its edges seem
like teasled wool, like tufts on barbs.
Then as the cloud spins thin
and drifts away in wisps, we glimpse
the sea below, the actual ocean,
wrinkled – Tennyson's word. I observe
only what I have words for – with tiny puckers plucked,
which indicate
small vessels urgent tugged from port to port.

A wavering line of sand fringes green and pewter –
when I see a shoreline I always think
of invaders running keels in,
leaping breast-high, thigh-deep,
Greeks, Vikings, Romans mostly;
a farm cart in Sicily showed
Caesar's legions in that act;
invading Britain, the coarse letters said.
Like others from the East, like all others;
but my folk landed dryshod.

Cloud draws its cover over.
Above, a level sky like any sky
over a plain. There are two skies,
earth's sky and ours:
the red horizon smudged, frayed,
against the west.

Down through mist.
Above, a band of gold
receding:
a map of roads below
of a strange solid country.

Out of the daylight now
lamps sparkle like stars
in an inverted firmament –
I've waited years to use that word –
the constellations too regular to be true.

Propellers rainbow:
the dark blades emerge
through flickering shutters.
Streetlights and dotted scribbles.
Close-meshed suburbs glow.
Long spangled roads belt over the dark land,
with here and there a blob of bloody light;
and tiny insects
with smears of light ahead, astern,
pulse and pause along dim arteries.

Our moth is gathered into
the airport's web and tent of light.
We replace the magazine
in its elastic net . . .
The engine alters.
Lettered lights instruct.

We are on the point
of returning
to ourselves.

ROTTERDAM

Out of the grey wet sand
the bright concourse of tall buildings,
neon-garlanded, with floodlit fountains,
thrusts away the vast anonymous sky.

The well-dressed shop windows
are full of expensive consumer goods.

A bastion of metal cargo-containers
has been erected along the dockside.

And in the small moat outside
the Boymans-Van Beuningen Museum
a gentle breeze wafts a blue plastic bucket
and a large red ball into a corner.

TO THE PEOPLE OF DRESDEN

Your famous city stood, plucked out of time,
a dream-pavilion set in porcelain,
where the masked dancers paced in stately mime
with grace no later age can now attain.
Then towards disaster all seemed swiftly drawn,
your cruel firestorm fuelling men's fears,
to shards all shattered, all those dancers gone,
in the dark Europe of my middle years.

But now that darkness breaks, and I have stood,
shouldered with thousands in your Altmarkt Square,
to swear my silent oath of brotherhood,
and join my lonely prayer to your vast prayer
that by the common will of common men
no war shall ever darken day again.

WINTER PARK

All growth securely grappled to the ground,
by frost-crisp paths I make my usual round;
and at the circular bed where roses stood
that now are stubbed to spiky stumps of wood
a young man raking takes the time to toss
some praise for hardy weather as I pass;
I call assent but slow no step to tell
that my own husbandry is going well.

ON THE PRESERVATION OF WORK SHEETS

It should not matter how I shaped my lines,
hit on a cadence; shuffled adjectives,
replaced a showy word with one that gives

a truer texture, or, precise, defines
a signal smudged by clumsy countersigns,
or altered phrase to mark a change of gear
when word proposing word at once combines
to make some level of intention clear.

Should I expose each shutter of my thought,
each accident of memory or of sense,
through which the structure to completion brought
is seen as weapon forged in self-defence?
No more absurd than that I'd hoard and store
the fringe of filings on the workshop floor.

DISSERTATION I

Tomorrow with his notes a man will come
enquiring when I wrote that verse or this,
where such and such an image sprouted from,
if I concur with his analysis,
the day, the hour, what infantile event,
and in what order should these carry weight;
so, explicating what I must have meant,
I'll flick my notebooks through to check the date.

I'll give what help I can. But humbly, pleased
that anyone should show the least concern
for words I named that secret springs released
out of the shadowy culverts of my mind,
eager for what I've sought so long to learn,
and anxious too for what we both may find.

DISSERTATION II

At least, with the dentist,
I am aware of the drill
spinning endlessly,
though the preliminary needle
cut the threads
of consequential pain.

But with the research student
in the next room, reading
the letters, the manuscripts,

I certainly feel no bone-tremor;
yet anxiety travels
along nerves not used to traffic.

I can rinse and spit out
the scorched gritty particles
but though my bone-structure is strong,
I bleed too easily.

IN RECOLLECTION OF DRUMCLIFFE, SEPTEMBER 1948

The years spin quicker since that day I stood
to watch the poet's coffin take to earth
a second time, in kinship's neighbourhood
which gave his proud imagination birth;
and my clenched homage knelt to cross and tower,
to those dark famous hills which, till time ends,
must wear the shapes conferred by vatic power,
the power that fleshed our legends and his friends.

Although I could not share his thoughts, and choose
instead a faith in man's progressive range,
finding his stance and temper alien,
I carry thence what I shall never lose,
his chanted cadence, and the right to change
the masks with which I face my fellow men.

FIRST HONEY

My mind drifts back to those far days that bred
the heart-light lyric leaping off the thought
some flicking twig or wing provoked unsought
and easily nested in a rhyme-rife head.
Now strangely, from youth's hopes and hazards free,
the verses come much slower, with a tone
closer to speech than song, their quality
of time's four seasons, this grave last alone.

Pulse-proven, wiser, maybe, but the mood
once lyric bright is now diffused and grey,
each blurred sun rises on a briefer day;
not green braird thrusting but rain-darkened corn;

so I look back with ready gratitude
to that first honey won from blossomed thorn.

RETREADED RHYMES

Henceforth my slow wits I must only spend
to phrase affection or to mourn a friend;
to state the convolutions of my thought
in quiet verse deliberately wrought,
leaving the coloured crags' romantic line
for humbler acre fairly mapped as mine;
stranger to passion, never strongly moved
by those emotions use has not approved;
responsive to the year's flow, spring to fall,
saluting winter at the end of all . . .

So ran my programme forty years ago,
in safe iambics, sotto voce, slow;
and since the butts are close, the circles wide,
I've kept on target, and am satisfied
when I recall behind the placid verse
a man still stands whose attitude declares
his loyalty to hope, unquenched belief,
despite the incidence of age or grief,
in men's rare-hinted possibility
of being just, compassionate and free.

I struck these verses also in a set
of plodding lines which offer comfort yet;
though pill-propelled, unsteady in my gait,
and conscious daily of my mortal state,
they sing their sense for ever in my head:
O windblown grass upon the mounded dead,
O seed in crevice of the frost-split rock,
the power that fixed your root shall take us back,
though endlessly through aeons we are thrust
as luminous or unreflecting dust.

LINES FOR A DEAD ALDERMAN

Justice is done in the end,
the rascal who had his day,
to party and prejudice friend,

lodged in non-partisan clay.
As the mourners drive away
they leave that bundle of lies
to the earthworms' enterprise.

But, Lord, it is long to wait
till the wrong that that man did
and the hurt born of his hate
lies under the coffin lid;
the earth may never be rid
of that wrong this side of time
if I let it tarnish my rhyme.

ST STEPHEN'S DAY

St Stephen's Day, the air is warm,
fair, early prelude to the spring,
though finches pick at withered haws
and stiff-necked swans beat leaden wing.

The old men bundled in their coats
creep out to greet the peeping sun,
as if, like jewel-headed toads,
they'd splintered winter's flinty stone.

from

THE DAY OF THE CORNCRAKE

POEMS OF THE NINE GLENS

1984

THE GENTLE BUSH

The gentle bush beside the well
of leaf and berry now is bare;
but you must let the neighbours tell,
with sceptic smile, of antics there.
It does not look an ancient tree:
most likely 'twas a passing bird
that dropped the seed unwittingly.
The man who piped the overflow,
and stepped the stones, and fenced the well,
must know if any man may know
but what he knows he does not tell.
Yet if you should, by lucky chance,
talk with him while the buckets fill,
observe his searching, anxious glance,
and with what quiet, furtive skill
he'll twine and weave the twigs in place
that none hang down to snap or break;
yet not a flicker on his face
admits it's for the gentry's sake.

FREEHOLD AND OTHER POEMS

FREEHOLD

I FEATHERS ON TURF

Now my October with the yellow leaf
spirts like the spring the sapflow of my grief,
for by the calendar I overtake
my father's years. The orphaned minutes make
my slow thought graver, my ambitious mind
content with less, more tolerant and kind
the words and gestures that unchecked before
gave angle to my noisy shadow. For
a purpose moulds me to its patient shape
that I must reach and measure, nor escape
along the random freshets of my youth,
a tempered channel narrowed to the truth
of human love, of quality defined
by the proved limits of a mortal mind;
a mind, the slave of time and place and chance,
that seeks a law for its continuance,
if not as individual, compact
of form and posture, feeling, thought and act,
at any rate, a thread of growing stuff
which lives because its nature's that of life,
not seven decades' span, but life that sends
its rippled circles to unmeasured ends.

I went again where I had found delight
in dawn's conjecture, where the strokes of light
woke, out of cloud, the known familiar place,
the fields, the trees, the river, and the pace
conditioned by them to a leisured grace.

Not I alone, but also one with me
whose voice and handclasp double all I see;
and now more dear since fewer claim my love,
and stemmed affection, urgently to prove
its undiminished power, seeks to give
a richer texture to the life we live,

so shot with chance, so perilously spent
on the flawed ice of mortal accident.

We'd walked these roads before with quick delight
at tilt of roof-line or design of gate,
bright smears of light on Garron, or on the sea,
and how the wind's remembered by the tree,
naming the wild flowers, watching from the rocks
the diving cormorants, and the busy flocks
of dunlin landing where the bog-brown Dall
cuts through the seashore with a lazy scrawl,
and leaves a mounded tongue of sand whereon
the patriarchal heron stands alone.

And having gone back to the city's grey
autumnal gloom, the roaring crowded day,
the winter evenings with the curtained light,
and the mad engines thumping through the night,
we knew that from that gentle interval
rich moments had returned at words' recall,
spoken or read, or when the mind was caught
adrift and idle from the leash of thought.

I've long had witness certain images –
bare country phrases, old men's memories,
worn hafts of axes, cottage ornaments,
tea canisters, old bindings, potted plants,
cloud colours, whorls of shell or stranded weed,
feathers on turf or gaping husks of seed –
mixed with the figures that my meshy brain
must in its knots and tangled loops retain,
can, when the hand is ready, prompt again
the quiet verses that have strength to give
some lasting reason why I like to live.

But what seemed always underpinned by doubt
was that, when beating showers had flattened out
our footsteps from the mud, and when the land
wore no more track of us than tide-washed sand,
one shred should linger, hint or breath or touch,
above the roads and rocks beloved by each;
that fisherman with one more line to throw
or pausing farmer glancing up from plough

might even recall a word of all we said
or sometimes think he saw us on the road.

We came again to see them stook the rows
up the steep glenside, where the scythesman mows
and the boy poles the toppling grain aside
that it fall rightly in the binders' stride.
We sought them at the crowded shippens where
the muttered warning kept the bargain fair,
and the gaunt lad drove back his black-faced flock
to the brown slope of tangled grass and rock;
but we were lonely still, unskilled to reach
across the thorny hedge of thought and speech
to the slow wisdom of the older way,
mere gapers idling through a holiday,
irrelevant as trail of smoke that shows
to men afield that still the ocean's traffic flows.

Some did remember, not with eagerness,
but with a friendly signal none the less,
such as one makes to those we're pleased to know
are still afloat on life's grey tidal flow,
but need not hear, because they have no use
for any of our unemphatic news.

Only the wild things, fuchsia, haw and hip,
admitted us to their companionship,
and proved to anxious eye and tongue anew
what bragging memory had claimed as true;
and the grave gannets in the choppy bay
gave their involved and rhythmical display,
as if, proud actors, they enjoyed our awe,
though not a wingbeat hinted that they saw.

The crowded gulls upon the spit of sand,
black-headed, common, herring, greater and
the lesser black-backed, facing out to sea,
stood round to be admired, then leisurely
made demonstration flourishes, taking off,
circling and settling in the swaying trough
of storm-brown water, or behind the spit
where the smooth river's cut a lake to fit
its bunkered course. Along the steep-dug sides
pied wagtails jerked between the wrack-marked tides,

and strayed rooks jostled, blacker in that light
than stirring mid the treetop stars of night.

But there was one we missed although we looked
in every elbow of the river, crooked
by bank of sand or bunker, that proud one,
the solemn heron always seen alone.
Affronted now we looked for him in vain,
and felt the poorer lacking his disdain.

So, ranging farther with a combing stride,
we sought new paths to key our slackened pride,
traced on the map the promise of the ground
and richer shapes, unhinted textures found.

Then, at the glenhead, up by Orra Lodge,
a gutted shell now, we'd the luck to dodge
the great black downpour that had threatened us
since an hour back we left MacCormick's house,
the farm at Brockaghs, with prophetic squalls
we stalked and hid from by the roofless walls
of an old cowshed, under a stone bridge,
in spiked discomfort of the last thorn hedge,
beside a turfstack, till the last dry spell
lured us unsheltered, cool and walking well
to the bare fenceless road. We'd hardly time
to find the shepherd's door shut and to climb
over the smashed porch-slab into the dry
wrecked safety of the Lodge, when the black sky
came down upon us, wiping out the world
as the mist's groping fingers caught and coiled
round peak and turfstack thrusting down the glen.

The battered husk wore evidence of men,
the hearth wrenched out, the boards prised up and gone,
the roof bare slates and rafters, the walls bare stone:
and resting grateful on a tilting plank,
we lapsed to silence, and the moment shrank
slow from my senses till I was no more
a timid creature tangled in a world at war,
but a free man set out of time and place
for whom event was braked to walking pace
that mind could measure, handle and assess,
dismiss from blessing or restrain to bless;

and in that moment's gasp, that mood intense,
a whirling focus of experience,
I knew with more than each thought-smothered sense.

That symbol holds. Although the year has run
to its grey ebb beneath the feeble sun,
low in the sky, a chill and pallid disc.
That house this world we know, yet in the husk
a war-purged passion stirs. That house my own
grief-gutted heart; the doorpost overthrown
when that firm pillar of the household fell,
and, with it, much that made life durable.
For though no angel then unsheathed his word
bright as the lightning, though I overheard
no distant spheres reverberating spin,
and had no vision with a wider span
than my lame thought could grasp as once before,
yet that stark symbol and that blessed hour
is, in some nature, bound and watershed
between the man I now am and the lad
I grew from, superseded; now, at last,
this is a wiser self, though surely cast
of a compacter substance, finding truth
in shards and rubble he'd not tamper with.

That symbol holds; a beacon in the mind
that lights the forward step, and yet behind
throws sharper and more searching beam upon
the way I'd travelled but had scarcely known.
So, now at leisure, when the teeming year
lurches across the lettered calendar,
I seek to set in ordered rhythmic line
the values I discover now are mine,
though these blurred couplets cannot but deny
the shifting textures and the subtle play
of overtone and colour that are the life
of these flat statements and their valid proof.

II THE LONELY HEART

My father was a city schoolmaster,
for forty years acclimatised to air
stale with hot breath, wet jerseys, chalk and crumbs,
in a tall building islanded in slums.

He schooled his chorus for the merry play
and led his grinning urchins up the hill
that five live senses might, united, fill
the smudgy symbols in the lesson book.
This was in the days before our fluent talk
was crammed with clichés cribbed from Homer Lane,
when the sworn totem was the falling cane.
His surly elders called him young and rash,
no teacher either, since he would not thrash,
for he'd no envy of the fat careers
that floated to success on tides of tears.

In all his ways a just and kindly man
who set his steps as if to some grave plan
for purposes beyond all argument;
if there were voices he did not recount
their orders, but continued in his part,
that secret warrant safe against his heart;
wrought hard and unequivocally stood
for quality of life and brotherhood,
without defiance, in all charity
towards those who in themselves were not yet free.

He sang old songs, and in his crowded days
had lifted baton in his Master's praise,
later content to span his octaves, though
he'd now and then rejoice in cello-bow;
with watercolours never more than fair
repeated themes with undiminished care;
played moderate golf on summer Saturdays,
and wrote reviews when he'd the urge to praise,
served on committees if he liked the cause,
but neither won nor wanted long applause;
spoke when chance granted, without eloquence,
warmly sincere, with gentle common sense,
for all that gave life richness and should again
be the accepted right of workingmen,
as he judged all men who are worth their salt.
If error seemed to triumph, then the fault
lay not in evil, but in ignorance,
and would come right in time. He looked askance
at angry theories set to overthrow
the good-mixed error at a single blow,
and counselled patience: those who have recourse

to force would find their own rash end in force:
and so he wore through life unblemished name,
lonely at heart and innocent of fame.

This written, I have told you nothing of
the greatest man of all the men I love;
his little jokes, his gestures, his affection
that shrank surprised behind his circumspection,
his gentle patience and his silences,
his scribbled notes and numbered summaries
forgot in pocket; and his joy when you
suddenly found that all the time he knew
what you by tedious thought had sorted out;
his quiet sense of being clear of doubt,
yet not dogmatic in the peace achieved;
he had no need to tell what he believed:
the vast and varied knowledge in his head,
though seldom seemed there leisure enough to read;
he rather learnt by breathing than intent,
and freely taking just as freely spent.

This was my father. I have understood
just how the meek, the merciful, the good,
possess the kingdom. And that fact is safe
from need of proof or danger of disproof.

This was my father. From his gentleness
that rose beyond success or unsuccess,
I know, though lonely, he was not alone,
and in this thronged world many another one
moves through the stir and stour unblemished too.
And when my faith in man is ebbing low,
I summon heart again at thought of him,
assured that goodness never wants a name.

For two dragged years a stricken man he lay,
when every hour was longer than he'd say;
all patiently enduring, he would take
stiff-fingered pen in hand for justice' sake.
And when his end was nearer than my thought
he rose and hobbled out to cast his vote
for honesty against that ribald clown
whose own hand clawed his frothy image down.
Yet though he lived and strove for brotherhood

some chilling ichor tincturing his blood
cast a remoteness round him to the end;
revered by hundreds, he had scarce a friend
to share the ultimate simplicities
that compass goodness with enduring peace.

Although well armoured by his innocence,
which was his firm defence
against life's endless frets and daily scores,
beneath that armour there were certain scars,
and I have known him hurt, though no complaint
was ever uttered. His remote restraint
I have no strength or will to imitate,
and those whose irking bondage makes them hate
the free man when they face him, makes them fear
the growing thing's live challenge, now and here,
shall find me rougher metal, till I win,
by time's kind mercy, his wise discipline.

In my best moments feeling justly proud,
I wait his smile and slow approving nod,
but suddenly I know he is not here,
and have small faith that he is anywhere,
and I must chalk the little victories
for life and art and human decencies
as if on blackboard in a public place,
for chance of sleeve or weather to efface,
and never know them radically defined
in the bright lens of his translucent mind.

I had known death before, my grandfather
stepped back from life, the one whose name I bear,
into the full sun of a summer day,
old, ripe and quiet, going on his way
to where his grey friends had already gone;
it seemed a thousand years to eighteen forty-one.

I was not sad, although between us two
more ties than those of blood his death withdrew.
He gave me much: he made me know my race,
filled out the empty names of man and place,
till, as the bright colours of a vivid eye
were painted over by rich memory,
I moved among the people of his mind:

his mother's parents, open-armed and kind
to the small orphan with his mother dead
from fever that the bitter famine bred;
his father, hook-nosed Mark, who packed his wares
in saddlebags and huxtered round the fairs;
the broad-brimmed elders, grave with yea and nay
as though each coming day were Judgment Day,
and the rash youngsters, sick with poverty,
who sought a fatter life beyond the sea,
and scrawled their spider's letters once a year
from the raw fenceposts of a new frontier.
These were his people, so he made them mine
by laying-on of hands, by word and sign;
a stubborn Irishry that would recall
the famine's curse, the farm that was too small,
yet with a faith protestant that denied
the hope of mercy to the papist side,
tongue-loose with stories of the Ninety-Eight,
yet proud the British Empire is so great,
despising royal pomp and rites of Rome,
but loving sashes, banners, fife and drum,
so tethered to antinomies it rocks
in seesaw straddle of a paradox.

Once in a seaside town with time to kill,
the windless winter-daylight ebbing chill,
the cafés shut till June, the shop blinds drawn,
only one pub yet open where a man
trundled his barrels off a dray with care,
and two men talking, small across the square,
I turned from broad street, down a red-brick row,
past prams in parlours and infrequent show
of thrusting bulbtips, till high steps and porch
and rigid statue signalised a church.
I climbed the granite past Saint Patrick's knees,
saw cross in stone, befingered, ringed with grease,
and water in a stoup with oily skin,
swung door on stall of booklets and went in
to the dim stained-glass cold interior
between low pews along a marble floor
to where the candles burned, still keeping pace
with ugly-coloured Stations of the Cross.
Two children tiptoed in and prayed awhile.
A shabby woman in a faded shawl

came hirpling past me then, and crumpled down,
crossing herself and mumbling monotone.

I stood and gazed across the altar rail
at the tall windows, cold and winter pale;
Christ and His Mother, Christ and Lazarus,
Christ watching Martha bustle round the house,
Christ crowned, with sceptre and a blessing hand.
I counted seven candles on the stand;
a box of matches of familiar brand
lay on a tray. It somehow seemed my right
to pay my penny and set up my light,
not to this coloured Christ nor to His Mother,
but single flame to sway with all the other
small earnest flames against the crowding gloom
which seemed that year descending on our time,
suppressed the fancy, smiled a cynic thought,
turned clicking heel on marble and went out.

Not this my fathers' faith: their walls are bare;
their comfort's all within, if anywhere.
I had gone there a vacant hour to pass,
to see the sculpture and admire the glass,
but left as I had come, a protestant,
and all unconscious of my yawning want;
too much intent on what to criticise
to give my heart the room to realise
that which endures the tides of time so long
cannot be always absolutely wrong;
not even with a friendly thought or human
for the two children and the praying woman.
The years since then have proved I should have stayed
and mercy might have touched me till I prayed.

For now I scorn no man's or child's belief
in any symbol that may succour grief
if we remember whence life first arose
and how within us yet that river flows;
and how the fabled shapes in dream's deep sea
still evidence our continuity
with being's seamless garment, web and thread.

O windblown grass upon the mounded dead,
O seed in crevice of the frost-split rock,

the power that fixed your root shall take us back,
though endlessly through aeons we are thrust
as luminous or unreflecting dust.

III TOWNLAND OF PEACE

Once in a showery summer, sick of war,
I strode the roads that slanted to Kilmore,
that church-topped mound where half the tombstones wear
my people's name; some notion drew me there,
illogical, but not to be ignored,
some need of roots saluted, some sought word
that might give strength and sense to my slack rein,
by this directed, not to lose again
the line and compass so my head and heart
no longer plunge and tug to drag apart.

Thus walking dry or sheltered under trees,
I stepped clean out of Europe into peace,
for every man I met was relevant
to the harsh clamour of my eager want,
gathering fruit, or leading horse uphill,
sawing his timber, measuring his well.
The crooked apple trees beside the gate
that almost touched the roadside with the weight
of their clenched fruit, the dappled calves that browsed
free in the netted sunlight and unhoused
the white hens slouching round the tar-bright sheds,
the neat-leafed damsons with the smoky beads,
the farm unseen but loud with bucket and dog
and voices moving in a leafy fog,
gave neither hint nor prophecy of change,
save the slow seasons in their circled range;
part of a world of natural diligence
that has forgotten its old turbulence,
save when the spade rasps on a rusted sword
or a child in a schoolbook finds a savage word.

Old John, my father's father, ran these roads
a hundred years ago with other lads
up the steep brae to school, or over the stile
to the far house for milk, or dragging the long mile
to see his mother buried. Every stride
with gable, gatepost, hedge on either side,
companioned so brought nearer my desire

to stretch my legs beside a poet's fire
in the next parish. As the road went by
with meadow and orchard, under a close sky,
and stook-lined field, and thatched and slated house,
and apples heavy on the crouching boughs,
I moved beside him. Change was strange and far
where a daft world gone shabby choked with war
among the crumpled streets or in the plains
spiked with black fire-crisped rafters and buckled lines,
from Warsaw to the Yangtze, where the slow-
phrased people learn such thought that scourge and blow
may school them into strength to find the skill
for new societies of earth and steel,
but here's the age they've lost.
                                        The boys I met
munching their windfalls, drifting homeward late,
are like that boy a hundred years ago,
the same bare kibes, the heirloom rags they show;
but they must take another road in time.
Across the sea his fortune summoned him
to the brave heyday of the roaring mills
where progress beckoned with a million wheels.

The bearded man who jolted in his cart
on full sack nodding, waking with a start,
giving his friendly answer to my call,
uncertain of the right road after all,
might have been he, if luck had let him stay
where no shrill hooters break across the day,
and time had checked its ticking. Had I passed
a woman by a gate, I should have paused
to crack about the year the Lough was hard
and safe as frozen bucket in the yard,
and fit to bear the revel and the feast
when merry crowds devoured the roasted beast
beneath the bright stars of a colder year
than any living man remembers here,
to ask if she had lost her mother too
from famine-fever, or if it were true
she bore my family name. There's scarce a doubt
she would have, or, at worst, have pointed out
a house whose folk did, for it's common there
as berries on the hedges anywhere.

I found my poet–parson and his fire
expecting me. When unobtrusive care,
that natural acceptance of a friend,
had eased my tired bones, and my weary mind
had stretched its knotted sinews, that still man
and his quick wife, the doctor, once again
confirmed intention, slowly making plain
that by the heart's blind wisdom I had found
my seeming-aimless feet on solid ground;
then, when good talk had brimmed my singing head,
the lamp, the shallow stairs, the friendly bed,
till chortling blackbird in the neighbour trees
woke me to sunshine and the cruising bees.

The next day, in the old cathedral town,
I saw my friend the painter, tall and brown,
his long skilled fingers on the handlebars,
weaving his high way through the close-parked cars.
I signalled, he dismounted leisurely.
The slow laconic words we always say
when we two meet were said again. We crossed
wide streets and narrow streets till we had passed
out of the town and over the old bridge,
above the sunken river thick with sedge.
He urged a detour to the rising lane
from which he'd made that drawing of the scene.
We stopped till I recalled, as best I could,
the bridge, the hedges and the skyline wood,
the squat cathedral tower, the headless mill,
as they'd been noted by his pencil's skill,
comparing his with earth's reality.
Resumed our journey then, our talk came free,
as each reported gay but urgently
what things he'd done worth doing, what he'd thought,
or read or heard, or what the times had brought
that showed once more how strangely parallel
the paths we find to life's rare miracle.
The long five miles of road to Killylea
held only half the things we had to say;
and once again the night was nearly gone
before the logs were ash and we were done.

Somehow that easy journey, every minute,
and every field and face and word within it,

not to be split or shredded line by line
to smooth equations easy to define,
has not the random shape of accident,
but the warm logic of a testament
by which since then my better moments move,
assured of certainties I need not prove.

Now and for ever through the change-rocked years,
I know my corner in the universe;
my corner, this small region limited
in space by sea, in the time by my own dead,
who are its compost, by each roving sense
henceforward mobilised in its defence,
against the sickness that has struck mankind,
mass-measured, mass-infected, mass-resigned.

Against the anthill and the beehive state
I hold the right of man to stay out late,
to sulk and laugh, to criticise or pray,
when he is moved, at any hour of day,
to vote by show of hands or sit at home,
or stroll on Sunday with a vasculum,
to sing or act or play or paint or write
in any mode that offers him delight.

I hold my claim against the mammoth powers
to crooked roads and accidental flowers,
to corn with poppies fabulously red,
to trout in rivers, and to wheat in bread,
to food unpoisoned, unpolluted air,
and easy pensioned age without a care
other than time's mortality must bring
to any shepherd, commissar, or king.

But these small rights require a smaller stage
than the vast forum of the nations' rage,
for they imply a well-compacted space
where every voice declares its native place,
townland, townquarter, county at the most,
the local word not ignorantly lost
in the smooth jargon, bland and half alive,
which wears no clinging burr upon its sleeve
to tell the ground it grew from, and to prove
there is for sure a plot of earth we love.

To Ulster then, my region, now I turn,
new to sworn service, with so much to learn
to school that service to its wisest use.

Now at my prime, my privilege to choose,
and so my choice; because of the good men
this region bred, not only of my kin
who earned their keep, whose sweat went back to her,
who sought no easy fame, who knew no fear,
and are resumed by earth uncelebrated
save in my thought which they themselves created.
Not only these but others loved or known
for quality of word or act alone,
craftsman or artist, orator or friend,
as each of these are those that to commend
were rough impertinence. They are secure
in all the modes by which our qualities endure,
in hearts that hold them, or in their own work,
till the next ice age and its creeping dark,
and even beyond, for when our folk survive,
crouched by some Nile, these elements will live
as symbols in their richly haunted dreams,
as we too share the images of times
sundered from us by barriers of flame
of other nations that have now no name.

Mine is historic Ulster, battlefield
of Gael and Planter, certified and sealed
by blood, and what is stronger than the blood,
by images and folkways understood
but dimly by the wits, yet valid still
in word and gesture, name of house or hill,
and by the shapes of men whose texture was
determined by the nature of the place,
flogged by the strong wind, soothed by the soft rain,
flushed by the April sunshine's gay champagne,
shod by the heather, heeled by the yielding moss,
till, wayward and persistent as the grass,
they kept their roots, or when chance drove them off,
held earth about them close and strong enough
to feed their stature with new skies to fill,
from Alexander Irvine back to Colmcille.

And we remaining here are what we are,
not by conjunction of this moon or star
scored on a tablet, drawn in desert sand,
but by the tilt and angle of this land,
last edge of Europe, cliff against the west
stemming the strong tides with its broken coast,
wedged in cleft-stick of sudden cloud and sun,
rimmed like a metal cup to measure the rain,
sodden and loaded with time's dripping weight,
chilled by the slow declension of the light,
when the great scab of ice withdrawing tore
the long glens sloping to the eastern shore,
for, after that, sick from the swamping wave,
the tall men scrambled, glad to be alive,
from their small vessels grounded in the reeds,
to light their fires and build their wicker sheds
on the safe flint-rich hills above the beast-
thronged forest and the bitter marish waste;
first landed of those driven refugee
by Europe's pulse thrust westward endlessly,
to yield a living space for men who came
with metal point and horse and lintelled tomb
from the wide Asian plains.
                                        Three hundred years
are long enough for these last wayfarers,
our fathers, now to be compacted here
of this live soil, these peoples, this bright air.
The limestone of these hills has sheathed our bones;
our names and texts are cut upon the stones:
the landscape and our thought so intermixed
our wits are jangled when the soil is vexed;
the earth goes sour when we have lost the sweetness
that is the flower and pollen of completeness.

But there is much to do before our pride
can move with mercy in its equal stride;
wet fields to drain, bare hills to plant with trees,
and power to gather from the plunging seas
and sprawling rivers, sagging walls to shore,
lost acres to resume, and skills restore,
and towns to trim to decency – and more,
bright halls for art and music, rambling parks
not fenced or gravelled by some board of works,
and simple trades to nurture, till again

potter and miller are familiar men,
and not mere names upon a crate or sack,
hoisted on lorries at the hooting dock.

And though we find our love in this deep well
mid rock and heather, let there be no wall
to shut the warm winds out that bring us word
how over Europe liberty has fared,
how in that valley or by that low shore
poor men make kindly laws to help the poor,
and quality is possible again
to meet the leaping hopes of earnest men.

I claim the birthright which I must defend
against the guile of foe and sloth of friend,
for one would bind us supine in the thrall
of ancient error and its crumbling wall,
the other in his dullness cannot see
the future gay with possibility,
and howls dismay at change, though it must come,
crests to its flood and lips into a foam.
Yet we shall ride the waters in their spite,
who thrash and wallow to the left and right,
drop gurgling down into the Romish pit,
or on a melting iceberg scold at it.
We shall drive on, obedient to the tide,
yet tacking as the current winds provide
to the safe haven of an ordered state,
rock-based and fertile, generously great,
and scaled to offer, for individual growth,
the peace of age, the ecstasies of youth.

But who am I to speak so in this wise,
consigning this and this as loyalties?
And by what right? Were it not better done
for me to listen like a grateful son,
and step with you and go where you would go
than drag you on a path you do not know?
I urge but this. When you have stood awhile
and watched the shadows running mile on mile
over the heather and the wind-bleached grass
where heroes strode, where heroes still may pass;
when you have flung your pebbles in the sea
from the black cliff; when, stepping leisurely,

you've come upon a grey-walled meeting house
where lichened headstones tilt in dumb carouse,
and know your people lie there, clay in clay;
when you have heard the loud drum far away
throb through the stillness of a summer night,
you too have this illimitable right.

Just so with me. Against this weight of pride
for years I'd set my wits, instead I'd tried
to wring a simple meaning out of sense,
equipping my slow mind for swift response
to painted panel or to printed book;
yet every road I travelled brought me back,
back to the sunlight on the glittering sod,
back to my fathers and their silent God.

ULSTER NAMES

I take my stand by the Ulster names,
each clean hard name like a weathered stone;
Tyrella, Rostrevor, are flickering flames:
the names I mean are the Moy, Malone,
Strabane, Slieve Gullion and Portglenone.

Even suppose that each name were freed
from legend's ivy and history's moss,
there'd be music still in, say, Carrick-a-rede,
though men forget it's the rock across
the track of the salmon from Islay and Ross.

The names of a land show the heart of the race;
they move on the tongue like the lilt of a song.
You say the name and I see the place –
Drumbo, Dungannon, Annalong.
Barony, townland, we cannot go wrong.

You say Armagh, and I see the hill
with the two tall spires or the square low tower;
the faith of Patrick is with us still;
his blessing falls in a moonlit hour,
when the apple orchards are all in flower.

You whisper Derry. Beyond the walls
and the crashing boom and the coiling smoke,

I follow that freedom which beckons and calls
to Colmcille, tall in his grove of oak,
raising his voice for the rhyming folk.

County by county you number them over;
Tyrone, Fermanagh . . . I stand by a lake,
and the bubbling curlew, the whistling plover
call over the whins in the chill daybreak
as the hills and the waters the first light take.

Let Down be famous for care-tilled earth,
for the little green hills and the harsh grey peaks,
the rocky bed of the Lagan's birth,
the white farm fat in the August weeks.
There's one more county my pride still seeks.

You give it the name and my quick thoughts run
through the narrow towns with their wheels of trade,
to Glenballyemon, Glenaan, Glendun,
from Trostan down to the braes of Layde,
for there is the place where the pact was made.

But you have as good a right as I
to praise the place where your face is known,
for over us all is the selfsame sky;
the limestone's locked in the strength of the bone,
and who shall mock at the steadfast stone?

So it's Ballinamallard, it's Crossmaglen,
it's Aughnacloy, it's Donaghadee,
it's Magherafelt breeds the best of men,
I'll not deny it. But look for me
on the moss between Orra and Slievenanee.

POSTSCRIPT, 1984

Those verses surfaced thirty years ago
when time seemed edging to a better time,
most public voices tamed, those loud untamed
as seasonal as tawdry pantomime,
and over my companionable land
placenames still lilted like a childhood rime.

The years deceived; our unforgiving hearts,
by myth and old antipathies betrayed,
flared into sudden acts of violence

in daily shocking bulletins relayed,
and through our dark dream-clotted consciousness
hosted like banners in some black parade.

Now with compulsive resonance they toll:
Banbridge, Ballykelly, Darkley, Crossmaglen,
summoning pity, anger and despair,
by grief of kin, by hate of murderous men
till the whole tarnished map is stained and torn,
not to be read as pastoral again.

COLONIAL CONSEQUENCE

The colony's so old it's out of touch
with much that's bruited in the Capitol.
The ports are silted up. The winds are such
that most who leave are driven to the west,
returning seldom if they come at all;
infrequent letters, tediously expressed,
yield year by year diminished interest.

But strangers from the mainland, eager men,
the latest jargon lively on the tongue,
here make their way among us; not as when
our fathers came to tame this land and till
and plant a thriving nation here among
the black-browed tribes whose remnants linger still
with random beacons on insurgent hill.

And briskly to their profit they attend,
stuffing their satchels while we stand and gape,
so drilled in old obedience we lend
the stranger's voice authority and awe,
and have among us some who seek to ape
his accent, seeing how all strangers draw
vast credit from this insubstantial law.

Yet we have seen them come and watched them go,
their flashing names forgotten in a year,
with not a shred of evidence to show
by what manoeuvres they achieved their score,
while out of that old superstitious fear

we greet the newest comers to our shore,
no whit the wiser than we were before.

NO CRESTA RUN

Now an elderly person,
living in a genteel old people's home,
he bores the other residents,
reading them the latest draft
of the letter he is going to send
to the head office of the company
which had employed him for years,
explaining why they must still need
his experience and expertise.

Seventy years ago I knew him,
the only son of the double house
opposite our terrace across the street;
a blond foal, seldom penetrating
the fringes of our rough herd.

That week of frost and snow
we polished slides
and shot on tin trays
down the steepest of our side streets.

Then the morning the thaw set in
he appeared, well muffled, carrying
a small toboggan in his arms
carpentered with clean slats of wood
and shod with shining strip of tin.

But it was too late.
The sled grated and ground
on the coarse road surface,
slewing repeatedly against the slushy kerb,
so disconsolately he picked it up
and carried it home.

THE WATERCOLOUR

I claimed this nearly forty years ago;
a few creased notes consoled my frugal friend,

a careful artist diligently slow
and concentrated on enduring end;
his tints not fugitive nor cheaply wrought
on tested paper of proved quality,
shaped by the rigours of his earnest thought,
its proper care has long devolved on me.

His honest hope respected, under glass
and never hung against a sunlit wall,
I spare a humbling glance each time I pass
its silent challenge in the shaded hall
and wonder who, if anyone, must be
my heir to this responsibility.

SUMMER ARCADY

The cottage garden owned a boxwood maze,
head-high, well trimmed, with paths clean swept and bare,
and often in those endless sunny days
when bathing, tennis bored, with hours to spare,
the laughing girls tripped out to frolic there
where John, who hovered eagerly for praise,
would hobble round intent that they should share
the splendour of his flowerbeds' summer blaze.

When every rose had yielded its old name,
each perfumed herb saluted, he would start,
with creaking knees, his old decrepit game,
and chase the squealing fillies for a kiss,
old randy bachelor with thumping heart,
crowing like Pan in sheer Arcadian bliss.

ART AND TECHNOLOGY

Tall lean young negroes in Paris
prance along the boulevards and streets,
attempting with apparently limited success
to sell leather handbags and satchels
and bone or ivory bracelets
to passing tourists.

Last year they could have been observed
presiding in the parks

over small herds of elephants of ebony
or blackened wood,
standing now above their wares,
and calling out to passers-by.
This too may be considered
to have some relation
to the folk-arts of African peoples.

In open spaces they may now be seen
demonstrating little elastic-powered birds
which flap and flutter in erratic scrolls,
often to drop into puddles or lose themselves
in the autumn foliage of chestnut and plane.
This may suggest that the higher technology
is coming to the aid of the Third World.

ROSEBLADE'S VISITANTS AND MINE

An elderly gentle clean-shaven man,
a parched saint with rippling locks,
he painted nineteenth-century watercolours
of ruined buildings and thatched barns
with careful competence.
He had learnt a lot from Cox, David Cox,
his secret way of laying washes
like thin waves over gritty sand.
Yes. Cox had shown him how.

How could he have learnt from Cox,
dead so long? A hundred years and more!
'He comes by night to show me.
They all come by night, all else asleep.
For they all come by night, the philosophers, the dreamers,
blessing, confessing, advising, warning, penitent.'
He had learnt so much, so much,
but was sworn to secrecy.

And Blake? Of course. I hadn't needed telling.
Shaw too, crying over that black girl.
A hundred others.

And Paine, I ventured, does he come too?
'Paine never comes; he knows that I don't like him.'

I too have my visitants
but Paine is of the second rank.
I'd thrown his name in
as a sort of challenge,
for it was likely that Roseblade
had heard of him and his unpopular opinions.
His response did not disappoint me.
Poor Paine, his bones in Cobbett's luggage.

My front-row visitants are William Morris,
Toland the Irish deist, Winstanley, Cobbett,
leading the crowded company.
They come by day, or night,
at appropriate moments,
having first at some time
stepped out of print,
the sturdy folk, the nameless and the named,
the vertical men who never genuflected,
the asserters, the protesters,
like that old Leveller who scratched his name
in the lead lining of the Burford font,
Anthony Sedley prisoner
sixteen hundred and fortynine.

AGE AND YOUTH

Once at a country halt – now closed for years –
I boarded a carriage with two passengers,
nuns by attire, an aged dozing nun,
and a frail novice. I sat opposite,
took out my book, and sought occasion fit,
when each contorted sentence was unspun,
to raise my gaze, as if involved in thought,
and comprehend this couple chance had brought
within the orbit and circumference
of my attention in this cabined space;
what trick of time set this face and that face
in wry conjunction, with which core of sense?

These two, the guarded and the guardian,
conscribed by edict of the Vatican
to token posture of security,
iconic, emblematic, Age and Youth;

though each weak visage marked and mocked the truth,
a coded signal with no ready key.
Age drifting towards a death long overdue,
Youth ebbing as all urge to live withdrew,
while, paradoxically, the ancient one
had slithered back to childhood's innocence
with slack-held beads, there sagged, with no defence
from time's brusque thrust, her faint companion.

TRYST

Coming up the green lane from the sea,
that bramble-trellised unfrequented lane,
on a hot summer Sunday afternoon,
we suddenly glimpsed a couple to our surprise,
a handsome tall young priest and a young nun
standing face to face, oblivious
of all around: the priest's blond head was bowed,
the nun's face uplifted; a romantic tryst,
life aping art, minor Pre-Raphaelite –
Halliday or Hughes? Most likely Arthur Hughes –
the sunlight flashing through the dappled leaves,
the convent's roof-tiles bright above the trees,
across the broad field at the lane's last gate.
Confer a title, explicate the theme:
illicit love at risk, a perilous moment
which mocked the vows; two hearts in jeopardy,
or simply Brother and Sister briefly held
in family bondage with some hint of treason.
Averting gaze in hushed embarrassment,
we hurried past, unanswered, deeply moved.

PORTSTEWART, JULY 1914

My cousin, four years taller than myself,
towed me, most willing, in his urgent stride
to pierrot concerts and to splashing games
and all the joys the holiday supplied:
the sunny basking picnic afternoons
among the sandhills' grass above the strand;
the floating hours when I was taught to row,
the thick oar steadied by my father's hand.

It was the red-mapped Empire's last July;
we saw our elders read and heard them say
that a daft bullet from a madman's gun
had sparked a war in Europe far away.
The photos in the daily newspapers
showed bishops on both sides accosting God,
demanding victory; though at that time
my faith was ill-defined, I thought that odd.

Once, early, leaning on the harbour wall,
we watched below the fishing boats come in,
the tying-up of ropes, the neat-reefed sails,
the loud unloading of the catch begin.

A man aboard the nearest, spotting us,
looked up and called, 'Here's something for your pan',
and stooped and grabbed a fish and tossed it up.
My cousin thanked the kindly fisherman.

We hurried home in haste to brag our prize,
our claim confirmed in loud false pantomime,
and looking closely at our grubby spoil,
my uncle said, 'You caught it just in time.'

HESITANT MEMORIAL

Some weeks ago I heard that you were dead –
I hadn't glimpsed your face these fifty years –
confused a little towards the end, they said.
I felt regret but no recourse to tears.

Yet we were sweethearts once when we were young,
linking and hugging, kissing, holding hands,
with tea in town, with screen's announcing gong,
nested in heather, lolling in Manx sands.

We were near-neighbours. Both our families
faced the same pulpit since our fathers' day.
A quiet comely lass, your qualities
matched expectation in a clenching way.

Our months of talk edged into plans, the ring,
and all seemed set for ever, till at last

with creeping filaments of misgiving,
affection flickered back into the past.

This mutual ebb and break incised no scar.
Now you, once loved, are gone, and I have sped
into a mesh of thought and action far
beyond the hearthside you inhabited.

So love is mortal too; and finally,
when memory's focus blurred, it left a sense
of some vestigial curiosity
occluded by a vague indifference.

BIFOCAL IN GAZA

Along my middle seventies my vision seemed
scummed over quickly with a thickening mist
as definition blurred, approximate,
a bathroom mirror clouded suddenly,
or a fogged windscreen when the wiper's stalled;
yet sight had been the axle of my being
which pivoted, propelled my spinning wits,
like that French poet and his visible world.

So this decay thrust into jeopardy
my passionate care for printed words and shapes
of coloured images those words evoked,
attempted to define, relate to living,
and set a launch pad for imagination.

Now I'd be left with memories alone
in beggared state, a disenfranchised man,
though by time's gift my memories are charged,
well nourished by the famous galleries,
among them Dresden, Beaubourg, Rotterdam,
the only gap left still was Franco's Prado.

I'd had some bother with my eyes before,
as edges, pigmentations frayed and faded
since hints in classroom days when blackboards baffled –
my father's pince-nez led the weak tradition,
his father'd been unspectacled to the last.

I'd stemmed this ebb to absolute defect
with well-tuned glasses every second year
till the optician, after the measured test
with slotted and turned lenses in steel frames,
could offer no pace forward and proposed
I'd seek some succour in the hospital.

So there the ophthalmic ward housed six of us,
that sullen fellow back from Ottawa,
the quarryman who loved the family farm,
the young truck driver who at least twice daily
would telephone his Lurgan betting shop,
two nameless workingmen who seldom spoke,
and me in the corner bed beside the window,
called, in my hearing, the old gentleman,
all here for cataract or retina detached,
the first my sentence, in my dimmer eye.

After the well-nursed waiting, temperature,
blood sample taken by cool-fingered girls
and hypertension measured, drops supplied,
then lifted neatly by a gentle team
to lie on trolley and watch ceilings pass
along, around those Kafka corridors,
first halt a pill to swallow, then a stab
among the brown spots of an old man's hand,
to waken, lost hours later, bedded safe
with padded weeping socket which still weeps.

Prescribed, awarded two thick panes of glass,
lucid low-domed circles ribboned round
with level glass to rim and fill the margins.
So with fixed gaze ahead at once I saw
colours forgotten, misinterpreted,
yellow to white transposed, each form defined
more sharply now, with unfamiliar brightness
garish as the Sunday supplements.
The television figures when I watched
were no mere miming shadows, I could judge
the politician's values by his eyes,
the living actors now become explicit,
the slightest gesture clearly registered.

And in the garden that year I observed –
whether because that spring was exceptional,

richer than any ever I had realised –
in steady focus clearly pigmented
the flourishing whin, my emblem, at the front door,
ebulliently golden, which, till now,
had eked its scattered flecks at any season,
the house-high hawthorn heaped with creamy blossom,
a Samuel Palmer *Shoreham Garden Tree,*
only to tarnish as its tiny petals
were squandered in a week; the harebells blue
among the grasses choking the rockery
my wife had built with stones from Garron's foot,
those harebells, still stem-rigid, though colour bleached
the swarming vetch, the invasive common daisies,
Chaucer-cheerful, metaphor of the people
never to be quelled, the militant dandelions
magnificently asserting, mocking the name
in childhood current, specific, pee-the-bed,
with odd mop-tufted evanescent heads.

So in the particularity of each
my sense expanded from the shrivelled state
I'd sunk into acceptance of, assumed;
now nature, long lulled background, had returned
to its thronged opulent vitality;
though it has been asserted, I've read somewhere,
that nature poets are shortsighted fellows,
like Tennyson, well known for his crannied flower.

Even the apple tree in the back yard
that lost its blossoms, frittered in the gusts
of April, far too fragile to endure
the bees' slow cruising plunder and its gain,
the smaller whin, here too, lavish in its scale,
and, over against the wall, the bramble roses
spurning the split lattice, spangled virgin-white
along the swaying swags, and the loosestrife –
seed-borne from whence? now planted here –
brought back the bombed sites of that second war,
and sweet pea, mauve and lavender, the leaves
cloaking the whiplash rods of the unpruned tree.

All this when standing looking, the still world
offered its essence to the still observer;
but when I shifted foot, unfocusing,

obedient to some moment's drift of whim,
out of the central circles' clarity
planes tilted, false perspectives interposed,
appearance shuffled like a pack of cards.
I'd strayed into an early Cubist phase
of those great facet-masters, Picasso, Braque,
where objects all can be identified
in spite of these distortions, flattened out,
not stripped of reference to familiar shapes
like those calculated grids of Mondrian.

So spectacled I could not move outside
where each next step provides its obstacles,
where kerbs confounded, switchback sidewalks heaved
and pavement flagstones with raised edges lurk
unwittingly to stub the creeping toe,
and all deceptive margins set at risk
my hesitant passage, hobbled by my years.

And indoors also when I shifted stance
the duvet billowed steeply, tables and chairs
engaged in slow pavane, door handles shrank
from fingers' reach, and oval cups declined
the pot's hot jet, indifferent to the aim.

Another session with the lettered screen,
read with diminished confidence as the next line
sank into smudges, undeciphered blurs,
and a tense passage with the piercing beams
as chin and brow were pressed unflinchingly
against the rigid armature when the orbs
were pierced and riddled by a lance of light.
Conferred by this with new bifocal lens
which set in order all my rocking world,
laying the pavement flat, all distances
assured, not reconnoitred doubtfully,
as the small circle nestled in the large
sank to the lower edge of the crystal womb
like some translucent embryo, frogspawn blob,
all former cheating margins washed away.

But, strangely now, the people in the street
were stilted shapes, small-headed, long of limb:
my Cubist world subsumed by Giacometti;

not like the rubber-jointed Mannerists
but firmly boned, like clothes pegs swathed and wrapped.
I envied them their steady balanced poise
and wondered had height changed in my dimmer years,
while my tense gaze was tethered to the past:
the younger certainly, I'd noticed that,
a consequence perhaps of the rationed years,
judged it some presage of the coming age.
When nations dwindle why should men grow tall?
A frantic paradox to wrestle with.

I like these taller people, though the old,
my generation, crouch and shuffle past
if they're still active, while they prop their chins
on stick or crutch, as they totter out of life.

I've seen now mankind's future, though I'd wish
they bodied that more flesh the Cretan gave,
conferring ecstasy on common limbs,
yet still as Calvert's *Bride,* intense as Blake's
demography of Heaven, flowing, rising.

So as I venture along the narrowing years
a brighter road than ever I have known
beckons my eager step now and tomorrow,
and I can only pray all senses join
in life more precious now, more perilous.

THE BLOODY BRAE

A DRAMATIC POEM

I wrote it over forty years ago,
laid it aside until the ink turned pale;
later they spoke it on the radio,
that verse-play cobbled from an island tale;
and when some players offered it a stage,
though planned for darkness and an empty scene,
I was not there. Now silent print on page,
it lay forgotten in a magazine.

It tells how once an old man sought a ghost,
a lass he slaughtered with his trooper's sword,
knowing his blackened soul forever lost
unless her mercy yield forgiving word,
for she was papist, he a protestant.
Four decades on, the heartbreak's relevant.

VOICES

MARY HILL	an old countrywoman
MARGARET HILL	her granddaughter
DONALD NIBLOCK	a young countryman
JOHN HILL	an aged man
MALCOLM SCOTT	a middle-aged soldier
BRIDGET MAGEE	a young countrywoman

Time: early seventeenth century, a January night
Place: a bare roadside above a cliff

MARY You have come far enough, Donald. It's downhill now,
and Margaret's all the staff I'll want from here.
I only needed your arm for the heavy brae.

MARGARET Aye, Donald, turn home now. You were neighbourly,
coming this long way back when you were tired
after the ploughing.

DONALD I will not go back
till I've convoyed you safe into the causey.
There's things are about in this place, queer freets and folk
I'd like no woman I care for to meet in the night.

MARGARET The long-nebbed ghosties hae no fear for me,
nor the grugach crying, nor the skeagh-bush.
I'd discourse any freet that crossed my path.
I'd even bide here till the lone man passes
that most folk run frae.

MARY You are over-ready
to laugh at these oul' witches of the world.
They're here, girl, full of mischief, spitting evil.
There's not a whinbush but may have its terror
that starts and darts away in the shape of a hare.

DONALD You hear your grannie, my bold Margaret.
So I'll not leave ye till I guard you home.

MARGARET I'm not affrighted, Donald, I'm braver than you.
I've seen you wait for company on the road
before you'd pass a tinker with his fire.

DONALD I was a cub of a lad then. It was natural,
for tinkers are known to steal a straying child.

MARY Aye, notable thieves and robbers, every one.
They will even change their own for another wean:
a tinker's family's a mystery to all but the Lord.

MARGARET You are rested rightly, Grannie; it's time to stir.
I've beasts to milk in the morn and the pot to boil
before the second cockcrow's warned the fox.

DONALD You are impatient. Let your grannie be;
the long brae's put a tether on her breath.
She's no young stirk to trot without a stop
from gate to gate. The night is warm and fine;
what wind is in it's in a friendly airt.

MARY Hear him, but never heed him, daughter dear.
It's not the love for me has stopped his step.
It's dark enough for him to hold your hand,
and I see nothing.

DONALD You shouldn't say the like.
If it was black as tar I wouldn't touch her.

MARGARET Well dare you, Donald Niblock. Stand at peace.

MARY Now, my young sweethearts, I am fit to rise.

DONALD I'll leave you at the far side of the burn.
You'll only be a beagle's gowl frae home.

MARGARET And then the long road back for a frightened man,
without a woman's stubborn shilty sense
to trot him steady by the whispering places,
the heifers nosing the bushes, the soughing trees,
the round stone falling with a spatter of mould,
and no one visible by, or maybe the chuckle
the wee burn makes in the sheugh, or the cough of a fox.

DONALD Och, Margaret, quit your gaming. I'm not afeared.

MARY Fear is a wholesome thing for a proud young man.
The Devil would never have fallen if he'd been afeared.
These freets are useful. We'd forget the past,
and only live in the minute, without their presence.
The place that lacks its ghosts is a barren place.
D'you think your father'd get such stooks of corn,
or fill the long pits with praties, or pull strong lint,
if ghosts, that were men once, hadn't given the earth
the shape and pattern of use, of sowing and harvest?
Our own best use may be as ghosts ourselves,
not little mischievous freets but kindly spirits.

DONALD But, Grannie, if the minister should hear you,
he'd name you from the pulpit to your shame.

MARGARET And rightly so, I never heard such talk
like the mad ravelings of a blackamoor,
not a good Christian.

MARY The Book is full of ghosts
passing through close-barred doors, and bringing peace.

DONALD But Saul was rebuked for wanting to speak with them.

MARY There were other ghosts than that.

MARGARET But, Grannie, think. There is Heaven and Earth
and Hell, and each is a place by itself. Deny me that.

MARY Heaven is here, and Hell is here beside it,
inside, round it, all throughother together.
It's only a ghost that knows the place it's in.

MARGARET Come on; you're deaving me with your daft words.

DONALD Wait, lass. I find your notions hard to follow.
I like my thoughts as straight as the haft of a rake.

MARY You'll maybe find the curve of a scythe makes sense
when you've handled it longer, Donald –

MARGARET Look, both of you!
Down there below and stirring in the bracken.
It is the lone old man that lives in the rocks.

DONALD Whist, now, and be you quiet till he passes;
no running out now with your foolish riddles.

MARY He'll maybe not pass, for I have heard tell
he stands about this place and talks to spirits.

MARGARET But he's no ghost.

DONALD He is so. He's no mortal man.

MARGARET He is. Like Saul, he bids them answer him.

MARY He is a living man, but ninety or over,
and crazed in his wits because of a cruel thing.

MARGARET What thing?

DONALD Whist, lassie. He is nearer now.

OLD MAN Malcolm! Malcolm Scott, are you here this night?
Dunwoody! Mitchell? Where are you, Simon Mitchell?
I thought tonight he might come when the moon was set.
I feared tonight they might come when the moon was set.
Malcolm! Malcolm Scott, can you hear my voice?
It's you I'm wanting, and no other man.
Oh closer, Malcolm, closer to the light.

SCOTT Hill! John Hill, by Heaven!
When came you among us, John? I missed you for years.

HILL Malcolm, I'm no ghost yet.

SCOTT Then what do you want?
It's ghosts want men and not men look for ghosts.

HILL I want you, Malcolm, for you can do for me
what I would do as a ghost for any man.

MARGARET Grannie, tell me which of them is the ghost.

MARY The one with the sword at his thigh. He is the ghost.

MARGARET He called him Hill, John Hill? Our name is Hill.

DONALD He wears the habit of a Cromwell trooper,
a trooper at the head of a penny ballad.
There's no Scott nearer here than Olderfleet, now.

HILL Malcolm, I think I am the last of the troop.

SCOTT You are, John. We have met and talked of you.
Mitchell came later than most. He spoke of you,
standing astride a cannon at Limerick.

HILL Limerick, Aughrim, it is hard to remember.
The older times are the days remembered clearest.

SCOTT He said you were old but strong; your hair was flying
into the smoke. He shouted before he fell.

HILL I did not hear him. He was no good friend.
But you were, Malcolm; you were my best friend.

SCOTT I am your friend, but what can I do now
that you, although an old man, cannot do?

HILL I will talk when I come to you, of the days I saw
after I left you. Now I must hurry my words.

DONALD Grannie, d'you think we'll see a Sabbath of ghosts?

MARY Donald, be quiet. I do not know what will happen.
There is no legend like this in the pedlar's book.

HILL Malcolm, I repent me for my actions.

SCOTT Now John, be wise. You were a worthy man,
a clean good horseman, and a fighting man;
your word had the sharp bright cutting edge of truth.

HILL Just so, my friend, this may have seemed to you.
But now I know my want was a deeper lack.
I was a fool and failed to push my thought
sheer to the roots of what I believed I was.

SCOTT If you were a fool, then we were greater fools.

HILL I think you are right in that, though foolishness
must cover us all in general damnation.

SCOTT You mock us, John, in flogging your tired wits.
I did not make the effort to break through
for you to mock at me for my foolishness,
from the precarious insolence of flesh.

HILL I mock at nothing. I am a guilty man.
This night, this place, and seventy years ago,
have left my forehead signalled with my guilt.

SCOTT This night and seventy years? You are doting, man.

HILL Think back; think hard. Let the far voice of the years
stir up and waken a ripple of muddy thought.

SCOTT This night and seventy years? This place? The skirmish!
I remember, John – I remember the little skirmish
when we drove the people over the Gobbins Brae.
Nothing in that. We were in vaster wars;
a brief patrol from Carrick, the work of a day.

HILL My life and my death were in it. My whole soul's fate . . .
I killed a woman here with her suckling child.

SCOTT I struck a dozen flatlings, keeping my edge
for two young men who turned with grappling hands.
I let the sea and the rocks decide on the others.

HILL I killed a woman, a comely woman and young,
in heat of frenzy with one stabbing thrust.

SCOTT You've let your pity drip upon your heart
until it's a sodden thing. You were harder than that
when you struck The O'Cahan down through the leather belts.

HILL That was fairer, Malcolm. He had horse and blade.
This woman carried a child in her white arms.

SCOTT It was your duty. God forgives all soldiers.

HILL For murder and torture, burning of kine and kirk?

SCOTT He forgives all soldiers, if they were ordered to it.

HILL My captain ordered. But it still was wrong.
Shall I limp back, rank by rank, to the general's tent,
to the King who signed his commission, the power that set

the King in authority, the stars, the sun,
seeking the primal wrong that made me its
weapon?
No, Malcolm. If this were, then man's not man,
but a round stone that travels where it's kicked –
I sometimes think a stone must know remorse.
There was a time once when stones near cried
out.

This is my country; my grandfather came here
and raised his walls and fenced the tangled
waste,
and gave his years and strength into the earth.
My father also. Now their white bones lime
the tillage and the pasture. Ebb and flow
have made us one with this.
For twenty years
I ran the loanens here and scoured the hills
for berries, snaring rabbits, guddling trout;
this land and I were one. My father's fields
marched with the native acres of Magees.

SCOTT Magees – they were the people we destroyed!

HILL I know. My father once gave his naked word
to shelter Magees in peril as they would him,
and did it, as they, too, in difficult times.
But that wild night of terror I forgot that oath.
The name of the girl I killed was Bridget Magee.

SCOTT It was the fortune of war. They were murderers.
What of Colkitto riding across the Route,
ravaging house and crop in his smoking track,
betraying the honest surrender of Kennedy's
men?
At Portna murdering eighty in their beds?

HILL They, too, were wrong. We did not right the
balance
by driving these harmless women over the cliff.

DONALD I know his story now. The massacre.

MARY I remember it well. As a wean of five or six
I hid in terror for fear the troopers mistake,
and goad us out like cattle over the rocks.
My uncle hid a family in his kiln.

He was a Hill who remembered the promised
word.

MARGARET This is a kinsman, then; I will speak with him.

DONALD Margaret, easy. There may be a time to speak,
but wait till the rough old soldier has gone
away.

SCOTT What would you have me do, John? It is over.

HILL It is not over. There's a wolf in the heart of man,
and violence breeds like the thistle blown over
the world.
Mercy's gone done and fellowship's flung in the
sheugh,
and every time he rises he's dunted back.
Hate follows on hate in a hard and bitter circle –
our hate, the hate I give, the hate I am given:
we should have used Pity and Grace to break
the circle.

SCOTT These are not words you were fond of when
you were young.
This talk of circles is like a juggler with rings,
but he'd have a better eye and catch them falling
while yours go spinning for ever over my head.

HILL The metal has cooled and set and is harder to
break:
whenever the Irish meet with the Planters' breed
there's always a sword between and black
memories for both.

SCOTT Black memories, John. You forget who began
the murder.
There'll be no rest till we drive them back to the
hills,
too scared to speak above a servile whisper.

HILL Malcolm; the old heart bitter and unforgiving.
I thought maybe the winds of death had chilled
the heady fevers of your turbulent youth.

SCOTT What, John? A renegade?

HILL I am beyond all names.
I flung them away as a swimmer will strip his
body

to let his limbs contend with the driving waters.
I am in smooth water now and sight the shore,
I only need a lamp to guide my landing –
that lamp is forgiveness, Malcolm, a golden light.
I hear the long waves batter and break on the rocks
and the hand which could hold that light would lift it up
if I could throw my voice above winds and water;
but I cannot alone; I need your help in the asking.

SCOTT Then ask me, John, for I am still your friend,
although your words and reasons dodge my grasp.

HILL My thought will twist within the firmest grip
like a diviner's hazel till it rest
where, if we dig, there is the water of life.

SCOTT Heth, John, you're in the water, above the water.
When you can sort it out, I may come back.

HILL Stay, Malcolm. I need you to listen;
your voice and face are a tether for my thought,
that otherwise runs loose like a calf at the fair,
lost among legs and sticks, moidered with orders . . .

SCOTT It's the creaking flesh that vexes you. When you are dead
you'll be free and clear in the strength of your bright prime,
drinking with soldiers, and crossing a ready blade
with the best swordsmen from the camps of the world,
taking a cut that is red but will not hurt,
and rising tomorrow, unmarked, to pierce his guard.

HILL So that's your Hell, to run for ever and ever
through the same dance of shadows, a jigging shadow.

SCOTT Hell? John, you're crazy. It's the soldier's Heaven.
The years have chilled your blood . . . you are old and cold,
mumbling of Mercy and Pity. These are words.
I made my choice with things, with swords and stirrups.
The things men choose come out of life with them.
It's thoughts and bodiless things that carry no ghosts.
You'll have me talking as foolish as yourself.
What was it, John, you thought that I could do?

HILL I thought you could go speak to Bridget Magee –

SCOTT I run among the Dead, boording this one and that,
like a packman or a beggar asking favour?

HILL And ask her to come some night to this lone place;
or, if she comes already, as I fear,
to make herself visible for a rushlight's length,
that I may plead the pardon I need to die.

MARGARET Think ye will he seek her out for his friend?

MARY I see a woman over my shoulder here.
Whist. She approaches slowly.

MARGARET Where, Grannie, where?

SCOTT We keep to our own kind where I am now;
the only women with us were always with us.

HILL But you could ask and find her. You know her name.

MARY Donald, can ye no see behind the man
the woman of the Magees they are speaking of?

MARGARET She's just the height of me, about my age.

SCOTT I'll run no lackey at your wheep and finger
after a country hussy. I'm away.

HILL Death has done little for ye, Malcolm Scott.
I'd often thought death quickened the seed in the ground,

and looked for the blossoming promised;
but you still writhe and twist in the dark mould.

BRIDGET John Hill! John Hill! I am Bridget Magee.

HILL You? Bridget Magee, but where is the child you
carried?

BRIDGET My child is not here. He is fulfilling life
in a way I am not sure of, in another place.
He's only the child again when I dream I dream.
I have not come to scare you. I heard your call.

HILL You heard? I knew that you, though invisible,
haunted this place as I have haunted it,
stepping the marches, each on his own side.
But though I called I felt I could not reach
to touch your pity without a go-between,
a ghost well known to me in life, and now
dead long enough to be acquaint with you.
Enough. You're here. I only ask for pardon.
Ye'll ken no quarter from which my deed was
good.
I murdered pity when I murdered you,
and reason and mercy and hope for this vexed
land.
There was time that mercy should have
appeared,
if ever, between the clashing of our peoples,
and from that mercy kindness seized a chance
to weave together the broken halves of this land,
to throw his shuttle across the separate threads,
and make us a glittering web for God's delight,
with joy in the placing of colours side by side.
That sword-thrust made our opposition for ever,
judged not me only but my kin and yours.

BRIDGET My pity stretches out to touch your arm.
Poor soldier. You were ordered and obeyed.

HILL No. No light that way, woman. The argument
leaps from my captain and beyond the King
to challenge God. Should I heap all on Him?
It was my act. I was not ordered to kill you,
with a sword-thrust thus, on a January night,
at this round boulder near the windy cliff.

I cannot be separated from this act
as a dancer doffs his coat for a different jig.

BRIDGET My native weakness stormed against you at first.
Savage in death I strode along the Gobbins,
crying my rage into a gale of gulls
against the sea's roar and the whetting tides.
I called on vengeance from the arid stars
until the tears of temper turned to pity.
Pity that I should die, that you should kill;
till I blamed God for ordering the world
to such a measure. That is over now.
For, after, in the time that has no years,
save on your side the march, I lived in thought
that those who died with me upon this cliff,
or at the tide's lip there, had narrowed harsh
into a fist of rage against the wrongers,
and lost the new scope offered to our grasp;
and dead, were less than the living, in gesture
 and grace,
although not cumbered now by the hesitant
 flesh
and the uncertain answers of hand or eye.
So I said: in this element of being
I must not stunt my branches with bitterness,
leaning for ever with this cruel wind.
The tree's way's leaf and blossom, blossom,
 fruit . . .
the dry twig's meant for burning. And my child
went from me slowly but with confidence.
And I would not hold him back, but prayed for
 him.

HILL I can say nothing. Yet of late I accused
a fellow ghost of yours – perhaps you saw us
in discourse here – that death had taught him
 nothing.
And I was grieved that death should make no
 change;
but now I know the fault was all in him.

BRIDGET So I came to your call, for this is the first
of all your pitiful nights you bid me come.
You called on this and this. They could not help,
for they'd refused the help of death itself.

Then only when your friend came, though
unchanged,
his hardness lit the candle in your heart
as flint sparks tow or pith, and by that light
you saw my waiting face as I'd seen yours.

HILL I am grown old now. I do not follow your
thought.
I only know I had no courage to call
for you at first. Yet I knew the bitter need.
I called on one of whom I had no fear.

BRIDGET I knew the need in your heart though you did
not speak,
as I know now the thresh and coil of your
hopes.
I'd wanted to come before this, but the need
was then no more than the yellow edge of the
leaf.
I came at last when every twig was naked.

DONALD Grannie, can she read the thoughts in my heart?

MARY I thought ye had some hint of the power o'
ghosts.

HILL You knew my need? I feared to utter it.
There is no pride like this, of asking forgiveness,
as if it were a right, or a debt you owed me;
but I have also schooled myself to forgive;
so like the ploughed field I await the sower.

BRIDGET You are a good man. I have watched you tend
the gull's hurt wing, have seen you ease the
yowe,
and the weak lamb that strayed on the slipping
turf.
I give the pardon I can. But I would give it
to a lecherous rascal whining at my feet.
Pardon like rain must fall on every face
that's lifted up towards it. It cannot be earned.
God is no huxter charging interest.

HILL Yet you forgive me. I am clean again,
can face the shadows now as once the cannon.

BRIDGET I have said that I pardon you. But the sword's
edge

is marked with blood for ever. I am dead
who might have mothered crowding
generations:
for good or ill you altered the shape of things.
You said there was a time for mercy once,
but every moment is the time for mercy.
You have narrowed your mercy round you
like a close blanket that you should have spread
over the shivering earth. You were kind and
gentle
with the suffering things that approached your
open door,
when you should have stormed singing through
this land,
crying for peace and forgiveness of man and
man,
nor vexed your lean years waiting for a ghost.

HILL I did what little I could. I meant to be kind.
Name me a man I wronged from then till now
and did not undo what I could.

BRIDGET You built your world as a child its castle of sand.
You said to this and this, 'I am kind and just.'
But to the worlds beyond, to the next townland,
'I am only a legend of a hermit in his cave.'

HILL I dreaded aright the bitter whip of your words,
and I cannot blame you for them. You do not
forgive.

BRIDGET This is not a lack of pity. Truth is free
from pity or fear. Truth is a lightning flash.

HILL What then to do with the narrowing years
ahead?
I had hoped to die with your blessing, being old
and tired.

BRIDGET First leave the cave. Christ's forty days will serve.
Go back to men. They will listen because of
your age.
The pointing child with the hoop, the leaning
woman
over the half-door, the man in the pratie field,
the shouldering crowds at the market, the
travelling tinker;

there are many to speak to, and your time is
short;
yet each must hear for himself and be satisfied.

HILL Woman of Ghosts, I cannot compass the world,
I am an old man now and my limbs are feeble.

BRIDGET I know. Then you must, as an urgent ghost,
wait restless with the knowledge in your hands,
till, here and there by chance, one turn from his
place
among the living to beg your strength and aid.
They will not turn too often for your comfort:
for few may remember to call you by your
name.

HILL I thought the blessed were free from bitterness.
You hold forgiveness out, then snatch it away.
You say that Heaven's no huxter, yet bargain
hard.

BRIDGET I have many things to lose and cast away
I cling to still, because of their memories.

HILL Another riddlemeree.

BRIDGET I go back to my place.
John Hill, as the woman you murdered, I forgive
you.

HILL Mercy. Heaven's Mercy's surely in that word;
and the strange things you said beyond my wit,
and so outside my responsibility.

DONALD He's like to fall. We must help him to his cave.

HILL Ghosts? Ghosts? Is this a trick? I am betrayed.

DONALD Ye are not. We are neighbours who chanced this
way,
and want to help you to your lonely bed.

HILL Ye came by here just now?

MARY This very minute.
And saw ye sitting faint on this hard rock.

MARGARET But we heard, or thought we heard, the sound
of voices.

HILL No, mistress. There was no sound save maybe myself;
an old man talking to himself. It was that ye heard.

MARGARET It seemed to be –

MARY Aye, that and nothing more.

HILL I have not far to journey from this place.
My home's in the rocks below there, in the bracken;
I am the foolish old man that lives in the cave.

DONALD Your step with mine, and we'll be safely there.

HILL Good night to ye, mistress, and God rest ye well.
It's a dark night for old folks to be abroad;
but the stars are aye the best in the birling year.

MARGARET Strange for a man to be talking of shining stars
a minute after he's spoke with a murdered ghost.

MARY It is not strange. It's the nature of this place
for a man to be talking fantastic. The rocks and stones,
the grass beneath us, are not plain natural things.
This is a fairy townland dropped out of time.
For all we know, we're maybe ghosts ourselves.

MARGARET Grannie, we are not ghosts. A thorn has jagged me,
and no ghost's wounded by a thing like that.

MARY There was a ghost once had his share of wounds;
but that was long ago, in another place.
And there's been talk enough of ghosts this night.

PART II

SELECTED UNPUBLISHED POEMS 1928–76

LITTLE SHIPS

O little ships that come and go
across the gleaming waters' breast
and reach Japan and Mexico,
will you not let me join your quest?

For I could pull harsh ropes or hold
the tugging wheel when seas run high
and when sleet whistles sharp and cold
I'd reef stiff sails against the sky.

And I'd be quite content to eat
the tinned salt beef, the thick grey bread
and lie awake in tropic heat
and have a hammock for my head.

O little ships that come and go,
can I not slip away with you
and see Japan and Borneo
and Madagascar and Peru?

POUR HÉLÈNE

from the French of Ronsard

When you are very old, by candleglow
  spinning beside the fire with wearied brain
  that rings and sings to many a memoried strain,
remember how I praised you long ago.
And then your servant, drowsily and slow,
  who dozes at her work, will wake again
  at my forgotten name and that refrain
wherewith for you I wrought Time's overthrow.

I shall lie deep in clay, a misty wraith,
  'neath myrtle shadows taking my repose,
  while you that crouch beside the flickering grate
will cry against your scorn for my young faith.
  Gather today life's ever-fading rose.
  Believe me, love, tomorrow is too late.

SONNET

There in the lonely quarry where at dawn
larks rise on jets of music out of sight,
we stood together in the warm spring night
with eyes turned to the hills whence day withdrawn
had made a fading primrose of the light.
There was no sound. The eager larks had gone.
The dark earth lay content. Thin, scattered, white,
the tattered banner of the clouds was blown
across the moon.
Then suddenly we heard,
low as a sob, the wind begin to cry
and weave a lyric more than any bird
has ever chanced on: mingled of the sky,
the dreaming land by urge of spring unstirred
and our new passion's quiet ecstasy.

SONNET

Our love is full of memorable things,
not the mad passions flaring and soon dead,
but quiet joy that weaves an endless thread,
dear moments rich with wisdom's traffickings:
Howth, say, in sunset when a lost lark sings,
the moon through Digswell trees that rises red
to torch the sheaves, reeds arching overhead,
stars perched on rigging, dawnchill stir of wings.

A thousand more whereof we share the life
given by old, forgotten, happy men
who knew the craft of chisel or of knife.
Nurtured on these our love gives back again,
must give – have we not felt it in the blood? –
new gentleness to stone, new strength to wood.

from TRISTAN: THE LAY OF THE GOATLEAF

for my wife

We too have gone down little roads in spring
from Strangford inland, slowly motoring,
have stopped while you stretched up to cut and take

the flowering goatleaf. I have lifted you
beyond the scathe of thorn for blossom's sake,
this shower of leafspilt rain or early dew,
and you have filled the car with golden whin
one night in April. Let me not begin,
for all your days with growing things are bright
till even ivy has its cool delight.

STONE

The font, the flint, the ammonite,
the pecten, crystal and the quern,
these please and tease the restless sight
while fancy matches shape in turn.

Out, weathered here they still endure
the incidence of frost and rain,
each in its shape and strength secure
from love's erosion, file of pain.

Of forms that flowered when earth grew cool
and blossomed to fantastic grace,
the crystal still is beautiful,
the bare flint shows a lovely face.

Of things laid down as life ran on
by quiet creatures in the dark,
the ammonite's the eldest son,
the pecten is the patriarch.

When men found will to master need
and gauged the sky and spring's return,
they prayed to God, they sowed the seed,
they carved a font, they left a quern.

And we for all our boasted pride,
our arrogance of hand or eye,
what shape of ours shall still abide
the indifferent favours of the sky?

AUTUMNAL

'Tis early dark. The lamps are lit.
A cold wind stirs the thinning trees.

Here in the lonely gloom I sit
and mouth my timid sophistries,

how autumn counts its laboured store
and winter's broom but clears the way
for spring's insurgent green once more
and sunshine of a summer day.

My wit insists the truth of this
would warm my heart, grudge no salute
to the snug egg, the chrysalis,
the seed within the fallen fruit.

But heart remembers spring by spring
the promise broken or deferred,
the yearly less exciting wing,
the dwindling joy of bud and bird.

Each year's a death. I grieve to see
th'acceleration of the cold:
the leaves but touch the shivering tree
with a green light and I am old.

LYRIC

Let this last lyric of a passing day
cry its slow fading way
into some lonely crevice of your mind.
Remote and strange, remember that its art
once held the heartbreak of another heart
whose world went dumb and blind.

Though time should crumble and the world should break,
disaster overtake
the friendly-gestured hand, the gentle word,
yet love and pity shall endure to be
the first green beacon on the barren tree
and the first wakened bird.

THE HOLLYHOCKS AGAINST THE WALL . . .

The hollyhocks against the wall,
like lantern-hung pagodas tall,

when a south-western wind begins,
sway courteously like mandarins:
but with a sudden splash of rain
are occidental once again
and stand with beaded drops of light
as cottage-homely and as bright
as when old Herrick made his rime
in England in King Charles's time.

TO ANY DWELLER IN LEWIS STREET

And do you know a man was born
in your short street of brick and slate
who made his life a simple chart
that he might keep inviolate

the clear precision of his sight
for curve of hill and field and tree
that he might set their colours down
with delicate economy?

Although tall chimneys hemmed him in
and gantries bound the sky with bars,
he came to his best years between
two pitiful disastrous wars:

and though the hearts of men were torn
he held his patient way alone
and while earth shuddered with despair
matched mass with mass and tone with tone.

SONNET

By the sea's edge, on gravel and on sand,
  I pace at leisure, marking out with care
  the steps of one unknown before me there
and weighing coloured stone with idle hand,
white flint or veined pebble that the land
  surrendered to the ocean's wear and tear,
  and by some magic I am pledged to share
in a vast peace I do not understand.

Tonight an empire lurches to decay,
  its mode of thought and living growing stale

yet free from gasping rumour of dismay
or threat of fate I careless pace the shore
where the great waters beat with endless roar
and Carthage is a clean forgotten tale.

GLENDUN

I saw the valley, patch by coloured patch,
potatoes, oats and grazing, flax and hay,
the whitewashed houses with rain-shabby thatch,
the bigger houses, slated blue and grey,
the shorn sheep nibbling round the mounds of gorse,
the red calves at the gate, the lonely horse,
and one man rowing slow across the bay.

I thought of Europe, of the bitter fate
that hung about us, ready to descend,
my generation cursed, unfortunate
and waiting for a miserable end,
each step regretted as it nearer came,
the uselessness of the apportioned blame,
my failure or the failure of each friend,

and walking in this valley in July
I made a prayer who do not often pray,
living by no revealed philosophy
but by slow knowledge scrabbled day by day,
that when fate strikes, God should in mercy spare
from the abysmal thralldom of despair
this little valley and this quiet day.

COBWEB

For fifteen days my cobweb spun
from Waterfoot to Cushendun
has caught and tethered many things
besides the flies' prismatic wings:

the finches crumbing round the door,
bright-coloured seeds of sycamore,
white bindweed's flower, the foxglove left
– of all but topmost bell bereft,
the wagtails darting on the sand,

the men who hauled the nets to land
with bladderwrack and crabs and fry,
the black calf's melancholy cry;

the boy who shouted he was fit
to handle horses, cuckoo spit
upon a weed with leaves gone red,
the rainbow's end on Garron Head,
the broken rainbow on the sea,
the shape of lightning-gutted tree,
the cream horse in the thistle field,
the nearhand cuckoo well concealed
but just like those I heard at home,
the spilt-milk pattern of the foam,
the geese that swaggered head in air
and Lurigedan always there,
save when a black cloud filled the glen
as ink fills up a fountain pen,
the skylarks singing in the sun,
the great red caves at Cushendun,
the house we passed one afternoon
where *fidil* scraped a rebel tune.

All these and more but over all
the sounds and scents of Cushendall,
the rooks asserting in the trees
the privilege of families,
the old familiar reek of peat
and Turnley's Tower where four roads meet.

Now I have marked and sorted these
in all their varied qualities,
I'll find a place to spread them out
against the hungry months of drought,
thanks to the cobweb net I spun
from Waterfoot to Cushendun.

I TALKED AND RAGED AND PLANNED . . .

I talked and raged and planned,
I praised where it was due,
I tried to understand
the scrannel modern crew,

till with the years I grew
a stranger in the land;

and now I turn within
and find in my own heart
the peace I longed to win
that armours me apart,
making my private art
my lonely discipline.

COMMENT ON VERSE

These are the surface shapes upon my mind,
straws floating mid reflections of the sky,
darting or cruising, indolently blind,
that leave no lasting angles in the eye.

The stones beneath, dark basalt, flint or lime,
scoured by the passing waters smooth and round
that wear the patient signature of time:
in their slow sculptured strength my peace is found.

SALUTE TO MATTHEW ARNOLD

None in these days shall crutch my limping faith
when violence overmasters gentleness,
when those who had capacity to bless
are smothered roughly in a common death.

I find no comfort in the carpenter,
the ease-renouncing prince, the courteous sage:
it was a leisured world assured their wage.
Now in an ebbing age
that scarce can tarry for appraising glance,
no little ranting master of despair
can fix its pity with his nervous lance:
but graven masters, eloquent and wise,
must surely phrase our frantic obsequies.

Not then for me the poet of the night,
dread-haunted, followed by the restless feet,
who cursed the bland illusion of the light

and gibbered at the shadows in the street,
nor him who by inversion of his faith
could find the satisfaction to blaspheme
and taunt indifferent, approaching death
to sate his terror with a cruel dream.

Rather I choose the calm defeated man
who from his anxious bitterness of heart
could grasp existence in a steady span,
assay it boldly with unflinching art
and patiently define
its endless flux in an immortal line.

VALEDICTORY LINES TO MY WEA STUDENTS

When darkness narrowed on our anxious days
and none dare hope beyond the midnight stroke,
we came together from our threatened ways,
two score of odd and ordinary folk,
eager to seize what comfort lay in art
for the vexations of the troubled heart.

We watched the subtle elements unfold,
the elegance of balance and design,
the warm romantic arabesque, the cold
precision of the thoughtful classic line,
the skill unerring and th'unflinching eye
that snatches wisdom from mortality.

The gentle monk of Florence, innocent,
the frantic Dutchman setting all on fire,
the banker's son, aloof and diligent,
who sought the cone, the cube, the cylinder,
Claude Monet, making even shadow bright,
and Rembrandt peering through the failing light;

the courtly painter to the Spanish king,
who drew his master and his master's fool,
the people's painter, Courbet, swaggering,
and cynic Degas at the dancing school:
these, these and many more, whose patient gaze
made permanent the pageant of their days.

Now, having argued and debated long,
we've grown a noisy company of friends,
no whit agreed on what is right or wrong
but somehow sorry that the session ends
where with opinion's privilege we were free
with the last gestures of democracy.

So, when the future opens at our feet,
let us go bravely on our careful ways,
secure above the terror of defeat
and the loud tumult of triumphant days,
wise in emotion, qualified by art
to the high purpose of the human heart.

I CANNOT MAKE A SONG TONIGHT . . .

I cannot make a song tonight.
The words are numb, my wits are dull.
I write and cancel what I write –
and yet my days are no less full
of thought, affection and delight
than when of old my singing heart
achieved the ecstasy of art.

And if I make another song
with rhythm to stanch the flow of time,
reverberant as a heathen gong
and rich as unforgotten rime,
to whom then should the grace belong
save unto her whose gestures give
mute evidence whereby men live?

SONNET

I think of Glasgow, where reluctantly
I had to pause and loiter for a train
to carry me from its black smoke and rain
to Portobello and the wind-whipped sea.
Later returning, one companioned me
who knew the place in childhood and again
was glad to greet it. Now these days remain
ambered in love for its stark poetry.

Wet street and gantry, chimney, gaslit close,
the piper in the alley pacing slow:
my native town a friendly kinship shews
in heart and feature. When I heard last night
that death had set its sober ways alight
I saw instead the flames in Sandy Row.

SAP IN THE STICKS AGAIN . . .

Sap in the sticks again
and birdsong growing clear,
but the fine drifting rain
retards the stripling year

as though the reluctant spring
feared what might yet befall
before the swallow's wing
shadow the sunlit wall.

THREE HORATIAN ODES

for R.P.M.

I

Already autumn silently
has come to sky and field and tree,
the leaves fall from the lime,
the oak's at golden prime.

Soon my October will be here
to mark the cresting of my year
and set me loose to find
hope in an older mind.

The reaper to the gleaning rooks
has left the fields. The tilted stooks
shadow the moonbright ground
where bivouac is found

for you and your fagged company
who narrow blurs of shadow lie
until dawn's chilly star
renews your blueprint war.

II

Since June was hot on head and hand
and thunder rocked the lush green land
   I've had no skill or time
   to flush my wits with rime.

Summer must not forego her praise
because she brimmed our eager days
   with certain gifts of eye
   not hers inherently.

But for that crop and harvest of
symbols and shapes that woke my love
   to ripen I must wait
   nor be importunate,

rather, because they were so new,
the pulse dare hardly swear them true,
   I must allow the mind
   to keep them undefined

and greet this season I have known
both text and texture of my bone
   with old accustomed phrase
   that served in safer days.

III

You mid the corn not yet asleep
a certain tryst with me may keep
   and not with me alone
   but many another one

who waking when the moon is high
sees in the bare, untroubled sky
   no warning sign of wars,
   only moon-blanchèd stars

and knows that age by bitter age
man here and there has [slought] his rage
   and reined his leaping fears
   to the slow-striding years

with stars for gauge, with seasons' ebb
and flow to map the patterned web

time holds a hooded chance
keep we but tolerance.

SONNET

Among the many selves that throng my flesh,
that clench the fist or urge the feet to run,
that peer in mirror every morning fresh
to search my face for whose mask lies thereon,
that jostle on the lips to say, unsay
the words that prompting circumstance demands,
but one recalls the body's built of clay
and one that clay is shapen well with hands.

And one's a child that whimpers quickly, bled
by jag or sting and quickly reconciled,
and one not yet the master gay and wise
in patience lets the [sagging] mutinies
in truculence and silence troop to bed,
forgives the braggart and enjoys the child.

DEDICATION

I have a certain skill in phrase,
can trace and space the stride of mood
and from the tumult of my days
beget my own beatitude.

For though the years have stripped my mind
of painted shrine and murmured creed,
the gay, unfettered senses find
the ritual that all men need,

not in the hallowed bread and wine,
the blessed relic or the bell,
but in the shaping of a line
that mystery makes a miracle.

ON THE CHOICE OF A TITLE

a rime for Estyn Evans

An earnest scholar skilled to weigh
from evidence of shard and bone

why creatures of a cruder day
left laboured rituals in stone,
took note of nimble peasant hands
and what they wrought at, page by page,
till, bound in bulk, the record stands
and lettered *Irish Heritage*.

Though what he wrote was rescued well
from progress and its daft machine
that nearer tolls the craftsman's knell,
to me that title still must mean
the coiling tangle of desire
that threshed across this windy stage
with breaking hearts or wits on fire –
that is the Irish Heritage.

The coarse buffoon with bawdy laugh
who moulds the mob with crafty hand,
the randy squire whose epitaph
is scrawled across a beggared land,
the poet's talk, the tenor's song,
the cattle dealer's storm of rage
when sober daylight proves him wrong –
this is the Irish Heritage.

The martyr, stubborn for his cause,
the rebel's final eloquence,
the waster wheedling your applause
and after pocketing your pence,
the man who faces death or kills
with only threadbare words for wage,
the dreamer walking in the hills –
this is the Irish Heritage.

SONNET

I thought tonight of all the lovers gone,
the tall, the proud, the swift of foot, the fair,
who strode the woods, or waking in the dawn
by some fern-feathered pool shook dewbright hair,
and how a bloody end was sure for each
because their love was far too weak to win

more than a mumbling poet's after-speech,
seeking a subject for his discipline.

Once arrogant in youth I set your name
with names that leap too easily from the tongue.
Forget the boast: it was a foolish game,
forgiven only when the heart is young.
Rather I'd pray our love last all our days
than be remembered in a poet's phrase.

PARAPHRASE OF VERSES BY MAYAKOVSKY

Rally and form in your squads,
no time to quibble or trifle,
this cackle's becoming a bore –
Comrade Rifle,
you have the floor.

No longer enslaved by the forces
of antediluvian gods,
palsied and thunder-bereft –
History, hustle your horses,
   Left,
   Left,
   Left.

PANGUR BAN

My wife's slick needles click and slide,
her fingers loop the dragging wool.
The pencil makes a scratching noise
across the paper on my knee.

The glove she knits will warm a hand
that time has chilled. The lines I write
can make no claim to any use
beyond a vain dexterity.

I TOLD MY HEART TO REST . . .

I told my heart to rest
and let the tempest rage,

because the happiest
of man's gay lineage
went by in quietness
to their appointed place,
slow-moving but to bless
with unobtrusive grace.

But then my mocking heart
rocked on a stricken sea
and though I moved apart
the tempest circled me
until I knew at last
that storm and I are one;
its rage shall not be past
till time and I are done.

ON THE USE OF DIALECT WORDS

I pluck words out of the speech of countrymen,
   not for their far-fetched joy or oddity,
   found-objects mounted for the gallery
and after tipped back in the bin again,
nor that I clutch them as an alien
   holds to the seal or stamp that marks him free
   to blunder in and rock the family
to mocking laughter, grief tapped now and then.

But somewhere in the shifting tides my heart
scarce holds from overlipping, there are things
which need such names to draw them to the light;
precision speeds my aim, and so outstart
from steaming flats the evidence of wings
and a deep world emerging into sight.

WITH A LITTLE BOOK OF POTTERY

for R.

Now you have found the clay to live
in shapes that clench around their use,
your spirit knows a moment's truce
with all that's sadly fugitive.

The fired clay may survive an age,
even as a shard in broken earth,
and glaze and texture have a worth
scarce troubled by an epoch's rage.

So, as the skill increasing flows
from clay to hand and hand to clay,
you'll find a surer means to say
the things I say in verse or prose.

FOR BUSHA

This is your own who patiently
stood by my side as time limped by,
and when I swithered in and out
through streams of hope and bogs of doubt,
watched the long, tedious vigil wear
from month to month to month and year to year
till faith became a token of
the perfect craftsmanship of love.

The words that hobble here or run
but hint the qualities of sun
and wind and landscape we have known,
the song, the leaf, the lake, the stone . . .
Of vanished moments this endures,
I cannot give what's also yours.

WHEN THE BELL RINGS IN THE STEEPLE . . .

When the bell rings in the steeple
all the clean-faced country people,
faith-constricted, briskly pass
on their way to morning Mass.
I still stand in jeopardy
under the unchristened tree.

THE PRIEST GOES THROUGH THE MOTIONS OF THE PLAY . . .

The priest goes through the motions of the play;
his skirts flounce out, his cuffs are lifted up;

the people stand and sing or kneel and pray,
but God's not in the wafer or the cup.

He asks no weekly miracle whose days
are fed on marvels from each eager sense,
who knows earth, fire and water, all are praise
and the bent grass blade all his evidence.

THIS IS NO LAND OF CONSTABLE AND CLARE . . .

This is no land of Constable and Clare,
of wheat and oak, of rich, use-mellowed things;
the red roofs drowsing in the summer air,
the slow-great river on whose dark glass swings
the laden barge, the farmsteads fat and brown,
wide-acred, deep in tides of ripening grain,
the towers and roses of the sooted town,
the nurtured woodland, the bloom-tunnelled lane.

This is a smaller country: little fields
with scattered houses and black mountain streams,
where even the rain-soft air a harshness yields
of ancient wars and violence, which gleams
and flashes off each grass blade, rock and tree,
and mocks the patient stride of history.

TO BE USED IN AN ADDRESS DELIVERED AT THE UNVEILING OF A PLAQUE COMMEMORATING 'GEORGE A. BIRMINGHAM'

Awhile caught in the bog of politics,
you let the arrows of your satire fly,
the placeman, the corrupt, and those that by
descent and dealing prosper, to transfix;
but these, well schooled in all evasive tricks
and carapaced in round hypocrisy
took no more heed of your sincerity
than should a rock chastised with little sticks.

So you unstrung your bow and bent your skill
to gentler humours on a smaller stage
and the swift years passed over you until

you had forgotten all your lonely rage,
content the crowded shelf your writings fill
should offer haven in an anxious age.

And so we laugh with you at prank and plight,
at kindly wit unbarbed by wits' conceit,
the little humours of the village street
that keep the last luckpenny warm and bright,
the parlour dramas played for our delight,
the small conspiracies whose sure defeat
brings grief to petty tyrants, in the neat
twist of the merry tale that makes all right.

Yet we remember, when the laughter dies
and the last page that raised it's turned away,
the lonely traffic of Atlantic skies
above the islands in the western bay,
and, nearer home, the windy spume that flies
high over Ballintoy and Ballintrae.

RESOURCE

In a wet season, when the tractor's bogged,
and the ripe corn is lodged with wind and rain,
after the first dry day the scythesman comes
and with him one to lift the stricken grain.

So too when ruin beats upon the state,
and the wry structure rocks in jeopardy,
we may remember half-forgotten skills,
and save ourselves by our simplicity.

VERS LIBRE

No verse is free that has been sweated for.
Simply, the rules are different,
the referee's whistle blows unexpectedly,
the ball bounces higher,
but the net's in the same place,
there, at the other end.

RITE

Friends, cousins, strangers saluted,
we edged to the ready place,
the proper masks of occasion
adjusted to each stiff face.

The clergyman's words were honest,
unmetrical, spare;
but recalling the morning my father died
I knew that nothing was there.

With webbing slipped under it, lowered
deep down into the ground,
the coffin answered the scumbled clod
with that hollow and mocking sound.

The gravedigger slowly stepped forward
and whispered, 'You're next of kin?'
At my nod, with the spade he proffered,
I tumbled the first earth in.

APPENDIX

I

UNCOLLECTED POEMS

1928–86

A LABOUR VICTORY

an election incident

At twelve the rain had gone and left a windy star-splashed sky;
We stood outside the polling booth and waited patiently . . .

At last a man came out and read a count of votes to us;
And someone groaned, and someone hissed, and some looked
   tremulous.

At one o'clock he came again and read another score;
And oh the shouts and oh the cheers that rose and ripped and tore!

The windy stars swung to and fro, the lamps below turned round,
The puddles laughed beneath our feet, and gaily heaved the ground.

A little child beside me then plucked at his mother's skirt –
A tiny tot, barefoot and cold, ragged, besmirched with dirt.

'Oh Ma, what's all the noise about?' The wrinkles on her brow
Smoothed out as she replied to him, 'Ye've got a friend in, now!'

THE SONG OF THE SHIPYARD MEN

Oh Jews, an' lords, an' moneymen,
   They're vampires one an' all.
They sen' us back tae work agen
   Until their profits fall.

For trade is brisk, an' cash is good,
   An' fortunes can be made.
So here us toils for daily food
   Till dividen's is paid.

But come the day when work gits slack,
   They banks their bloody roll;
Us till the streets just trudges back,
   An' lines up for the dole.

THE SONGS I SING

I might have writ of Belmarie
and shining men in mail

and frosty starshine on the sea
and all the joys of Gall and Gael.
I might have made my melodies
of faery lore and spell,
and lived through lovely lethargies
of amaranth and asphodel.
I might have sung of spring and fall,
of summer's ripened fruit;
I might have made my madrigal
upon an olden borrowed lute.
But time and all-directing fate
have caught me in their net
and days and deeds confederate
have laid on me a heavy debt.
I weave the sum of homely things
into a homely song,
an angry shouting man that clings
to beauty 'spite an age's wrong.

THE EX-SERVICEMAN

Work for my living? Would to God I could;
  But work is scarce, and I must be content
  Who in Britannia's khaki armament
Went out to save the wide world's brotherhood.

Since then for four long years I, too, have stood
  In queues to take the gen'rous money sent
  By a kind-hearted, grateful government
To buy me boots and give my fam'ly food.

And I am grateful, too, when in the street
  I see a limousine purr gently by,
    To know that by the valour of my friends,

Who, with me, on the pavement, stamp cold feet,
  This man can go to work without a sigh,
    And without worry draw his dividends.

NEW JERUSALEM

He stood – a bitter scolding man,
ravaged by cruel years –

and pictured out a poet's plan,
calling up angry tears.
The party, gathered in the rain,
mumbled applause – and then
forgot their worklessness and pain,
became enchanted men.
I saw eyes flash with hidden fire,
and knuckles whiten hard,
for they beheld their hearts' desire,
and it was closely barred.

He ceased: the fists relaxed, and we
prepared to hurry home.
The Chairman mutter'd, 'Half-past three,
next Sunday; try an' come.'

TO A MODERN IRISH POET

You drowsed my senses by your misty kings,
  dream-drunken ladies languid as the noon,
until I deemed no other songbird sings,
  save nightingale in twilight to the moon.

You came with your strange, wistful, trembling verse,
  beguiled me for a while in quaint deceit;
and I forgot th'oppressor's blow and curse,
  the muffled tread of workless in the street.

A silver trumpet, or a golden thong,
  these are the harmonies loved of thy muse.
'Tis better done to beat from bitter wrong
  a flaming slogan's challenge, fit for use!

TO THE MEMORY OF JAMES CONNOLLY

A dozen years have passed since then,
  The memory has died away
Of Connolly and the martyred men
  Who rose on Easter Day.

When I was six years old I heard
  Connolly address a Labour crowd –

I cannot recollect a word
  Yet I am very proud –

As one who stood upon the edge
  Of Galilee to watch the ship
That waders pushed beyond the sedge
  While bright oars flash and dip;

But not indeed as one who stood
  Among the crowd on Calvary
To see Christ die for Brotherhood,
  As Connolly died for me.

PAPER BANNERS

to certain working-girl pickets
seen in Dublin

At noon I passed and saw you there,
Girls striding slowly up and down,
Your paper banners in the air,
The weary air of Dublin town.

When I returned in time for tea
You held your ranks unbroken still –
A sober chiding 'twas for me
That seeks to lessen human ill.

My life is spent in futile play,
In daily strategies of brain,
And seldom does there come a day
When I remember wrong and pain.

But you go crying through our night,
Hoarse little victims of such wrong,
Rallying workers to their fight.
O noble sisters, take my song.

OMENS AND AUGURIES

Last night from Troy's high battlements
  I saw a falling star,
Where shone above the Grecian tents
  The moon's gold scimitar.

Tonight I saw a falling star
O'er roofs and chimneypots.
I wonder who the pedants are
That weave Time's dusty plots.

ASHES IN THE WIND

Isis is dead: her fame is hid
Under the dust of centuries,
As sand piles o'er a pyramid
Choking the well's encircling trees.

Helen is dead, and windy Troy's
But heapèd stone and tufted grass,
Where singing shrill brown Arab boys,
Trudging beside their camels, pass.

IN PRAISE OF ELISABETH

Had I a golden-broidered life?
Was mine a red and velvet death?
Did Marlowe feel my shining knife,
In thy dead days, Elisabeth?

And did I play an ebon lute
In company of Campion,
Casting it down and leaving mute
My madrigals when Ben was gone?

And to thee brought a negro boy
With ivory teeth and tales of death?
Ah, surely, surely I had joy
In thy dear days, Elisabeth.

NETTLES OF OFFENCE

One had a fair body,
One a lovely face,
And I loved each because of this –
Because of their high grace.

Each in her love for me
   Plucked nettles of offence . . .
While one lies robed in flame, one is
   Shod with impenitence.

IN THAT FAIR AND PLEASANT LAND . . .

'In that fair and pleasant land
Lo, He sits on God's right hand.'
So Parson said: it worried me,
Remembering the Trinity,
How God the Father, God the Son,
And God the Spirit are but one!

The explanation must be that
His God is quite an acrobat.

COLNEY HATCH

I will put Truth in a box because
They say Truth's dynamite,
Then I will sap and mine Earth's walls
And set the fuse alight.

Then I will run away and hide,
Stopping my ears with wool . . .
And when th'explosion's over, come
And build Earth beautiful.

TIMBER

Whether sunshine, snow, or rain,
Caesar now and Charlemain
Sleep and will not wake again.

Sandstorms sweep o'er Babylon:
Thistles cover Marathon:
Sheba's dead, and Solomon.

Winds fret through the creaking trees,
Gusty with ten centuries . . .
Trees are more than dynasties.

YOUNG WOMANHOOD

Young girls alone are lovely,
  Fresh saplings in the wind.
The grace of each young body
  Is pleasing to my mind.

Their faces and white bodies
  Heal up the hurt of Time,
Till old immortal ladies
  Walk forth again in rime.

IRON AND STONE

Old metal princes, copper-coloured, cool,
  With pointed feet and faces set and hard,
Lie sleeping in the twilight beautiful,
  Above the pebble-paven palace yard.

Stern kings of icy stone stand in a row,
  For time has dried the sap from out their veins,
And age's dust has grimed their beards of snow,
  Down in the dawn-grey vault's green-guttered drains.

MISTER FAINTHEART MIDDLECLASS

When I see workless men I hurry by
Lest I should seem to mock their wretchedness,
For food, and fire, and roof and books have I,
And comfortable dress . . .

They stand together in the rain and spit
Upon the greasy pavement of the street,
And mutter sporting gossip and make wit
Of dull, obscene deceit . . .

I dare not tell them that I have a plan
To bring a certain end to their distress,
To give them food and shelter, every man,
And comfortable dress.

ON HEARING A TRAVELLER'S TALE OF THE ALPS

He said you should not give a shout
  Among the snowbound Alpine hills,
  For fear some angry spirit spills
An avalanche from his redoubt.

I thought how good it would be if
  I might go shouting through the town,
  Tempting that spirit to cast down
His avalanche from Heaven's cliff

To smother up the things I hate,
  Bottling from sight Time's cruel face
  Till men upon our débris base
A kinder, fairer, nobler state.

A FATHER EXPLAINS

My son and I went for a walk –
Oh God, how little children talk!
We saw a man stand in the street
In rags and stamping slush-cold feet,
And farther on another man
Was begging – so the child began:
'Who's that man in the gutter, Dad?
Why does he look so glum an' sad?
Why's he lame, an' where's his leg?
An' does he always have to beg?
What's he wearing medals for?' –
Be quiet, child. He won the War!

MOTIVES

Cleopatra dead and famous,
  Wanton Helen, bane of Greece,
Rise ye never now to shame us
  In our pitiable peace.

Wars we know and battle glories
  Waged for colonies and spoil,

Troy and Pompeii are dull stories
To the lords that fight for oil.

ANY RICH SUBURBAN CHURCH

Last Sunday afternoon I went
And climbed a soapbox in the rain,
And spoke to my strange regiment
Of tattered men about their pain.

Returning home, dead-tired, for tea,
I passed a church at half-past six –
Parked motors in their panoply
Switched back my thoughts to politics.

Next Sunday I will go again
And summon my strange regiment,
And march them to that hallowed fane –
And there will be – an accident!

HYMN

Noon in an English county,
We scare the grazing flocks;
God bless the redcoat riders;
God help the hunted fox.

Moonlight in Monte Carlo,
Daybreak on Matterhorn.
God bless the winter tourists;
God help the gutter-born.

THE RANK-AND-FILER

I knew him well, and yet I did not know
The inner splendour of his shining heart,
The bitter triumph won from bodily smart,
Half baffled by hard circumstance's blow:

For he was poor and ill and tramped the street
Daily in search of work to feed his child;

Yet still his stormy soul unreconciled
Took hope from every falter and defeat.

One winter night among the dispossessed,
I stood beside him while a scolding man
Stormed Heaven with his cries Promethean,
And fired a torch within each hearer's breast.

We sauntered home when that hoarse man was done,
By crooked alleys to his mean abode.
At the street's end we stopped: his features glowed.
As he remarked, 'Big job before us, son!'

FOR CERTAIN SUBSCRIBERS TO THE MINERS' FUND

Oh you are kind and lavish with your pence.
You answer these appeals most handsomely,
And for a while are happy to agree
In this support to broadcast eloquence.

The season's talk of brotherhood, good sense
Gladdens your hearts as you sit down to tea
Or swallow port wine, cocktails . . . As for me,
God knows I hate your very insolence.

Is it today our shoes begin to leak?
Is it tonight our grates are bare and cold?
Is it just now . . . or only just this week?
No, curse you! We have known these things of old.

This charity shall not wipe out the wrong
When dawn breaks, lark-filled with the workers' song.

SUBURB

There is a villa avenue
Where motors rest at every gate;
I often take a short cut through
And envy those so fortunate:

For well I know a smoky slum
Where very seldom does there chance

Another vehicle to come
  Save accident's hoarse ambulance.

ARISTOCRATIC AREA

I know a quiet avenue,
  Trim-plotted, lined with beeches tall,
Where sudden sunlight flashing through
  Made splendid the last pomp of fall.

There is one thing I mean to do:
  When spring runs down this leafy length
I'll gather in this avenue
  The slum folk in their ragged strength.

LIMITATIONS

I sought to put the sunshine in a song,
  Green open fields and sheep that do their will,
And high waves, and a wind that sings along
  To laugh its heart out up a misty hill:

And hours of happy ease beneath a tree,
  Hearing the thick boughs mutter like far surf,
And easy tramps with minds and legs carefree
  Over green miles of undulating turf.

But all I get in my hard-textured song
  Is dust and muffled drums of our defeat,
And hungry men that dumbly suffer wrong,
  And barefoot children in the smoky street.

EQUALITY

With equal largesse spends the sun,
  An equal system sways the seas,
And shall man prove the foolish one
  To break the law that masters these?

Shall we profane attempt to bind
  Our fellows in unequal yoke?

Oh hasten lest too late we find,
  Sun, stars, and seas their law revoke.

EPITAPH FOR A GARDENER

Life limited his scope to this small plot,
  This tiny triumph over weed and rock,
Wherein he planted mint and bergamot
  And those gay steeples of the hollyhock.

But now, if God has planned hereafter well
  And does things nobly for the newly dead,
This old man tends great banks of asphodel
  And amaranthus blossoms bed on bed.

THE SIMPLE-MINDED CHRISTIAN

When workless men walk down the street
In ragged clothes, on ill-shod feet,
And beggars rake the bins for meat,
The Christian should not drink or eat.

When children cry aloud for bread
In slums disease-inhabited,
And mothers wish that they were dead,
The Christian should not go to bed.

TWO SONNETS ON THE FREE STATE CENSORSHIP BILL

I

Grim Dean, who sleeps within his pulpit's shade,
  Canst thou rise up to say the bitter thing
  Or pen the words that hiss and stab and sting
And flay the foul flesh of the Pope's brigade?
Ah, no! Thou sleepest: and the glories fade
  From off the altar, and the censers swing;
  The mystic smoke climbs up in clouds that cling
About the temples of the priestly trade.

O Swift, these tricksters in thy famous town
  Have laid a plot to fetter our free minds,
  And bring again the chainèd Bible days.

And later, doubt not but the martyr's gown
  Of living flame, the white-hot iron that blinds,
  Shall be brought back to better Heaven's praise!

II

Oh, ban the books and save the children's lives,
  And cut the heart out of the sceptic's rage;
  Erase the angry word that mars the page,
That sears the soul, yet in its searing shrives.
Go bind our dreaming spirits in steel gyves,
  Since freedom's dead in this still darker age;
  Lest we forsake the dictates of the sage
And play with ethics of the herds and hives.

O worthy purpose, O most noble plan,
  O holy Churchmen who will save our youth
From all the bitter blasphemies of man,
  And lead them gently in the ways of truth!

Your God grant pardon . . . my wild rage outran
  Christ's love and saw ye perish in red ruth.

SILVER WAS THE BARBÈD HOOK . . .

Silver was the barbèd hook
  Dropped into the silver stream,
As the silver stream was shook
  To allure the silver bream.

Silver shone the broad-faced moon
  When I hooked the silver fish;
And a silver queen will soon
  Sup it from a silver dish.

THE REBEL

I died, a follower of Cade,
In Kent for liberty.

When thousands on the barricade
Were murdered, there was I.
With Sacco and Vanzetti too,
The chair became my throne
In Russian cells the knout I knew,
Where frost cuts to the bone.
Indeed, on skull-shaped Calvary,
Impenitent we hung
And talked of Zion, he and I
Who had to die so young.
O Christ, of friendless men the friend,
O Harrower of Hell,
I stand, thy kinsman to the end,
Teaching men to rebel.

MATHEMATICS

Can those old dusty learned men
  That talk of pi and calculus
Wake up to red-blood life again,
  And think quite like the rest of us?
    And can they stop awhile to laugh
    Who live in diagram and graph?

Or is their function on this globe
  To seek the underlying laws,
Giving their hearts to pry and probe
  Time's ultimate and starry cause?
    Or would life seem more plain to me
    If I knew trigonometry?

THE MONARCH

His fingers tangled in his beard,
  The old king brooded on his throne:
The little hunchback smirked and leered,
  And mumbled in a monotone . . .

The king stood up and clapped his hands:
  A slave in satin shuffled in . . .
Ere dark they cried throughout his lands,
  'The king has thought of a new sin.'

NEBULA

Who knows yon star that blinks at us
May have gone out these hundred years,
And yet it shone on Darius
As he stood in his wood of spears.

Mayhap a lonely man looked out
From his snow cabin in the north,
And like light snowflakes shed his doubt,
And girt his shoes and hurried forth.

Who knows but it is similar
With those that have a faith in God,
And he is but a blind bright star
Whose heat would not burn up a sod.

IMMORTALITY

Talk turned this evening on the end of man,
And if there is survival after death:
So I perforce then heatedly began
To quarrel with the old established faith:
'Where are the dead? . . . Their bodies rot, we know.
This Christian Heaven can't be in the sky.
To what far star then do the spirits go?'
So they in turn rebuked me heatedly:
'Oh look around, see all the woe and pain
That clouds the days of this our earthly life.'
One answered, 'Christ the Lord will come again
And bring an age of gold to end our strife.
God will have mercy on His people yet:
He will adjust th'innumerable scores.'
'But sir,' I cried, 'You do, it seems, forget
He had no mercy on the brontosaurs.
Shall we not vanish also from the earth
Leaving white bones to show what once was man
To some new creature of a greater birth
That follows us as we the saurian?'

SONNET

I have no time to worship. I must live:
The days in which we move are marred with wrong.

Shall I be craven then and fail to give
Hard blow for blow, and bitter song for song?
I know that breath is light and fugitive,
That Art's eternal and may well prolong
The shaken echoes beaten from Life's gong
By hands that seize on man's prerogative.

But what is there to worship if I would?
The cell and star are both beyond my ken:
The best I know is human brotherhood,
The dearest things enslaved and broken men.
So, if you will, call my hoarse, crying wrath
An act of worship in a newer faith.

WILLOW PATTERN

Pagoda princes in blue silk
  Move past like hesitant gazelles,
Through blossoms blown as white as milk
  Where winds are drowsy, full of bells.

A melancholy mandarin
  Like peacock spreads his starry dress,
While, softly plucked, a mandolin
  Shakes through the moonlit loveliness.

Two satin lovers by the sea
  Wait for the gold-sailed lacquer boat,
And beat their white hands aimlessly
  As lotus blooms beside them float.

AESTHETE'S RENUNCIATION

Had I the time I'd like to see
The great white horse of Westbury.
I'd like to walk through old Madrid,
And gaze on Pharaoh's pyramid:
Eat curried rice in dim Hong Kong
While coolies row me with a song:
And hear the bulbul in the trees
Walking alone in Persian peace:
On Tartar steppes drink wild mare's milk,

And rustle through Canton in silk:
And stand before bright tapestries
Of Paris clasping Helen's knees.
Then I would saunter home to tell
How sunlight strikes Rome's capital,
And how the camel bells swing low
When hunchbacked sandhills rise and go
At bidding of the bitter East.
And what dead kings loved for the feast –
Pink peacocks' tongues and nests of birds,
And pearl-rich wine, and crystal curds,
But each dish with its subtle scent
Black cooks distilled for ornament
And how van Eyck is better than
The famousest Italian.
But though I'd like to do and say
These things, today is still today:
And men tramp hungry down the street,
In ragged clothes, on ill-shod feet,
And little children cry for bread
In dens disease-inhabited.
And women sell their bodies white
To leering men by cold lamp light:
And honest people go to work
In wet bleak winter twilight's dark,
While other folk sail south for France
And in the moonlight drink and dance:
While pasteboard kings and tipsy lords
Stamp on the stage and clash their swords.
And my poor people are forgot,
Are left to starve and die, and rot.
So the time's not ripe for me to see
That great white horse at Westbury,
And till my people rise and strike
I dare not see the things I'd like.
So I shall stay at home and shout
Until this thing will come about:
Then I and they will go and see
The galleries of Italy.

SONNET

Since brooding men put beauty in a rime
And fixed it there for ever by their skill

There is no need for any daffodil
To wither when spring withers with old time.
Though beauty be intangible as the chime
Of mellow silver bells from some high hill,
It is our privilege, with ink and quill,
To hoard it up against an age's crime.

And if my name be known awhile to men
It shall not be because of flaming deeds,
But rather as a rude and artless pen
Cut in bleak season from the whistling reeds
Wherewith the spirit of the years wrote down
The half-created beauty that else had flown.

THE NOVICE

The weary novice thumbed his beads,
Yawned gently, blew his candle out.
'No doubt the holy icon bleeds.
No doubt.' He said again, 'No doubt.
But then I saw the priest come out,
Rubbing a dark stain from his hands,
And there before the shrine, devout,
A worshipper still praying, stands.'

MARCH DAY

I never heard the birds until today:
  A sparrow-heavy bush, a busy tree,
  A sunny morning full of melody,
And crocuses that stab the frozen clay:
These seemed to throng the landscape. Far away
  The hills were greener than they used to be
  When mist drew trailing veils in front of me
And late-lit lamps glowed gold in dawn's thick grey.

These birds, that were my pensioners and worse,
  Have now forsaken my crumbed windowsill,
And here about the sky blithe songs rehearse
  To win again quick phrasing, slur, and trill.
I take the hint, and stretch my limbs in verse
  To be prepared for spring's first daffodil.

SONG FOR MAY DAY

Today you wear your ribbon red to symbolise your brotherhood
With all the workers of the earth whose veins run red with common
  blood.
And I salute you, comrades all, as one salutes forgotten friends,
Stung by the spring to wakefulness, and turned from Life's ignoble
  ends.
But in my dreams I see a host of hero martyrs who are dead:
John Brown, James Connolly, and Christ, for you I wear my ribbon
  red.

DUSTY ROADS

'I heard a lark, I heard a thrush,
I heard a starling on a bush . . .'

A voice was ringing through the wood,
In a bright glade the singer stood.
I asked him where he had been born:
He said mid fields of springing corn.
I asked him what his age might be:
He said just half that old oak tree.
I asked him how he earned his meat:
He said there's turnips, apples, beet,
And water running, running still
From tip to toe of every hill.
I asked him where he travelled to:
He said perhaps the west wind knew.
I asked him if he'd take me there:
He said: 'You'd be content to share
The hedge's shelter from the rain,
The berries in the rutted lane,
The haystacks in the ghostly moon,
The dusty highway at the noon,
The smoky fire, the stars at night,
The fir trees' moan, the dawn's grey light,
The stolen fowl, the begged-for eggs,
The steep hills and the weary legs,
The workhouse ward, the daily bath,
The cinders on the prison path,
The policeman's fist, the whipping sleet,
The thin man praying in the street?'

As I was making up my mind
He vanished quicker than the wind.
But in the morning air so still
I heard him singing down the hill:
'I heard a lark, I heard a thrush,
I heard a starling on a bush.'

PENDRAGON

The wizard touch of Merlin's gone:
King Arthur sleeps in Avalon,
And Jennifer is half forgot –
Save as a rime for Camelot.
The tide flows through dead Iseult's tress
Five fathoms deep in Lyonesse,
But when the midnight waters stir
I see the old Excalibur.

PEACE PACT

You bring the hawthorn and laburnum back,
  And they bring you, for it was during May
My citadel gave in to your attack,
  And draped its streets with flags for holiday.

You were repulsed. Another foeman came,
  Putting a deeper bondage on the place.
But when the hawthorn burns with white-hot flame
  The treaty's threatened by your mocking face.

OPHELIA

In the fine rain small birds made merry din
  When she turned down the lane towards the river.
Then gusts of March blew down, and in the thin
  And delicate sunlight set the rushes ashiver.

The sun grew strong, the rain wore off, and she,
  Bending above her rake, began her labour.
Sleek crows beat past, and somewhere in a tree
  A hidden bird made melody her neighbour.

She did not come to help him with the cows
   In the far meadow when her father shouted.
He only startled thrushes from the boughs
   Who fled like frightened fledglings cuckoo-routed.

In the cold dawn small birds made merry din
   When tanned men searched the willow-bordered river.
And when the wind blew back the rushes thin
   They found her drowned where salleys creak and shiver.

SARCOPHAGUS

They bound her in white linen, smeared rich spice
Over her cold limbs: closed her sleeping eyes,
Tied back her jet-black hair in two broad bands,
And on her small breasts laid her small brown hands.
They laid her gently in a cushioned sleep
In a long box, set with great pearls the deep
Sea yielded up to flashing naked men,
For she was dead and would not wake again.

She was a Pharaoh's daughter, young and very fair.
Oh Isis, how the sunlight on her hair
Struck gold from ebon, till like Danaë
She stood flame-cinctured to her marble knee.

A tall man came and counted out some gold,
And led me to the tomb. He was too old
To weep that beauty dies away to dust.
He pointed to the box and said. 'You must
Paint on this side and this. Her father was
A Pharaoh, and for her in kindness has
Ordained this burial in sculptured stone.
And say, He is the greatest Pharaoh known:
The strongest ruler since Osiris here
Put empire on the desert, and put fear
On the dusk dwellers by the palm-skirted Nile,
And dread in every mud-drowsed crocodile.'

He went away. I took the colours and drew,
Not what the tall man said, but what I knew.
So I shall die tomorrow when he comes
To drive the demons off with little drums.

NO COMMENT!

'Come, George. Champagne and oysters,
A rubber – and then to bed,'
Said one of the never hungry
To one of the overfed.

A sick girl coughed in a doorway:
A beggar sang in the street:
And children crawled in the gutter
Looking for something to eat.

Then at a windy corner
A thin man shook his fist,
The sergeant nibbled his pencil,
And wrote – 'A Communist.'

But all the time I was dreaming
Of a new day breaking red,
When no one is ever hungry
And there are no overfed.

TWO SONNETS

I THE LITTLE BOURGEOIS IS UPSET

A woman rapped my door tonight and stood
Nursing a baby in the stinging rain.
Its face was twisted as it were in pain,
And sick through lack of sunshine, clothes, and food.
She asked me for a copper, 'or as good,
A slice of bread to give the cryin' wean'.
I gave her both, told her to call again:
With cold blue lips she thanked me, said she would.

So I went back and sat before the fire,
Lit up my pipe, and tried to read a book.
The wind and rain outside became a storm.
I drew the blinds, and heaped the fuel higher,
But could not free my mind from her thin form,
And that poor baby's pitiable look.

II HE SUGGESTS A SOLUTION

So I have written this that men may know
Comfort and warmth are curses till we make

A new bright world for little children's sake,
And pleasant paths where they may come and go,
Yet feel no cold when winter brings the snow,
Nor suffer thirsts in summer none can slake.
For is the earth not ours if we but take?
And what is there that we must overthrow?

A handful, here and there, of insolent men
Whose word rules when the people starve or eat,
Who call in at their offices at ten,
And leave their motors purring in the street.
By God it's simple – just as you'll say when
Their little world will crash about your feet.

THE DOCTOR MUSES

Last night I stood beside a woman's bed,
  A candle in a bottle gave us light,
But when the child came it was cold and dead;
  The father shouting ran into the night.

If it had lived there would have been no heat;
  The grate was empty. Even slums are cold
When dawn slips silver-sandalled down the street,
  And turns the gutters to bright streams of gold.

Prize pups have better chances than a child
  Who stupidly selects a dirty slum
To be born in. Why, not a month ago
  A duchess had a baby – Clynes went wild,
And all the papers made a splendid show,
  And only filthy Communists were dumb.

FAIR GAME

A man stopped me in a lane:
  'For Crissake give us a smoke.
My belly's rumblin' wi' hunger,
  I'm on the road, and broke.'

Over the hedges I saw
  While he was lighting up
A fat gamekeeper striding along
  With double-barrel and pup.

'He's goin' ta look at the pheasants,'
The tramp said, blowing rings.
I coughed and meekly suggested
How much we bungle things.

With features puckered and puzzled
He waited till I had done:
I wish you'd seen his face when I said,
'We ought to have that gun.'

THE GOLDEN BOY

A king, the story oft was told,
Whose passion was for pageantry,
Coated a boy with molten gold
To bear torch for his company.

The living lad beneath the flow
That hardened to a golden crust
Soon died – hence men will ever know
The curse of gold, that monarch's lust.

Today I passed two hundred men,
White with the dust of coarse cement,
And that old legend dreamed again
As coughing, slow they homeward went.

IN MEMORIAM: D.H. LAWRENCE

born 11 September 1885
died 2 March 1930

For Lycidas the laurel is not sere,
Though he who wove that garland long is gone;
The white moon rises for Endymion,
Though Shelley's cloud and skylark many a year.
By splendid singing one in days more near
Has been raised to that galaxy alone,
Though his young body lies beneath a stone
By the sea-battered cliffs of Skyros sheer.

And you, shall you go out into the dark
Without the tribute of one feeble song?

Your titan gestures, stern, tremendous, stark,
Your wounded challenge to the starry sky,
Have turned my mind to brood on ancient wrong,
And from that brooding I have made this cry.

THE MAD APPLEGROWER

It breaks my heart to sell this fruit:
  For twenty year I've knowed each tree,
Have cared for bark, and branch, and root,
  And lived with them right happily.

But till I fill a sock with gold
  I must do this, betray my trees,
For I am nigh four score years old,
  And mortal stiff about the knees.

Happen I'll fill that sock this year . . .
  No apples after that I'll sell,
But call my friend the gamekeeper
  To make the cider he makes well.

Then I will take the old coach road
  To where that orchard blooms in spring,
And draw to town a merry load
  That is not meant for marketing.

THE PALMIST

She read my hand and told me patent lies:
The little truth she said was in my face.
One can't disguise one's feelings when a word,
Uttered by chance or craft, probes memory.

Said I was disappointed: and in love,
Would get some money from America,
And must beware a tall strange man in grey.

But then she said, 'Your lover is untrue,
And even now is kissing someone's hair' –
How could she know that he was fond of hair,
And kissed mine till it fell in a black flood.
God! how I hate her for her second sight.

APPARITION

I stood at twilight on a mound:
  The grass was wet beneath my feet:
A dripping moon rose wet and round,
  And winds blew faint horns of retreat.

A shape of mist with shield and spear
  Stood in the bracken to his knees.
I raised my hand to call him near . . .
  He trailed his spear into the trees.

I turned me lonely to my hut;
  The curtained candle seemed a star.
It may have been Cuchullain, but
  I think 'twas only Concobar.

EASTER TUESDAY

I carefully let Easter pass this year
  Without a thought of Calvary's bare hill,
  being intent on bird and daffodil,
and April skies with one cold star and clear,
I watched the red-tipped daisies peep and peer
  out of the fresh thick grass, and skylarks fill
  the air with fluttered chorusing until
I felt myself a similar sonneteer.

But yesterday a man went up the street
  singing a rebel song of Easter Week,
    and the old unquiet woke within my head.
I saw again the blood bedabbled feet,
  and all the horror that I dared not speak,
    and knew that Christ and Connolly were dead.

PRACTICAL MYSTICISM

Gaze at a fire till it grow cold and far:
Look at the moon till it rush hot and near:
  Then suddenly space widens, and you are
  Naked and lonely on a tumbling star,
Your throat sore bruisèd by thin hands of fear.

Look at a tree, climb each bent twig in thought,
   Delve mole-like with the writhing of each root.
Then suddenly the earth and stars are caught
In a live mesh, and in one pattern wrought
   Till God and you are one with seed and fruit.

Then having done these things go back to men,
   Live quietly the fag end of your days:
Speak not above a whisper, only then
To urgent folk who will not come again
   And need your comfort, hunger for your praise.

ARITHMETIC

Six larks are not so sweet as one,
or fingers were not made to count.
I lay on bracken in the sun
and watched the urgent songsters mount
till there were dozens in the sky,
crowding it with monotony.

But striding through the beaded grass
I heard a corncrake call its mate:
the echoes seemed to pass and pass
across two hedges and a gate –
'twas faëry almost – then I knew
one corncrake's not as good as two.

THE LAST CRUSADE

As I stood alone on a windy mound
   and counted the stars in the sky,
a horseman came riding northward bound,
   but he slackened his pace at my cry.

'Oh where do ye ride? Oh where do ye ride,
      that the rein is loose in your hands?'
'To preach the word of Christ,' he cried,
   'to the dwellers in heathen lands.'

A year and a day plodded past me there
   as I stood on the mound alone,

when the horseman came back with the wind in his hair,
  but his face was as white as a bone.

'Oh where do ye ride with the clenchèd fist?
  Oh where do ye ride again?'
'To deliver the broken body of Christ
  from the hands of Christian men.'

BRADFORD MILLIONAIRE

With rolled umbrella, little bowler hat,
  and spats to hide superfluous patterned socks,
he walks oblivious to both owl and bat,
  and never hears the sirens on the rocks.

Trees arch his heaven, limit his low sky,
  His cellars echo to the scurrying rat,
And when a God-drunk poet lurches by
  he never even lifts his little hat.

CHANT FOR THE FIVE-YEAR PLAN

Let the engines roar. Let the engines roar.
We must make far more. Let the engines roar.
Let the shuttles sing. Let the shuttles sing.
And the hammers ring. Let the derricks swing.
Shoulder to shoulder, woman and man,
another heave for the five-year plan
five-year FIVE-YEAR FIVE-YEAR PLAN.

Pull down the slums. Give the factories room.
Comrade, comrade, back to your loom.
Build bright houses with plenty of room.
No more cramping in the dirt and the gloom.
Way for the tractor. Ten miles of wheat,
and children crying for bread in the street.
Shoulder to shoulder, woman and man,
another heave for the five-year plan
five-year FIVE-YEAR FIVE-YEAR PLAN.

Marx was a man with a big black beard,
he's dead many years, but his name is feared:

though not because of his menacing look,
but because of the words that he wrote in a book.
Ilyich Lenin was small and square,
but he bored through the Czar with his gimlet stare.
And now he sleeps in the Kremlin Wall,
Ilyich Lenin, square and small . . .

But if he should find us standing there
he'd bore us through with his gimlet stare.
And Marx would shout, 'You forgot to look
at the thick black type in the big red book.'
So comrade, comrade, back to your loom.
Let the engines roar. Give the factories room.

We must not stop till Russia's all wheat,
and children are singing for joy in the street.
We must not stop till every man
is part of the World's Great Five-Year Plan.
We must not stop till the Earth is Free
of War and Hate and Poverty.
Till the World is free. Till the World is Free.
Let the engines roar. Let the engines roar
from the Urals' crags to the Baltic's shore.
Shoulder to shoulder, woman and man,
another heave for the five-year plan
five-year
FIVE-YEAR
FIVE-YEAR
PLAN.

ADMONITION TO SCIENCE

Though you breed men to better tree and root,
and bundle clouds up for the ripening
of dull unpoppied corn and hard bright fruit,
or bid the earth tilt carefully to spring:

though you build starcinct palaces of gold,
drape topaz walls with tapestries of light,
or with undreamed-of braziers banish cold,
and shape of sunbeams torches for the night:

what shall't avail? The Incas of Peru
had kindly laws and moved with quiet grace,

accepting moon and thunder, since they knew
no tense abstraction can unbaffle space.

OF A PROFESSOR

When he is dead
I shall remember affectionately the swing of his cape
and the shape
of his head.

NOTE ON INTELLECTUALS

I passed a Poet in a dismal street
and envied him his proud and happy air.
He saw no oily gutter at his feet,
nor feared the sickly harlot's hungry stare.

Then in a nearby window hung a cage.
A prisoned skylark made my anger wake.
I slowed my pace to share the Poet's rage:
but he strode on . . . intent upon his Blake.

THE TERRIBLE CHOICE

Shalt thou be dug or left as pasture land
Where meditative cattle chew the cud,
For the green corn of the mind on either hand
Is choked by the passionate poppies of the blood?

Before the urgent roots or seedlings start
Choose thou, and keep allegiance strong and whole:
Jesus, the singing shepherd of the heart,
Or Tolstoy, stubborn ploughman of the soul.

ATLAS

Take off your hat five minutes every day:
play Atlas for a while till you regain
the balanced horror of the universe
just resting on your back and pivoted
where your heels hit the uncomplaining ground.

That's why earth's greatest men walked slowly so
with heads bent forward, eyes fixed on the dust.
It's not the scampering ant bewitches them,
nor yet the grass blades jostling for the sun,
But th'imminent weight of heaven's secrecy,
the whole tremendous bulk of intangible law,
that bows them down. They hardly even smile
lest that dislodge a meteor or a star.

When you play Atlas, your mind's muscles knotted
and straining underneath the focused force,
I'd have you do it joyfuller than they.
Go move your feet to some trochaic measure,
and now and then toss up the burden from
your aching shoulders . . . that is, if you dare.
And your reward? The Pole Star in your hair.

SEASON'S RETURN

I saw the spring's first daffodil today,
with scudding sky of blue for overarch:
as I strode down my long accustomed way,
knowing in bone and sinew it was March,
and somewhere tassels jangled from the larch.

But I was sad, for heel and toe denied
the dizzy liquor of the morning air:
and all my gay and seasonable pride
was salted with a powder of despair
for I was growing old and did not care.

For I was growing old, and daffodils
were jargoning for other men than me.
The gorse's golden smoulder on the hills
when hawthorn hedges break in foamy sea
will sting strange lads to fresher poetry.

PIONEER

A warm spring day . . . the end of March:
Light grey down on the tasselled larch,
Buds shewing on the scraggy trees,

And clouds on splendid voyages
Across a vacant sky of blue.
The green grass bright with breaking through
The cleansing moisture of the earth.
But like a gesture of deep mirth
In small bedraggled garden mean
There stands the spring-caught evergreen.

FOR A MILD SEASON

Do not be eager, spring, to come:
  This weather may betray you still.
Frost yet may strike the thrushes dumb,
  And snow storm over that green hill.

Be tardy in thy burgeoning,
  And bid the trees be patient yet,
Lest winter take thee on the wing,
  And spring bring more than spring's regret.

MORNING HYMN

I cannot think men wholly lost
When I walk in the early frost.
Indeed our New Jerusalem
Shall rise to guard and shelter them
Built on bright hints from frost at morn
When everything is newly born,
When trees cut clearly in the air
Look far more delicate and rare,
And grass-blades sheathed in silver mail
Stand dagger-edged against the snail.
Our hearts beat quicker, and our feet
Make laughing echoes down the street:
Our touch is keener, and our eyes
Greeting the earth meet Paradise.
But bravest hint, the blood-red sun
His banner lifts for everyone.

VALUES

When on the banks of winter trees strip bare
  yet dread the plunge and huddle shivering,

I judge each gesture with a critic's care,
  nor prophesy a subterranean spring.

Each season is enough. Tomorrow's thought
  will shatter today's empetalled retinue.
A glint of sun on streaming branches caught
  is now and ever worth just that to you.

MAUBERLEY'S SON: A SUMMARY

At twenty-five or a little later he had decided
that thought to be useful must not be profound,
and spent a wet Saturday afternoon deriding
the critics who disliked his (ours, yours, anybody's) imitations of
  Ezra Pound.

Consequently he had never troubled to master
the scribble on the hare's shoulder blade, or the ogham on slates,
that has replaced the elegant Rosicrucian alabaster,
and makes any mountain less permanent than senator Yeats.

But morality had never been in question.
He had grown up a shoot of a Fabian tree:
swop metaphor . . . drunk skim milk from the breasts of
a granddaughter of Delacroix' liberty.

So not yet had the high seriousness,
the stiff bleak spirit that breaks before it bends,
left him sitting in thin rain on a misty bus-top
rather than talk at corners with literary friends.

Fortunately the Anglo-Catholic god of Mr Eliot
was no more real to him than Bernard Shaw,
and certainly had not that soap-and-water smell, or
the frosty brightness of late-Victorian eternal law.

So there was, at any rate, hope for him even if Lenin
had not yet ruined his style with allusions to Plekhanov,
for when a hungry crowd of unemployed men trailed
by, with torn flags, he had the decency to avert his face and cough.

ART'S DUPED RIDDLE

Though time be blocked in coloured squares
and fame's a greasy fingerprint,

perpetually rat-riddled stairs,
move under me with shrill creak's hint.

So I know well, though sick with space,
and dizzy on the rope-swung void,
a blind man heard men praise a face
and beauty's endlessly betroyed.

EGYPTIAN NIGHT

Weary with travel, hungry and afraid,
Joseph and Mary with their little son
came to the dark bulk of the resolute Sphinx,
and halted in the shadow, strength all gone.
Then night woke with her kind old comrade stars
who had convoyed their fearful journeying:
and Joseph, who had spread their scanty rags,
hobbled the ass, drew water from a spring,
and lay down on a bag of straw, and snored.
But Mary, when the frightened child made cry,
thanked Yahweh that her breasts had not yet failed,
and hummed a Galilean lullaby.
There in the lonely strange Egyptian night
the mysteries of time are met as one –
the circling legion of th'unfathomed stars,
the wind-scarred woman–beast, and Mary's son.

TIPHEAD

'Today we have each our Waste Land'

As I came through the desert on my right
dry bones of Eliot bleaching to the moon
and moss-dark hieroglyphs on rain-grey stone
where lizards crawled and bats whirred all the night.
As I came through the desert on my left
a ruined curate on a pinchbeck cross:
as I came through the desert thus it was,
of spear sponge nails thorn coronet bereft.

Here we come gathering nuts in may nuts in may nuts in may
here we come gathering nuts in may
on a cold and frosty morning.

This is that fiddle which for eighteen pence
I bought and played, when young and lacking sense.

A mudguard like a lonely roman arch
rests on a pile of rusted hoops and springs:
a poster preaching Mrs Robin's Starch
shakes ragged corners.
                                        Judah's shattered kings,
left on the hills or hanging by the hair,
are not more tragic.
                                    Bovril bottles stare
brown-socketed red eyes.
                                            The Jew has not
yet seen the profit in the reeking heap.
Warm winds from slob lands sweep the vacant lot.
The thin cat shakes a tin and goes to sleep.

Yet with this mortar I must brick my life,
paint cave wall, decorate bone hilted knife.

PRELUDE TO CONSTERNATION

Duty shunned, signals drunk:
lamplighter missed blind alley,
or pointsman laughs with girl.

Already in the valley
the cottages are sunk
under white-flagged whirl.

Rats gnawed dyke or prop.
None heard leak's sharp drop.
Though men scream from bus top
blind man strikes wheel. Goods train
head on roars in fogged brain.

ANTI-PROMETHEAN ODE

Leave now the crest of thought's high secrecy,
and the scarce breathable air.
Come down, come back to familiar hillock and tree,
and there

take your inviolable share.
You cannot dare
to stand a whole day poised against the sun,
letting the unappeasable eagle tear
your quivering entrails with harsh talon and beak.
Nor then, the self-appointed penance done,
would you have skill and language so to speak
of the adventure that men should
walk kindlier, follow more lasting good,
and build again ramparts of brotherhood.

Come down, come back: the mountain crags are bare,
and only once a lost lark scaled the air.
Did you not hear him, crying his dismay,
and heading for the cloud-patched fields below?
Too late returning he had missed his way
when overtaken by the plunging dark.
And when dawn came you found him, songless, stark,
shut-eyed upon a slipping ledge of snow.

Come down, come back: the winter of the heart
must break into a blossoming of joy.
That night's cold loneliness was all your part.
Time's secret is not vanquished thus.
The universe is not a ten years' Troy,
but stormed by sudden sallies glorious.
Troy even itself fell not without a trick.
Back then to fields and habitable places,
swift blossom-shattering showers and streaming faces.
For humble prose
of cart and street and steeple
forego the frenzied rhetoric
of toppling crags and elemental skies.
Go back and use your eyes
on hedge-hid speedwell or clipped garden rose,
on hearts and faces of dull common people.

MORNING MOMENT

I stood and gazed. The hills were hid in mist
save where a narrow avenue of wind
had tunnelled through and left a core of green,
two fields, a tree clump, and a glittering cottage,

backed by the sky's half-circle of blue light.
And as I stood I strove to make a phrase
that would embrace the magic of the thing,
the imminence of wonder, the delight,
the inescapable sense of time at work,
shaping an instant of significance:
a poet's birth, a saviour's revelation,
or an old man who had loved the grass and sky,
and known the skill and attitude of trees,
and now, grown drowsy, sees for the last time
the blue and green that nourished his endeavour,
and will lap round his everlasting rest.

DEFEAT

So from defeat I learn
The stress and strain of bone,
The twigs that smoke or burn,
The stone remaining stone
No matter what way thrown.

I shall go forth from thence
Aware of entity,
And to life's imminence
And tumult, I shall be
At once both rock and tree.

EPITHALAMION

O who will share with me
  The traffic of my heart?
The stripping of the tree:
  The frost that splits apart:
The winds that craze the boughs:
  The snow that breaks the branch:
Dry seasons ruinous:
  Night's sable avalanche:

Bleak dawn: the sun at noon
  By cloud unreckoned blurred:
Rain at the harvest moon,
  And lilt of larks unheard?

Yet for her comfort there
  Shall sometimes fall and rest
The high stars of the air
  Upon her rainchill breast.

MATIN SUR LE PORT

from the French of Albert Samain

Slowly the sun from the mist arises,
  Gilds the old tower and the tips of the spars,
And, with a touch on the shadowy waters,
  Meshes the sea in a mail of stars.

Suddenly struck by a distant glitter
  The marble domes and the arches gleam,
And in the clear air of the morning's splendour
  A spiced wind weaves an adventurous dream.

HOST

Set the tall white candles burning,
Bring white linen from the chest:
Let thy table gleam with silver
When Lord Love shall be thy guest.

But the door bolt to in silence,
Draw the gusty curtains thin:
Speak no word above a whisper
When Queen Sorrow would come in.

Take no thought of lighted window,
Lay no dishes, sweep no floor,
When that old blind beggar Fortune
Taps the pavement to thy door.

PRELUDE TO AN ODE FOR BARNUM

So to the tented ground where showmen come
On festive eve I wandered dismally,
Saw rusty-coated barker with a drum,
And heard the dreary burden of his cry.

Then under canvas flap that hid the sky,
But let the wind's four little brothers in,
I gaped at freaks and monsters strange as sin.

The Human Seal who balanced on his nose
A paper spill and juggled ball and stick;
The Tattooed Lady with too little clothes;
The Spotted Lady sure to make you sick;
The India-rubber Man whose only trick
Was pulling up the skin from's pimply chest;
And La Belle Eve, Miss Blackpool, fully dressed.

The stench of shawls and dirty bodies round,
The stale tobacco and the blue thick air,
The spittle-slippery puddles on the ground,
Conspired to fill my belly with despair.
So staggering out and round I knew not where
I came upon a sideshow and went in
And gaped at freaks and monsters strange as sin.

The Grocer with his fingers changed to cheese;
The Boxing Bishop with Short Talks to Men;
The Politician's barefaced policies
That broncoed up and billowed down again;
The Bearded Banker snarling in his den;
The Spotted Spaniard who three times a week
Sells submarines and zeps to Turk and Greek.

The Smallest Whiskey Drinker on the Earth;
The Tallest Bible-Reader in Brazil;
The only Nazi who has given birth
To babies that saluted her with 'Heil';
The Bankrupt Yankee who once bought the Hill
Called Calvary: in transit both were broken,
And there's no cross or Christ in all Hoboken.

The team of Fasting Men who sit upon
A pile of loaves and die by dull degrees –
This was perhaps the Greatest Piece of Fun –
Though four Protectors nearly bettered these
Who, building Tariff-walls on bleeding knees,
Stopped now and then to notice with a sigh
Birds, bees, and clouds float taxless through the sky.

The Greatest Thrill for half a century
Was where a young man knelt and laid him down
For tank to crush, shell smash, and fire to play,
Till there was nothing left save dust of bone.
Then, at a given signal, with a gun
Another lad with glory on his face
Stepped from the crowd and knelt in the same place.

So neat the action, and so humorous
The slick performance, from the Golden Band
That blared above the racket and the fuss
To well-groomed Dutchman with fat jewelled hand
Who sold the Music, Tanks, and owned the land
The Show was built on, I crept to the door
And laughed and laughed until my eyes were sore.

POEM

My name is Revolution – let me speak.
You find in me no feathery sentiment.
Not pity makes me base upon the weak
the tiptoe hope of half a continent,
but law that's shaped of changelessness and change;
the alternation of the upward slope;
the spiral core of being taut to range
back on itself and yet, surmounting hope,
reach levels that deny the limited
validity that once was broadest day;
th'insurgent bud that thrusts aside the dead,
the daffodils' negation of the clay.
Choose then the little choice that is your own:
death's rigid circle, life's inverted cone.

AQUARIUM

Let wonder leave us for another place,
trees bud for nurture of themselves alone;
be no rock split or turned: let stone be stone
black with the hearth fires of a beaten race.
Poised in the sunlit quiver of the case,
the smooth fish mocks the fret of troubled bone,
turns tail on twitching features not its own,
and moves superb on any plane of grace.

Learn that, if it be possible, and try
new scopes of motion. Death is in the old.
No feathered rescues trumpet from the sky.
No truth remains so having once been told.
Though tides of being swing unhurriedly,
to strike, who knows, sunk shaft of shattered gold.

SWAN'S NEST

The way I go is by a mere,
  With osiers breaking light in green;
Where in the autumn of the year
  The nine great floating swans were seen.

But when the pond was frozen grey,
  And grey the sky as wing of goose,
Stiff-necked, four rose and swung away,
  Their parents' home no further use.

With splash of February sun,
  When blue ripped through the whirling sky,
I saw two flying after one,
  Toward where the northern mountains lie.

The two deserted parents then,
  Unvexed by loss, and satisfied,
Built up the low, round nest again
  On grass bank at the waterside.

The mother coiled her wing and head,
  As if to sleep away the spring;
But once or twice she rose to spread
  The loving still, but weary wing.

A month I've paid them closer heed
  And studied with what elegance
The old swan steers through rush and reed,
  Dreaming of nine great floating swans.

MOURNE MOUNTAINS

But these are not my hills, they are too high:
they have not been, since ice ground slowly over,

abased to any force beneath the sky;
they are too harsh for me to be their lover.
The broad stone winking with the flattened stream,
the sheer cliff barren and the timeless peak:
not even sharp against the sun's last gleam
can I find comfort in them I may speak:
for they are from a world beyond my reach,
not the warm human world of broken earth,
the hand-chipped flints along the gravel beach,
the tilted dolmen and the baked clay hearth.
I do not fear a bare land but a high:
the curlew-whistling moors have no affright:
the bog-brown trout stream twisting hurriedly
can flash no terror in the failing light.
But the cold summit harried by the rain,
smothered in cloud or bannered far with snow,
has all the high sublimities of pain
I leave for braver hearts than mine to know.

FOR DEIRDRE

I would have her go to school
at the crag-fed mountain pool;
learn the best arithmetic
with ten pebbles and a stick;
know by climbing hill and tree
the gestures of geography;
master grammar's hardest word
in the deft phrases of a bird;
know a splashed stone's widening rings
more account than kings and kings;
and a bobbing scut in sight
more than all the verse men write;
love rock's edges; and in frost
find the pattern I have lost.

Then, her body disciplined
by the sweet rigours of the wind,
taught by water, ice, and fire,
what is possible desire,
taught by water, fire, and ice,
want of thought the only vice,

may she leave the oldest school
happy, strong, and beautiful.

OCTOBER'S CHILD

I watch the stack tilt on the garth fulfilled,
rooks in the stubble, rooks appeased fly home,
the burst sack drip till half its gold is spilled,
the swathe uncut from whence the lithe hares come,
and know the secret worth of being born
when the full can brims up its purple foam,
and clustered haws weigh down the splintered thorn.

I came in the full ripeness of the year.
My mother held me from the lamb's first bleat,
past bluebell days and blossoming of pear,
through sultry noons of rose and meadowsweet,
over the ridge of summer till she came
weary to gaze upon the ample wheat
kindled with poppies to a sudden flame.

Then when men's harvests filled the motey barn,
and hope rejoicing blessed the laden ark,
she brought me whimpering in a twilit morn
to follow candles in the crowding dark
and nursed me warm when time was dumb with snow,
and rocked me quiet when the trees were stark
that woke when I began a year ago.

So, though I love the seasons in their turn
for sake of her that bore me glad through each,
when the heaped leaves are swept and set to burn
I touch a magic deeper than my speech:
there is a strength and richness and an end
no other season's fledglings ever reach.
The year's fulfilment knows them not as friend.

My child, if I should ever father one,
let it be born at stripping of the tree,
in mellow warmth of an October sun
in well-tilled quarter of this north country,
and let the full year tincture every thought,

not summer's pride or spring's green urgency
but careful harvest to completion brought.

SEEDING TIME

This is the season of the thistledown,
tilted on whin, or not yet broken loose,
waiting the destined wind that, hatched behind
the cold hills of the west, is hurrying
to its appointed moment. From the beech
the green husk patters; from the sycamore
the scimitars spin down. Earth earns again
what was so lavish spent in flower and leaf.
And I, a barren summer in my pouch,
walking in dread of frost's grey penury,
already find my hands too small to cup
the cloud of clustered berries in my grasp.

FLIGHT

The three swans broke the water with a splash,
Dragging black feet and stretching urgent necks,
Beating great shining wings and flapping clear
To gleam and flash their silver in the sky,
March-tousled, grey, and blowing near to rain.
I paused to marvel, hearing in the wind
The whistle of their flight. They headed straight,
Across the curve and hollow of my path,
For the lead level of the upper lake
That slaps for ever on its flat wet stones.
When they were past I fumbled with my thought.
They are not lovely. Feather-balanced skill
Is beautiful to see, but this mere instinct,
This natural motion and form's a lesser thing.
I do not praise the stone for being stone.
I think them so remembering a poem,
And the clear phrase that leapt beyond the brush
Of whirring wing into a timeless sky
Beyond life's screaming hands and drumming fear.
They prey on darting fish, they hatch and die,
Fly so about the business of their hunger,
No cumulance of wisdom handed on.

They are lovely only in the dream-slaked mind . . .
So ran my thoughts, the scotching arguments
Clipping into the context, and my mind
Proud in its disillusion, proud and poor.
But sudden beat of pinions again;
I raised my solemn face. Again the three
Came whistling down the long slant of the land,
Bright in the troubled air and shadowless,
And I rejoiced in the wide-angled form,
My heart plucked from its pity, set aflame
With something out of time and out of space.

ULSTER WINTER (1942)

The army lorry, cold, anonymous,
Straining its plates and groaning heavily,
Bore me at speed along the winter road
Between black hedges under a grey sky.

Low on the left a flooded bog was fenced
With dark-tipped flags that here and there had gone
All over-ripe and harried by the wind
Into gay flaunting tufts of thistledown.

And on the right the higher ground assumed
The attributes of hills: the cresting trees,
Bare now and grey with evening's drifting mist,
Were vexed by starlings in daft companies.

Then, at a sudden corner, hedges gave
A grass bank topped by line of oak and beech
Above red arcs of wet decaying leaves,
And veined with ivy high as hand could reach.

I glanced at the young soldier by my side,
Gripping the wheel with a grubby-knuckled hand,
A cockney by his tongue, and wondered if
I spoke my thoughts he'd even understand.

For I am native, though my fathers came
From fatter acres over the grey sea:
The clay that hugs the rows of exile bones
Has shaped my phantom nationality.

FOR ONE WHO DID NOT MARCH

What bannered pardon slapping on the mast
shall wait the crooked heels of those who come?
There will be saws to tooth, and much to happen
before the flicked switch steers the tired cows home :
and one will hide behind a limping fable,
or point to card or table's alibi ;
or bluffing out the sequence smear the pity
in littered laurels and brass finale.

My hope is other, will accept the cynic,
the envy for the luck, the limbs entire,
be scarce and quiet, pocketing the gibe,
glad of the bitter hours I was awake,
for so I must contain as bottle takes
the fluent water and confers a shape.

ROLL CALL

I name my comrades, though they may not know
towards what adventure we together go.

First then, the artists that good fortune brought
within the narrow focus of my thought.
One, the dynamic symbolist, because,
while I but half discern his nature's laws,
he gives with lavish fist and will not stay
content with revelation yesterday,
still pressing out the frontiers of his mind
and leaving me amazed to drag behind,
enlarged and troubled, yet rejoiced to know
his quality before the trumpets blow.

And, peer with him, the tall dark painter who
no careless line or lazy contour drew,
who sees life steadily, asserting still
the heart-uplifting structure of a hill
against the peevish threat and sullen whim
that makes a crazy quagmire of the time.
This man the most, for his enriching mind
began with art and now involves mankind;
for hand and mind and picture integrated

necessitate an attitude created
from pulse's truth and time's wise evidence
from sun and soil and rightly measured stance.
So, he has found that those that would achieve
the durable in art, must first perceive
that art's the colour on the lips of life;
and that a sick mind with sick world at strife
can only breed ephemeralities,
contorted forms pigmented with disease.
For men engaged in plundering the earth
may only bring a monstrous art to birth;
this he has learned with clear unflinching eye,
and turned again to art and husbandry
to practice proved by precept and by guild,
for none can harvest where he has not tilled.

Another too, a brave far-travelled man,
by choice dramatic critic, with sharp pen
for social wrong, who now in sickness lies
immobilised awhile, must lend the cause
his sense and courage that his patient mind
may draw this blunt arc to the perfect round.

And after these: the voluble architect
who knows this country so, he can direct
your questing steps, in any lane or town,
to sill or door inherently our own,
and dreams of Ulster cleanly built and well,
with church and farm and workingmen's hotel,
discreetly using style and scale and site
to better life and keep tradition bright:
my father's friend, the country schoolmaster
who gives so much, by simply taking care
not to offend the least, and rightly earns
reward abundant in the gay returns
his children make with graver and with pen,
picture or poem fresh as a petalled whin
or thrush in hedge or dripping moss on stone
where, with small thunder, the dark stream drops down:
the poets now in Ulster fully ripe;
that still man I have praised, whose hanging pipe
and tweedy gestures cover up the press
and hurtling force of his bold images
that crash his words together till they break

with harsh new light that strikes us wide awake;
I owe his thought much thanks but not his style:
next the grave lad with disconcerting smile,
the country town solicitor whose verse
touches new richness, as the drifting years
kindle his wisdom to a friendly blaze
we marvel one so young can be so wise:
and one in friendship older, who by war
finds his shy spirit suddenly mature,
although as yet his harvest has been small,
each poem's sharp and individual,
cool as a brook, as winter sunshine brief,
tart as a berry, naked as a leaf:
and that fine woman with the gentle skill
for roses, words and friendship most of all:
and with these too, the rocking novelist
who lifts a sod up in his peasant fist
and shews the threads, the stems, the webs of dew,
till quickened sense regards the earth anew;
and any other whose thought finds its name
in honest story or in lilting rime
that, ready on the tongue or in the heart,
may tell of what allegiance it is part:
and in the van, that scholar who is deft
in quern and thatch and many a rural craft,
who by his honest and well-furbished mind
has shewn my generation where to find
the loyalties a people needs to live
and where its shrunk and battered roots survive
in our thrawn mesh of time-lag and decay,
and green shoots groping toward the coming day:
and one to whom a heart-roll or a cross
of woven rushes means a living place;
and that shy lord who has a friendly grip
for joiners, sculptors and men who handle sheep;
and the good woman with the merry eyes,
whose family, for near three centuries,
has tilled the well-named fields, who brings each year
the last sheaf of the harvest in with care;
and others, farmers' daughters, sons, I've heard
in dusty gas-lit schoolroom breathing hard,
grope through debate uncharted towards a plan
whereby man's name's spelt full as husbandman;
all parish chroniclers, or men who keep

old books and pamphlets for companionship,
or by pursuit of plants or ammonites
find mask to dig for fundamental roots,
nor press their wisdom into shrivelled notes:
the hiker leaning on the dry-stone wall
to watch the slow wings pass behind the hill
across the wind-scooped valley, or who turns
down any steep road in the rocky Mournes,
his tired heels beating out a marching tune
that ends with Bloody Bridge or Slievenaman.

These are my comrades though they may not know
to what adventure we together go
and if I asked them, would be sure to find
some other motive closer to the mind
that they can argue. Yet behind their words
some logic like the will that bids the birds
sing in December's sticks, or build in spring,
or punctually in autumn loosen wing
to cross the waters according to their kind,
moves to a purpose in each wakened mind,
to its degree, to hoard the cherished past
that not one valid quality be lost
for lack of love; to guard the growing ends
with whispered warning, warm protective hands;
to win a landskip equal to the love
his heart is big with – for no man can live
to his full height to whom no mountain burn
has chuckled welcome and has bade return;
to take the present for an urgent text
to draw an order out of, that the next
gay generation may not find their house
cold and unfriendly and anonymous,
but rather know the lines that we have planned
as folk ways fit for heart and head and hand
till joy and mercy again possess the land.

ULSTERMAN

Far back the shouting Briton in foray,
the sullen Roman with his tramping host,
the fair beard plaited in the Saxon way,
the horned prow torching terror to the coast:

then the dark chaunting Kelt with cup and cross,
the red Scot flying from a brother slain,
the English trooper plowing whin and moss,
the gaunt Scot praying in the thin grey rain.

These stir and mingle, leaping in my blood,
and what I am is only what they were,
if good in much, in that where they were good –
a truculent and irritable heir.

Kelt, Briton, Roman, Saxon, Dane, and Scot,
time and this island tied a crazy knot.

THE PLOUGHMAN

Up the steep brae the ill-matched horses climb,
turn at the furrows' end, in shadow stand,
before the slack reins loose within the hand
are tugged, and they go down another time.
From fronting hill, I watch the pantomime,
and catch, at wind's whim, the abrupt command
that guides the stumble down the clodrough land,
intent to twist the symbol into rime.

This man will later sow and, lucky, reap,
talk crops and horses, drinking at the fair,
will build a skill from weather, soil and spade.
Like him, I too shall rise and eat and sleep;
may neither ever find the earth less fair,
nor wish we had been taught another trade.

WILL

It is a matter for the human will
and will's the thing we cannot answer for;
the senses may go grazing, or we may till
the stubborn clods of our nature and be sure
of some crop sprouting; and the open heart
can always snatch some wonder from the air
that for a while may set our steps apart
from the swift jostling hurry to despair.

But will rocks idly, like a tethered skiff,
unoared or captained, settling slowly down,

who, given the habit and the practised hand,
could carry easily past the burnished cliff,
between the washed reefs, and the spray-cowled stone,
that safely we might come to our own land.

PERIODICITY

First day and night alarmed the child's salt eye:
night cold to wake in, not the close dark womb,
and spaced with noises, sometimes your own cry:
and day that tiptoed from the toy-stacked room.

The seasons told by holidays and games;
the kite, the egg, the hoop, the wading sea,
by loaves piled in the church porch, and by names
on parcels hanging from a grocer's tree.

This takes a while to learn, and as you learn
you too are changing into someone else:
then years appear, the date they say you were born,
the new year strange upon the tongues of bells.

Known once as feelings, known by senses now,
the celandine in sleet, the sun-warmed wall,
the smell of fog, the bitter taste of snow,
the evening shouts that greet the fielded ball.

These teem and throng the slow congested mind,
intrude on themes where they've no speaking part.
Compelled to check them, I can only find
the brave pace of a disregarded heart.

SHEEP FAIR

The gawky lad strides round the auction pen,
swinging his ashplant, with a hushing noise
keeping the crazed sheep circling, as the bids –
a knuckled finger or a jerky nod –
push the slow price by shillings toward the pound.

The auctioneer leans from his plinth and asks:
'Are they in the market, Paddy?' The shambling lad
shakes a grave head, a grave self-conscious head,

flushing a little since his mountain lambs
look small and sickly to his own sad eyes.

STALLION

Caught in a wedge of clanging trams and cars
that screeched their comfortable arrogance,
boys shouting shrilly of this morning's wars,
and crooners touting queues for penny glance,
a man strode anxious, dragging frothy bit
as the brown stallion with the long white nose
battered the squaresets with sharp, itching feet,
or veered like wind-slapped schooner tugging loose.

Then I remembered from the whin-gay ridge,
pausing with you to watch the sleek mare run
to toss mane-tasselled gaze above the hedge
and whinny to the passing stallion
as proud boy bobbed on him across the ditch
and foolish foal lay kicking in the sun.

WINTER DAY

When sun was winter high
and trees stood tall and bare
great flocks of rooks came by,
bright in the shining air.

And though the light was wan,
a stack men forked apart
shewed colour till it shone
like bullion on the cart.

The year had just begun
to break frost's discipline
with flecks of gold upon
the dark green spikes of whin.

Sleek starlings in a crowd
massed for the sunset flight:
the wet earth newly ploughed
was gashed with silver light.

AWARENESS OF TIME

Awareness of time has always been
the chief quality of a certain type of mind:
gardeners have it, and cricketers and some librarians.
Time past surviving not only in the compost
time present not contained only in the leaf turning
but threefold moment in report recognition response.

Eliot for instance in our day
attempts to digest the published assertions
of astronomers and theologians
through the juices and truces of Rome and heraldry

Sir Thomas Browne was another
baroque with trumpet sensitive
to the incised shard in the mould
and the hare's foot in the cupboard

and Morris at his loom
or prodding his stick in the black-letter vat
would call out to Chaucer in the next room
to fetch him Anti-Duhring from the top shelf

Most men need a song or a stone to invoke it
a list of names or a yellow envelope

In Ireland here it is a different matter;
the past persists in every knuckle and sinew,
drips from the eaves to run its lithe ivy over
the white shavings on the floor;
the future can find no crevice to enter by
and cannot be heard at the door
for the din of the keening host.

I walk along a road or over a bank of earth
down a green path between black water pits
but I never walk alone.
Even the man I meet on the crest of the mountain road
in tatters undated, unimplicated in time,
is mustered with fellows, hero, sidhe and ghost,
the foot-loose poet, the itinerant navvy,
Cromwellian soldier or peasant on the quay
watching the full-blown hull diminish to the west,

and the tonsured mason chipping out
the sustaining hand under the arm of the cross;
here in the Irish earth they are heaped together;
here in the Irish twilight they whisper together.

THE LINT PULLING

I

The neighbours gathered to pull the lint
at Ballinaglass that August day,
till there were a dozen or fourteen in't,
enough for a jury, enough for a game;
in neither case will you look for pay,
and pulling the lint, it is much the same.

You come to return a debt you owe
for a day last week or a day to come,
for your lint or hay, or because you know
the duties of kinship and common thrift,
or now that the weather's quarrelsome
there's a chance that maybe you'll need a lift.

The bands of spritt made the day before
are flung in a heap near the open gate:
each puller gathers the best of a score,
takes off his jacket, and bends to begin:
someone is always a little late:
and the quick clean pullers are six foot in.

With a left-hand drag and the right wrist's pull
the light stalks lie on the bent left knee:
the back not raised till the crooked arm's full
or the first pile laid on the waiting band:
a good beet's ready with four or three,
and twisted tight with a well-schooled hand.

The knot's the same for a sheaf of corn:
a spiral twist and it pushed beneath,
then the lifted beet is given a turn
and tossed right back with the knot below.
The stalks by now are as rough as teeth,
as you strive to keep in an even row.

But the gang sags out in a ragged line;
the three best men are always abreast.
The ripe talk ripples its seasoned wine;
the tang of gossip, the old man's crack,
the loud advice, the predicted jest
that brings th'expected answer back.

We are moving across the wind-combed crop;
behind each puller a straggle of beets,
the fewest behind the fellow who'd stop
to go to the sheugh where his jacket lies,
for the long grass there is the best of seats
when his smoke has scattered the midges and flies.

A handful of drops will patter the leaves,
or a shadow pass over the greyish green.
A man looks up and, aloud, believes
we'll soon be in for the tail of a shower.
Then the hills are hid by the mist between
and the tired boy hopes it will last an hour.

Shawled with coats or under the hedge,
the crowd of us wait for the rain to pass.
A line of light on Tievebulliagh's edge
gives warning the shower is near its end;
and the thick boots bleached by the dewy grass
plod out to the lint, and the stiff backs bend.

We've crossed the field to the other side;
a good clean third of the work is done –
well, near a third, for it's not so wide,
here at the lower end of the field,
as we all march back in the singing sun,
discussing the possible size of the yield.

So by the evening with sun and shower,
we've most of an acre pulled of the two,
and throats are dry and my hands are sore:
it's time already to stop for tea;
someone is calling us down by the bru;
the loose beets are knotted hurriedly.

We stand to reckon the work we've done,
and measure the time it will take to end,

then stride unhasting, one by one,
to the case of stout in the lee of a rick;
if any bend now then a backward bend,
the bottle held by the cool smooth neck.

Then down the road to the whitewashed house,
the kitchen is full, when we enter, of folk;
the women with kettles and cups, and those
who finished their bottles with neater skill
are seated now in the gloom and the smoke,
and quieter far than out on the hill.

The first relay are already begun,
already calling the second cup,
or putting on caps to shew they have done;
I see the fire shine on an old man's head,
the stab at the jam pot to finish it up,
the knuckles clenched round the griddle bread.

When each has eaten he rises and goes
at his own pace to the waiting lint,
though the thought's unspoken, each one of us knows
tomorrow will be a different day,
and the evening light should be better spent
than talking of war or the price of hay.

It is uphill now for the lint unpulled:
the day crowds in and time grows short:
the talk dies down. We are grim and schooled
in a harsh routine of pull and bind,
with scarce a hint now of the early sport,
and the leisured pace of the rural mind.

This lint is heavier now and thick;
the redshanks bright with its lance-like leaf,
the jangling seed-heads tangle and stick
as the hands drag slow from the drier soil:
but we crest the hill with a deep relief
to the last thin strip of our day-long toil.

With quickened step and a surer knack,
I have learned at last what they tried to explain:
to avoid the ache of the breaking back
you must catch well up on the stubborn stalk;

but the best of advice is always in vain
to one who'd gallop before he could walk.

The lint to be taken has narrowed in;
the pullers are shoulder to shoulder now,
till even laggards like me begin
to feel we are worth our place on the side.
I let the strong stalks cling by the bough,
and fill the fourth of a beet at a stride.

We reach the grass of the ditch at last;
the lint is pulled, we have finished the day.
The stout's brought up and the bottles are passed,
frothing and shining, from hand to hand.
The pipes are filled and the match-flames sway
in the light cool airs of the twilit land.

We talk of the work and are satisfied
with a good job done. But we do not let
a single remark be taken for pride,
for life is hard, and there's more to do
and greater things to accomplish yet
before the rest of the harvest's through.

Then we rise for home and mutter good night
to those who are going the other way;
but step to the dub in the last of the light
to judge if it's big enough for the job.
I shut my mouth. I have nothing to say.
My sinews scream and my hot palms throb.

We walk then, three of us, slowly now,
two turn to the left and bid one good night;
there's little discussion between the two.
We say goodbye at his loanen end,
and I watch him lurching out of my sight,
the tall hill-farmer, my glensman friend.

I go on alone with wearisome tread,
splashing the slunks at the heavy brae:
it's downhill now with trees overhead,
the road for thought if your mind still stirs.
I fumble for rimes in a clumsy way,
but the facts still stick with the hooks of burrs.

Here are no fine gestures; the kind that set
the ploughman, the sower, stark on the hill
in large symbolical silhouette,
for a film or a poster or well-cut print.
We have done a job with degrees of skill
and Jamie MacDonnell has pulled his lint.

II

I have given no space to the men who wrought,
their quality, size, condition, or faith;
in another poem I might have caught
the telltale phrase, the revealing look.
The lint is no symbol of life or death.
I am stating facts, not padding a book.

I might have talked of the meadowsweet,
or the fuchsia bright in the dark green hedge,
the alternations of cold and heat
as the shadows patterned the vivid glen;
those joys of sense that are more than a wage
to the artist-part in the hearts of men.

I might have turned to the spinning wheel
and the ancient loom on the cottage floor,
and given a hint of the pleasure I feel
for the Rhyming Weavers I ferret out –
Herbison, Carson, Campbell, and Orr,
their moments of ecstasy, ages of doubt.

I might have argued a scholarly case
for the custom of morrowing, obsolescent;
how the larger unit has given place
to a bleaker life and a poorer tradition,
and lacking the strength of the family peasant,
society swiftly invites perdition.

But these are the thoughts of a leisured man
with time to remember, time for research –
I hope some day to achieve a plan
will bring all these within proper bound;
a common ethic, a common church,
a commonwealth on the common ground.

But lint is a labour that year by year
in hundreds of fields in this land of ours
is tackled by thousands who never appear
in an honours list or the daily press.
The angry synods of clashing powers
have no agenda for items like this.

And none who do it enjoy the job –
like building a rick or reaping the corn:
drawing lint in a cart to the dub
has a certain dignity closer to these;
but no man or woman ever was born
went pulling the lint in an effort to please.

Though progress marches by steel and oil
and the lonely hills are electrified
and engines take the weight of the toil,
this job is left in the rural scene
where the cunning of man has never applied
the friendly aid of a good machine.

You may ret by acid or scutch by steam
or spin your threads in a tower of glass
to a cable's strength or the weight of a dream,
but back of the chemist's instrument
and subtle equation of tension and mass,
it's the hands of men that pull the lint.

THE LIVING LANDSCAPE

Somehow for me, at this slow hour and in this mood,
there is a state my senses know as certain good
in looking across a glen and naming a house
from a man once spoken to or seen at a fair:
for this implies not a hard and populous
city where folk buy coloured tickets for the air
and then return dog-tired to lie thick upon stone;
nor this denial of man as animal,
lipping the rough and the smooth and walking tall
over the wind-lit grasses or small and alone
across a black bog under a low roof of sky,
but rather a polar pull that is belted by
ropes of knowledge or kinship which articulate
the sap and the seasons of the Natural State.

THE FARMER'S SECOND SON

The farmer's second son has just left school,
and is a man now, following the plough
with help at awkward corners, harrowing
and opening the long potato drills,
and running after sheep across the mountain.
The books are shut for ever. From now on
he'll learn in that slow cumulative way,
by eye and gesture and a well-cocked ear
that listens to the old, the peasant way,
enough to fill his days with ready labour,
his nights with quiet dreams to last his life,
and hand on store of sense and ease of heart
to a vexed age sick for the lack of both.

THE LIFTING

They gathered from half the countryside,
Two parishes long, nine townlands wide;
Some came by lorry, and six by train,
From over the mountain, from down the lane,
Up from the shore, or along the glen,
From each wee town came a flaught of men.
They gathered in from far and wide
To wake the decent man who had died.
The kindly old craytur who lived alone
With neither chick nor child of his own;
For he had willed it the master should take
His stocking of guineas to cover the wake,
And word had gone round and orders were sent
Till every penny was squarely spent.

So they sat in the house, on tables and chairs,
On the windowsill and the wooden stairs,
Till all was throng, then out in the yard
They sat on the turfsack, and up on the tarred
Roof of the shed where he'd kept his cow,
But they'd sold the beast; there was none there now.
They sat and smoked, for tobacco in pounds,
From hand to hand, kept making the rounds.
They smoked and they cracked of the decent man,
And the fairs he attended, the roads he ran,

And never a man, on road or at fair,
Had as kind a heart as the dead man there.
One boiled the pot and thought of tea
But the canister seemed to be far away;
So they drew the cases of drink from the room
To the bright white faces that grinned in the gloom,
And the bottles glugged and drink was spilled
And the man that spilled it nearly killed.
To fill the glasses in all those hands
Had cleared the bars of the five townlands.
They had great songs that none knows now
And stories that lifted the weightiest brow.
But the quick hours passed with the crack so fine,
They'd have drunk his memory in turpentine.
So when morning came they were all on the floor,

Or stiff on the midden fornenst the door;
Till by twelve o'clock and the time to lift,
There wasn't a dozen with strength to shift,
And none could find it in his heart
To look for a slipe or go for a cart;
But the five bold men with the clearest wits
Hoisted the coffin by starts and fits,
And carried it down to the Low Road slaap,
Where the minister waited stiff in his trap.
They might have laid his boards on the seat,
But an act like that admitted defeat;
So they took their turns and carried it high.
But the way was long and the work was dry,
For the burying ground was the most of a mile
On the other side of McClenagan's stile,
So someone thought they should ease the load
With a quick, cool drop on the country road.

When they reached the house they left their friend
In his coffin propped at the gable end,
And they went inside and called a round
For the sake of the man going underground,
And the weight of him, and the length of the way,
And the time of year, and the hour of the day.
So one by one the party diminished,
Till two were left when the last round finished;
If there had been three the minister might
Have made a fourth for the lift all right:

But the clergyman was a notionate chap –
The coffin was there but not the trap;
For the time was a kick off a quarter to eight,
And he wouldn't bury a body that late.
So they went in again, in honour bound,
To wait till the other porters came round.
And what with words, and what with blows,
It soon was time for the house to close.
So one by one they were laid along
The side of the sheugh in a sodden throng.
At half-past ten they began to stir
And call for the trysted minister,
And swither deep in despair and doubt
To go back home or to see it out.
By twelve o'clock they lifted again
And turned off the road up Meeting-house Lane;
But the gate was chained, and the sexton's door
Was the most of a mile away or more.

So they climbed the wall, and with peching care
Handled the coffin fair and square,
And stepping slow over mound after mound
Came to the gaping hole in the ground,
And laid their load in the open clay
And kicked the clods in and shauchled away.
But the lonely moon shining over the wall
Gave never a hint that she saw at all
Somebody buried without a word,
Save the fearsome hoot of a startled bird.

EVENING IN SPRING

The evening angelus has blessed the land
with the broad gesture of its warm bronze hand,
and children's voices rising without words
are gay and lonely as diminished birds.
The sun's slant light has polished blade and leaf
and now retreats, content to gild the sheaf
of tall Australian wheat a world away:
but now this sabbath-season of the day
puts on that benediction like a prayer
which draws the last rook home through shining air,
unyokes the plough-team, leaves the furrows brown

for frosty wind to crust a lighter tone;
and men close gates and, slow, afoot, awheel,
approach the peace slow drifts of smoke reveal.
The cattle grazing on the sloping ground
drag their long shadows fainter round and round.
The hilltops darken sharp against the sky,
and the lost corncrake's never-ending cry
rasps through the rushes to the first pale star.
The swerving curlew calling from afar
insists on kingdoms unadventured still
and wonder braver than the flagging will
has gauge or grasp for. The admonished heart
now knows the pulse of which it is a part,
from blessing as to blessing it shall move,
in widening circles of ascending love.

CITY MORNING

Sun on the city morning high on walls,
drips down the awnings, carpets flat the corners;
flower sellers fill their tins at public fountains,
and dustmen empty bins in the hooded cart:
shop doors have the blank, just-wakened look;
the figures in the windows tilted stiff
as if surprised at their revel and ashamed
of the coarse glances which will harry them;
but the bare streets are clean and ready for feet.

The invisible elastic bands which scattered
the rocking buses last night to the suburbs
now twang them back to the centre, full of faces,
which also drank of sleep, and now are people
for a short while, until by ten o'clock
an ordinary day contains their gestures
as a thick meadow the small and taller weeds.

AUTUMN VALLEY

Across the lock-smoothed river you may see
three dabchicks with a wide and pleated wake
jerk toward the farther bank: the evening sky,
a gentle-graded luminous haze that ends

in a cool yellow backcloth for the trees
still leafed enough to mark broad silhouette:
the hollows in the wide fields brimmed with mist
obscure and aid the fading day to hide
the stooky stubble and the reaped bare earth.
Peace offers its hushed blessing to the heart,
its coil of trouble narrowed to the night
that wears the little stars like points of dew
webbed on a sheltered and unshaken whin;
an autumn sunset closes round the mind.

SEASON'S END

High on our hill a vast cloud laps us round,
pours down the Glens and masks the roaring sea:
a light wind shakes the branch with pattering sound,
and close at hand the brook runs endlessly.
The fine rain falls or ceases, but the day
lies like a nation, all its will subdued;
the glittering berries on the hawthorn spray,
the pale leaves drifting through the dripping wood
are autumn's parody: for never again
shall the live seasons move in ritual:
time is consumed and over; joy and pain
clenched and compounded in the curlew's call.

REAL ESTATE

He walks his fields, and every glance
has use and purpose in it,
as though off every thorn or barb
he plucked the wool to spin it.

I crop these fields that he marks out
for tilling or for grazing;
my harvest never lessens his,
however long my gazing.

For I still leave the wisps of wool –
the world and all within it:
I merely take the memory home
and seek the words to spin it.

DICHOTOMY

Given a crisp leaf or a lichened strip
of rotten bark, I fill my brooding mind
with little hills and great hills to the west,
ploughed land and brairded corn and corn in stooks,
and all the traffic of the striding year,
with those that labour in it through the light,
the bell at noon, the gilt cup lifted up,
and the slow stories webbing stone to stone:
but half my life sprawls imageless and bare;
I have no symbol for this clay-red town,
its painted gables and its marching feet,
and the thronged, anxious lives its walls contain.
Yet till I name it, I must never speak
the full truth that my heart is eager with.

THE CEILIDHE

Tonight beside this hearth the farmer sat,
thumbing the grains into the well-charred bowl,
and drawing from his memory's depths a shoal
of full-charged phrase my leached wits marvelled at:
reaping and threshing and the ancient use,
here in the Glens, with crop and stock and tool;
the tricks of craft not taught in any school,
and in the young men's hands now slack and loose.

And as he travelled broadcast in his thought,
I paced the furrows of another trade;
the quiet art by which the mood is caught
and the slow labour till the poem's made,
and somehow knew the wages we are paid
still earn the peace no progress ever bought.

THE BELFASTMAN

In this my valley how should I revolt
against the stream that is the pulse of it,
against the great hills rounded to the north
and the wide east from which each dawn is lit?
Should I go there, the sea would change my tongue
and the lip hardly know its syllable;
west lies the sod we sought and travelled from,

its falling petals always spell farewell.
This then is home; its clay has clenched my foot,
its angry factions jangle in my heart,
and I must wait until the bells clash past,
before I hear the patient birdsong start.

CORNCRAKE

In meadow ribbed with secret bog
the corncrake hidden deep in grass
ventriloquist that never tired
played all his tricks till I should pass:
from mound to mound with careful tread
I followed where my hearing led.

So for a minute's breathless space
the heavens crammed with troubled stars
burning to birth or slowing down
with shouting men and flaming wars
had narrowed to the interval
'twixt step and call and step and call.

INTERVAL

The tired boy dreams of rabbits
in all the snares he set
this morning on the mountain –
he dare not count them yet.

He will not know till Sunday
and this is Friday night:
tomorrow lifting praties
will take up all the light.

So he must thole the waiting
and dream as best he can,
for that's the half-sad wonder
of being boy and man.

THE THRESHER

Clouds from the west have covered the sun
and chill gusts ripple the puddled lane,

but the tractors throb and the long belts run
as the flanks of the thresher grumble and strain,
for half of the stacks have still to be done
before the light dies in a flurry of rain.

So the busy man on the top of the stack
tosses the sheaves with a steady throw,
and none of his mates has a minute to slack
as the bales run out in an endless row,
    and the clean grain bulges the open sack
    and chaff drifts round like a golden snow.

PRO TANTO QUID RETRIBUAMUS

Turn back in thought to when a little town
at Long Bridge end, this city wore the name
of Northern Athens, with no irony
staining that title, for along its streets,
High Street, Ann Street, round the Linen Hall,
men walked, of many skills and sciences,
scholars, orators, philosophers,
physicians, poets of no meagre fame.

And now today remember that although
their names have withered from the common mind,
within these walls about us their bright hopes
have found their lasting home and covenant.

The common names of these uncommon men
should ring and sing like lilt of balladry:
Thompson, Tennent, Crozier, Patterson;
and yet there is no ballad of their names,
for we have lost the ear for public song.

Yet if a man should try, as I have tried,
to set the story in deliberate verse
as a preserving amber, not the chill
and acrid spirit of uncoloured prose,
how could he wake the fancy, overwrought
with tedious marvels of these latter days?

How could he stir the mind with chronicles
of artefacts and fossils, crumbling bones,
when all may crumble through our cleverness?

Let me be brief; speak quickly of the years
when that first ardour dwindled, and the dust
fell steadily of dancing mask and drum,
all, all grew stale and, as this city threw
its clay-red gables at the leafy lanes,
all seemed consumed by progress of that sort
the men who kept the ledgers reckoned with.

Yet of the few, one watched the gull's white wing
over the deepened channel, and one crammed
his swinging vasculum with moss and lichen;
another bribed the ploughman for the axe
his slow share jolted to the furrow's crest,
and kept and labelled till, his hoard complete,
he left the scarcely heeding town his heir,
though from Broughshane, among the copper beeches.

And in another street, a clean, broad street,
where once was huddle of old crooked walls,
the Public Library, new built, gave roof
to painted canvas and to plaster Greek,
here space was yielded for such gifts as his.

O sandstone walls, I bless you as I pass,
for there, for me, for thousands, hope began
among your books, along your galleries,
reading the live words, seeing the bright shapes
that carry man's condition out of time.

And even the spattered wounds across your face
are symbol that the quiet values last
beyond man's hate enduring, and the worm
of evil coiling in the human heart.

But all stood still waiting on the bold design
till one rose up, a bearded, noisy man,
bidding the City's Mayor and Councillors
assume a stewardship proper to their right,
and others, later, rallied to his side;
but it was long before the voice and pen
achieved their purpose. Then, so long delayed,

the civic gesture met the people's need,
and borough and society were linked.

And so together, clear-eyed and awake,
they summoned men whose craft it was to tend
the crowded objects fifty years had flung
into the dusty corners, mapping out
a bold and ample project to display
a people's treasures to a people's gaze;
choosing as plinth the slope of that long hill
where once the sweet stream ran – Stranmillis still –
beside the Friar's Bush and the grassy mounds.

But war came on the straining Commonwealth,
and men put by the blueprints to survive,
and that hoarse man was dead full twenty years
before the stones in structure placed began
to mould the floors and open galleries.

The tardy hour we now commemorate
fell in the twilight of an ebbing day,
when the wheels, turning slowly, paused and stopped,
and men with empty pockets stood at corners;
then the full project, trimmed to meet the moment,
was carried forward to a half-completion,
set the high columns fronting to the trees,
and left the bare bricks toothed along the flank.
And so it stands, Stranmillis, the sweet stream
of knowledge trickling where a flow should be,
so closely walled the spring is overbrimmed.

But in the span of years, of twenty-five
eager and moving, anxious, busy years,
gashed midway through with the dark pass of war,
those summoned to the service serving long,
and others later beckoned serving still,
in their known several ways, this heritage,
have, by the nature of the causes served,
made life the richer for this hill-rimmed city.
A child may grasp what once a scholar dragged
slow inch by inch towards the light of truth:
a man, a woman may equip the sense
with images of meaning and delight;

and all may learn, if willing, how this land
through pacing centuries has taken shape
from rock, from plant, from creature, from man's act
to be their native place, the place called home,
and loved most truly when best understood.

To mind and heart is offered nurturing
for all who come. And not with pomp we say:
of man and nature: man the artificer
for use, for comeliness; of nature bold
in stone and ore, or frail as gossamer;
here is some tally of that story told:
for man, for nature is our quest and care:
man wilful; nature bound to rule and law;
the fossil in the rock, the wing in air,
the blunted weapon and the cross of straw.

Of man who fashions out of coloured clay
shapes that contain and carry life beyond
the small vexations of our anxious day,
bright as the sunrise, fresh as bracken frond,
herewith the witness that man's stripling hope
find sod and sustenance for its bravest scope.

HERE AT THE TIDE'S TURN

Here at the tide's turn of the moving year
feeling and thought are poised like the stiff leaves
which wait the word to fall and so resume
the cycle-sequence which is more than they,
yet has no other meaning than they give.

The stacks are grey now in the clover green
where once the sweet hay under the wind's thumb
shewed changing nap and texture to the light:
the pale blunt stubble glitters in the sun
as black rooks paw and peck the tufted stooks.

So I must wait as ripening berries wait,
as the crouched shadows wait for the full moon,
as the hill waits for heather's grains of light
to give a colour to its withered name,
for autumn on my tongue to find its speech.

MARY'S LULLABY

for an old Irish air

I rock Thee to sleep now, My King and My Baby,
I and no other, Thy Mother, a maiden:
I'll lay Thee to rest in the warmth of the manger,
On straw that's as soft as the feathers of angels;

To and fro, lu la lo,
To and fro, My Darling,
To and fro, lu la lo,
Marvel of All Marvels.

Ride, My Love, wide on the tide of Thy Slumber
While the rough shepherds, bewildered with wonder,
Enter to gaze on Thee, pray to Thee, seeking
The Blessing and Peace which Thou hast in Thy Keeping;

To and fro, lu la lo,
To and fro, My Darling,
To and fro, lu la lo,
Marvel of All Marvels.

Sleep, My Heart, sleep, for there's comfort in sleeping
While round Thy Cradle the four kings are kneeling;
Thou art Their Master, of Monarchs Most Holy,
Yet I, a poor maiden, have mothered Thy Glory;

To and fro, lu la lo,
To and fro, My Darling,
To and fro, lu la lo,
Marvel of All Marvels.

OVERTURE FOR AN ULSTER LITERATURE

Listen, and you shall hear above the storm
the new songs strengthen with the growing light.
The Welsh have started well; the lyric stories,
and jolting poems reach to grasp their truth.
Scotland has its poets by the dozen
as various as the birds of an April dawn.

They have their advantages. Wales is a nation:
the rocky chapels are older than our spires.

Scots is as old as English; there was Dunbar,
and golden tongues before we were begot;
and the Gaelic holds its ceilidhe in the islands.
But we have a newer lease and far to run.

Our speech is a narrow speech, the rags and remnants
of Tudor blades and stiff Scots covenanters,
curt soldierly despatches and puritan sermons,
with a jap or two of glaar from the scroggy sheugh,
the crossroads solo and the fair-day ballad.

But even this bare tongue will serve our purpose
if we're obedient to the shape of the land,
to the shifty weather with its crazy habit,
cold and dry in the spring, wet in the summer,
dry again at the heels of the Lammas floods.

We can make something of it, something hard
and clean and honest as the basalt cliffs,
patchy with colour like the coast in July,
bold as Slieve Bernagh and the bald Mourne peaks,
flat and reflecting as a Lough Neagh sunset,
as nourishing as potatoes out of the mould,
maybe not more shapely than the potato.

We are a little people, but we will be heard,
for we are lucky, can wither, grow or die,
but the great have no alternative to dying
into a drab anonymity of words,
dated with tags of slang and bureaucrat's jargon,
where no man has room or skill to raise his voice
as of a person calling across a field.

A RHYME FOR CHRISTMAS MORNING

Today our thoughts, flower, leaf and stem,
Are rooted firm in Bethlehem,
In that triumphant Christmas morn
When Mary's little Son was born.
There in the corner hushed and dim,
The manger, where she cradles him;
And with old Joseph leans to see
The wonder of the Mystery:

The Ox, the Ass, that gentle pair;
The huddled figures kneeling there –
Among the crowding angels' wings
We sort the shepherds from the kings;
For we know how the scene must look
From Christmas card and picture book,
And some have learnt it on their knees,
And some in foreign galleries.

But though that scene returns again
To comfort weary-hearted men,
We somehow wrap it up with things
That blur our sharp imaginings;
With silver strings on packages,
And coloured lights on spangled trees,
With holly leaves and mistletoe,
And heaps of artificial snow.

But there's no harm in these, you say,
It's good to pluck a single day
Out of the sad year's grimy round,
And make it an enchanted ground.

Then to your presents, toys and games,
The paper hats, the pudding's flames,
But spare a thought, when all is done,
For Mother Mary's little Son.
Remember how the story tells
That He began His miracles
By turning water into wine;
And take this as a certain sign
That He liked company and friends.

But yet, before the story ends,
Remember how He had to die,
A Lonely Man on Calvary,
To be the first Proof positive
That by Love only Man shall live.

LINES ON THE OPENING OF THE BELGRADE THEATRE

As yet this playhouse has no memories,
but time must earn them, yielding us a share,

who tread this broad stage first, intent to please,
and you who first attend, expectant, there.
So, sixty years from now, some lad grown old
may tell with pride how he was here to see
the first bright scene within these walls unfold
like dawn athwart the spires of Coventry.

Some say this city breeds prosaic men,
without tradition, sceptic of the arts;
the wrench, the ratchet, rather than the pen
relieve the coiled intentions of their hearts:
but in this playhouse time can give the lie
to the rash judgement. Has there been an age
when hearts were chill to warm words' artistry,
projected living from the peopled stage?
Here we have now this edifice designed
for all dramatic traffic, framed and lit
for any dance of language, limb or mind,
the clown, the lover or the man of wit.

This is no upstart town: in ancient days
the Corpus Christi guildsmen roared their lines;
from Gosford Street to Bishop Street their plays,
in vivid pageant, smote the Philistines;
and when the guilds went down, poor mummers came
in booth and shed, to dare the groundling's call,
or shod in stouter buskin strode to fame
in old Saint Mary's multi-purpose hall.
If you should scan the annals, year by year,
you'd find no easy target set for scorn,
but proudly point the finger, saying, Here
was Siddons married, Ellen Terry born.

Let these remembered burgeon in our thought
till drama fills its place within our lives.
As men of Athens, Shakespeare's London, wrought,
so nurtured, many a gesture that survives
the drive and drift of time, and still is part
of what, for good, man yet may claim as his –
the power and pathos of the playwright's art;
and may our city find its heart in this,
as loyally these walls safe home provide
for poets' craft, for actors' discipline;

and a great audience, generations wide,
achieve enhancement of their days therein.

POEM

Consider Wordsworth in his withered age,
his high song over in ten eager years,
the chill words spilled upon the barren page
that offer boredom's armistice from tears:
yet the old hand set long in habit now,
must rime and stanza every trivial dawn,
must lift the silver locks and press the brow,
contemplative although the gleam is gone.

Admit the pity, bidding others rise
with face and gesture flushed with burning youth
and pass their images before your eyes,
interrogating each for utter truth –
the seaborne Shelley, and the coughing lad,
the ranting gauger, and the limping lord,
and Owen whispering to the deaf and mad
with blood-smeared lip his pitiable word.

These by the leaping levels of their blood
could pour no more into the glutted horn,
for they had travelled every altitude
potential in the stars when they were born.
The end of each lay coiled within the glass.
Whose fault the crystal held a central flaw?
Through what more convolutions could they pass?
Who heard the watcher mumble what he saw?

What then of those who had the will to end
the reiveless complications of the cord –
the poisoned Chatterton without a friend,
the drug-sick poet leaping overboard?
The death within those wills but planted firm
the maggot in the music: you shall see
the lovely architecture of the worm
in coral cast of white sterility.

This way or this: to take what fate may grant;
a singing summer and a barren fall
and empty winter nights when ignorant

the heart owls round its own memorial;
or the pale face that winces at defeat
and will not brace the logic of despair:
or gay among the masks that throng the street,
the merry eyes of one who does not care
because he knows by heart his span and reach
and estimates the chances time may give.
The crafty seaman by the bloody ditch
heard dead men's drivel and preferred to live.

A COUNTRY WALK IN MAY

for E.N.C., E.E., and R.H.

Car parked on gravel near the Castle Gate,
where, though still early, visitors in spate
unloaded picnic basket, stool and rug,
let loose the children, leashed the leaping dog,
we left the bustling caravanserai,
equipped with sticks in the old walkers' way,
crossed the hot concrete where the muddy ford
once lapped the axles, now with ledge and board
boxed back and groined for safety; to the right,
tree-darkened path swung up an easy height,
roofed by close branches, floored with leafy mould,
from whence, a meadow's breadth away, the old
red walls of Kenilworth against the sky
took the full sunlight with unshuttered eye.

We four who stepped in file, by circumstance
linked for our project, scarce would earn a glance
from any passer-by, yet to explain
our brief conjunction in this Warwick lane,
on this bright Sabbath at the close of May,
would need a tedious essay, turn away
my pen from its straight task, which is to note
our day in ready couplets you might quote,
lacking a snapshot's handy reference,
to make some point of fact or quickened sense.

Then let these flat words serve to spell the list:
my wife, myself, our friend the botanist,
our other friend the sculptor. Stated so,
the coarse-meshed words let half the meanings go,

and all the colour with it. Yet if I
set down my observations honestly,
the words I handle and the tricks of style,
not only those contrived with hidden smile,
but the more blatant I'm not conscious of,
should, by addition and subtraction, prove
some sort of portrait-sketch, which, by degrees,
may focus into conversation piece.

For nearly thirty years my chosen part
has been to play the middleman in art;
not one of those sleek creatures, tall and bland,
who lisp in jargon and on the carpet stand,
with long nose in the glossy catalogue
to document the very latest vogue
for rubber-jointed minor Mannerist,
or metal-twister shinning up the list.

I stretch my hands to make a friendly bridge
between the man whose blessed privilege
is to be born an artist and the rest
born uncreative, but with latent zest
for texture, colour, pattern, tone and line,
a hunger they are skill-less to refine,
but I may help to, if I can engage
the interest behind the doubt or rage,
and hold it, till the dawning answer breaks
in burnt siennas and in crimson lakes,
and the broad landscape of the human heart
finds aptest image in the forms of art.

My wife abides, she even shares my hope
for the new age, with more expansive scope
than this, of people innocent and gay,
whose life and labour will be prayer and play,
beyond the Affluent Society,
which must fall back like any tidal sea,
and, gasping, leave upon the empty strand
the baffled folk who failed to understand,
who bed so early now, and rise betimes,
adore the telly and the ice-cream chimes,
lust after gadgets, as do mice for cheese,
which wash, dry, heat in several ways, and freeze,

but most for cars that glitter in the park,
with curved back window like a Noah's Ark.

The sculptor, a newer friend's an Englishman,
makes subtle verses which both think and scan,
plays the recorder, loves an argument,
planned out this walk, and, for his own content,
traced it on map and, yesterday, on ground,
that hedge or brook or fence be nowhere found
impassable. In this precaution find
some indication of his ordered mind.

The botanist's also a bookman, in himself
a geiger counter over sod and shelf,
stuffed with quaint facts, a lodestone for the odd
in colophon, in finial, or in pod.

They've this in common: neither gears his gait
to the brash rush of this Tombola State;
neither, with blazer nor with artist's beard,
nor with the camera's adjuncts bandoliered.

The sculptor's English, but we other three
are Irish of the Planters' polity;
not black-browed, moody Gaels, addicted much
to the soft answer and the easy touch,
the spume of spangled words, the sidelong glance
that masks the peasant's eye to the main chance,
the ready oath, the blessing on the lip,
the fingered cards, the signalled fellowship,
the patriot's passion, the malicious jest
which cuts the deepest what is loved the best;
though generations of that earth and air
have predicated that we too must share
the best and worst alike, for till we die,
will it or not, we're of the Irishry.

In Midland precinct or suburban lane,
each moment makes our wide divergence plain
from these good-hearted, cocksure, talkative,
more-tolerant-than-any-race-alive,
brave, cosy, but inhospitable folk,
who gape at wit and roar at every joke,

God's Englishmen.
Yet such the trick of fate,
it's their exceptions that have made them great:
Blake, Darwin, Wesley, Newton, Shakespeare, Wren;
there's no John Bull among these Englishmen.

My wife and I meet our fourth summer here,
where my trade prospers, in an atmosphere
more friendly to my independent mind
than that brusque canton we have left behind,
and, through the months, we've grown to like the scene
where the clay is redder and the grass as green.

The botanist is here, as he has come,
an annual migrant to our exile-home,
with news and gossip of sea-severed friends,
and how time blunts them to his baffling ends.
With broader aim than this, one might engage
in a minor Canterbury Pilgrimage,
with some apt story tied to tongue of each,
in character, with fitting turn of speech,
that, taken in relation, should supply
a paradigm of our society.
But since Dan Chaucer's old account book closed,
the peering Wordsworth's shadow's interposed,
and folk have walked, sans benefit of shrine,
for nature's sake alone, or to combine
ozone for lungs with images for sense
that urban life denies th'intelligence.

That journey nears its end, which was begun
when that gaunt poet sought the rising sun,
but hints and rumours linger in the blood,
and stubbornly we claim it still is good
to feel the turf beneath our plodding feet,
an exercise that's all but obsolete
in this mad age of hurried ends and means
the goggled Vikings of the loud machines
best symbolise, who dream their state of grace
astride the atom streaking into space.

Pause and draw breath: these couplets have outrun
the friendly task I set my heart upon.

It is their nature obstinate to prove
and slot for ever in satiric groove.
Betrayed from my intention, tempted by
that old tradition, I have let them fly
after the shifting targets of my wit
which shew no scar when they are squarely hit,
but jig and beckon still and mock my shot
and still shall posture when I am forgot.

Instead of panting in the headlong race,
I should have curbed my verses to the pace
of Browne's or Crabbe's, which closer match the stride
of one who danders through the countryside,
with time to dally, time to see and hear
and taste and smell and touch the varied year.

At the lane's end a weathered wooden gate
gave us the freedom of the country straight;
we stood on sunny turf and gazed in peace
on undulating acres, with great trees
securely moated in their pools of shade,
on a broad landscape centuries have made
and left that making roundly evident
in tended pasture, in controlled extent
of wood and tillage, to the horizon's bound;
the gauze-blue heat-haze swathing veils around
each trim receding tier of field and tree;
a comfortable landscape, certainly,
known from the paintings, sober, nurtured, rich,
yet never mine at heart.

The whin-bright ditch
across the sloping moss of the long hill;
the twisty trout-brown stream, from sill to sill
of gleaming rock, that jostles chattering;
the curlews swerving overhead in spring,
out of the mountain mist; in grey of dawn
the whinchat breaking from the cannavaun,
the dry-stone wall topped by wind-slanted thorn,
between the heifers and the hutted corn,
and that sharp heathered cone, from whence, they say,
one saw the sun dance on an Easter Day:
this is my landscape. Though our fields are small,
cupped in steep glens, this roughness edges all

with timelessness and sadness, shewing man
against all odds, a small precarious clan.
Here, in the English heart of Warwickshire,
though you'll find all a safe man should desire
to keep him lifelong in good countenance,
no skeagh-bush will threaten, no sun dance.

In the great field we entered, grazing sheep,
new-shorn, the lambs well grown, alert to keep
their distance, drifted off without stampede:
the legs, the nose, bespoke their Leicester breed;
but, when I looked more closely, hoped-for trace
of mountain blood in blackness round the face
recalled the running dogs, the shouting man,
where my scant knowledge of that kind began.

When distance was established, silently
the grazing was resumed, but ear and eye
kept twitching vigil, slowly as we moved,
our purpose feared, our presence unapproved.

With careful haste, we shouldered under wire,
and struck a rougher ground with hazel, briar,
in tangled growth, at heart of which a pool,
among the willows, shewed remote and cool –
for water's precious in this Midland plain,
a river name's conferred on every drain –
brick-littered Sherborne and the tyre-choked Sowe
are instances the gazetteers allow –
it seldom runs, but oozing, half inert,
its body sludge, its surface slime and dirt,
only at weirs to loveliness may come
in tumbling billows of detergent foam,
such as on Stratford's Avon flake and fly
to make a little winter in July,
and scorch the leaves to autumn where they cling,
or through twigs flicker like a dove's white wing.

But here, surprised, among the quiet trees
still with reflections of romantic peace,
its depth unguessed, to the last raindrop full,
it seemed a legend rather than a pool,
and I should glimpse, had I the time to spare,
the Salmon of All Knowledge lurking there.

Across the fence which guards its open edge,
the botanist reached to pluck and shew us sedge;
sheer gain for me who'd lumped all sedges with
the thin rush Irish peasants used to pith,
with strong thumbnail, for wick. The sculptor made
the Keats quotation, then we three displayed
the attention which our ignorance required,
three-sided stem examined and admired.

Then, pacing farther, shewed us Sauce Alone,
giving the other names by which it's known,
the smell when crushed, the flavours in the taste;
we mused on all the plants allowed to waste,
that once sat stewing on the witch's stove,
simples for sprains and remedies for love.

He'd lag behind, and, when we'd make a stand,
he'd hurry after, bearing in his hand
a twig, a single leaf, a bead of fruit,
or some long trailing thing with nasty root.
From some such pause and sweeping scrutiny,
he followed, laden with Dog's Mercury,
a stranger to us, never found at home,
save in an herbal, or some humbler tome.

Our track turned right. An ancient red-brick house
peered at us from the left through leafy boughs.
This is the country's image and motif,
the old warm brick, the new sun-dappled leaf.
At Cotswold stone I marvel and admire,
but brick and leaf for me is Warwickshire.
Your black and white is seldom more than quaint –
I'll shew you houses so contrived with paint.
The yeoman's honesty is in the clay,
and Joseph Arch is never far away.

But slipping tiles and shattered panes of glass
and every crevice lodged with ragged grass
pronounced defeat. We murmured our regret
and fancied use and purpose even yet.

Along a meadow bordered by a brook,
where two lads, squatting, watched the trailing hook,
looked round to ask the hour, we made our way;

stopped to remark a fallen tree which lay
like sprawling monster on a patch worn bare
by cleg-irked cattle drawn for comfort there.

Here each of us sought out, and shewed the rest,
that part or play of parts which sparked the best
analogy to sculptured stone or wood;
the writhen torso and the roughly thewed
limbs of a giant, the mask, the knuckled fist,
Laocoon or Milton's Agonist,
owl's puckered eye, fish-flank, smooth snout of beast,
the styles of Moore and Lipchitz not the least.

For man the savage knew by head and heart
a spirit animated every part
of dead or living nature: rock and tree
had valid place in his cosmology,
and he would pay, with sacrifice and prayer,
due worship to whatever brooded there.

Now we, set free from superstitious awe,
conversant with the latest natural law,
feel promptings in our bosoms urgently
to fix some meaning on the shapes we see.
Thought spins full circle. Content spoke in form.
We grope for meaning through th'atomic storm
which our reality has now become,
while all stand waiting for the threatened bomb.

The sculptor by his craft consistently
named shape and shape from his vocabulary,
sweated from tool and hand through eager years;
but we, whose sculpture's come by eyes and ears,
snatched rasher names, yet each of these was true,
our hearts bared by the parallels we drew.

We left the tumbled tree and paced the stream,
now wider, shallower here, with frequent gleam
of light on ripple scumbled over stones;
climbed barricaded stile and stood at once
in a little field with hawthorn blossom walled;
the sheep, in heavy fleece, moved off and called,
and, over all, the sky, bare blue and bright,
was swiftly heightened by the billowy white

of full-rigged clouds that bundled from the east:
each white of whiteness, blossom, cloud and beast,
offered too much to overloaded sight;
I thought of sunspots, liver fluke and blight.

Instinctive, shamed by opulence, I run
to the dispetalled from the fully blown,
and would have all things safely stripped to scale,
for much of me is sure that men must fail;
and so life's teeming riches run to waste,
while we starve proudly in the best of taste.

With the drowsy sweetness of that blossom brimmed,
we trod a short path, hung about and dimmed
with elder bushes hardly yet in flower.
Then, as with flinging open of a door,
we stepped out into the sun on laboured earth.
The distant fence that belted its hot girth
held back the hazy woodlands from the scene,
and, through the powdery clods, no tip of green
spiked out to sign what crop was planted there,
with such precision, concentrated care,
for each ridge of the endless parallels,
deep-drilled, clean-weeded, spoke of nothing else
than sheer delight in demonstrated skill.
So far, we'd come through fields where no men till,
that this vast measured desert seemed designed
proudly to bring technology to mind.
Led by a furrow, striding in a file,
dust on our shoes, it seemed a quarter-mile
before we footed grass: no swath to spare
for furtive corncrake or diverting hare.

Economy was all. My cynic wit
imagined what potatoes might be fit
for this accouchement, soapy, tasteless, clean;
no Champions with gilgowans gold between,
no Arran Victors floury on the plate.
With crooked smile I climbed the rigid gate.

Relief came when we took a right incline
by bank of grass, surmounted with a line
of alders, beeches, oaks, where, in the shade,
the straggling bluebells innocently made

the coolness visible. A toppled tree
clutched earth in taloned roots for us to see
what little grip it had upon the ground,
when slow erosion of the seeping pond
had worked against its weight. That field we marched,
upon our left was corn, still light and parched,
but, here and there, a daring bluebell thrown,
as seed from safety, sadly drooped alone.

The sculptor thought us late. Our lagging stride
which hauled slow dragnet through the countryside
had braked our progress, which, by this time, should
have set us waiting near an open wood,
cut through by quiet byroad, where his wife
with infant and with basket would arrive
in punctual car, to park beside the road.
He'd planned us there first, handy to unload.
But we were half a mile at least away,
the sun at noon's height, fulcrum of the day.

So, inch to step, we marched who strolled before,
up narrow lane, passed man at cottage door,
flung quick salutes, and took another gate,
and blundered into pens iron-corrugate,
empty of beasts, tarred tenements of tin.
Cackle of fowl unseen, that friendly din,
alerted us, and waking no alarm,
we threaded through the suburbs of the farm.

A worn track sloping hurried us away
down twenty yards, then left, its rutted clay
surfaced by rubble of stones, and some of these
roused time-consuming curiosities;
for they were black as coal, seemed diamond-hard,
and disengaged, shewed stubborn disregard,
when tried beneath my knife-point, to all hurt.
Was this, we wondered, outcrop, shovelled dirt,
from near-hand quarry? We were firmly held
by mystery not easily dispelled.
The puzzle daunted but we dared not lag,
till, heaped unspread, a pile suggested slag
by cinder-like excrescence, change of hue
from black to grey that merged in palest blue;
slag lorried from some furnace, ancient kil'

or glasshouse rubbish? Say from where you will,
Keresley, Binley Pit or Newdigate,
the answer to that query still must wait.

But when the track turned back to honest earth,
my blunt-toe's shuffle hit on something worth
another moment's notice, for my look
disclosed, half buried, a rusted reaping hook,
flat-pressed in dirt. The hilt of splitting wood,
picked up and hefted, proved its balance good
as any hook flung at the Platted Hare,
when harvest home was all the country's care;
for this was smaller than the sort in use
along the hedgerows still. Could one refuse
to carry it away nor let it lie
and with it half our human history?

The sculptor headed on and whistled back
that we were waited for. There was no lack
of friendliness to greet us when we met;
and, without fuss, the roadside meal was set
with salad, sandwiches, white wine and cans of beer,
the first alfresco banquet of our year.

That bottle safely drained of its last drop,
the gear was stowed when all was gathered up,
and so we parted. Off the black car went;
strapped in her chair, the child sat, too intent
on the vast moving world before her eyes
to spare a single smile for our goodbyes.

The road was our road till we'd turn again
towards the red castle in the flat green plain;
so heels that gritted harshly bore us on,
past high and narrow house, it looked, of stone,
which, by proportion rather than by grace,
shewed Regent breeding in its pallid face.
This flanked a red-brick yard elaborate
with turret, niche, and arch we failed to date.

The wayside grass was lush, with, here and there,
the pink Red Campion; in Warwickshire –
its flora poor the botanist opined –
this ranks among the gayest flowers you'll find.

The sculptor then confessed that he confused
the Ragged Robin with it, still unused
to fine distinctions in his botany.
In this he comes a trifle after me,
but not far after: all my married life
I've leaned for confirmation on my wife,
who loves wild flowers and herbs, and cherishes
the smallest mosses in their crevices,
and has a way with growing things, denied
its full fruition by her being tied
to my flat-dwelling sedentary trade.

When their distinctions had been sharply made,
from names of wild flowers our quick chatter sped,
like darting finches in a thistle bed,
to clerihews, one new, the sculptor's own,
then flickered round to Emily Dickinson
by way of Zen and Beat and Kerouac,
till shadow, leaf and petal brought us back
to nature as a theme for poetry.
This prodded out old memories for me;
I told how something Havelock Ellis wrote
which mentioned stitchwort forced me to take note
of that small shapely flower which fails to claim,
by reason of its 'unattractive' name,
much place in verse, and how I searched for it,
and, long years after, found its image fit
with celandine, wood sorrel, violet,
in batch of country verses green and wet
I made about a glen in County Down.

Your nature poets mostly live in town;
the native countryman will value most
those things he knows the price of and the cost;
he has no time for things he cannot use;
his names for flowers and birds are vague and loose.
I've known one long and well, and to his mind
finches and crows comprise the feathered kind:
this is of course the reason why John Clare
of countrymen and poets is most rare.

The sculptor then remarked that he had found,
in recent months, his taste swing slowly round
from verse begotten only in the head,

to slow descriptive lines which come instead
within the limits of experience,
from each clear-channelled and well-focused sense.

He broke off here, to head us to the right,
where surf of tall cow parsley hid from sight
a modest wisp of track, so deeply grassed
that, without signal, we had surely passed.
We struck through whipping twigs and slapping leaves
for thirty yards of effort, till our sleeves
were cuffed with burrs and laced with gossamer.
Small rods of sunlight pierced the swaying air,
and somewhere in the branches overhead
a genial chiffchaff sang his limited
but penetrating comment on the day,
and cuckoo-echo sounded far away.

We swung a wide gate on a field of grain,
pale in heat. Far down the rippling plain
the castle lifted up its warm stone face
out of the blue-green waves of hazy space:
newly abandoned structure, ruin or rock,
each separate meaning signalled from that block;
but nature, too, may be ambiguous,
the knowing botanist reminded us.

Across the field, close to the high thorn hedge,
the sculptor led us down the furrow's edge,
and suddenly a strange unlikely cry
came from above us, and as suddenly
a sparrowhawk broad-pinioned broke in view,
crying his private purpose as he flew
out and across the field, intense and slow,
as if in search of something there below;
some creature in the corn where it was high
as striding thigh, some bird too scared to fly
that crouched for safety, strove to lie concealed.
Out and across, back and across the field,
the tireless hawk wove his relentless way.

This gave that tang of terror to the day,
that hint of violence which pricks the mind
alert to the dark forces fierce and blind,
which lurk to strike, or so my fancy turned.

But my harsh image was as swiftly scorned,
my wife asserting that this cruise and cry
was nothing more than ancient strategy
to catch and draw unwelcome interest
farther and farther from imperilled nest;
and as each run and sweep made clear to me
the savage motive, all the more would she
insist my error, calling to her aid
those frantic sleights that oystercatcher made,
a box of tricks from her ancestral store,
to guard her low nest on the Rathlin shore.

We left the hawk still crying, launching now
on wider sweep, less certainly, as though
our failure to respond had foiled his aim,
as out and through another field we came
to where on lower ground, the histories say,
the castle's moat a lake defensive lay
that now is tufted marsh, uneven, drained
by narrow ditches, where there still remained
a few rush-bordered pools with yellow flags,
broad-bladed over the dark sodded quags.
Along ditch-ridges to a level square –
for jousts or pleasance, chronicles declare –
we passed and waited till you reached to seize
a splaying sheaf of leaves, the irises
half opened, not full yellow in the flower.

Then a fenced path, the first for many an hour
brought quickened step into the final stretch.
The left-hand fence-bank, thick with grass and vetch,
gave its White Campion to the botanist.
Across the wire, corn sown with miser's fist
and sprouting thinly, some small poppies shewed,
not those great flounces by the Flemish road
recalled through thirty years, when poppies still
stood as an emblem of the common will
to hold the murdered men in memory
that self-determined peoples should be free.

A weed of cultivation was the phrase,
the botanist said, which best described its ways.
Here, where the scant corn proves the soil is poor,

the poppy can but be a miniature;
when earth is rich and corn is strong indeed,
though splendid, still the poppy is a weed.

Is this a symbol of complexer kind
for the bright fabrications of the mind?
And are men's arts mere poppies in the corn,
without the tillage never to be born,
the weeds of cultivation? Or are these,
we know now, portents of the world's disease –
the spattered pigment and the tortured wire,
the crusted cinders of the impending fire –
and the true arts are still the healthy grain,
as men to thrive must find them once again?
Then, by this logic, love the growing tree;
the rotted trunk's romantic agony
can never be of any mortal use,
occasion merely for aesthetic self-abuse.

The strong thought shook me, so I thrust it by,
and followed up the steep lane hurriedly.
Some noisy figures passed me, who, far less
than drifting feather, stirred my consciousness,
were vague, diffuse, less real to my sense,
than any pickle of experience
the walk had brought us. Moving slower now,
we topped the last ledge of the grassy brow
that banks the castle wall, and, from afar,
among the clustered cars we saw the car.

FOR R.S. THOMAS

Voice of one across the water, high
mid taller hills than mine, yet speaks
the obligations and the distances
the turning season makes

of earth and weather here where I am known
to dog and master on the road,
over a tide of heather, between
a descending and a rising cloud;

for though we huxter at a different fair
and mouths open with another sound,

the fancies in the lonely skulls sap up
through bone that's rooted to the ground.

HOSPITALITY: FOR E.K.

When he clambered down from the bus
with his parcel under his arm,
I brought him to the cottage;
then my wife showed him his room.

And when tea was ready
he came down at my call,
his shirt open at the neck,
his gym shoes freshly whitened.

But before taking his seat at the table,
he drew himself solemnly up to
his full five feet two, and blurted:
'One thing we must get straight,
when do you want me to go home?'

PROLOGUE FOR AN EVENING AT THE WHITEFRIARS

14 MAY 1970

We bid you welcome to this ancient house,
and pray you stay awhile, to share with us
well-spoken verse, fine prose, rare melodies
from tune books and anthologies
whose words and music echo these brave walls.
But first, I ask your leave to tell
brief snatches of what here befell,
as from a dream, bright fragments one recalls.

AD 1342

The Benedictines, by the Swanswell Pool,
had held, two hundred years, unquestioned rule
over the Prior's half of this thriving town,
and brought it high renown,
if not for sanctity, at least for wealth,
through charters forged by abbot's guile.
Franciscans, too, in humble style,
Christ's Kingdom later sought to bring by stealth.

Then a third order, Carmelite by name,
as mendicant as their brown brethren, came
to wait beside the town, for charity
and alms against their penury;
here, for their use, John Poultney built this house,
the White Friars Church, and, for a shrine,
the Lady Tower, where, by that sign,
pilgrims and merchants should prove generous.

Strict and austere and sparing in their praise
of all save worship and Our Lady's Grace,
their dormitory windows splayed to catch
dawn's hint, that they might leap to match
the hours of light with measured discipline;
when no bell called to church,
each would, the cloister pacing, search
his secret heart for seed of joy within.

AD 1538

Hurt by Pope Clement's unresponsive words
to his demands, and urged by upstart lords,
Henry decreed the Roman Church be stripped
of crozier, chalice, manuscript.
The Friary doors were locked, its strongbox taken,
the dozen left, of its old team,
shocked out of their monastic dream,
expelled unpensioned, man-and-God-forsaken.

John Hales arrived, that complicated man,
land-hungry scholar, limping Puritan:
he cruised these counties in his master's pay,
to let no profit drift astray:
saw Whitefriars, liked it, bought it for his own;
against its chill domestic dearth,
installed a hospitable hearth,
and cut new windows in the weathered stone.

AD 1552

His fortunes faltered in young Edward's reign.
Before the old faith shuffled back again,
he shipped abroad and did not pause to mark
the martyrs' progress to the Park,

by Mary ordered, Spain's admiring tool.
In exile plotting, on her death,
returned to serve Elizabeth,
regained this house, reorganised his school.

17 AND 18 AUGUST, AD 1565

The Queen rode into Coventry with grace
to rest with Hales her host, two busy days
of pageantry and homage. He was proud
to see her greet the shouting crowd
from his own casement, his most regal guest.
The Council, his sworn enemies,
must nod embarrassed courtesies,
long-winded John Throgmorton, and the rest.

19 AUGUST, AD 1642

From Whitley, Charles bade Coventry submit;
within the New Gate none would hear of it,
but mustered men and women, staves and stones.
The King announced attack at once,
the muzzles volleyed and the missiles sped.
With clumsy aim, through nearby wall,
a random bounding cannonball
struck Lady Hales and one old woman dead.

AD 1717

The last Hales here, Tory Sir Christopher,
died, mid his debts; the place was sold to clear
the burden, passing on from name to name,
till, tenantless, lean squatters came,
set up their looms, to wrestle from their trade
a scant existence, furtive, free
from tithe and comfort equally,
of every unfamiliar step afraid.

AD 1804

The French wars dragged. Depression sapped the town:
the poor's distress brought troops to beat them down.
Appointed for their care, Directors sought
a hostel where they might be taught
obedience, diligence, humility.

The distant owner rushed to sell
this cold dilapidated shell
to be the paupers' House of Industry.

And so, plain food, hard beds and baths were quick
to school the able-bodied, brace the sick,
but, lest in pampered idleness they'd stray,
a brisk contractor filled the day
with genial taskwork for their ready fingers.
These left no ghosts. Beds, baths are gone.
No sign or trace on tile or stone
of Mr Bumble or carbolic lingers.

Our grateful thanks to those who gave the word
that these worn stones be dressed, these beams restored,
to those whose care and craftsmanship made sure
these walls a longer while endure
and time's decay be stayed. For to this place
all Coventry henceforth may come,
where many races find a home,
to glimpse the story of the English race.

CHRISTMAS EVE

At ten o'clock on Christmas Eve
I thanked my host and took my leave,
And shut the gate and hurried down
The lane that leads out of the little town.

Snow fell lightly with never a noise,
Making the houses look like toys:
The windows shining like coloured paper –
Lanterns lit with a single taper.
When snow lay inches, inches thick,
And the steelshod heels made now no click,
The wind came up and cleared the sky
With a gusty broom and a housewife's eye.
The stars were shining knockers bright
Across the great hall door of night.
The trees in the fields stood still as stone:
A far dog barked alone . . . alone . . .

At Ballykimmer the old church clock
Crashed at the half like a trusty lock.

I passed one man: his brisk good night
Lifted my steps and made them light.
At Curry's Corners my watch face showed
Eleven o'clock . . . and half the road,
As distant carols stirred and died
On the frosty rim of the countryside.
At a quarter to twelve a sudden sound
Rang in the air and all around.
Between two stars that sang and shone
An angel trumpeted a mellow tone.
Behind him far and behind the stars,
Seraphim steered their meteor cars:
White-gleaming traffic of wings and feet
Glittered along the golden street,
And golden voices and golden lutes
And dulcimers and golden flutes –
Oh, high sky crying violins
Awoke the coda that begins
With golden instruments, golden throats
And mountain-rocking organ notes . . .

This Christmas morn
Rejoice O men
To Man is born
The Child again.

Then I saw the Mother sitting on the Throne,
And a little laughing baby that held her as his own.
Then I saw the Stable, and the shepherds kneeling there,
And old bewildered Joseph with the starlight in his hair,
And the cattle in the corner and the crib among the hay,
And the droop-eared little donkey with melancholy bray.

But when I heard that sudden bray
The vision vanished clean away:
And heaven shut; and the music died
And I stood alone on the white hillside.

At ten past twelve I reached the town;
The snow was slushy, trampled down
To ribs of white in a sea of brown.
And at the end of the glimmering street
A sleet-scummed puddle splashed my feet.

And at the corner near my door
I saw them standing, singing, there,
A shabby remnant of the city's poor
Beneath the streetlamp's windy flare.

A big boy thumped on a thundering drum,
And the echoes volleyed their Kingdom Come;
A half-starved cat crept frightened out
By the hoarse hosanna gospel shout;
A drunk man lurched from an entry's dark
Into the lamp light's yellow arc;
And a man with snow-flaked tufted hair
Held up a fat white hand for prayer.
A heavy-footed policeman paused on his beat,
Beamed at the crowd and rocked on his feet.
And the big boy pounded his thundering drum,
Till the tall walls clattered with Kingdom Come.

And as I turned the key in my door
A tiptoe angel stepped before;
For in every house that Christmas morn
The laughing hope of the world was born.

IN THE LUXEMBOURG GARDENS

In the Luxembourg Gardens today
scattered idlers are sunning themselves
on the green metal chairs
round the glowing flowerbeds.

The pond has been drained,
and a dozen young men in overalls
are raking and scraping the slimy bottom.
A young man on a metal stepladder
is thrusting a long pole
down the fountain's dry gullet.

On the wire-fenced tennis court
players are lobbing balls
lackadaisically over the sagging net.

A fresh breeze is rustling the leaves
of plane and chestnut.

Pigeons purposefully but with little profit
patrol the grit at our feet.

As a tall grey clean-shaven man
strides along a path twenty yards away,
my friend, sitting beside me, remarks,
'That looks like Sam Beckett.'

AN INCIDENT

The family clambered into the crowded bus;
the mother, hatless, wrestled with a push-car,
a sleeping child cocooned; the long-haired father
hoisting a two- or three-year-old. Aboard
he set the boy down, warmly clad and clean,
who jostled with the car, was ordered off,
clung to his mother's coat. She found a seat.
The restless child grabbed, spun around a post
with stumbling speed. The seat next me then vacant,
the father bade him sit there. He refused,
demanding his paternal lap. He climbed content.
The father hugged him gently, and turned to me:
'Sure we were all like that when we were young',
his actual words, a true pentameter.

THE ANGLO-IRISH ACCORD

These days the air is thick with bitter cries,
as baffled thousands dream they are betrayed,
stripped of the comfort of safe loyalties,
their ancient friends considered enemies,
alone among the nations and afraid.

And those who now most loudly mouth their fears
are webbed in spirals of rash verbiage
which, coarse with coloured epithets, appears
a rhetoric of cudgels, torches, spears,
loaded with vivid enmity and rage.

This land we stand on holds a history
so complicated, gashed with violence,
split by belief, by blatant pageantry,
that none can safely stir and still feel free
to voice his hope with any confidence.

Slave to and victim of this mirror hate,
surely there must be somewhere we could reach
a solid track across our quagmire state,
and on a neutral sod renew the old debate
which all may join without intemperate speech.

THE MORTAL PLACE

Now it has come to this, the little glen
within the tree-groined slope of the quarried hill
where we lit our twig-fires some Saturdays,
on flat ground near the stream we paddled in,
a few months since was nest of a hid body,
a Catholic shot by gunmen never named.

The gate which leads to that glen steps off the road
that is a highway now with frequent cars,
but once a country lane. Here then it was
my mother pushed my pram, where once I spoke
my first recorded words observing the lough –
ship, boat, water – saluting the distant port
below us, south in the sunny valley.
A new estate swarms up the rising ground;
there in her house, in her bed, a young woman was shot,
her only crime to marry outside her faith.

From nearer home peal out familiar names
of streets beside our terrace, chiming names,
a litany of Dargle, Annalee,
Avonbeg and Roe,
the two last resonant in anxious bulletins;
I knew them for the world
I spent my childhood in;
each street distinct in name and character:
Roe Street was mostly warders, pensioners;
a quiet street, we tied strings to their knockers,
on dark November evenings rapped secure,
but Dargle Street was rougher. You stepped with care.
In Annalee Street a pale baker lived
who went to work each evening, his sons my friends;
a Russian family, Jews, on the other side,
the small father bearded. They paid boys
to light their fires on Saturday, their Sabbath.
But Avonbeg Street housed my two best friends,

John Ives, his father coachman to Miss Bruce,
legginged he went through the door in the wall
of Thorndale there across our avenue;
and Walter Murphy, a grim widow's son,
who took his snapped forearm with quiet courage.
Here we played mostly at the gable end
our striking, running, vaulting games which chalked
the passing seasons, known by our local names
such as 'piggy' for 'tipcat' in the English books,
for them recruited by our coded call.
The street sloped upward from our avenue
to meet its parallel in Manor Street,
equipped with shops you'd need at any time
whose names I still remember, druggist, grocer,
confectioner, baker, draper, by their wares.
From Dargle Street to Roe Street windows blazed
with sight's delight, with treasures pence could buy
when you had coppers, or on bidden errand,
each character with individual faces
dwindling at each end with strangers' houses.

Now just last week a taximan who lived
in Manor Street was gunned remorselessly,
and in between the streets,
Roe Street and Avonbeg, a wall's being raised
to hold the tribes apart. For in recent years
there's been a drift of folk from distant places
for kinships, friendships, comfort, security;
to paraphrase those words of Baudelaire,
a town's more mortal than a people's fears.

A LITTLE PEOPLE

We are a little people, in this island
would be outnumbered by an older stock
whose history's too confused to understand,
whose faith's deep-grounded on an ancient rock.
In this north-eastern corner not outfaced,
we've hugged our sod for nigh four hundred years,
since the last ripples of migration placed
our grip upon this soil that once was theirs.

Here we have our own tribal rituals –
bonfires and banners, drums, fifes, marching men –

which every year each summer season calls
the ancient standards to unfurl again
for battles when we won our victories
for the free spirit and the open mind –
names only now blown upon the breeze,
their valiant freedoms blurred and ill-defined.

Yet for an age we saw ourselves a part
of a world-striding empire's endless prime,
great ships, fine linen shewed our skill and art
that should, we thought, outlast the drift of time.

But now that empire–Commonwealth runs down;
new flags, new faces fill the halls of state
and in embattled company alone
we misbelieve these vagaries of fate.
Those happier decades we were dominant,
but now that mastery has flaked away,
those trades and crafts which fed us have grown scant;
too many waken to a workless day.
So some would pray our shrunken empire hold
us closer to her flank beside the throne
and others, rasher, summon us to fold
our thin cloak round us close and stand alone.

Among that other tribe, a myth-crazed clan,
oath-bound to serve their dream of nationhood,
cower in their covens secretly to plan
their future's chart in scrawls of tears and blood.
Hence sorely challenged by their doubts and fears,
our public men spin out a skein of words
which lashing towards disaster's shores appears
a storm of hissing snakes and croaking birds.

From this fraught language as sure consequence
sparks fall like tinder on the gaping streets,
where baffled wits ignite to violence
as frightened face its mirror image meets.

A certain way to boost our enemies
or rub the friendship off what friends we had:
that ancient Greek philosopher was wise –
whom the gods would destroy they first make mad.

So now intransigently negative
our threadbare lexicon provides no scope
should one of our nay-sayers dare to give
some gentler phrase of mercy, grace or hope.

That only hope now is to tame our tongues,
trim them to truth, for all within the place
endure the same indignities and wrongs,
the common fortune of our human race
and all must need, in tolerance combined,
a steady purpose to achieve, extend
employment, bodily nurture, peace of mind,
when each may grasp his neighbour's hand as friend.

SONNET

When I have read your hard and lively words
I know your landscape stripped to wave and stone;
the knuckled fingers dealing the stiff cards,
insisting player and the game as known:
unreasoned violence may charge the crowds,
you name the current and the killing power;
will meditate upon the scattered shards
mortality must make of any flower.

When I have read your words, no more alone,
I pace the chill flints and the sucking clay,
companioned in a place inhabited
so long by ghosts, well crutched in what you say
in answer for the living to the dead,
and in no other voice than this, your own.

APPENDIX II

CHRONOLOGICAL LIST OF POEMS, BY DATE OF COMPOSITION

The following is an attempt, using Hewitt's notebooks and other sources, to list all the poems in the present volume chronologically by date of composition. Where the information in Hewitt's notebooks is incomplete or contradictory, I have used the symbol (?) to indicate speculative datings.

1927

October–November(?)	The songs I sing
October–November(?)	To a modern Irish poet
late 1927(?)	The ex-serviceman
late 1927	Mr Faintheart Middleclass
late 1927	The song of the shipyard men

1928

18 January	A Labour victory
20 January	New Jerusalem
7 February	Ashes in the wind
15 February	The golden boy
March	In praise of Elisabeth
March–April(?)	In that fair and pleasant land . . .
1 April	Silver was the barbèd hook . . .
12 April	Paper banners
20 April	Omens and auguries
28 April	On hearing a traveller's tale of the Alps
1 May	Song for May Day
	To the memory of James Connolly
8 May	Nettles of offence
9 May	The rebel
10 May	Colney Hatch
14 May	Timber
23 May	A father explains
7 June	Immortality
14 June	Sonnet ('I have no time to worship. I must live . . .')
15 June	Young womanhood
13 July	Equality
7 August	Epitaph for a gardener
18 September	Pendragon

20 September	Iron and stone
	Limitations
26 September	Suburb
27 September	Morning hymn
4 October	The rank-and-filer
17 October	Aristocratic area
25 October	Two sonnets on the Free State Censorship Bill
4 November	Nebula
6 November	Willow pattern
10 November	Mathematics
13 November	Little ships
19 November	Aesthete's renunciation
21 November	Any rich suburban church
25 November	Christmas Eve (revised November[?] 1977)
26 November	The simple-minded Christian

1929

4–17(?) January	For certain subscribers to the miners' fund
30 January	Motives
	Hymn
18 February	March day
22 February	Dusty roads
4 March	Pioneer
8 March	The monarch
	The novice
9 May	Sarcophagus
13 May	Sonnet ('Since brooding men put beauty in a rime . . .')
29 May	Peace pact
August	The palmist
29 December	St Stephen's Day (revised July 1943)

1930

1 March	Practical mysticism (*see also* 1 March 1931)
30 March	Ophelia
31 March	Pour Hélène
11 April	In memoriam: D.H. Lawrence
28 April	Easter Tuesday

28 May	Arithmetic
11 September	No comment
15 September	The doctor muses
20 September	Fair game
	Two sonnets
29 September	The mad applegrower
	Apparition
7 October	The last crusade
3 November	Chant for the five-year plan

1931

1 March	Practical mysticism (possibly 1 March 1930)
17 March	Season's return
30 April	New Jerusalem 2
15 May	Note on intellectuals
29 June	Providence
	Ecce homo
21 July	Atlas
28 July	Bradford millionaire
30 September	Values
28 October	Admonition to science
18 December	The terrible choice
late 1931(?)	Of a professor

1932

2 February	For a mild season
3 February	Ireland
9 February	Host
29 March	Egyptian night
18 April	Mauberley's son: a summary
5 May	Mary Hagan, Islandmagee, 1919 ('finished' 1968; revised 20 March 1973)
	Anti-Promethean ode
24 May	Scissors for a one-armed tailor
10 June	Art's duped riddle
17 August	Providence 3
19 August	The hired lad's farewell
17 September	Tiphead
16 November	Prelude to consternation
20 November	Morning moment
24 November	Defeat (revised March–October[?] 1964)

19 December	Epithalamion

1933

11 April	Sonnet ('There in the lonely quarry where at dawn . . .')
27 April	The touch of things
2 September	Epitaph to a man not dead
14 September	Sonnet ('Our love is full of memorable things . . .')
21–8 September	Tristan: the lay of the goatleaf
11 November	For Deirdre
23–4 December	Prelude to an ode for Barnum

1934

15 January	Matin sur le port
July–September	Providence 2

1935

9 May	Aquarium ('Let wonder leave us for another place . . .')
30 September	The return
22 November	An Island folk tale

1936

16 March	Poem ('My name is Revolution – let me speak . . .')
30 April	Swan's nest
28–9 May	MacDonnell's question
15 July	Ulster names (revised 14–15 July 1949)
27–8 August	The Bloody Brae (opening section)
August–September	The Bloody Brae
16 September	Leaf
17 September	October's child
22–3 November	Frost (revised July 1943)
26 November	Lyric ('Let but a thrush begin . . .')

1937

20 February	The ruins answer (revised March 1937, March 1939, 6 August 1944, and 6 August 1980)
March	The ruins answer (revised)

22 April	Ghosts
12 June	This then my country
27 June	Hay
3 August	Stone
19 August	Mourne Mountains
	Autumnal
22 August	The listener
9 September	The neglected lane
17 September	The descent
19 September(?)	Load
14 October	Ulsterman

1938

11 January	From the Chinese of Wang Li Shi
15 January	The storm
30 March	Alien harvest
	I turned my touch to Campion . . .
7 April	Flight
11–14 April	The Curfew Tower (revised summer[?] 1980)
21 April	Lyric ('Let this last lyric of a passing day . . .')
26 May	Stallion
9 September	Sonnet in autumn

1939

30 January	Winter day ('When sun was winter high . . .')
1 February	Freehold (revised 13 September 1942, October and 3 December 1945, and completed and revised January–February 1946)
March	The ruins answer (revised)
20 August	Boy seen in a bus journey
24 August	August 1939
29 September	The hollyhocks against the wall . . .
9 November	Camaradas y compañeros
25–9 November	The portrait
30 November	S.S.K.
11 December	R.P.M.
21 December	W.R.R.
29 December	R.K.
	On a country bus forty years ago

1940

12 January	Minor poet's dilemma
12–15 January	The little death
26 January	Sunset
1 February	Mirror
20 March	Summer Arcady
3 May	Epitaph for a conscript
8–9 May	Antrim April
9 May	The mask
11 May	Interim
24 May	Corncrake
5 June	To any dweller in Lewis Street
16–20 June	In a suburban avenue
2 July	Glendun
3 July	Sonnet ('By the sea's edge, on gravel and on sand . . .')
6 July	Ocean, 1940
12 July	Grey and white
13 July	Cobweb
16 July	Glenarriffe and Parkmore
20 July	Poem ('Consider Wordsworth in his withered age . . .')
6 September	I talked and raged and planned . . .
24 November	Comment on verse
30 November	Salute to Matthew Arnold
6 December	Valedictory lines to my WEA students
13 December	I cannot make a song tonight . . .
17 December	The witch
18 December	New Jerusalem 1

1941

19 March	Sonnet ('I think of Glasgow, where reluctantly . . .')
21 March	Breastplate
24 March	Sap in the sticks again . . .
23 June	Triad ('Three things that men might scorn . . .')
13 September	Three Horatian odes
19 September	Sonnet ('Among the many selves that throng my flesh . . .')
25 September	The lifting
1–2 October	Dedication ('I have a certain skill in phrase . . .')

2 October	The little lough
6 November	Triad ('Three sounds of peace and rich increase . . .')
27 December	The beastie
	The Christmas Rhymers, Ballynure, 1941 (revised 25 July 1982)

1942

4–5 January	On the choice of a title
16 January	Calling on Peadar O'Donnell at Dungloe
3 February	Sonnet ('I thought tonight of all the lovers gone . . .')
7 March	In The Rosses
19–22 March	Once alien here (revised April 1945)
21 March	The lyric sonorously rhymed . . .
	Passion
24 March	Ulster winter (1942)
25 March	Roll call (originally part of Freehold – revised 17 September 1942)
8 May	The little glen
8 September	Seeding time
	September lull
	The brothers
	The alder stick
	The Glens
13 September	Freehold (revised)
17 September	Roll call (revised)
23 December	Skypiece
29 December	The happy man
	East Antrim winter

1943

28 January	On a January train journey
4–5 February	Paraphrase of verses by Mayakovsky
23 April	Now in the spring
April–May	Conacre (revised June 1943)
June	Conacre (revised)
2 July	Second front: double summertime, July 1943
July	St Stephen's Day (revised)
	Frost (revised)
24–7 October	Sonnets in October
25 October	For one who did not march

27 October	Sonnets in October 2
18–24 November	Minotaur
20 November	A great headmaster
20–2 November	November wood
5 December	The splendid dawn
	Pangur Ban
27 December	The souterrain
30–1 December	The swathe uncut

1944

10 January	Lost *Argo*, Islandmagee, summer 1919 (revised 16 April 1979)
29 May	Poem in May
19 July	Turf-carrier on Aranmore (revised May 1960)
24 July	Function
26 July	First corncrake
6 August	The ruins answer (revised)
8 September	I turn to trees
16 September	Lyric ('Chestnut and beech . . .')
17 September	Swan
11 October	Because I paced my thought
26 October	To Robert Telford Hewitt
11 November	Two Irish saints
25 November	Away match: June 1924
1 December	Awareness of time
2 December	From a museum man's album
13–23 December	Collector's choice (revised November 1964)
28 December	I told my heart to rest . . .

1945

April	Once alien here (revised)
23 May	Sonnet ('When I have read your hard and lively words . . .')
28 July	Grief ('When men lie down for ever . . .')
6 August(?)	Sheep fair (*see also* 6 September 1945)
8 August(?)	Here at the tide's turn (*see also* 8 September 1945)
6 September(?)	Sheep fair (possibly 6 August 1945)
8 September(?)	Here at the tide's turn (possibly 8 August 1945)

27 September	I write for . . .
2 October	Autumn valley
October	Freehold (revised)
2 December	Nourish your heart
	Emily Dickinson
3 December	Freehold (revised)

1946

January–February	Freehold (completed and revised)
25–6 April	Sparrowhawk
26 April	April awake
	Mist
27 April	The ploughman
14 June	The booleys
17 August	City morning
21 August	Will
26–8 August	The house on the hill
2 September	The green shoot (revised late 1963[?], early 1964[?])
12 September	The tinker's answer (revised 28 November 1963)
September(?)	Overture for an Ulster literature (revised early[?] 1955)

1947

28 January	First snow in the Glens
28–9 January	Periodicity (possibly 1946)
11–12 May	The ballad ('I named a ballad round a sparking fire . . .')
13 May	Summer park
	If I should be remembered after this . . . (dedicatory poem to this volume, finished on this date)
14 May	Blessing
	Colour (revised 28 May 1949)
	Mother and son
16 May	Expectancy
10 October	Salute
11 October	Footing turf

1948

5 January	Encounter, nineteen twenty

24 April	The farmer's second son
26–7 April	On the use of dialect words
27 April	Cold warrior: Anzac Day, 1946
28 April	Revenant
	Agenda
21 August	First honey
22 August	The ceilidhe
24–8 August	The lint pulling
29 August	Landscape
	The living landscape
30 August	With a little book of pottery
21 October	Gathering praties
23 October	Bleeze
	Autumn gale
	Interval
4 November	For Busha

1949

27 January	Raindrop
16–17 April	Ars poetica
19 April	Evening in spring
28 May	Colour (revised)
17 June	I've known her turn from bitter phrase . . . (revised 14 August 1949)
29 June	The ram's horn
3–4 July	Homestead (*see also* 10–13 July and 14 August 1949)
6 July	The crossing
10–13 July	Homestead (*see also* 3–4 July and 14 August 1949)
12 July	July (revised 14 August 1949)
14–15 July	Ulster names (revised)
14 August	Homestead (*see also* 3–4 July and 10–13 July 1949)
	Haymaking in the low meadow
	I've known her turn from bitter phrase . . . (revised)
	July (revised)
21 October	Grief ('I thought when the grave was sodded . . .')
13 November(?)	My father's ghost (*see also* 13 December 1949)
4 December	Vigil

13 December(?)	My father's ghost (possibly 13 November 1949)
29 December	The gentle bush
30 December	For any women who pass this house
30 December–5 January 1950	The colony (revised January 1950)
31 December–1 January 1950	O country people
late 1949(?)	Winter day ('From the first light when in the upland field . . .')

1950

5 January	Man fish and bird
6 January	The colony (revised)
23 April	The stoat
28 May	May altar
10 June	The watchers (revised 23 November 1950)
10 July	Dichotomy
30 August	Season's end
	Failed image
31 August	Corridor (revised 30 November 1963)
1 September	Fame
1–2 September	Sunset over Glenaan
28 October	William Conor RHA, 1881–1968 (*see also* 23 November 1950)
23 November	William Conor RHA, 1881–1968 (second sonnet finished[?], revised[?])
	The watchers (revised)

1951

15 February	The old mill-race
7 April	Instead of an elegy
	Late spring
8–9 April	A rhyme for Blake
27 May	The bell
25 July	Real estate
	The clink of rhyme
26 July	The true smith of Tieveragh
29 July	When the bell rings in the steeple . . .
	The priest goes through the motions of the play . . .
3 August	The gap

7 August	The free foot
	The volunteer ('For his long working life an engineer . . .')
9 August	This is no land of Constable and Clare . . .
13 August	Torcello
13–16 November	To be used in an address at the unveiling of a plaque commemorating 'George A. Birmingham'
12 December	For R.S. Thomas

1952

17 March	Folk custom
26 March	For R.
14 April	Easter flock (revised November–December 1962[?])
18 May	Company
18 July	Garron Top
15 September	Hedgehog
26 October	The shortened day
28 October	Rite, Lubitavish, Glenaan
	B.O.W.
1 November	Halloweve: a Glensman speaks
2 November	The fairy thresher (completed and revised 22 March 1973)

1953

22–3 March	A country walk in March
23 March	The braes o' Layde
	The Hen and the Cock: a Glens folk rhyme
5 April	The Belfastman
12–13 April	The wake
13 April	Glenaan
	Mid-April
10 August	My father's death in hospital
29 August	The little house
3 September	Resource
4 September	The owl
13 September	Lines for a dead alderman
17–18 September	For a September afternoon of unexpected brightness (revised 22 July 1962)

29 September	The Glens of Antrim
1 October	A father's death
	Colonial consequence
21 December	Bandstand
21–4 December	The child, the chair, the leaf
22 December	The tumbling spore
27 December	Cushkib Fair
29–30 December	The threshing
31 December	The thresher

1954

6 June	Black and white
7–12 June	The blossomed thorn
late June–12 July	Pro tanto quid retribuamus
28–9 July	The man from Malabar
30 July	The spectacle of truth
31 July	Lilibulero
14 August	Name and number
15–16 August	October-born
16–19 August	Sonnets for Roberta (1954) (sonnets 1–3; *see also* 27 April 1956)
25–6 October	The Municipal Gallery revisited, October 1954 (revised 23 December 1954)
16–17 November	Mary's lullaby
2–3 December	The twisted heart
22–3 December	The heart of joy
23 December	The Municipal Gallery revisited, October 1954 (revised)
	A rhyme for Christmas morning

1955

early 1955(?)	Overture for an Ulster literature (revised)
1 February	The habit of mercy
20 February	Survival
21 February	The lettered snow
23–4 February	Substance and shadow (finished 26 July 1955)
25 February	Old men sitting
18 April	April
April–May(?)	A local poet (revised August 1975)
25–6 July	The spring restored (revised June 1975)
26 July	Substance and shadow (finished)
16 August	Ossian's grave, Lubitavish, County Antrim

20–1 August	The response
14 September	The frontier
October–November	Those swans remember
15–16 December	The fairy-man at Layde

1956

3 February	The sheep skull
10 April	Spring of the year
27 April	Sonnets for Roberta (1954) (sonnets 4–5; *see also* 25–6 October 1954)
31 August	The hill-farm

1958

February	Lines on the opening of the Belgrade Theatre
11 April	Jacob and the angel
12 June	Irish glass (revision of earlier poem, date unknown; revised July–August 1962[?] and August 1975)
24–5 June	The mainland
26–30 June	The last call (revised July 1962[?])
2 July	An Irishman in Coventry (revised September 1958)
September	An Irishman in Coventry (revised)
3 December	J.B. Shelton (1876–1958), the Coventry antiquarian
29 December	This Antrim air in summer

1959

19 February	To the people of Dresden (revised 4 January 1982)
22 April	The knife

1960

28 April	My own and not my own
19 May	Nicolai, courier in Belgrade
May	Turf-carrier on Aranmore (revised)
1–17 June	A country walk in May (revised 22 June, 29 June and July–August 1960)
22 June	A country walk in May (revised)
29 June	A country walk in May (revised)

20–1 July	Mass
21 July	Chinese fluteplayer
July–August	A country walk in May (revised)

1962

15 July	Whit Monday (revised 20 September[?], 20 November[?] 1962)
22 July	For a September afternoon of unexpected brightness (revised)
July(?)	The last call (revised)
July–August(?)	Irish glass (revised)
10 August	The glen of light
10–11 August	Palimpsest
20 September(?)	Whit Monday (revised)
20 November(?)	Whit Monday (revised)
November–December(?)	Easter flock (revised)

1963

28 November	The tinker's answer (revised)
30 November	Corridor (revised)
late 1963–early 1964(?)	The green shoot (revised)

1964

11–13 March	The end of the world
March–October(?)	Defeat (revised)
27–8 October	A birthday rhyme for Roberta
24–5 November	The wheel
November	Collector's choice (revised)

1965

28–30 May	'Dedication' ('I owe much thanks to players everywhere . . .')
	In recollection of Drumcliffe, September 1948
6–7 June	Country talk
16–20 July	The modelled head
18 July	Lake Bled, Slovenia
20–1 July	The word
13 December	Poetry, then . . .
14 December	The poet's trade
15–16 December	The pet shop

17–20 December	My grandmother's garter
21 December	Eager journey
22 December	A Victorian steps out
28 December	With E.M.F. on 28th December 1965

1966

2 October	Mykonos (revised 28 November 1966)
21 November	Betrayal
22 November	No second Troy
22–3 November	Aquarium ('A challenge to my verbalising mind . . .')
23–4(?) November	The search
28 November	Mykonos (revised)
29 November	Old Corinth
	Mycenae and Epidaurus
	Delos
29–30 November	The reference
30 November–1–2 December	Vida, Mykonos
1 December	After reading *Sonnets* by Rev. Charles Turner (1864) and *The New Day*, sonnets by Dr T. Gordon Hake (1890)
15 December	Drypoint
28–9 December	Cape Sunion

1967

January(?)	Hand over hand
5 February	Pavane for a dead professor
13 March	Hospitality: for E.K.
17 April	To Piraeus
2–4 December	Erice, western Sicily
4 December	Montelepre
21 December	Vers libre

1968

4–5 January	The Long Bridge
7 January	From the Tibetan (revised February–May 1968)
February–May	From the Tibetan (revised)
23 May	Suburban spring in Warwickshire
24–6 May	The Blue Lias Inn

1 June	Prague, or Novotny, if you remember him
1–2 June	Legend in his own lifetime
9–10 June	Compton Wynyates, Warwickshire
14 October	For a moment of darkness over the nations
	Rotterdam
18–19 November	Gloss, on the difficulties of translation
1–2 December	Et tu in Arcadia vixisti
16–17 December	Monastery, Tourliani, Mykonos
22–8 December	Carol singers

1969

3–4 February	W.R. Rodgers (1909–1969)
27–8 February	An hour with E.M.F. at ninety (*see also* 4 March 1969
4 March	Remembering a conversation: Itzik Manger at the PEN Conference, Edinburgh, 1950
	An hour with E.M.F. at ninety (*see also* 27–8 February 1969)
5 March	Peter Peri (1899–1967) (revised June 1970)
13–18 March	Variations on a theme (*see also* June 1978)
29 March	On reading Wallace Stevens' *Collected Poems* after many years
29–30 March	Rome Sunday, June 1960
24 July	The moon (revised 29 May 1970)
25–6 August	In this year of grace
26 August	The iron circle (revised 30 May 1970)
26–8 August	A Belfastman abroad argues with himself
27 August	Memorandum for the moderates
28–31 August	An Ulsterman in England remembers
1 September	Fables for Stormont
2 September	The dilemma (revised 29 September 1969)
	An Ulster landowner's song
8–9 September	Street names (revised 10–11 December 1969)
9 September	A minor Victorian painter
13 September	The well-intentioned consul
14 September	The boat-builder's caulking irons

14 September	The tribunes
	Exile
15 September	Parallels never meet
	The coasters
18–19 September	'The Lass of Richmond Hill', or The Royal Garden Party
23–5 September	An Ulsterman (revised 12 October 1969)
26 September	Prime Minister
26–7 September	Agitator
26–8 September	Demagogue
27 September	The hedgehog: for R.
28 September	Minister
29 September	The dilemma (revised)
9 October	A neighbour's funeral
12 October	An Ulsterman (revised)
13 October	I wrote it over forty years ago . . .
21–2 October	Conversations in Hungary, August 1969
23 October	A mobile mollusc
	Administration
27 November	The faded leaf: a chapter of family history (revised 19–20 June 1973)
10–11 December	Street names (revised)

1970

24 February	First funeral
5 March	The turban
8 March	Rite
29–30 March	The riders
March	Prologue for an evening at the Whitefriars
29 May	The moon (revised)
30 May	The iron circle (revised)
June	Peter Peri (1899–1967) (revised)
13 August	Middle Infant
	Miss Murdoch
25 August	The distances
	St Rosalie: Monte Pellegrino

1971

17 January	First ride
18–19 January	The scar
20 January	The test
	Executives third tier

27–9 January	Strangers and neighbours
22–5 February	The watercolour
27 February	Memorial service
17 May	In a Lurgan pub
17–18 May	Dungannon cattle market
27–8 May	Disaster on the box
29 May	My Uncle
7–10 June	By air to Birmingham on a mid-June morning (revised 23 March 1973)
16–17 August	Bogside, Derry, 1971
22–8 September	Clogh-Oir: September 1971
30 November	The path ahead
27 December	The Burnt Post
	The Roman fort
28 December	William J. McClughin (1900–1971)
30–1 December	A difficult man

1972

4–6 February	Neither an elegy nor a manifesto
8 February	Mosaic

1973

12–13 March	North-west passage: an old man dying
14–15 March	Nineteen sixteen, or The terrible beauty
15 March	Agrigento, Sicily (revised)
20 March	Mary Hagan, Islandmagee, 1919 (revised)
22 March	The fairy thresher (completed and revised)
23 March	Art room in a city school (revised January 1974)
	By air to Birmingham on a mid-June morning (revised)
23 April	The King's horses
5–6 June	On the Grand Dublin Canal: musing on the 'two nations' theory
6 June	On the canal
16 June	Dissertation I
18 June	Dissertation II
	At Shottery, Anne Hathaway's cottage
19 June	For Roberta in the garden (revised 24 July 1982)
19–20 June	The faded leaf: a chapter of family history (revised)

22 July	The geriatric ward
	Fontanel
	Glendun on a wet July day
31 October	On reading Terence de Vere White on Landor
1 November	The Lagan in October
7 November	On the preservation of work sheets
23 November	The mile-long street

1974

16–19 January	Art room in a city school (revised)
7 February	Dedication of 'The Rhyming Weavers'
15–16 April	Cultra Manor: the Ulster Folk Museum
20 May	For any Irishman
26–7 May	The fool's cap (revised 4 February 1975)
23 November	November park
24 November	Winter park
3 December	The drift of petals
4 December	E.H. (1877–1958)

1975

4 February	The fool's cap (revised)
25 February	On choosing some verses for my sister's cremation
11–13 April	A great event
13 April	Orientations
14 May	Northern spring
	I remember
14–19(?) May	Diptera
19 May	Below the Mournes in May
25–6 May	On Colinward: the scattering
30 June	A seaside town
	Roseblade's visitants and mine (revised early 1986[?])
June	The spring restored ('revised after 20 years')
4 July	The last summer, for Roberta (1975)
	The college fence
4–9 July	As you like it
18 July	The man from the mountains
August	Irish glass (revised)
	A local poet (revised)

1 October	The romantic
early October(?)	1957–1972

1976

5 July	The bombed public house
7 July	Moscow moment
23 July	Carnations (revised 7 February 1979)
25 August	The ballad ('When I sought out the Cottage Hospital . . .')
27 August	The seedsman (J.H., 1841–1922)
August–September	For Jean (revised 23 August 1982)
9 December	The iron pot

1977

March	In the Lenin Library, Dushanbe
November(?)	Christmas Eve (revised)

1978

June	Postscript to Variations on a theme (*see also* 13–18 March 1969)
16 October	October sonnets 1
16–17 October	October sonnets 2
17–18 October	October sonnets 3
18 October	My grandfather dies, 1923
19 October	The unnecessary dread
	My Uncle Willy (revised 4 February 1979)
21–2 October	My Uncle Johnny
23 October	Uncle Dick and Aunt Bertha
24–5 October	The volunteer ('My father's closest brother of his three . . .')
25–6 October	My Brooklyn uncle
31 October–1 November	Lonsdale Street
1 November	The magician
	The breach
1–2 November	Consequences
2–3 November	Orchard country
3–4 November	Scottish interlude
4 November	Teetotal master
5 November	The return (1885)
7 November	Jenny Geddes
14 November	Year of Grace and my great-grandfather

15 November	My great-grandfather's refusal
	My Aunt Sarah and Uncle Joe
	My Grandmother Robinson
18–21 November	My father's voice
21 November	The Teacher's Residence
	96 Clifton Park Avenue and the Robinsons
	Grandfather Robinson dies in 1898
	The scattering
22–3 November	The house at Ballyholme (revised 20 January and 28–9 June 1981)
24 November	Carson at Six Roads End
	The tricycle (revised 17 July 1979)
25 November	Ellendene
	What little happened there
	Balloons and wooden guns
26 November	Aunt Cis and Uncle Tom
27 November	Uncle Sam and Aunt Edie
	My sister
27–9 November	Methodists
28–9 November	Outside the creeds
29 November	Paid quarterly
	The Irish dimension
30 November	Portstewart, July 1914 ('Portstewart. Nineteen fourteen. Willie's clutch . . .')
11 December	First letters
12 December	My naming
13 December	The doctor's bag
	The wedding present
13–14 December	Portraits on the walls
20 December	Scarlatina
31 December	The dry summer, Islandmagee, 1921

1979

4 January	October sonnets 4
	October sonnets 7
	Brown's Bay, Islandmagee, spring 1917
5 January	Music lessons
11 January	I learn about art
16 January	A holy place
17 January	A dominie's log
18 January	My father
18–19 January	An eye for colour
19 January	The way to school

20 January	My mother
	I go to school
	Our Sunday School teacher (revised 19 January 1981)
21 January	Domestic help
	The one I loved
22 January	October sonnets 5
23 January	October sonnets 6
24 January	My widowed mother
25 January	My first reported words
	My parents' courtship
	The double-ended tram
	Leaving for holiday
27 January	The Troubles, 1922
	After the fire
	The prisoners on the roof
28 January	Two spectres haunt me
	On Dunmore's waste
28–9 January	The river streets
29 January	Our avenue
	Reading
	The school upstairs
29–30 January	The big room
30 January	My teachers
	Those morning walks
31 January	Who was C.B. Fry?
1 February	His Majesty's Inspectors
3 February	My future wife
4 February	Going to church
	Evangelist
	Isaac McKeown
	My Uncle Willy (revised)
7 February	Free Mason
	The open eye
	I lie alone
	Carnations (revised)
	The YCVs and the Ulster Division (revised 15 July 1979)
8 February	Folk for tea
	First pantomime (revised 24 May 1979)
9 February	The filled stocking
	The carol singers from the church
	Late spring, 1912
	21st September 1912

9 February	The King concerned
	I still had a friend
10 February	Bangor, spring 1916
11 February	My father's mother
12 February	The 'forty-four hours' strike, 1919
13 February	Going up to Dublin
14 February	The names we used
15 February	Encounter with R.J. Welch, the antiquary
17 February	Lead soldiers and regimental uniforms
24 February	Sanctuary
6 March	The dustcart
16 April	Lost *Argo*, Islandmagee, summer 1919 (revised)
24 May	First pantomime (revised)
29 June	A happy boy
7 July	The Eleventh Night
15 July	The YCVs and the Ulster Division (revised)
17 July	My grandmother's restlessness
	The tricycle (revised)
31 July	A case of mistaken identity
July(?)	The Twelfth of July
late August	This narrative

1980

3 January	The psychometrist's remarkable forecast
6 August	The ruins answer (revised)
summer(?)	The Curfew Tower (revised)
27 November	For stonecutters (revised 12 January, 16 March, and 12 April 1981)

1981

12 January	For stonecutters (revised)
17 January	The Covenanter's grave
19 January	Our Sunday School teacher (revised)
20 January	The house at Ballyholme (revised)
7 February	At the newsagent's
8 February	Style (rewritten from an earlier draft, date unknown)
16 March	For stonecutters (revised)
12 April	For stonecutters (revised)
26 April	A house demolished
28–9 June	The house at Ballyholme (revised)

1982

4 January	To the people of Dresden (revised)
June	Retreaded rhymes
24 July	For Roberta in the garden (revised)
25 July	The Christmas Rhymers, Ballynure, 1941 (revised)
23 August	For Jean (revised)
12 September	In the Luxembourg Gardens (revised 29 September 1982)
25 September	Art and technology
29 September	In the Luxembourg Gardens (revised)

1984

19 January	No Cresta Run
15 May	Postscript, 1984 (to Ulster names)

1985

March	Portstewart, July 1914 ('My cousin, four years taller than myself . . .')
27 April	An incident (revised May 1985)
April	Hesitant memorial
May	Age and youth
	An incident (revised)
4–5 June	Tryst
July	Bifocal in Gaza
5 August	Bifocal in Gaza
21 August	Bifocal in Gaza
4 September	Bifocal in Gaza
24 September	Bifocal in Gaza

1986

early 1986(?)	Roseblade's visitants and mine (revised)
13–14 March	The Anglo-Irish accord
19 June	A little people
August	The mortal place

NOTES
TO
PARTS I AND II

EDITOR'S NOTE

The notes which follow are, for the most part, textual rather than explanatory and are based primarily on the forty-seven numbered manuscript notebooks of poems and other notebook material that John Hewitt bequeathed to the University of Ulster at Coleraine. I have given, where possible: the number of the notebook(s) in which each poem is transcribed, with page references and dates; details of periodicals, anthologies and other compendiums in which particular poems were published; and page references for the individual book and pamphlet collections by Hewitt in which particular poems appeared. I have not attempted to document Hewitt's many manuscript revisions, but where he revised poems already published in periodicals and elsewhere for inclusion in his books and pamphlets, I have, in as many cases as possible, recorded these changes.

More detailed information about the anthologies and other compilations in which Hewitt's work is included will be found under 'Anthologies, Textbooks and Other Compendiums' in the Select Bibliography.

It may be useful at this point to give a brief account of Hewitt's notebooks. An unpublished poem entitled 'Desk' (notebook 44, pp. 103–6, 15.10.36) contains the following picture of the poet at work:

I have written on shining tables beside flowers
I have torn out a cigarette packet
and written on the plain side of the carton
I have written on the backs of envelopes and
election addresses

But as against this seeming carelessness
I have always copied the verses out
in a neat and regular series of exercise books
like this.

The accumulation of this neat and regular series of exercise books can be traced over the years in interviews and elsewhere. Geoffrey Taylor, in his introduction to *No Rebel Word* (1948), for example, refers to the 'eighteen or twenty fat shiny-black note-books' that contain Hewitt's 'collected works' and laments the 'rather casual attitude of the poet himself. For, once a poem was safely fair-copied into the current black note-book, he was inclined to leave it there.' In an interview with Dan Casey in *Quarto* (vol. 7 [1980–1], pp. 1–14) Hewitt states: 'I have about thirty notebooks of handwritten verse, fair copy of the poems I wrote, with the dates they were composed'; and in conversation with Neil Johnston (*Belfast Telegraph*, 13 April 1983) he reveals that 'every poem [I have] ever written has been transcribed neatly into notebooks which [I] keep in a metal strongbox in [my] study. There are 33 of them now, all dated and with an index at the back, giving the number of lines written per month.' Talking to Sam

McAughtry later that year (*Irish Times*, 25 July 1983), Hewitt remarks: 'I'm a neat and tidy person by nature. Here, in this deed box, I have kept in notebooks all the poetry I've ever written, beginning with Book 1 in 1924. Now I'm at Book 33.' The terms 'every' and 'all' are exaggerations; Hewitt was extremely prolific and there is evidence that many of his poems were not transcribed into the notebooks at all and that the notebooks themselves were subjected to a weeding process over the years; nevertheless, the notebooks described below contain, in addition to virtually all of Hewitt's published verse, some three and a half thousand unpublished poems. It is clear that some of the notebooks in the final numbering previously belonged to a different series, or even more than one series; for example, notebook 43 in the list given below was previously designated 'Book XXXI'.

What follows is a summary of the final series, numbered 1 to 47 (N = notebook). In most cases the datings are those provided by Hewitt on the first page of the relevant notebook; in the few cases where these are incomplete (notebooks 21, 22 and 40), or not strictly accurate (notebooks 20 and 23), I have made corrections. I have also added notes that clarify the contents of notebooks 10, 18, 19 and 27.

N1	prose pieces and sketches, 1926
N2	poems, 1924–July 1927
N3	poems, 1927–19 March 1928
N4	poems, 2 October–22 December 1928
N5	poems, 30 March–31 July 1928
N6	missing (possibly poems, August–November 1928)
N7	poems, 1928–39
N8	'Collected Free Verse of John Hewitt, 1925–June 1929'
N9	poems, December 1928–December 1930
N10	'The Red Hand: a poemosaic' (a sequence of untitled poems numbered I to LXXXVII, with a further twenty-five pages of untitled, unnumbered poems)
N11	poems, January 1931–November 1932
N12	poems, December 1931–April 1932
N13	poems, 1932–9
N14	poems, May–October 1932
N15	poems, November 1932–April 1933
N16	poems, May–December 1933
N17	poems, January–December 1934
N18	sonnets, lyrics and epigrams (selected from earlier notebooks)
N19	lyrics, 1927–34 (selected from earlier notebooks)
N20	poems, January 1935–July 1936
N21	poems, September–December 1936
N22	poems, January–December 1937
N23	poems, January 1938–March 1939
N24	poems, April 1939–March 1940
N25	poems, October 1940–December 1941
N26	poems, April–September 1940
N27	a selection of poems by Hewitt's friends – Patrick Maybin, Patric Stevenson and Colin Middleton

N28 poems, January–June 1942
N29 poems, June 1943–November 1944
N30 poems, December 1944–September 1946
N31 poems, September 1946–April 1949
N32 poems, June 1949–September 1950
N33 poems, September 1950–November 1952
N34 poems, December 1952–March 1955
N35 poems, March 1955–December 1958
N36 mainly a workbook for *Loose Ends* (1983)
N37 poems, January 1959–December 1965
N38 poems, October 1966–September 1969
N39 poems, September 1969–May 1971
N40 poems, June 1971–October 1975
N41 selection of poems dating from 1946 to 1977–8(?), not previously published; mainly a workbook for *The Rain Dance* (1978)
N42 poems, July 1946–August 1976
N43 poems, July 1976–May(?) 1984
N44 'The Better Poems of John Hewitt' (selected from fourteen other notebooks and arranged chronologically, in reverse, from June 1938 to January 1933)
N45 'The Better Poems of John Hewitt' (selected from the periods late September 1939 to June 1938; late December 1932 to early 1927; November 1939 to December 1939; to February 1940)
N46 'The Better Poems of John Hewitt' (selected from the period April 1940 to November 1943)
N47 'The Better Poems of John Hewitt' (selected from the period November 1943 to August(?) 1947)

To this list should be added a separate notebook, designated 'Book XXXII', which contains poems written between March 1985 and September 1986, many of which were published in *Freehold and Other Poems* (1986); and an unnumbered notebook containing a transcription of the poem *Conacre.* There are also several unnumbered, undated prose notebooks among Hewitt's papers, as well as two notebooks which (like N27 above) contain transcriptions of poems by Hewitt's friends, Colin Middleton, Patrick Maybin and others.

The notebooks listed above frequently end with a tally of lines written during the period covered, and several contain other interesting material. N46, for example, concludes with an extensive selection of prose quotations on the subject of poetry, drawn from the work of more than thirty poets and critics, and at the end of N44 Hewitt lists eleven poets whose 'influence . . . can be observed' in the notebook (W.B. Yeats, Robert Frost, Edward Thomas, Gerard Manley Hopkins, Gordon Bottomley, W.H. Auden, C. Day Lewis, Stephen V. Benét, Archibald MacLeish, Humbert Wolfe, Walter de la Mare).

Hewitt's method of dating poems varies from notebook to notebook, and also within individual notebooks; sometimes he gives only the year of composition, sometimes the month and year, and – most frequently – the exact date(s) also. As is apparent from the summary above, the numerical ordering of the notebooks is often, but not always, exactly chronological, partly because of Hewitt's habit of periodically making notebook selections of what he regarded as the 'better' poems written over a number of years. Where a poem appears in more than one notebook, I have listed the notebooks in numerical order. Where the dating of a particular poem is confirmed in more than one notebook, I have recorded this dating only once; where conflicting dates are given, I have recorded all the variations. *See also* Appendix II, a tentative chronological listing, by date of composition, of all the poems in the present volume.

Though primarily textual, the notes do, however, include a considerable body of explanatory and background material. Much of this is, again, drawn from the notebooks, in which Hewitt often notes, for example, the setting of a particular poem, or provides information relevant to the content. The other principal sources are Hewitt's unpublished autobiography 'A North Light'; the autobiographical essay 'Planter's Gothic', reprinted in *Ancestral Voices: The Selected Prose of John Hewitt* (ed. Tom Clyde, 1987); Hewitt's prose journalism; various albums and scrapbooks of cuttings among the Hewitt papers in both the University of Ulster at Coleraine and the Public Record Office of Northern Ireland; profiles of and interviews with Hewitt; proof copies of several of Hewitt's books, annotated by the poet, usually with dates of composition and information relating to setting; copies of published books and pamphlets in which Hewitt has recorded similar information; the notes and glossaries Hewitt provided for some of his books; typescripts of broadcast talks and features; Hewitt's own library, now housed at the University of Ulster at Coleraine; diaries relating to the Hewitts' travels abroad, now part of the Hewitt collection in the Public Record Office of Northern Ireland; miscellaneous letters and manuscripts in the same collection; conversations with people who knew Hewitt and were informative about the background to particular poems, and several conversations I myself had with Hewitt over the years. References to Hewitt's 'papers' are to material located in the University of Ulster at Coleraine, unless otherwise indicated.

The autobiography 'A North Light', subtitled 'Twenty-five years in a Municipal Gallery', was a particularly useful source of information. It is, for the most part, an account of Hewitt's lifelong devotion to art, from his earliest years through his period as assistant in the Belfast Museum and Art Gallery to his appointment as art director of the Herbert Art Gallery and Museum in Coventry (1957). Some of this material was incorporated into Hewitt's monographs *Colin Middleton* (1976), *Art in Ulster I* (1977) and *John Luke 1906–75* (1978), some reworked as articles for periodicals and as radio features. In addition to the many chapters on art and artists, there are portraits of writers such as Brendan Behan, F.L. Green and Shelley Wang, chapters relating to the socialist summer schools attended by the Hewitts in the 1930s, accounts of regionalism, the war years in Northern Ireland, the magazine *Lagan* and the Hewitts' trips abroad for PEN conferences in, for example, Vienna, Venice and Amsterdam. I have also made use of the numerous manuscript and typescript drafts of 'A North Light' among Hewitt's papers, including chapters omitted from the final typescript.

Throughout the notes I have used the following abbreviations:

NRW	*No Rebel Word*
T	*Tesserae*
CP	*Collected Poems 1932–1967*
DC	*The Day of the Corncrake: Poems of the Nine Glens*

PG	*The Planter and the Gael: Poems by John Hewitt and John Montague*
UR	*An Ulster Reckoning*
OMT	*Out of My Time: Poems 1967–1974*
SOT	*Scissors for a One-Armed Tailor: Marginal Verses 1929–1954*
CF	*The Chinese Fluteplayer*
TE	*Time Enough: Poems New and Revised*
RD	*The Rain Dance: Poems New and Revised*
KS	*Kites in Spring: A Belfast Boyhood*
S	*The Selected John Hewitt* (ed. Alan Warner)
M	*Mosaic*
LE	*Loose Ends*
F	*Freehold and Other Poems*

I have used the abbreviation 'pub.' to indicate a poem's first publication and the abbreviation 'rep.' to indicate all subsequent reprintings, except those in Hewitt's own books and pamphlets.

PART I

COLLECTED POEMS
1929–86

CONACRE, privately published, Belfast, 1943.

p. 3 *Conacre*: N28, pp. 133–55, with title 'Lysis', April and May (1943), revised in June; N46, pp. 187–91; p. 203, discarded lines from first draft. Among Hewitt's papers there is an ms. dated 23.3.43 that begins: 'I sometimes wonder why I do not find/the prompting satisfactions that my mind . . .' Rep. *Poetry of the Present* (1949), p. 110; *Poètes d'Irlande du Nord* (1991), p. 26 (extract): *CP*, p. 33; *S*, p. 15 (extract).

In a letter to John Montague in the spring of 1964, Hewitt states: '*Conacre*, my wife, then working in the Censorship, had printed as a brochure for Christmas. I sent around copies and got some interesting comments from Read, Church, Massingham. Later, when Grigson asked me for something for *Poetry of the Present*, I sent *Conacre* on spec and he put it in.'

In an interview with Dan Casey, Hewitt remarks:

> *Conacre* was written in 1943. It was a long poem and there was no chance of it being published. My wife suggested we have it printed and used as a Christmas card. Some years later Geoffrey Grigson was doing an anthology and he asked me to send him some verse. I sent him a couple of shorter poems and *Conacre*. I was surprised and delighted when that appeared in his anthology in 1949. It was a beginning, you see. It had been written at the time we were cut off by the war. You couldn't take holidays outside the North of Ireland. You had to get special permits even to cross the border because you were going into a neutral country. I felt very enclosed and segregated, and then my thinking turned inwards. From that and from my reading I developed a concept of regionalism. It was a reaction to the isolationism of the war years (*Quarto*, vol. 7 [1980–1], pp. 1–14).

Among Hewitt's papers is a copy of the first printing of *Conacre*, with the following note on the reverse of the title page:

> This poem was printed by Thomas Johnston, Great Victoria Street, Belfast, in September, 1943: the first printing consisted of 100 copies; of these, 40 were sold by D.A. McLean, Bookseller, Union Street and Howard St. at 1/- each; the second printing consisted of 100 copies; of these, about 70 were sold as before. Less than 20 copies of both printings are now (12.4.44) in my hands: the rest were given away. The only review was by Geoffrey Taylor in *The Bell*, March, 1944.

The second printing contains corrections of two misprints, 'breathe', p. 1, l. 13 and 'zest', p. 8, eighth line from bottom; and also the change of the word 'blackberry' for 'blaeberry', p. 4.

There is a further note, dated 27.5.48: '2 copies remain in my hands, this and one other first printing inscribed to my wife.' Among the pages of this copy, Hewitt has placed the printer's two invoices, with receipts attached. (A further invoice from the same printer, dated 30.12.44, is for the printing of *Compass: Two Poems*, Hewitt's next pamphlet publication.) The inside back cover of this copy of *Conacre* has a number of handwritten notes recording the use of quotations from the poem in Ethel Mannin's *Bread and Roses* (Macdonald, 1944, p. 136) and Tom Harrisson's articles 'Ulster Outlooks I' (*Cornhill Magazine* [May 1944], p. 80) and 'Ulster Outlooks II' (*Cornhill Magazine* [November 1944], pp. 87–8); the setting of a passage from the poem in the Matriculation Examination in English, Queen's University Belfast, 21 May 1945; the inclusion of the entire poem in Geoffrey Grigson's *Poetry of the Present* (Phoenix House, 1949, pp. 110–20); and the use of a fragment of the original ms. in the Ulster Book Exhibition at the Belfast Museum and Art Gallery, May 1951, as part of the Festival of Britain.

COMPASS: TWO POEMS, privately published, Belfast, 1944. This booklet consists of a dedicatory poem to Hewitt's father, titled 'To Robert Telford Hewitt', 'The Return' (dated 1935), and 'The ruins answer' (dated 1937, 1939 and 1944). Hewitt reprinted 'The ruins answer' in *No Rebel Word* (1948), p. 53, but revised it extensively in August 1980 for inclusion in *Mosaic* (1981), p. 24. I have printed the final version on p. 324 of the present volume, and the version that appeared in *Compass: Two Poems* and *No Rebel Word* in the Notes, p. 629.

p. 13 'To Robert Telford Hewitt': N29, p. 169, 26.10.44, with title 'Dedication for sea anchors', and a note to the effect that 'Sea anchors' was a 'discarded title used for booklet *Compass*'.

p. 13 'The return': N10, pp. 24–5, part XXV of 'The Red Hand: a poemosaic'; N13, pp. 32–45, September 1935; N20, pp. 29–43, 30.9.35; N44, pp. 135–45. In an interview with Dan Casey, Hewitt states: 'I wrote a longish poem, called "The Return", that describes a holiday my wife and I spent in 1935 on Rathlin Island. We came back to local riots in Belfast, so for me the island community seemed to be above the conflict of our days' (*Quarto*, vol. 7, [1980–1]). Hewitt gives an account of this holiday in chapter 11 of his unpublished autobiography, 'A North Light'. The poem also draws on Hewitt's trip to Bristol in 1935 on a Museums Association course, described in chapter 19 of 'A North Light'; Hewitt describes how he went on

> an excursion to visit the archaeological site of Meare Lake Village, a milestone in my imaginative journey, for there I underwent some sort of mystical conversion, a true turning towards, and away from; not to be expressed in orthodox religious terms, but rather, an upspringing of self-realisation . . . I had been away alone before this. But Paris, London, Liverpool are cities, autonomous, their meaning contained within themselves. Bristol was the Wills Tower at the University and Burke's Statue where the trams spun round and St Mary's Radcliffe [*sic*] and Chatterton and the bridge slung high and the Severn Sea; it was, in a way, a microcosm of England, the first England to salute me in street, road, tree, hill and not by the smeared fragments of these drawn across the window of the train. When I returned to my own country, I noticed the difference, the change in my thought and feeling, and also 'The return' came out of it. In something like 200 lines I summarised the year past, plucking out the

emotive images from my experience. The first complete year of married life – it was, in its way, leaving my wife for the first time which emphasised the aloneness of my Bristol journey – in which we had together spent a holiday on Rathlin Island, another allegory there, had become deeply involved in the Peace Movement, in that work for the Council of Civil Liberties; it was also the year of Mussolini's assault on Abyssinia, when we saw the match struck and the fuse began to spark and splutter toward the inevitable. Yet Meare and its moral of man's persistence in the things his hands had made, and Rathlin with its momentary crystallisation of human life in a naturally circumscribed context offered me points to spin my threads between, so that I achieved a sort of humanist aesthetic.

NO REBEL WORD (*NRW*), published by Frederick Muller, London, 1948, with an introduction by Geoffrey Taylor. Dedicated: 'For My Mother and My Wife'. I have included all the poems in this collection, except 'Townland of peace', extensively revised for *Freehold and Other Poems* (1986), 'The Glens', revised for *The Selected John Hewitt* (1981), and the final poem, 'The ruins answer', extensively revised for *Mosaic* (1981).

In a letter to John Montague in the spring of 1964, Hewitt has this to say about *No Rebel Word*:

> The title, a quotation from a sonnet of mine, was deliberately ambiguous, meaning no word leaping or tugging out of the consigned order, and at the same time no word by a rebel, asserting as it were that I was no rebel whatever folk might think. I corrected the page proofs in 1947 and it was published a year after. So by that time my interest had appreciably diminished. In addition, it contained nothing written after 1944, so that it was far away from my active thought. The price 7/6 I thought too much then. It sold about 150 copies, got some good reviews (*Irish Times*, *Tribune*, *TLS*). It has now only the relevance of a period piece, being in fact 18 years old.

In N31, p. 88, there is an untitled, unpublished poem, dated 2.12.48, which comments ruefully on the extent to which *No Rebel Word* was ignored.

p. 20 'The touch of things': N13, pp. 3–4, April 1933; N15, pp. 147–8, 27.4.33; N44, p. 187. Pub. *Listener*, 24 January 1934; in this version, l. 3 reads: 'have reacht rich ecstasy by merely thought'. *NRW*, p. 9.

p. 20 'Once alien here': N28, pp. 35–6, 19–22.3.42; N46, p. 147, with note 'revised April 1945'. Pub. *Lagan*, no. 3 (1945), p. 5. Rep. *Little Reviews Anthology* (1946), p. 154; *New Irish Poets* (1948), p. 94; NI GCE 'A' level English Literature, Paper III (1969), pp. 3–4; *The Wearing of the Black* (1974), p. 6; *Community Forum*, vol. 4, no. 1 (1974), p. 10; *Poets from the North of Ireland* (1979), p. 27; *Contemporary Irish Poetry* (ed. Bradley, 1980), p. 110; *Across the Roaring Hill* (1981), p. 8; 'John Hewitt 1907–1987' (a memorial broadsheet published by the Arts Council of Northern Ireland, 1987); *Contemporary Irish Poetry* (ed. Bradley, 1988) p. 104; *Poets from the North of Ireland* (1990), p. 33; *The Field Day Anthology of Irish Writing* (1991), p. 164. *NRW*, p. 10. Lines from the poem were quoted by Taoiseach Jack Lynch at a dinner of the South Louth Comhairle Ceantair, Fianna Fáil, at the Fairways Hotel, Dundalk, 28 May 1971.

p. 21 'Glenarriffe and Parkmore': N26, pp. 133–7, 16.7.40; N46, pp. 48–51. *NRW*, p. 12.

p. 23 'The splendid dawn': N29, pp. 71–2, 5.12.43, with note: 'In Larne station, 4.XII.43'. Note in Hewitt's proof copy of *NRW*: 'Larne, after a lecture the previous evening'. Pub. *Irish Times*, 11 November 1944. Rep. *Poems from Ireland* (1944), p. 30. *NRW*, p. 15.

p. 24 'Antrim April': N26, pp. 14–15, 8–9.5.40; N46, p. 3. Note in Hewitt's proof copy of *NRW*: 'At Clady House, Dunadry, with Patrick Maybin'. *NRW*, p. 16.

p. 24 'Poem in May': N29, pp. 112–14, 29.5.44. Note in Hewitt's proof copy of *NRW*: 'Cavehill, Belfast Castle Estate'. Pub. *Northman*, centenary number (1945), p. 8. Rep. *New Irish Poets* (1948), p. 90. Part of this poem was quoted by Howard Sergeant in *The Cumberland Wordsworth* (Williams and Northgate, 1950, pp. 25–6). *NRW*, p. 17.

p. 26 'The little glen': N28, p. 45, 8.5.42; N46, p. 151. Note in Hewitt's proof copy of *NRW*: 'Near Carnalea, Co. Down'. Pub. *Ulster Voices* (Summer 1943), p. 1. *NRW*, p. 19. Hewitt refers to his use of the term 'stitchwort' here in 'A country walk in May'.

p. 26 'First corncrake': N29, pp. 135–6, 26.7.44. Note in Hewitt's proof copy of *NRW*: 'Near the Giant's Ring, Ballylesson'. Pub. *Irish Harvest* (1946), p. 52. Rep. *New Irish Poets* (1948), p. 9; *Chorus* (1969), p. 45. *NRW*, p. 20.

p. 27 'The alder stick': N28, p. 56, 8.9.42; N46, p. 159. Fourth line revised 30.12.42 (*see* N28, p. 56). Note in Hewitt's proof copy of *NRW*: 'Portnagolan, Cushendall'. *NRW*, p. 21.

p. 27 'September lull': N28, p. 49, 8.9.42; N46, p. 153. Note in Hewitt's proof copy of *NRW*: 'Portnagolan Cottage'. Pub. *Poetry Scotland*, no. 1 (1944), p. 52, with title 'The lull'; in this version l. 5 reads 'until the last rook leaves the empty sky'. *NRW*, p. 24.

p. 28 'I turn to trees': N47, p. 38, 8.9.44. Pub. *The Bell*, vol. 15, no. 5 (February 1948), p. 3. *NRW*, p. 25.

p. 28 'November wood': N29, pp. 51–2, 20–2.11.43; N47, p. 7. Note in Hewitt's proof copy of *NRW*: 'Cavehill'. *NRW*, p. 26.

p. 29 'East Antrim winter': N28, p. 93, 29.12.42; N46, p. 170. Note in Hewitt's proof copy of *NRW*: 'Doagh, Co. Antrim'. Pub. *Northern Harvest* (1944), p. 89. *NRW*, p. 27.

p. 29 'The hired lad's farewell': N10, pp. 62–4, part LXXII of 'The Red Hand: a poemosaic'; N13, pp. 26–31, August 1932; N14, pp. 110–15, 19.8.32; N45, pp. 92–5, with note: 'Written in memory of days on Islandmagee with Sandy Noble of Ballycarry village at the farm of [illegible] July/August 1921'. Note in Hewitt's proof copy of *NRW*: 'Islandmagee, Co. Antrim, a holiday in July and August, 1921'. Pub. *New Northman*, vol. III, no. 3 (Summer 1935), p. 4. Rep. *The Bell*, vol. 3, no. 3 (December 1941), pp. 177–9; *Irish Poems of Today* (1944), p. 17. *NRW*, p. 28. Sandy Noble is also referred to in 'The dry summer, Islandmagee, 1921' (*KS*, p. 54).

In a portrait of Geoffrey Taylor, poet and editor of *The Bell*, originally intended for inclusion in 'A North Light', Hewitt describes this poem as 'a long, slow, Frostian slab of blank verse'.

p. 32 'The brothers': N28, pp. 53–4, 8.9.42; N46, pp. 158–9. Note in Hewitt's proof copy of *NRW*: 'Cushendall'. Pub. *Northern Harvest* (1944), p. 88. *NRW*, p. 31.

p. 32 'Minotaur': N29, pp. 59–64, 18–24.11.43, with note: 'A memory of Burtonport, July, 1943'. Note in Hewitt's proof copy of *NRW*: 'Burtonport, Co Donegal'. Pub. *Lagan*, no. 2 (1944), pp. 18–20. *NRW*, p. 32; *CP*, p. 26; *S*, p. 70.

In chapter 24 of his unpublished autobiography, 'A North Light', Hewitt, describing two visits to The Rosses, County Donegal, during the Second World War, records how a 'neighbourly officer, on coastal watch inspection, packed us into Willy Bonar's boat for the island-and-rock-threading voyage to Aranmore'; on this visit the Hewitts stayed at the tailor's in Burtonport. *See also* Hewitt's Donegal poems 'The little lough' (*NRW*, p. 40); 'In The Rosses' (*SOT* [p. 3]), 'Turf-carrier on Aranmore' (*CP*, p. 31). Other memories of Donegal occur in *Conacre*, p. 11.

p. 35 'The witch': N46, pp. 78–9, 17.12.40. Note in Hewitt's proof copy of *NRW*: 'Brown's Bay, Islandmagee. A holiday in the Spring of 1917'. Pub. *The Bell*, vol. 15, no. 5 (February 1948), pp. 5–6. Rep. *Happenings 2* (1972), p. 87; *Witches and Charms and Things*, extract (1973), p. 10. *NRW*, p. 35; *CP*, p. 18; *S*, p. 65. *See also* 'Brown's Bay, Islandmagee, spring 1917' (*KS*, p. 50).

p. 36 'The swathe uncut': N29, pp. 92–3, 30–1.12.43; N47, pp. 19–20. Pub. *The Bell*, vol. 15, no. 5 (February 1948), pp. 3–4. Rep. *New Irish Poets* (1948), p. 93; *Poetry of the Present* (1949), p. 109; *Mentor Book of Irish Poetry* (1965), p. 156; *The Field Day Anthology of Irish Writing* (1991), p. 164. *NRW*, p. 37; *CP*, p. 30; *S*, p. 59.

p. 37 'Lyric' ('Let but a thrush begin . . .'): N7, p. 9, November 1936; N21, p. 123, 26.11.36; N44, p. 91. Pub. *New Northman*, vol. VI, no. 2 (Summer 1938), p. 42. Rep. *The Flowering Branch* (1945); *New Irish Poets* (1948), p. 93; *Hibernia* (July 1955), p. 20; *Mentor Book of Irish Poetry* (1965), p. 159; *Les Lettres nouvelles* (March 1973), pp. 152–3, in English and French. *NRW*, p. 38; *CP*, p. 14.

p. 37 'Hay': N7, p. 8, June 1937; N22, p. 48, 27.6.37; N44, p. 59, with note: 'Mowing of golf links, Westland Road'. Pub. *Poems by Ulster Poets* (n.d., 1937[?], 1938[?]). Rep. *The Bell*, vol. 2, no. 4 (July 1941), p. 14. *NRW*, p. 39.

p. 37 'The little lough': N25, pp. 123–4, 2.10.41, with title 'The little lough that has no name'; N46, p. 119, with note: 'Memory of Donegal (Burtonport)'. Pub. *Observer*, 12 July 1942. Rep. *Fifteen Poems* (1942), p. 4; *New Irish Poets* (1948), p. 88; *Belfast Telegraph*, 20 February 1954; *Contemporary Irish Poetry* (eds Greacen and Iremonger, 1959), p. 76; *Poètes d'Irlande du Nord* (1991), p. 20. *NRW*, p. 40; *CP*, p. 21; *S*, p. 58.

In the *Observer* version l. 9 begins 'will stilt on darkly', and l. 16 reads 'your pale face gazing where the stiff rods grow'. Hewitt reads this poem on the gramophone record *Poetry of Ireland*, vol. 2, in the Poetry of the British Isles series, Beltona Records (Decca), 1959.

p. 38 'Lyric' ('Chestnut and beech . . .'): N29, p. 160, 16.9.44; N47, p. 41. *NRW*, p. 41.

p. 38 'Sonnet in autumn': N23, p. 89, 9.9.38; N45, p. 73, 9.8(?).38; September probably correct. Pub. *Fifteen Poems* (1942), p. 5. *NRW*, p. 42.

p. 39 'Sonnets in October': N29, p. 21, 24/26/27.10.43 (first sonnet), p. 22, 27.10.43 (second sonnet); N46, pp. 213–14. *NRW*, p. 43; *CP*, p. 25. In *CP* the sonnets are printed without breaks between octaves and sestets.

p. 40 'Leaf': N7, p. 3, September 1936; N21, p. 8, 16.9.36; N44, p. 113. Note in Hewitt's proof copy of *NRW*: 'Crumlin Road, Belfast'. Pub. *New Northman*, vol. VI, no. 2 (Summer 1938), p. 42, with title 'Fall of the leaf'. Rep. *The Bell* (January 1941), p. 90; *New Irish Poets* (1948), p. 92; *Mentor Book of Irish Poetry* (1965), p. 157. *NRW*, p. 44; *CP*, p. 15.

The *New Northman* version uses the forms 'tir'd', 'fir'd', 'wither'd' and 'washt'. In the *New Northman* and *Bell* versions, ll. 15–16 read: '. . . in the green and blue/and delicate gold of the sky'.

p. 40 'Load': N7, p. 6, October(?) 1937; N22, p. 119, 19.9.37; N44, p. 33, 19.9.37, with title 'Last load' in all three notebooks. Pub. *The Bell*, vol. 2, no. 6 (September 1941), p. 3. Rep. *Irish Poems of Today* (1944), p. 16; *1000 Years of Irish Poetry* (1947), p. 738; *Ulster Education* (December 1953); *Wolfhound Book of Irish Poems for Young People* (1975), p. 47; *The Crock of Gold* (1984); p. 73. *NRW*, p. 45.

p. 40 'Frost': N7, p. 10, November 1936; N21, p. 110, 22–3.11.36; N44, p. 95. First stanza revised July 1943. Pub. *Irish Jewry* (January 1937), p. 6. Rep. *Now in Ulster* (1944), p. 37; *New Irish Poets* (1948), p. 88; *New York Times Book Review*, 28 November 1948; *Mentor Book of Irish Poetry* (1965), p. 160; *Andersonstown News*, 12 November 1977, as part of a review of Hewitt's work; *The Field Day Anthology of Irish Writing* (1991), p. 163. *NRW*, p. 46; *CP*, p. 13; *S*, p. 57.

In the version in *Irish Jewry* the first stanza reads as follows:

> With frost again the thought is clear and wise,
> That rain made dismal with a mist's despair,
> Life leaps along the lashes of the eyes;
> A tree is truer for its being bare.
> The shapes that sag from neon-dizzy skies,
> Fold back to girder in the dawn-sharp air.

p. 41 'The mask': N46, p. 4, 9.5.40. Note in Hewitt's proof copy of *NRW*: 'Westland Road'. *NRW*, p. 47.

p. 41 'The happy man': N28, p. 89, 29.12.42; N46, p. 168. Pub. *The Bell*, vol. 15, no. 5 (February 1948), p. 4. *NRW*, p. 48; *CP*, p. 24; *S*, p. 108.

p. 42 'This then my country': N10, pp. 33–4, part XXXVIII of 'The Red Hand: a poemosaic'; N22, pp. 44–5, 12.6.37; N44, pp. 60–1. Pub. *The Bell*, vol. 15, no. 5 (February 1948), pp. 4–5. *NRW*, p. 49.

p. 42 'Ghosts': N13, pp. 17–18, April 1937; N22, pp. 35–6, 22.4.37; N44, pp. 64–5. Note in Hewitt's proof copy of *NRW*: 'Grandfather John Hewitt 1841–1922. Uncle John Robinson 18?–1918'. *NRW*, p. 50; *CP*, p. 16.

p. 43 'The little death': N24, pp. 129–38, 12–15.1.40, with title 'Reverie and recollection', part of which became the elegy for Shelley Wang; N45, pp. 187–93, part of longer poem with title 'Hold memory!', the remainder of which is unpublished. Note in Hewitt's proof copy of *NRW*: 'Part of a long poem on people and events'. Pub. *New Statesman and Nation*, 20 April 1940, with subtitle, 'In memory of Shelley Wang, Chinese writer, died Honan, July 1939 (from a longer poem)'. *NRW*, p. 51; *CP*, p. 20.

The *New Statesman* version reads as follows:

> I cannot cheat my thought I remember too well
> his bland smooth face by that hearth, his cigarettes,
> his explanation of the characters,
> the firm fist with the brush held vertical,
> his glinting glasses laminated thick,
> his way of speaking of his early days,
> his wise grandfather, poetry, and tea,
> Confucius, soya beans, and Mao Tse Tung . . .
>
> He was a restful man, a quiet scholar,
> compact of wisdom courage tolerance,
> a gentle poet even of our hills
>
> making a vivid stanza as he pass'd,
> disliking our coarse literal art's conceit,
> and setting style and reason against despair.
>
> For all his greatness life could offer him
> only a little death in a vast campaign,
> a manuscript unpublisht, and a book
> of badly printed verse on wartime paper.
> Yet I do not think he would have understood
> that sick word failure. There are other words.

The second stanza refers to Shelley Wang's poem about the Mourne Mountains, translated by Hewitt; *see* 'From the Chinese of Wang Li Shi' (*CF*, p. 6; *M*, p. 45).

Hewitt met Shelley Wang at the summer school of the Independent Labour Party at Welwyn Garden City, 1933. The Chinese poet came to Belfast to speak at a public meeting on Aid for China in the Ulster Hall on 12 January 1938, and stayed with the Hewitts for about ten days. The two poets corresponded for a time and Wang sent Hewitt a booklet of verses in Chinese and English from Chungking. Hewitt read of Wang's death behind Japanese lines in the *Daily Worker* in 1939. There is an account of Shelley Wang and his visit to Belfast in chapter 17 of Hewitt's unpublished autobiography, 'A North Light', and there are several unpublished items in the notebooks relating to Wang: N23, pp. 78–9, September 1938, translations of three of Wang's poems; N45, p. 55, 4–5.11.38, long poem with title 'Traveller: a mosaic', section 9, pp. 61–3, of which is based on a talk with Shelley Wang.

p. 44 'Interim': N46, p. 5, 11.5.40. The first ten lines of this poem, with three minor emendations, recur in 'Retreaded rhymes' (*LE*, p. 50). *NRW*, p. 52.

THOSE SWANS REMEMBER: A POEM, privately published, Belfast, 1956.

p. 45 'Those Swans Remember': N35, pp. 38–49, October–November 1955. In a letter to John Montague in the spring of 1964, Hewitt comments:

Those Swans Remember is an attempt to draw out and together the three strands of my thought and feeling: the Irish, the European, the Christian [that]

linked the dark Aegean to the Moyle
oaring the whistling winds and crossing slow
the painted roof of Michaelangelo [*sic*]
past Tara's grass and the wrecked Trojan spoil . . .

It was also in some sense a deliberate attempt to go beyond my usual flat plain manner of statement. If the Yanks and the English brought out their obscure poems I felt that I would shew 'em that an Irishman could be just as baffling and opaque. I had this printed but distributed casually.

In a manuscript note among his papers, Hewitt comments: 'I have estimated that this [poem] would require several score of references ranging from the Book of Kells to the tapestries in the Cluny Museum.'

TESSERAE (*T*), published by Festival Publications, Queen's University of Belfast, Belfast, 1967, as one of a series of six poetry pamphlets; the other poets were Laurence Lerner, John Montague, Norman Buller, Arthur Terry and Norman Dugdale. *Tesserae* contains a selection of poems written between November 1966 and February 1967. The visit to Greece and the Cyclades recorded in several of them took place in the autumn of 1966.

I have included all the poems in the pamphlet, with the exception of 'After reading *Sonnets* by Rev. Charles Turner (1864) and *The New Day*, sonnets by Dr T. Gordon Hake (1890)', which was extensively revised for *RD* (1978).

The pages of *Tesserae* are unnumbered. I have provided numbers in square brackets [pp. 1–11] for those pages on which poems are printed.

p. 51 'Hand over hand': N38, p. 29, January(?) 1967. *T* [p. 1]; *CP*, p. 140.

p. 51 'Betrayal': N38; pp. 4–5, 21.11.66. *T* [p. 2]; *CP*, p. 132; *PG* [p. 13]; *S*, p. 84. *See also* 'The one I loved' (*KS*, p. 24). The subject of these poems and of 'No second Troy', is Hewitt's nanny, Mrs Thompson, or as the young Hewitt, struggling with his pronunciation, called her, 'Maw Tawson'.

p. 52 'No second Troy': N38, pp. 6–7, 22.11.66. *T* [p. 3]; *CP*, p. 133; *PG* [p. 13]; *S*, p. 85. *See also* 'The one I loved' (*KS*, p. 24).

p. 52 'Pavane for a dead professor': N38, pp. 30–1, 5.2.67. with title 'For an extinct professor'. *T* [p. 4]; *CP*, p. 141.

p. 53 'Vida, Mykonos': N38, p. 24, 30.11.66 to 1–2.12.66. Pub. *Irish Times*, 11 February 1967. *T* [p. 5]; *CP*, p. 138.

p. 54 'Mykonos': N38, p. 1, 2.10.66; pp. 14–15, rev. 28.11.66. *T* [p. 6]; *CP*, p. 134.

p. 55 'Delos': N38, p. 19, 29.11.66. *T* [p. 7]; *CP*, p. 137.

p. 55 'Mycenae and Epidaurus': N38, pp. 17–18, 29.11.66. *T* [p. 8]; *CP*, p. 136.

p. 56 'Cape Sunion': N38, p. 28, 28–9.12.66. *T* [p. 9]; *CP*, p. 139.

p. 56 'Old Corinth': N38, p. 16, 29.11.66, with title 'Korinth'. *T* [p. 10]; *CP*, p. 135.

COLLECTED POEMS 1932–1967 (*CP*), published by MacGibbon and Kee, London, 1968, with the dedication 'For Roberta' and the following foreword:

> This gathering of poems has been arranged chronologically from the earliest, 'Ireland' (1932): some have been revised, some shortened in the process and given new titles.
>
> Fourteen have been taken from *No Rebel Word*, which, although published in 1948, took in nothing written later than the first half of 1944. Ten come from the pamphlet, *Tesserae* (Festival Publications, 1967). *Conacre*, privately printed in 1943, was included in *Poetry of the Present* (1949), Geoffrey Grigson's anthology.
>
> Most have appeared in a diversity of periodicals such as the *Listener, New Statesman, Times Literary Supplement, Outposts, Poetry Ireland,* the *Irish Times, Massachusetts Review,* and a number figure in about two dozen anthologies, British and American, from *Poems of Tomorrow* (1935) to *The Mentor Book of Irish Poetry* (1965): some have found place in textbooks, in BBC Schools Programmes or have been broadcast by the BBC and Radio Éireann.
>
> Half a dozen, 'The Glens', 'Turf-carrier on Aranmore', 'O country people', 'The owl', 'Hedgehog', 'The swathe uncut', have travelled farthest and have been used most often. While I am grateful that this should have been so, it might well happen that anyone who has heard or read a couple of these only, would think of me as a nature poet. That I am, by birth, an Irishman of Planter stock, by profession an art gallery man, politically a man of the Left are circumstances no less relevant in the conditioning of my response to experience. Many of the nature poems originated in frequent sojourns in the Glens of north-east Antrim over a period of almost twenty years. A break in this and in much else occurred when I settled in the English Midlands in the spring of 1957.

I have included all the poems in this volume with the exception of those that Hewitt reprinted unchanged from *Conacre, No Rebel Word* and *Tesserae.*

p. 58 'Ireland': N12, pp. 89–90, 3.2.32; N13, pp. 1–2; N45, pp. 111–12. Pub. *Listener*, 18 May 1932. Rep. *Poems of Tomorrow* (1935), p. 52; *Contemporary Irish Poetry* (eds Greacen and Iremonger, 1959), p. 73; *Contemporary Irish Poetry* (ed. Bradley, 1980), p. 107; *Faber Book of Poems and Places* (1980), p. 304; *Contemporary Irish Poetry* (ed. Bradley, 1988), p. 101; *Ireland in Poetry* (1990), p. 66. *CP*, p. 11.

In the *Listener* version, l. 12 reads 'and happy to stride over sterile acres'; l. 17 reads 'on half a dozen turf and a black bog'; and the final stanza begins 'So we are bitter and are dying out/in terrible sourness in this lonely place'.

p. 59 'Turf-carrier on Aranmore': N29. pp. 120–2, 19.7.44; N37, pp. 17–18, rev. version, May 1960; N47, pp. 27–8. Note in Hewitt's proof copy of *CP*: 'Donegal'. Pub. *Irish Writing*, no. 6 (November 1948), pp. 29–30, with title 'Aranmore'. Rep. *New Poems 1961* (1961), p. 42; *Listening and Writing*, BBC Radio for Schools (Summer 1964), p. 4; *Modern Poems Understood* (1965), p. 69; *Listening and Writing*, BBC Radio for Schools (1967), p. 4; *Poems to Read Aloud* (1967), p. 161; *Voices: The First Book* (1968), p. 36; *Adventures in English* (1972), p. 58. *CP*, p. 31; *S*, p. 67.

In the version published in *Irish Writing*, l. 4 reads 'to fetch more turf to top the stack'; l. 8 reads 'and find some topic to discuss'; ll. 18–19 read 'the string that braced the splintered creel,/the bare, rubbed flank, the hooves unshod'; l. 23 reads 'the land that bears such boys and beasts'.

p. 59 'Swan': N29, pp. 161–2, 17.9.44; N47, p. 42. Pub. *Poetry Ireland*, no. 1 (April 1948), p. 13. Rep. *British Weekly*, 24 May 1951; *New Poems 1954* (1954), p. 138; *New Statesman and Nation*, 16 February 1962. *CP*, p. 46.

p. 60 'Because I paced my thought': N29, p. 165, 11.10.44; N47, p. 43. Pub. *Irish Times*, 26 March 1949, with title 'Poem'. Rep. *Sphere Book of Modern Irish Poetry* (1972), p. 128; *Ten Irish Poets* (1974), p. 26; *Poets from the North of Ireland* (1979), p. 36; *Contemporary Irish Poetry* (ed. Bradley, 1980), p. 108; *Sunday Tribune*, 5 July 1987, with an appreciation of Hewitt by Seamus Heaney; *Contemporary Irish Poetry* (ed. Bradley, 1988), p. 102; *Poets from the North of Ireland* (1990), p. 41; *The Field Day Anthology of Irish Writing* (1991), p. 164. *CP*, p. 47; *S*, p. 53.

I recall discussing the last stanza of the poem with Hewitt, who mentioned that the image in l. 13 is drawn from William Morris; that l. 14 refers to summer schools of the kind that the Hewitts took part in between the wars; and that the concluding line refers to Vasari's account in his *Lives of the Artists* of how, when the Florentine painter Cimabue finished a work for the local church, it was carried there in celebratory procession by the community.

The *Irish Times* version begins 'Because I pace my thought by the natural world/the earth organic, renewed with palpable seasons'; ll. 7–8, and ll. 10–12 are punctuated as direct speech.

p. 61 'Two Irish saints': N29, pp. 177–8, 11.11.44, with titles 'St Patric' and 'Columcille'; N47, pp. 48–9. Both poems pub. *Irish Times*, 19–20 April 1946; 'Saint Patrick' pub. *British Weekly*, 7 December 1950. *CP*, p. 48; *S*, p. 19.

In the *Irish Times* version of 'Saint Patrick', ll. 5–6 read 'brought Christ to Eirinn better than the others/who, baffled, oared the yeasty billows' wake'; ll. 7–8 of 'Columcille' read 'the knuckled swift intolerance, the lips/too ready with the raspt and bleeding words'; and l. 13 has 'spadesman, mason'.

p. 61 'From a museum man's album': N30, pp. 1–6, 2.12.44, with title 'Museum pieces'; N47, pp. 56–9. Pub. *The Bell*, vol. 15, no. 6 (March 1948), pp. 3–4, omitting final section of ms. version. Rep. *Oxford Book of Twentieth Century English Verse* (1973), p. 427. *CP*, p. 50; *S*, p. 96.

In the *Bell* version, ll. 3–4 read 'although often with the damp maps of wallpaper/and the pickle of plaster on the shelf'; l. 27 reads 'when then was out of fashion but now is in fashion again'; l. 37 has 'popular handbooks'; the lines 'that is, all except the green-bound Chaffers/which came to us with the ceramics' are not included at the end of the second section; the third section begins 'Another, a spinster' and l. 55 (l. 57 in *CP* version) has 'died of fever'.

p. 63 'The green shoot': N30, pp. 140–2, 2.9.46, with title 'The frozen sod'; N37, pp. 80–1, rev. version, probably late 1963–early 1964. Pub. *The Bell*, vol. 15, no. 6 (March 1948), pp. 5–6, with title 'The frozen sod'. Rep. *Imagi*, vol. 5, no. 3 (1951), with title 'The frozen sod'; *Outposts*, no. 61 (Summer 1964), p. 11, with title 'The green shoot'. *CP*, p. 53; *PG* [p. 4]; *S*, p. 35.

The version in *The Bell* and *Imagi* reads as follows:

When I was small, if chance should bring a priest
once in a while along the quiet street
I'd run beside him, pull my schoolcap off,
and fling it on the ground and stamp on it.

I've caught my enemy, a message-boy,
and gripped his jersey and admonished him
first to admit his faith, and, when he did,
repeatedly to curse the Pope of Rome.

This was before I'd found the stilts of thought,
and, close to ground, knew puddles offered most;
for you could launch your fleet of paper boats
and seize an Empire, or, entranced by frost,

break little panes of ice to show the world
a bright blurred dance of crooked house and wall.
The frost was better than the dirty snow
which turned to slush the minute that it fell,

and licked the fingers with its dripping flame
like petrol from a lighter. Years before,
when I came in from play one Christmas Eve,
my mother bathed me at the kitchen fire,

and wrapped me in a blanket for the climb
up the long stairs to bed, we turned and heard
the carol singers somewhere in the dark,
their voices sharper, for the frost was hard.

My mother carried me along the hall
into the parlour, where the only light
upon the patterned walls and furniture
was from the yellow lamp across the street;

and there looped round the lamp, the singers stood,
their faces lifted to the lively stars,
singing a song I liked, until I saw
my mother's lashes were all bright with tears.

Out of this mulch of ready sentiment,
gritty with blades of flinty violence,
I am the green shoot asking for the flower,
soft as the feathers of the snow's cold swans.

p. 64 'First snow in the Glens': N31, pp. 6–7, 28.1.47. Pub. *Irish Writing*, no. 7 (February 1949), p. 65. Rep. *British Weekly*, 28 December 1950; *New Poems 1952* (1952), p. 31; *Poètes d'Irlande du Nord* (1991), p. 22. *CP*, p. 55; *S*, p. 55. In the *Irish Writing* version, l. 12 ends 'the bare thorn hedge'.

p. 65 'Blessing': N31, p. 17, 14.5.47. Pub. *Dublin Magazine*, vol. XXVII, no. 1 (January–March 1952), p. 2. Rep. *Digraphe*, no. 27 (June 1982), p. 22, in French and English. *CP*, p. 56.

p. 65 'Colour': N31, p. 19, 14.5.47; emended 28.5.49. Pub. *Irish Times*, 13 September 1947, with title 'May colour'. *CP*, p. 57; *DC* (1984), p. 70.

In the *Irish Times* version, which is in the form of three quatrains, l. 2 has 'because of the celandine'; l. 4 has 'bearded green'; and l. 10 reads 'the cherry and blackthorn bless'.

Rose McDonnell was the daughter of Patrick McDonnell, Hewitt's neighbour in the Glens of Antrim. She figures also in the poems 'Bleeze' and 'May altar', and her father is referred to again in 'The gap'.

p. 65 'Revenant': N31, pp. 44–5, 28.4.48. *CP*, p. 58; *S*, p. 112.

p. 66 'Agenda': N31, pp. 46–7, 28.4.48. *CP*, p. 59.

p. 67 'Landscape': N31, p. 63, 29.8.48. Pub. *Tribune*, 18 February 1949. Rep. *Irish Times*, 29 October 1949. *CP*, p. 60.

p. 67 'The ram's horn': N32, p. 2, 29.6.49. Pub. *New Statesman and Nation*, 20 May 1950. Rep. *New Poems 1952* (1952), p. 30; *New Poets of Ireland* (1963), p. 43; *Sphere Book of Modern Irish Poetry* (1972), p. 129; *Faber Book of Irish Verse* (1974), p. 300; *Poets from the North of Ireland* (1979), p. 36; 'John Hewitt 1907–1987' (a memorial broadsheet published by the Arts Council of Northern Ireland, 1987); *Poets from the North of Ireland* (1990), p. 41; *Poètes d'Irlande du Nord* (1991), p. 24. *CP*, p. 61; *S*, p. 56.

p. 68 'The crossing': N32, pp. 3–4, 6.7.49. Pub. *Irish Times*, 27 March 1954. *CP*, p. 62.

p. 68 'Homestead': N32, pp. 18–26, 3–4.7.49, 10–13.7.49, 14.8.49, with title 'The habitation'. Another projected title was 'The house that Jack built'. Dated 3–4.7.49, 10–18.7.49 and 14.8.49 in Hewitt's proof copy of *CP*; the 10–18 dating here seems to be an error. Pub. *The Bell*, vol. 18, no. 1 (April 1952), pp. 8–12. *CP*, p. 63.

The version in *The Bell* is subtitled 'Oisin's Grave, Lubitavish, Co. Antrim'; l. 16, omitted from the *CP* version, reads 'to the stout assertive writer busy with faces'.

Writing to John Montague in the spring of 1964, Hewitt comments that 'Homestead' forms part of a trilogy with *Conacre* and *Freehold* but because it 'was not in couplets and was rather short when it appeared in *The Bell*, nobody noticed the linkage'.

Among Hewitt's papers is a typescript entitled 'The dispute of Big Denis Lavery and the blind Gilmhuire McCartan', with the note: 'The above literal translation has been made from the version of the poem written down by Patrick Pronty in April 1769, O'Laverty Mss., no. K, unpaginated, preserved in St Malachy's College. A longer and more complete version of the poem has been published with notes by T. F. O'Rahilly in *Measgra Danta*, pt. 1, pp. 8–14 and 67–8.'

p. 72 'O country people': N32, pp. 54–7, 31.12.49, 1.1.50. Dated 31.12.49, 3.1.50 in Hewitt's proof copy of *CP*. Pub. *Dublin Magazine* (April–June 1950), pp. 4–5. Rep. *Concord of Harps* (1952), p. 20; *Outposts*, no. 22 (1952), pp. 2–3; *New Poems 1953* (1953), p. 86; *An Anthology of Commonwealth Verse* (1963), p. 143; *Mentor Book of Irish Poetry* (1965), p. 157; *Poems from Ireland* (1972), p. 60; *Ten Irish Poets* (1974), p. 24; *Poets from the North of Ireland* (1979), p. 31;

Soft Day (1980), p. 25; *Ireland in Poetry* (1990), p. 158; *Poets from the North of Ireland* (1990), p. 37. *CP*, p. 69; *S*, p. 63.

In the *Dublin Magazine* version, l. 43 reads 'there'd still be strata neither'd ever reach'.

p. 73 'Man fish and bird': N32, pp. 58–63, 5.1.50, with note: 'This poem was "given" to me in a more immediate sense than any since my surrealist experiments of years ago; even they, I believe, were more consciously imposed than this. Apart from one slight alteration in the days' order the intelligence intruded very little.' This note is dated 6.1.50. Pub. *Massachusetts Review*, vol. 5, no. 2 (Winter 1964), pp. 338–40. *CP*, p. 71.

p. 76 'The colony': N32, pp. 50–3, 30.12.49–5.1.50; pp. 65–72, rev. 6.1.50. Pub. *The Bell*, vol. 18, no. 11 (Summer 1953), pp. 33–7. Rep. *Pace*, vol. 4 (Spring 1972), p. 5 (extract); *Community Forum*, vol. 4, no. 1 (1974), pp. 11–12; *Irish Times*, 16 November 1985, as part of series on the Anglo-Irish summit; *The Field Day Anthology of Irish Writing* (1991), p. 165. *CP*, p. 75; *PG* [p. 17]; *S*, p. 21.

The editorial in the *Irish Times* on 25 March 1972 was headed 'Not outcast on the world'; 'The colony' was also quoted in a speech by Taoiseach Jack Lynch to the Society of the Friendly Sons of St Patrick in the Convention Room, Civic Centre, Philadelphia, 17 March 1971; in 'National identity and the Irish question', Father John Brady SJ, *The Month*, a review of Christian thought and world affairs (September 1974), pp. 701–3; and in *Peace, the Work of Justice, Addresses on the Northern Tragedy 1973–79*, Bishop Cahal B. Daly (Veritas Publications, 1979, pp. 15–16).

In a letter to John Montague in the spring of 1984, Hewitt describes the poem as 'strongly tinctured with Edwin Muir's influence'.

p. 79 'The stoat': N32, pp. 89–90, 23.4.50. Pub. *Massachusetts Review*, vol. 5, no. 2 (Winter 1964), p. 337. Rep. *Hundsrose: Neue Irische Gedichte* (1983), p. 124. *CP*, p. 80; *S*, p. 60.

p. 80 'The watchers': N32, pp. 102–3, 10.6.50. Rev. 23.11.50. Pub. *New Statesman and Nation*, 23 December 1950. Rep. *New Poems 1952* (1952), p. 30; *New Poets of Ireland* (1963), p. 41. *CP*, p. 81; *PG* [p. 12]; *S*, p. 62.

p. 81 'Corridor': N32, pp. 114–15, 31.8.50; N37, pp. 78–9, 30.11.63, rev. version. *CP*, p. 82.

p. 81 'A rhyme for Blake': N33, p. 16, 8.4.51. Dated 9.4.51 in Hewitt's proof copy of *CP*. *CP*, p. 83.

p. 82 'The gap': N33, p. 43, 3.8.51. Pub. *Listener*, 23 April 1964. Rep. *New Poems 1965* (1966), p. 84; *Speak to the Hills* (1985), p. 178. *CP*, p. 84; *DC* (1984), p. 70.

p. 82 'Torcello': N33, p. 72, 13.8.51. Pub. *Time and Tide*, 14 January 1956. *CP*, p. 85.

Torcello, situated on the Lagoon in Venice, is the location of a cathedral and the eleventh-century church, Santa Fosca. The Hewitts were in Venice for a PEN conference in September 1949.

p. 83 'Hedgehog': N33, p. 143, 15.9.52. Pub. *Time and Tide*, 21 August 1954. Rep. *New Poems 1958* (1958) p. 47; *New Poets of Ireland* (1963), p. 41; *Poems of Today* (1963), p. 60; *The Animal Anthology* (1966), p. 116. *CP*, p. 86.

p. 83 'Rite, Lubitavish, Glenaan': N33, pp. 151–2, 28.10.52, with title 'Rite'. Pub. *Irish Times*, 28 February 1953, with title 'Rite'. Rep. *Mentor Book of Irish Poetry* (1965), p. 159, also with title 'Rite'. *CP*, p. 87.

In the *Irish Times* version, l. 5 reads 'And let no patriot decry'; l. 7 reads 'for I still hold the faith was here'; ll. 9–12 read 'The healing well was known to me,/the magic of the thorn,/the menace of the cursing stones,/long years ere I was born'; and l. 14 reads 'I aimed my hook with care'.

The 'platted hare', also mentioned in 'A country walk in May', refers to the harvest ritual of cutting the last sheaf, or hare, by throwing reaping hooks at it.

p. 84 'A country walk in March'; N34, pp. 15–19, 22–3.3.53, originally titled 'O Lord how manifold'. Pub. *Times Literary Supplement*, 29 April 1955. *CP*, p. 88. The 'quiet botanist' is Hewitt's friend E. Norman Carrothers, also one of the ramblers in 'A country walk in May'; there is a portrait of Carrothers, originally intended for inclusion in 'A North Light', among Hewitt's papers.

p. 86 'The owl': N34, pp. 45–6, 4.9.53. Pub. *Irish Times*, 19 September 1953. Rep. *New Poems 1960* (1960), p. 63; *New Poets of Ireland* (1963), p. 42; *The Animal Anthology* (1966), p. 105; *Understanding and Appreciation: Book I* (1967), p. 27. *CP*, p. 91; *S*, p. 61.

In the *Irish Times* version, which takes the form of eight quatrains, l. 23 reads 'the feathered stump beside the tree'.

p. 87 'For a September afternoon of unexpected brightness': N34, p. 48, 17–18.9.53 with title 'For a September day', and note 'revised 1962'; N37, p. 68, 22.7.62, rev. version. *CP*, p. 93; *S*, p. 103.

p. 87 'The tumbling spore': N34, p. 62, 22.12.53. Pub. *New Statesman and Nation*, 27 February 1954. *CP*, p. 94.

p. 87 'The child, the chair, the leaf': N34, pp. 63–6, 21–4.12.53, with subtitle 'The cripple child'. Pub. *Outposts*, no. 50 (Autumn 1961), pp. 3–5. Rep. *Best Poems of 1961* (1962), p. 65. *CP*, p. 95; *S*, p. 110.

p. 89 'The spectacle of truth': N34, pp. 96–8, 30.7.54. Pub. *A Winter Harvest* (1956), p. 12. Rep. *New Poems 1960* (1960), p. 61; *Contemporary Irish Poetry* (ed. Bradley, 1980), p. 111. *CP*, p. 98. This poem was prompted by Hewitt's visit to Amsterdam in 1954 for the PEN conference; in chapter 35 of 'A North Light' titled 'Amsterdam, 1954', he records: 'The tall tower of the dark Westerkerke across the canal, with men at a canvas-canopied stall eating herring, in the foreground, and a flowery barge slowly floating past in the middle distance lodged itself in my imagination until, two months later, I made the first draft of a poem "The spectacle of truth" ' (p. 184).

p. 90 'The Municipal Gallery revisited, October 1954': N34, pp. 105–7, 25–6.10.54, pp. 122–3, 23.12.54. Pub. *A Winter Harvest* (1956), p. 13. *CP*, p. 100; *S*, p. 27.

p. 92 'The twisted heart': N34, pp. 110–11, 2–3.12.54. Pub. *Outposts*, no. 49 (Summer 1961), p. 1. *CP*, p. 102.

p. 92 'The heart of joy': N34, pp. 116–18, 22–3.12.54. Rep. *Irish Poetry of Faith and Doubt* (1990), p. 89. *CP*, p. 103.

p. 93 'The habit of mercy': N34, pp. 137–8, 1.2.55. Pub. *Poetry Ireland*, no. 1 (Autumn 1962), pp. 27–8. *CP*, p. 105; *S*, p. 109.

p. 94 'Ossian's grave, Lubitavish, County Antrim': N35, pp. 19–20, 16.8.55, with title 'Oisin's grave, the horned cairn at Lubitavish, Co Antrim'; N37, pp. 19–20, May 1960, rev. version. Pub. *Acorn*, vol. 1, no. 2 (Spring 1962), p. 3. *CP*, p. 106; *DC* (1984), p. 70.

p. 95 'The response': N35, pp. 30–1, 20–1.8.55. *CP*, p. 107. The dedication is for Jill and Brenda Stewart, daughters of the Hewitts' friends Jim and Sophie Stewart.

p. 96 'The frontier': N35, p. 35, 14.9.55. Pub. *Poetry Ireland*, no. 1 (Autumn 1962), p. 28. Rep. *Coventry Evening Telegraph*, 29 August 1968; *Les Lettres nouvelles* (March 1973), pp. 152–3, in English and French; *Faber Book of Irish Verse* (1974), p. 300. *CP*, p. 108. The poem was prompted by travel through the French and Swiss Alps.

p. 96 'Jacob and the angel': N35, pp. 90–1, 11.4.58. Ms. version contains four stanzas, the last of which is the basis for the published poem. Pub. *Poetry Ireland*, no. 1 (Autumn 1962), p. 27. *CP*, p. 109.

p. 96 'The mainland': N35, pp. 95–6, 24–5.6.58. Pub. *Acorn*, vol. 1, no. 1 (Winter 1961), p. 7. Rep. *Outposts*, no. 68 (Spring 1966), p. 7. *CP*, p. 110.

p. 97 'An Irishman in Coventry': N35, pp. 99–101, 2.7.58; rev. September 1958. Pub. *New Statesman and Nation*, 16 May 1959. Rep. *Standard*, 5 June 1959; *Guinness Book of Poetry 1958–59* (1960), p. 70; *Coventry Evening Telegraph* (extract), 29 August 1968; *Sphere Book of Modern Irish Poetry* (1972), p. 130; *Angry for Peace* (1973), p. 7 (extract); *Faber Book of Irish Verse* (1974), p. 301; *Ten Irish Poets* (1974), p. 21; *A Prose and Verse Anthology of Modern Irish Writing* (1978), p. 233; *Poets from the North of Ireland* (1979), p. 28; *Contemporary Irish Poetry* (ed. Bradley, 1980), p. 109; *Soft Day* (1980), p. 27; *Mainichi Daily News* (Japan), 1984; *Contemporary Irish Poetry* (ed. Bradley, 1988) p. 103; *Poets from the North of Ireland* (1990), p. 34. *CP*, p. 111; *PG* [p. 5]; *S*, p. 25.

Interviewed by the *Standard* (5 June 1959), Hewitt comments:

> 'It is a good thing for an Irishman to leave home because he can then see the things in perspective which normally obscure, if not distort his vision. One can only be aware of one's roots when they are at a distance, not round one's neck. The situation stated in the poem revolves around the contrast between the sense of social urgency demonstrated in a progressive community such as Coventry, which has attracted people from all quarters of these islands, giving the city a cosmopolitan flavour. This is in vivid contrast to the ingrown parochialism of the Irishman in his native habitat. The opening phrase in the poem is significant, for although Coventry has had many material successes in various forms, an outsider from a conservative and provincial setting is immediately struck and delighted by the general social tolerance shown in the city. In such a climate, emotions, ideas and beliefs are accepted for what they are and are never challenged on mere obscurantist grounds.'

See Hewitt's article 'Godiva rides again in a new Coventry', *Belfast Telegraph*, 20 September 1957, and his essay 'Coventry, the tradition of change and continuity' in *Coventry: The Tradition of Change and Continuity* (1965), pp. 1–13.

p. 98 'The knife': N37, pp. 5–6, 22.4.59. Pub. *Listener*, 10 October 1963. *CP*, p. 113.

p. 99 'Mass': N37, p. 52, 20–1.7.60. Hewitt's notes in his proof copy of *CP* read: 'Wellinhall [*sic.* Willenhall is a housing estate in Coventry]. Attended a wedding of a young Irish RC Pat Powell at church in new housing estate'. Pub. *Kilkenny Magazine*, no. 10 (Autumn–Winter 1963–4), p. 32. *CP*, p. 115.

p. 99 'Whit Monday': N37, p. 60, 15.7.62. Rev. 20.11.62. Dated 15.7.62, 20.9.62 in Hewitt's proof copy of *CP*. Pub. *Kilkenny Magazine*, no. 10 (Autumn–Winter 1963–4), p. 32. Rep. *Celebration: A Salute to a Visiting Artist* (*Pope Paul VI*) (1979), p. 28; *The Deer's Cry* (1986), p. 232. *CP*, p. 116. This poem arose out of Hewitt's visit to Poland in June 1962; in a copy of a letter to a Polish friend, dated 12 July 1962, in the Public Record Office of Northern Ireland, Hewitt recalls 'watching the little girls in their confirmation dresses climbing the hill to the church – was it Jedrzejow?'

p. 100 'Collector's choice': N37, pp. 100–2, with cancelled title 'The picture', with date November 1964 and note: 'Drastic revision and recast of portion of longer poem "Exposition", 13–23.12.44'. Dated 13–23.12.44, rev. November 1964, in Hewitt's proof copy of *CP*. *CP*, p. 117.

p. 101 'The wheel': N37, pp. 103–5, 24–5.11.64. *CP*, p. 119. *See also* the group of poems in *KS* that form an extended portrait of Hewitt's Uncle Sam: '21st September 1912', 'First pantomime', 'The magician', 'The breach' and 'Consequences', and the introductory notes to *KS* in the present volume. The 'book on aeroplanes' was *British Aircraft, 1809–1914* by Peter Lewis (1962).

p. 102 'Lake Bled, Slovenia': N37, p. 121, 18.7.65. *CP*, p. 121.

p. 102 'The modelled head': N37, pp. 125–6, 16–20.7.65. Rep. *A Poet's Pictures: A Selection of Works of Art Collected by John Hewitt (1907–1987)* (Shambles Art Gallery, 1987, p. 15). *CP*, p. 122. The poem refers to the *Portrait of John Hewitt, 1965* in polyester resin by Eric J. Elmes, head teacher of sculpture and model-making, Coventry Art School, 1951–62.

p. 103 'The word': N37, pp. 127–8, 20–1.7.65. Quoted in full in a review of Hewitt's work, *Andersonstown News*, 12 November 1977. *CP*, p. 124.

p. 104 'The pet shop': N37, pp. 136–7, 15–16.12.65. The pet shop referred to was situated in Gresham Street in the Smithfield area of Belfast; it closed down in February 1991. *CP*, p. 125.

p. 105 'My grandmother's garter': N37, pp. 138–40, 17–20.12.65. *CP*, p. 126; *PG* [p. 12]. George MacDonald (1824–1905) was a poet, preacher, lecturer, novelist and writer of children's stories; John Greenleaf Whittier (1807–92) was an American poet.

p. 106 'Eager journey': N37, pp. 141–2, 21.12.65. Pub. *Irish Times*, 17 June 1967. Rep. *Ten Irish Poets* (1974), p. 23. *CP*, p. 128. *See also* 'Grandfather Robinson dies in 1898' (*KS*, p. 7).

p. 107 'A Victorian steps out': N37, pp. 143–4, 22.12.65. Pub. *Ten Irish Poets* (1974), p. 24. *CP*, p. 129.

p. 108 'With E.M.F. on 28th December 1965': N37, p. 145, 28.12.65. *CP*, p. 131. *See also* 'An hour with E.M.F. at ninety' (*OMT*, p. 22). Hewitt first met E.M. Forster when Forster came to Belfast to deliver an address (*see Threshold*, no. 28 [Spring 1977], pp. 3–6) at the unveiling of a memorial plaque for the novelist Forrest Reid on 10 October 1952. At the request of a mutual friend, Hugh Meredith, the Hewitts provided a meal for Forster at their flat in 18 Mountcharles, Belfast; the literary company on that occasion included Philip Larkin, George Buchanan and Roy McFadden. Hewitt often visited and read to Forster when the novelist stayed with his friends Bob and May Buckingham in Coventry.

p. 108 'To Pireus': N38, pp. 39–41, 17.4.67. *CP*, p. 143.

THE DAY OF THE CORNCRAKE: POEMS OF THE NINE GLENS (*DC*), published by the Glens of Antrim Historical Society, n.p., 1969, and dedicated 'To the memory of my friend Geoffrey Taylor (1900–1956), poet, anthologist, gardener, who approved many of these poems: "Watch your syntax, John".' Hewitt wrote the following foreword:

> Once nearly every townland had its poet. At the time of their greatest flourishing, one hundred and fifty years ago, each carried the name of his locality like a badge of nobility; Orr of Ballycarry, Campbell of Ballynure, Herbison of Dunclug. Rooted men, they wrote in the vernacular, and their verses, convivial, satirical, sentimental, frequently taking occasion from current or recent events, had a clear social function. The last diminishing traces of this tradition lingered on into this century, and, in the Antrim Glens within living memory, were represented in the rhymes of James Stoddard Moore and Daniel McGonnell. But this kind of composition could not long outlast the decline of the social order which needed it.
>
> The other tradition, the relation, with some topographical accuracy, of a poem to a named place, which began in England in the early seventeenth century, was late in emerging in Ireland. Not until 1811, in William Hamilton Drummond's '*Giant's Causeway*', do we find reference to
>
> Garron's bastion cliffs the waves repel
> Or fair Glenariff winds her wizard cell.
>
> Moira O'Neill's *Songs of the Glens of Antrim* (1900), therefore, was a unique event in our literary history. But, although highly popular for over thirty years, the book by now has lost much of its momentum, perhaps due to the limitations in the social background of the author.
>
> Since then good poems about the Glens have come from the powerful American poet Robinson Jeffers who spent some time at Knocknacarry in the nineteen thirties, from Louis MacNeice, with a couple on Cushendun, and from Roy McFadden, again a handful only, but of fine quality.
>
> It will be obvious to any reader of the verses gathered here that they relate to the years just after the last war, before the rapid leap in technology changed the pace of rural life, when traditional usages and customs were still practised or vividly remembered. Many of the people mentioned who were then old are now dead, and the young have learned new rhythms. So, apart from any other interest they might have, I hope that these verses may summon up the day of the corncrake and the whin-fed mare, to those who have experienced it, and to those who have not.

Hewitt also appended the following note:

> With the exception of 'Country talk', written in 1965, these poems come from the decade 1946–56, the bulk from the four years' period 1949–53, although several have since been extensively revised.
>
> Sixteen were printed in the following journals, some of which are now defunct: the *Belfast Telegraph*, the *Irish Press*, the *Irish Times*, *The Bell*, *Dublin Magazine*, *Irish Bookman*, *Rann* and *Tribune*; and 'The wake' was reprinted in the *Ulster Folk Museum Year Book 1966/67*, in the account of the re-erection of Daniel Hyndman's house at Cultra, at the opening of which, in August, 1965, I read 'Cushkib Fair'.
>
> Not included here, other Glens poems may be found in *No Rebel Word* (1948) and in *Collected Poems 1932–1967* (MacGibbon and Kee 1968).

I have included all the poems from this edition, with the exception of 'The free foot', revised for *Mosaic* (1981), 'The gentle bush', amended for the second edition of *The Day of the Corncrake* (1984), and 'Black and white', amended for *The Chinese Fluteplayer* (1974). The poems 'The booleys', 'Black and white' and 'The bell' are omitted from the 1984 edition.

p. 110 'Late spring': N33, pp. 11–12, 7.4.51; N41, pp. 81–2. *DC* (1969) p. 7; *DC* (1984), p. 11.

p. 110 'April awake': N30, p. 107, 26.4.46, with note 'From Tiveragh, Cushendall'; N47, p. 94. Pub. *Irish Bookman*, vol. 1, no. 10 (June 1947), p. 32. *DC* (1969), p. 7; *SOT* [p. 11]; *DC* (1984), p. 12.

p. 111 'Haymaking in the low meadow': N32, pp. 30–4, 14.8.49. Pub. *Rann*, no. 9 (Summer 1950), pp. 6–7. Rep. *The Nine Glens* (1974), p. 77. *DC* (1969), p. 8; *DC* (1984), p. 12.

p. 112 'Footing turf': N31, p. 28, 11.10.47. Pub. *Irish Times*, 22 November 1947. Rep. *Tribune*, 14 January 1949. In the *Tribune* version the last line reads 'shone on the harvesters' and 'footing turf' is glossed: 'placing the cut "peats" in little stacks to dry out'. *DC* (1969), p. 9; *DC* (1984), p. 15.

p. 112 'Sunset over Glenaan': N32, pp. 122–4, 1–2.9.50. Pub. *Dublin Magazine*, vol. XXVI, no. 3 (July–September 1951), pp. 1–2. *DC* (1969), p. 10; *DC* (1984), p. 15.

p. 114 'Gathering praties': N31, pp. 81–3, 21.10.48. Pub. *Poetry Ireland*, no. 9 (January 1950), pp. 19–20. Rep. *Ten Irish Poets* (1974), p. 22; *Antrim Coast and Glens* (1990), p. 40 (extract). *DC* (1969), p. 12; *DC* (1984), p. 16.

p. 115 'May altar': N32, p. 93, 28.5.50. *DC* (1969), p. 14; *DC* (1984), p. 19.

p. 115 'Country talk': N37, pp. 116–17, 6–7.6.65, with title 'Glens talk'. Pub. *Irish Press*, 31 August 1968, with title 'Irish country talk'. *DC* (1969), p. 14; *DC* (1984), p. 20.

p. 116 'The booleys': N30, pp. 118–19, 14.6.46; N47, pp. 102–3. *DC* (1969), p. 15.

p. 117 'The ballad' ('I named a ballad round a sparking fire . . .'): N31, pp. 13–14, 11–12.5.47. Pub. *Irish Times*, 27 December 1947. Rep. *Tribune*, 21 April 1950. In the *Tribune* version, l. 13 ends 'in a house' and the final line ends 'and of shame'. *DC* (1969), p. 16; *DC* (1984), p. 20.

p. 117 'The wake': N34, pp. 25–6, 12–13.4.53. Pub. *Rann*, no. 20 (June 1953), pp. 15–16. Rep. *Irish Press*, 27 April 1968; *Ulster Museum Year Book 1965/66*, p. 10; *The Nine Glens* (1974), p. 113, with subtitle 'Written on the occasion of the death of Dan Hyndman'; *Antrim Coast and Glens* (1990) p. 32. *DC* (1969), p. 16; *DC* (1984), p. 23. Hewitt notes in *DC* (1969) in an afterword that the poem was reprinted in the *Ulster Folk Museum Year Book* [1966–7] 'in the account of the re-erection of Daniel Hyndman's house at Cultra'.

p. 118 'Glenaan': N34, p. 28, 13.4.53. *DC* (1969), p. 17; *DC* (1984), p. 23.

p. 118 'Instead of an elegy': N33, pp. 9–10. 7.4.51, with title 'Daniel O'Loan'. Pub. *Irish Press*, 26 July 1969, with title 'Daniel O'Loan: instead of an elegy'. *DC* (1969), p. 18; *DC* (1984), p. 24.

p. 119 'The volunteer' ('For his long working life an engineer . . .'): N33, pp. 52–4, 7.8.51. Originally titled 'Epilogue' in ms. *DC* (1969), p. 18; *DC* (1984), p. 24.

p. 120 'Halloweve: a Glensman speaks': N33, pp. 158–9, 1.11.52, with title 'The fairy hill'. *DC* (1969), p. 20; *DC* (1984), p. 61.

p. 121 'Company': N33, pp. 136–7, 18.5.52. Pub. *Rann*, no. 20 (June 1953), p. 15. *DC* (1969), p. 15; *DC* (1984), p. 61.

p. 121 'For any women who pass this house': N32, p. 47, 30.12.49. Pub. *Tribune*, 26 May 1950. Rep. *Irish Times*, 2 February 1952. The *Tribune* version begins 'This shuffling fellow, old John William Greer'. *DC* (1969), p. 21; *DC* (1984), p. 62.

p. 122 'Cushkib Fair': N34, pp. 67–70, 27.12.53. Rep. *The Nine Glens* (1974), p. 84. Hewitt notes in *DC* (1969) in an afterword that he read this poem in August 1965 at the opening of Daniel Hyndman's house, re-erected at the Ulster Folk Museum, Cultra. *DC* (1969), p. 22; *DC* (1984), p. 62.

p. 123 'The bell': N33, p. 21, 27.5.51. Pub. *The Bell*, vol. 19, no. 1 (December 1953), p. 145. *DC* (1969), p. 24.

p. 124 'The hill-farm': N35, pp. 70–1, 31.8.56. *DC* (1969), p. 24; *DC* (1984), p. 65.

p. 125 'The braes o' Layde': N34, p. 22, 23.3.53, with title 'Danegeld' and note: 'Based on a story from Michael J. Murphy, 21.3.53'. *DC* (1969), p. 25; *DC* (1984), p. 65.

p. 125 'Fame': N32, pp. 116–21, 1.9.50. Pub. *The Bell*, vol. 16, no. 4 (January 1951), pp. 12–14. *DC* (1969), p. 26; *DC* (1984), p. 68.

THE PLANTER AND THE GAEL: POEMS BY JOHN HEWITT AND JOHN MONTAGUE (*PG*), published by the Arts Council of Northern Ireland, Belfast, 1970, to accompany a programme of readings by the two poets in November 1970 in a number of towns in Northern Ireland. The following poems are reprinted from Hewitt's *Collected Poems 1932–1967* (1968): 'Once alien here', 'The green shoot', 'The Glens', 'An Irishman in Coventry', 'The watchers', 'My grandmother's garter', 'Betrayal', 'No second Troy' and 'The colony'. Two are reprinted in later collections with emendations: 'The man from Malabar' in *Mosaic* (1981) and 'Conversations in Hungary, August 1969' in *An Ulster*

Reckoning (1971), though it is the original form of the latter that appears in *Out of My Time* (1974). *See* notes below. 'The Long Bridge' and 'The search' are reprinted in *Out of My Time*, with the addition of dedications, and I have included them with that collection.

The pages of *The Planter and the Gael* are unnumbered. I have provided numbers in square brackets [pp. 1–19] for those pages on which poems are printed.

p. 129 'Gloss, on the difficulties of translation': N38, p. 99, 18–19.11.68, with title 'Gloss'; rev. version pp. 101–2, 2.12.68. Pub. *Irish Press*, 15 March 1969. Rep. *Digraphe*, no. 27 (June 1982), pp. 20–1, in English and French. *PG* [p. 8]; *OMT*, p. 19. In *OMT* Hewitt provides the note: 'See *Early Irish Lyrics*, edited by Gerard Murphy, 1956, p. 6'. Hewitt reviewed this book in the *Belfast Telegraph*, 6 October 1956. There is an ms. among Hewitt's papers on which he has transcribed versions, from the Irish, of the original, by K. Jackson, Robin Flower, Gerard Murphy, Myles Dillon and John Montague; the last version is Hewitt's own, which forms the opening three lines of 'Gloss, on the difficulties of translation'.

This poem was one in a series of poster/poems produced by the Arts Council of Northern Ireland in 1985; the image was by Wendy Dunbar.

p. 129 'Conversations in Hungary, August 1969': N39, p. 39, 21.10.69, section 1, with title 'August at Balaton'; pp. 40–1, 22.10.69, sections 2 and 3, with title 'Explaining the Ulster question'. Pub. *Hibernia*, 1 May 1970. Rep. *UR* (1971) with a number of emendations: in section 2, l. 13 'Christians' becomes 'Christian', and in section 3, ll. 6–8 read: 'close-heeled in hope, as by the Furies paced;/blight in the air and famine's after-taste,/from fear, guilt and frustration never free'. In *OMT* (1974), however, the version printed is that from *PG*. *PG* [p. 19]; *UR*, p. 14; *OMT*, p. 25; *S*, p. 36.

This poem is quoted in *The Break-up of Britain* by Tom Nairn (1977, p. 224).

AN ULSTER RECKONING (*UR*), privately published, Belfast, 1971, with a dedication to 'John Montague, a practical friend', and the following foreword, dated April 1971:

> In the verse-play *The Bloody Brae*, written in 1936 but not performed or published until twenty years later, and the 'parable-allegory' 'The colony' (1953), I thought that I had expressed my attitude to the major problem of my native province as accurately as I could. In the years after, for this seemed the mood, an apparent softening of the hard lines and a growing tolerance between the two historic communities pointed towards a more mature and responsible society.
>
> But the tragic events since October 1968 have ruined that prospect. To one living outside Ireland the impact of the terrible days of August, 1969, was heartbreaking. As I could not readily walk among the barricades with my white flag, I found release for my sense of frustration in verse.
>
> Except for 'Conversations in Hungary', written in late October, the rest of the pieces gathered here came in September, 1969, with revisions later. More than half have appeared in *Tribune*, *Hibernia*, the *Irish Times* and

the *Irish Press*, and in the magazines *Ariel*, *Threshold*, and in *The Planter and the Gael*, *Exercises in Practical Criticism* (1971) and *Poems from Ireland* (New York).

In an article in *Poetry Ireland* seven years ago, John Montague described me as 'the first (and probably the last) deliberately Ulster Protestant poet'. That designation carries a heavy obligation these days.

Of the twenty poems in the original edition, the only one I have not included is 'Conversations in Hungary, August 1969', previously printed in *The Planter and the Gael.*

p. 132 'An Ulsterman': N39, p. 24, 23–5.9.69; final version, 12.10.69, with titles 'Birth right/An Ulsterman'. Rep. *Here in Ulster*, BBC Schools Booklet (Spring 1971); *Pace*, vol. 4, no. 1 (January 1972), p. 20; *Community Forum*, vol. 4, no. 1 (1974), p. 10; *Irish Times*, 17 June 1974, with title 'An Ulsterman (1969)'; *The Wearing of the Black* (1974), p. 81; *Pace*, vol. 10, no. 1 (Spring 1978), p. 2. *UR*, p. 3.

p. 132 'The dilemma': N38, p. 148, 2.9.69; rev. version N39, p. 31, 29.9.69, with title 'Ulsterman's dilemma'; further rev. p. 79, 31.5.70. Rep. *Community Forum*, vol. 4, no. 1 (1974), p. 10; *The Wearing of the Black* (1974), p. 8; *A Prose and Verse Anthology of Modern Irish Writing* (1978), p. 232. *UR*, p. 3.

p. 133 'An Ulsterman in England remembers': N38, pp. 145–6, 28–31.8.69, with title 'Inheritance'. Pub. *Tribune*, 26 September 1969. Rep. *The Wearing of the Black* (1974), p. 9. In the *Tribune* version, l. 24 is followed by four lines later omitted: 'There was that other, threshing in arrest,/the four who carried, swung, and rammed his head/against a handy corner, and the red/blood dribbled down his chin – across his chest'. *UR*, p. 4.

Some of the incidents referred to in this poem figure in a number of others: see, for example, 'Encounter, nineteen twenty' (*TE*, p. 19); and the following poems in *KS*: 'The Troubles, 1922' (p. 58), 'The prisoners on the roof' (p. 58), 'A case of mistaken identity' (p. 59), 'After the fire' (p. 59) and 'Two spectres haunt me' (p. 60).

p. 133 'In this year of grace': N38, p. 141, 25–6.8.69. Pub. *Irish Times*, 3 January 1970. Rep. *Poems from Ireland* (1972), p. 62; *Angry for Peace* (1973, octave only, untitled), p. 7; *The Wearing of the Black* (1974), p. 76. *UR*, p. 5.

p. 134 'Street names': N39, p. 1, rev. 11.12.69; p. 2, 8–9.9.69. Ms. version among Hewitt's papers, dated 10–11.12.69, with title 'The people of the Shankill Road'. Pub. *Aquarius*, no. 4 (1971), p. 42. Rep. *The Wearing of the Black* (1974), p. 11. *UR*, p. 5.

p. 134 'An Ulster landowner's song': N38, pp. 149–50, 2.9.69. Pub. *Tribune*, 26 September 1969. Rep. *Ten Irish Poets* (1974), p. 27. *UR*, p. 6. Note in Hewitt's annotated copy of *UR*: 'Chichester-Clarke'.

p. 135 'Fables for Stormont': N38, p. 147, 1.9.69. *UR*, p. 6.

p. 135 'The coasters': N39, pp. 15–19, 15.9.69. Pub. *Threshold*, no. 23 (Summer 1970), pp. 26–8. Rep. *Alliance* (January 1972), p. 5; *The Wearing of the Black* (1974), p. 154; *Hundsrose: Neue Irische Gedichte* (1983), p. 121. *UR*, p. 7.

p. 137 'Memorandum for the moderates': N38, p. 143, 27.8.69, with title 'Advice to the moderates'. Pub. *Irish Times*, 31 January 1970. *UR*, 9.

p. 138 'The tribunes': N39, p. 9, 14.9.69. Pub. *Irish Press*, 1 November 1969. *UR*, p. 9. Note in Hewitt's annotated copy of *UR* glosses 'the young men/who had spoken for freedom in the marketplace' with the initials 'P.D.', that is, the People's Democracy movement.

p. 138 'The well-intentioned consul': N39, pp. 7–8, 13.9.69. Pub. *Irish Press*, 1 November 1969. *UR*, p. 10. Note in Hewitt's annotated copy of *UR* glosses 'the ailing aged consul' as 'Brookebrough [*sic*]'; the line 'that he had sent and received emissaries' with the note 'Lemass'; and the 'Western Quarter' as 'Falls Rd'. Presumably the consul of the title is Captain Terence O'Neill.

p. 139 'Parallels never meet': N39, pp. 13–14, 5.9.69. Pub. *Ariel* (an Anglo-Irish number), vol. 1, no. 3 (July 1970), p. 77. Rep. *Exercises in Practical Criticism* (1971), p. 19. *UR*, p. 11.

p. 140 'Prime Minister': N39, p. 25, 26.9.69, with titles 'Major James Dawson Chichester-Clark' and 'Prime Minister: from Ulster portraits'. Pub. *Hibernia*, 10 October 1969. *UR*, p. 12. This poem was published in *Hibernia* with 'Demagogue', 'Minister' and 'Agitator' (*see below*) under the general title 'Four Northern portraits'.

p. 140 'Demagogue': N39, p. 26, 26–8.9.69, with titles 'Rev Ian Paisley' and 'Demagogue'. Pub. *Hibernia*, 10 October 1969. *UR*, p. 12.

p. 141 'Minister': N39, p. 28, 28.9.69, with titles 'Brian Faulkner' and 'Minister'. Pub. *Hibernia*, 10 October 1969. *UR*, p. 13.

p. 141 'Agitator': N39, p. 27, 26–7.9.69, with titles 'Bernadette Devlin' and 'Agitator'. Pub. *Hibernia*, 10 October 1969. *UR*, p. 13.

p. 141 'Exile': N39, p. 10, 14.9.69. *UR*, p. 15.

p. 141 'A Belfastman abroad argues with himself': N38, p. 144, 26–8.8.69, with title 'An Ulsterman abroad argues with himself'. Rep. *The Wearing of the Black* (1974), p. 13. *UR*, p. 16. In Hewitt's annotated copy of *UR*, he glosses the 'evil man' as 'Paisley' and '. . . that little clan/who later marched for justice' as 'People's Democracy'.

p. 142 'The iron circle': N38, p. 142, 26.8.69; rev. version N39, p. 77, 30.5.70. Rep. *The Wearing of the Black* (1974), p. 17. *UR*, p. 16. The poet W.R. Rodgers (1909–69) is also the subject of 'W.R. Rodgers (1909–1969)' (*OMT*, p. 21), 'W.R.R.' (*SOT* [p. 8]), and is referred to in *Freehold:* 'III Townland of peace' (*F*, p. 12), and 'Roll call' (Appendix I of the present volume). *See also* Hewitt's review of Rodgers's *Collected Poems* (*Irish Press*, 15 January 1972).

THE CHINESE FLUTEPLAYER (*CF*), privately published, Lisburn, 1974, in a limited edition of two hundred copies. The booklet was designed and printed by Tomorrow's Press, 6 Carrisbrook Park, Lambeg, Lisburn, and the cover design, by George Morrow, is based on a bronze figurine, *The Chinese Fluteplayer*, owned by Hewitt. I have included all the poems from this booklet, with the exception of 'Vigil', which appears in slightly amended form in *Mosaic* (1981, p. 48), and the untitled lyric that begins 'Leafing through a book on Oriental art', which is reprinted in *Mosaic* (p. 47), with the title 'Sunset'.

The pages of *The Chinese Fluteplayer* are unnumbered. I have provided numbers in square brackets [pp. 1–13] for those pages on which poems are printed.

p. 144 'Spring of the year': N35, p. 61, 10.4.56. *CF* [p. 2].

p. 144 'Black and white': N34, pp. 77–8, 6.6.54. Pub. *Belfast Telegraph*, 3 July 1954. *DC* (1969), p. 19; *CF* [p. 3]. In the *Belfast Telegraph* version the poem is printed without stanza division; l. 4 reads 'and drifted slow to the waiting stone'; and l. 7 begins 'he may never'. In the *DC* version, ll. 5–8 read 'And, though that blackbird, all summer through,/should sing so long as there's light to see,/he will never fling a song as bright'.

p. 144 'Sparrowhawk': N30, p. 102, 25–6.4.46; N47, p. 91. Pub. *Irish Times*, 22 January 1949, in the form of two quatrains. Rep. *British Weekly*, 28 February 1952. *CF* [p. 4].

p. 145 'The storm': N23, p. 5, 15.1.38, with note 'a poem in the Chinese manner'; N44, p. 28. *CF* [p. 5]; *M*, p. 46. In his unpublished autobiography 'A North Light' (chapter 17, 'The Taste of Mayors'), Hewitt refers to the influence on his work of Arthur Waley's *One Hundred and Seventy Chinese Poems* (1918):

> Exactly how much my own verse owes to it would be hard to define. Certainly the quiet, undramatic tone, the even texture, the significant abstraction from experience of natural phenomena, the awareness of landscape and man-in-landscape, these are qualities which I admired and which I must half-consciously have attempted to reproduce.

p. 145 'From the Chinese of Wang Li Shi': N7, p. 30, January 1938; N10, p. 98, part of 'The Red Hand: a poemosaic'; N23, p. 2, 11.1.38, with note: 'a poem composed this morning on a visit to the Mourne Mountains and translated in the evening'. Pub. *New Northman*, vol. VI, no. 3 (Autumn 1938), p. 87, with title 'The Mourne Mountains: a poem' and signed 'Shelley Wang 11th January, 1938'; Hewitt's name does not appear. Rep. *New Statesman and Nation* (November 1938), with title 'The Mourne Mountains'; *Belfast Telegraph*, 20 March 1954, with title 'The Mourne Mountains (from the Chinese of Shelley Wang)' and signature 'Shelley Wong [*sic*]. Translated by John Hewitt'. Rep. *Poètes d'Irlande du Nord* (1991), p. 30. *CF*, [p. 6]; *M*, p. 45. This poem is referred to in 'The little death', Hewitt's elegy for Shelley Wang (*NRW*, p. 51). *See also* note on 'The little death', p. 579.

p. 145 'August 1939': N18, p. 14, with title 'September before war'; N24, p. 51; N45, p. 7, 24.8.39. *CF* [p. 7].

p. 145 'Chinese fluteplayer': N37, p. 54, 21.7.60. Pub. *Common Ground Quarterly* (Winter 1983), p. 11. Rep. *Poètes d'Irlande du Nord* (1991), p. 30. *CF* [p. 9]; *M*, p. 44.

p. 146 'The lyric sonorously rhymed . . .': N28, p. 33, 21.3.42; N46, p. 145. Pub. *Ulster Voices* (Summer 1943). *CF* [p. 10].

p. 146 'I turned my touch to Campion . . .': N7, p. 5, March 1938; N18, p. 33; N23, p. 18, 30.3.38; N44, p. 18. *CF* [p. 11]. Thomas Campion (1567–1620) was a poet, musician and doctor, whose published works included four Bookes of Ayres and *Observations in the Art of English Poesie.*

p. 146 'I've known her turn from bitter phrase . . .': N32, p. 27, 17.6.49/14.8.49, with title 'Lyric'. *CF* [p. 12].

p. 147 'For R.': N33, p. 114, 26.3.52. Pub. *The Bell*, vol. 19, no. 1 (December 1953), p. 143, with title 'Poem for R.'. *CF* [p. 13].

SCISSORS FOR A ONE-ARMED TAILOR: MARGINAL VERSES 1929–1954 (*SOT*), privately published, Belfast, 1974: a booklet of sixteen pages in a limited edition of two hundred copies, and dedicated 'For Eileen [Mackie], Norman [Todhunter] and Deirdre [Todhunter]'. The foreword reads as follows:

> The old Irish scribes used sometimes to write brief snatches of verse on the margins of their taskwork. So in a not dissimilar manner these little pieces came to me usually when I had something larger in hand, prompted by a word, a sudden thought, or simply the clink of a rhyme.
>
> They were written years ago, the most recent in 1954, the earliest in 1929, but I have given a date only when it has some relevance. Some of them were printed in the *Irish Times*, the *Belfast Telegraph* or in the long defunct *Bell*, the *Irish Bookman*, *Ulster Voices*.

I have included all the poems in this booklet, with the exception of 'April awake', published earlier in *DC* (1969, p. 7), and 'St Stephen's Day' revised for *LE* (p. 52).

The pages of *Scissors for a One-Armed Tailor* are unnumbered. I have provided numbers in square brackets [pp. 1–13] for those pages on which poems are printed.

p. 148 'Survival': N34, p. 139, 20.2.55. *SOT* [p. 1].

p. 148 'The listener': N22, p. 101, 22.8.37. Rep. *UCD Broadsheet*, no. 7 (1979). *SOT* [p. 1].

p. 148 'Name and number': N34, p. 103, 14.8.54. *SOT* [p. 1].

p. 149 'Ecce homo': N45, p. 124, 29.6.31. *SOT* [p. 2].

p. 149 'Providence 1': N11, p. 87, 29.6.31; N18, p. 46; N19, p. 26. *SOT* [p. 2].

p. 149 'Providence 2': N17, p. 132, July–September 1934, as part of long sequence 'Uladh', later called 'The Red Hand: a poemosaic'. *SOT* [p. 2].

p. 149 'Providence 3': N14, p. 109, 17.8.32; N18, p. 17, with title 'The angle'; N19, p. 18; N45, p. 96, with title 'The angle' and note: 'after fishing from a [boat(?), rock(?)] off Ramsay, Isle of Man'. *SOT* [p. 2].

p. 150 'In The Rosses': N28, p. 26, 7.3.42. *SOT* [p. 3]; *S*, p. 17.

p. 150 'Passion': N28, p. 34, 21.3.42; N46, p. 146. *SOT* [p. 3].

p. 150 'Triad' ('Three things that men might scorn . . .'): N25, p. 93, 23.6.41. *SOT* [p. 3].

p. 150 'Triad' ('Three sounds of peace and rich increase . . .'): N25, p. 132, 6.11.41, with title 'Rann'. Rep. *UCD Broadsheet*, no. 5 (1975). *SOT* [p. 3].

p. 151 'New Jerusalem 1': N18, p. 8, dated 1941; N25, p. 43, 18.12.40; N46, p. 81, 18.12.40, with title 'Stanzas'; the first of these stanzas became the final poem. *SOT* [p. 4].

p. 151 'Epitaph for a conscript, 1940': N26, p. 9, 3.5.40. *SOT* [p. 4].

p. 151 'Cold warrior: Anzac Day, 1946': N31, p. 43, 27.4.48, with title 'To Churchill'. *SOT* [p. 4]. Anzac Day is 25 April. On the same page of N31 is a further (unpublished) attack on Churchill titled 'To the same on Anzac Day'.

p. 151 'New Jerusalem 2': N11, p. 46, 30.4.31, with title 'Epigram'; N18, p. 19; N19, p. 25. Pub. *Labour Progress* (December 1943), with title 'Note for planners'. *SOT* [p. 4].

p. 151 'Minor poet's dilemma': N18, p. 22, 1940; N24, p. 126, 12.1.40; N45, p. 180. *SOT* [p. 4].

p. 152 'Lilibulero': N34, p. 99, 31.7.54. *SOT* [p. 5].

p. 152 'Second front: double summertime, July 1943': N46, p. 205, 2.7.43, with title 'Second front: before the invasion of Sicily'. *SOT* [p. 5].

p. 152 'Breastplate': N18, p. 6; N25, p. 78, 21.3.41; N46, p. 96. Pub. *Belfast Telegraph*, 26 December 1953. *SOT* [p. 5].

p. 152 'Grief' ('I thought when the grave was sodded . . .'): N32, p. 35, 21.10.49. *SOT* [p. 6].

p. 153 'Emily Dickinson': N30, p. 80, 2.12.45; N47, p. 84. *SOT* [p. 6]; *S*, p. 106.

p. 153 'Grief' ('When men lie down for ever . . .'): N30, p. 60, 28.7.45. *SOT* [p. 6].

p. 153 'Mother and son': N31, p. 18, 14.5.47. *SOT* [p. 7].

p. 154 'Boy seen in a bus journey': N24, p. 45, 20.8.39, with title 'For a boy seen yesterday on a bus'. *SOT* [p. 7].

p. 154 'Epitaph to a man not dead': N16, p. 80, 2.9.33, with title 'Epitaph on a man not dead'. *SOT* [p. 7].

p. 154 'R.K.': N18, p. 20, dated 1939, with title 'R.T.'; N24, p. 111, 29.12.39, with title 'R.T.'; N45, p. 173, with title 'R.T.'. *SOT* [p. 8].

p. 154 'W.R.R.': N24, p. 103, 21.12.39, with title 'Portrait: WRR'; N45, p. 173. *SOT* [p. 8]. The subject of the poem is the poet W.R. Rodgers. *See also* 'The iron circle' (*UR*, p. 16); 'W.R. Rodgers (1909–1969)' (*OMT*, p. 21); *Freehold:* 'III Townland of peace' (*F*, p. 12), and 'Roll call' (Appendix I of this volume).

p. 154 'S.S.K.': N24, p. 88, 30.11.39, with title 'Messenger'. *SOT* [p. 8]. The subject of the poem is Samuel Somerset Keith, Roberta Hewitt's stepfather, who figures also in 'The Long Bridge' (*OMT*, p. 12).

p. 155 'B.O.W.': N33, p. 152, 28.10.52. *SOT* [p. 8]. The subject of the poem is Bruce Wallace, d. 1939, prominent member of the Congregational Movement, who edited the Labour newspaper the *Belfast Evening Star* in 1890, was an early member of the Fabian Society and a participant in the Garden City Movement, co-founding Letchworth with Ebenezer Howard. *See* Hewitt's prose appreciation 'Bruce Wallace of Limavady: an Ulster pioneer of socialism, died recently', *Irish Workers' Weekly*, 10 June 1939.

p. 155 'R.P.M.': N18, p. 20, dated 1939; N24, p. 94, 11.12.39; N45, p. 171. *SOT* [p. 8]. The subject of the poem is Hewitt's friend R. Patrick Maybin.

p. 155 'Mirror': N45, pp. 182–3, 1.2.40. *SOT* [p. 9].

p. 155 'Scissors for a one-armed tailor': N45, p. 101, 24.5.32, with two notes: 'Evelyn Gardens. This tramp called later at Westland Drive'; 'Scissors for a one-armed tailor. Springs in shoe heels to assist walking'. *SOT* [p. 9].

p. 156 'In a suburban avenue': N26, p. 59, 16–20.6.40. *SOT* [p. 9].

p. 156 'Ocean, 1940': N18, p. 9, with title 'Ocean'; N46, p. 31, 6.7.40, with title 'Ocean'. *SOT* [p. 10].

p. 156 'Grey and white': N18, p. 9, dated 1940; N26, p. 113, 12.7.40; N46, p. 31. *SOT* [p. 10]; *S*, p. 75.

p. 156 'Mist': N30, p. 103, 26.4.46. *SOT* [p. 10].

p. 157 'On a January train journey': N28, p. 103, 28.1.43; N46, p. 174, with title 'From a train by the banks of the Foyle'. Pub. *Ulster Voices* (Summer 1943). Rep. *UCD Broadsheet*, no. 5 (1975). *SOT* [p. 10]; *S*, p. 74.

p. 157 'Now in the spring': N28, p. 132, 23.4.43; N46, p. 186. *SOT* [p. 11].

p. 157 'April': N35, p. 4, 18.4.55. *SOT* [p. 11].

p. 157 'Mid-April': N34, p. 29, 13.4.53. *SOT* [p. 11].

p. 158 'July': N32, p. 29, 12.7.49, rev. 14.8.49. *SOT* [p. 12].

p. 158 'Skypiece': N28, p. 87, 23.12.42. Rep. *UCD Broadsheet*, no. 5 (1975). *SOT* [p. 12].

p. 158 'Winter day' ('From the first light when in the upland field . . .'): dated 1949 in one of Hewitt's annotated copies of *SOT*. Rep. *Common Ground Quarterly* (Winter 1983), p. 11, with title 'Winter'. *SOT* [p. 12].

p. 158 'Alien harvest': N18, p. 23; N23, p. 20, 30.3.38; N44, p. 18. *SOT* [p. 13].

p. 158 'Bleeze': N31, p. 87, 23.10.48. *SOT* [p. 13].

p. 159 'Raindrop': N31, p. 98, 27.1.49, with title 'For certain reviewers'. Pub. *The Bell*, vol. 19, no. 1 (December 1953), pp. 143–4, with title 'For certain reviewers'. *SOT* [p. 13].

p. 159 'I write for . . .': N30, p. 73, 27.9.45; N47, p. 80. Rep. *UCD Broadsheet*, no. 5 (1975); *Poets from the North of Ireland* (1979), p. 27; *Across the Roaring Hill* (1981), p. 1; *Poets from the North of Ireland* (1990), p. 33. *SOT* [p. 13]; *S*, p. 81.

The poem also provided the title for *Across a Roaring Hill: The Protestant Imagination in Modern Ireland* (eds Gerald Dawe and Edna Longley, Blackstaff Press, 1985) and *Across the Roaring Hill: An Impression of Ulster Compiled from the Work of the Province's Writers* (comp. David Grant, 1981).

OUT OF MY TIME: POEMS 1967–1974 (*OMT*), published by Blackstaff Press, Belfast, 1974, with the following preface:

> These two score poems have been taken from the verse I have written in the last seven years, from December 1967 to May 1974. They reflect in varying degrees my sojourn in the English Midlands until August 1972, my travels abroad, the impact of the troubled times in Northern Ireland, and my life as an older man in my native country.
>
> Just over half of them have appeared in the journals the *Listener*, the *New Statesman*, *Country Life*, *Ariel*, *Aquarius* (London), the *Irish Times*, the *Irish Press*, *Hibernia*, the *Honest Ulsterman*, *Threshold*, and the anthologies *Soundings '72*, *Choice* (1973), *Ten Irish Poets* (1974), in the Arts Council booklet *The Planter and the Gael* (with John Montague, 1970), or have been broadcast by the BBC and RTE.

I have included all the poems in this volume, with the exception of 'Gloss, on the difficulties of translation', and 'Conversations in Hungary, August 1969', which appeared originally in *The Planter and the Gael* (1970). Hewitt provides notes on nine of the poems in *Out of My Time*; I have reprinted the notes for eight of these; for notes on 'Gloss, on the difficulties of translation' and 'Conversations in Hungary, August 1969', see p. 593 of the present volume.

See Hewitt's contribution to the *Poetry Book Society Bulletin*, no. 91 (Christmas 1976), reprinted on p. 605 of this volume, for his comment on the ideas expressed in the title *Out of My Time*.

p. 160 'The search': N38, pp. 9–11. 23–4.11.66. The poem is, however, dated 1967 in *OMT.* Pub. *Honest Ulsterman*, no. 4 (August 1968), p. 4. Rep. *Ariel*, vol. 1, no. 3 (July 1970), p. 78; *Poetry Dimension Annual 3* (1975), p. 79; *Poets from the North of Ireland* (1979), p. 35; *Poets from the North of Ireland* (1990), p. 40. *PG* [p. 9]; *OMT*, p. 9. The dedication is for Shirley and Darryl Mackie, Hewitt's niece and her husband. Hewitt provided the following notes:

> 'city older by centuries': Coventry charter 1345;
> 'market town': Belfast charter 1613;
> 'landmarks are yours': a mason with my name lived in the Burges, Coventry in the 14th century. Another John Hewitt was property master of the Coventry Guilds' Mystery Plays in the 16th century. I would like to imagine that his son or grandson came with the Planters and settled in Co. Armagh;
>
> 'circle of stones': for me the archetype of this is the Rolright Stones on the border of Oxfordshire, mingled with the recollection of 'Ossian's Grave', Glenaan, Co Antrim.

p. 161 'Erice, western Sicily': N38, pp. 46–7, 2–4.12.67, with title 'Erice'. Pub. *Irish Times*, 7 September 1968. *OMT*, p. 10. Prompted by the Hewitts' visit to Sicily, October 1967.

p. 161 'Montelepre': N38, pp. 48–9, 4.12.67. Pub. *Irish Press*, 31 August 1968. *OMT*, p. 11. The Hewitts visited Montelepre in Sicily on 11 October 1967.

p. 162 'The Long Bridge': N38, pp. 64–5, 4–5.1.68. Pub. *Irish Times*, 24 February 1968. *PG* [p. 9]; *OMT*, p. 12. The dedication is for Hewitt's nephew Keith Millar, the 'grandson of the old man' referred to in the poem. Hewitt provides the following notes:

> Built in 1682, rebuilt as Queen's Bridge [Belfast] in 1943.
>
> 'The grandson of the old man': Samuel S. Keith (1858–1955), born in Ballymacarret [*sic*].

See also 'S.S.K.' (*SOT* [p. 8]).

p. 163 'From the Tibetan': N38, pp. 67–8, 7.1.68; pp. 70–1, revisions carried out February–May 1968. Pub. *Honest Ulsterman*, no. 1 (May 1968), p. 14. Rep. *Ten Irish Poets* (1974), p. 28; *Poets from the North of Ireland* (1979), p. 32; *Poets from the North of Ireland* (1990), p. 38. *OMT*, p. 13.

p. 164 'Carol singers': N38, p. 106, 22–8.12.68. Rep. *Four Seasons* (1983), p. 173; *The Irish Christmas Book* (1985), p. 165; *Irish Poetry of Faith and Doubt* (1990), p. 90. *OMT*, p. 14. The dedication is for Hewitt's niece, Deirdre Todhunter.

p. 164 'Legend in his own lifetime': N38, pp. 85–7, 1–2.6.68, with title 'Legend'. *OMT*, p. 15. The subject of the poem is 'Paddy' Blair Mayne, DSO (3 bars), Croix de Guerre, Légion d'Honneur, former Irish and British Lions rugby international and member of the SAS. He was born in 1915 and killed in a car accident at Newtownards, County Down, 14 December 1955.

p. 165 'Suburban spring in Warwickshire': N38, pp. 72–3, 23.5.68, with title 'Suburban spring'. Pub. *Irish Times*, 2 August 1969, with title 'Suburban spring'. Rep. *Four Seasons* (1983), pp. 41–2. *OMT*, p. 17. The dedication is for Lilac, who wrote numerous letters to Hewitt in the 1960s and 1970s and whose identity he himself never knew.

p. 166 'Compton Wynyates, Warwickshire': N38, p. 91, 9–10.6.68. Pub. *Irish Times*, 8 March 1969. *OMT*, p. 18. The dedication is for Hewitt's friends Beatrice and Ralph Meredith.

p. 166 'Et tu in Arcadia vixisti': N38, p. 100, 1–2.12.68. Pub. *Irish Times*, 13 September 1968. Rep. *Choice* (1973), p. 41; *Poets from the North of Ireland* (1979), p. 39; *The Long Embrace* (1987), p. 32. *OMT*, p. 20.

In *Choice* the poem is accompanied by the following introductory note:

> This sonnet was written at the beginning of December 1968, but the original experience had occurred one morning in September 1934 in the street below our hotel-window in Paris where my wife and I were staying. During the intervening years 'the idea' had never offered itself as a possible poem, and for ten days before the writing of it and for the fortnight after I was not visited by any other verse. It may be, although I cannot be positive, that I had some months or weeks earlier read the essay by the Art Historian, Erwin Panofsky, entitled '*Et in Arcadia: Poussin and the Elegiac Tradition*'.
>
> A surprise for me, outside my more usual logically-ordered, low-charged descriptive manner, I enjoyed the tricks it seemed to play with the sonnet-form in its shuttling back and forth in time against the orthodox armature of the three-quatrains and the closing couplet. I was pleased with the run of internal rhymes, 'played', 'splay', 'strayed'; 'classic', 'pastoral'; 'beside', 'tideless'; and with the assonances and alliterations – every single line threaded with one or more sibilants like a sustained whisper and by the contrast of the quiet-back-street in a busy city with the unpeopled Mediterranean shores, although Greece is now the police-state of the usurping Colonels, and Sicily, once the home-ground of Theocritus, is now the island of the Mafia and that brave reformer Danilo Dolci – circumstances which give a dash of irony to the idyll convention.
>
> When, a couple of years ago, I read in a Sunday newspaper, Hemingway's account of the same piping goatherd, I realised with deep satisfaction that my memory had not played me false. I have, I believe, written better, perhaps more popular poems, but this has a unique place in my affection, a self-contained, precious moment in my shared past, something given, not earned.

The incident that prompted this poem occurred during the Hewitts' honeymoon in Paris in September 1934; Hewitt also gives an account of it in his unpublished autobiography 'A North Light', describing the experience as 'the stuff of a poem which I have never dared to write, a Joycean epiphany'.

p. 167 'W.R. Rodgers (1909–1969)': N38, p. 111, 3–4.2.69, with title 'W.R. Rodgers d. California 1.2.69'. Pub. *Irish Times*, 15 February 1969. Rep. *Listener*, 20 February 1969; *Poetry Book Society Bulletin*, no. 61 (Summer 1969), p. 4, at the end of a short prose piece titled 'Hewitt on Rodgers'. *OMT*, p. 21. *See also* 'The iron circle' (*UR*, p. 16); 'W.R.R.' (*SOT* [p. 8]); *Freehold*: 'III Townland of peace' (*F*, p. 12), and 'Roll call' (Appendix I of the present volume).

p. 167 'An hour with E.M.F. at ninety': N38, p. 117, 28.2.[69]–4.3.69. Ms. among Hewitt's papers dated 27.2.69. Pub. *Listener*, 13 March 1969, among the letters to the editor. *OMT*, p. 22. The dedication is for May and Robert Buckingham, 11 Salisbury Avenue, Coventry, friends of Forster's in his later years, and of the Hewitts. *See also* 'With E.M.F. on 28th December 1965' (*CP*, p. 131).

Lines 11–13 of the *Listener* version read: ' "Had Clark forgotten?" I remembered three/good reasons why that culture stayed at home,/marvelling greatly that we still should find'.

p. 167 'A minor Victorian painter': N39, pp. 3–4, 9.9.69, with title 'Idyl [*sic*]: John Anderson ARCA 1835–1919'. Pub. *Country Life*, 8 August 1974. Rep. *Poems of Warwickshire* (1980), p. 44. *OMT*, p. 23. In *OMT* Hewitt provided the following note: 'John Anderson (1835–1919), head of Coventry Art School for many years. Based on a letter by a former pupil, *Coventry Herald*, 8 January 1920'.

p. 168 'A neighbour's funeral': N39, pp. 34–7, 9.10.69, with title 'Death of a neighbour'. *OMT*, p. 24.

p. 169 'First funeral': N39, pp. 53–4, 24.2.70. *OMT*, p. 27; *S*, p. 92.

p. 169 'The moon': N39, p. 78, 29.5.70, with note: 'Discovered the substance and octette [*sic*] of this dated 24.7.69 among my papers. Finished 29.5.70'. Further note: 'Sestet rewritten 12.7.74'. Rep. *Poets from the North of Ireland* (1979), p. 38; *Voices of Today* (1980), p. 97. *OMT*, p. 28.

p. 170 'Middle Infant': N39, p. 82, 13.8.70. Rep. *Voices of Today* (1980), p. 3. *OMT*, p. 29. The dedication is for Hewitt's sister, Eileen (Todhunter). Miss McCleery also figures in 'I go to school' (*KS*, p. 37).

p. 170 'The riders': N39, pp. 61–2, 29–30.3.70. *OMT*, p. 30.

p. 171 'The turban': N39, p. 57, 5.3.70. Pub. *Aquarius*, no. 4 (1971), p. 43. Rep. *Poems of Warwickshire* (1980), p. 65. *OMT*, p. 31.

p. 171 'The distances': N39, p. 86, 25.8.70. Pub. *Soundings '72* (1972), p. 26. Rep. *Digraphe*, no. 27 (June 1982), p. 25, in English and French; *Poètes d'Irlande du Nord* (1991), p. 22. *OMT*, p. 32; *S*, p. 104.

p. 172 'St Rosalie: Monte Pellegrino': N39, pp. 84–5, 25.8.70. Pub. *Soundings '72* (1972), p. 25. *OMT*, p. 33. The version in *Soundings '72* takes the form of seven quatrains; l. 5 begins 'The sunlit candles were bought in'; l. 14 begins 'spinning of flames' (misprint?); and the penultimate line refers to the 'glass-box'. The Hewitts visited Monte Pellegrino in Sicily on 1 October 1967.

p. 173 'Disaster on the box': N39, pp. 121–2, 27–8.5.71, with title 'Disaster'. Rep. *Lines Review*, no. 52–3 (May 1975), p. 48. *OMT*, p. 34.

p. 173 'William J. McClughin (1900–1971)': N40, p. 19, 28.12.71, with title 'I.M. W.J. McC 1900–1971'. Pub. *Threshold*, no. 25 (Summer 1974), pp. 9–10, under title 'Two artists' (with 'The Lagan in October – remembering Frederick W. Hull'). *OMT,* p. 35. *See also* 'A difficult man' (*LE,* p. 7).

p. 174 'My Uncle': N39, pp. 123–4, 29.5.71. *OMT,* p. 37.

p. 175 'The Burnt Post': N40, p. 14, 27.12.71. *OMT,* p. 36.

p. 175 'The Roman fort': N40, p. 17, 27.12.71, with title 'The Lunt fort'. *OMT,* p. 38. The dedication is for Peggy and George Johnson. In *OMT* Hewitt provides the note: 'The Lunt, Baginton, Warwickshire; see *Transactions of the Birmingham Archaeological Society,* vol. 83, 1965'.

p. 176 'Bogside, Derry, 1971': N40, p. 7, 16–17.8.71, with title 'Bogside'. Rep. *The Wearing of the Black* (1974), p. 51; *Across the Roaring Hill* (1981), p. 26. · *OMT,* p. 39. Quoted in full, with comments, in *We Irish: Selected Essays of Denis Donoghue: Vol. 1* (1986), p. 186.

p. 177 'The scar': N39, p. 99, 18–19.1.71. Pub. *Irish Press,* 10 June 1972. Rep. *Ten Irish Poets* (1974), p. 26; *The Wearing of the Black* (1974), p. 4; *Poets from the North of Ireland* (1979), p. 29; *Soft Day* (1980), p. 26; *Contemporary Irish Poetry* (ed. Bradley, 1988), p. 105; *Poets from the North of Ireland* (1990), p. 35; *Poètes d'Irlande du Nord* (1991), p. 28. *OMT,* p. 40.

In *OMT* Hewitt notes: 'My grandfather John Hewitt, born in 1841 in Co Armagh, told me how his mother died in the Famine year, 1847.' N44, pp. 120–1, contains an unpublished poem titled 'The Famine', dated 28.5.36, which includes the lines:

> My grandfather
> was six years old.
> His mother caught the fever
> over the halfdoor of her little house
> from a poor starveling begging a pinch of tea.

See also 'Orchard country' (*KS,* p. 19).

p. 177 'Clogh-Oir: September 1971': N40, pp. 11–12, 22–8.9.71. Pub. *Irish Press,* 10 June 1972. *OMT,* p. 41. The dedication is for Roberta Hewitt. In *OMT,* Hewitt notes:

> 'One of the Three Sacred Stones': 'the other two are the Stone of Destiny in Westminster, and the Crom Cruach, now lost.' *Macartan's Cathedral, Clogher,* 1970, p. 5.
>
> 'Ailech [*sic*]': . . . 'the chief king of the Northern Ui Neill was called the king of Aileach, near Derry, which was occupied by the kings of that line as late as the 10th century.' *Phases of Irish History* by Eoin MacNeill, 1968, pp. 184–5.

p. 178 'Mary Hagan, Islandmagee, 1919': N14, pp. 7–8, 5.5.32, with title 'Mary Hagan: memory of summer 1921' (substantially different from final published version); N40, p. 43, 20.3.73, with title 'Islandmagee, 1921 (Mary Hagan)' and note 'Finished 1968'. Pub. *Irish Press,* 16 February 1974, with title 'Islandmagee, 1921: a boyhood heroine'. *OMT,* p. 43; *S,* p. 69. In *OMT,* Hewitt notes: '"Granuaile": the famous 16th century pirate queen, Grace O'Malley of Mayo'.

p. 179 'The fairy thresher': N40, pp. 44–8, with note '1st draft 2.11.52'. Completed and revised 22.3.73. Rep. *Antrim Coast and Glens* (1990), p. 31 (extract). *DC* (1984), p. 66; *OMT,* p. 44.

p. 181 'Art room in a city school': N40, p. 49, with title 'Art room in a Coventry school', and note 'revised and finished 23.3.73'; p. 89, with note: 'Drastically revised 17.1.74'; p. 90, note 'Art room again revised', 19.1.74. Ms. among Hewitt's papers dated 16.1.74. *OMT,* p. 48, where it is dated 1973.

p. 182 'On the Grand Dublin Canal: musing on the "two nations" theory': N40, p. 61, 5–6.6.73, with title 'On the Grand Canal'. Pub. *Irish Times,* 23 February 1974, with title 'On the Grand Canal: thinking of the "two nations"'. Rep. *The Wearing of the Black* (1974), p. 1. *OMT,* p. 49. The dedication is for Anne and Dermod Carty; Anne Carty was Hewitt's niece by marriage. In *OMT,* Hewitt notes: ' "Black Pig's Dyke": an earthen rampart, the extant remains of a continuous line of defence from the Irish Sea in the east to Donegal Bay in the west. See MacNeill, *op cit,* p. 131 and Heslinga: *The Irish Border as a Cultural Divide,* 1971, p. 110.'

p. 182 'On the canal': N40, p. 62, 6.6.73. Pub. *New Statesman and Nation,* 8 March 1974. *OMT,* p. 50. The dedication is for Hewitt's brother-in-law, Norman Todhunter.

p. 183 'At Shottery, Anne Hathaway's cottage': N40, pp. 66–7, 18.6.73, with title 'At Shottery'. *OMT,* p. 51. The dedication is for Hewitt's friends Peggy and Joe Spiers. *See also* Hewitt's prose piece 'At the shrines of the Bards', *Belfast Telegraph,* 14 November 1959.

p. 184 'The geriatric ward': N40, p. 76, 22.7.73, with title 'In a geriatric ward'. Rep. *Lines Review,* no. 52–3 (May 1975), p. 50. *OMT,* p. 52.

p. 184 'The King's horses': N40, pp. 55–6, 23.4.73. Pub. *Irish Press,* 22 November 1973. Rep. *Poetry Dimension 2* (1974), p. 199; *Lines Review,* no. 52–3 (May 1975), p. 49; *Poets from the North of Ireland* (1979), p. 34; *Hundsrose: Neue Irische Gedichte* (1983), p. 119; *Ireland in Poetry* (1990), p. 31. *OMT,* p. 53.

p. 185 'Glendun on a wet July day': N40, p. 77, 22.7.73, with note: 'The glen of the cuckoo'. *OMT,* p. 54. The dedication is for Peggy and Andrew Millar, Roberta Hewitt's sister and her husband.

p. 185 'On reading Terence de Vere White on Landor': N40, p. 82, 31.10.73. Pub. *Irish Times,* 15 December 1973. Rep. *Digraphe,* no. 27 (June 1982), p. 24, in English and French. *OMT,* p. 55; *S,* p. 102. *See* Terence de Vere White's 'Following the Parker pen', a review of *Landor: A Biographical Anthology* by Herbert van Thal (*Irish Times,* 20 October 1973).

p. 186 'The Lagan in October': N40, pp. 83–4, 1.11.73, with title 'The Lagan: recalling F.W. Hull'. Pub. *Threshold,* no. 25 (Summer 1974), pp. 9–10, under title 'Two artists' (with 'William J. McClughin [1900–1971]'). *OMT,* p. 56.

p. 187 'Cultra Manor: the Ulster Folk Museum': N40, p. 93, 15–16.4.74. Ms. among Hewitt's papers with title 'For JK', dated 15.4.74. Rep. *Across the Roaring Hill* (1981), p. 9. The dedication is for Hewitt's friends and neighbours, John and Renee Kilfeather. *OMT,* p. 57; *S,* p. 38.

p. 187 'Dedication of "The Rhyming Weavers" ': N40, p. 91, 7.2.74. *OMT,* p. 58. *Rhyming Weavers and Other Country Poets of Antrim and Down,* edited and introduced by John Hewitt, was published by Blackstaff Press in November 1974; *OMT* appeared in October that year.

p. 188 'Neither an elegy nor a manifesto': N40, pp. 28–31, 4–6.2.72. Pub. *Alliance* (June 1972). Rep. *The Wearing of the Black* (1974), p. 145; *Across the Roaring Hill* (1981), p. 42. *OMT*, p. 59; *S*, p. 44.

TIME ENOUGH: POEMS NEW AND REVISED (*TE*), published by Blackstaff Press, Belfast, 1976. I have included all forty poems from the original volume and incorporated Hewitt's explanatory notes.

Time Enough was a Recommendation of the Poetry Book Society, Christmas 1976. In the *Poetry Book Society Bulletin*, no. 91 (Christmas 1976), Hewitt writes:

> The title of my last book of verse, *Out of My Time*, expressed several ideas; first, the colloquial usage for the completion of an apprenticeship; secondly, that by not strenuously endeavouring to be 'modern', concerned with the momentary modes, the verse is 'out of date' in style; thirdly the title also suggests that the themes have been taken from my experience of this time, these years.
>
> My *Collected Poems* included verse written from 1932 to 1967; *Out of My Time* draw its contents from poems of the period 1967 to 1974. Of the present volume almost half was written in 1974 and 1975, up to the death of my wife in October. Thereafter I found myself unable to do any new work, so I turned to fill the hours when I should have been at my desk to revising earlier poems, whether printed in journals or still in manuscript. The revision has been in varying degrees. Thus a poem written in 1958 has received a final clinching stanza after 17 years; another took 20 years to recast. I have not, as previously, set the poems in chronological order, for they all make clear to me things I have learned in the passage of the years and can fairly be considered verses which in my sixty-ninth year represent my moods, thoughts, imaginings, recollections, now.
>
> In a review of *Out of My Time*, my fellow Ulster poet and friend, James Simmons, remarked that 'lack of consistent style is Hewitt's style', an estimate I do not dispute. I have always taken verse-forms and devices as a kit of tools, each implement appropriate to the task in hand, not as a similar line of soup-cans on a conveyor belt with only their labels changed. In my half-century of reading extensively in contemporary English verse, I have observed fashions come and go, and have seen the decay or tarnishing of popular reputations – who now remembers Alfred Noyes, Henry Newbolt, Humbert Wolfe, John Freeman, Edward Shanks? – but I do not like to see any garment discarded which still has some wear in it.
>
> Most of the poems are concerned with my family, my childhood, my schooldays, with country places and the folk who live in them, and with certain people who have interested me by some quirk of character or individual word or gesture.

p. 190 'A birthday rhyme for Roberta': N37, pp. 96–8, 27–8.10.64, with title 'On the occasion of my 57th birthday'. The third and fourth stanzas of the ms.

version are the basis for the finished poem. Rep. *Poets from the North of Ireland* (1979), p. 40. *TE*, p. 1.

p. 190 'Substance and shadow': N34, p. 146, 23–4.2.55, with title 'Affirmation'; N35, pp. 8–9, with title 'Shadow and stone', and note: 'Begun 23.2.[55]: worked over more than usual. Finished 26.7.[55]'. Pub. *New World Writing* (1956), p. 102, with title 'Shadow and stone'. Rep. *Poets from the North of Ireland* (1979), p. 37; 'John Hewitt 1907–1987' (a memorial broadsheet published by the Arts Council of Northern Ireland, 1987); *Poets from the North of Ireland* (1990), p. 42; *Poètes d'Irlande du Nord* (1991), p. 26. *TE*, p. 2. In the version in *New World Writing*, the first section reads:

> There's little richness in the images
> I parry time with in my mind's defence –
> a gannet's plunge, all creatures' secrecies,
> bred of their single nature's innocence:
> a spider's tangle on a bracken frond;
> the certain journey of the homing rooks;
> a blossomed thorn; a heron by a pond;
> or silver thistles in the tilted stooks;
> a lonely moorland boulder, lichen-stained;
> the spark of sun on dripping icicles:
> the substance and its meaning both contained
> in colour, shape and texture, nothing else.

The last two lines read:

> the meaning and the matter break adrift
> that rightly should be clenched in chiseled stone.

p. 191 'The sheep skull': N35, p. 53, 3.2.56. Pub. *A Winter Harvest* (1956), p. 15. Rep. *Massachusetts Review*, vol. 5, no. 2 (Winter 1964), p. 341; *Soft Day* (1980), p. 28. *TE*, p. 3; *S*, p. 76.

p. 191 'Function': N29, p. 130, 24.7.44; N47, p. 31. Pub. *Tribune*, 8 October 1948. *TE*, p. 3. The *Tribune* version reads as follows:

> No longer now the attitude, the duel,
> the cloak Byronic, the impasto sky,
> the wind-waved locks, the nimbus guarantee,
> the gaunt brow mooning up the misty hill.
> The poet now must tread the common level,
> be member of board, council, sub-committee,
> move his brief resolution audibly,
> dissect his syntax in the lecture hall;
>
> must also potter, listening intent,
> chalk up the score of human rights and wrongs,
> know without proof what is significant
> in buyer's thumb or drover's gift of tongues;
> yet find his softest pitch, for all his care,
> in parachuting seed and punctual star.

p. 192 'The fool's cap': N40, pp. 104–5, 26–7.5.74; rev. 4.2.75. Pub. *Cyphers*, no. 1 (June 1975), p. 25. Hewitt provides the note: 'James Ensor, 1860–1949.

Famous Belgian Expressionist'. (Some biographical dictionaries give the year of Ensor's death as 1947.) *TE*, p. 4.

p. 193 'The spring restored': N35, pp. 5–7, 25–6.7.55; N40, pp. 128–30, with note: 'Revised in June 1975 after 20 years'. *TE*, p. 5.

p. 194 'A seaside town': N40, p. 132, 30.6.75. *TE*, p. 7.

p. 195 'In a Lurgan pub': N39, p. 118, 17.5.71, with title 'In a Lurgan bar'. *TE*, p. 8.

p. 195 'Dungannon cattle market': N39, p. 119, 17–18.5.71. *TE*, p. 8.

p. 196 'J.B. Shelton (1876–1958), the Coventry antiquarian': N35, p. 105, 3.12.58, with title 'To the memory of John B. Shelton, the Coventry antiquarian'. Pub. *Coventry Evening Telegraph*, 5 December 1958, with title 'To the memory of John B. Shelton' and signed 'Anon'; in that version, l. 3 has 'rich in spoons and nails'; l. 7 has 'the broken pot, the pointed bone'; l. 10 has 'with a lavish hand'; and l. 14 reads 'barns stacked high with sacks of clean-threshed grain'. *TE*, p. 9.

p. 196 'Peter Peri (1899–1967)': N38, p. 118, 5.3.69, with title 'Peter Peri – Sculptor and Communist, 1899–1967', and note 'Revisions in next notebook, June 1970'; N39, p. 80, June 1970, with title 'Peter Peri, Sculptor, Quaker, Socialist, 1899–1967'. *TE*, p. 9. Hewitt provides the note: 'Peter Peri: For an excellent description of Peri and his studio see John Berger's *Selected Essays and Articles* (1974).' Peri was friendly with the Hewitts and sometimes stayed with them in Coventry.

p. 197 'Nicolai, courier in Belgrade': N37, p. 16, 19.5.60, with title 'Nicolai'. Pub. *Irish Times*, 12 July 1975. *TE*, p. 10.

p. 197 'Remembering a conversation: Itzik Manger at the PEN Conference, Edinburgh, 1950': N38, p. 116, 4.3.69, with title 'To the memory of Itzik Manger, recalling a conversation in Edinburgh'. Pub. *Honest Ulsterman*, no. 22 (March–April 1970), p. 15, with title 'Remembering Itzik Manger and a conversation in Edinburgh years ago'. Rep. *Poetry Book Society Bulletin*, no. 91 (Christmas 1976). *TE*, p. 10. Hewitt provided the notes: 'Itzik Manger, 1901–1969. For a sensitive evocation of Manger in Edinburgh see Dan Davin's *Closing Times* (1975); Marc Chagall, born 1887. Great imaginative Russian-Jewish painter'. (Some biographical dictionaries give Chagall's birth year as 1889.)

p. 198 'Strangers and neighbours': N39, pp. 106–10, 27–9.1.71. Pub. *Honest Ulsterman*, no. 42–3 (March–July 1974), pp. 27–30. *TE*, p. 11.

p. 200 'As you like it': N40, pp. 136–9, 4–9.7.75. Pub. *Honest Ulsterman*, no. 50 (Winter 1975), pp. 138–40. *TE*, p. 14; *S*, p. 99.

p. 202 'The last call': N35, p. 98, 26–30.6.58; N37, p. 65, with title 'The old collector (a revision of An Old Man)'. Probably rev. July 1962. *TE*, p. 16.

p. 202 'The fairy-man at Layde': N35, p. 50, 15–16.12.55, with title 'The whisper: for MJM'. *TE*, p. 16; *DC* (1984), p. 5, alongside the Second Foreword and followed by the note: 'These verses are dedicated to the memory of the late Patrick McDonnell and Pat O'Loan, and to our greatest listener, Michael J. Murphy.' In *TE*, Hewitt provided the following notes: ' "skeagh-bush", a fairy thorn; "forth", an earthen fort, a fairy habitation; "hungry grass", grows on bad, starved land where, if one walks, one becomes faint and hungry; "freets and ferlies", spells and marvels; "grugach", a banshee, or premonitory supernatural female'.

p. 203 'The Hen and the Cock: a Glens folk rhyme': N34, p. 23, 23.3.53, with title 'The cock and the hen' and note: 'Based on a folk rime from Patrick MacDonnell, Senior, 21.3.53'. *TE*, p. 17.

p. 203 'An Island folk tale': N10, pp. 59–60, part LXX of 'The Red Hand: a poemosaic'; N20, p. 59, 22.11.35, with title 'The ballad of the changing of a name of a Rathlin homestead'. *TE*, p. 17.

p. 204 'Nineteen sixteen, or The terrible beauty': N40, p. 42, 14–15.3.73, where it is wrongly noted as appearing in *OMT*. Pub. *Pace*, vol. 6, no. 4 (Winter 1974–5), p. 30; this version is in the first person: l. 1 reads 'First, as a boy of nine, I heard our teacher'; l. 7 ends 'told us'; l. 12 ends 'half our country's youth'; l. 14 reads 'I caught no hint I'd cast an ageing eye'; l. 16 reads 'or unattended cars, as I edge by'. *TE*, p. 18. *See also* 'Bangor, spring 1916' (*KS*, p. 47).

p. 204 'Encounter, nineteen twenty': N31, p. 32, 5.1.48. Pub. *Irish Times*, 3 April 1948, with title 'Encounter'. *TE*, p. 19; *S*, p. 32. In the *Irish Times* version, l. 1 has 'sodden ball'; l. 5 'seeing his sharp face'; l. 8 reads 'the age of hate that waits each growing child'; l. 9 has 'Fear sent each reeling'; and l. 10 has 'in darkness since'. *See also* 'An Ulsterman in England remembers' (*UR*, p. 4), 'A local poet' (*TE*, p. 36), and 'Two spectres haunt me' (*KS*, p. 60).

p. 205 'For any Irishman': N40, p. 94, 20.5.74. *TE*, p. 19; *S*, p. 31.

p. 205 'Northern spring': N40, pp. 120–1, 14.5.75. *TE*, p. 20.

p. 206 ' "The Lass of Richmond Hill", or The Royal Garden Party': N39, pp. 21–3, 18–19.9.69. *TE*, p. 21; *S*, p. 39. Hewitt provides the following notes: '"that other June day", 7 June 1798, Battle of Antrim; "James Hope" 1764–1846, weaver, see R.R. Madden's *United Irishmen*; "Leonard McNally" 1752–1820, songwriter and barrister, see Madden'. The garden party referred to in the poem was at Parliament House, Stormont, in 1951; Hewitt gives an account of it in a chapter entitled 'Donegore', originally intended for inclusion in 'A North Light'.

p. 207 'Irish glass': N35, pp. 93–4, with note: 'This has been by me for years. Finally[?] tidied up 12.6.58'; N37, pp. 66–7, a revised, undated version, possibly July–August 1962; N40, pp. 147–9, August 1975, revised with additional stanza. *TE*, p. 22.

p. 208 'My father's death in hospital': N34, pp. 39–40, 10.8.53, with title 'Sonnets on my father's death'. *TE*, p. 24. *See also* 'A father's death' (*RD*, p. 32), and the fourth of the 'October sonnets' (*M*, p. 38).

p. 209 'My father's ghost': N32, p. 41, 13.11.49 (possibly an error for 13.12.49). *TE*, p. 25; *S*, p. 88.

p. 209 'E.H. (1877–1958)': N40, p. 110, 4.12.74. Pub. *Irish Times*, 12 July 1975. *TE*, p. 25; *S*, p. 89. The subject of the poem is Hewitt's mother, Elinor. *See also* 'First letters' (*KS*, p. 27), 'An eye for colour' (*KS*, p. 32), and 'My mother' (*KS*, p. 32). There is an untitled ms. among Hewitt's papers, dated 5.3.69, which begins: 'I never loved my mother well enough,/ took her as landscape, larder, lexicon,/ but gave obedience [cancelled] affection to that other one'.

p. 210 'The drift of petals': N40, p. 109, 3.12.74. *TE*, p. 26.

p. 210 'A great event': N40, pp. 112–13, 11–13.4.75. *TE*, p. 26.

p. 211 'The mile-long street': N40, pp. 87–8, 23.11.73. Pub. *Poetry Supplement of Poetry Book Society* (Christmas 1974). Rep. *New Poems 1975* (1975), p. 131; *Thirty Years of the Poetry Book Society 1956–1986* (1988), p. 116. *TE*, p. 27. *See also* 'The way to school' (*KS*, p. 37).

p. 212 'I remember': N40, p. 122, 14.5.75. *TE*, p. 28.

p. 212 'The college fence': N40, pp. 133–4, 4.7.75, with title 'At the morning break'. *TE*, p. 28.

p. 213 'Diptera': N40, p. 123, undated, but placed between poems dated 14.5.75 and 19.5.75. Pub. *Gown Poetry Supplement* (May 1976); in this version, l. 4 reads 'switching his long-shafted net' (possibly a misprint). *TE*, p. 29.

p. 213 'Away match: June 1924': N29, pp. 189–91, 25.11.44, with title 'The cricket match'; N47, p. 47, with title 'Cricket match Betjemanesque', finished pp. 53–4. *TE*, p. 30; *S*, p. 90.

p. 215 'The faded leaf: a chapter of family history': N39, pp. 48–9, 27.11.69, with title 'My other grandmother'; N40, pp. 69–74, with title 'The fading leaf: a chapter of family history', and note: 'An old draft much revised and completed 19/20.6.73'. N8, pp. 17–19, contains an unpublished poem, titled 'Hic jacet', dated 1929, in which a visit to his grandfather's grave prompts Hewitt to a meditation on the motto 'we all do fade as a leaf'. *TE*, p. 31. In *TE*, Hewitt provides the following notes:

> 'Charles Bradlaugh, 1833–1891, leading Victorian freethinker'; 'Charles G. Gordon, 1833–1885. The Prime Minister was popularly believed to have delayed rescue operations when Gordon was captured in the Mahdi's Rebellion'; 'General Tom Thumb, Charles Stratton, 1838–1883, famous American midget toured by P.T. Barnum'; 'Sir Redvers Henry Buller, VC (1834–1880). *Britannica* generously records that he "proved unsuccessful as Commander-in-chief in Boer War" '. [Sir Redvers Henry Buller was, in fact, born in 1839 and died in 1908.]

Much of the family history in this poem figures also in *KS*, particularly in the poems 'My father's mother' (p. 15), 'Scottish interlude' (p. 20), 'Teetotal master', (p. 20), 'The return (1885)' (p. 21), 'Jenny Geddes' (p. 21). The line 'when the ship's siren rocked the Broomielaw' recurs verbatim in 'The return (1885)'.

p. 218 'A mobile mollusc': N39, p. 45, 23.10.69. Pub. *Gown Poetry Supplement* (May 1976); in this version, l. 2 reads 'a man who never failed to speak his mind'. *TE*, p. 35.

p. 218 'Orientations': N40, p. 116, 13.4.75. *TE*, p. 35.

p. 219 'Nourish your heart': N30, p. 79, 2.12.45; N47, p. 83. *TE*, p. 36.

p. 219 'A local poet': N40, p. 146, August 1975, with title 'A local historian', a revision of 'Poet in Ulster' (1955). Pub. *Irish Times*, 11 June 1955, with title 'Poet in Ulster'. Rep. *Poets from the North of Ireland* (1979), p. 41; *Poets from the North of Ireland* (1990), p. 44. *TE*, p. 36; *S*, p. 113. The *Irish Times* version reads as follows:

> I have peopled your roads with heroes
> and stepped aside on the grass

to let the headlong chariots through
and the kings in their coaches pass.

I have walked the ways of my kindred
when the fruit-hung trees swung low,
when the rooks rose out of the furrows,
and the whin blossomed out of the snow.

I have followed your rimes and stories
through a thousand books and more,
and hoked for the broken couplets
among the straws on the floor.

And now, with no wage for my labour,
I stand where the four winds cross,
and my heart's with the lonely heron
and the curlew high on the moss.

THE RAIN DANCE: POEMS NEW AND REVISED (*RD*), published by Blackstaff Press, Belfast, 1978. I have included all forty-five poems from the original edition, as well as incorporating, where appropriate, the alphabetical 'Glossary of vernacular words, North-east Antrim' and the notes to individual poems which Hewitt provides. At the end of the volume Hewitt states: 'A number of these poems, since revised, appear in the *Irish Times*, *Irish Press*, *Dublin Magazine*, *British Weekly*, *Time and Tide*, *Poetry Quarterly* and *Tribune*.'

The Rain Dance was a Christmas Recommendation of the Poetry Book Society in 1978. In the *Poetry Book Society Bulletin*, no. 99 (Christmas 1978), Hewitt writes:

> Throughout 1977 I was engaged in writing a couple of books on local art and had little time for original verse, so, in the lull after, I turned to the refurbishing of poems which seemed to be waiting for, and worth, improvement. *The Rain Dance* therefore includes not only pieces written since my last book but others published in journals or still in manuscript from previous decades which have been subject to varying degrees of revision.
>
> Now over 70, I have been reading and writing verse seriously for over fifty years, and in that time have been aware of and laid open to the fluctuations of fashion. As a student, with no living poet in my text-books, I plunged into Shelley, Whitman, Rossetti and Morris, first encountering contemporary poetry in the booklets of Benn's *Augustan Poets*. I can still repeat without effort bits of Drinkwater, de la Mare, Flecker. This phase seems to have ended with the brutal and unjust demolition of Humbert Wolfe's *Uncelestial City* (1930). Gordon Bottomley has, for me, lasted longer, perhaps because we corresponded and I met him once.
>
> So I threaded my way or lurched among the trends and tendencies. The books on my shelves then became those of Eliot, Pound and, after *New Signatures* (1932), Day-Lewis, Auden, Tessimond. My friend Bertie Rodgers shot ahead in brief incandescence among the romantics where I could not follow; but, by 1939, with Waley's translations of *170 Chinese*

Poems (seventh printing) I learned to step with care and keep my voice down.

Somewhere along the way I had found Frost and Edward Thomas and Andrew Young and Edwin Muir, and had come to terms with the later Yeats whose *The Tower* (1928) had so jolted and disconcerted me. Then, in 1946, I came upon R.S. Thomas with eager delight, in his *Stones of the Field.* A loop-line led me to the Irish, to Padraic Colum, F.R. Higgins and Austin Clarke. In recent years I have found nourishment in the English Philip Larkin, the Scottish Edwin Morgan and the Welsh Leslie Norris, and in my junior fellow Ulstermen, Heaney, Mahon, Longley, Ormsby and Muldoon. Now, in my verses, a reader may discover hints of these conditioning enthusiasms.

p. 221 'For a moment of darkness over the nations': N38, p. 95, 14.10.68, with title 'In a moment of darkness over the nations'. *RD*, p. 1.

p. 221 'The romantic': N40, p. 150, 1.10.75; N41, p. 19. *RD*, p. 1; *S*, p. 114.

p. 221 '1957–1972': N40, p. 151, early October 1975; N41, p. 18. *RD*, p. 2. Hewitt moved from Belfast to Coventry in 1957 to become Art Director of the Herbert Art Gallery and Museum; he retired in 1972 and returned to Belfast.

p. 222 'November park': N40, p. 106, 23.11.74; N41, p. 33. *RD*, p. 2; *S*, p. 115. The setting of the poem is Musgrave Park, Belfast, which was opposite the Hewitts' house in Stockman's Lane.

p. 222 'My own and not my own': N37, pp. 14–15, 28.4.60, with title 'This, with time'; N41, pp. 2–3. *RD*, p. 3.

p. 223 'The end of the world': N37, pp. 89–90, 11–13.3.64, with title 'Moraine'; N41, pp. 14–15, with titles 'Moraine/The end of the world'. *RD*, p. 4.

p. 224 'After reading *Sonnets* by Rev. Charles Turner (1864) and *The New Day*, sonnets by Dr T. Gordon Hake (1890)': N38, p. 23, 1.12.66. *RD*, p. 5. This is an extensively revised version of the poem of the same title in *Tesserae* (1967), which runs as follows:

> Sonnet, beloved of doctors, clergymen,
> by skill, by daily habit, not averse
> to small-scale essays of a leisure pen,
> I too have slipped my pence in your tight purse.
>
> Keeper of art, my working will's involved,
> by private thought, by public exposition,
> in facing questions never to be solved –
> humility the primary condition.
>
> So little room or urge this use affords
> for patterned stanzas' complicated trope,
> or any large design's sustained concern,
> that to the sonnet's riming net of words,
> as the day ebbs, instinctively I turn
> to what I'd hold of reverie or hope.

p. 224 'Rome Sunday, June 1960': N38, p. 138, 29–30.3.69, with title 'Rome, June, 1960'. Rep. *The Deer's Cry* (1986), p. 232. *RD*, p. 6.

p. 224 'William Conor RHA, 1881–1968': N33, p. 4, 28.10.50 (first sonnet); p. 7, 28.10.50/23.11.50 (second sonnet); N41, p. 79 (first sonnet), p. 80 (second sonnet). Rep. *Pace*, vol. 11, no. 1 (Spring 1979), p. 9. *RD*, p. 7. Hewitt notes in *RD* that the first sonnet was published in the CEMA catalogue for an exhibition of recent paintings and drawings by William Conor, November 1950, where it was dated 28 October 1950. Pub. also *British Weekly*, 26 April 1951, with title 'To Conor'; that version reads as follows:

So, Conor, take our thanks for what you've done;
not by those harsh abstractions of despair
that find the teeming earth no longer fair,
and paint a disc when we would feel the sun;
nor by pursuit of fantasies that run
in private labyrinths and mazes where
the lonely man must find but few to share
the secret truth his agonies have won.

Not these for you. But rather by your skill
the leaning woman over the half-door,
the labouring horse that struggles up the hill,
the pity and the laughter of the poor,
move the dull heart and prop the flagging will,
by mercy made more gentle than before.

Hewitt glosses 'Islandmen' as 'workers in Harland and Wolff's shipyard at Queen's Island, Belfast'.

Of Hewitt's many writings about William Conor and his painting, the most notable is 'Conor's art', in *Conor* by Judith C. Wilson (Blackstaff Press, Belfast, 1981, pp. 107–27).

p. 225 'Aquarium' ('A challenge to my verbalising mind . . .'): N38, p. 8, 22–3.11.66. *RD*, p. 8.

p. 226 'The poet's trade': N37, p. 135, 14.12.65; N41, pp. 58–9. *RD*, p. 9. Hewitt refers to a boyhood ambition to be a missionary in a number of prose works and poems: *see*, for example, 'The open eye' (*KS*, p. 43).

p. 226 'Poetry, then . . .': N37, pp. 132–4, 13.12.65; N41, pp. 55–7. *RD*, p. 9.

p. 227 'Ars Poetica': N31, pp. 117–21, 16–17.4.49; N41, pp. 115–19. Pub. *Dublin Magazine* (July–September 1949), pp. 4–6; in this version, l. 1 reads 'Strip bare the thought till every word is proved'. *RD*, p. 11.

p. 230 'On reading Wallace Stevens' *Collected Poems* after many years': N38, p. 137, 29.3.69, with title 'On glancing through Wallace Stevens' *Collected Poems* after many years'; N41, p. 49. *RD*, p. 14.

p. 230 'October-born': N34, pp. 100–2, 15–16.8.54; N41, pp. 67–9. *RD*, p. 14.

p. 231 'The Glens of Antrim': N34, p. 49, 29.9.53. Rep. *Antrim Coast and Glens* (1990), p. 11. *RD*, p. 16; *DC* (1984), p. 11. Hewitt glosses 'lint' as 'flax'.

p. 231 'The glen of light': N37, p. 70, 10.8.62; N41, p. 52. *RD*, p. 16.

p. 232 'Garron Top': N33, pp. 139–40, 18.7.52. Pub. *Time and Tide*, 3 September 1955. *RD*, p. 17. Hewitt glosses 'moss' as 'moor, rough pasture or bogland', and 'wallstead' as 'ruined dwelling, a roofless structure'.

p. 232 'Easter flock': N33, pp. 125–6, 14.4.52; N37, pp. 63–4, with title 'The safe pasture (a revision)'. Probably November–December 1962. *RD*, p. 18. Hewitt glosses 'lap' as 'armful of grass or hay rolled in bundle to shed rain before stacking'.

p. 233 'The blossomed thorn': N34, pp. 80–1, 7–12.6.54, with title 'The hawthorn tree'; N41, pp. 63–4. Pub. *Irish Times*, 31 July 1954, with title 'The hawthorn tree'. *RD*, p. 19. The *Irish Times* version reads as follows:

> The lateness of the season here
> allows the thorn to blossom now;
> in opulent and brief career
> each single bough is bent on show.
> Once walking with unquiet mind
> I saw one bush of all in flower
> that had a beauty of a kind
> my senses had no measure for.
> As gazing at it long I stood
> a strange awareness stirred within,
> not just of flesh becoming wood
> and prickling where the buds begin,
> but of a flowing universe
> that poured and streamed towards the tree,
> drawn with a magnet's silent force
> into that one reality.
> The running earth, the rushing sky
> seemed thrusting into twig and spray:
> to save my small identity
> I had to turn and walk away.

p. 234 'Failed image': N32, p. 112, 30.8.50; N41, p. 11. *RD*, p. 20.

p. 234 'The threshing': N34, p. 72, 29–30.12.53; N41, p. 6. *RD*, p. 20.

p. 234 'The lettered snow': N34, pp. 140–1, 21.2.55; N41, pp. 70–1. Pub. *Irish Times*, 14 January 1956. *RD*, p. 21. The *Irish Times* version reads as follows:

> We spend our swift years learning how to read
> the languages our travelling senses need,
> first sentences, then clustered syllables,
> then, with assurance, the brief sign that tells
> a family's, a people's history
> in tilt of stone or silhouette of tree.
>
> But this day walking in the sunlit snow,
> we traced a page as yet we hardly know;
> the pace of boot and shoe, the clean tyre's tread
> were easily identified and read;
> the jogging bullock's splay, the deep-plunged track
> of the quick dog that leapt and bounded back:
> then, with more study and close scholarship,
> we scrutinised the blurred hoof's plodding grip,

and argued round the little slithered lane
from hedge to stack which looped and came again,
and postulated field rats as the cause,
confirmed by crisp cast of the small-toed paws:
but what the bird we have no skill to guess,
that crossed this sward, the brittle wilderness,
and where it flew to, where it nestled warm
in last night's bitter east of driving storm,
though the whole story's here in cuneiform.

p. 235 'The tinker's answer': N31, pp. 1–4, 12.9.46; N37, pp. 75–7, rev. version 28.11.63; N41, pp. 94–7. *RD*, p. 22. Hewitt glosses 'brae' as 'small hill, slope of hill' and 'piggy' as 'tipcat, in England'.

p. 237 'The true smith of Tieveragh': N33, pp. 26–30, finished 26.7.51; N41, pp. 83–7, subtitled 'To the memory of Pat O'Loan, carpenter'. *RD*, p. 24; *DC* (1984), p. 76. Hewitt provides the following notes:

'True Smith of Tieveragh', Struthers Moore, colloquial form of name of James Stoddard Moore, otherwise known as 'Dusty Rhodes', the tramp poet;

'Yeos'; the yeomanry used to suppress insurrection of the United Irishmen in 1798;

'*The Irish Times*', issue of 27 December 1947 [the reference is to Hewitt's poem 'The ballad', pub. *Irish Times*, 25–7 December 1947, and rep. *Tribune*, 21 April 1950. *DC* (1969), p. 16; *DC* (1984), p. 20];

'booklet', *The Life and Poetry of James Stoddard Moore, the Glens of Antrim Poet* by Robert McCahen, printed by the *Northern Constitution*, Coleraine (n.d. *c.* 1925);

'ballad', its title in booklet is 'Robert Kennedy, a Tale of 1798'.

Hewitt also glosses 'gleed' as 'a glowing coal', 'sock' as 'ploughshare', 'gentle' as 'fairy', 'airt' as 'direction', 'rolling' as 'drunk, staggering', and 'gentle bush' as 'fairy thorn'.

Paul Nietsche (1885–1950) was a German-born painter who came to Northern Ireland about 1926 and made his home there.

p. 239 'The seedsman (J.H., 1841–1922)': N43, p. 7, 27.8.76, with title 'John Hewitt, seedsman, 1841–1922, John Hewitt, reader, 1907–'. Pub. *Irish Press*, 20 November 1976. *RD*, p. 27. In the *Irish Press* version, ll. 2–3 read 'the myriad grass-heads, stiff and mummified/by the long season's drought, brought back to mind'; ll. 6–7 read 'like bush, like hedge, a landscape's property;/a skill I envied and can never share'; l. 9 begins 'Then suddenly recalled'; ll. 13–14 read 'of a rich word-hoard, vivid long ago/when seasons marked the time and all was slow'.

Hewitt's grandfather John is also the subject of a number of poems in *KS*: 'Orchard country' (p. 19), 'Scottish interlude' (p. 20), 'Teetotal master' (p. 20), 'The return (1885)' (p. 21), and 'Jenny Geddes' (p. 21). *See also Freehold*: 'III: Townland of peace' (*F*, p. 12).

p. 239 'The boat-builder's caulking irons': N39, pp. 11–12, 14.9.69, with titles 'Tool box' and 'Boat builder'; the fourth section of this is the basis for the published poem; N41, p. 34. Rep. *Poetry Book Society Bulletin*, no. 99 (Christmas 1978). *RD*, p. 28.

p. 240 'First ride': N39, pp. 97–8, 17.1.71; N41, pp. 40–1. *RD*, p. 28.

p. 241 'Miss Murdoch': N39, p. 81, 13.8.70; N41, p. 39, with title 'Miss Mary Murdoch'. *RD*, p. 29. Miss Murdoch also figures in 'The school upstairs' (*KS*, p. 39), and 'My teachers' (*KS*, p. 40).

p. 241 'The beastie': N25, p. 162, 27.12.41; N41, p. 120. Rep. *All Shy Wildness* (1984), p. 30. *RD*, p. 30.

p. 242 'Summer park': N31, p. 16, 13.5.47, with title 'Park'; N41, p. 100. Pub. *Irish Times*, 19 June 1948, with title 'City park'. Rep. *Tribune*, 15 April 1949. *RD*, p. 31. In his 'Ulster commentary', broadcast NI Home Service, 16 June 1950, Hewitt includes the entire poem, with the comment that it is set in Botanic Gardens, Belfast. The *Irish Times* version reads as follows:

> When unexpected sun beat on the stones
> the people leaked into the evening park
> cramming the benches, nodding to the flowers
> or flat on grass drew lids against the light:
> the rolling children's voices ran like hoops
> over the shadows of the chestnut's leaves;
> the old men left the shelter and the draughts
> to play the last game over sticks in dust;
> and on the rough slope where the tarmac ends
> the football bounced erratic on dry clay:
> assertive finches independent sang;
> and one high blackbird in a conifer
> said without words what everybody felt . . .
> and some sat happy smiling at the world.

p. 242 'A father's death': N34, pp. 54–5, 1.10.53; N41, pp. 61–2. Rep. *Poets from the North of Ireland* (1979), p. 30; *Poets from the North of Ireland* (1990), p. 36. *RD*, p. 32.

p. 243 'On choosing some verses for my sister's cremation': N40, pp. 111–12, 25.2.75, with note: 'Written the day before my sister's cremation'; N41, pp. 30–1. *RD*, p. 33.

p. 243 'On Colinward: the scattering': N40, pp. 126–7, 25–6.5.75; N41, pp. 25–6. *RD*, p. 34.

p. 244 'Below the Mournes in May': N40, pp. 124–5, 19.5.75; N41, pp. 27–9. *RD*, p. 35.

p. 245 'The Blue Lias Inn': N38, p. 76, 24–6.5.68; N41, pp. 43–4. *RD*, p. 36.

p. 246 'Monastery, Tourliani, Mykonos': N38, pp. 103–5, 16–17.12.68. Rev. 11.1.69; N41, pp. 46–8. There is an undated ms. among Hewitt's papers with the title 'The Greek Orthodox Monastery of Tourliani, Anomera[?], Mykonos'. *RD*, p. 37.

p. 247 'The man from the mountains': N40, pp. 141–3, 18.7.75; N41, pp. 20–2. *RD*, p. 39.

p. 248 'In the Lenin Library, Dushanbe': N43, pp. 15–17, March 1977. Pub. *Gown*, 28 April 1977. *RD*, p. 41. Among Hewitt's papers is a cutting of this poem in which he has substituted 'mountains' for 'mountain-river' in the penultimate stanza.

p. 250 'Camaradas y compañeros': N24, pp. 74-5, 9.11.39; N45, p. 166. *RD*, p. 43.

p. 251 'Sonnets for Roberta (1954)': N34, p. 127, 16.8.54 (first sonnet); p. 128, 16.8.54 (second sonnet); p. 129, 19.8.54 (third sonnet); N35, p. 65, 27.4.56 (fourth sonnet); p. 66 (fifth sonnet); N41, p. 73 (first sonnet); p. 74 (second sonnet); p. 75 (third sonnet); p. 77 (fourth sonnet); p. 78 (fifth sonnet). First two sonnets rep. *Poets from the North of Ireland* (1979), p. 39; first two rep. *The Long Embrace* (1987), p. 32; first two rep. *Poets from the North of Ireland* (1990), p. 43. *RD*, p. 44; *S*, p. 95 (first two).

p. 253 'The shortened day': N33, p. 145, 26.10.52; N41, p. 5. *RD*, p. 47; *S*, p. 77.

p. 253 'The last summer, for Roberta (1975)': N40, pp. 134–5, 4.7.75; N41, pp. 23–4. *RD*, p. 47.

p. 254 'Old men sitting': N34, p. 149, 25.2.55; N41, p. 121. Pub. *Irish Times*, 8 September 1956, with title 'Poem'. *RD*, p. 48. The *Irish Times* version reads as follows:

> Shew me a man who's suddenly at peace
> with a game, a gadget, or merely listening
> to others talking, to the band in the park,
> he is himself, no more nor less than that.
>
> Yet see the same man talking, at the bar,
> or walking where he's known; he's another person:
> watch how the eyes behind his eyes behave;
> a crouched observer spying out the land.
>
> He's stranger, friend, a wit, professional,
> sportsman or artist, any but himself:
> each mask's a trick he's hardly conscious of,
> or only sometimes where it's not often used.
>
> But old men sitting may not be at peace;
> they are already absent from themselves:
> when their eyes moisten it is the east wind,
> or a speck of dust that smarts a small boy's eye.

p. 254 'Expectancy': N31, pp. 20–1, 16.5.47; N41, pp. 101–2. Pub. *Irish Times*, 2 August 1947. Rep. *Poetry Quarterly* (Winter 1949–50); *British Weekly*, 29 November 1951. *RD*, p. 49; *S*, p. 116.

KITES IN SPRING: A BELFAST BOYHOOD (*KS*), published by Blackstaff Press, Belfast, 1980. I have included all 107 sonnets from the original volume.

A number of Hewitt's prose writings provide invaluable background and complementary material for this set of poems, in particular 'Planter's Gothic, an essay in discursive autobiography', published in three instalments in *The Bell* (1953), under the pseudonym 'John Howard' (*see* Select Bibliography, 'Selected Articles and Reviews, and Other Prose Writings') and reprinted in *Ancestral Voices: The Selected Prose of John Hewitt* (ed. Tom Clyde, 1987, pp. 1–33).

Hewitt also recalls his childhood in a BBC broadcast for schools in the Today and Yesterday in Northern Ireland series, transmitted 9 May 1975.

Among Hewitt's papers are a number of unpublished manuscripts relating to *Kites in Spring*. One is a draft foreword:

> I had written no new verse since March, 1978, and by mid-October I was feeling rather depressed; in a few days I should be approaching the third anniversary of my wife's death, my wife for over forty years; by the end of the month I should be entering my 72nd year. So it was perhaps natural that I should brood on the idea of death, at the dismal outset of winter, in a deeply riven and violent society, tortured by a cruelly remembered past.
>
> By chance, on 16 October, I began versing again, with a sonnet and a half on the theme of death as I had known it in my days. Within four weeks I had written 25 sonnets, by the New Year 52, their subjects gradually developing into a series on my parents' families and my own childhood, turning back to a past which had seemed more secure.
>
> I have confined myself to the traditional fourteen lines, packing them with what I believe are factual statements or references, or accurate, so far as I know, undoctored memories, a highly [constricting] exercise. With no enthusiasm or capacity for large rhetorical gestures and with no space for the flourishes, the ornaments of poetry, I do not think that I have indulged in any elaboration of expression or padding-out of my lines.
>
> Consequently it might be asserted that these quatorzains are really prose, or, at best, since they scan and rime, no more than verse, but frequently the statement or development of a particular item may involve a serious breach of the sonnet device, paying little or no attention to the relationship between the octave and the sestette [*sic*], either technically or emotionally, and taking liberties with the Petrarchan and Shakespearean models, treating them as stanzas in a loosely narrative meditation.
>
> I can claim no more for them than that this series records an Ulsterman's childhood in the first decades of this century and of the families from which he sprang [the next few words are illegible]. It is my hope that the compressions of the form and the precision of the words I have been compelled to use may have been able to generate some light and warmth, as the vigorously rubbed sticks of the aborigine may start his little fire of dead leaves and [handily] gathered twigs.
>
> The events to which reference is made generally occurred up to 1922 when I was 15 years old. [Hewitt cancels the preceding sentence.] The public events in the biographical narrative came to an end in (had all happened by) 1922 [and] the last [illegible] is devoted to the deaths of several of the individuals mentioned.

Another manuscript, dated 7 April 1979, takes the form of a commentary introducing and linking four of the sonnets, prepared, perhaps, for radio or a public reading:

> During last year I had no impulse to write any verse. Then suddenly, in mid-October, I started on what proved a lengthy sequence of short poems, each of them of fourteen lines. At that time I was in a very serious, not to say sombre mood, for the third anniversary of my wife's death was

approaching, and I myself was coming to my seventy-first birthday, both occasions for solemn thought.

But as the little poems kept coming almost unbidden – they number 115 to date – their elegiac tone lightened and they became plain memories of my childhood years and probings into the early origins of my firmly held beliefs and prejudices. And it became clear that it was to my parents, to my paternal grandfather, and to one of my uncles, that my debt was deepest.

This uncle, my father's youngest brother, I once was delighted to discover, has his tiny corner in a printed source, in a book entitled *British Aircraft 1809–1914,* for on page 309 there is a photograph of and a note on the Hewitt ornithopter constructed by S.R. Hewitt in 1908 – an ornithopter is the technical name for an aeroplane with flapping wings like a bird.

I never saw that ornithopter, for I was only one in 1908, but later I heard of it and can recollect clearly having its steering wheel pointed out to me, as it rested on the high shelf of the kitchen among the big brass pans in my grandfather's house, where my uncle also lived.

So, naturally, Uncle Sam figures now in a number of these little poems which I have written this winter.

The first that I shall read tells how I, as a very small boy, was brought into his enthusiasm for flying machines. [What follows is an early, untitled version of the poem which became '21st September 1912' (*KS*, p. 17)]:

My Uncle Sam who loved all aeroplanes
took me one day to see who'd win the race
from Dublin, but rough winds and scudding rains
knocked any finish clearly out of place.
One later Saturday, we took our stand,
hedge-high, to watch a monoplane display
at the Balmoral Showgrounds close at hand –
where we then stood is all built-up today.

Diving and climbing, swinging quickly round,
the spellbound monoplane seemed magical:
sudden it slipped; a stiff wing stabbed the ground.
At home then when the evening paper came,
its stop-press gave the airman Astley's name,
reporting he had died in hospital.

Strange now to think that because it was a wet stormy day there was no race! And for the second event, after I had written of it, I went to the Reference Library to check the date, and there from a newspaper cuttings book I found that Harry Astley had been killed on the 21st September 1912.

My grandfather's house, where I saw that ornithopter steering wheel, was an Aladdin's Cave to me in those days. I can still, in my mind's eye, see its rooms, its furniture, the marvellous objects which seemed to fill its every crevice or corner, that rich accumulation of my uncle's and my grandfather's passions.

Here's a poem about that house. [What follows is an early untitled version of the poem which became 'Lonsdale Street' (*KS*, p. 16)]:

My father's youngest brother stayed at home
with his old father when the others left.
I can recall the treasures in each room
although the house is gone, the street bereft
of all but name: that rarest of bazaars –
huge lolling conch-shells; chair of prairie grass
twisted in coils; newts, lizards tanked in glass;
live pigeons in the attic; snakes in jars;
the Orange sash, the Volunteer shako,
the phonograph with spinning cylinders,
the stamps, the butterflies, all disappeared
into the limbo where such treasures go,
gone too that wheel with which my uncle steered
his fabled ornithopter – gone for years.

The sash had been my grandfather's, for when he lived in Glasgow he had been Master of his Lodge; the shako his too when he had been in the Volunteers in the eighteen sixties, facing the supposed threat of the French Emperor, Louis Napoleon. But the interest in living things, in natural history, was my uncle's; and that led him out of doors to enrich his collections, a pleasure I often shared. [What follows is an early, untitled version of the poem which became 'The magician' (*KS*, p. 18)]:

This uncle was my eager Prospero,
that house his island-dukedom. Thence I shared
his marvels and his magic. We would go
with netted rods and jam-jars well prepared
to pace the towpath by the drifting stream
or stride through the heather for the furtive moth.
I gaped to see his magic-lantern beam
colour with life the hoisted table-cloth.

His nimble fingers thrilled the mandolin,
or strummed banjo. Once, with a pointed blade,
he gouged a fist-size eagle from tough oak.
He glittered through my days, a paladin,
in all accomplished, nature's tricks his trade
till one sad day for me that dream-spell broke.

That breach in the family was like an amputation for me. In another poem I wrote fifteen years ago I referred to it in these terms –

. . . I took the side
duty ordered, as if the flesh were cut
with a quick knife. And so, with one hand since,
I have explored the surfaces of life.
['The wheel', *CP*, p. 119]

But in this recent sequence I have more to say about my uncle. [What follows is an early, untitled version of the poem which became 'Consequences' (*KS*, p. 19)]:

Our houses parted as that shutter fell
in this same town. Not once I'd pace again
close on his heels, along a tufted lane
net at the ready. Nevermore he'd spell
Darwinian theory from some mollusc's shell
nor trace fierce logic in the spider's skein.
Yet from that teeming mind there must remain
much which has made and kept me infidel.

He taught in Sunday school, had been expelled
for heresy, since Darwin's was his book;
from thence his reading went from bad to worse.
So though I lost him early I have held
close to that sceptic and enquiring look
at the old riddle of the universe.

p. 256 'A happy boy': N43, p. 141, 29.6.79. *KS*, p. 1.

p. 256 'This narrative': N43, p. 147, with note 'last week in August '79'. *KS*, p. 1.

p. 257 'The unnecessary dread': N43, p. 26, 19.10.78. *KS*, p. 2.

p. 257 'My Uncle Willy': N43, p. 27, 19.10.78; p. 112, rev. version, 4.2.79. *KS*, p. 2.

p. 258 'My Uncle Johnny': N43, p. 28, 21–2.10.78. Pub. *Hibernia,* 20 September 1979, untitled. *KS*, p. 3.

p. 258 'Uncle Dick and Aunt Bertha': N43, p. 29, 23.10.78. *KS*, p. 3.

p. 259 'Year of Grace and my great-grandfather': N43, p. 43, 14.11.78, with note '1859'. *KS*, p. 4.

p. 259 'My great-grandfather's refusal': N43, p. 44, 15.11.78, with notes '1859' and 'The ould orange flute'. *KS*, p. 4.

p. 260 'My Grandmother Robinson': N43, p. 46, 15.11.78, with note '*c.* 1915'. *KS*, p. 6.

p. 260 'The Teacher's Residence': N43, p. 48, 21.11.78, with title '96 Clifton Park Avenue, 1884' and note '1880 +'. *KS*, p. 6.

p. 261 '96 Clifton Park Avenue and the Robinsons': N43, p. 49, 21.11.78, with note '1888?'. *KS*, p. 7.

p. 261 'Grandfather Robinson dies in 1898': N43, p. 50, 21.11.78, with note '1898'. *KS*, p. 7. *See also* 'Eager journey' (*CP*, p. 128).

p. 262 'The scattering': N43, p. 51, 21.11.78, with note '1898–'. *KS*, p. 8.

p. 262 'My parents' courtship': N43, p. 94, 25.1.79. *KS*, p. 8.

p. 263 'The wedding present': N43, p. 71, 13.12.78. *KS*, p. 9.

p. 263 'Uncle Sam and Aunt Edie': N43, p. 61, 27.11.78, with note '1919'. *KS*, p. 9.

p. 264 'Aunt Cis and Uncle Tom': N43, p. 59, 26.11.78, with note '1912'. *KS*, p. 10.

p. 264 'Ellendene': N43, p. 56, 25.11.78, with note '*c.* 1916'. *KS*, p. 10. *See also* 'The house at Ballyholme' (*LE*, p. 29).

p. 265 'What little happened there': N43, p. 57, 25.11.78, with note '1916'. *KS*, p. 11.

p. 265 'Carson at Six Road Ends': N43, p. 54, 24.11.78, with note '*c.* 1913 –14'. *KS*, p. 11.

p. 266 'My grandmother's restlessness': N43, p. 144, 17.7.79. *KS*, p. 12.

p. 266 'The tricycle': N43, p. 55, 24.11.78, with note '*c.* 1920'; p. 145, rev. 17.7.79. *KS*, p. 12.

p. 267 'Balloons and wooden guns': N43, p. 58, 25.11.78, with note '1907–1930'. *KS*, p. 13.

p. 267 'The volunteer': ('My father's closest brother of his three . . .'): N43, p. 30, 24–5.10.78, with note '*c.* 1875–1917'. *KS*, p. 13. There is a typescript of this poem among Hewitt's papers with the title 'Alexander Horne Hewitt 1878–1917, London Artists' Rifles'. N40, pp. 144–5 has an unpublished poem entitled 'November 1917' dated 17–18.7.75 about the death of Hewitt's Uncle Sandy in France.

p. 268 'My Brooklyn uncle': N43, p. 32, 25–6.10.78, with note '*c.* 1895'. *KS*, p. 15.

p. 268 'My father's mother': N43, p. 130, 11.2.79, with note '1870'. *KS*, p. 15.

p. 269 'My Aunt Sarah and Uncle Joe': N43, p. 45, 15.11.78, with note '*c.* 1890'. *KS*, p. 16.

p. 269 'Lonsdale Street': N43, p. 33, 31.10.78–1.11.78, with note '*c.* 1912'. *See* Notes, p. 619, for an earlier version of this poem. *KS*, p. 16.

p. 270 '21st September 1912': N43, p. 126, 9.2.79. *See* Notes, p. 618, for an earlier version of this poem. *KS*, p. 17.

p. 270 'First pantomime': N43, p. 122, 8.2.79; p. 139, rev. 24.5.79. *KS*, p. 17.

p. 271 'The magician': N43, p. 34, 1.11.78. Pub. *The Writers: A Sense of Ireland* (1980), p. 58, where it is described as 'from a sequence "My Uncle"'. *See* Notes, p. 619, for an earlier version of this poem. *KS*, p. 18.

p. 271 'The breach': N43, p. 35, 1.11.78, with note '*c.* 1915'. *KS*, p. 18. The widow courted by Hewitt's grandfather was named Mrs Spratt.

p. 272 'Consequences': N43, p. 36, 1–2.11.78, with note 'Ernest Haeckel: *The Riddle of the Universe* in paperback was on his shelves.' Pub. *The Writers: A Sense of Ireland* (1980), p. 59, described as 'from a sequence "My Uncle"'. *See* Notes, p. 620, for an earlier version of this poem. *KS*, p. 19.

p. 272 'Orchard country': N43, p. 37, 2–3.11.78, with note '*c.* 1917'. *KS*, p. 19.

p. 273 'Scottish interlude': N43, p. 38, 3–4.11.78. *KS*, p. 20.

p. 273 'Teetotal Master': N43, p. 39, 4.11.78, with note '*c.* 1860'. *KS*, p. 20.

p. 274 'The return (1885)': N43, p. 40, 5.11.78, with note '1880?'. *KS*, p. 21.

p. 274 'Jenny Geddes': N43, p. 41, 7.11.78, with note '1916+'. *KS*, p. 21.

p. 275 'The doctor's bag': N43, p. 70, 13.12.78, with note '1907'. *KS*, p. 22.

p. 275 'Methodists': N43, p. 63, 27–9.11.78. *KS*, p. 22. The 'kindly backwoods pastor' was Rev. John Walton. His son, E.T.S. Walton, attended Methodist College, Belfast (1915–22) while Hewitt was a pupil there, later played a part in the splitting of the atom and shared the Nobel Prize for Physics with Sir John Douglas Cockcroft in 1951.

p. 276 'Outside the creeds': N43, p. 64, 28–9.11.78, with note '1907'. *KS*, p. 23.

p. 276 'My naming': N43, p. 69, 12.12.78, with note '1907'. *KS*, p. 23.

p. 277 'Domestic help': N43, p. 88, 21.1.79. *KS*, p. 24; *S*, p. 82, where it is dated 1978.

p. 277 'The one I loved': N43, p. 89, 21.1.79. *KS*, p. 24; *S*, p. 83, where it is dated 1978. *See also* 'Betrayal' and 'No second Troy' (*CP*, pp. 132 and 133).

p. 278 'The names we used': N43, p. 133, 14.2.79. *KS*, p. 25.

p. 278 'My first reported words': N43, p. 93, 25.1.79. *KS*, p. 25. *See also* 'The mortal place' (Appendix I of the present volume).

p. 279 'Folk for tea': N43, p. 121, 8.2.79. *KS*, p. 27.

p. 279 'First letters': N43, p. 68, 11.12.78, with note '*c.* 1910'. *KS*, p. 27. *See also* 'E.H. (1877–1958)' (*TE*, p. 25).

p. 280 'The double-ended tram': N43, p. 95, 25.1.79. *KS*, p. 29.

p. 280 'Scarlatina': N43, p. 73, 20.12.78, with note 'Sir Edward Creasy: *Ten Decisive Battles of the World*'. *KS*, p. 29.

p. 281 'Sanctuary': N43, p. 136, 24.2.79. *KS*, p. 30.

p. 281 'My father's voice': N43, p. 47, 18–21.11.78, with note '1873–1945'. These dates refer to the birth and death of Hewitt's father, Robert Telford Hewitt. *KS*, p. 30.

p. 282 'My father': N43, p. 82, 18.1.79. *KS*, p. 31.

p. 282 'A holy place': N43, p. 80, 16.1.79, with note, 'F.J. Gould: *Children's Book of Moral Lessons*'. *KS*, p. 31.

p. 283 'An eye for colour': N43, p. 83, 18–19.1.79. *KS*, p. 32.

Ouida was the pseudonym of the popular novelist Marie Louise de la Ramée (1839–1908); Marie Corelli was the pseudonym of the popular novelist Mary Mackay (1855–1924); Sir Thomas Henry Hall Caine (1853–1931) was an English novelist, many of whose novels were set on the Isle of Man.

p. 283 'My mother': N43, p. 85, 20.1.79. *KS*, p. 32.

p. 284 'My sister': N43, p. 62, 27.11.78, with note '1902–1975'. These dates refer to the birth and death of Hewitt's sister, Eileen. *KS*, p. 34.

p. 284 'Portraits on the walls': N43, p. 72, 13–14.12.78, with note '*c.* 1910'. *KS*, p. 34.

p. 285 'I learn about art': N43, p. 79, 11.1.79, with note 'W.E. Sparkes' and a list of painters and paintings: 'Landseer: *The Bay Mare;* Turner: *The Last of the Fighting Temeraire*; da Vinci: *The Last Supper;* Michelangelo: *Sistine Sybils*'. *KS*, p. 35. *See also* section 8 of 'Variations on a theme' (*M*, p. 18).

In 'How it all started: an autobiographical talk', adapted from chapter 1 of Hewitt's unpublished autobiography, 'A North Light', and broadcast by BBC radio in June 1964, Hewitt recalled:

On my father's bookshelves was a large bound volume of *The Art Teacher's Monthly*, for what year I never noticed, and in this, issue by issue, someone called W.E. Sparkes contributed an article on a famous painting, always accompanying it with a diagrammatic analysis of the composition. So even before I could read comfortably I could grasp the structure of such works as *The Last Supper* with its radiating lines of perspective which could be extended to converge in the central figure, as *The Last of the Fighting Temeraire* with its sagging tent-rope rhythms of hull-rigging and tug-funnel. So, too, Landseer's *The Bay Mare* and Michelangelo's *Prophets* and *Sybils* were, in monochrome, part of the furniture of my mind. When I saw *The Bay Mare* in Burlington House in Derek Hill's Landseer Exhibition early in 1961 and in the May of that year, the Sistine Chapel, I could not help thinking on each occasion that it had all been a long way round. Indeed, the principles underlying these analyses are still the spine and bone of my aesthetics, as natural and as easily acquired and firmly maintained as my Belfast accent and my lurching gait.

p. 285 'Lead soldiers and regimental uniforms': N43, p. 135, 17.2.79. *KS*, p. 35.

p. 286 'Leaving for holiday': N43, p. 96, 25.1.79. *KS*, p. 36.

p. 286 'Late spring, 1912': N43, p. 125, 9.2.79, with title 'Spring, 1912', and notes 'March 1912' (Scott's death) and 'April 1912' (sinking of *Titanic*). *KS*, p. 36.

p. 287 'I go to school': N43, p. 86, 20.1.79. *KS*, p. 37.

p. 287 'The way to school': N43, p. 84, 19.1.79. *KS*, p. 37.

p. 288 'The school upstairs': N43, p. 105, 29.1.79. *KS*, p. 39.

p. 288 'The big room': N43, p. 106, 29–30.1.79. *KS*, p. 39.

p. 289 'My teachers': N43, p. 107, 30.1.79. *KS*, p. 40.

p. 289 'His Majesty's Inspectors': N43, p. 110, 1.2.79. *KS*, p. 40.

There is a portrait of William J.M. Starkie in his daughter Enid Starkie's autobiography, *A Lady's Child* (1941), which was reviewed by Hewitt in *The Bell*, vol. 3, no. 5 (February 1942), p. 402. In 'Planter's Gothic III: an essay in discursive autobiography', *The Bell*, vol. 18, no. 12 (Autumn 1953), pp. 94–103, Hewitt comments:

> When in recent years I read Enid Starkey's [*sic*] excellent autobiography, *A Lady's Child*, I realised the difficulty of the transition from the public to the private face and back again. Her father was not particularly loveable, as she describes him, but she could hardly have been aware of how, for several generations, his features and the horrid mask of a repressive institution so merged as to be indistinguishable one from the other.

Starkie was the last Resident Commissioner of Education for Ireland under British rule.

p. 290 'A dominie's log': N43, p. 81, 17.1.79, with note: 'On 23.1.79, walking along Ormeau Avenue, I saw a couple of buses draw up at the Corporation Public Baths and parties of little schoolgirls dismount and go in.' *KS*, p. 41.

In 'Planter's Gothic III: an essay in discursive autobiography', *The Bell,* vol. 18, no. 12 (Autumn 1953), pp. 94–103, Hewitt writes:

> In 1916 A.S. Neill [1883–1973], now justly celebrated for his educational experiments, published his first book, *A Dominie's Log*, and my father reviewed it with quiet enthusiasm in a monthly journal, and, as volume followed volume, *A Dominie Dismissed* [1917], *A Dominie in Doubt* [1921], *A Dominie Abroad* [1923], *The Problem Child* [1926] and so on I was able to keep track of that fecund and fertilising mind. I still possess some of the books with my father's underlinings and marginalia and can remember how well he retold many of Neill's anecdotes in the correct vernacular pronunciation.

In the poem Hewitt omits *A Dominie's Five* (1924).

p. 290 'Those morning walks': N43, p. 108, 30.1.79. *KS*, p. 41; *S*, p. 86.

p. 291 'Who was C.B. Fry?': N43, p. 109, 31.1.79, with note 'R.C. Trench: *The Study of Words*. Bernard Palissey. See *Self-Help*, Samuel Smiles.' *KS*, p. 42; *S*, p. 87.

In 'How it all started: an autobiographical talk' BBC radio, June 1964, Hewitt states: 'What I learned [about art] I picked up from books at home; for artists' biographies discovering the much-jeered-at Samuel Smiles' *Self-Help* to be a treasure island of which Cellini and Palissey were as heroic denizens as Arkwright and Stephenson.'

Charles Burgess Fry (1872–1956) was an English sportsman and writer who represented Britain in soccer, cricket and athletics and was, for a time, world record-holder for the long jump; Jack London (1876–1916), was an American novelist and socialist.

p. 291 'Going to church': N43, p. 113, 4.2.79. *KS*, p. 42.

p. 292 'The open eye': N43, p. 117, 7.2.79. *KS*, p. 43.

p. 292 'Evangelist': N43, p. 114, 4.2.79. Rep. *Irish Poetry of Faith and Doubt* (1990), p. 90. *KS*, p. 43.

p. 293 'Isaac McKeown': N43, p. 115, 4.2.79. *KS*, p. 44.

p. 293 'Our avenue': N43, p. 103, 29.1.79, with notes 'Dr Wilson. W.J. McGuffin'. *KS*, p. 44.

p. 294 'The Twelfth of July': I cannot find this poem in N43 or in any other notebook. Probably written July 1979. *KS*, p. 45.

p. 294 'The Eleventh Night': N43, p. 142, 7.7.79. *KS*, p. 45.

p. 295 'The river streets': N43, p. 102, 28–9.1.79. *KS*, p. 46. *See also* 'The mortal place' (Appendix I of the present volume).

p. 295 'Portstewart, July 1914' ('Portstewart. Nineteen fourteen. Wille's clutch . . .'): N43, p. 67, 30.11.78, with note '1914'. *KS*, p. 46.

p. 296 'The YCVs and the Ulster Division': N43, p. 120, 7.2.79; p. 143, recast 15.7.79. *KS*, p. 47.

p. 296 'Bangor, spring 1916': N43, p. 129, 10.2.79, with title 'Spring 1916'. *KS*, p. 47.

p. 297 'I still had a friend': N43, p. 128, 9.2.79. *KS*, p. 49. *See also* 'The house at Ballyholme' (second sonnet, l. 4, *LE*, p. 29).

p. 297 'The filled stocking': N43, p. 123, 9.2.79. *KS*, p. 49. A version of this incident is incorporated in Hewitt's 'Ulster commentary', broadcast 19 December 1950.

p. 298 'The carol singers from the church': N43, p. 124, 9.2.79. *KS*, p. 50.

p. 298 'Brown's Bay, Islandmagee, spring 1917': N43, p. 77, 4.1.79, with title 'Brown's Bay 1915'. *KS*, p. 50.

p. 299 'Lost *Argo*, Islandmagee, summer 1919': N43, p. 138, 16.4.79. The poem incorporates revised material from an unpublished poem, 'The yacht', N47, p. 21, 10.1.44. *KS*, p. 51.

p. 299 'The dustcart': N43, p. 137, 6.3.79. *KS*, p. 51.

p. 300 'The "forty-four hours" strike, 1919': N43, p. 131, 12.2.79, with title 'The Forty-Four, 1919'. *KS*, p. 53.

p. 300 'Reading': N43, p. 104, 29.1.79. *KS*, p. 53.
The library referred to is the North Belfast Branch Library, Oldpark Road. Among the writers referred to are Robert Michael Ballantyne (1825–94), author of *The Coral Island* (1857) and George Alfred Henty (1832–1902), best known for adventure stories for boys, such as *Under Drake's Flag* (1883) and *With Clive in India* (1884).

p. 301 'Music lessons': N43, p. 78, 5.1.79. *KS*, p. 54.
Paolo Tosti (1846–1916) was an Italian-born composer and singing teacher.

p. 301 'The dry summer, Islandmagee, 1921': N43, p. 74, 31.12.78, with title 'Islandmagee, 1921'. *KS*, p. 54.

p. 302 'My future wife': N43, p. 111, 3.2.79, with title 'Summer 1921'. *KS*, p. 55.

p. 302 'Free Mason': N43, p. 116, 7.2.79. *KS*, p. 55.

p. 303 'Paid quarterly': N43, p. 65, 29.11.78, with note '*c*. 1919'. *KS*, p. 56.

p. 303 'The Irish dimension': N43, p. 66, 29.11.78, with note '*c*. 1920'. Pub. *Hibernia*, 20 September 1979, untitled. Rep. *The Writers: A Sense of Ireland* (1980), p. 57, described as 'from a sequence "The Troubles 1922"'. *KS*, p. 56; *S*, p. 16. *See also* Hewitt's article 'The family next door', *Evening Press*, 17 August 1970, and *Threshold*, no. 23 (Summer 1970), pp. 14–19.

p. 304 'The King concerned': N43, p. 127, 9.2.79, with title '22nd June 1921'. *KS*, p. 56.
Jan Christiaan Smuts (1870–1950) was a South African statesman who was a member of the Imperial War Cabinet during the First World War.

p. 304 'Going up to Dublin': N43, p. 132, 13.2.79. *KS*, p. 57.

p. 305 'The Troubles, 1922': N43, p. 97, 27.1.79, with title '1922'. *KS*, p. 58.

p. 305 'The prisoners on the roof': N43, p. 99, 27.1.79. Pub. *The Writers: A Sense of Ireland* (1980), p. 57, described as 'from a sequence "The Troubles 1922"'. *KS*, p. 58.

p. 306 'A case of mistaken identity': N43, p. 146, 31.7.79. Pub. *The Writers: A Sense of Ireland* (1980), p. 58, described as 'from a sequence "The Troubles 1922"'. *KS*, p. 59.

p. 306 'After the fire': N43, p. 98, 27.1.79. *KS* p. 59; *S*, p. 34.

p. 307 'Two spectres haunt me': N43, p. 100, 28.1.79. Rep. *That's Life: Einführungskurs Englisch Sek. II* (1984), p. 41. *KS*, p. 60; *S*, p. 33. The 'cycling sergeant' was named Fisher. *See also* 'An Ulsterman in England remembers' (*UR* p. 4), and 'Encounter, nineteen twenty' (*TE*, p. 19).

p. 307 'On Dunmore's waste': N43, p. 101, 28.1.79. *KS*, p. 60.

p. 308 'My grandfather dies, 1923': N43, p. 25, 18.10.78. *KS*, p. 61.

p. 308 'Carnations': N43, p. 11, 23.7.76, with note '1922'; p. 119, 7.2.79, with note '1922'. *KS*, p. 61.

p. 309 'I lie alone': N43, p. 118, 7.2.79, with note '1922'. *KS*, p. 63.

THE SELECTED JOHN HEWITT (*S*), edited and with an introduction by Alan Warner, published by Blackstaff Press, Belfast, 1981. It reprints sixty-eight poems drawn from Hewitt's books and pamphlets to *Kites in Spring* (1980), as well as an extract from *Conacre* and one from the verse play *The Bloody Brae*. Hewitt revised his poem 'The Glens' specially for this edition: *see* the note which follows.

p. 310 'The Glens': N28, pp. 57–8, 8.9.42; N46, pp. 160–1. Pub. *The Bell*, vol. 6, no. 3 (June 1943), pp. 210–12. Rep. *Irish Poems of Today* (1944), p. 15; *New Irish Poets* (1948), p. 87; *A New Romantic Anthology* (1949), p. 130; *Contemporary Irish Poetry* (eds Greacen and Iremonger, 1959), p. 75; *New Poets of Ireland* (1963), p. 40; *Penguin Book of Irish Verse* (1970), p. 346; *Penguin Book of Irish Verse* (1981), p. 364; *Ireland in Poetry* (1990), p. 10; *Poètes d'Irlande du Nord* (1991), p. 18. *NRW*, p. 11; *CP*, p. 23; *PG* [p.5]. In all these versions, ll. 19–20 read:

> I fear their creed as we have always feared
> the lifted hand between the mind and truth.

In Hewitt's interview with Dan Casey (*Quarto*, vol. 7 [1908–1], pp. 1–14), Hewitt comments:

> 'When I wrote that it seemed true to me. I wanted no bar on my thinking. I admitted no censorship of my thought by anyone. But I found that I was giving offence to kindly and gentle Catholics. And looking back on the poem, when I was working over the selection with Alan Warner, I realised that those were arrogant lines. And so I've revised it and, when it appears in *Selected Poems*, the word "truth" will be omitted, or I'll replace it with "lifted hand against unfettered thought", which represents my thinking more exactly. The criticism was valid I think.'

In a letter to John Montague in the spring of 1964, Hewitt remarks:

> Why was I not in the *Oxford Book* [*of Irish Verse*, 1958, eds Donagh MacDonagh and Lennox Robinson]? I was invited and submitted stuff. Lennox told me that I was in with one or two pieces; he wasn't sure. When Mary O'Malley tackled MacDonagh he just said that he lost my stuff and forgot all about it. Years ago when Jack Sweeney was recording poets reading their verse, he came to Belfast with MacDonagh to tape Roy [McFadden] and me. After I had read 'The Glens', that poem with the line 'the lifted hand between the mind and truth', MacDonagh said 'John,

you're a bloody Orangeman'. I think that was consciously or unconsciously at the back of it.

Hewitt had already used the phrase 'unfettered thought' in 'The dilemma', *UR*, p. 3.

MOSAIC (*M*), published by Blackstaff Press, Belfast, 1981. I have included thirty-four of the thirty-seven poems in the original volume. Hewitt reprints, without emendation, 'Chinese fluteplayer', 'From the Chinese of Wang Li Shi' and 'The storm' from *The Chinese Fluteplayer* (1974), and I have placed those three poems in the appropriate place in the present volume. *See also* the note, p. 629, on 'The ruins answer'.

p. 311 'Dedication' ('I owe much thanks to players everywhere . . .'): N37, p. 114, 28–30.5.65. Pub. in the programme for the laying of the foundation stone of the new theatre at Ridgeway Street, Belfast, by Austin Clarke, 12 June 1965, with title 'For Mary O'Malley and the Lyric Players'. Rep. *Lyric Theatre 1951–68,* and *a needle's eye* (1979), p. 47. *M*, p. 1. In the version in *a needle's eye* l. 2 begins 'who've set'; l. 3 begins 'that I have shed'; l. 4 reads 'in rapt occasion of a richer kind'; l. 8 has 'cracking wheels'; l. 10 reads 'and set among the best of their own kind'; l. 11 begins 'the little band'; l. 14 reads 'the Theban monarch's terror, gouged and blind'. This earlier version is quoted in full in *The Theatre in Ulster* by Sam Hanna Bell (Gill and Macmillan, 1972, p. 123).

p. 311 'The path ahead': N40, p. 13, 30.11.71. *M*, p. 2.

p. 311 'Style': N43, p. 155, 8.2.81, with note 'rewritten extensively from earlier draft'. Pub. *Quarto*, vol. 7 (1980–1), p. 15. Rep. *Common Ground Quarterly* (Winter 1983), p. 11. *M*, p. 3. In the *Quarto* version, l. 1 has 'coloured words' and l. 4 'textures strange and new'.

p. 312 'For stonecutters': N43, p. 150, 27.11.80; later version 12.1.81; further version 16.3.81; p. 157, rev. version, 12.4.81. Pub. *Quarto*, vol. 7 (1980–1), p. 16. *M*, p. 4. In the *Quarto* version, l. 3 reads 'define with kerb the viewer's stance'; l. 5 'cut deep or shallow as required'; and the final line has 'the metaphor'.

p. 312 'The iron pot': N43, p. 12, 9.12.76. *M*, p. 5.

p. 313 'Fontanel': N40, p. 75, 22.7.73, with title 'On reading Michael Longley's shorter poems'. Pub. *Fortnight*, no. 178 (October–November 1980), p. 21, with title 'On reading Michael Longley's shorter poems'.
M, p. 6. The *Fortnight* version reads:

> This bearded fellow, laughing,
> friendly, fond of jazz,
> a witty mimic,
> seems to be a large,
> an affable extrovert.
>
> Nevertheless he clenches
> the convolutions of his thought,
> and will not liberate

his wren, his badger, to follow
their hinted purposes outside
the coded casket of
his intricate syllables.

I want for the badger to lurch
over to nuzzle my boot
offering to share his secret,
and the wren to contract
till it split open, explode in
a featherstorm of canticles.

p. 313 'Mosaic': N40, p. 27, 8.2.72. Pub. *The First Ten Years: Dublin Arts Festival Poetry* (1979), p. 23. Rep. *Quarto* (Winter 1987–8), p. 20. *M*, p. 7.

p. 314 'Memorial service': N39, pp. 115–16, 27.2.71, with title 'Sunset and evening star, or please be in your place by 10.45 a.m.'. *M*, p. 8.

p. 314 'Prague, or Novotny, if you remember him': N38, pp. 83–4, 1.6.68, with title 'Novotny'. *M*, p. 9.

p. 315 'Moscow moment': N43, p. 4, 7.7.76. *M*, p. 10.

p. 316 'Agrigento, Sicily': N40, pp. 40–1, with note 'found in notebook, revised 15.3.73'. *M*, p. 11.

p. 317 'The man from Malabar': N34, pp. 94–5, 28–9.7.54; N41, pp. 65–6. Pub. *Irish Times*, 21 August 1954, with title 'The drum and the song'. Rep. *Common Ground Quarterly* (Winter 1983), p. 11. *PG* [p. 8]; *M*, p. 12. In the *Irish Times* version, ll. 13–14 read 'a narrow jungle track,/a six-note village mode'; and l. 18 has 'strange alien cry'.

p. 317 'The Covenanter's grave': N43, p. 151, 17.1.81, with title 'The grave of the Reverend Adrian Crawford'. *M*, p. 13. Hewitt tells this story in prose in a chapter entitled 'Donegore', originally intended for inclusion in 'A North Light'.

p. 318 'Variations on a theme': N38, pp. 127–36, 13–18.3.69, with title 'The mini-skirt: a digression'; N43, pp. 17–19, final part, with title 'Postscript to Variations on a Theme' and note '1st week in June 1978'. Pub. *Threshold*, no. 31 (Autumn–Winter 1980), pp. 31–5. *M*, p. 14. Compare section 8 and 'I learn about art' (*KS*, p. 35).

'Boucher's pink rococo dame' refers to the painting *Louise O'Morphi sur un divan* by François Boucher (1703–70); Otterlo is the location of the Kröller-Müller Museum, situated sixty miles from Amsterdam; Pieter Jansz Saenredam (1597–1665) was a Dutch painter; Jean-Baptiste Siméon Chardin (1699–1779) was a French painter; Jan Vermeer (1632–75) was a Dutch painter; Oskar Kokoschka (1886–1980) was a painter of Czech and Austrian parentage who spent his formative years in Vienna; Nicolas Poussin (1593/4–1665) was a French painter; Samuel Palmer (1805–81) was an English landscape painter; Jack Butler Yeats (1871–1957) was an Irish painter; Giovanni Battista Cinna, known as Cinna da Conegliano (*c.* 1459–*c.* 1517) was a Venetian painter; Erwin Panofsky (1892–1968) was a German art historian; Ernst H. Gombrich (1909–) is a British art historian and scholar; and Bernhard Berenson (1865–1959) was an art historian, best known for *The Italian Painters of the Renaissance* (1930).

p. 322 'Our Sunday School teacher': N43, p. 87, 20.1.79, with title 'The Ethopian eunuch', and notes 'Miss Robertson. Rev. J.C. [G?] R. John Charles M.A.'; p. 152, rev. version, 19.1.81. *M*, p. 20.

p. 322 'The psychometrist's remarkable forecast': N43, p. 148, 3.1.80, with title/note 'My mother takes me to Mrs Smeltzer, the psychometrist'. *M*, p. 21. *See also* Hewitt's 'How it all started: an autobiographical talk', BBC radio, June 1964:

> Sometime in the spring or summer of 1916, when I was not yet nine years old, and when we were living with my maternal grandmother in Bangor, Co. Down, for some obscure reason or on a sudden impulse – she was a woman of impulse – my mother took me to a clairvoyante or, to be more precise, what we should now call a psychometrist, a Mrs Smeltzer, for 'a reading'. When I was introduced, the lady, tall, English, grey, serious, asked me for something from my person. I unlatched and gave her my belt, one of those striped canvas-elastic belts with the catch shaped like a snake. She held this in her hands on her lap and closed her eyes. After an enormous silence, she began, slowly and then with greater vigour, to describe forms which hovered about me. My mother recognised from the description that her father, dead nearly twenty years before, was one of them. They all communicated goodwill toward me and offers of help 'from their side'. Then Mrs Smeltzer said 'I see pencils and brushes and things. The boy's future will be bound up in Art. Yes. They are nodding approval.'

The concluding lines of the poem refer to the fact that Hewitt's father and mother, and his mother's elder sister and eldest brother, were or had been teachers. Hewitt himself, having spent two years at Stranmillis College, Belfast, was qualified to teach.

p. 323 'A great headmaster': N29, p. 50, 20.11.43, with title 'On a great headmaster' and note 'James Watson Henderson M.A., Headmaster, Methodist College, Belfast'. *M*, p. 22.

p. 323 'A house demolished': N43, p. 158, 26.4.81, with title 'The demolition of 96 Clifton Park Avenue'. *M*, p. 23.

p. 324 'The ruins answer': N7, pp. 42–6, dated February 1937/March 1939, with title 'Prelude to decision'; N22, pp. 6–11, 20.2.37, with title 'Phalanx' and note 'Rev. March '37. Rev. fully March 1939'; N29, pp. 137–42, finished 6.8.44, with notes: 'A new draft of a poem first written in early spring 1937, recast in 1939, called variously "Phalanx" or "Prelude to decision". Latest version printed as second part of *Compass*, 1944.' Further note: 'There is a later draft still'; N43, p. 149, additional stanzas for original version 6.8.80. First published version appeared as second part of *Compass* (1944); second published version appeared in *No Rebel Word*, p. 53. *M*, p. 24.

The version in *Compass* and *No Rebel Word* reads as follows:

> What now for future's Europe; where they wait
> the hoped event that must for most be late;
> and even those not yet involved with death
> draw harsh and crippled breath

till all can turn to life released again,
slow and repetitive in word and thought,
loving the gestures by our fathers taught,
essaying simple clumsy gestures of our own?

To let this be, to bring again the life
unregimented lazy talkative;
to build a world where one might catch a glance
and, eager, stop to dance,
sure of the guarantee of friendly touch
there will be found no twist of tongue or heart;
where none chides him who walks apart
because they know by now his silence makes them rich:

can we presume a politicians' peace,
tooled with grave saws and text-book instances,
ordered statistical benevolent
on listed precedent,
and not then find the avalanche of time,
tilting its course these hundred years,
and greased to skidding by our cynic fears,
will leave the crowded valley only its white name?

To bring this good life? Must we lean on prayer
to some grey shadow that we hope will care;
or by submission of our personal
peevish erratic will
to some tall-pyloned steady discipline,
charged by a class or one man's brilliant mind?
The ruins answer: Truth is found
in random blowing seed and not in lettered stone.

The lichened Christ, so pierced by theory
we miss the timber of the riddled tree,
or hoisted so above our fumbling reach
we have no strength to touch
the human comfort of his wounded side,
cannot draw out from any face
the sweat of glory and the light of grace
and must stand powerless till we choose a wiser road.

Shall science then release a rule of light,
laying its harness on the shuddering might
of pounding waters, to eliminate
indifference to fate?
Weigh well the proffered evidence: the skill
that only knows the scalpel's way to truth
may heal the sore upon the broken mouth,
but leave the loosened tongue a crazy dream to tell.

Can art make certain justice moves in men?
Art can but jig according to the tune:

this man had fist to chisel and to break
dumb stone awake,
a lecher-king's whim cracked him to his best;
and this tore music from the thunder once
at order of a frothy prince;
this graven sonnet was a noisy coward's boast.

These all are at time's mercy, good or bad
as foolish man's divided heart may bid;
so long forgotten now the loving will,
you cannot hope to tell
what lease you or your children may expect
for this imperilled tenancy.
Already the sour fields in sickness lie,
gutted by reckless passion, savaged by neglect.

Alone you cannot stem the tide of drought.
Walk soberly upon your rented plot
and set the ways in order; tend with care
what roots or blossoms there:
be happy to achieve a rounded shape
for hours and pulses of your family;
graft your brave fancies to a fruiting tree,
and bid the slow thought bulge like autumn-drowsy grape.

Hope hard for this. But if disaster come,
falling like flame or summoned by no drum,
the high wall can no more than bramble hedge
turn terror's frosty edge.
There still may gape your hearth against the moon,
not by man's hate, nor bomber's load.
See the long field that crammed the threshing shed
where the grey rush resumes its rank dominion.

To win the life our aching needs define
we must pace humbly to an older shrine;
we must unbuckle our stiff arrogance,
and grip each spinning chance
to offer texture to the actual sense,
bidding the heart rehearse within the dream
the proven password and the proper name
whereunder, singing, life's gay images advance.

We must seek back for any clue of worth
to keep beneath our feet a friendly earth,
wherefrom, for all our notions, we derive
the right to live,
which will withdraw that right if we forsake
the wisdom of the seasons' round,
and bank instead on a system slickly planned
meekly to offer less than it intends to take.

For the bare mind, unable to devise
the sphere of truth from what each sense supplies,
shifts its rough freightage so, that way or this
by switching emphasis,
till the tense balance shivers out too far,
and the bow plunges as we try by talk
to bluff the wave to wash us past the rock,
too ignorant to trust a vindicated star.

We shall not gain that equipoise unless
we learn to answer blessing – and to bless,
else on a dusty cinder man shall wait
the clout of fate,
too sick to mark the mocking epitaph;
'All these long years within the swineherd's hut
their brittle logic never would admit
the anxious father's welcome and the fatted calf.'

p. 327 'The neglected lane': N13, pp. 11–12, with title 'The lane', dated September 1937; N22, pp. 108–9, 9.9.37, with title 'The lane'; N44, p. 39, with title 'The lane' and note: 'My first colloquial blank verse, catching, to my surprise, something of the tone of Edward Thomas. Lane was at back of Cavehill.' *M*, p. 29.

p. 328 'On a country bus forty years ago': N24, p. 113, 29.12.39; N45, p. 176, with title 'Sonnet: bus journey' and note 'Larne to Carnlough'. *M*, p. 30.

p. 329 'The Curfew Tower': N7, pp. 51–5, April 1938, with title 'Turnley's Tower'; N23, pp. 35–40, 11–14.4.38, with title 'Turnley's Tower'. There is an ms. version among Hewitt's papers, described as 'second version' and dated 1980. *M*, p. 31; *DC* (1984), p. 73.

p. 333 'October sonnets': N43, p. 22, 16.10.78 (first sonnet); p. 23, 16–17.10.78 (second sonnet); p. 24, 17–18.10.78 (third sonnet); p. 75, 4.1.79 (fourth sonnet); p. 76, 4.1.79 (seventh sonnet); p. 90, 22.1.79 (fifth sonnet); p. 91, 23.1.79 (sixth sonnet). First sonnet rep. *Common Ground Quarterly* (Winter 1983), p. 11. *M*, p. 37.

In relation to the fourth sonnet, *see also* 'My father's death in hospital' (*TE*, p. 24), and 'A father's death' (*RD*, p. 32). In relation to the seventh sonnet, *see also* 'North-west passage: an old man dying' (*LE*, p. 1), and the note on this poem, p. 633.

p. 335 'The free foot': N33, p. 51, 7.8.51. Pub. *Irish Times,* 12 July/30 August 1952, with title 'Sonnet'. *DC* (1969), p. 11; *M* p. 41. In the version in *DC* (1969), l. 2 begins 'thrusting sudden'; ll. 6–8 read 'or once, when we were out, through scarfing airs/of daybreak striding, to inspect the snares/with which he pegged the sleeping neighbourhood'; l. 9 begins 'Now you may hear him'; l. 10 begins 'dog or that child'; l. 12 ends 'for all your own lack'.

p. 336 'Salute': N31, p. 27, 10.10.47; N41, p. 103, with titles 'Salute' and 'Recognition'. Pub. *Irish Times,* 17 January 1948. *M*, p. 42.

p. 336 'The little house': N34, p. 43, 29.8.53. Pub. *Irish Times,* 31 October 1953. Rep. *Common Ground Quarterly* (Winter 1983), p. 11. *M*, p. 43.

p. 337 'Sunset': N24, p. 139, 26.1.40. First pub., untitled, in *CF* [p. 8]. *M*, p. 47.

p. 337 'Vigil': N32, p. 36, 4.12.49. *CF* [p. 1]; *M*, p. 48. In the *CF* version, l. 1 has 'wait for meaning'.

LOOSE ENDS (*LE*), published by Blackstaff Press, Belfast, 1983. I have reprinted all forty-two poems, including the dedicatory poem, from the original volume, and incorporated below the notes provided by Hewitt at the end of the volume.

p. 338 'For Jean': N43, p. 8, between poems dated 27.8.76 and 15.9.76, with title 'Lines to a friend (Jean Craig)'; rev., p. 164, 23.8.82. There is an unnumbered ms. notebook among Hewitt's papers that contains various drafts of this poem, dated 28–9.8.76. Pub. *Irish Press*, 20 November 1976, with title 'Lines to a friend'. Dedicatory poem to *LE*.

The *Irish Press* version reads as follows:

> Dear girl, dream-daughter of my widowed age,
> my lost youth beckoned, comely substitute
> for one who was the anchor of my days
> and cornerstone of all I strove to build,
> now riven from me roughly out of time;
> or so I figured in my loneliness,
> calling these masks out of my fantasy –
> too great a weight for any face to wear.
>
> Yet I should be absolved, for it was you,
> known since your birth, your parents were our friends,
> your brother, sisters threaded through our lives;
> imagination claimed you next of kin,
> you with the candid eyes, the ready song,
> who sparked the tinder in my withered heart.

p. 338 'North-west passage: an old man dying': N40, pp. 34–5, 12–13.3.73, with title 'North-west passage'. The dying man is Andrew Millar (1896–1974), who was married to Roberta Hewitt's sister, Peggy. *LE*, p. 1. Rep., with questions, NI GCE 'A' level English Literature, Paper III (1986), p. 2. *See also* the seventh of the 'October sonnets' (*M*, p. 40).

p. 339 'The reference': N36, pp. 27–9, 1966, with title 'The militant'; N38, pp. 20–2, 29–30.11.66, with title 'For R.P. (Reg Perry)'. *LE*, p. 2. Reg Perry was a social worker and probation officer whom the Hewitts knew in Coventry at a time when they acted as short-term foster parents for a number of teenage children.

p. 340 'The portrait': N24, pp. 84–6, 25–9.11.39, with title 'Retreat'. Hewitt notes: '"a crayon portrait by a hand I knew" – William Conor, RHA (1881–1968)'. *LE*, p. 4.

p. 342 'A difficult man': N40, pp. 22–3, 30–1.12.71. *LE*, p. 7. The subject of the poem is Hewitt's friend, the painter William J. McClughin. *See also* 'William J. McClughin (1900–1971)' (*OMT*, p. 35). The lecture on shadow was given in the summer of 1936 during a walk from Donegore Hill to Ballyclare.

p. 343 'Drypoint': N36, pp. 30–1, with title 'An artist: SBMcC'; N38, pp. 26–7, 15.12.66, with title 'S.B.McC'. *LE*, p. 8. The subject of the poem is Samuel B. McCreery, who figures also in an unpublished poem, N45, p. 45, 30.1.39, with the title 'To the [strange] memory of S.B. McCreery, died 11.11.38'. In his article 'Artist, actor, teacher, friend', *Belfast Telegraph*, 6 July 1957, Hewitt writes as follows:

> Samuel B. McCreery, who died in 1938 in his middle twenties, was a student at the College of Art. A tall gaunt fellow with a slight stoop accentuated by his hanging tie, I found him as difficult to deal with as any of his fellows. His painting was, naturally, immature – Frank Brangwyn was his idol. His rather cubist wood carvings held promise, but in his drypoint etchings he showed true ability.
>
> A solitary person, given to long walks to which his long legs were well adapted, he used often to carry a copper plate in his pocket, upon which he would draw swiftly a subject that caught his attention. One print of a sow from his hand is as good of its kind as anything I know.
>
> Perhaps fired by the example of some other folk he met in our house, he suddenly took to verse writing. These verses had a clear spare visual quality and a surprising modernity of form. Just at that time I was literary editor for a certain short-lived journal [*Irish Jewry*], and, thinking to please Sam – for, in my experience, poets love to see their work in print – I put a couple of his tiny poems into my columns, without the formality of asking the poet's permission.
>
> This was, of course, very wrong and discourteous of me. I should have had better manners, but I thought he would be pleasantly surprised. But it was I who was surprised; for, a day or two after publication, Sam strode in, walked round the living-room, lifted down the paintings he had lent us, bundled them up with the wooden figures, and marched out with his cargo, mumbling. I never saw him again. And when a year or so later I learned of his death I felt the finality of it with some remorse.
>
> I still keep his little imagist poem, 'The nest', safe in my private anthology:
>
> I found
> the nest
> belonging to the hen
> that laid away
> thirteen eggs
> all pointing in
> beneath a rusty plough.

p. 344 'The test': N39, pp. 100–1, 20.1.71, with title 'The man from Bangalore'. *LE*, p. 10.

p. 345 'Calling on Peadar O'Donnell at Dungloe': N28, pp. 13–14, 16.1.42, with title 'Remembered from August in West Donegal'; N46, p. 136, 16.1.42, with title 'Peadar'. Pub. *The Bell*, vol. 4, no. 4 (July 1942), p. 232, with the title 'Peadar O'Donnell'. Rep. *The Best from the Bell* (1978), p. 88; *Contemporary Irish Poetry* (ed. Bradley, 1988), p. 106; *Fortnight*, no. 290 (December 1990), in a special supplement on the work of Sam Hanna Bell, Joseph Tomelty and Peadar O'Donnell. *LE*, p. 12.

The version in *The Bell* reads as follows:

> I remember walking through the August twilight
> along the narrow lane from house to house
> the boys still playing hurley loud and shouting
> and a black calf that turned with mournful cry.
>
> It seemed the long way round that we had taken
> over a rough ground higher than the bog.
> Three fields away white foam was on the breakers.
> Storm's opposition made us both dog-tired.
>
> Then darkness came and window after window
> held out its yellow candle. We went on
> slow pacing now and painfully admonished
> by gulls that cried above the water's din.
>
> We reached the three small houses and the gate
> that faced them where the drive turned to the right.
> It was too late to make a call we argued;
> there was no blink of light in any room.
>
> But half-way down the drive we saw the writer
> still working in the garden with his wife.
> I shouted and he straightened up to answer
> and in the gloom his fine head glimmered white.

p. 346 'The ballad' ('When I sought out the Cottage Hospital . . .'): N43, pp. 5–6, 25.8.76, with note/title 'Mrs Stone, or You've made my day'. There is a version of this poem in an unnumbered ms. notebook among Hewitt's papers, with the title 'The made day' (cancelled) and 'You've made my day', dated 25.8.76; there is another undated version in the same notebook, with the title 'Mrs Stone, or the made day'. *LE*, p. 13. Hewitt's note in *LE* identifies the ballad as ' "The man from God knows where", from *The Coming of the Earls* (1918) by Florence L. Wilson'.

p. 347 'The clink of rhyme': N33, pp. 24–5, 25.7.51, with title/note 'An exercise in Standard Habbie (my first attempt)'; N36, pp. 16–17, 1951, with title 'An exercise in Standard Habbie'. *LE*, p. 15. Hewitt glosses 'caillaigh' as 'an old woman'.

p. 348 'Folk custom': N33, pp. 112–13, 17.3.52; N36, p. 8. *LE*, p. 16.

p. 349 'MacDonnell's question': N10, p. 26, part XXVII of 'The Red Hand: a poemosaic'; N20, p. 136, 28–9.5.36, with title 'Sorley Boy'. *LE*, p. 17. Hewitt notes:

> Sorley Boy (1505–1590), Chief of Clandonnell.
>
> The massacre on Rathlin took place in 1575.
>
> Sir Arthur Chichester (1563–1625), Governor of Carrickfergus, Admiral of Lough Neagh, one of the leading organisers and the chief beneficiary of the Plantation of Ulster. His funerary monument was commissioned and

probably delivered during his lifetime. His elder brother Sir John was killed in a skirmish at Altfrackin, near Carrickfergus, in 1597; Sir James MacDonnell was poisoned in 1601.

p. 349 'The house on the hill': N30, pp. 128–32, with title 'The house at Leamore', 26–8.8.46; N47, pp. 107–10, with title 'The house at Liamore'. *LE*, p. 18. The house is Glenville, near Cushendall. Hewitt notes: ' "mass upon a rock", "the altar in the woods" – Glendun; "kinsman with another crew" – Sir Roger Casement'.

p. 352 'This Antrim air in summer': N35, p. 115, 29.12.58; N41, p. 76. *LE*, p. 21.

p. 352 'Autumn gale': N31, p. 85, 23.10.48; N36, p. 20, with title 'An autumn moment'. *LE*, p. 22.

p. 352 'The old mill-race': N33, p. 20, 15.2.51 (this may be an error for 15.4.51), with title 'The weir at Edenderry'; N36, p. 18, with title 'The old weir' and '(?)Mill Race'. *LE*, p. 23.

p. 353 'The descent': N22, p. 112, 17.9.37; N44, p. 36. *LE*, p. 24.

p. 353 'The souterrain': N29, p. 87, 27.12.43; N47, p. 17. *LE*, p. 25. Hewitt notes: 'underground stone-built passage and chamber, near Doagh, in the valley of the Sixmilewater, where many of these have been found'.

p. 354 'Palimpsest': N36, p. 24, 1962; N37, p. 72, 10–11.8.62. *LE*, p. 26; *DC* (1984), p. 77. Hewitt glosses 'wallstead' as 'roofless ruin of house or cottage' and notes: ' "tree-dark glen", the upper reaches of the Glens now undergoing afforestation'.

p. 354 'The Christmas Rhymers, Ballynure, 1941': N43, p. 163, 25.7.82, with title 'For Christmas Rhymers, Ballynure, 1941' and note 'First draft 1941'; N46, p. 127, 27.12.41, with title 'Sonnet: Christmas Rhymers' and note: 'Jane Millar said something like this. JM died autumn 1943, aged 80.' Pub. *Labour Progress* (December 1943), with title 'The Christmas Rhymers'. *LE*, p. 27. Hewitt notes: 'substance of this from an old Ballyeaston woman in 1941'; ' "The Doctor, Darkie and Wee Divil Doubt", characters from mummers' play performed in S.E. Antrim'.

The version in *Labour Progress* reads as follows:

(In parts of South-East Antrim, at Christmas, lads dress up and go about the countryside performing their traditional play in farmhouses. The substance of the following was told me by an old woman of that locality, in December, 1941.)

The Christmas Rhymers came this year again;
  Mere boys they were, and hammered on the door
With 'We're the Rhymers. Open up before
  Wee Devil Doubt has counted up to ten,
Or we'll do mischief.' So I barged them then,
  From upstairs window, though my heart was sore
For those that ranted on the kitchen floor,
  And are not here now, being fighting men.
And as they tiptoed back along the lane,
  A straggling disappointed regiment,

Without a word – Saint George and Humpy Jack,
The Doctor, Devil Doubt, and all their train,
I knew that more than Christmas Rhymers went
Into the shadows never to come back.

p. 355 'Encounter with R.J. Welch, the antiquary': N43, p. 134, 15.2.79, with title 'Meeting R.J. Welch for the first time'. *LE*, p. 28. Hewitt notes: 'Robert Welch (1859–1936), geologist, photographer'. Welch, who lived for some sixty years at 49 Lonsdale Street, was a familiar figure to Hewitt from boyhood.

p. 355 'The house at Ballyholme': N43, pp. 52–3, 22.11.78, basis of first sonnet; 23.11.78, basis of second sonnet; rev. p. 153, 20.1.81; p. 160, 28.6.81; p. 161, 29.6.81. *LE*, p. 29. The poem refers to the home at Bangor, County Down, of Hewitt's maternal grandmother and his experiences there are also the subject of the following poems in *KS*: 'Ellendene', 'What little happened there', 'My grandmother's restlessness', 'The tricycle', 'Bangor, spring 1916' and 'I still had a friend' (which deals with the 'mitching' incident referred to in l. 4 of the second sonnet).

p. 356 'My widowed mother': N43, p. 92, 24.1.79, with title '1877–1958' and note 'St Gerard's R.C. Church, Antrim Road'. *LE*, p. 30.

p. 356 'Bandstand': N34, p. 61, 21.12.53, with title 'The bandstand'. *LE*, p. 31.

p. 357 'For Roberta in the garden': N40, p. 68, 19.6.73, with title 'For Roberta'; N43, p. 162, rev. 24.7.82, with title 'For Roberta in the garden'. Rep. (in English) in Japanese newspaper, *Mainichi Daily News*. *LE*, p. 32.

p. 357 'The hedgehog: for R.': N39, pp. 29–30, 27.9.69; N41, p. 35. *LE*, p. 33.

p. 357 'At the newsagent's': N43, p. 154, 7.2.81, with title 'Inadvent'[?], 'In Advent'[?]. *LE*, p. 34. The newsagent's is in Balmoral Avenue, Belfast.

p. 359 'The bombed public house': N43, p. 3, 5.7.76. *LE*, p. 36. Rep. *The Pure Drop* (1987), p. 43. The playwright is Brendan Behan (1923–64); *see also* chapter 36 of 'A North Light' (pp. 195–8), titled 'Brendan Boy'. The foreign poet is the Russian, Yevgeny Yevtushenko, who visited the Department of Slavonic Studies at Queen's University Belfast and the Club Bar, University Road, on 17 October 1975.

p. 359 'Executives third tier': N39, p. 102, 20.1.71; N41, p. 2. Pub. *Honest Ulsterman*, no. 70 (November–December 1981), p. 51. *LE*, p. 37.

p. 360 'Administration': N39, p. 46, 23.10.69. *LE*, p. 38.

p. 360 'By air to Birmingham on a mid-June evening': N40, pp. 50–4, 23.3.73, with note 'from draft 7/10.6.71'. *LE*, p. 39.

p. 362 'Rotterdam': N38, p. 97, 14.10.68, with title 'Rotterdam, or monopoly capitalism'; N41 p. 45, with title 'Europort'. *LE*, p. 42.

p. 363 'To the people of Dresden': N32, p. 32, 19.2.59, with title 'Dresden'; N36, p. 34, rev. 4.1.82; N37, p. 4, with title 'For the people of Dresden'. German translation pub. *Stadt und Gemeinde*, vol. 3, no. 4 (1959), p. 11, with account of Hewitt's visit to Dresden. *LE*, p. 43. Rep. *Pace*, vol 17, no. 2 (Summer–Autumn 1985), p. 8, with note: 'This sonnet was written after the poet had taken part in a peace demonstration in Dresden in February, 1959, on the anniversary of the Allied raids, 13–14 February, 1945; he was there with others to represent the bombed city of Coventry, where he was Director of the Art Gallery and Museum.' Hewitt provides a similar note in *LE. See also* Hewitt's article 'A Dresden notebook: some aspects of art under Communism', *Threshold*, vol. 3, no. 2 (Summer 1959), pp. 47–60.

p. 363 'Winter park': N40, p. 108, 24.11.74. *LE*, p. 44.

p. 363 'On the preservation of work sheets': N40, p. 85, 7.11.73. *LE*, p. 45.

p. 364 'Dissertation I': N40, p. 64, 16.6.73, with title 'Being made a subject for research. For Brian Bidwell' (should be Bruce Bidwell). *LE*, p. 46.

p. 364 'Dissertation II': N40, p. 65, 18.6.73, with title 'Dissertation'. Pub. *Poetry Ireland Newsletter*, no. 3 (March 1983). *LE*, p. 47.

p. 365 'In recollection of Drumcliffe, September 1948': N37, p. 113, 28–30.5.65. Printed in the programme for the laying of the foundation stone of the new theatre at Ridgeway Street, Belfast, by Austin Clarke, 12 June 1965. Rep. *Lyric Theatre 1951–68* and in *a needle's eye* (1979), p. 47; in these versions, l. 7 begins 'will wear'; l. 9 has 'his thought'; l. 11 begins 'and find his stance'; and l. 13 begins 'his chaunted cadence'. *LE*, p. 48.

p. 365 'First honey': N31, p. 57, 21.8.48; N36, p. 21. *LE*, p. 49.

p. 366 'Retreaded rhymes': N43, p. 159, June 1982, with title 'Addendum to ['Interim'] in *No Rebel Word'. See* note on 'Interim', p. 580. Hewitt notes: 'The first ten lines are from "Interim" (*No Rebel Word*, 1948); the last five lines from "Freehold" in *Lagan*, 1946.' Rep. *Andersonstown News*, 11 June 1983. *LE*, p. 50. In the version of 'Interim' in *NRW*, the first line reads 'Henceforth my slow skill I must only spend'; l. 8 has 'to those emotions'; and l. 9 has 'spring and fall'.

p. 366 'Lines for a dead alderman': N34, p. 47, 13.9.53, with title 'Comment for a councillor'. Pub. *Honest Ulsterman*, no. 2 (June 1968), p. 10, with title 'Elegy for an enemy'. *LE*, p. 51. The version in the *Honest Ulsterman* reads as follows:

> Justice was done in the end:
> the rascal that in his day
> walked with the Town as his friend
> slipped quickly into the clay,
> and the mourners drove away
> to board-room, office or game;
> the moss crawls over his name.
>
> But, Lord, it is long to wait
> till the evil that man did
> with the hurt born of his hate
> lies under his coffin-lid;
> the earth may never be rid
> of his malice this side of time
> if I let it tarnish my rime.

The alderman is Percy Tougher, Unionist chairman of the committee which denied Hewitt the directorship of the Belfast Museum and Art Gallery in 1953. *See* Hewitt's articles 'From chairman and committee men, Good Lord deliver us', *Honest Ulsterman*, no. 6 (September 1968), pp. 16–22, rep. *Ancestral Voices: The Selected Prose of John Hewitt* (ed. Tom Clyde, 1987), pp. 48–55; and

'The family next door', *Evening Press,* 17 August 1970, rep. *Threshold,* no. 23 (Summer 1970), pp. 14–19.

p. 367 'St Stephen's Day': N9, p. 127, 29.12.29; N19, p. 49; N36, p. 38; N45, p. 137, 29.12.29, with notes: 'after a walk round Westland Road' and 'revised July 1943'. *SOT* [p. 12]; *LE,* p. 52. Rep. *Contemporary Irish Poetry* (ed. Bradley, 1988), p. 106. The version in *SOT* reads:

> St Stephen's Day: the sun was warm;
> it seemed a prelude of the spring,
> though robins pecked at withered haws
> and stiff-necked swans were on the wing.
>
> The old men bundled in their coats
> hop blinking out to catch the sun,
> as though like jewel-headed toads
> at last they'd split chill winter's stone.

THE DAY OF THE CORNCRAKE: POEMS OF THE NINE GLENS (*DC*), published by the Glens of Antrim Historical Society, n.p., 1984, with paintings by Charles McAuley, an introduction by Jack McCann and the following foreword by Hewitt:

> This is not an exact reprint of the first edition; three poems have been omitted and eight added, released from copyright or taken from later books published by the Blackstaff Press. By far the most obvious and significant change is in the twenty-five reproductions of paintings by Charles McAuley, the Glensman artist.
>
> I cannot here offer a comprehensive essay on Art in the Glens of Antrim. It is sufficient to remark that by the second decade of the century James Humbert Craig (1878–1944) had developed a pictorial mode for representing the landscape of fields, rivers, hills, headlands, shore and clouds over them in a widely acceptable yet sensitive manner, for he knew the Glens well and had a cottage for thirty years at Cushendun. His response in less professional hands became something of a convention, a style ready made for the range of subjects. Indeed Craig himself, now and then answering popular expectations, fell into a slacker realisation of his visual experience, all the easier to imitate.
>
> Charles McAuley, when he began to paint, had some advice from Craig. It was inevitable that the lad should have been attracted to and influenced by the current convention. But it became increasingly evident that as a Glensman born and bred he should take the landscape as his own terrain, inhabited by folk he knew and belonged to. His growing awareness was not merely graphic but demographic. This has made him for me the authentic regional artist, the painter who belongs to and finds his themes in a known place. Nowadays with the rapid flow of international styles succeeding each other, this is a distinctive title one can seldom confer. To share a book with him, then, is a satisfaction and a pleasure which could never have entered my mind when, over forty years ago, I first stopped to

see through the window of his house in Shore Street that tall young man working at his easel.

The three poems not reprinted from the first edition of 1969 are 'The booleys', 'Black and white' and 'The bell'. The eight poems added to the first edition are 'The fairy-man at Layde' (rep. from *TE*, p. 16), 'The Glens of Antrim' (rep. from *RD*, p. 16), 'Colour' (rep. from *CP*, p. 57), 'The gap' (rep. from *CP*, p. 84), 'Ossian's grave, Lubitavish, County Antrim' (rep. from *CP*, p. 106), 'The Curfew Tower' (rep. from *M*, p. 31), 'The true smith of Tieveragh' (rep. from *RD*, p. 24) and 'Palimpsest' (rep. from *LE*, p. 26).

p. 368 'The gentle bush': N32, pp. 38–9, 29.12.49. Pub. *Irish Times*, 18 February 1950. Rep. *British Weekly*, 2 August 1951; *Belfast Telegraph*, 2 October 1954. *DC* (1969), p. 13; *DC* (1984), p. 19. In the 1984 edition of *DC* Hewitt omitted l. 5 of the original version, which read 'yet who can say? So they have heard'.

FREEHOLD AND OTHER POEMS (*F*), published by Blackstaff Press, Belfast, 1986, with the dedication 'For Deirdre and Shirley, Eileen's daughters' (Hewitt's nieces, Deirdre Todhunter and Shirley Mackie). I have reprinted all the poems from this volume, including the dramatic poem *The Bloody Brae*, and incorporated, where appropriate, the notes and glossary provided by Hewitt at the end of the volume.

p. 369 *Freehold:* this poem was conceived as a sequel to *Conacre* (1943), and material later incorporated in or adapted for the final version is to be found in a number of Hewitt's notebooks. N13, pp. 70–2, February 1939, poem with title 'Chapel dusk' became part of *Freehold*: 'II The lonely heart'; N23, pp. 154–6, 1.2.39, 'Chapel dusk', with note: 'Visit to chapel in Warrenpoint, January, 1939'; N28, pp. 73–5, 13.9.42; pp. 76–8, with title 'Feathers on turf', material used in 'Roll call', with note: 'Fragments of a projected long poem, written 25.3.42, mislaid until 17.9.42', and a further note: '*The Bell*, 1944, August [error], modified into couplets for *Freehold*'; N30, p. 81, 3.12.45, with title 'Fragment for long poem'; pp. 86–96, with title 'Fragments for a long poem' and note 'written in October [1945(?)]'; p. 97 has note: 'The rest of *Freehold* was written and the whole revised during January and February [1946]. This included the recasting of "Chapel – country town" and "Townland of peace" in couplets'; N45, p. 39, 1.2.39, 'Chapel dusk', with note: 'Modified in couplets for *Freehold* section "The lonely heart" ', and further note, 'Written after a visit to Rostrevor and Warrenpoint'; N46, pp. 164–5, 13.9.42, with title 'Feathers on turf' and note 'with emendations and extension in "Freehold", 1946'.

The first section of *Freehold* to be published was the opening seventy-eight lines (approximately) of 'Townland of peace', which appeared in *The Bell*, vol. 9, no. 1 (October 1944), pp. 10–12; this section also appeared in *No Rebel Word*, p. 22 (*see* notes below). The entire poem was published in *Lagan*, vol. 2, no. 1 (1946, described as no. 4 on front cover), pp. 23–44; in this version, section III, 'Townland of peace', was recast in couplets (*see* notes below) and there was a fifth section, with the title 'Roll call', which I have reprinted in Appendix 1 of the present volume.

p. 369 'I Feathers on turf': in the version published in *Lagan*, l. 20 begins 'that lives'; l. 45 ('the patriarchal heron stands alone') is followed by twenty-two lines omitted from the final version:

> We'd learned from men on roads and men at gates,
> but most from one man sitting by his nets
> on the bare stretch of turf above the sand
> where the broad rowboats snuggle to the land
> like sucking pigs against the friendly sow:
> that lads these days will never learn to row
> like those fine crews that kept for twenty years
> their graceful and unbeatable careers
> coached by the doctor; how that field of grain
> was ricked too soon, far better risk the rain
> than build before it's dry; and how a tinker played
> a nasty trick once, after he had made
> a still-worm for a farmer back a bit,
> by sneaking to the police with word of it;
> and how an old account book long since lost
> told of the watchmen paid to tramp the coast
> and keep all beggars out; and how to-day,
> what with the prices and the subsidy,
> men get so greedy that they over-use
> the flax-dams dug for crops not half the size,
> rushing the buckled cartloads in and out
> and never giving the water time to rot.

Line 92 (l. 70 in final version) begins 'about the roads'; l. 140 (l. 118 in final version) is followed by four and a half lines omitted from final version:

> stiff with conceit, when once or twice provoked
> still in his agitated motion cloaked
> with a certain dignity as though he went,
> in tall Miltonic idiom, to prevent
> our coming. [Now we looked for him in vain . . .]

In a copy of *Lagan* among Hewitt's papers, he annotates l. 23 ('I went again . . .'), 'Cushendall', and l. 125 ('Then, at the glenhead . . .'), 'Glendun'. *F*, p. 1.

p. 373 'II The lonely heart': in the *Lagan* version, l. 6, omitted from the final version, reads 'and saw no evil in their being gay'; l. 31 (l. 30 in final version) has 'watercolour'; l. 61 (l. 60 in final version) has the error 'place achieved'; l. 116 (l. 115 in final version) reads: 'stepped back from life with no reluctant stare'; ll. 204–13, omitted from the final version, read:

> and know the Cross inviolable part
> in the high wisdom of the dreaming heart,
> that gave its comfort before Christ was born,
> or made men pots of clay to store the corn;
> and that the murdered god who rose in spring

offers forgiveness to our misgiving;
and that the rich earth-mother still can bless
if we regard her not with wantonness;
and that the blessed water yet has power
to still our fevers, wash our spirits pure . . .

Line 215 (l. 204 in final version) ends 'that ocean sways'. Hewitt incorporated the final five lines of this section in 'Retreaded rhymes' (*LE*, p. 50).

In *F*, p. 70, Hewitt provided the following notes on this section: ' "my father", Robert Telford Hewitt (1873–1945); "Homer Lane", pioneer of "free schools" (d. 1925); "my grandfather", John Hewitt (1841–1922)'.

In a copy of *Lagan* among his papers, Hewitt makes the following annotations:

l. 1 '1873–1945 Agnes St. Mixed P & S'

ll. 83–5 (final version) 'General Election 1945. Churchill?'

l. 114 (final version) 'John, 1841–1922'

l. 150 (final version) 'Warrenpoint. This is recast of blank verse poem'

F, p. 6.

p. 379 'III Townland of peace': the blank verse version of the first seventy-eight lines, published in *NRW* (p. 22), reads as follows:

Once walking in the country of my kindred
up the steep road to where the tower-topped mound
still hoards their bones, that showery August day
I walked clean out of Europe into peace:
for every man I met was relevant,
gathering fruit or shouting to his horse,
sawing his timber, measuring his well.
The little appletrees with crooked arms
that almost touched the bright grass with the weight
of their clenched fruit, the dappled calves that browsed
under the melting sunlight of the orchard,
the white hens slouching round the rusty trough,
the neat-leafed damsons with the smoky beads
the rain had failed to polish, and the farms
back from the road but loud with dog and can
and voices moving, spelt no shape of change,
belonging to a world and to an age
that has forgotten all its violence,
save when a spade rasps on a rusty scabbard.

Old John, my father's father, ran these roads
a hundred years ago, before the Famine,
up the steep brae to school or through the gap
to the far house with milk, or dragging slow
to see his mother buried at Kilmore.
I ponder, walking steadily, my aim
to stretch my legs beside a parson's fire
in the next parish. As the road goes by

with house and hedge and tree and stook-lined field
and apples heavy on the crouching boughs
I move beside him. Change is far away,
where a daft world gone shabby makes its war
among the crumbled streets or in the plains
that show black fire-crisped rafters and smashed hearths
from Poland to the Yiang-tse, where the people,
slow-phrased, are whipped and beaten into thought
that well may shoulder continents for power
and new societies of steel and truth;
but here's the age they've lost.

The boys I met
munching their windfalls, coming late from school,
are like that boy a hundred years ago;
the same bare kibes, the same drab heirloom rags,
but they must take another road in time.
His fortune summoned him across the sea
to the brave heyday of the smoking mills.
The bearded man who jolted in his cart,
giving his friendly answer to my word,
uncertain if my track were right or left,
might have been he, if luck had left him here
or time had checked its ticking. Had I passed
a woman by a gate I should have paused
to crack about the year the Lough was frozen
and merry crowds devoured the roasted ox
beneath the bright stars of that coldest winter,
to ask if she had lost her mother too
from fever that the Famine bred, or if
she bore my family name. There's every chance
she would have, for the name is common there
as berries in the hedges anywhere.

In the version of this which appeared in *The Bell*, vol. 9, no. 1 (October 1944), pp. 10–12, l. 1 has 'county of my kindred'.

Hewitt recast the blank verse version in rhyming couplets for the publication of *Freehold* in *Lagan*; in this version, l. 2 begins 'I marked the roads'; ll. 23–5, omitted from the final version, read: 'each in its orbed climate safe from rain,/ the sudden hedgegap that bespeaks a lane/to farm unseen . . .'; l. 105 (l. 103 in final version) has 'a drawing of the scene'; l. 157 (l. 155 in final version) reads 'county at the least'.

In *F*, p. 70, Hewitt provides the following notes for this section:

'Townland of peace': the first section, then unrhymed, appeared in *The Bell*, vol. 9, no. 1 (October 1944);

'my poet parson', W.R. Rodgers (1909–1969), then minister of Cloveneden Presbyterian Church, Loughgall;

'my friend the painter', John Luke (1906–1975), then living at Knappagh, Co. Armagh.

In a copy of *Lagan* among his papers, Hewitt annotates as follows:

> This is a recast of blank verse poem of same name, published in *Bell*.
>
> l. 2 'Co Armagh';
>
> l. 81 (l. 79 in final version) 'W.R. Rodgers';
>
> l. 86 (l. 84 in final version) 'M.H. Waddell';
>
> l. 95 (l. 93 in final version) 'John Luke'.

Lines 127–34 and ll. 143–60 were published as a separate three-stanza poem, with the title 'The regionalist', in *Irish Times*, 25 February 1956; in this version, l. 21 (l. 155 in final version) has 'county at the least'.

See also Hewitt's monograph *John Luke (1906–1975)* (Arts Councils of Ireland, 1978, pp. 48–50); Hewitt refers here to a letter from John Luke, dated 19 August 1943, inviting the Hewitts to visit the painter at Knappagh, County Armagh:

> In the event this proved a significant venture. As my wife was at work in the Censorship, I left a day or two before her. I took the train to Portadown, and then walked, with some assistance from a ride on a hay-float, to Loughgall, where my friend W.R. Rodgers, the poet, was minister of Cloveneden Presbyterian Church. Staying the night with him and his wife, Marie, in the spacious book-scattered manse, next morning he drove me into Armagh where, as pre-arranged, I met Jack.
>
> As the part of Armagh county I had travelled through was indeed 'the country of my kindred' – my greatgrandfather Mark, and my grandfather John, as a boy, had lived near Kilmore where the churchyard holds the bones of generations of Hewitts – the whole episode came out first as 'Townland of peace' in blank verse, and later, worked in couplets, formed a section of a long poem, *Freehold*, printed in *Lagan*, 1946, from which I quote the closing lines.

F, p. 12.

p. 383 'IV The glittering sod' in the *Lagan* version, ll. 25–8, which are omitted from the final version, read:

> My region's Ulster. How can we afford
> to take the shouting politician's word,
> map-makers' frenzy, who with crazy line,
> cut off three counties history marked our own?

Line 70 (l. 66 in final version) has 'this people'; l. 85 (l. 81 in final version) has 'the Board of Works'; ll. 134–48, which are omitted from the final version, read as follows:

> When, basking in the hay, through thorny gap
> you've glimpsed the farmer in his Sunday trap;
> or at the bar in some bare crossroads pub
> you've heard a thatcher talking of his job;
> when you have paced a tinker down the hill
> and heard his story; when you've drunk your fill
> from roadside trickle, or from strawbound pump,
> or kicked your ragball on the tiphead dump

and stood on cinders later to advise
the errant referee; or when your eyes
have warmed your heart at names like Templeton,
Toland or Hope, your fate's already spun.
You cannot break the web; you must declare,
in shrill allegiance to this crowded air,
the heritage to which you're lucky heir.

Lines 157–62, omitted from the final version, read:

Wherefore I pray your silence, till my verse
has hobbled through its unfamiliar course,
secure in knowledge that the load it bears
has somehow relevance to your affairs,
though my slack couplets have less skill to please
than Maro's nice encomium of bees.

In a copy of *Lagan* among his papers, Hewitt annotates the references to 'Templeton,/Toland or Hope' as follows: ' "John Templeton, Ulster botanist, 17??–18??"; "John Toland, Derry, philosopher 1669–1722"; "James Hope, Antrim, United Irishman 1764–1847[?]'.
F, p. 17.

p. 386 'Ulster names': N10, pp. 11–13, part X of 'The Red Hand: a poemosaic'; N20, pp. 157–9, 15.7.36, with title 'Antrim names'; N32, pp. 15–17, 14–15.7.49, with title 'The Ulster names', and note 'began as a recasting of an old poem. Stanzas 1 and 2 are fairly close to 1st version'; N44, p. 117. Pub. *Irish Red Cross Annual* (1950), p. 43. Rep. *Belfast Telegraph*, 11 June 1953; *Within Our Province* (1972), p. 5; *Rich and Rare* (1984), p. 138; *Bitter Harvest* (1989), p. 11 (with 'Postscript, 1984'). *F*, p. 25. Hewitt's note in *F*, p. 70, incorporates most of this information. On the back of an ms. version among Hewitt's papers is a note to the effect that the poem was 'first prompted by Stephen Vincent Benét's "American Names" '.

p. 387 'Postscript, 1984': N43, p. 169, 15.5.84, with title 'Postscript to Ulster names'. *F*, p. 26. Hewitt's note in *F*, p. 70, states that this poem was prompted by reading 'Ulster names' in *Rich and Rare* (Ward River Press, 1984).

p. 388 'Colonial consequence': N34, pp. 50–1, 1.10.53, with title 'Gentlemen adventurers, or The old Virginian'; N37, pp. 61–2, undated, with title 'The island (a revision)'. *F*, p. 28.

p. 389 'No Cresta Run': N43, p. 167, 19.1.84. *F*, p. 29. An ms. version among Hewitt's papers identifies the subject of the poem as George Laurie (who lived at 103 Clifton Park Avenue).

p. 389 'The watercolour': N39, p. 112, 22–5.2.71; N41, p. 4, with title 'Custodian'. *F*, p. 30. The painting referred to is probably *Sawmills* by W.J. McClughin.

p. 390 'Summer Arcady': N24, p. 159, 20.3.40; N41, p. 12; N45, p. 186, with title 'Sonnet: Pan' and note: 'memory of visit to old man near Donaghadee, Co. Down, *c.* 1918'. *F*, p. 31.

p. 390 'Art and technology': N43, p. 165, 25.9.82. *F*, p. 32. Hewitt's last three visits to Paris were in 1981, 1982 and 1983, in the company of John and Renee

Kilfeather. In his memoir 'Remembering John Hewitt', *Threshold*, no. 38 (Winter 1986–7), pp. 31–6, John Kilfeather records how Hewitt 'would go and watch the Algerians selling paper birds in the Tuileries Gardens', adding, 'He made a poem of this.'

p. 391 'Roseblade's visitants and mine': N40, p. 131, 30.6.75, with title 'The old mystic'. Rev. early 1986(?). *F*, p. 33. An ms. note among Hewitt's papers reads 'William Roseblade – a Coventry artist; his work is represented in the Herbert Art Gallery and Museum in the city.' In *F*, p. 70, Hewitt provides the following notes: ' "Toland, the Irish deist", John Toland (1670–1722). His most famous book, *Christianity Not Mysterious* (1696), was burned by the common hangman'; "Winstanley", Gerrard Winstanley (1609–*c.* 1660), leader of the Diggers or True Levellers'. Other references in the poem are to William Morris (1834–96), Victorian poet and socialist, William Cobbett (1763–1835), satirist and polemicist, and David Cox (1783–1859), landscape painter.

p. 392 'Age and youth': ms. notebook XXXII, May 1985, with title 'In a railway train'. *F*, p. 35.

p. 393 'Tryst': ms. notebook XXXII, 4–5 June 1985. *F*, p. 36. Rep. *Bitter Harvest* (1989), p. 13.

p. 393 'Portstewart, July 1914' (My cousin, four years taller than myself . . .'): ms. notebook XXXII, March 1985. *F*, p. 37.

p. 394 'Hesitant memorial': ms. notebook XXXII, April 1985. *F*, p. 38. The poem refers to Dorothy Roberts, to whom Hewitt was engaged about 1930. An ms. note among Hewitt's papers reads: 'I was engaged to Dorothy R– (1911–1984) in [or about?] the spring of 1930', and a further note 'The church was Agnes St. Methodist.' An ms. draft of the poem, dated 17–18.4.85, has the title 'Sad enough' and the note 'Dorothy 1911–84'.

p. 395 'Bifocal in Gaza': ms. notebook XXXII, July–August 1985. Various ms. versions among Hewitt's papers, dated 5.8.85, 21.8.85, 4.9.85 and 24.9.85. Pub. *Threshold*, no. 36 (Winter 1985–6), pp. 14–18. *F*, p. 39. Hewitt provides the following notes in *F*, p. 70: ' "that French poet", Theophile Gautier (1811–72); "the Cretan", El Greco, pseudonym of Domenicos Theotocopoulos (*c.* 1541–1614)'.

p. 400 'I wrote it over forty years ago . . .': N36, two drafts on unnumbered pages, the second dated 1969; N39, p. 38, 13.10.69. *F*, p. 46.

p. 400 *The Bloody Brae: A Dramatic Poem:* N21, pp. 151–4 (opening section), 27–8.8.36. *F*, pp. 45–69. Hewitt's note in *F*, p. 70, states that *The Bloody Brae*

> was written in 1936 under the influence of Gordon Bottomley's verse plays. It was broadcast in January 1954, on the BBC Northern Ireland Home Service, performed by the Lyric Players in March 1957 and printed in *Threshold* in Autumn, 1957 [vol. 1, no. 3 (Autumn 1957), pp. 14–32]. *See* D.H. Akenson, *Between Two Revolutions* (Ontario, 1979) for an informed reference to the legendary and largely fictitious event which is supposed to have taken place in Islandmagee, Co. Antrim, in January 1642.

In a letter to John Montague in the spring of 1964, Hewitt writes that *The Bloody Brae* was

> written in 1936 something in the style of Gordon Bottomley's verse plays. (We corresponded and, later, met.) It lay around until 1953, when I suddenly came on it and thought from the look of it that it might be suitable for radio. It was broadcast from Belfast in January 1954, and got a good response in press and among listeners. Later, Mary O'Malley gave it its first stage-production in 1957 which I did not see, being already in England. She then suggested its publication in *Threshold* twenty-one years after it had been written. I think you might be able to date the B.B. by the similarity in the texture of its verse with that of 'The return' (1935) of the previous year.

Much of the glossary provided by Hewitt in *F*, p. 71, relates to *The Bloody Brae*:

'airt'	direction, point of the compass
'birling'	whirling
'boording'	entering into conversation
'burn'	brook or small stream
'causey'	cobbled or hard-beaten area around house
'grugach'	banshee
'guddling'	catching [fish] by hand
'heavy brae'	steeply rising ground
'moidered'	confused
'sheugh'	ditch
'shilty'	pony
'skeagh-bush'	fairy thorn
'stirk'	young bullock or heifer
'wean'	young child
'wheep'	whistle
'yowe'	ewe

PART II

SELECTED UNPUBLISHED POEMS
1928–76

p. 419 'Little ships': N45, p. 150, 13.11.28, with note: 'I have heard that this has been used in elementary school or schools.' This suggests that the poem was published, but I have been unable to trace any such publication.

p. 419 'Pour Hélène': N7, p. 56, March 1930; N9, p. 152, 31.3.30; N18, p. 51; N45, p. 136. Translated from the French of Pierre de Ronsard (1524–85).

p. 420 'Sonnet' ('There in the lonely quarry where at dawn . . .'): N15, p. 142, 11.4.33; N44, p. 191.

p. 420 'Sonnet' ('Our love is full of memorable things . . .'): N16, p. 88, 14.9.33; N44, p. 180. In the summer of 1933, Hewitt and his wife Roberta attended the summer school of the Independent Labour Party at Welwyn Garden City; the conference house was in the Digswell woods, where, Hewitt records in his unpublished autobiography, 'A North Light', 'I had my first acquaintance with the tame and orderly English countryside.'

p. 420 'Tristan: the lay of the goatleaf' (extract): N16, pp. 104–14, first part, 21–8.9.33; second part, 12.10.33; N44, pp. 173–9. This extract consists of ll. 136–45 of a 175-line poem in which Hewitt interweaves the story of Tristan and Isolt (*sic*) and a love poem to his wife Roberta.

p. 421 'Stone': N22, pp. 54–5, 3.8.37; N44, p. 57.

p. 421 'Autumnal': N22, pp. 92–3, 19.8.37; N44, p. 45.

p. 422 'Lyric' ('Let this last lyric of a passing day . . .'): N7, p. 2, dated April 1938, with title 'The passing mask'; N23, p. 53; 21.4.38; N44, p. 7.

p. 422 'The hollyhocks against the wall . . .': N45, p. 3, 29.9.39.

p. 423 'To any dweller in Lewis Street': N18, p. 12, 1940, with title 'To any dweller in Harrybrook Street'; N26, pp. 38–9, 5.6.40; N46, p. 14. Hewitt's friend, the painter John Luke (1906–75), was born at 6 Lewis Street, Belfast.

p. 423 'Sonnet' ('By the sea's edge, on gravel and on sand . . .'): N26, p. 86, 2.7.40; N46, p. 30.

p. 424 'Glendun': N26, p. 89, 3.7.40; N46, p. 31.

p. 424 'Cobweb' ': N26, pp. 121–6, 13.7.40, with title 'I spy'; N46, pp. 20–1.

p. 425 'I talked and raged and planned . . .': N18, p. 35, 1940; N26, p. 163, 6.9.40; N46, p. 60.

p. 426 'Comment on verse': N25, p. 17, 24.11.40; N46, p. 67.

p. 426 'Salute to Matthew Arnold': N25, pp. 20–1, 30.11.40; N46, pp. 70–1.

p. 427 'Valedictory lines to my WEA students': N25, pp. 24–6, 6.12.40; N46, p. 74.

p. 428 'I cannot make a song tonight . . .': N18, p. 36, 1940; N25, p. 28, 13.12.40; N46, p. 77.

p. 428 'Sonnet' ('I think of Glasgow, where reluctantly . . .'): N25, p. 68, 19.3.41; N46, p. 94.

p. 429 'Sap in the sticks again . . .': N18, p. 5, 1941; N25, p. 82; N46, p. 101, 24.3.41.

p. 429 'Three Horatian odes': N25, pp. 95–9, 13.9.41; N46, pp. 104–6. The dedicatee is R. Patrick Maybin, who served with the Royal Medical Corps in Africa and Italy during the Second World War.

p. 431 'Sonnet' ('Among the many selves that throng my flesh . . .'): N25, p. 110, 19.9.41; N46, p. 114.

p. 431 'Dedication' ('I have a certain skill in phrase . . .'): N18, p. 3, 1941; N25, p. 125, 1–2.10.41; N46, p. 120.

p. 431 'On the choice of a title': N28, pp. 7–8, 4–5.1.42, with title 'On the choice of titles'; N46, p. 134. The poem was prompted by the title of E. Estyn Evans's book *Irish Heritage* (1942). The first two stanzas were quoted by Dr R.A. Gailey in the Estyn Evans Lecture, March 1989, pub. as ' "Such as pass by us daily": the study of folklife', *Ulster Folklife*, vol. 36 (1990), pp. 4–42.

p. 432 'Sonnet' ('I thought tonight of all the lovers gone . . .'): N28, p. 21, 3.2.42; N46, p. 140.

p. 433 'Paraphrase of verses by Mayakovsky': N28, p. 116, probably 4–5.2.43; N46, p. 180.

p. 433 'Pangur Ban': N29, p. 70, 5.12.43; N47, p. 10.

Pangur Ban (that is, 'white Pangur') is 'The lithe white cat/that rubbed its shoulder on the scribe's worn shoe/till he thrust by the missal he was at/ and jotted down those stanzas, sharp and true,/on cats and poets' referred to in 'Those swans remember'. The stanzas, written in Irish, are preserved in a ninth-century manuscript of the monastery of St Paul in Carinthia, southern Austria.

p. 433 'I told my heart to rest . . .': N30, p. 31, 28.12.44; N47, p. 69.

p. 434 'On the use of dialect words': N31, p. 41, 26–7.4.48.

p. 434 'With a little book of pottery': N31, p. 64, 30.8.48.

p. 435 'For Busha': written for and inscribed by Hewitt in Roberta Hewitt's copy of *No Rebel Word*, signed 'Johnny, 4.XI.48'. 'Busha' was a family name for Roberta Hewitt.

p. 435 'When the bell rings in the steeple . . .': N33, p. 39, 29.7.51.

p. 435 'The priest goes through the motions of the play . . .': N33, p. 40, 29.7.51.

p. 436 'This is no land of Constable and Clare . . .': N33, p. 65, 9.8.51.

p. 436 'To be used in an address delivered at the unveiling of a plaque commemorating "George A. Birmingham"': N33, pp. 100–1, 13–16.11.51. 'George A. Birmingham' was the pseudonym under which the Reverend James Owen Hannay (1865–1950) wrote numerous popular novels and other works, such as *An Irishman Looks at His World* (1919); he was rector of Westport, County Mayo, for over twenty years. The commemorative plaque was unveiled at his birthplace, 75 University Road, Belfast, on 19 November 1951, and these two sonnets were read as part of Hewitt's address on the occasion; the second was quoted in full as part of a comment on the unveiling, *Northern Whig and Belfast Post,* 20 November 1951.

p. 437 'Resource': N34, p. 44, 3.9.53.

p. 437 'Vers libre': N38, p. 58, 21.12.67.

p. 438 'Rite': N39, pp. 58–9, 8.3.70, with title 'At my father's graveside'; N41, p. 38, with title 'In a country graveyard'.

NOTES
TO
APPENDIX I

UNCOLLECTED POEMS
1928–86

p. 441 'A Labour victory': N3, pp. 161–2, with title 'Victory, 18.1.28'. Pub. *Irishman*, 18 February 1928.

p. 441 'The song of the shipyard men': N3, p. 138, probably late 1927. Pub. *Irishman*, 25 February 1928.

p. 441 'The songs I sing': N3, pp. 114–15, probably late 1927, with title 'Invictus'. Pub. *Irishman*, 10 March 1928.

p. 442 'The ex-serviceman': I have not been able to find this poem in any of Hewitt's notebooks. Probably late 1927. Pub. *Irishman*, 10 March 1928.

p. 442 'New Jerusalem': N3, pp. 165–6, 20.1.28. Pub. *Irishman*, 17 March 1928.

p. 443 'To a modern Irish poet': N3, p. 116, probably late 1927, with title 'To a modern poet from a Jacobin'. Pub. *Irishman*, 17 March 1928.

p. 443 'To the memory of James Connolly': N5, p. 99, 1.5.28, with title 'To the memory of James Connolly, executed 12th May, 1916 in Dublin'. *Irishman*, 12 May 1928. (*See also* N9, p. 78, 26.4.29, for an unpublished sonnet with the title 'To the memory of James Connolly, patriot and martyr, murdered by English soldiers, May 10th 1916'.) The correct date of Connolly's execution is 12 May 1916.

p. 444 'Paper banners': N5, p. 64, 12.4.28. Pub. *Irishman*, 12 May 1928. Rep. *Watchword*, 8 November 1930.

p. 444 'Omens and auguries': N5, p. 80, 20.4.28, with title 'Omens'. Pub. *Freethinker*, 10 June 1928.

p. 445 'Ashes in the wind': N3, p. 177, 7.2.28, with title 'Queen's'. Pub. *Freethinker*, 17 June 1928.

p. 445 'In praise of Elisabeth': N3, p. 217, March 1928, with title 'In praise of good Elizabeth'. Pub. *Northman*, vol. 1, no. 6 (June 1928), p. 19, signed J.H.H.

p. 445 'Nettles of offence': N5, p. 112, 8.5.28; N18, p. 50; N19, p. 31; N45, p. 161. Pub. *Northman*, vol. 1, no. 6 (June 1928), p. 26, signed J.H.H.

p. 446 'In that fair and pleasant land . . .': I have not been able to find this poem in any of Hewitt's notebooks. Probably March–April 1928. Pub. *Freethinker*, 5 July 1928.

p. 446 'Colney Hatch': N5, p. 126, 10.5.28. Pub. *Freethinker*, 22 July 1928.

p. 446 'Timber': N5, p. 134, 14.5.28; N19, p. 34; N45, p. 160. Pub. *Northman*, vol. 2, no. 1 (December 1928), p. 9, signed J.H.H. Rep. *Everyman* (December 1928).

p. 447 'Young womanhood': N5, p. 211, 15.6.28; N18, p. 49; N45, p. 158. Pub. *Northman*, vol. 2, no. 1 (December 1928), p. 9, signed J.H.H.

p. 447 'Iron and stone': N5, p. 40, 20.9.28. Pub. *Northman,* vol. 2, no. 1 (December 1928), p. 31, signed J.H.H.

p. 447 'Mister Faintheart Middleclass': N3, p. 130, late 1927, with title 'Are you asham'd?'; N45, p. 163, dated 1927, with note: 'The title was quoted against me during a lecture, W.C.L.C[?] that winter [?].' Pub. *Irishman*, 5 January 1929.

p. 448 'On hearing a traveller's tale of the Alps': N5, p. 89, 28.4.28. Pub. *Irishman*, 26 January 1929.

p. 448 'A father explains': N5, p. 168, 23.5.28. Pub. *New Leader*, 8 February 1929. In a poetry scrapbook among Hewitt's papers, he notes that this was the 'first poem I ever got paid for'. The payment was 7s.6d.

p. 448 'Motives': N9, p. 14, 30.1.29. Pub. *Irishman,* 16 February 1929.

p. 449 'Any rich suburban church': N4, p. 105, 21.11.28. Pub. *Irishman*, 23 February 1929.

p. 449 'Hymn': N9, p. 15, 30.1.29. Pub. *Irishman*, 2 March 1929.

p. 449 'The rank-and-filer': N4, p. 10, 4.10.28, with title 'To Paddy O'C.'. Pub. *Irishman*, 2 March 1929.

p. 450 'For certain subscribers to the miners' fund': N9, p. 9, January 1929, probably 4–17.1.29. Pub. *Irishman,* 2 March 1929.

p. 450 'Suburb': N5, p. 45, 26.9.28. Pub. *Irishman*, 9 March 1929.

p. 451 'Aristocratic area': N4, p. 48, 17.10.28, with title 'Malone Park'. Pub. *Irishman*, 16 March 1929.

p. 451 'Limitations': N5, p. 42, 20.9.28. Pub. *Irishman*, 19 March 1929.

p. 451 'Equality': N5, p. 236, 13.7.28. Pub. *Irishman*, 23 March 1929.

p. 452 'Epitaph for a gardener': N5, p. 13, 7.8.28; N19, p. 29; N45, p. 152, all with title 'The gardener'. Pub. *Everyman*, 30 March 1929.

p. 452 'The simple-minded Christian': N4, p. 118, 26.11.28, with title 'A simple Christian sings his song'. Pub. *Irishman*, 6 April 1929.

p. 452 'Two sonnets on the Free State Censorship Bill': N4, pp. 58–9, 25.10.28. Pub. *Freethinker*, 26 June 1929.

p. 453 'Silver was the barbèd hook . . .': N5, p. 53, 1.4.28, with title 'Silver'. Pub. *Northman*, vol. 2, no. 3 (June 1929), p. 14, as part of a prose piece titled 'The legend concerning the beggar and the brothers'.

p. 453 'The rebel': N5, p. 125, 9.5.28. Pub. *New Leader*, 23 August 1929, under pseudonym 'John H. Hurst'.

p. 454 'Mathematics': N4, p. 82, 10.11.28. Pub. *Northman*, vol. 2, no. 4 (December 1929), p. 41.

p. 454 'The monarch': N9, p. 46, 8.3.29, the first of a sequence of seven poems titled 'Little tales of the Dark Ages' (*see also* 'The novice'). Pub. *Northman*, vol. 2, no. 4 (December 1929), p. 41.

p. 455 'Nebula': N4, p. 69, 4.11.28. Pub. *Freethinker*, 3 November 1929.

p. 455 'Immortality': N5, p. 201, 7.6.28; N45, p. 159. Pub. *Freethinker*, 10 November 1929.

p. 455 'Sonnet' ('I have no time to worship. I must live . . .'): N5, p. 208, 14.6.28. Pub. *Freethinker*, 28 November 1929.

p. 456 'Willow pattern': N4, p. 73, 6.11.28; N45, p. 151. Pub. *Northman*, vol. 2, no. 5 (March 1930), p. 20.

p. 456 'Aesthete's renunciation': N4, pp. 99–102, 19.11.28, with title 'The dilettant [*sic*] studies M. C.H.[?] but remaineth impenitent to the end'. Pub. *Northman*, vol. 2, no. 5 (March 1930), p. 26.

p. 457 'Sonnet' ('Since brooding men put beauty in a rime . . .'): N9, p. 88, 13.5.29. Pub. *Northman*, vol. 2, no. 5 (March 1930), p. 30.

p. 458 'The novice': N9, p. 46, 8.3.29, the third in a sequence titled 'Little tales of the Dark Ages' (*see also* 'The monarch'). Pub. *Northman*, vol. 2, no. 5 (March 1930), p. 35.

p. 458 'March day': N9, p. 22, 18.2.29, with title 'Sonnet on February'; N45, p. 143, with note: 'Evelyn Gardens'. Pub. *Everyman*, 31 March 1930.

p. 459 'Song for May Day': N5, p. 98, 1.5.28. Pub. *Vanguard* (May 1930), under pseudonym 'John Horne'.

p. 459 'Dusty roads': N9, p. 28, 22.2.29. Pub. *Northman*, vol. 2, no. 6 (June 1930), p. 23.

p. 460 'Pendragon': N5, p. 38, 18.9.28. Pub. *Northman*, vol. 2, no. 6 (June 1930), p. 27.

p. 460 'Peace pact': N9, p. 108, 29.5.29, the third in a sequence of love poems titled 'Challenge: a lyric sequence', the other four unpublished; N19, p. 46, with title 'Peace pact'. Pub. *Northman*, vol. 2, no. 6 (June 1930) p. 28.

p. 460 'Ophelia': N9, p. 151, 30.3.30; N19, p. 50. Pub. *Northman*, vol. 2, no. 6 (June 1930), p. 36.

p. 461 'Sarcophagus': N7, pp. 27–8, dated May 1929; N9, pp. 86–7, 9.5.29; N45, p. 141. Pub. *Northman*, vol. 2, no. 6 (June 1930), p. 43.

p. 462 'No comment!': N9, p. 170, 11.9.30, with title 'Propaganda'. Pub. *Workers' Voice*, 30 September 1930, under pseudonym 'John Thorne'.

p. 462 'Two sonnets': N9, pp. 174–5, 20.9.30. Originally titled 'Mendicant 1/11'. Pub. *Workers' Voice*, 27 September 1930, under pseudonym 'Jack Horne'.

p. 463 'The doctor muses': N9, p. 172, 15.9.30. Pub. *Workers' Voice*, 4 October 1930, under pseudonym 'J. Horne (Belfast)'.

p. 463 'Fair game': N9, p. 173, 20.9.30. Pub. *Workers' Voice*, 1 November 1930, under pseudonym 'John Horne'.

p. 464 'The golden boy': N3, p. 190, 15.2.28. Pub. *Watchword*, 15 November 1930.

p. 464 'In memoriam: D.H. Lawrence': N9, p. 155, 11.4.30. Pub. *Northman*, vol. 3, no. 2 (March 1931), p. 4.

p. 465 'The mad applegrower': N9, p. 180, 29.9.30, with title 'The old applegrower'. Pub. *Northman*, vol. 3, no. 2 (March 1931), p. 11.

p. 465 'The palmist': N9, p. 116, August 1929, with title 'At the gypsy queen's red tent'. Pub. *Northman*, vol. 3, no. 2 (March 1931), p. 20.

p. 466 'Apparition': N9, p. 180, 29.9.30. Pub. *Northman*, vol. 3, no. 2 (March 1931), p. 22.

p. 466 'Easter Tuesday': N9, p. 160, 28.4.30. Pub. *Northman,* vol. 3, no. 3 (Summer 1931), p. 22.

p. 466 'Practical mysticism': N11, p. 7, 1.3.30 (error?); N18, p. 48, 1931; N19, p. 24, 1931; N45, p. 127, 1.3.31. Pub. *Northman,* vol. 3, no. 3 (Summer 1931), p. 36.

p. 467 'Arithmetic': N7, p. 14, May 1930; N9, p. 161, 28.4.30 (error?); N45, p. 133, 28.5.30. Pub. *Northman,* vol. 3, no. 3 (Summer 1931), p. 37.

p. 467 'The last crusade': N9, p. 190, 7.10.30, with title 'Christendom and heathenry'. Pub. *Northman,* vol. 3, no. 3 (Summer 1931), p. 37.

p. 468 'Bradford millionaire': N11, p. 112, 28.7.31. Pub. *New Age,* 22 October 1931.

p. 468 'Chant for the five-year plan': N9, pp. 203–5, 3.11.30, with title 'A chant for the workers of the world, on the 13th anniversary of the Revolution'; N45, p. 130, with title, 'The five year plan: a chant for the workers of the world'. Pub. *Northman,* vol. 3, no. 4 (Winter 1931), p. 34. In letter to John Montague in the spring of 1964, Hewitt remarks: 'I wrote my chant for the Soviet Five Year Plan in the Vachel Lindsay manner.'

p. 469 'Admonition to science': N11, p. 176, 28.10.31; N45, p. 118. Pub. *Northman,* vol. 3, no. 4 (Winter 1931), p. 35.

p. 470 'Of a professor': I have not been able to find this poem in any of Hewitt's notebooks. Probably late 1931. Pub. *Northman,* vol. 3, no. 4 (Winter 1931), p. 35. The subject of the poem is R.M. Henry, Professor of Latin at Queen's University Belfast and brother of the painter Paul Henry. Chapter 13 of Hewitt's unpublished autobiography 'A North Light' is titled 'The Henrys'.

p. 470 'Note on intellectuals': N11, pp. 58–60, 15.5.31, third part of a six-part poem titled 'Thursday is polling day', the remaining five parts unpublished. Pub. *Northman,* vol. 3, no. 5 (Spring 1932), p. 29.

p. 470 'The terrible choice': N12, p. 22, 18.12.31; N45, p. 116. Pub. *Northman,* vol. 3, no. 5 (Spring 1932), p. 29.

p. 470 'Atlas': N11, p. 104, 21.7.31. Pub. *Northman,* vol. 3, no. 5 (Spring 1932), p. 33.

p. 471 'Season's return': N11, p. 10, 17.3.31. Pub. *Northman,* vol. 3, no. 5 (Spring 1932), p. 37.

p. 471 'Pioneer': N9, p. 40; N45, p. 142, 4.3.29, with note: 'Evelyn Gardens [next word illegible] with Fortwilliam Terrace and Salisbury Avenue'. Pub. *Everyman,* 31 March 1932.

p. 472 'For a mild season': N7, p. 12, February 1932; N12, p. 85, 2.2.32, with note: 'Evelyn Gardens'. Pub. *Everyman,* 31 March 1932.

p. 472 'Morning hymn': N5, p. 46, 27.9.28, with title 'Caravan in the frost'. Pub. *Everyman,* 8 September 1932.

p. 472 'Values': N11, p. 150, 30.9.31, with title 'Obiter dicta'; N18, p. 45; N45, p. 121. Pub. *Adelphi,* vol. 5, no. 2 (November 1932), p. 80.

p. 473 'Mauberley's son: a summary': N12, pp. 144–6, 18.4.32. Pub. *Adelphi,* vol. 5, no. 2 (November 1932), p. 122.

p. 473 'Art's duped riddle': N14, p. 43, 10.6.32; N18, p. 42; N45, p. 100. Pub. *Adelphi*, vol. 5, no. 3 (December 1932), p. 209.

p. 474 'Egyptian night': N12, p. 132, 29.3.32; N45, p. 106, with note: 'I had a brief but amusing correspondence with A.R. Orage on this poem and my use of substitution. Some time after this was written I was shown a small painting on the subject, by J.R. White, in the house of his friend Mrs Beresford. The painting was by, I think, a female relation of Mrs B.' Pub. *New English Weekly*, 2 March 1933.

p. 474 'Tiphead': N13, pp. 78–9, September 1932; N14, pp. 133–4, 17.9.32; N45, pp. 86–7. Pub. *Twentieth Century* (March 1933), p. 24.

p. 475 'Prelude to consternation': N15, p. 20, 16.11.32. Pub. *Twentieth Century* (June 1933), p. 256.

p. 475 'Anti-Promethean ode': N7, pp. 38–40, May 1932; N14, pp. 9–11, 5.5.32; N45, p. 103. Pub. *Listener* (Poetry Supplement), 12 July 1933.

p. 476 'Morning moment': N15, p. 24, 20.11.32, with title 'Early morning in November'; N45, p. 78, with note: 'Cavehill Road bus-stop'. Pub. *New Britain*, 20 September 1933.

p. 477 'Defeat': N7, p. 13, November 1932; N15, p. 27, 24.11.32; N37, p. 91, rev. version, 1964 (probably between March and October); N45, p. 77. Pub. *Listener*, 8 November 1933. Rep. *Poems of Tomorrow* (1935), p. 54.

p. 477 'Epithalamion': N15, p. 43, 19.12.32; N18, p. 40; N45, p. 76. Pub. *Sunday Referee*, 14 January 1934.

p. 478 'Matin sur le port': N17, p. 6, 15.1.34, with title 'From the French of Albert Samain'. Pub. *Sunday Referee*, probably early 1934, where it won a consolation prize for translation.

p. 478 'Host': N7, p. 11, February 1932; N12, p. 93, 9.2.32; N18, p. 43; N45, p. 108, with note: 'I heard blind man's stick on pavement in front of City Hall on a day when the draw for the Irish Sweepstake was taking place.' Pub. *Observer*, 2 September 1934.

p. 478 'Prelude to an ode for Barnum': N16, pp. 182–5, 23–4.12.33, with title 'Grotesque carnival'; N44, pp. 166–8. Pub. *Adelphi*, vol. 9, no. 6 (March 1935), pp. 351–2. In letter to John Montague in the spring of 1964, Hewitt refers to this poem as showing the influence of W.H. Auden.

p. 480 'Poem' ('My name is Revolution – let me speak . . .'): N7, p. 62, March 1936, with title 'Revolution'; N20, p. 95, February(?) 1936(?); N44, p. 128, 16.3.36, with title 'Revolution'. Pub. *Adelphi*, vol. 13, no. 1 (October 1936), p. 37.

p. 480 'Aquarium': ('Let wonder leave us for another place . . .'): N20, p. 7, 9.5.35; N44, p. 150. Pub. *Adelphi*, vol. 13, no. 1 (October 1936), p. 48.

p. 481 'Swan's nest': N7, pp. 21–2, April 1936; N20, pp. 123–4, 30.4.36, with note 'See *Swans in the City*, 12 November, 1935'; N44, pp. 124–5. Pub. *Irish Jewry* (Spring 1937). Hewitt compiled a scrapbook of cuttings, titled 'Verse from The Forum, spring 1937'; on 18 May 1943, he wrote the following note in the inside front cover:

In the spring of 1937 Louis Barnett started a monthly newspaper, *Irish Jewry*. I was editor of a literary supplement called 'The Forum', and packed it with my friends' work. I also wrote reviews, art and film criticism, short stories under pseudonyms. This scrapbook is made up of the verse which was printed in it. During the assembling of the material for the third number the Rabbi butted in, and our scheme was shattered. By this time my friend Jim Mackinlay had assumed the Forum editorship, but owing to the Rabbi's interference the whole journal fizzled out. I later discovered that Louis had sold his interest to his patron, whose name I forget; and that another contributor had been paid well for his articles on music!

These comments are followed by notes on contributors to the *Forum*:

Edward (Malachy) (O') Boyle has since contributed to 'Northern Harvest', 1944.

Samuel McCreery, an etcher and woodcarver, died, I think, on 11th November 1937. His poems here appeared without permission, and were the cause of a breach between us. At the moment I possess several of his prints. [*See* the poem 'Drypoint' in the present volume and the notes on the poem.]

James Gildea I have lost sight of. He about this time had a fine story broadcast entitled 'Curls'.

Ruby Black is the maiden name of my wife. This poem ['A surrealist poem'] was later reprinted in the *New Northman* under the editorship of Robert Greacen from whom she received a most encouraging letter!

John Luke is now represented in the Belfast Gallery by a portrait and a landscape and now is painting subtly, slowly and magnificently.

W.J. McClughin has given up painting.

During the same period I was also literary editor of the 'Irish Democrat'. O'Boyle also contributed, I think.

p. 481 'Mourne Mountains': N7, pp. 23–4, August 1937; N10, pp. 28–9, part XXX of 'The Red Hand: a poemosaic'; N22, pp. 84–5, 19.8.37; N44, p. 48. Pub. *Poems by Ulster Poets* (undated, but Hewitt has handwritten '1937 or 38' on his own copy). Rep. *Belfast Telegraph*, 28 August 1954.

p. 482 'For Deirdre': N7, pp. 17–18, November 1933, with title 'For my niece'; N16, pp. 141–2, 11.11.33; N44, p. 169, with title 'Deirdre'. Pub. *New Northman*, vol. VI, no. 2 (Summer 1938), p. 60. The poem is for Hewitt's niece, Deirdre Todhunter.

p. 483 'October's child': N7, pp. 31–2, September 1936; N21, pp. 13–15, 17.9.36; N44, p. 111. Pub. *Poetry Review* (November–December 1941), p. 342.

p. 484 'Seeding time': N28, p. 50, 8.9.42; N46, p. 156. Pub. *The Bell*, vol. 5, no. 4 (January 1943), p. 314. Rep. *Tribune*, 22 October 1948.

p. 484 'Flight': N13, pp. 15–16, April 1938, with title 'Flight of swans'; N23, pp. 30–1, 7.4.38; N44, pp. 14–15. Pub. *Lagan*, no. 1 (1943), p. 73.

p. 485 'Ulster winter (1942)': N28, pp. 39–40, finished 24.3.42, with title 'Winter in Armagh'; N46, p. 148. Pub. *Labour Progress* (January 1944).

p. 486 'For one who did not march': N29, p. 19, 25.10.43, with title 'Roll call' (not to be confused with fifth section of *Freehold*; *see* note below); N46, p. 212. Pub. *Lagan*, no. 3 (1945), p. 51.

p. 486 'Roll call': N28, pp. 76–8. with note 'Fragments of a projected long poem, written 25.3.42, mislaid until 17.9.42'. Fifth section of *Freehold*, pub. *Lagan*, vol. 2, no. 1 (1946, described on front cover as no. 4), pp. 23–44, but omitted from version of *Freehold* in *Freehold and Other Poems*.

In an annotated copy of *Lagan*, vol. 2, no. 1 (1946), Hewitt identifies the cast of the poem: the 'dynamic symbolist' is Colin Middleton; the 'tall, dark painter', John Luke; the 'brave, far-travelled man', H.S. Kennedy (1906–46); the 'voluble architect', Denis (O'Dea) Hanna; 'my mother's friend, the country schoolmaster', R.L. Russell; 'that still man I have praised', W.R. Rodgers; 'the grave lad with disconcerting smile', Roy McFadden; 'one in friendship older', R. Patrick Maybin; 'that fine woman with the gentle skill', May Morton; 'the rocking novelist', Michael McLaverty; 'that scholar who is deft', E.E. Evans; 'one to whom a hearth-roll or a cross . . .', T.G.F. Paterson; 'that shy lord', Lord Antrim; 'the good woman with the merry eyes', Mrs Beatty, 'the pursuer of plants or ammonites', E.N. Carrothers.

In *John Luke (1906–1975)* (1978), p. 50, Hewitt writes: 'A later section in *Freehold*, subtitled 'Roll call', listing those Ulstermen I considered representative of the best values of my Region . . . had a passage summarising, without naming him, those which John Luke stood for.' Hewitt goes on to quote the relevant lines of 'Roll call'.

p. 489 'Ulsterman': N7, p. 66, October 1937; N22, p. 131, 14.10.37, with title 'Ulsterman speaks'; N44, p. 31. Pub. *Labour Progress* (January 1946). Rep. *Irish Times*, 26 October 1946.

p. 490 'The ploughman': N30, p. 108, 27.4.46; N47, p. 95. Pub. *Irish Bookman*, vol. 1, no. 10 (June 1947), p. 32.

p. 490 'Will': N30, p. 124, 21.8.46; N47, p. 106. Pub. *Irish Bookman*, vol. 1, no. 10 (June 1947), p. 33.

p. 491 'Periodicity': N31, pp. 8–9, 28–9.1.47; N36, pp. 22–3, dated 1946(?); N41, pp. 92–3, undated. Pub. *The Bell*, vol. 15, no. 6 (March 1948), p. 6. Rep. *British Weekly*, 3 July 1952.

p. 491 'Sheep fair'; N30, p. 61, 6.9.45(?), with note: 'Waterfoot sheep fair'; N47, p. 76, 6.8.45(?). Pub. *Rann*, no. 1 (July 1948), p. 3.

p. 492 'Stallion': N7, p. 69, May 1938; N23, p. 65, 26.5.38; N44, p. 3. Pub. *Irish Times*, 16 October 1948.

p. 492 'Winter day' ('When sun was winter high . . .'): N7, p. 16, January 1939; N23, pp. 143–4, 30.1.39, with note: 'After visit to Rostrevor, Co. Down'. Pub. *Tribune*, 10 June 1949. Rep. *British Weekly*, 28 February 1952.

p. 493 'Awareness of time': N30, pp. 8–11, 1.12.44; N47, pp. 60–2. Pub. *Poetry Ireland*, no. 3 (October 1948), pp. 6–7. Rep. *Q*, no. 11 (Hilary term 1955), p. 34.

p. 494 'The lint pulling': N31, pp. 65–76, 24–8.8.48; N41, pp. 104–14. Pub. *Ulster Young Farmer* (October 1948). Pub. separately as an offprint. Hewitt introduced the poem to his readers as follows:

Last August I went a day lint-pulling, for the first time in my life, an experience I advise for any Ulsterman who thinks farmers grumble too much, or who writes letters to the newspapers or makes speeches about Ulster's exports. The experience would give his words a touch of reality and a tang of authority, and he might find the wings of his eloquence clipped a little, if he ever realises that his words represent at bottom, labour, organisation, rain and wind, stiff backs, sore hands.

Being a poet, I have tried to phrase and describe my experience honestly and directly, without the obvious reliefs of fine decorative writing or comic incident. I have used the exact terms as I heard them from my fellow-workers, whether dialect or idiom; and to ease the monotony of the rime-pattern, I have deliberately, here and there, put in a rime which is inexact, like 'rick' and 'neck', 'house' and 'those', or 'press' and 'this'.

I offer this set of rimes then, as a specimen of the kind of writing of which we will require a large outpouring before we can be sure we have the basis for a strong Ulster tradition of poetry true to our activities, feelings, thought and speech: the kind of poetry which must emerge from many levels and sources, surely among these, from the Young Farmers of this region.

Writing to John Montague in the spring of 1964, Hewitt describes the background to the poem:

> In 1948 the editor of *The Ulster Young Farmer* asked me to do a series of articles buckshee, to give a bit of literary tone to his journal. In my Regionalist ardour I seized the chance, wrote five articles on the appreciation of poetry, on our folk tradition, and inviting verse, gave careful criticism. Then, to wind up the series, I wrote this as an example of what could be done to record in verse a normal agricultural activity. The editor gave me a bundle of offprints.

p. 499 'The living landscape': N31, p. 62, 29.8.48. Pub. *Irish Times*, 18 December 1948.

p. 500 'The farmer's second son': N41, p. 33, 24.4.48, with title 'For Patrick McDonnell Junior of Cloughglass'. Pub. *Envoy* (December 1949).

p. 500 'The lifting': N25, p. 115, 25.9.41; N46, pp. 116–18. Pub. *Brave Crack* (1950), p. 92. Rep. *The Pure Drop* (1987), p. 22.

A 'slipe' is a wooden platform without wheels, like a sledge, used for carrying turf on a bog; a 'slaap' is a gap in a hedge; and 'shauchled' means 'shuffled'.

p. 502 'Evening in spring': N31, pp. 122–3, 19.4.49. Pub. *Envoy* (January 1950).

p. 503 'City morning': N30, p. 123, 17.8.46; N47, p. 105. Pub. *Tribune*, 21 April 1950.

p. 503 'Autumn valley': N47, p. 81, 2.10.45. Pub. *Irish Times*, 21 October 1950.

p. 504 'Season's end': N32, p. 111, 30.8.50. Pub. *Irish Times*, 6 January 1951.

p. 504 'Real estate': N33, p. 23, 25.7.51, with note 'The lodge' (the Hewitts' cottage at Cushendall). Pub. *British Weekly*, 13 December 1951.

p. 505 'Dichotomy': N32, p. 110, 10.7.50. Pub. *Irish Times*, 11–12 April 1952.

p. 505 'The ceilidhe': N31, p. 58, 22.8.48. Pub. *Rann*, no. 20 (June 1953), p. 11.

p. 505 'The Belfastman': N34, p. 30, 5.4.53. Pub. *Irish Times*, 18 July 1953. Rep. *Belfast Telegraph*, 28 November 1953.

p. 506 'Corncrake': N26, p. 29, 24.5.40; N46, p. 7. Pub. *The Bell*, vol. 19, no. 1 (December 1953), p. 144.

p. 506 'Interval': N31, p. 86, 23.10.48, with title 'Interval: for Patrick'. Pub. *The Bell*, vol. 19, no. 1 (December 1953), p. 144.

p. 506 'The thresher': N34, p. 73, 31.12.53. Pub. *Irish Times*, 8 May 1954.

p. 507 'Pro tanto quid retribuamus': N34, pp. 82–93, June 1954, finished 12 July 1954, with notes: 'This opening later discarded. Full and corrected version. An abbreviated form was used at opening of Exhibition 10.VII.1954.' A speech in verse delivered by Hewitt during the Silver Jubilee celebration of the Belfast Museum and Art Gallery, 10 July 1954. The extract printed here, about three-quarters of the full text, pub. *Belfast Telegraph*, 17 July 1954, with marginal notes: the one 'who watched the gull's white wing' is Sir R. Lloyd Patterson (1836–1906), who wrote *Birds of Belfast Lough*; the collector of moss and lichen' is S.A. Stewart (1826–1910); the one who 'bribed the ploughman for the axe' and so on is Canon Grainger (1830–91), rector of Broughshane, 1890; the Public Library was built in 1888; the 'spattered wounds' on the library's face were caused during the Blitz in 1941; the 'bearded, noisy man' is William Gray (1830–1917), who secured the adoption by the corporation of the Museums and Gymnasium Act (1891) in 1909; the 'civic gesture' refers to collections given to the city in 1910; the men 'whose craft it was to tend/the crowded objects' are Arthur Deane and J.A.S. Stendall; the 'tardy hour we now commemorate' occurred in 1929.

Hewitt refers to the occasion and the poem in his unpublished autobiography, 'A North Light' (p. 182):

> I celebrate the contribution to [the museum idea] of William Thompson, pioneer naturalist, Emerson Tennent, Dickens's friend and historian topographer of Ceylon, Crozier, associate of Sir John Franklin and collector of penguin skins, and Robert Patterson, ironmonger and Fellow of the Royal Society . . . I spoke . . . of the long struggle of William Gray to force the Municipality to adopt the existing legislation. And in a paragraph I reminded my hearers that after twenty-five years the building was still far from complete, that it had been started as relief work in the Depression and left when that Depression persisted. I also made a little allusion to the Irish origin of the very name Stranmillis. ['Stranmillis' is derived from an Irish phrase meaning 'sweet stream'.]

The unpublished section of the poem (ll. 13–78) reads as follows:

The preacher with a knack for making sense
of hieroglyphic puzzles, and the brisk
shortsighted little minister who charmed
his swarming boarders, englished Latin verse,
and turned his couplets of geology,
the gentle farmer with an eager eye
for leaf and bird, or fish upon the slab;

the busy doctor with an hour to spare
for ammonites or harpers, and the stout
church organist who jotted down their tunes;
the honest painter, Bishop Percy's friend,
and his boy genius whose far-fabled gifts
were spoken of in the metropolis;
all these were ours, and round them kindly men
who shared their rising fortunes with the town,
filling the blankleaves at the ledger's end
with tags of Pliny, Plutarch, Cicero.

Powered by their words a generation grew,
some kin of the great names, like Drummond's brother,
ship's surgeon, fever-doctor, pamphleteer;
some further fired by the fanatic Ure[?],
glib Scots performer in the lecture hall,
with sparking batteries and array of glass;
some, pupils of the teacher-dramatist
who set their little trophies on his desk,
the flints and shells he'd schooled them well to find:
these, with their fellows from the mills and stores,
spancelled by fortune to the family gear,
mustered their solemn company of eight
in Dr Drummond's house, and, minuting
proposals, propositions, resolutions,
formed their society, our fountain head.

And out of that grave play of mind with mind,
the need to ask, the need to satisfy
the leaping questions, they conjoined their strengths
to master Nature. Soon their labours brought
such wealth of wonder, such an urge to share
that wonder with their fellows yet untutored
in the bright marvels of the teeming earth,
that they in compact found a plot of land
near the new college where the fields began,
and raised a comely and capacious house
to hold and show all evidence of order
in shells and pebbles of the varied shore,
in leaves and insects never named before
by any skilled to know and tabulate,
adding to these the leaf-shaped metal blade,
the broken shard, the twisted ring of gold
and the gold crescent; for they held of man
that he was also under Nature's law.

And through the long years of the new Queen's reign,
when most were vowed to commerce, some remained
not wholly captive to the turning wheels,
but grave and whiskered now and grown sedate,

keeping their verses in a private drawer,
still held some heart of passion to enlarge
the hoard of knowledge. One far-wandering man
plucked trophies from the vast Pacific seas,
the chieftain's carved staff, the flat jade club,
and the great cloak a bankrupt monarch sold.
Another went to bear the seals of state
where Adam's foot still marks the pilgrim's hill,
enriched with painted dancing-masks and more,
the lettered cases and the numbered shelves.
And one shipped home a mummy from the Nile;
unwrapped by scholars, she was goggled at
by Easter Monday hundreds. To this day
a child will lisp to ask where she may lie,
that little daughter of great Ammon's priest.
And one who walked into the wasted snows
and came no more to speak of what befell,
edging Antarctic ice in early years,
packed back the dry skins of those lurching birds
that lord the berg and floe where no man lives.
Another, a lean man with a poet's face,
found all he sought for humbly by the flat
and reedy loughside, or among the hills,
and now is famed, twin-star, with Templeton.

p. 510 'Here at the tide's turn': N30, p. 63, 8.9(?).45; N47, p. 78, 8.8(?).45 (probably September). Pub. *Irish Times*, 9 October 1954. Rep. *The First Ten Years: Dublin Arts Festival Poetry* (1979), p. 22.

p. 511 'Mary's lullaby': N34, pp. 108–9, 16–17.11.54. Pub. *Belfast Telegraph*, 24 December 1954.

p. 511 'Overture for an Ulster literature': N30, pp. 143–5, probably September 1946, with title 'Overture regional'. Pub. *Poetry Ireland*, no. 1 (April 1948). pp. 13–14, with title 'Overture for Ulster regionalism'; *Q*, no. 11 (Hilary term 1955), p. 28. The *Poetry Ireland* version reads as follows:

Listen, and you shall hear above the storm
the new songs strengthen with the growing light.
The Welsh have started well; the lyric stories,
the jolting poems reach to grasp their truth.
Scotland, going a long time now with M'Diarmid,
has room for Drinan's salty lilt and Young's
polyglot gallimaufries on the pipes.

They have their advantages. Welsh is a language:
the rocky chapels are older than our spires.
Scots is as old as English. There was Dunbar;
and the Gaelic holds its ceilidhe in the islands.
But we, we are not Gaels: they have their ghettoes
and will be later than we to find a mode,
mode for translated thought, for the Gaeltacht shrinks.

Our speech is a narrow speech, the rags and remnants
of Tudor rogues and stiff Scots Covenanters,
curt soldierly dispatches and puritan sermons,
with a jap or two of glaar from the tangled sheugh,
the cross-roads solo and the penny ballad.

But even this starved thing will serve our purpose
if we're obedient to the shape of the land,
to the shifty weather with its crazy logic:
cold and dry in the spring, wet in the summer,
dry again at the heels of the Lammas floods.

We can make something of it, something hard
and clean and honest as the basalt cliffs,
patchy with colour like the coast in July,
bold as Slieve Bernagh and the bald Mourne peaks,
flat and reflecting as a Lough Neagh sunset,
as nourishing as potatoes out of the clay,
maybe not more shapely than the potato.

We are a little people, but we will be heard,
for we are lucky, can either grow or die,
but the great have no alternative to dying.

p. 512 'A rhyme for Christmas morning': N34, pp. 119–21, 23.12.54. Pub. *Belfast Telegraph*, 24 December 1955. Rep. *Coventry Evening Telegraph*, 21 December 1957.

p. 513 'Lines on the opening of the Belgrade Theatre': N35, pp. 75–7, February 1958, with title 'Prologue to be spoken at the opening of the Belgrade Theatre in March'. Pub. *Birmingham Post*, 28 March 1958; *Coventry Evening Telegraph*, 29 March 1958; programme for *Half in Earnest: A Musical Adaptation of Oscar Wilde's 'The Importance of Being Earnest'* at Belgrade Theatre, p. 3.

p. 515 'Poem' ('Consider Wordsworth in his withered age . . .'): N26, pp. 138–40, with title 'Mortality and age'; N46. pp. 52–3, 20.7.40. Pub. *Contemporary Irish Poetry* (eds Greacen and Iremonger, 1959), p. 74.

p. 516 'A country walk in May': N37, pp. 21–49, 1–3, 7–17.6.60, with note 'Finished 22.6.60'. Among Hewitt's papers, however, is an ms. third(?) draft of the poem, with the title 'The country walk: near Kenilworth', and the following notes: 'First Draft, 1/17.6.60, 549 lines; Second Draft, 22.6.60, 526 lines; Third Draft, 29.6.60, 527/535 lines; Fourth Draft, July–August 1960, 548 lines'. Pub. *Threshold*, vol. 4, no. 2 (Autumn–Winter 1960), pp. 17–35, with the following notes:

> The walk took place on the forenoon and afternoon of 29th May, 1960. The participants were E. Norman Carrothers, the botanist, Eric Elmes, the sculptor, my wife Roberta, and myself.
>
> *Tombola state:* Tombola, a game of chance popular in Midland Workingmen's Clubs;
>
> *Planter's polity:* that is, descendants of the English and Scots families who were settled in parts of the province of Ulster in the early 17th century;

Chaucer's old account book: Chaucer held several offices, e.g. Controller of the Customs of the Port of London, Clerk of the King's Works;

Browne's: William Browne (1591–1645?). Author of *Britannia's Pastorals*;

Cannavaun: Irish for bog-cotton or cotton-grass;

Hutted corn: corn sheaves built into small stacks;

Heathered cone: Tieveragh, 'a volcanic neck', near Cushendall, Co Antrim;

Sun dance: Daniel Hyndman (d. 1953) of Cushkib, Cushendall, claimed to have observed this occurrence, which is well-known in Irish folklore;

Skeagh-bush: hybrid Irish and English, dialect for 'fairy thorn', a hawthorn with magical properties;

Mountain blood: black-faced mountain sheep, a popular breed in mountainy districts of Co Antrim;

Salmon of all knowledge: in Irish mythology this fabulous creature subsists on the nuts which drop into the pool from the Nine Hazel Trees which grow beside it;

Sauce alone: garlic-mustard, or Jack-by-the-Hedge;

Joseph Arch: pioneer organiser of agricultural labourers (1826–1919), born and buried at Barford: held celebrated rally at Wellesbourne, both in Warwickshire;

Gilgowans: corn marigolds;

Kil': vernacular pronunciation of 'kiln';

Keresley, Binley, Newdigate: colleries of the Coventry area;

Platted hare: obsolete harvest-ritual of cutting the last sheaf, which was known in Ireland as the Hare or Cailliagh, by throwing reaping hooks at it;

Kerouac: Jack Kerouac, American writer of the Beat Generation;

Havelock Ellis: The Dance of Life (1926), p. 155;

Romantic agony: Mario Praz: *The Romantic Agony* (new edition, 1960).

A manuscript of this poem among Hewitt's papers contains variations of some of the above notes, notes relating to lines and references not included in the published version of the poem, and the following additional notes relevant to the published version:

Kenilworth: 'one of the most splendid and picturesque wrecks of castellated strength to be found in any English county'; *The Beauties of England and Wales*, vol. XV, p. 34;

Cleg-irked: tormented by horse-flies;

Moore: Henry in this context, not George or Thomas;

Lipschitz [sic]: Russian-born sculptor, long-resident in USA;

Sedentary trade: W.B. Yeats: 'This sedentary trade', *The Tower*;

Skeaping's Horse: wooden horse by English sculptor, at present on loan from Tate Gallery to the Herbert Art Gallery, Coventry;

Feathered kind: a cliché of English XVIIth century verse. A. Philipson: 'and fostered by the feather'd kind', *The Fable of Thule* (1748);

The castle's moat: 'The fine lake, which formerly ornamented three sides of the castle, and was the scene of much pageantry during Queen Elizabeth's visit, is now nearly dried up, and has long ceased to be an attractive object', *The Beauties of England and Wales*, vol. XV, Warwickshire (1814), p. 42.

The poem in which Hewitt first refers to 'stitchwort' is 'The little glen'.

p. 530 'For R.S. Thomas': N33, p. 109, 12.12.51, with title 'On reading "An acre of land" by R.S. Thomas, received today'. Pub. *Outposts*, no. 57 (Summer 1963), p. 16.

p. 530 'Hospitality: for E.K.': N38, p. 36, 13.3.67, with title 'E.K. The guest'. Pub. *Honest Ulsterman*, no. 2 (June 1968), p. 9. The subject of the poem is an acquaintance of the Hewitts, named Eric Knipe.

p. 531 'Prologue for an evening at the Whitefriars': N39, pp. 65–71, March 1970. Pub. in the form of a programme. The fourteenth-century Whitefriars monastery in Coventry was reopened in May 1970, after renovation; the first function there was an evening of Elizabethan and Jacobean music and poetry, staged by the Friends of the Herbert Art Gallery and Museum, for which Hewitt provided this prologue.

p. 534 'Christmas Eve': N4, pp. 112–16, 25.11.28, with title 'Christmas (in style of Lindsay)'; N7, pp. 47–50; N45, pp. 146–9, with note: 'written one Sunday when home (Evelyn Gardens) from Stranmillis Training College. This earned £1 from AE, £3.3.0 from BBC, £4.4.0 from *Radio Times*. I had brief correspondence with C.H. Vane regarding the modified spelling. AE warned me against Vachel Lindsay's overpowering influence.' Pub. *Northman*, vol. 2, no. 4 (December 1929), pp. 25–6. Rep. *Irish Statesman*, 21 December 1929; *Radio Times*, 18 December 1931; *Ulster Tatler* (rev. version) (December 1977), p. 50. *The Second Irish Christmas Book* (earlier version) (1986), p. 74.

The earlier version reads as follows:

There is a time for the crying thin,
The lyric tone of the violin.
There is a time for the hammerd song
Of the canebangd drum and the brasslungd gong.

At ten o'clock on Christmas Eve
I thankt the host and took my leave,
And slammd the door and hurried down
The lane that leads to the little town.
Snow fell lightly with never a noise,
Making the houses look like toys:
The windows shining like colord paper
That one holds up before a taper . . .
When snow lay inches, inches thick
And steelshod heels made now no click
The wind came up and cleard the sky
With a gusty broom and a huswife's eye.
The stars were shining, knockers bright,
Across the great halldoor of night.

The trees in the fields stood still as stone,
A far dog barkt alone . . . alone . . .
A late man passt at an open gate,
Cruncht on the snow, and went thro' the gate.
Then on alone I went . . . I went . . .
The stars stood still in their regiment.

At Crowcopse Manor the old churchclock
Crasht at the half and wakend a cock.
At Deadman's Hollow my watch face showd
Eleven o'clock . . . and half the road . . .
A quarter to twelve and I heard a sound,
It rang in the air and all around . . .
Between two stars that sang and shone
An angel trumpeted a mellow tone.
Behind him far, and behind the stars
Seraphs ran in their flaming cars:
And golden wings and golden feet
Glitterd along the golden street,
And golden voices and golden lutes
And dulcimers and golden flutes . . .
O High sky crying violins
Woke the Coda that begins
With golden voices and golden throats
And deep earthshaking organ notes
  This Christmas morn
  To you is born
  A Christ again,
  Rejoice, O men.

Then I saw the mother sitting on the throne,
And a little laughing baby that held her as his own . . .
Then I saw the manger and the shepherds kneeling there:
And old bewilderd Joseph with the starlight in his hair:
And the cattle in the corner, and the crib among the hay,
And the droopeard little donkey with melancholy bray . . .
But when I heard that sudden bray
The picture vanisht clean away,
And heaven shut, and the music died . . .
And I stood alone on the white hillside.

At ten past twelve I reacht the town,
The snow was trampled, slushy, and brown:
And at the end of the little street
A sleet scummd puddle soakt my feet.
And at the corner near my door
I saw them standing, singing there,
A shabby host of the weak and poor
Beneath a streetlamp's windy flare.

A big boy beat on a thundering drum,
And a thin man screecht of the Kingdom Come . . .
And a redfaced man, coverd over with braid,
Knelt in the slush, and prayd . . .
A halfstarvd cat crept frightend out
By the hoarse hosanna gospel shout:
A drunk man lurcht from an entry's dark
Into the lamplight's windy arc:
And a hungry boy with his papers unsold
Blew his fingers that were red with the cold . . .
And a flatfoot policeman trundled on his beat
With a deepchest cough and stamping feet . . .
AND A BIG BOY BEAT ON A THUNDERING DRUM,
AND A THIN MAN SCREECHT OF THE KINGDOM COME . . .

p. 536 'In the Luxembourg Gardens': two ms. versions among Hewitt's papers, one dated 12.9.(82), the other 29.9.82. Pub. *Gown* (1986), p. 22.

p. 537 'An incident': ms. notebook XXXII, May 1985; two ms. versions among Hewitt's papers, one dated 'April', the other 27.4.85. Pub. *Gown* (1986), p. 22.

p. 537 'The Anglo-Irish accord': ms. notebook XXXII, 13–14.3.86, with title 'Written for the People's Conference'. Pub. *The Dissenter: Journal of the New Ireland Group* (Summer 1986), p. 1. Rep. *Fortnight* (November 1986), p. 7; *Fortnight*, a special supplement titled 'Free thought in Ireland', no. 297 (July–August 1991), p. 9.

p. 538 'The mortal place': ms. notebook XXXII, August 1986. Pub. *Threshold*, no. 37 (Winter 1986–7), pp. 10–11. *See also* 'My first reported words' (*KS*, p. 25) and 'The river streets' (*KS*, p. 46).

p. 539 'A little people': ms. notebook XXXII, 19.6.86. Pub. *Threshold*, no. 37 (Winter 1986–7), pp. 11–13.

p. 541 'Sonnet' ('When I have read your hard and lively words . . .'): N30, p. 40, 23.5.45, with title 'To Roy McFadden on reading his *Flowers for a Lady*'. Pub. *Threshold*, John Hewitt edition, no 38 (Winter 1986–7), p. 13.

SELECT BIBLIOGRAPHY

BOOKS AND PAMPHLETS

POETRY

Conacre, privately published, Belfast, 1943
Compass: Two Poems, privately published, Belfast, 1944
No Rebel Word, Frederick Muller, London, 1948
Those Swans Remember: A Poem, privately published, Belfast, 1956
Tesserae, Festival Publications, Queen's University Belfast, Belfast, 1967
Collected Poems 1932–1967, MacGibbon and Kee, London, 1968
The Day of the Corncrake: Poems of the Nine Glens, Glens of Antrim Historical Society, n.p., 1969
The Planter and the Gael: Poems by John Hewitt and John Montague, Arts Council of Northern Ireland, Belfast, 1970
An Ulster Reckoning, privately published, Belfast, 1971
Out of My Time: Poems 1967–1974, Blackstaff Press, Belfast, 1974
Scissors for a One-Armed Tailor: Marginal Verses 1929–1954, privately published, Belfast, 1974
The Chinese Fluteplayer, privately published, Lisburn, 1974
Time Enough: Poems New and Revised, Blackstaff Press, Belfast, 1976
The Rain Dance: Poems New and Revised, Blackstaff Press, Belfast, 1978
Kites in Spring: A Belfast Boyhood, Blackstaff Press, Belfast, 1980
The Selected John Hewitt, edited and with an introduction by Alan Warner, Blackstaff Press, Belfast, 1981
Mosaic, Blackstaff Press, Belfast, 1981
Loose Ends, Blackstaff Press, Belfast, 1983
The Day of the Corncrake: Poems of the Nine Glens (revised edition), Glens of Antrim Historical Society, n.p., 1984
Freehold and Other Poems, Blackstaff Press, Belfast, 1986

AS EDITOR

The Poems of William Allingham, edited and with an introduction by John Hewitt, Dolmen Press, Dublin, 1967
Rhyming Weavers and Other Country Poets of Antrim and Down, edited and with an introduction by John Hewitt, Blackstaff Press, Belfast, 1974

PROSE

Colin Middleton, Arts Council of Northern Ireland, Belfast, 1976
Art in Ulster 1, Blackstaff Press, Belfast, 1977
John Luke 1906–1975, Arts Councils of Ireland, Belfast and Dublin, 1978
Ancestral Voices: The Selected Prose of John Hewitt, edited and with an introduction by Tom Clyde, Blackstaff Press, Belfast, 1987

SELECTED ARTICLES AND REVIEWS, AND OTHER PROSE WRITINGS

This section is heavily indebted to Tom Clyde's 'The prose writings of John Hewitt: a bibliography, with an introduction and an appendix comprising a selection of his works', unpublished MA thesis, Queen's University Belfast, 1985. I have concentrated on material of literary interest and included only a small fraction of Hewitt's numerous writings on art and artists. Also omitted are his letters to the press and his short stories; the best of the latter are reprinted in *Ancestral Voices: The Selected Prose of John Hewitt*, ed. Tom Clyde, Blackstaff Press, 1987.

'Vachel Lindsay', *Northman*, vol. 3, no. 5 (1932) p. 30
'Bohemian on the boulevard: a memory of Nineteen Thirty', *New Northman* (February 1937)
'George William Russell ("AE")', *Quarterly Notes* (Belfast Museum and Art Gallery [BM & AG]), no. 53 (June 1937), pp. 8–10
'William Butler Yeats 1865–1939', *Quarterly Notes* (BM & AG), no. 60 (March 1939), pp. 6–7
'Portrait of Dr Alexander Irvine', *Quarterly Notes* (BM & AG), no. 63 (December 1939), pp. 1–5
'A newspaper of 144 years ago', *Quarterly Notes* (BM & AG), no. 63 (December 1939), pp. 8–10 (about the *Northern Star*, June 1795)
'Dr Thomas Munro 1759–1833', *Quarterly Notes* (BM & AG), no. 63 (December 1939), p. 10
'"A lad was born in Kyle": Robert Burns, the people's poet', *Trade Union Searchlight* (March 1940), pp. 11–12. Continued *Trade Union Searchlight* (April 1940)
Review of *Willow Leaves: Lyrics in the Manner of the Early Chinese Poets* by John Irvine, *The Bell*, vol. 3, no. 5 (February 1942), p. 101
Review of *Lost Fields* by Michael McLaverty, *The Bell*, vol. 4, no. 4 (July 1942), pp. 303–4
Review of *Irish Heritage* by Estyn Evans, *The Bell*, vol. 4, no. 5 (August 1942), pp. 371–4

'Some observations on the history of Irish painting', *Lagan*, no. 1 (1943), pp. 93–9

'Painting in Ulster', in *Northern Harvest: An Anthology of Ulster Writing*, ed. Robert Greacen, Derrick MacCord, 1944, pp. 140–7

'Under forty: some Ulster artists, a personal essay', in *Now in Ulster*, comps Arthur and George Campbell, n.p., 1944, pp. 13–35; reprinted in *Ancestral Voices: The Selected Prose of John Hewitt*, ed. Tom Clyde, Blackstaff Press, 1987, pp. 108–21

'James Hope, weaver of Templepatrick', *Northern Star*, vol. 5, no. 1 (January 1944), pp. 6–12; extract reprinted in *Ninety-Eight*, ed. Seamus McKeanney, n.p., 1948, under pseudonym 'John McHugh'

'The bitter gourd: some problems of the Ulster writer', *Lagan*, no. 3 (1945), pp. 93–105

Review of *Odd Man Out* by F.L. Green, *Lagan*, no. 3 (1945), pp. 128–30

'Les arts en Ulster pendant la guerre', *La France Libre*, vol. 12, no. 69 (15 July 1946), pp. 234–8

'Regionalism: the last chance', *Northman*, vol. 15, no. 3 (Summer 1947), pp. 7–9; reprinted in *Ancestral Voices: The Selected Prose of John Hewitt*, ed. Tom Clyde, Blackstaff Press, 1987, pp. 122–5

'A study of William Carleton', *Irish News*, 31 December 1947

Review of *Rural Life in Northern Ireland* by John M. Mogey, *The Bell*, vol. 16, no. 1 (April 1948), pp. 69–73

'Poetry and you', *Ulster Young Farmer*, vol. 2, no. 8 (May 1948), pp. 21–2

'What is poetry?', *Ulster Young Farmer*, vol. 2, no. 9 (June 1948), pp. 19–20

'Programme for poetry', *Ulster Young Farmer*, vol. 2, no. 10 (July 1948), pp. 14–16

'Three letters on poetry writing', *Ulster Young Farmer*, vol. 2, no. 11 (August 1948), pp. 14–17

'Hints of the proper craft – some examples of fine poetry', *Ulster Young Farmer*, vol. 2, no. 12 (September 1948), pp. 16–19

'"True to our thought and speech"', *Ulster Young Farmer*, vol. 3, no. 1 (October 1948), pages unnumbered

Untitled article on contemporary Scottish poetry, *Poetry Ireland*, no. 5 (April 1949), pp. 25–7

'Ulster poets 1800–1850', privately published text of a paper read to the Belfast Literary Society, 2 January 1950

'Poetry and Ulster: a survey', *Poetry Ireland*, no. 9 (January 1950), pp. 3–10

Review of *Poems 1938–49* by Robert Lowell, *Rann*, no. 10 (Autumn 1950), pp. 9–10

'Some notes on writing in Ulster', *Ulidian* (Michaelmas 1950), pp. 12–13

'Painting and sculpture in Ulster', in *The Arts in Ulster: A Symposium*, eds Sam Hanna Bell, Nesca A. Robb and John Hewitt, Harrap, 1951, pp. 71–95; reprinted in *Ancestral Voices: The Selected Prose of John Hewitt*, ed. Tom Clyde, Blackstaff Press, 1987, pp. 87–107

Review of *Wild Earth* by Padraic Colum, and *Reservations* by Valentin Iremonger, *Irish Writing*, no. 14 (March 1951), pp. 65–6

Review of *Ulster Folklore* by Jeanne Cooper Foster, *The Bell*, vol. 17, no. 6 (September 1951), pp. 63–4

Review of *Rainer Maria Rilke: His Life and Work* by F.W. van Heekiksheuzen, *The Bell*, vol. 18, no. 1 (April 1952), p. 55

'The lonely furrow', *British Weekly*, 26 June 1952 (about the poetry of R.S. Thomas)

Review of *Mourne Country* by Estyn Evans, *The Bell*, vol. 18, no. 4 (July 1952), p. 246

'R.N.D. Wilson: an obituary', *Dublin Magazine*, vol. 28, no. 2 (1953), pp. 54–5

'The course of writing in Ulster', *Rann*, no. 20 (Spring 1953), pp. 43–52; reprinted in *Ancestral Voices: The Selected Prose of John Hewitt*, ed. Tom Clyde, Blackstaff Press, 1987, pp. 64–76

'Planter's Gothic: an essay in discursive autobiography', *The Bell*, vol. 18, no. 8 (Spring 1953), pp. 497–510, under pseudonym 'John Howard'; reprinted in *Ancestral Voices: The Selected Prose of John Hewitt*, ed. Tom Clyde, Blackstaff Press, 1987, pp. 1–15

'Planter's Gothic II: an essay in discursive autobiography', *The Bell*, vol. 18, no. 10 (Summer 1953), pp. 605–12, under pseudonym 'John Howard'; reprinted in *Ancestral Voices: The Selected Prose of John Hewitt*, ed. Tom Clyde, Blackstaff Press, 1987, pp. 15–23

'Planter's Gothic III: an essay in discursive autobiography', *The Bell*, vol. 18, no. 12 (Autumn 1953), pp. 94–103, under pseudonym 'John Howard'; reprinted in *Ancestral Voices: The Selected Prose of John Hewitt*, ed. Tom Clyde, Blackstaff Press, 1987, pp. 23–33

'The strange durability of Walter de la Mare', *Belfast Telegraph*, 21 November 1953

'We are marking our place in literature', *Belfast Telegraph*, 7 December 1953

Review of '*Collected Poems* of James Stephens', *Belfast Telegraph*, 15 March 1954

'American scholar's study of W.B. Yeats', *Belfast Telegraph*, 7 August 1954 (review of *The Identity of Yeats* by Richard Ellmann)

'The letters of Yeats', *Belfast Telegraph*, 13 December 1954

'The songs of Moira O'Neill', *Belfast Telegraph*, 12 March 1955

'Distinctive and correct use of language', *Belfast Telegraph*, 2 April 1955

'Poetry is another American export', *Belfast Telegraph*, 9 April 1955

'Words preferred to stone: Canadian poet's *Titanic* disaster tribute more durable than any monument', *Belfast Telegraph*, 23 April 1955 (about *The Titanic* by E.J. Pratt)
'Lyric thoughts of the early Irish poets', *Belfast Telegraph*, 6 October 1956 (review of *Early Irish Lyrics*, edited and translated by Gerard Murphy)
'Artist, actor, teacher, friend', *Belfast Telegraph*, 6 July 1957 (about W.R. Gordon, S.B. McCreery and others)
'Godiva rides again in a new Coventry', *Belfast Telegraph*, 20 September 1957
'Alexander Irvine and his legend', *Belfast Telegraph*, 2 November 1957
'Recent verse by Irish poets', *Threshold*, vol. 2, no. 2 (Summer 1958), pp. 70–5 (review of books by Thomas Kinsella, Patrick Galvin and Ewart Milne)
'Irish poets learn your trade', *Threshold*, vol. 2, no. 3 (Autumn 1958), pp. 62–71; reprinted in *Ancestral Voices: The Selected Prose of John Hewitt*, ed. Tom Clyde, Blackstaff Press, 1987, pp. 77–86
'Selection of Irish Verse has some gaps', *Belfast Telegraph*, 30 October 1958 (review of *The Oxford Book of Irish Verse*, ed. Donagh MacDonagh)
'Journey of discovery into the literature of Ulster', *Belfast Telegraph*, 24 November 1958
'A Dresden notebook – some aspects of art under communism', *Threshold*, vol. 3, no. 2 (Summer 1959), pp. 47–60
'Poetry review', *Threshold*, vol. 3, no. 2 (Summer 1959), pp. 92–6 (review of six collections, including *Forms of Exile* by John Montague)
'The poetry of Patrick MacDonagh', *Threshold*, vol. 3, no. 3 (Autumn 1959), pp. 50–4
'Men from the fields', *Threshold*, vol. 4, no. 2 (Autumn–Winter 1960), pp. 61–7 (review of *The Poet's Circuits* by Padraic Colum)
'The cobbler's song', *Threshold*, vol. 5, no. 1 (Spring–Summer 1961), pp. 42–51 (about the poetry of Patrick Kavanagh)
'The longest campaign', *Threshold*, vol. 5, no. 1 (Spring–Summer 1961), pp. 58–64; reprinted in *Ancestral Voices: The Selected Prose of John Hewitt*, ed. Tom Clyde, Blackstaff Press, 1987, pp. 126–32
Review of *From 'The Prelude'*, ed. H.S. Taylor, *Threshold*, vol. 5, no. 2 (Autumn–Winter 1961), p. 86
'Coventry, the tradition of change and continuity', in *Coventry, The Tradition of Change and Continuity*, Coventry Corporation, 1965, pp. 1–13
'T.S. Eliot', *Belfast Telegraph*, 9 January 1965
'The progress of a poet', *Belfast Telegraph*, 19 May 1966 (review of *Death of a Naturalist* by Seamus Heaney)

'An idealist in action', *Belfast Telegraph*, 8 April 1967 (about George Russell/AE)
'Another look at William Allingham', *Belfast Telegraph*, 6 January 1968
'Secular burial', *Honest Ulsterman*, no. 2 (June 1968), pp. 6–9 (extract from an unpublished autobiography, 'A North Light'); reprinted in *Ancestral Voices: The Selected Prose of John Hewitt*, ed. Tom Clyde, Blackstaff Press, 1987, pp. 34–7
'Alec of the Chimney Corner', *Honest Ulsterman*, no. 4 (August 1968), pp. 5–12 (extract from an unpublished autobiography, 'A North Light'); reprinted in *Threshold*, no. 35 (Winter 1984–5), pp. 40–6, and in *Ancestral Voices: The Selected Prose of John Hewitt*, ed. Tom Clyde, Blackstaff Press, 1987, pp. 38–47
'From chairmen and committee men, Good Lord deliver us', *Honest Ulsterman*, no. 6 (September 1968), pp. 16–22 (extract from an unpublished autobiography, 'A North Light'); reprinted in *Ancestral Voices: The Selected Prose of John Hewitt*, ed. Tom Clyde, Blackstaff Press, 1987, pp. 48–55
'Poet's report', *Irish Press*, 1 February 1969 (review of *Modern Poetry* by Louis MacNeice)
'The family next door', *Threshold*, no. 23 (Summer 1970), pp. 14–19; reprinted *Evening Press*, 17 August 1970
'No rootless colonist', *Aquarius*, no. 5 (1972), pp. 90–5; reprinted in *Ancestral Voices: The Selected Prose of John Hewitt*, ed. Tom Clyde, Blackstaff Press, 1987, pp. 146–57
'Late starter', *Irish Press*, 15 January 1972 (review of *Collected Poems* by W.R. Rodgers, and *W.R. Rodgers 1909–69* by Darcy O'Brien)
'The folded dream: the printed words of AE', *Arts in Ireland*, vol. 1, no. 3 (1973), pp. 49–52
'The arts and the Troubles', *Irish Times*, 13 June 1973
'James H. Cousins, 1873–1956', *Irish Press*, 21 July 1973
'The troubled world of Padraic Fiacc', *Belfast Telegraph*, 11 August 1973 (review of *Odour of Blood* by Padraic Fiacc)
'Stereoscopic Ireland', *Irish Press*, 27 April 1974 (review of *From the Jungle of Belfast* by Denis Ireland)
'Austin Clarke 1896–1974', *Threshold*, no. 25 (Summer 1974), pp. 3–6
'Clarke memorial', *Irish Press*, 20 July 1974 (review of *Irish University Review*'s Austin Clarke special issue)
'The centaur at the house of prayer: the poetry of Austin Clarke', *Honest Ulsterman*, nos. 44–5 (August–October 1974), pp. 64–8
'The forgotten tradition', *Hibernia* (11 October 1974), p. 15 (on working-class poetry)
'Rhymer and poet', *Hibernia* (24 January 1975), p. 19 (review of *The Bard of Thomond* by Frank Hamilton, and *Francis Ledwidge: Complete Poems*, ed. Alice Curtayne)

'Where I was born', in *Today and Yesterday in Northern Ireland*, BBC Radio 4, Teachers' notes (Summer 1975), p. 5
'Permanent Yeats', *Irish Press*, 11 November 1976 (review of *Yeats* by Frank Tuohy)
'John Hewitt writes . . .', *Poetry Book Society Bulletin*, no. 91 (Christmas 1976) (*Time Enough* was a Poetry Book Society Recommendation)
'George Russell (AE)', in *Harold Balfour*, a commemorative pamphlet of the Ulster Agricultural Organisation Society, Portadown, 1977
'John Hewitt writes . . .', *Poetry Book Society Bulletin*, no. 99 (Christmas 1978) (*The Rain Dance* was a Poetry Book Society Recommendation)
Contribution to 'The war years in Ulster, 1939–45; a symposium', *Honest Ulsterman*, no. 64 (September 1979–January 1980), pp. 24–7
Foreword to *As I Roved Out* by Cathal O'Byrne (facsimile edition), Blackstaff Press, 1982
Foreword to *Morning in Belfast* by Dennis Greig, Pretani Press, 1983
'"The Northern Athens" and after', in *Belfast: The Making of the City, 1800–1914*, J.C. Beckett *et al.*, Appletree Press, 1983, pp. 71–82
'Good times, lean times: the passing caravan', *Belfast Review*, no. 5 (Winter 1983), pp. 21–3

ANTHOLOGIES, TEXTBOOKS, AND OTHER COMPENDIUMS

Poems of Tomorrow: An Anthology of Contemporary Verse, chosen from the *Listener* by Janet Adam Smith, Chatto and Windus, 1935, pp. 52–4
Poems by Ulster Poets, n.p., n.d. (copy among Hewitt's books dated, in his hand, '1937 or 38')
Fifteen Poems, Socialist Party, Belfast, in aid of the Russian Red Cross, 1942, pp. 4–5
Irish Poems of Today, chosen from the first seven volumes of *The Bell*, ed. Geoffrey Taylor, Irish People's Publications/Secker and Warburg, 1944, pp. 15–20
Northern Harvest: An Anthology of Ulster Writing, ed. Robert Greacen, Derrick MacCord, 1944, pp. 88–9
Now in Ulster, comps Arthur and George Campbell, n.p., 1944, p. 37
Poems from Ireland, poems drawn from the *Irish Times*, ed. Donagh MacDonagh, *Irish Times*, 1944, p. 30
Poetry Scotland, no. 1, ed. Maurice Lindsay, William MacLellan, 1944, p. 52
The Flowering Branch, ed. John Irvine McCord, n.p., 1945

Irish Harvest: A Collection of Stories, Essays and Poems, ed. Robert Greacen, New Frontiers Press, 1946, pp. 52–3
Little Reviews Anthology, ed. Denys Val Baker, Eyre and Spottiswoode, 1946, p. 154
1000 Years of Irish Poetry, ed. Kathleen Hoagland, Devin-Adair, 1947, p. 738
New Irish Poets: Representative Selections from the Work of Thirty-Seven Contemporaries, ed. Devin A. Garrity, Devin-Adair, 1948, pp. 87–94
A New Romantic Anthology, eds Stefan Schimanski and Henry Treece, Grey Walls Press, 1949, p. 130
Poetry of the Present: An Anthology of the Thirties and After, comp. Geoffrey Grigson, Phoenix House, 1949, pp. 110–20
Brave Crack: An Anthology of Ulster Wit and Humour, H.R. Carter, 1950, pp. 92–4
Concord of Harps: An Irish PEN Anthology of Poetry, Talbot Press, 1952, pp. 20–1
New Poems 1952: A PEN Anthology, eds Clifford Dyment, Roy Fuller and Montague Slater, Michael Joseph, 1952, pp. 30–2
New Poems 1953: A PEN Anthology, eds Robert Conquest, Michael Hamburger and Howard Sergeant, Michael Joseph, 1953, pp. 86–7
New Poems 1954: A PEN Anthology, eds Rex Warner, Christopher Hassall and Laurie Lee, Michael Joseph, 1954, p. 138
A Winter Harvest: A Folio of New Poems from the North of Ireland, ed. Andrew Molloy Carson, Emerald Press, 1956, pp. 12–15
New World Writing (tenth Mentor selection), New American Library, 1956, p. 152
New Poems 1958: A PEN Anthology, eds Bonamy Dobree, Louis MacNeice and Philip Larkin, Michael Joseph, 1958, p. 47
Contemporary Irish Poetry, eds Robert Greacen and Valentin Iremonger, Faber and Faber, 1959, pp. 73–9
The Guinness Book of Poetry 1958–59, Putnam, 1960, p. 70
New Poems 1960: A PEN Anthology, eds Anthony Cronin, Jon Silkin and Terence Tiller, Hutchinson, 1960, pp. 61–3
New Poems 1961: A PEN Anthology of Contemporary Poetry, eds William Plomer, Anthony Thwaite and Hilary Corke, Hutchinson, 1961, pp. 42–3
Best Poems of 1961 (Borestone Mountain Poetry Awards, 1962), Pacific Books, 1962, pp. 65–6
An Anthology of Commonwealth Verse, ed. Margaret J. O'Donnell, Blackie and Sons, 1963, p. 143
New Poets of Ireland, ed. Donald Carroll, Alan Swallow, 1963, pp. 40–3
Poems of Today (fifth series), comp. Margaret Willy, published for the English Association by Macmillan, 1963, p. 60
Listening and Writing, BBC Radio for Schools (Summer 1964), p. 4

The Mentor Book of Irish Poetry from AE to Yeats, ed. Devin A. Garrity, New American Library, 1965, pp. 156–60
Modern Poems Understood: A Selection, ed. C.W. Gillam, Harrap, 1965, pp. 69–70
The Animal Anthology, comp. Diana Spearman, John Baker, 1966, p. 105, pp. 116–17 (royalties devoted to work of Fauna Preservation Society)
New Poems 1965: A PEN Anthology of Contemporary Poetry, ed. C.V. Wedgwood, Hutchinson, 1966, p. 84
Listening and Writing, BBC Radio for Schools (Summer 1967), p. 4
Poems to Read Aloud, ed. Edward Hodnett, W.W. Norton, 1967, p. 161
Understanding and Appreciation: Book I, ed. B.J. Pendlebury, Nelson, 1967, pp. 27–8
Voices: An Anthology of Poetry and Pictures: The First Book, ed. Geoffrey Summerfield, Penguin, 1968, pp. 36–7
Chorus: An Anthology of Bird Poems, comp. Susanne Knowles, Heinemann, 1969, p. 45
Lyric Theatre 1951–1968, Lyric Players Theatre, *c.* 1969–70, pages unnumbered
The Penguin Book of Irish Verse, ed. Brendan Kennelly, Penguin, 1970, p. 346; second edition, 1981, p. 364
Exercises in Practical Criticism, comp. John O'Neill, Robert Gibson and Sons, 1971, pp. 19–21
Here in Ulster, BBC Radio for Schools, 1971
Adventures in English, ed. Patrick Murray, Educational Company, 1972, pp. 58–60
Happenings 2: New Poems for Schools, eds Maurice Wollman and Alice Austin, Harrap, 1972, pp. 47, 87
Poems from Ireland, comp. William Cole, Thomas Y. Cromwell, 1972, pp. 60–2
Soundings '72, ed. Seamus Heaney, Blackstaff Press, 1972, pp. 25–6
The Sphere Book of Modern Irish Poetry, ed. Derek Mahon, Sphere, 1972, pp. 128–30
Within Our Province: A Miscellany of Ulster Writing, ed. Sam Hanna Bell, Blackstaff Press, 1972, pp. 5–6
Angry for Peace (vol. 9, no. 1, in Risk series), ed. Rex Davies, World Council of Churches, 1973, p. 7
Choice: An Anthology of Irish Poetry Selected by the Poets Themselves, with a Comment on their Choice, eds Desmond Egan and Michael Hartnett, Goldsmith Press, 1973, pp. 40–1
The Oxford Book of Twentieth-Century English Verse, comp. Philip Larkin, Clarendon Press, 1973, pp. 427–9
Witches and Charms and Things, comp. C.G. Stokes, Collins, 1973, p. 10

The Faber Book of Irish Verse, ed. John Montague, Faber and Faber, 1974, pp. 300–1

The Nine Glens, Maureen Donnelly, *Newtownards Chronicle*, 1974, pp. 77–8, 84, 113

Poetry Dimension 2: A Living Record of the Poetry Year, ed. Dannie Abse, Abacus, 1974, p. 199

Ten Irish Poets, ed. James Simmons, Carcanet Press, 1974, pp. 21–8

The Wearing of the Black: An Anthology of Contemporary Ulster Poetry, ed. Padraic Fiacc, Blackstaff Press, 1974, pp. 1–2, 4, 6, 8, 9, 11–12, 13, 17, 51, 76, 81, 145–6, 154–5

New Poems 1975: A PEN Anthology of Contemporary Poetry, ed. Patricia Beer, Hutchinson, 1975, p. 131

Poetry Dimension Annual 3: The Best of the Poetry Year, ed. Dannie Abse, Robson Books, 1975, p. 79

The Wolfhound Book of Irish Poems for Young People, eds Bridie Quinn and Seamus Cashman, Wolfhound Press, 1975, p. 47

Blueprint (a series of four reference books for use in secondary school assemblies, religious education and liberal studies classes etc.), general ed. John Bailey, Book I, Stainer and Bell, 1976, pp. 188–9

The Best from The Bell: Great Irish Writing, ed. Sean McMahon, O'Brien Press, 1978, pp. 88–9

A Prose and Verse Anthology of Modern Irish Writing, ed. Grattan Freyer, Irish Humanities Centre, 1978, pp. 232–3

Celebration: A Salute to a Visiting Artist (Pope Paul VI), ed. Jim Fitzgerald, Veritas, 1979, p. 28

The First Ten Years: Dublin Arts Festival Poetry, eds Peter Fallon and Dennis O'Driscoll, Dublin Arts Festival, 1979, pp. 22–3

Poets from the North of Ireland, ed. Frank Ormsby, Blackstaff Press, 1979, pp. 27–41; second edition, 1990, pp. 33–44

Contemporary Irish Poetry, ed. Anthony Bradley, University of California Press, 1980, pp. 107–13; second edition, 1988, pp. 101–7

The Faber Book of Poems and Places, ed. Geoffrey Grigson, Faber and Faber, 1980, pp. 304–5

Poems of Warwickshire, ed. Roger Pringle, Roundwood Press, 1980, pp. 44, 65

Soft Day: A Miscellany of Contemporary Irish Writing, eds Peter Fallon and Sean Golden, University of Notre Dame Press, 1980, pp. 25–8

Voices of Today: An Anthology of Recent Verse, comp. F.E.S. Finn, John Murray, 1980, pp. 3, 97

The Writers: A Sense of Ireland, eds Andrew Carpenter and Peter Fallon, with photographs by Mike Bunn, O'Brien Press, 1980, pp. 57–9

Across the Roaring Hill: An Impression of Ulster Compiled from the Work of the Province's Writers, comp. David Grant, 1981, pp. 1, 8–9,

9–10, 26, 42–5 (anthology programme for a presentation by Cambridge Mummers, Edinburgh Fringe Festival, April 1981)

Four Seasons, comps Edward Phelps and Geoffrey Summerfield, Oxford University Press, 1983, pp. 41–2, 173–4

Hundsrose: Neue Irische Gedichte, eds Eva and Eoin Burke, Maroverlag, 1983, pp. 119–26

All Shy Wildness: An Anthology of Irish Animal Poetry, ed. Robert Johnstone, illus. Diana Oxlade, Blackstaff Press, 1984, p. 34

The Crock of Gold (Rainbow Reading Programme, Stage Four, Book Two), Fallons, 1984, p. 73

Rich and Rare: A Book of Ireland, ed. Sean McMahon, Ward River Press, 1984, pp. 138–9

That's Life: Einführungskurs Englisch Sek. II, ed. Klaus Hinz, Ferdinand Schöningh, 1984, p. 41

The Irish Christmas Book, ed. John Killen, Blackstaff Press, 1985, p. 165

Speak to the Hills: An Anthology of Twentieth-Century British and Irish Mountain Poetry, eds Hamish Brown and Martyn Berry, Aberdeen University Press, 1985, p. 178

The Deer's Cry: A Treasury of Irish Religious Verse, ed. Patrick Murray, Four Courts Press, 1986, p. 232

The Second Irish Christmas Book, ed. John Killen, Blackstaff Press, 1986, pp. 74–6

The Long Embrace: Twentieth-Century Irish Love Poems, ed. Frank Ormsby, Blackstaff Press, 1987, pp. 32–3

A Poet's Pictures: A Selection of Works of Art Collected by John Hewitt (1907–1987), Shambles Art Gallery, 1987, p. 15

The Pure Drop: A Book of Irish Drinking, ed. John Killen, Blackstaff Press, 1987, pp. 22, 43

Thirty Years of the Poetry Book Society 1956–1986, ed. Jonathan Barker, Hutchinson, 1988, p. 116

Bitter Harvest: An Anthology of Contemporary Irish Verse, comp. John Montague, Charles Scribner's Sons, 1989, pp. 11–14

Antrim Coast and Glens: A Personal View, Cahal Dallat, Countryside and Wildlife Interpretation series, HMSO, 1990, pp. 11, 22, 28, 30, 31–3, 34, 40

Ireland in Poetry, ed. Charles Sullivan, Harry N. Abrams, 1990, pp. 10, 31, 66, 158, 173

Irish Poetry of Faith and Doubt: The Cold Heaven, ed. John F. Deane, Wolfhound Press, 1990, pp. 89–90

Literature in Projects, ed. A.J.M. van Eijk, Wotters-Noordhoff-Longman, 1990, pp. 120–2

The Field Day Anthology of Irish Writing, vol. III, general ed. Seamus Deane, associate ed. Andrew Carpenter, Field Day Publications, 1991, pp. 163–5

Poètes d'Irlande du Nord (bilingual), ed. Colin Meir, Amiot-Lenganey, 1991, pp. 18–31

SELECTED BROADCASTS

Hewitt contributed poems, commentary and reviews to a large number of radio programmes. I have selected from those he wrote in their entirety, or which were devoted largely to his work. The date given in each case is that of first transmission.

'Samuel Ferguson', Northern Ireland Home Service (NIHS), 11 August 1946
'The poetry of Robinson Jeffers', NIHS, 3 January 1947
'Writing in Ulster, no. 15: Francis Davis, the Belfastman', NIHS, 4 February 1948
'Pictures', NIHS, 1 March 1948
'Place and folk: John Hewitt discusses various definitions of regionalism and outlines the regional idea in connection with landscape, history and culture in Ulster', NIHS, 19 April 1949
'Ulster commentary', NIHS, 7 November 1949
'Ulster commentary', NIHS, 2 December 1949
'Ulster commentary', NIHS, 13 January 1950
'Eye and image: John Hewitt discusses the teaching of art with Kathleen Bridle and Dan O'Neill', NIHS, 31 January 1950
'Ulster commentary', NIHS, 10 March 1950
'Ulster commentary', NIHS, 21 April 1950
'The country poets of the north: a talk about northern folk poets of the nineteenth century', Radio Éireann, 16 May 1950
'Ulster commentary', NIHS, 16 June 1950
'Ulster commentary', NIHS, 19 December 1950
'Ulster commentary', NIHS, 15 February 1951
'The Lavery exhibition', NIHS, 3 May 1951
'John Hewitt: Ulster poet on his life and work', BBC Radio 4, 26 September 1961
'How it all started: an autobiographical talk', NIHS, 1 April 1965
'John Hewitt' (Hewitt is interviewed on Ulster's identity and reads from his work), BBC Radio 4, 29 September 1970
'Davis, Mangan, Ferguson', BBC Radio Ulster, 19 October 1974
'Poets on poetry: Hewitt', Radio Éireann, 18 February 1975
'The Rhyming Weavers', BBC Radio Ulster, 13 April 1975
'Today and yesterday in Northern Ireland: John Hewitt recalls his childhood', BBC Northern Ireland schools broadcast, 9 May 1975

'Poems plain: John Hewitt and Desmond O'Grady', RTE Radio 1, 11 December 1978

'John Hewitt' (Hewitt reads from *The Selected John Hewitt*), BBC Radio Ulster, 9 August 1981

'Explorations II: John Hewitt', (Hewitt is interviewed by Geoffrey Summerfield and reads from *Kites in Spring* and *Mosaic*), BBC Radio Ulster, 23 March 1982

'Voices of the north, no. 5: John Hewitt and Frank Ormsby', RTE Radio 1, 30 January 1983

'Poetry patterns: John Hewitt' (Hewitt reads from and discusses his collection *Loose Ends*), RTE Radio 1, 5 July 1983

RECORDINGS AND FILM

Poetry of Ireland, vol. 2 in the Poetry of the British Isles series, Beltona Records (Decca), 1959. (An anthology of work by Irish poets, read by Richard Hayward, John Hewitt and Eithne Dunn. Hewitt reads his own poem 'The little lough' and also the following: 'Kilcash' by Frank O'Connor; 'Outcast', 'Dust' and 'Reconciliation' by AE; 'Carrickfergus' by Louis MacNeice; 'Armagh' by W.R. Rodgers; and sections 3 and 4 of 'Vacillation' by W.B. Yeats.)

I Found Myself Alone, made by Landseer Productions for the Arts Council of Northern Ireland, 1978 (a film about Hewitt and his work)

Substance and Shadow, Audio Arts, 1980. (A cassette recording of Hewitt reading his poems: 'The little lough'; 'Turf-carrier on Aranmore'; 'Because I paced my thought'; 'From a museum man's album'; 'O country people'; 'The colony'; 'The ram's horn'; 'The watchers'; 'The gap'; 'The spectacle of truth'; 'An Irishman in Coventry'; 'The knife'; 'The search'; 'Et tu in Arcadia vixisti'; 'The moon'; 'The scar'; 'On the canal'; 'The King's horses'; 'Substance and shadow'; 'A birthday rhyme for Roberta'; and 'A local poet'.)

ABOUT JOHN HEWITT: SELECTED ARTICLES, INTERVIEWS, PROFILES, REVIEWS AND OTHER ITEMS

Baird, Brian. 'The right to change the masks: a note on the poetry of John Hewitt', *Ulster Tatler* (November 1983), pp. 70–3

Banyard, Margaret. 'An Ulster poet: John Hewitt', *Acorn*, no. 7 (Autumn 1964), pp. 9–10

Boland, Eavan (ed.). 'The clash of identities I', *Irish Times*, 4 July 1974

Boland, Eavan (ed.). 'The clash of identities II', *Irish Times*, 5 July 1974
Boland, Eavan. 'Hewitt the outsider', *Irish Times*, 26 July 1986 (review of *Freehold and Other Poems*)
Boland, Eavan. 'John Hewitt, an appreciation', *Irish Times*, 30 July 1987
Brown, Terence. 'John Hewitt: an Ulster poet', *Topic: A Journal of the Liberal Arts*, no. 24, (Fall 1972), pp. 60–8
Brown, Terence. 'John Hewitt: land and people', in *Northern Voices: Poets from Ulster*, Gill and Macmillan, 1975, pp. 86–97
Brown, Terence. 'The poetry of W.R. Rodgers and John Hewitt', in *Two Decades of Irish Writing*, ed. Douglas Dunn, Carcanet Press, 1975, pp. 81–97
Brown, Terence. 'John Hewitt', in *Dictionary of Literary Biography*, vol. 27, 'Poets of Great Britain and Ireland, 1945–60', ed. Vincent B. Sherry, Gale Research Company, 1984, pp. 149–55
Brown, Terence. 'A secular imagination', *Threshold* (Hewitt edition), no. 38 (Winter 1986–7), pp. 4–5
Brown, Terence. 'The poet's shadow', *Fortnight* (Hewitt supplement), no. 275 (July–August 1989), p. vii
Burnside, Sam. 'Preparing lonely defences', *Fortnight* (Hewitt supplement), no. 275 (July–August 1989), p. iii
Campbell, Arthur. 'Art in the war', *Honest Ulsterman*, no. 84 (Winter 1987), pp. 13–14
Campbell, John. 'The John Hewitt I knew', in *Waterfront: A Dockside Literary Publication*, North Belfast History Workshop, 1990, pp. 6–9
Casey, Dan. 'The doyen: a *Quarto* interview with the Belfast poet, John Hewitt, December 4, 1980, the New University of Ulster', *Quarto*, vol. 7 (1980–1), pp. 1–14
Clarke, Austin. 'Nature and art', *Irish Times*, 12 February 1949 (includes review of *No Rebel Word*)
Clyde, Tom. 'The prose writings of John Hewitt: a bibliography, with an introduction, and an appendix comprising a selection of his works', unpublished MA thesis, Queen's University Belfast, 1985
Craig, Patricia. 'John Hewitt: a vertical man', *Honest Ulsterman*, no. 84 (Winter 1987), pp. 3–7
Craig, Patricia. 'Finding hope in the weavers', *Fortnight* (Hewitt supplement), no. 275 (July–August 1989), p. vi
Dawe, Gerald, and John Wilson Foster. *The Poet's Place: Ulster Literature and Society, Essays in Honour of John Hewitt 1907–87*, Institute of Irish Studies, Queen's University Belfast, 1991.
Devlin, Paddy. 'No rootless colonist', *Threshold* (Hewitt edition), no. 38 (Winter 1986–7), pp. 22–3
Doyle, Rosemarie. 'John Hewitt, the author and poet', *Irish Times*, 15 March 1980

Durcan, Paul. 'Hewitt's achievement', *Cork Examiner*, 29 April 1980 (review of *Kites in Spring*)
Evans, John. 'Now poetry is what I'm about, John Evans: profile of John Hewitt', *Coventry Evening Telegraph*, 29 August 1968
Fiacc, Padraic. 'An Ulsterman's search for identity', *Hibernia* (26 April 1974), p. 11
Foster, John Wilson. 'The landscape of the Planter and the Gael in the poetry of John Hewitt and John Montague', *Canadian Journal of Irish Studies*, vol. 1, no. 2 (November 1975), pp. 17–33
Foster, John Wilson. '"The dissidence of dissent": John Hewitt and W.R. Rodgers', in *Across a Roaring Hill: The Protestant Imagination in Modern Ireland*, eds Gerald Dawe and Edna Longley, Blackstaff Press, 1985, pp. 139–60
Gorman, Damian. 'For believers in mankind . . . the alternative', *Irish News*, 25 November 1986 (part of the Religion and Non-belief series: 'Part one: living without a God')
Greacen, Robert. 'John Hewitt: a personal tribute', *Ulster Tatler* (November 1983), p. 74
Greacen, Robert. 'John Hewitt, a memoir', *Honest Ulsterman*, no. 84 (Winter 1987), pp. 8–9
Grennan, Eamon. Review article on Hewitt's *Out of My Time* and *Time Enough*, *Éire–Ireland* (Summer 1977), pp. 143–51
Heaney, Seamus. 'The poetry of John Hewitt', *Threshold*, no. 22 (Summer 1969), pp. 73–7 (review of *Collected Poems 1932–1967*); reprinted in Heaney's *Preoccupations: Selected Prose 1968–1978*, Faber and Faber, 1980, pp. 207–10; reprinted *Threshold* (Hewitt edition), no. 38 (Winter 1986–7), pp. 38–41
Heaney, Seamus. 'John Hewitt, 1907–1987: the universal poet. An appreciation', *Sunday Tribune*, 5 July 1987
'"I would make amends by fraternising": profile, John Hewitt', *Northern People*, 18 March 1983
Johnston, Neil. 'John Hewitt . . . talks to Neil Johnston', *Belfast Telegraph*, 13 April 1983
Johnstone, Robert. 'Portrait gallery: John Hewitt, a Protestant atheist', *Fortnight* (November 1977), p. 5
Kearney, Timothy. 'Beyond the Planter and the Gael: an interview with John Hewitt and John Montague', *Crane Bag*, vol. 4, no. 2 (1980–1), pp. 85–92
Kiely, Niall. 'John Hewitt, northern poet of Planter stock', *Irish Times*, 23 April 1977
Kilfeather, John. 'Remembering John Hewitt', *Threshold* (Hewitt edition), no. 38 (Winter 1986–7), pp. 31–7
Levine, Ketzel. 'A tree of identities, a tradition of dissent: John Hewitt at 78', *Fortnight*, no. 213 (4–17 February 1985), pp. 16–17

Longley, Edna. 'Progressive bookmen: politics and northern Protestant writers since the 1930s', *Irish Review*, no. 1 (1986), pp. 50–7
McAughtry, Sam. 'The McAughtry profile: trying to make sense of the north', *Irish Times*, 25 July 1983
McFadden, Roy. 'Bard from the north', *Hibernia* (October 1968), p. 14 (includes a review of *Collected Poems 1932–1967*)
McFadden, Roy. 'No dusty pioneer', *Threshold* (Hewitt edition), no. 38 (Winter 1986–7), pp. 6–12
McKeown, Ciaran. 'John Hewitt: appreciation', *News Letter*, 29 June 1987
Mackle, Henry. 'A personal appreciation of John Hewitt', *Honest Ulsterman*, no. 84 (Winter 1987), pp. 10–12
Midgley, John. '"Creed without claws, faith without fetters"', *Belfast Review*, no. 2 (Spring 1983), pp. 24–5
Montague, John. 'Regionalism into reconciliation: the poetry of John Hewitt', *Poetry Ireland*, no. 13 (Spring 1964), pp. 113–18; reprinted in *The Figure in the Cave and Other Essays*, ed. Antoinette Quinn, Lilliput Press, 1989, pp. 147–53
Montague, John. 'Spiritual maverick', *Threshold* (Hewitt edition), no. 38 (Winter 1986–7), pp. 17–18
Mooney, Martin. 'Ancestral voices', *Threshold* (Hewitt edition), no. 38 (Winter 1986–7), pp. 24–6 (review of *Ancestral Voices: The Selected Prose of John Hewitt*)
Mooney, Martin. '"A native mode": language and regionalism in the poetry of John Hewitt', *Irish Review*, no. 3 (1988), pp. 67–74
Morrow, John. 'John Hewitt', *Honest Ulsterman*, no. 85 (Summer 1988), pp. 27–8
Mullan, Fiona. '"Paved unerring roads": the poetry of John Hewitt', *Threshold*, no. 36 (Winter 1985–6), pp. 30–43
Olinder, Britta. 'The poet's trade: John Hewitt's view of his own poetry', *Papers from the First Nordic Conference for English Studies*, Oslo, 1981, pp. 148–61
Olinder, Britta. 'John Hewitt: Ulsterman of Planter stock', in *Studies in Anglo-Irish Literature*, ed. Heinz Kosok, Bouvier Verlag Herbert Grundmann, 1982, pp. 376–89
Olinder, Britta. 'John Hewitt's Belfast', in *The Irish Writer and the City*, ed. Maurice Harmon, Colin Smythe, 1984, pp. 144–52
Ormsby, Frank. 'John Hewitt: the yearnings of a restless nature', *Belfast Telegraph*, 4 July 1987
Sealy, Douglas. 'An individual flavour: the collected poems of John Hewitt', *Dublin Magazine*, vol. 8, nos 1–2 (Spring–Summer 1969), pp. 19–24
Smyth, Damian. 'Speaking a common tongue', *Fortnight* (Hewitt supplement), no. 275 (July–August 1989), p. ii

Taylor, Geoffrey. 'The poetry of John Hewitt', *The Bell*, vol. 3, no. 3 (December 1941), pp. 229–31

Taylor, Geoffrey. Introduction to *No Rebel Word*, Frederick Muller, 1948

Wallace, Martin. 'A poet and his past: profile, John Hewitt', *Belfast Telegraph*, 15 March 1957

Warner, Alan. Introduction to *The Selected John Hewitt*, Blackstaff Press, 1981, pp. 1–11

Warner, Alan. 'The poetry of John Hewitt', in *Studies in Anglo-Irish Literature*, ed. Heinz Kosok, Bouvier Verlag Herbert Grundmann, 1982, pp. 368–75

Warner, Alan. 'John Hewitt: honest Ulsterman', *Threshold* (Hewitt edition), no. 38 (Winter 1986–7), pp. 1–3

Watts, Geraldine. 'Utility clashes with emotion', *Fortnight* (Hewitt supplement), no. 275 (July–August 1989), p. v

INDEX OF TITLES

INDEX OF FIRST LINES